ENGLISH RECUSANT LITERATURE
1558–1640

Selected and Edited by
D. M. ROGERS

Volume 164

MATTHEW WILSON
Christianity Maintained
1638

OLIVER ALMOND
The Life and Gate
of Christianitie
1614

MATTHEW WILSON

Christianity Maintained
1638

The Scolar Press
1973

ISBN 0 85967 126 7

Published and Printed by The Scolar Press Limited
20 Main Street, Menston, Yorkshire
England

NOTE

The following works are reproduced (original size), with permission:

1) Matthew Wilson, *Christianity maintained*, 1638, from a copy in the Community Library, Mount Street, London, by permission of the Librarian.

References: Allison and Rogers 893; STC 25775/5149.

2) Oliver Almond, *The life and gate of christianitie*, 1614, from a copy in the library of Ushaw College, by permission of the President.

References: Allison and Rogers 14; STC 11.

CHRISTIANITY
MAINTAINED.
O R

A Diſcouery of ſundry Doctrines tending to the Ouerthrovve of
Chriſtian Religion:

Contayned in the Anſwere to a Booke entituled,
Mercy and **Truth**, *or*, Charity maintayned by **Catholiques**.

Bringing into captiuity all Vnderſtanding vnto the **Obe-**
dience of Chriſt. 2. Cor. 10. 5.

What is more contrary to Fayth, *then not to belieue any thing,*
to which Reaſon cannot reach? S. Bernard. Epiſt. 190.

Permiſſu Superiorum. **1638.**

TO THE
HIGH AND MIGHTY
PRINCE,
CHARLES
King of *Great-Brittaine*, *France*,
and *Ireland*, &c.

May it pleafe your Moſt Excellent Maieſty,

Y Prefumption vvere not eafily excufable (a *Moſt gracious Soueraigne*) in fly-ing to the Sanctuary of your Maiefty, for the pro-tection of this poore Treatife, if the great importance of the Caufe, vvherof

I vvrite,

I vvrite, did not change my *Feare* into *Hope*, and raife vp my *Hope* as high as *Confidence*, that *Chriftianity Maintay-ned*, by vvhat pen foeuer it be perfor-med, needeth not feare to find benigne acceptance from fo Gracious and Great a King as you are; vvho glory more in that moft Sacred Name of being a *Chri-ftian*, then in that moft ancient Stocke of R oyall Progenitours, vvhich fo glo-rioufly adornes the Diademe of your Sacred Maiefty. For I do not in this oc-cafion pretend to act either the Offen-fiue or Defenfiue part of any one parti-cular R eligion, honoured vvith the Name of *Chriftianity*; but I only come in the generall Name of a *Chriftian* Church, vvithout treating vvhether it be *Latin* or *Greeke*, *Eaft* or *VVeft*, of *England*, or of *Rome*: and therefore I cannot defpayre of being gracioufly admitted by your Maiefty.

My *Scope*, and *VVorke*, as I am fay-ing, is only to maintaine the authority
.of

of Holy Scripture, the Myftery of the Bleffed Trinity, the Deity of our Bleffed Sauiour, the infallibility of his Apoftles, the povver of his Miracles, the neceffity of his Grace, and of the abfolute Certainty of Chriftian Fayth; againft an Aduerfary, vvho feeketh to turne the *diuine beliefe* of Chriftians into *humane Opinion*: (a) Who teacheth that our affurance of holy Scripture, & of all the verityes contained therein, is but (b) *probable*, and *credible*; and confequently fuch as may vvell be falfe: Who continually vrgeth, (c) *that God*, as fure, *as he is good*, neither doth, nor can require of Chriftians an *infallible, and certainly vn-erring Beliefe* of his vvord; That men, neither are bound, nor can belieue diuine Reuelations (d) further then they are made apparent & euident to them; and that it fufficeth vnto Saluation *to belieue the Gofpell* (e) *as vve do other Stories*; as much as vve do (f) *Cefars Commentaries*, or *the Hi-*

(a) *Pag.* 36. & 37. & *pag.* 112. n. 154.

(b) *Ibid.*

(c) *Pag.* 112. lin. 3.

(d) *Pag.* 330. lin. 13. 25. 33.

(e) *Pag.* 37. lin 20. & fequ.

(f) *Pag.* 327. n. 5. lin. 28.

* 3 *ftory*

story of Salust: Who proclaimes (g) the Apostles, vvith the vvhole Church of their time, to haue erred in matters of fayth, euen after they had receiued the Holy Ghost; That after their Deaths, (h) the vvhole Church vvas presently infected vvith vniuersall Errour; and that the vvhole Church of the (i) Gentils may fall avvay into Infidelity: Who shutteth (k) the gates of *Mercy* against penitent sinners: Finally vvho openeth an easy vvay for the deniall of all those maine points of Christianity aboue mentioned, as it vvill appeare in this ensuing Treatise.

Vouchsafe therefore, *Most gracious Soueraigne*, to consider hovv Christianity is impugned by some, euen in this your Kingdome, and the inconueniences and dangers thereof; and preuent both them, and such others of the selfe same kind, as may grovv greater if they be not preuented, by your Zeale and Care. I cannot doubt, but that your
Ma-

(g) Pag. 144.n.31.

(h) Pag. 292.infine & 293. initio.

(i) Pag. 338.lin.5.

(k) Pag. 292. & 393.

Maiefty vvill do it euen for the Piety of the thing it felfe, though my Aduerfary (vvho yet pretends that he is vvholy of your Maiefties Religion) giues you a more particular offence , by departing from the very doctrines, vvhich you be-lieue . For befides diuers other fingle differēces, he neither allovves the *Nine and thirty Articles ,* vvhich your Maie-fty, in your Royall Declaration , affir-mes to containe the true Doctrine of the Church of *England;* nor holds he the *Succefsion of Bishops* to be neceffary in *Pag.* 356. *& feqs.* Gods Church; vvhich experience tea-ches to tend exprefly to the confufion of the faid *Church ,* and deftruction of *Monarchy.*

And though God hath made your Maiefty moft happy, both in a Royall Confort, of fingular and rare endovv-ments both of Body and Mind, & vvith a plentifull and moft hopefull Iffue, (vvhich vvith my hart I begge may euen laft to the very end of the vvorld) and

and vvith an Obedient & Loyall People, and vvith povver both at land and
fea, and vvith times both of Plenty and
Peace, vvhilft almoft all your Neighbours are in vvarre and vvant; yet nothing vvill euer be more able, to efta-
blish You in all thefe Felicityes, nor to
auert all difafters from your *Maiefty*,
then not to permit, that there be any
conniuence at fuch enormous Errours
as thefe, vvhich partly openly, & partly
couertly, are vented againft Chrift our
Lord, and all Chriftian Fayth.

The God of Heauen preferue your
Maiefty in all Health and Happineffe,
to his greateft Glory, your Maieftyes
ovvne Felicity, and to the ioy & comfort of all your Kingdomes.

Your Maiefties moft humble, and moft
obedient loyall fubiect,

I. H.

To the Chriſtian Reader.

ONDER *not* (Chriſtian Reader) *That I entitle this Little Treatiſe,* Chriſtianity Maintained. *I giue it that Name, becauſe that is the thing which I endeauour heer to make good, againſt one who ouerthrows* Chriſtianity, *not by remote Principles, or ſtrained Inferences, but by direct aſſertions, & cleere deductiōs, naturally flowing from diuers of his doctrines: which if it be made appeare, I cannot but hope, that all who take comfort in the glorious, and moſt happy name of* Chriſtian, *will giue me* the right hands of fellowſhip *in this Common Cauſe. Ancient Pacianus ſayes* (a) *of euery orthodoxe belieuer, that* Chriſtian is his name, Catholicke his Surname. Catholicke *cannot be conceiued without* Chriſtian . *But* Chriſtianity *ſo long as it is maintained, wil afford ſome common Principles of beliefe, which may direct men to find, that* one Catholicke *Church of Chriſtians, by meanes whereof* our Lord *hath decreed to giue* Grace and Glory. *Let therfore neither preiudice auert, nor priuat reſpects diuert the good Readers vnderſtanding from weighing in an equal ballance that which is herce layd before it. God forbid any*

(a) *Epiſt. ad Sem-* pro**.**

Chri-

Christian, should exceed the desperate folly of the Iewes, who would not depose their priuat quarells, euen while they were circled with a hostile army of Romans : *or be lesse aduised then the* Romans, *who tooke occasion to make peace at home, by the prouocations of the Enemy abroad, iudging it wisedome to be swayed with feare of greater euill, especially when they could do it, vnder the honourable title of* a Common

(c) Liu.
lib. 2.

(c) good. *In which respect, I lay aside, and as it were forget at this present, the Surname of* Catholicke, *while my scope is to maintaine* Christianity .

1. *But I must notwithstanding by the way desire thee, by example of this Man whose errours I vndertake to discouer, that thou wilt be pleased, to reflect vpon the misery into which they do bring themselues, who forsaking in truth that glorious* Surname, *content themselues with the only name of* Christians. *For consequently hauing lost the* Guift, *and* Light *of supernaturall and infused* Faytn, *which in their* Christendome *they receaued, they lye so open to all manner of deceites, that though they be warned of them, they runne vnawares into them: because not regarding, or not esteeming and weighing the necessity and importance of a* Guide, *they follow the* Eye *of their owne* Reason *only, which is too short-sighted to preserue them from falling into the manifold pitfalls, which lye on all sides of* Christian Fayth, *as we learne by all those, who in all ages haue swarued from it.*

2. *This Man, as the world knowes, had warning abundant, in a little Treatise called,* The Direction, *that he*

Direct.
ca. 4. per
totū.

should not goe a destructiue way tending to the ouerthrow of all Religion, no lesse then of Catholicke Doctrine. *How little he hath obserued it, will appeare by the ensuing discourse, penned to the like intent, and to no other,*

other, then , I dare say,the Direction *was, to wit , to preuent,or rather now, to discouer* Socinianisme *couertly cree-
ping into this Kingdome vnder the shrowde of* Naturall
Reason. *The venome of which Sect being still, as it seemes,
growing, or as I may say , compounding , it is no wonder
if the enemy of mankind doth vse all his art to make that
Treatise more and more odious, by which it began to be detected.*

3. *For to what other purpose doth this man in his preface* The Di-
say,against all Truth , and against the word of the letter, rection
that the Author of the Direction *, fastens the (a) im-* falsified.
putation of Atheisme and Irreligion vpon all wise (a) *Pre-*
and gallant men that are not of our owne Religion: *fat. n.7*
and this in a different letter, as the very words of the Di-
rector,*who yet hath neither any such words or sense. And
againe, that (b)* as the Samaritans saw in the Disci- (b) *Pre-*
ples coûtenances, that they meant to goe to Hierusa- *fat.n.20*
lem,so you pretend it is euen legible in the forheads
of those men, that they (that is some Protestants of
worth, and learning and auctority too) are euen going, nay making hast to Rome : *words set downe in a
different letter,and in the same context with the other words
of the* Direction,*which yet hath not any one such word, or
syllable. And the Author was farre from presuming to med-
dle with the intentions of those persons, with whom this
man would make him odious.*

4. *He neither commended, nor discommended, nor so
much as considered their* vicinity *to vs . His purpose was
to shew that for want of some* publicke infallible Authority *,they could not possibly auoyd frequent variations, by
which whether they fell to come neerer to vs , or to go further from vs, was not materiall to his purpose. Let altars be*

demo-

demolished to morrow, let pictures be defaced, let all that is done be vndone; These last alterations will prooue his intent as strongly as the others can, wherein they happen to agree with vs. For his scope being to discouer the impietyes of the Socinians, *and to preuent the hurt of foules by forewarning them of the danger ; to this end he declared some of the reasons for which this Sect disperseth it selfe , and is able to do it, by working vpon the minds of diuers Protestants . The chiefest he affirmed to be the want of a publicke infallible Iudge of Controuersyes, without which they are left to their owne priuate spirit , or wit, and discourse , which must of necessity bring forth a multitude of differences , altercations, and alterations, and end in* Socinianisme, *the quintessence whereof is to resolue* Fayth into Opinion, *or into euery mans owne* Reason *and* Persuasion *. Now to shew that for want of some liuing* Guide, *alterations in matters of* Fayth *and* Religion *must needes be frequent , he alleadged such instances, as lay open to the knowledge, and euen to the eye of euery man, and might afford a more sensible demonstration of what he intended to euince: Yet so, that (as I said before) his Argument receaued strength , not from their comming neere to vs , but from their altering from themselues . From thence to inferre, that they must intend* Popery, *because they happen to agree with vs in some things or rather seeme to agree, but indeed differ ; is iust as if one should say : The first* Protestants *in England , intended to persist in* Papistry, *euen when they purposed the contrary, yea euen when they did actually depart from vs : Because (forsooth) they were not so furious against euery particular doctrine of* Catholicks, *as some others were .* And I wonder how these men dare belieue the B. Trinity, *and other principall mysteries of* Christian Fayth *, since they must by this*

meanes

meanes agree with Papists, and so may feare least themselues be in a way to Popery.

5. Others are apt to belieue on the contrarie side, that the Directour was so farre from hoping that Protestants would become Catholicks by these degrees, as that he rather feared it might be a cause of some temptation to Catholicks, and a setling of Protestancy more effectually then could haue been performed either by the feruour of Zelots, or feare of Death, or any other meanes. And therfore I make bold to say, that although we Catholicks, his Maiesties most humble and loyall subiects, should be most vnworthy and vngratefull creatures, if we did not with deepest thankefulnes acknowledge our infinite obligation to the tender Clemency of our dread Soueraigne : Yet I may truly say (if such a Truth may be spoken without offence) that by many degrees They are more vnreasonable, and vnthankefull, who are vnquiet, because the most moderate, that is, the most powerfull meanes which can be thought of, are put in execution, for establishing that which they pretend to desire, I meane the Protestant Religion; vnlesse indeed they desire Protestancy should perish, if it do not in all respects perfectly and punctually sute with their humours. For it is a true saying ; Moderate things may last, but no Violence can long endure.

6. This then was the Directours intention, free from all malignity, and directed only to matters of Religion, and good of soules in the manner declared aboue. Which to be true, I haue heard him affirme most seriously by all that can be feared, or hoped for in the next life, for all eternity ; and therefore he could not but be sorry, that any writing of his was interpreted to an other meaning, of which if he had but once imagined his words to haue been capable, himselfe without so much as hearing any plea of defense, would haue been

the

the first to haue sentenced them to be destroyed, and all me-
mory of them to be forgotten. And he hopes that vpon this
sincere declaration it will be belieued, that if he erred, it was
against his owne intention, and not, amore erroris, fed errore amoris (*as Blessed* S. Austine *speakes*) not by any
loue to errour, but by an errour of loue, *to the eternall*
good of soules , by preuenting the daunger of their falling
into precipices of Socinian *doctrines.*

Lib. 22.
Ciuit.ca.
6.

7. *But the foule Imputation wherewith, euen in the Epi-*
stle Dedicatory to the Kings most Excel. Maiesty , this man
is bold to calumniate the whole Order of Iesuites *, with in-*
tent doubtlesse to make the Directour, *and his endeauours*
hatefull , (*tearming it ,* that Order which enuenomes
poifon it felfe, and makes the Roman Religion more
malignant and turbulent then otherwife it would be:
whole very Rule and Doctrine obliges them to make
all men, as much as lyes in them, fubiects vnto Kings,
& feruants vnto Chrift no further then it fhall pleafe
the Pope) *is a most virulent slaunder , and most vniust*
vntruth. For the cleering whereof, though we might content
our selues either with his ignorance of our Order , Rule,
and Doctrine ; *or with the guiltinesse of his owne Con-*
fcience, in regard, that probably he cannot choofe but know,
that the intent of them, and our proceedings , are nothing
fuch as he proclaymes them : yet I thought fit here to touch
briefly fome grounds, whereby his Maiesty chiefly, and all o-
thers may receaue fatisfaction, that there is no fuch thing in
our Order, Rule, *and* Doctrine, *as this man is pleafed to*
cast vpon it.

8. *And first (in regard, by what he fayth in his Pre-*
face, of the fourth Vow *which the* Iefuits *make of* fpeciall obedience to the Pope, *proper to their* Order *, it*
feemes,

seemes, that which *he doth vent in his Epiftle* Dedicatory, *hath relation to that* VOW *) it is to be* vnderftood, *that, that* Fourth VOW *is* wholy circa Milliones, concerning Milliones, *in order to the help of foules, as the words of that* Vow *expreßely fpeake, and their* Confti- *Conftit. part.5: cap. 13. L. C.* tutions *declare thus :* Tota intentio huius Voti Obediendi Summo Pontifici fuit, & eft circa Milliones, & fic intelligi oportet literas Apoftolicas, vbi de hac Obedientia loquutur, in omnibus quæ iuſſerit Summus Pontifex,& quocunq miſerit &c. The whole intention of this Vow to obey the Pope,was, & is concerning Miſsions, and ſo the Apoſtolicall Letters are to be vnderſtood, where they ſpeake of this Obedience, in all things which the Pope ſhall commaund, and whitherſoeuer he ſhall ſend &c. *As for their* Rules *in generall, they are confirmed by the fame* Authority, *which confirmed the Rules of all Religious Orders,and there is nothing in them* which *is not moft holy,and* which *hath not been accounted fuch, euen by our Enemies : or if there be any thing to be found in them other*wife, *let this man produce it if be can. They are not fo hard to come by, but that S. Paules Churchyard may oftimes afford them.* Doctrine *their Order approoues none but* what *is taught by other Catholicke Diuines,as hath been often demonftrated againft fuch as this man is. And therefore* we *hold our felues bound in all ducty to be, and to profeffe our felues to be, as loyall fubiects to the foueraigne* Maieſty of our King,*as louing and tender to*wards *his* Sacred Perſon, *as refpectfull and dutifull to his* Commaunds, *as any other of his fubiects of* what *profefsion foeuer; and to be bound alfo to teach all other fubiects, that the fame fubiection is due,not only* for feare,*but* for Conſcience *alfo,by the law of* God, *of* na-

B *ture,*

ture, *and* of Nations. *This we shall be ready to make good at all times; as also to giue his* Maiesty *full satisfaction, by what meanes his* Maiesty *shall be pleased to appoint , in any particular point of* Doctrine, *or* Practise, *which is, or may be imputed to our* Rule, *or* Order.

9. *It were ouer great boldnesse to appeale in this to the liuing testimony of him , who in his experience abroad hath beene acquainted with more* Communities *of our* Order, *then this man hath beene with* Persons *in his late changes when he professed himselfe a* Roman Catholicke, *and conuersed with diuers of vs : And by the equall hand which he carryeth towards all sorts of persons, obligeth all without preiudice to any. His* Maiesty *may be pleased to vse what meanes in his Royall wisedome he shall thinke best. And if he should thinke it fit to pitch vpon such a* Testimony *, we should esteeme our selues happy in the choyce ; notwithstanding that* M. Chillingworth *may conceaue otherwise, in regard that he wil needs haue it, that* Signor Con *hath prohibited the Directour from writing bookes any more, or at least,* hath reason to do it.

Pref. n.
25.

10. *But he must know , that we are of a different disposition from the* Socinians, *and therefore though that Person were not of that eminent* Integrity, Piety, Wisedome, Modesty, *and all kind of worth as he is, who by so many wayes hath obliged many great Persons to our nation, and howerly receiues a most gracious regard from those whose iudgment and example all should dread, we esteeme it a great happinesse to be subiect to all lawfull* Auctorities. *And whatsoeuer our skill be in* Logicke, *yet by Gods grace we will alwayes in hart, word, and deed maintaine these to be good and lawfull Arguments:* A Person of so eminent wisedome as he is whom this man names, *aduises me not to write; Therefore it is fittest*

teſt *for me not to write. And this other: A Perſon endued
with Authority,* commandes *me not to write: Therefore it
is not only* fit*, but* neceſſary *for me not to write. But this
Logicke is no Philoſophy with* Socinians, *who will haue no
Maiſters but themſelues, euen in matters concerning the
eternall ſaluation of their ſoules, and will one day find to
their coſt, that Holy* S.Bernard *vttered a moſt important
Truth when he ſaid*: Qui ſe ſibi Magiſtrum conſtituit,
ſtulto ſe Diſcipulum ſubdit. He who will be his owne
Maiſter, ſhall be ſcholler to a foole. *But it is time for me
to take vp & conclude this Preface with this caueat, that I
would not haue the Reader coceiue that in this litle volume I
haue touched all this mans Doctrines which tend to the ouerthrow of* Chriſtianity, *but only ſuch as were moſt obuious.
Nor is it my purpoſe at this time, exactly to cofute his grcuds
or anſwere his obiections, which may be done hereafter. My
maine buſines is to demonſtrate, that vnder the Name of*
Chriſtians, *he vndermines* Chriſtianity, *and ſetles* Soci-
nianiſme. *Which is the cauſe that mooued me to ſet forth
this short Treatiſe for a preſent Antidote, till a larger anſwere can be published. For who will aduenture vpon food if
he know it is mixed, and euen incorporated with deadly poi-
ſon? This is the ſcope of this Treatiſe, whereto I hope all
Chriſtians will concurre.* Socinians *are but an aggregate of*
Iewes, Manicheans, Arians, *and other condemned ſects,
which all good* Chriſtians *ought to deteſt. I hartily with
their Conuerſion: yet if they will obſtinately reſiſt, in deſpite
of their inuentions the words of the Apoſtle will be verified,*
Ieſus Chriſt yeſterday, and to day, the ſame alſo for
euer. *And they ſhall giue a fearefull account for their contempt of al Churches, and errours againſt* Chriſtian Fayth,
when repentance will nothing auaile: Euen at that day, when

Hebr. 13.
8.

B 2

AS

Lib. 5. de
fide c. 7. *as* S. Ambrose *grauely fayth* : The Iew fhall perforce acknowledge whom he crucified;when the Manichean
fhall adore whom he belieued not to haue come in
flefh; when the Arian fhall confeffe him to be omnipotent whom he denied. *And I may adde; when all good*
Chriftians *shall ioyfully behold him, whofe* Fayth *they laboured to* Maintaine.

The Doctrines confuted in the enfuing Treatife.

T *He firft Doctrine.* That Fayth neceffary to Saluation is
not infallible. *Chap.* 1.
The grounds of this Doctrine lead to Atheifme. *Chap.*2.
*The fecond Doctrine.*That the affurance which we haue of
Scriptures is but morall. *Chap.*3.
The third Doctrine. That the Apoftles were not infallible
in their Writings, but erred with the whole Church of
their tyme. *Chap.* 4.
The fourth Doctrine , Iniurious to the miracles of our Sa-
uiour,and of his Apoftles. *Chap.*5.
The fifth Doctrine . By refoluing Fayth into Reafon,he
deftroyes the nature of Fayth, and Beliefe of all Chriftian
Verities. *Chap.* 6.
The fixt Doctrine , Deftructiue of the Theologicall Ver-
tues of Chriftian Hope, and Charity. *Chap.* 7.
The feauenth Doctrine, Takes away the grounds of Ra-
tionall Difcourfe. *Chap.* 8.
The eight Doctrine , Opens a way to deny the B. Trinity ,
and other high myfteries of Chriftian Fayth. *Chap.* 9.
The ninth Doctrine , Layes grounds to be Conftant in no
Religion. *Chap.* 10.
The tenth Doctrine , Prouides for the impunity,and pre-
feruation of whatfoeuer damnable Errour againft Chri-
ftian Fayth. *Chap.* 11.
The Conclufion.

CHRIS-

CHRISTIANITY

MAINTAINED.

OR

The difcouery of fundry Doctrines tending
to the Ouerthrow of Christian
Religion.

The firft Doctrine.

*That Fayth neceſſary to Saluation is not
Infallible.*

CHAP. I.

CHRISTIAN *Fayth* being the foundation of *Hope*, the eye of *Charity*, the
leſſer light appointed for the night
of this world, the *Way* to Heauen;
if this *Foundation* be faulty, this *Eye*
deceitfull, this *Light* an Eclypſe to
it felfe, this *way* erroneous; our *Hope*,
Charity, *Light*, *Happineſse*, and all *Christianity* muſt

B 3   end

end, in worse then nothing, in euerlasting *vnhappines*.
For as *S. Thomas* said to our Sauiour, (a) *We know not whither thou goest, and how can we know the way?* So what will it auaile vs to know *whither we goe*, if we follow a misleading *way*, the Direction of a *Fayth* weake, waueriug, and subiect to Errour? such is Christian Fayth in this man's iudgment deliuered in the *Doctrine* with which I thought fit to begin, in regard it is the substance, and summe of that which he deliuers, and labours to prooue through his whole booke; and is persuaded, that it is of great and singular vse, and demonstrable by vnanswerable arguments.

2. I must confesse, it is of great vse to ground *Socinianisme*, which, as the (b) *Direction* fortold, reiecteth *infallible* supernaturall infused *Fayth* from being necessary to saluation: and maketh our *Christian Fayth* of the Gospell, and of Christ Iesus our Lord and Sauiour to be a meere *human opinion*, resolued into the authority of men, of no greater certainty then other *human Traditions and Histories* knowne by report. Hence the saying in *Charity Maintayned* (*that an absolute certainty of Fayth is necessary to Saluation*) he taxeth deeply as (c) *most pernicious and vncharitable*; and elswhere (d) as a *great errour of daungerous & pernicious consequence*; yea pag. 57. thus he writeth: *Men being possessed with this false principle (that Infallible Fayth is necessary) and that it is in vaine to belieue the Gospell of Christ with such a kind, or degree of assent as they yield to other matter of Tradition; and finding that their Fayth of it is to them indiscernable from the beliefe they giue to the truth of other Stories, are in daunger not to*
belieue

(a) Io.
14.5.

(b) Cap.
1.p.7.

(c) Pag.
328.
(d) Pag.
325.n.3.

beliene at all &c. It is true, that (pag. 36. n.8.) he ſayth *We cannot ordinarily haue any rationall and acquired aſſent, more then morall founded vpon credibilities*, wherby ſome may conceiue, that beſides *human and rationall Fayth*, he ſuppoſes and requires *Diuine Fayth*, which is a pure, ſincere, firme adheſion to Gods word, not cauſed by reaſon and diſcourſe, but infuſed by the Holy Ghoſt's inſpiration into a belieuing ſoule. But in truth he diſclaimes from any *neceſsity* of Diuine Fayth, or any diuine light aboue the light of meere reaſon, and will haue men to be ſaued by the natiue forces of human, rationall, and fallible Fayth. *Men* (ſayth he) (f) *are vnreaſonable; God requires not any* (f) *Vbi thing but reaſon; They pretend that heauenly things cannot* ſupra pa: *be ſeene to any purpoſe, but by the midday-light : but God* 36. n. 8. *will be ſatisfyed, if we receiue any degree of Light which makes vs leaue* the works of darkneſſes. *They exact a certainty of Fayth aboue that of ſenſe and ſcience: God deſires only that we belieue the concluſion, as the premiſſes deſerue,* wherof in rationall Fayth one is euer weake, credible, and not infallible. And againe pag. 112. n. 154. *Neither God doth, nor man may require of vs, as our duety, to giue a greater aſſent to the myſteries of our Fayth, then the motiues of credibility (* which are fallible *) deſerue.* This is his doctrine, which he deliuers often, & makes vſe thereof to reiect the infallible Authority *of Gods Church:* ſo prophane, impious, & vnchriſtian, as I wonder that a man profeſsing himſelfe a Chriſtian, durſt venture to vent the ſame in print, in a Chriſtian country. For is the certainty of the Fayth which Chriſtians yield to the truth of the Goſpell, to the life of Chriſt Ieſus our Lord and Sauiour, to the

hiſto-

Chap. 1. histories of holy Scripture, of no greater *discernable certainty*, then the beliefe we yield to humane traditions? I appeale to the conscience of euery true Christian, whether he do not most cleerely discerne his assent to the Truths of holy Scripture, to be superiour, and incomparably more firme, then his beliefe of meere humane storyes. That the Serpent spake vnto Eue, and persuaded her to eat of the forbidden tree; that our first Parents were naked, and did not perceiue it till they had eaten of the forbidden apple; these storyes & other the like would any Christian beleiue them, yea would they not laugh at them, as they doe at *Æsops* Fables, were they not of more credit with them, then *Cæsars* Commentaries, or *Salusts* histories, as this man * saith, they are not? That God requires not any thing of vs but only reason; That he exacts no more then that we beleiue the misteries of Christian Fayth, with a human fallible assent; That diuine illumination aboue the reach of the light of reason is not necessary, that men may *beleiue* as they ought, *to please*, and *satisfy* God; That God is satisfied with any degree of light, with the meere light of naturall Reason, and with the weake and wauering Fayth, which reason standing vpon probabilities can ground; These be strange and dismall positions, and such as ouerthrow Christianity, as is euident by many reasons. I will point at a few.

* *Pag.*
327. n. 5.

3. First it is against holy Scripture. *Fayth*, sayth *S. Paul, is the substance of things to be hoped for, the argument of things not appearing:* or, as the translation receiued in England hath it, *the euidence, or ground or confidence of things not seene.* All which signify a firme,

(g) Heb.
II. v. I.

cer-

certaine,and as I may fay *fubstantiall Fayth,* much different from whatfoeuer affent,if it be only probable.
For as *S. Bernard* difputing againft *Abailardus* (who
likewife taught that *Fayth* was but *Opinion*) fayth touching this definition of *S.Paul* (By the nameof *Substance* we are determined to fome *certaine* and *fetled*
thing, & *Fayth* is not *Opinion* but *Certainty:*) *Audis* (h)
(fayth this Saint) *Substantiam? Non licet tibi in fide
putare,vel difputare pro libitu, non hac illacq̗, vagari per
inania opinionum, per deuia errorum. Substantiæ nomine,
aliquid tibi certum, fixumq̗ præfigitur. Certis clauderis fi-
nibus,certis limitibus coarctaris. Non est enim fides æstima-
tio fed certitudo. Doest thou heare the name of Substance?
It is not lawfull for thee in Fayth to thinke or to difpute at
thy pleafure, nor to wander hither and thither,through the
emptines of opinions,or ftraying errour. By the name of fub-
stance, fome certaine and fetled thing is appointed thee.
Thou art fhut vp within certaine bounds,and confined within limits which are certaine. For Fayth is not an opinion but
a certainty.* This is alfo prooued by the words of the
fame Apoftle: (i) *Although we,or an Angell from Heauen euangelize to you,befide that which we haue euangelized
to you, be he anathema* : and where he fayth, (k) *That by
two things vnmooueable,whereby it is impofsible for God to
lye,we may haue a most strong comfort.* For how can it be
most strong if it be groūded only vpon probabilities,as
this man fayth our *Fayth* and *comfort* is? The falfhood
whereof is yet further declared by the fame Apoftle
*Ep. 1. ad Theffal.cap. 2.v. 12. When you had receiued of
vs the word of the hearing of God, you receiued it not as the
word of men, but (as it is indeed) the word of God.* And
*S. Bernard Ep.*190. alleageth *S.Paul* to the fame purpofe,

(h) *Epist.*
190.

(i) *Gal.* 1.
v. 8.
(k) *Heb.*
6.*v.* 8.

C

poſe, in this manner. *Scio cui credidi, & certus ſum, cla-mat Apoſtolus (1. Tim. 1.) & tu mihi ſubſibilas, Fides eſt æſtimatio? tu mihi ambiguum garris, quo nihil eſt certius?* But this Truth being certainly belieued by all *Chriſtians*, it will be needleſſe to alleadge more texts of Scripture in confirmation of it. *D. Potter* (in whoſe behalfe you ſtept forth) doth euidently contradict your doctrine, when he teacheth (1) that the chiefe ground of *Chriſtian Fayth* is *diuine Reuelation*, and that *nothing but this can erect an act of ſupernaturall Fayth; which muſt be abſolutely vndoubted, and certaine, and that without this, Fayth is but opinion or perſuaſion , or at the moſt an acquired human beliefe.* And Doctour Hooker (whom you alleadge pag. 325. for your opinion)in his Eccleſiaſticall Policy pag. 117. writes moſt ex-

,, preſſely in theſe words : The greateſt aſſurance ge-
,, nerally with all men, is that we haue by plaine aſpect
,, and intuitiue beholding &c. Scripture with Chriſtian
,, men being receiued as the word of God, that, for
,, which we haue probable, yea that which we haue ne-
,, ceſſary reaſon for , yea that which we ſee with our
,, eyes, is not thought ſo ſure ; as that which the Scrip-
,, ture of God teacheth, becauſe we hold, that his ſpeach
,, reuealeth there what himſelf ſeeth, and therefore the
,, ſtrongeſt proofe of all, and the moſt neceſſary aſſen-
,, ted vnto by vs, which doe thus receiue the Scripture,
  is the Scripture.

4. If we haue recourſe to reaſon, grounded on prin-ciples, which no Chriſtian denyes, this doctrine like-wiſe cannot be tolerated. For if a Chriſtian be not *certaine* that his beliefe is true, he may according to your owne confeſſion doubt, whether it be not falſe

Accor·

(1)Pag. 143.

According to your owne confeſsion,I ſay, ſeeing
your ſelfe goe about to prooue (m) that Chriſtian (m)*Pag.*
Fayth cannot be abſolutly certaine; becauſe if it were 326.*n.4.*
ſo,it would follow,that any leaſt *doubting* though reſiſted and *inuoluntary,*would deſtroy it ; which manifeſtly declares, that doubting can well conſiſt with
that ſort of *vncertaine* Chriſtian *Fayth* which you goe
about to vent. If once way be giuen for Chriſtians to
fall vpon doubting of their Fayth, why may not they
put themſelues vpon an examination in good earneſt,and as doubting of the grounds thereof? And if
this kind of examinaⁱion be lawfull, who can diſ-
commend an alteration, if they chance to find cauſe?
as it is very poſſible they may,if their firſt aſſent was
not infalliblꞓ? How then could *S. Paul* ſo abſolutely *Gal.1.8.*
ſay : Although we, or an Angell from Heauen ſhould
euangelize to you,beſide that which we haue euangelized, be he *anathema?*

5. But let vs goe a ſtep further. This Aſſertion giues way to belieue,that the contrary *to Chriſtian Fayth*
retaines ſome probability,in regard that no high degree of probability can of it ſelfe wholy deueſt the
oppoſite part of all probability, this being excluded
by *certainty* alone : Miſtake me not, as if I meant that
the probability of one ſide were ſufficient to beſtow
probability on the other. This only I ſay,that whoſoeuer belieues any poïnt only with probability, hath in
his vnderſtanding no preſent diſpoſition which of it
ſelfe is repugnant to probability for the contrary
ſide. And if Chriſtians muſt be of this diſpoſition in
their beliefe,they can haue no ſetled or firme reſolution,neuer to imbrace the contrary of that which for

C 2   the

the preſent is their beliefe, which ought notwithſtanding to be the reſolution of euery true Chriſtian
belieuer.

6. This is not all. If we follow this doctrine, this
other vnchriſtian Conſequence cannot be auoided:
That one may be ſaued, though he belieue ſome ſect
contrary to *Chriſtian Religion,* as Iudaiſme, Turciſme,
Paganiſme, or Atheiſme, with as great, or greater probability, then he belieues the articles of *Chriſtian
Fayth* . For proofe I need alleadg nothing beſide what
(n)Pag. your ſelfe ſuggeſt. In one place you tell vs, that *(n)*
37. *any fayth if it be but a graine of muſtardſeed, if it worke by
loue, ſhall certainly auaile with God, and be accepted of him.*
In another *(o)* you endeauour to prooue, that a pro-
(o) Pag. bable perſuaſion, and *hope of infinite and eternall happi-
327. neſſe, prouided for all thoſe that obey Chriſt Ieſus, may be
able to ſway our will to Obedience, and encounter with all
thoſe temptations, which fleſh and bloud can ſuggeſt to auert
vs from it.* Ioine theſe two doctrines togeather, & the
iſſue will be; that any probable beliefe of Chriſtian
verities, or euen of a God, muſt ſuffice to ſaluation,
as enabling vs to *worke by loue.* Now it is cleere that
your *graine of muſtardſeed,* your *any probable perſuaſion
or hope,* are verified in any low degree of probability
of fayth in Chriſt, or God; and yet they do not exclude equal or greater probability in behalfe of the
contrary part (for example that Chriſt is not the
Sauiour of the world, or that there is not a God:)
whence it followes that a man may attayne ſaluation, though he belieue with equall or greater probability, that Chriſt is not the Sauiour of the world, or
that there is not a God, then is that wherewith he belieues

Iieues the ſame, and all other myſteries of Chriſtian
Fayth.Whether this tend not to Iudaiſme,Turciſme,
Paganiſme, or Atheiſme, and to the ouerthrow of all
Chriſtianity, I need not ſay.

7. Moreouer, who can oblige any vnderſtanding
man, to dye for auerring the Truth of that Fayth,
wherof he proclaymes himſelfe to haue no certainty? And you,O glorious Martyrs of Chriſt our Lord,
did rather ſpill, then ſhed your bloud , if you were ſo
prodigall therof, for a truth not certainly belieued to
be ſuch. This is the very ſame argument,which melli-
fluous *S. Bernard* brings againſt *Petrus Abailardus,*
a Progenitour of the *Socinians*, who in thoſe dayes
taught, that Chriſtian *Fayth* was but *opinion,*and not
infallibly certaine:(p)*Stulti ergo Martyres noſtri* (ſayth (p) *Epiſt.*
this Saint)*ſuſtinentes tam acerba propter incerta, nec du-* ¹⁹⁰.
bitantes ſub dubio remunerationis præmio durum per exi-
tum diuturnum inire exilium. S Paul ſayth,(q) *Scarce for* (q)*Rom.*
a iuſt man doth any dye. And we may ſay,who will giue ⁵.⁷.
his life for a Truth? and moſt of all,who will not only *giue* his life,but thinke himſelfe *bound* vnder paine
of eternall damnation to lay it downe in teſtimony
of that, which for ought he certainly knowes, may
prooue to be an vniuſt, and vntrue thing ? Was the
precious bloud of Chriſt our Lord,which by infinite
degrees excelled that of Martyrs, ſhed in ſuch abundance for purchaſing probabilities ? or for the impe-
tration of Grace, to enable his ſeruants to dye for the
truth of things,which in fine they eſteemed but probable ?

8. Far be it from the harts of Chriſtians to belieue,
and their tongues to profeſſe, that a God of infinite
wiſe-

wifedome and goodneffe, would oblige himfelfe to
reward men with euerlafting happines, for imbracing the myfteries of Chriftian Fayth, which may
once proue falfe, and to adiudge men to endles torments, for adhering to the contrary, which in the
end may be found true, if Chriftian Fayth can poffi-
bly be falfe, as falfe it may be, if it be but probable.

9. Neuer could any doctrine be offered to the fonnes of Adam more plaufible, then that our beliefe of
Heauen and Hell is but an opinion in it felfe, and no
way certayne, concerning things of another world;
whereas worldly pleafures, are in prefent poffeffion
and certaine. If the greateft certainty wherewith all
Chriftians hitherto haue belieued their fayth to a-
bound, hath not byn able to ftay the cariere of mens
licencioufneffe; what fhall we now expect, but, that
flattered by this doctrine, they, who before did runne,
will now fly, after the Idols of whatfoeuer may appeare to their foules or bodies, obiects of delight?

10. No leffe liberty doth this doctrine affoard for
belieuing, then it doth for liuing, giuing fcope to A-
poftafyes, and endleffe changes of Religions, as this
man's fourefold alteration makes manifeft, if all be
true which is reported of him. In which inconftancy
(r) Prefa. notwithftanding he feemes to glory, ftiling it (r) *his*
n. 5. *Conftancy in following that way to heauen, which for the*
prefent feemes to him the moft probable. But of this more
hereafter.

11. I will doe him the fauour to fuppofe that he
holds no Religion more certainly true then that of
Chriftians, which yet to him being not certaine,
what remaines in his perfuation and *doctrine*, but that
for

for matters of fayth and Religion, God hath prouided
no certainty on earth? which is not only of very ill
confequence, as I haue faid, amõgft Chriftians themfelues, but expofeth Chriftian Religion to contempt
among the enemies thereof, and disbelieuers of it:
which this man it feemes doth not value a hayre; but
meafuring euery body by himfelfe, taxeth Chriftians
generally to be of the like weakenes, vngrounded-
nes, & vnfetlednes in their beliefe: *For*, fayth (s) he, (s) *Pag.*
men may talke their pleafure of an abfolute & moft infalli- 327. *n.* 5.
ble certainty, but did men generally belieue, that obedience to
Chriſt were the only way to prefent and eternall felicity, but
as firmely and vndoubtedly, as that there is fuch a Citty as
Conſtantinople, but as much as Cæfars Commentaries or the
hiſtory of Saluſt, I belieue the liues of moſt men both Papiſts
and Proteſtants would be better then they are. I leaue the
Cenfure of this Doctrine to others: I only note, firft
how poore a conceit this man himfelfe hath, & endeauoureth to inftill into others of the ground or ad-
hefion, which Chriftians vndoubtedly haue in their
beliefe, making it no more folid or firme, then the beliefe of Cæfars Commentaries &c. And fecõdly that
it may perchance be his fortune to be really forbidden to write any more bookes, if he can make no better confequences, then to conclude the want of *Fayth*,
or *firmeneffe of Fayth* in Chriftians, from the faults in
their liues, feeing there may be in a manner infinite
other caufes, why they do not liue, as they moft firmely belieue they fhould.

12. This therefore, you fee is his *doctrine* concerning
Chriſtian Fayth; that it is weake, and weakely grounded; that it is refolued into the authority of men, as
the

the beliefe of Conſtantinople, and Cæſars Commentaries ; that a Chriſtian may really and deliberatly
doubt of the points of his fayth, and yet be a Chriſtian (that is) faythfull. But that which doth moſt
manifeſtly diſcouer the impiety of this doctrine, and
of this his manner of arguing, is, that the reaſons by
which he pretends to maintayne it, induce plaine A-
theiſme, that is, they conclude as well, that men can
haue no certaine beliefe, knowledge, or aſſent that
there is a God, or that we are *certaine*, that *Chriſtian
Fayth* is euen ſo much as *probable* ; which now I am
going to ſhew.

The Grounds of this Doctrine leade to Atheiſme.

CHAP. II.

1.   **I** Said in the former Chapter that if a Chriſtian
be not certaine that his beliefe is true, he may
according to this mans owne côfeſſion doubt
whether it be not falſe. I pleaded his Confeſſion,
vpon an Argument of his which perhaps ſeemed to
him a great ſubtilty, and hard to be anſwered, but is
indeed a meere toye, and if it prooue any thing, it
prooues the Title of this Chapter to be true. *If,* ſayth
he (t)*this Doctrine,* of the abſolute certainty of Chriſtian Fayth *were true, then ſeeing not any the leaſt doubting can conſiſt with a moſt infallible certainty, it will follow, that euery leaſt doubting in any matter of Fayth though
reſiſted and inuoluntary, is a damnable ſinne, abſolutly de-
ſtructiue, ſo lo g as it laſts, of all true, and ſauing Fayth.*
Doth

(t) *Pag.* 326.

Doth not this Sophifme tend alfo to prooue , that if one be tempted with *inuoluntary* doubts againft the Truths I fpake of , he muft forfeit his *certainty* that there is a God, or that Chriftian Fayth is *certainly* probable, and fo either incurre damnation without his owne fault, which is impofsible , or attaine heauen without any certaine beliefe or knowledge that there is a God, or that Chriftian Fayth is *certainly* probable.

2. As for the argument it felfe, it is of no moment. It doth not diftinguifh betwixt the *Habit* of Fayth, whereby Chriftians are permanently denominated *Faithfull* , and which remaines euen when we are a fleepe, and the *Act* or exercife thereof, which may be hindred by many good employments , as ftudy or ferious attention to any bufineffe, without the leaft preiudice to the *Habit* of which we are depriued only by *Voluntary* errours or doubts againft it , not by thofe which are *inuoluntary* and *refifted*. If this anfwere giue not fatisfaction , let him either afford a better againft his owne obiection, or elfe profeffe , that he doth not certainly belieue there is a God , or that he is not certaine, that Chriftian Fayth and Religion is fo much as *probable* . And by the way me thinks he fhould reflect, that if he thinke *euery Act* deftroyes the *cōtrary habit*, and in that refpect no *doubting* may confift with the habit of infallible fayth , then the Doctrine of Catholicke Diuines , that euery voluntary Act of Herefy or Infidelity is deftructiue of the habit of *Fayth*, fhould not in reafon and true confequence be tearmed by him (v) *a vaine and groundleffe fancy.* (v) *Pag.*

3. An other argument to prooue the fallibility of *368*.

D   Chri-

(w)Pag. 326. Chriſtian *Fayth*, in effect is this: (w) We pray for the increaſe and ſtrengthning of our *Fayth* : Therefore our *Fayth* is not *infallible*. You might as well argue: We may pray for a high degree of happines in heauen: Therefore euery Saint in heauen is not perfectly happy. Do you not know, that there may be intenſion of degrees , euen in qualities which haue no mixture of the contrary? No light includes darknes, yet one light may be greater then another. Thus the moſt imperfect acte of fayth , is *moſt certaine* in the moſt perfect *kind* of certainty, though not moſt *certaine* in the moſt perfect *degree* of certainty : and we may well belieue that the leaſt degree of *Chriſtian Fayth* is incompatible with any deliberate and not reſiſted doubt, or vncertainty, and yet pray for the increaſe thereof. If you deny this, then tell me whether you may not pray for the increaſe of your beliefe of a God , and his Attributes, and for the ſtrengthning of it againſt all temptations (riſing either from the ſuggeſtions of the enemy , or from the weakeneſſe of mans vnderſtanding in order to ſo high miſteryes) as alſo of *your certainty* that Chriſtian Religion is probable in the higeſt degree of probability ; and when you haue granted that you may, as I hope you will , then you will haue anſwered your owne argument, vnleſſe you will acknowledge your ſelfe not to be *certaine* that there is a God, or that Chriſtian Religion is probable.

4. A third reaſon wherby he endeauours to prooue that *Chriſtian Fayth* is not abſolutely *certaine*, is this in (x) Pag. 326. ſubſtance: That ſeeing , as *S. Iohn* aſſures vs , (x) *our Fayth is the victory which ouercomes the world* ; if our

Fayth

Fayth be a certaine infallible knowledge, our victory ouer the world muſt of necefsity be perfect, and it ſhould be impoſſible for any true belieuer to commit any deliberate ſinne; How this doth follow I cannot perceiue, no more then one can inferre that Chri-ſtians cannot commit as grieuous ſinnes as men that reiect Chriſtianity, becauſe the beliefe of Chriſtians is true, and the beliefe of others is falſe. The Angels in heauen and Adam in Paradiſe, were indued with infallible Fayth, yea and with Euidence, in the opi-nion of diuers good Diuines; and yet the Angels and Adam ſinned deliberatly, and damnably. Fayth doth direct, but not necefsitate the will, which ſtill remay-ning free, may chooſe good or euill. If he will ſtill maintayne the argument for good, then he muſt be conuinced to ſay, that he doth not with *certainty* be-lieue a God, or that vertue is to be imbraced, becauſe he can doubtleſſe commit deliberate ſinnes againſt God, and vertue.

5. Not vnlike to this is another reaſon, *(y)* That *Charity* being the effect of *Fayth*, if our *Fayth* were perfect, *Charity* would be perfect, & ſo no man could poſsibly make any progreſſe in it. Giue me leaue to ſpeake to your ſelfe; do you not ſee, that by this rea-ſon, if you belieue in God with certainty, your loue of God muſt be perfect without poſsibility to make any progreſſe in it; which becauſe it is falſe, it muſt fol-low, by force of your Argument, that you do not with certainty belieue a God. But as for the reaſon in it ſelfe, becauſe it concernes more then your ſelfe, I muſt tell you that it doth falſly ſuppoſe that *Charity* is both an immediate, and neceſſary effect of *Fayth*,

(y) Ibid.

without

without interuention of *Freewill*, which may refuſe
to follow the direction of Fayth, and either wholy
ceaſe to loue God ,or loue him,now more, now leſſe.
And therefore no wonder, if vpon a falſe ſuppoſall,
that follow which is alſo falſe.

6. This is not a time to enter into long diſcourſes,
how you confound *certainty* with *perfection*, as if becauſe Fayth is abſolutely *certaine*, but yet *obſcure*, it
muſt be alſo abſolutely *perfect*, which is a great miſtake, for it wants the perfection of *euidence*, & hath
a *poſsibility* annexed to it, that it may be both reſiſted,
and reiected. But it will not be vnpleaſant notwithſtanding,nor vntimely to ſtand a while, and ſee how
exceſſiuely confident you are of the ſtrength and
force of the foreſaid Arguments, and the content-
ment which you take in them. Thus you ſpeake of

(z) *Pag.*
326.327.

them: *(z) Theſe you ſee are ſtrange and portentous conſe-
quences,and yet the deduction of them is cleere and apparent, which ſhewes this doctrine of yours (you meane
our doctrine of the infallibility of Chriſtian Fayth)
which you would faine haue true , that there might be ſome
neceſsity of your Churches infallibility, to be indeed plainly
repugnant, not only to Truth, but euen to all Religion and
piety, and fit for nothing but to make men negligent of making any progreſſe in Fayth , or Charity. And therefore I
muſt intreat and adiure you , either to diſcouer vnto me
(which I take God to witneſſe I cannot perceiue) ſome fal-
lacy in my reaſons againſt it , or neuer hereafter open your
mouth in defence of it.* I anſwere, it ſeemes to me, that
your *reaſons* are already ſufficiently prooued to be *fal-
lacyes*,ſince from them either nothing can be deduced
for your purpoſe,or elſe you muſt acknowledge your
ſelfe

felfe to haue no *certainty* that there is a God, that vertue is to be imbraced, or that Chriftian Fayth is euen
probable .

7. And yet I adde, that you muft in another refpect alfo folue your owne obiections. Remember thefe
your words: (zz) Yet all *This I fay not, as if I doubted* (zz) Pag.
that the fpirit of God being implored by deuout, and humble 36. 37.
prayer, and fincere obedience, may and will by degrees ad-
uance his feruants higher, and giue them a certainty of ad-
herence, beyond their certainty of euidence. And els where:
(a) *Gods fpirit if he pleafe may work more, a certainty of ad-* (a) Pag.
herence beyond certainty of euidence. Now you cānot de- 112.
ny but that thefe men may be tempted againft their
Fayth by *inuoluntary doubting*; that they may increafe
in it; that they may commit fome deliberat finne; and
may make daily progreffe in Charity and good workes, euen by the greater increafe of their Fayth : and
yet you graunt them a certainty of adherence, beyond
their certainty of euidence. And fo in this cafe your
felfe muft anfwere your owne arguments, and confeffe them to be but fallacies. Euen your maine reafon, that Chriftian *Fayth* can be endued with no
ftronger certainty then the probable motiues on
which it relyes, by this felfe fame inftance is proued
a *Sophifme.* For now you grant a *certainty* of Fayth
not without probable arguments of credibility, yet
not for them, it being more certaine then they are;
and therefore you are ftill put vpon a necefsity of anfwering your owne arguments . And whereas pag.
330. you make a fhew of anfwering this particuler
obiection, really you do not anfwere but plainly contradict your felf, labouring to prooue that it is impof-

fible

fible that there fhould be a certainty of adherence
beyond the certainty of euidence, as the Reader may
cleerly fee, and fhall be demonftrated in due time.

8. One thing more I muft not let paffe, and it is,
That whereas you fay, We would fayne haue Chriftian Fayth belieued to be infallible, *that there might
be fome necefsity of our Churches infallibility*; it feemes
you are apt inough to yield infallibility to Gods
Church, if once it be granted that Chriftian Fayth
is infallible. And with good reafon . For feeing you
teach that vniuerfall Tradition and other arguments
of credibility, cannot produce an infallible beliefe of
holy Scripture, and of the myfteries belieued by Chriftians; it muft follow, that fome other infallible meanes muft be found out for the propounding to vs the
holy Scriptures: which other infallible meanes euen
according to your perfuafion, being not Scripture it
felfe, nor euery mans priuate fpirit, there remaynes
only the authority of the Catholicke Church, which
as an inftrument of the holy Ghoft, may be an infallible propounder both of Scripture and all diuine verities . Wherein there is a large difference betweene
the Church and other Iudges. Thefe in their fenten-
ces or determinations intend not to deliuer points of
infallible Fayth, as the Church muft intend, and do it,
if once it be granted, that from her we muft receiue
holy Scriptures, and belieue them with a certaine and
infallible affent of Chriftian *Fayth.*

The

The ſecond Doctrine.

*That the aſſurance which we haue of
Scriptures, is but morall.*

CHAP. III.

1. **T**His man magnifies holy Scriptures in many places, as the only thing on which he
relyes his Saluation; but whoſoeuer ſhall
walke along with him from place to place, & marke
well his wayes, will find that they lead to the quite
contrary, and ſhew that he neither doth value them
to their right worth, nor doth lay any other grounds,
but ſuch as are more apt to breed diſeſteeme then
eſteeme of them. This may be ſeene, in that he teacheth, (b) That our aſſurance that the Scripture hath (b) *Pag.*
been preſerued from any materiall alteration, and 141. &
that any other booke of any profane writer is incor- 62.
rupted, *is of the ſame kind and condition, both morall aſ-
ſurances.*

2. If this may be allowed, it muſt neceſſarily follow that the aſſurance which we haue of Scripture
muſt in degree be much inferiour to the aſſurance
which we haue of ſuch bookes of prophane Authors
as haue a more full teſtimony and tradition of all
ſorts of men, to wit, Atheiſts, Pagans, Iewes, Turkes
& Chriſtians; wheras the bookes of holy Scripture,
are either vnknowne, or impugned by all except
Chri-

Chriſtiās, & by ſome alſo who would beare the name of Chriſtians, and conſequently the morall aſſurance of them, and of the incorruptedneſſe of them, is the much the leſſe, and of leſſe morall credit. And by ſo ſame reaſon whoſoeuer builds vpō this mans groūds, cannot haue ſo great aſſurance that there was a Ieſus Chriſt, that he had diſciples, and much leſſe that he wrought wonderous things, and leſſe then this, that thoſe wonders were true miracles; as that there was a Cæſar, Alexander, Pompey &c. or that they fought ſuch battailes, and the like. For theſe things deſcend to vs by a more vniuerſall tradition, then the former. Do not your ſelfe ſpeake thus? *We haue as*

(c) Pag. 116.

great reaſon to belieue there was ſuch a man as Henry the Eight King of England, as that Ieſus Chriſt ſuffered vnder Pontius Pilate. You ſhould haue ſaid; we haue greater reaſon to belieue it, if we conſult humane inducements only, and conſequently if Chriſtian Fayth be not abſolutely infallible, euen aboue the motiues of credibility, we are more certaine that there was a King *Henry*, then a *Ieſus Chriſt*: A thing which no true Chriſtian can heare without deteſtation.

3. That which followes out of the ſame 116. page, is of the like nature, laying a ground for vnwary people to reiect Scripture; For, hauing ſpoken of ſome barbarous Nations, that belieued the doctrine of Chriſt, and yet belieued not the Scripture to be the

(d) Pag. 116.

word of God, (d) for they neuer heard of it, and *Fayth comes by hearing*; you adde theſe words : *Neither doubt I, but if the bookes of Scripture had byn propoſed to them by the other parts of the Church where they had been before receiued, and had been doubted of, or euen reiected by thoſe*
barba.

barbarous nations, but ſtill by the bare beliefe, and practiſe of Chriſtianity they might be ſaued, God requiring of vs vnder paine of damnation, only to belicue the verities therein contained, and not the diuine authority of the bookes Where-in they are contained.

4. If this be granted, why might not any Church haue reiected the Scriptures being propoſed by other parts of the Church? And why may not we do ſo at this day? Nay ſeeing *de facto* we know the verities of Chriſtian Fayth by Scripture only, according to your doctrine; we cannot be obliged to belieue the Scriptures, becauſe the verities therein contained are neceſſary to be belieued, (for this very neceſsity you cannot belieue, but by belieuing aforehand the Scripture) but contrarily you may reiect the verities themſelues, if you be not preobliged to belieue the diuine authority of the bookes wherein they are contained.

5. Againe, you ſay that Scripture is the *only Rule* of Chriſtian Fayth, (e) yet it is not neceſſary to Saluation to belieue it *to be a rule of Fayth, no nor to be the Word of God.* The firſt part of this doctrine is the ſcope of your whole ſecond Chapter. The ſecond is taught purpoſely, and at large in the ſame Chapter (f) *pag.* 116. *n.* 159. Ioyne theſe two aſſertions, and the Conclufion will be; That we are not obliged to receiue that which is the only ordinary meanes of attayning Chriſtian Fayth, namely the Scriptures. And therefore in the ordinary way, we cannot be bound to imbrace Chriſtian Fayth, ſeeing it cannot be compaſſed without the meanes to attaine to it. For how can one be obliged to attayne an end, and yet be left free to reiect the only meanes of atchieuing that end? I am the

(e) Cap. 2. per totum.

(f) Pag. 116.

E   freer

freer to make this queſtion, becauſe you concurre
with me in the anſwere,when you ſay : *(g) It was ne-*
ceſſary that God by his prouidence ſhould preſerue the Scrip-
ture from any vndiſcernable corruption, in thoſe things
which he would haue knowne;otherwiſe it is apparent it had
not been his will that theſe things ſhould be knowne, the on-
ly meanes of continuing the Knowledge of them being peri-
ſhed. Now is it not in effect all one, whether the Scripture haue periſhed,or whether it be preſerued, if in
the meane time we be not bound to belieue, that it is
the Rule of Fayth,and word of God? Nay, ſeeing as
things now ſtand we may find the verityes contayned in Scripture, ſufficiently expreſſed in innumerable other bookes,we may at this preſent in conformity to your doctrine reiect all the holy Scripture, con-
tenting our ſelues with the contents thereof taken
from other Authors,and not from the writers of the
Bible .

6. The Doctrine which he carryeth through his
whole Booke , but particularly inſiſteth vpon in his
third Chapter,that we cannot learne from Scripture
it ſelfe that it is Canonicall, but only from Tradition of men , deliuering it from hand to hand ,is no
leſſe iniurious and derogatiue to holy Scripture then
the former , ſpeaking of men in his ſenſe, that is, not
as endued with any infallible afſiſtance of the holy
Ghoſt (which Catholicks belieue of the Church)but
only as wiſe, or many men,or for the like human qua-
lifications;for to this effect he ſayth: *(h) Tradition is a*
principle, not in Chriſtianity, but in Reaſon , not proper to
Chriſtians, but common to all men. This is certainly the
right courſe to blaſt the Authority of holy Scripture,
not

(g) *Pag.*
16.

(h) *Pag.*
72.n.511

not to maintaine it. For beſides that which I haue
touched already, that by this meanes we are not ſo
certaine of Scripture, as of profane bookes , he muſt
come at length to reſolue the beliefe of Scripture into
the Tradition or Authority of Pagans, Iewes, Turkes,
or condemned Hereticks, as well as of true Chriſtiãs.
For ſeeing errours againſt fayth , or Hereſies cannot
in his principles be diſcerned but by Scriptures ; before they be receaued, the teſtimony of one man concerning the admittance of them muſt weigh as much
as of another, and be conſidered only as prooceeding
from a number of men, be they faythfull or Infidels,
true Chriſtians or condemned Hereticks.

7. And further according to the ſame principles he
muſt acknowledge, that he belieueth ſome parts of
Canonicall Scripture with a more firme aſſent, then
others, to wit, as they haue been deliuered with more
or leſſe generall conſent, or haue been more or leſſe
once queſtioned: which is to depriue Canonical Scripture of all Authority . For if once we giue way to
more or leſſe in the behalfe of Gods word , we ſhall
end in nothing. And this hath the more force in this
mans doctrine, who profeſſeth that the greateſt certainty which he hath of any part of Scripture, is within the compaſse of probability. What certainty then
ſhall thoſe Scriptures haue, which participate of that
probability in a leſse and leſse degree, according as
they haue been deliuered with different tradition and
conſent. How this doctrine will ſound in the eares of
all true Chriſtians, I leaue to be conſidered, conten-
ting my ſelfe to oppoſe your Aſſertion with the diſcourſe of *D. King,* afterward Biſhop of *London,* in the
E 2 begin-

beginning of his *firſt Lecture* vpon *Ionas*, where a-
mongſt other things he ſayes: *Compariſons betwixt Scripture and Scripture are both odious and daungerous. The
Apoſtles names are euenly placed in the writings of the holy foundation. With an vnpartiall reſpect haue the children
of Chriſts family from time to time, receiued, reuerenced, &
imbraced the whole volume of Scriptures.* You on the o-

(i) *Pag.*
67.n.36.

ther ſide ſpeake in a different ſtrayne and ſay thus: *(i)
I may belieue euen thoſe queſtioned Bookes to haue been
written by the Apoſtles, and to be Canonicall: but I cannot
in reaſon belieue this of them ſo vndoubtedly, as of thoſe
bookes which were neuer queſtioned.* And elswhere: *The
Canon of Scripture, as we receiue it, is built vpon vniuerſall
Tradition. For we do not profeſſe our ſelues ſo abſolutly and
vndoubtedly certaine, neither do we vrge others to be ſo, of
thoſe Bookes which haue byn doubted, as of thoſe which neuer haue.* By this meanes what will become of the E-
piſtle of *S. Iames,* the ſecond Epiſtle of *S. Peter,* the ſecond and third of *S. Iohn,* the Epiſtle to the *Hebrewes,*
and the *Apocalyps of S. Iohn?* And what part of Scripture hath not been queſtioned by ſome, and thoſe
ſome ſo many, as would haue made vs doubt of the
works of *Tully* or *Liuy &c.* if they had affirmed them
not to haue been written by ſuch Authours? And the
only doubting of *Eraſmus,* or ſome ſuch other about
the workes of ſome Fathers, hath cauſed them to be
queſtioned by diuers, vpon much weaker grounds, as
difference of ſtiles, or the like.

(k) *Pag.*
69.n.45.

     8.   In another place you tell vs *(l)* that to receiue
a Booke for Canonicall, it is inough to haue *had atteſtation though not vniuerſall, yet at leaſt ſufficient to make
conſidering men receiue them for Canonicall, which were*

(l) *Pag.*
68.n. 43.

ſome-

ſometimes doubted of by ſome, yet whoſe number and au-thority was not ſo great, as to preuaile againſt the contrary ſuffrages. Obſerue vpon what inextricable paſſages, and leſſe degrees of probability this man doth put vs in our beliefe of holy Scripture. Firſt we muſt ſettle our Fayth on *men*; then on *conſidering* men, though the conſent be not vniuerſall;thirdly vpon the grea-ter and more preualent number and authority of ſuf-frages, as if the greater number alone, without in-fallible aſſiſtance of the holy Ghoſt, were a ſufficient ground for Chriſtian Fayth. You deny (pag. 68. n. 42.) that the Controuerſy about Scripture is to be tryed by moſt voyces, and yet what is your greater number, but moſt voyces? And as for greater *Autho-rity*, what can you meane thereby, except perhaps greater learning, or ſome ſuch quality, nothing pro-portionable to that *Authority*, on which Chriſtian Fayth muſt relye?

The third Doctrine.

That the Apoſtles were not infallible in their writings, but erred with the whole Church of their time.

CHAP. IIII.

1. IT can be no wonder that he ſhould ſpeake meanly of the neceſſity, and infallibility of holy Scripture, ſince he labours to faſten er-rour vpon the Canonicall writers, and deliuerers thereof the *Apoſtles* themſelues, and the *whole Church*

of

of their time. And this cōcerning an Article of Fayth
of higheſt conſequence and moſt frequently reuealed
in holy Scripture, the deniall whereof had byn moſt
derogatory from the glory of our Sauiour, and from
the abundant fruit of his ſacred Paſsion: to wit, that
the Ghoſpell was to be preached to all nations. You

(m) Pag. ſhall receiue it in his owne words: (m)*The Church may*
287. n. 21. *ignorantly disbelieue a Reuelation , which by errour ſhe*
thinkes-to be no Reuelation. That the Goſpell was to be prea-
ched to all Nations , was a Truth reuealed before our Sa-
uiours Aſcenſion in theſe words; Goe and teach all nations.
Math. 29. 19. Yet through preiudice , or inaduertence, or
ſome other cauſe the Church disbelieued it, as it is apparent
out of the 11. and 12. Chapter of the Acts, vntill the conuer-
ſion of Cornelius. And that the Apoſtles themſelues
were inuolued in this ſuppoſed errour of the moſt
primitiue Church, he deliuers without ceremony in

(n) Pag. another place : (n) *That the Apoſtles themſelues euen af-*
144. n. *ter the ſending of the holy Ghoſt were, and through inaduer-*
31. *tence, or preiudice continued for a time , in an errour repug-*
nant to a reuealed Truth, it is, as I haue already noted, vn-
anſwerably euident from the ſtory of the Acts of the Apo-
ſtles. Is not this to ouerthrow all Chriſtianity? If the
Bleſſed Apoſtles on whom Chriſtians are builded, as
vpon their foundation (*Epheſ.* 2.) were obnoxious
to *inaduertence,* to *preiudice*, to *other cauſes* of errour;
what certainty can we now haue ? The Apoſtles
might haue written what they belieued, and ſo we
cannot be ſure but what they haue written may contain ſome errour proceeding from *inaduertence, preiu-*
dice, or ſome other cauſe. If they euen after the receiuing of the holy Ghoſt, and with them the whole
                                                    Church

Church of that time, could either forget or tranſgreſ-
ſe ſo freſh a Commaund, impoſed by our Sauiour
Chriſt for his laſt farewell at his Aſcenſion; it will be
obuious for aduerſaries of Chriſtian Religion to ob-
ieⅆ,that perhaps they haue byn left to themſelues, to
obliuion, inaduertence, and other humane defeⅆs in
penning the Scripture. If they erred in their firſt
thoughts, why not in their ſecond? With the aſsiſtan-
ce of the holy Ghoſt they can erre in neither, without it, in both.

2. The Obieⅆion which he brings is not hard to
ſolue. *S.Peter* himſelfe neuer doubted. That viſion was
ſhewed to him, and he declared it to the conuerted
Iewes for their ſatisfaⅆion, as it happened in the
Councell held by the Apoſtles,about the obſeruation
of the law of *Moyſes*; which ſome Chriſtians conuerted from Iudaiſme did much vrge. But neither the
Apoſtles, nor the other Chriſtians had any doubt in
that matter: as likewiſe in our preſent caſe, not all the
Church,but only ſome Zealous for the Iewes did oppoſe themſelues to *S.Peter.* For before the conuerſion (o) *Com.*
of *Cornelius* other Gentils were become Chriſtians,as *in Aⅆ.*
(o)*Cornelius à Lapide* with others affirmes & proues. *cap.*10. *poſt verſ.*
For which reſpeⅆ the text expreſsely declares, (p) 48,
that they who were offended with *S.Peter were of the* (p) *Aⅆ.*
circumciſion, that is Iewes made Chriſtians. *c.11.v.2.*

3. He goes on in this conceit, and addes a point
no leſse daungerous then the former.*The Apoſtles Do-*
*ⅆrine ,*ſayth he, (q) *was confirmed by miracles , therefore* (q) *Pag.*
it was entirely true ,and in no part either falſe, or vncertain. *144. n.* 31.
I ſay in no part which they deliuered conſtantly, as a certaine
diuine truth, and which had the atteſtation of diuine mira-
cles.

cles. Thus you ſee he couertly calls in queſtion all the
Apoſtles writings, and layes grouds to except againſt
them. For if once we giue way to ſuch diſtinctions,
and ſay that the Apoſtles are to be credited only, in
what they *deliuered conſtantly as a certaine diuine Truth*;
we may reiect in a manner all Scripture, which ſcarce
euer declares, whether or no the writers thereof did
deliuer any thing, as a certaine diuine Truth; and
much leſſe that they remained conſtant in what they
deliuered by writing. Or if it ſhould expreſſe theſe
particulars, yet we could not be obliged to belieue it,
if once we come to deny to the Apoſtles an vniuerſall infallibility. For what reaſon can this man giue,
according to theſe grounds of his, why they might
not haue erred in that particular declaration?

4. And beſides, will he not oblige vs to belieue with
certainty any thing deliuered by the Apoſtles which
had not *the atteſtation of diuine miracles?* It ſeemes he
will not, and thereby in effect takes away the beliefe of very many myſteries of Chriſtian Fayth and
verities contayned in holy Scripture. For that mira
cles were wrought in confirmation of euery particular paſſage of Scripture, we cannot affirme neither
out of holy Scripture it ſelfe, nor any other credible
argument: rather the contrary is certaine, there being
innumerable verityes of the Bible which were neuer
ſeuerally confirmed in that manner, and yet it were
damnable ſinne to deny them. And moreouer where,
or when did the Apoſtles particularly prooue by miracle, that their writings were the word of God? Thus
you ſee into what plunges he brings all Chriſtians by
his owne *Inconſtancy*; from which certainly ariſeth
this

this itching deſire of his to put conceites into mens heades, as if the Apoſtles alſo might haue byn various in their writings and not conſtant.

5. I cannot omit another diſtinction preiudiciall to the infallibility of the Apoſtles & of their writings, which he deliuereth in theſe words: (r) *For thoſe things which the Apoſtles profeſſed to deliuer, as the Dictates of human reaſon, and prudence, and not as diuine Reuelations, why ſhould we take them as diuine Reuelations? I ſee no reaſon, nor how we can do ſo, and not contradict the Apoſtles and God himſelfe. Therefore when S. Paul ſayes in the* 1. *Epiſt. to the Corinth.* 7. 12. *To the reſt ſpeake I, not the Lord. And againe : Concerning virgins I haue no commaundment of the Lord, but I deliuer my iudgment. If we will pretend that the Lord did certainly ſpeake what S. Paul ſpake, and that his iudgment was Gods commandment, ſhall we not plainly contradict S. Paul, and that ſpirit by which he wrote which mooued him to write; as in other places diuine Reuelations, which he certainly knew to be ſuch, ſo in this place his owne Iudgment touching ſome things, which God had not particularly reuealed vnto him*. This doctrine is ſubiect to the ſame iuſt exceptions, which were alleadged againſt the former For if once we deny vniuerſall infallibilty to the Apoſtles, we cannot belieue them with infallibility in any one thing, but ſtill we may be doubting whether they ſpeake out of their owne ſpirit, and not by diuine Reuelation, though they ſhould euen declare in what ſort they intend to ſpeake, becauſe we may feare they are deceiued in thoſe very declarations. And as you will perhaps ſay, they write Diuine Reuelations, except in things which they profeſſe to deliuer *as the Dictates of human*

(r) *Pag.* 144. *n.* 32.

human reafon and prudence ; another will fay that they muft or may be vnderftood to deliuer *the dictats of human reafon and prudence*, whenfoeuer they do not in expreffe tearmes profeffe to deliuer diuine Reuelations, which is very feldome; the ordinary cuftome of holy Scripture being to deliuer verityes without any fuch qualifying of them. And if *S. Paul* when in the Epiftle and Chapter by you cited *v.*40. fayes of himfelfe, *I thinke that I alfo haue the fpirit of God*, might be deceiued in that thought of his ; we may alfo fay he might be deceiued, euen when he affirmes that he writes by the fpirit of God ; and much more may we doubt, when he expreffes no fuch thing, as commonly neither he, nor any other Canonicall writers doe.

6. In the words which you cite : *To the reft fpeake I, not the Lord, S. Paul* treates of a very important matter, that is, of the wiues departing from her husband, or the husbands from his wife. Wherein if *S. Paul* were fubiect to errour, he might chance to haue taught a point of great Iniuftice, againft the command of our Sauiour declaring the very Law of nature, *What God hath ioyned together let not man fepa-* (s) *Mat.* rate (s). And as for the words you alleadge in the fe-
19. 6. cond place : *Concerning virgins I haue no commandment of our Lord, but I deliuer my Iudgment*, the Apoftle afterwards within the compaffe of the felfe fame difcourfe, fayes that a man finnes not if he marry; wherin if *S. Paul* may be deceiued, as fpeaking out of his owne fpirit, as you fay he doth in fome precedent words ; you will not only want this text to prooue with certainty, that marriage is lawfull, but whenfoeuer marriage is allowed in any other place of
Scrip-

Scripture (as *Hebr.* 13. *v.* 4. *Marriage is honourable in all*) you haue put into the mouthes of the old and mo-derne heretiques, who impugned the lawfullnes of marriage, a ready anſwere that thoſe texts of Scrip-ture, were but the Dictats of human reaſon and pru-dence, wherein the writers of Canonicall Scripture might be deceiued.

7. The other words, *Speake I, not the Lord,* ſhew only that our Sauiour left power for the Apoſtles, and his Church to aduiſe, counſaile, ordaine, or commaund ſome things, as occaſion might require, which him-ſelfe had not commaunded, or determined in parti-cular: which truth if you hold to be only a *Dictate of human reaſon,* you open a way for refractary ſpirits to oppoſe the ordinances of their Superiours and Pre-lats, in things not expreſſely commaunded by our Lord.

8. The laſt Words *v.* 25. *Concerniug virgins I haue no commandment of the Lord, but I deliuer my Iudgment,* which we tranſlate, *but I giue counſaile,* prooue indeed our Catholicke Doctrine concerning workes of ſu-pererogation, or Counſayles, in regard that the Apo-ſtle in this place perſuades virginity as the better, but commaunds it not as neceſſary: Yet they do in no wiſe imply any doubtfulneſſe or fallibility in the A-poſtles; neuer any hitherto beſides your ſelfe, offering to anſwere our argumét by ſaying, the Apoſtle wrote only the dictate of human reaſon, or prudence, and ſo might be deceiued. Which anſwere had been very obuious, if they had preſumed to be ſo bold, as you are, with the Apoſtles, and therefore it is a ſigne that no man beſides your ſelfe durſt deliuer this doctrine.

9. Cer-

9. Certainly if the Apostles did sometimes write by the motion of the holy Ghost, and at other times out of their owne priuate Iudgment or spirit; though it were granted that themselues could discerne the diuersity of those motions or spirits (which one may easily deny, if their vniuersall infallibility be once impeached) yet it is cleere that others, to whom they spake or wrote, could not discerne the diuersity of those spirits in the Apostles. For which cause learned Protestants acknowledge, that although ech mans priuate spirit were admitted for direction of himselfe, yet it were not vsefull for teaching others. Thus you say (pag. 141.) A supernaturall assurance of the incorruption of Scripture may be an assurance to ones selfe, *but no argument to another*. And as you affirme (t) *that bookes that are not Canonicall may say they are, and those that are so, may say nothing of it :* so we cannot be assured that the Apostles deliuer diuine Reuelations, though they should say they doe; nor that they deliuer not such Reuelations though they say nothing thereof, if once we deny their vniuersall infallibility.

(t) Pag. 62.

10. Now I beseech the good Reader to reflect vpon this mans endeauours to ouerthrow the holy Scriptures, and Christianity, and to what at last he tends by these degrees. First he sayth, our beliefe that Scripture is the word of God exceedes not probability. 2. Amongst those Bookes which we belieue to be the word of God, we belieue some with lesse probability then others. Thirdly we may be saued though we neither belieue that Scripture is the Rule of Fayth, nor that it is the word of God . Fourthly, our assurance that Scripture or any other Booke is corrupted, is of the

the ſame kind and condition, both , *only morall aſſu-*
rances.Fifthly the writers of holy Scripture might erre
in things which they deliuered not conſtantly,or not
as diuine Reuelations, but dictates of human reaſon,
or if they deliuered any doctrine not confirmed by
miracles. Sixtly,vpon the ſame ground he might ſay
that the Apoſtles were infallible only when they deliuered things belonging to Fayth,Piety,or Religion,
& not when they wrote things meerely indifferent,
or of no great moment in themſelues, as ſome *Soci-*
nians (u) eyther grant , or care not much to deny.
And then further it will be left to euery mans iudgement, what is to be accounted a matter of moment : And ſoone after it will be ſaid, that to ſearch
whether the doctrine of the Bleſſed Trinity, for example, be contained in Scripture, or no,is not much
neceſſary ; ſince a man without knowledge of that
ſpeculatiue doctrine, may belieue and loue God , as a
chiefe *Socinian* teaches (w),and your ſelfe affirme (x)
that any Fayth if it worke by loue ſhall certainly auaile with
God, and be accepted of him . And then will ſome ſay ;
Why may not a man loue *God* though he erre in the
doctrine concerning *Chriſt* deliuered in Scripture ? &
ſo it will not be neceſſary to belieue that the Apoſtles were infallible in penning the Scripture,but only in articles abſolutely neceſſary to loue God,and to
haue a generall ſorrow for all our ſinnes.And ſince to
loue God & haue contrition for our ſinnes , a probable beliefe will ſerue according to your(y) Principles,
what need we any infallible Scripture at all , but only ſome motiues ſufficient to produce a probable aſſent that there is a God , whether it be by Scripture

(u) *Vol-*
kel.l.5.c.
5.*Dom.*
Lopez de
Autho-
rit.ſac.
Script.

(w) *Iren.*
Philaleth.
diſſerta-
tione de
Pace Ec-
cleſiæ.
(x) *Pag.*
37.

(y) *Pag.*
327.

belie-

belieued to be only a probable writing, or by naturall diſcourſe, or any other meanes, as you teach, that
one is not bound to belieue the Scripture to be the
word of God, but may be ſaued, if by other meanes,
for example, preaching, he attaine the knowledge of
(z) Pag. the verityes contayned in Scripture *(z)*. And thus
116. you ſee to what hauock theſe things lead, not only
touching Chriſtianity, but of all Religion.

***

The fourth Doctrine.

Iniurious to the miracles of our Sauiour, and of his Apoſtles.

C H A P. V.

r. THE Diſciple is not aboue his Mayſter:
& we may not wonder that a man ſhould
be free with the Apoſtles, if he ſpare not
Chriſt himſelfe. To the end that the entrance might
be proportionable to the building which he was rai-
ſing, he plants in his Preface a Tenet, which cannot
but be as ſtrange to all conſiderate Chriſtians, as it is
dangerous to the weake. It ſeemes he was not able to
deny, that true miracles haue been wrought by members of our Catholicke Church : He comes therefore
to this deſperate euaſion, and giues vs theſe wordes
(a) Pref. in print : *(a) It ſeemes to me no ſtrange thing, that God*
P. 43. *in his Iuſtice ſhould permit ſome true miracles to be wrought*
to delude them who haue forged ſo many, as apparently the
Profeſſours of the Roman doctrine haue to abuſe the world.

I ſhall

I ſhall wrong the Readers vnderſtanding, if for his
ſake I ſhall ſtand to dilate vpon that, which is very
cleer; that by this meanes the miracles of our Bleſſed
Sauiour, and his Apoſtles cannot be knowne to be
inducements to truth, but may haue been ſnares to
entrap the behoulders in pernicious errours. To
what end then doth *S. Paul* prooue his miſſion by miracles? (b) *Signa Apoſtolatus mei facta ſunt ſuper vos, in* (b) *2.Cor.*
omni prudentia, in ſignis, & prodigijs & virtutibus. To *12.12.*
what end did our Bleſſed Sauiour aſſigne miracles, to
confirme the preaching of his Apoſtles? *Signa autem*
eos, qui crediderint, hæc ſequentur: In nomine meo dæmo-
nia eijcient &c. (c). To what purpoſe did he ſend this (c) *Marc.*
meſſage to *S. Iohn Baptiſt, Cæci vident, claudi ambulant* *vlt.v. 17.*
(d)? To what end did he ſay (e) *ſi opera non feciſſem in* (d) *Mat.*
eis, quæ nemo alius fecit, peccatum non haberent? *11.*
  2. Many other texts might be alledged. Theſe (e) *Ioan.*
will ſatisfy euery good Chriſtian that belieues the *15.24.*
Scriptures. But I confeſſe, neither theſe or any other
places of Scripture can prooue any thing with this
man, who by affirming that true miracles may be
wrought to delude men, doth depriue the Apoſtles
of all authority which they could gayne by working
miracles, and conſequently leaues men free from any
obligation to belieue that their writings were infallible. And then to what purpoſe doth he tel vs in the
ſame place, that the Bible hath byn *confirmed with thoſe*
miracles, which were wrought by our Sauiour Chriſt and his
Apoſtles, ſince thoſe very miracles might by the ſame
ground, be deluſions rather then confirmations? If
true miracles may now be wrought in puniſhment
of Chriſtians for forging falſe miracles, as you pretend;

tend; what certainty can you giue a man that our Sauiour & his Apoſtles did not the like, in puniſhment
of the Iewes and Gentils for Idolatry, Irreligiouſneſſe
and other grieuous ſinnes, which are neuer wanting
in the world, and may be puniſhed in the manner
you ſpeake of, if once this aſſertion be admitted, that
True miracles may be wrought to delude men?

   3. But though by this impiety you depriue Scripture of all authority, and cannot conſequently be
perſuaded to any thing by Scripture: yet there remaines one powerfull authority to conuince you euen in
this your tenet. It is your ſelfe. For thus you ſpeake
to vs vpon another occaſion : *(f) If you be ſo infallible,*

(f) Pag.
144. n.31.

as the Apoſtles were, ſhew it as the Apoſtles did. They went
forth (ſayth S. Marke *) and preached euery where, the*
Lord working with them, and confirming their words with
ſignes following. It is impoſsible that God ſhould lye, & that
the eternall Truth ſhould ſet his hand and ſeale to the con-
firmation of a falſhood, or of ſuch doctrine, as is partly true
and partly falſe. The Apoſtles doctrine was thus confirmed,
therefore it was intirely true, and in no part either falſe or
vncertaine. Is it not cleere by theſe words that ſince
the Doctrine of the Roman Church hath byn confirmed by true miracles (as you affirmed in your
Motiue, and for ought I can perceiue, deny it not in
your anſwere) ſhe muſt be the true Church ? For
euen againſt your ſelfe, when you ſpeake not in oppoſition to the Roman Church, you confeſſe that the
eternall Truth cannot confirme a falſhood with true
miracles. Or if in oppoſition to our Church you will
recall what you deliuer in your Booke, and be con-
ſtãt to that which you ſay in your Preface in anſwere

to

to your *Motiue*; I muſt ſtill be enforced to affirme that you prepare a way to the ouerthrow of Chriſtianity, by euacuating the efficacy of miracles wrought by Chriſt our Lord, his Apoſtles, and all holy men, in confirmation of Chriſtian Religion.

4. And to the end the Reader may not thinke I am too rigorous in preſſing you vpon this one paſſage, vpon which you were thruſt by a hard neceſſity of anſwering your owne motiues; I challenge you vpon this other wherein you ſay: *(g) For my part I profeſſe, that if the Doctrine of the Scripture were not as good, and as fit to come from the fountaine of goodneſſe, as the miracles by which it was confirmed were great, I should want one maine pillar of my Fayth, and for want of it, I feare should be much ſtaggered in it.* Catholickes are moſt certaine that the doctrine of the Scripture is as good, as the miracles by which it was confirmed were great. But this certainty we do not ground vpon our owne Knowledge or Iudgment, framed by conſidering the Doctrines in themſelues, as if we ſhould *be ſtaggered* if we could not find them to be ſuch independently of miracles; but, becauſe they are confirmed by miracles, or otherwiſe teſtifyed to be good, by them, to whom we muſt ſubmit: whereas your way of beliefe leaues a man in a diſpoſition to be perpetually altering opinions, accordingly as the ſame things may ſometimes appeare true, and other times falſe; which diuerſity of iudgments you muſt according to this your doctrine follow, euen againſt any point confirmed by miracles, if it chance to ſeeme not true to your vnderſtanding, which is the part and proper diſpoſition of a *Socinian*.

(g) Pag. 69. n. 47.

The

The fifth Doctrine.

By resoluing Fayth into Reason , he destroyes the nature of Fayth and beliefe of all Christian verityes.

C H A P. V I.

1. THe source whence all the aforesaid and in-numerable other pernicious sequels do fol-low, Gentle Reader, is , that according to this mans doctrine, *Christian Fayth* must be resolued into the euidence of naturall *reason,* not as preparing or inducing vs to belieue, but as the maine ground, & strongest pillar of our Fayth , and in a word, as the conclusion depends on the premises. And to this pur-pose he builds much vpon this axiome: *(h) We cannot possibly be more certaine of the conclusion, then of the wea-ker of the premises; as a riuer will not rise higher then the fountaine from which it flowes.* Hence in the same place he deduceth that the certainty of Christian *Fayth* can be but *morall,* and not absolutely *infallible .* With this principle is connexed another , vnlesse you will call it the same more expressely declared and applyed. And it is this : If vpon reasons seeming to my vnder-standing very good, I haue made choyce of a Guide or Rule for my direction in matters of Fayth; when afterward I discouer that this Guide or Rule leades me to belieue one or more points , which in the best iudgment that I can frame, I haue stronger reasons to

(h) Pag. 36.n.8.

reiect,

reiect, then I had to accept my former Rule; I may and ought to forſake that Rule as falſe & erroneous: otherwiſe I ſhould be conuinced not to follow reaſon, but ſome ſetled reſolution to hold faſt whatſoeuer I had once apprehended. What followes from this vaſt principle, but that if holy Scripture (for example) propound things ſeeming more euidently cōtrary to reaſon, or my opinion, more plainly contradicting one another, then the inducements which firſt mooued me to belieue Scripture were ſtrong & conuincing; I muſt reiect the Scripture, as an erroneous Rule, and adhere to my owne Reaſon and diſcourſe as my laſt and ſafeſt guide. This certainly doth follow. Eſpecially if we remember another principle that the motiues, for which we belieue holy Scripture, are only probable, for ſo they muſt in all equity giue place to reaſons ſeeming demonſtratiue & conuincing, as there will not want many ſuch againſt the high miſteries of Chriſtian Fayth, if once we profeſſe that our aſſent to them muſt be reſolued into naturall diſcourſe. How farre diſſonant this is from the receiued perſuaſion and tenet of all Chriſtians, that their Fayth is not reſolued into Reaſon but Authority, it is eaſy to ſee by the effects. For why do *Socinians* and ſuch like deny the miſteryes of the Bleſſed Trinity, the Deity of our Bleſſed Sauiour, and diuers other verityes of Chriſtian Fayth, but becauſe they ſeeme manifeſtly repugnant to reaſon?

2. It cannot be doubted but that any one to whom the ſaluation of his owne ſoule is deare, will be wary in admitting doctrines deliuered in a Booke, if with Truth it may be affirmed, that the Author in point of

G 2   be-

beliefe is certainly no good Chriſtian, as one who
denyes the Diuinity of Chriſt our Lord, and the moſt
Bleſſed Trinity, which are miſteryes moſt proper to
Chriſtian Fayth, and moſt hatefull to Iewes and
Turkes. For what authority can he challenge with
any iudicious Chriſtian, in matters concerning
Fayth, who confeſſedly erres in the prime articles of
Chriſtian Fayth? as we feare euen a ſound man, if we
thinke he come from the peſt-houſe; and none will
truſt the Diuell though transfigured into an Angell
of light. For which cauſe ſpirituall men bid vs examine, not only what motions we find in our ſoule,
but alſo from what roote they proceed.

3. I wil not take vpō me to ſay what you are, or what
you are not, but in matters cōcerning articles of fayth
(i) *Præ-
fat. n. 5.* we ought to ſpeak plainly. You tell vs (i) that you belieue *the Doctrine of the Trinity, the Deity of our Sauiour,
and all other ſupernaturall veritye reuealed in Scripture.*
The queſtion is not, whether you belieue ſome kind
of Trinity, nor whether our Sauiour be God in ſome
ſenſe by participation, as Dauid ſayes, *I haue ſaid, you
are Gods* (*Pſal.* 81. 6.) and in that ſenſe that they are
contayned in Scripture: But the queſtion is whether
you belieue thoſe miſteryes, as they are generally belieued by Chriſtians, and expreſſed euen in the 39.
Articles of the Engliſh Church: or whether you belieue that in this ſenſe they are reuealed in Scripture.
Be pleaſed then to declare your ſelfe, whether you belieue, that *in the Godhead there be three Perſons of one
ſubstance, Power, and Eternity, the Father, the Sonne, and
the Holy Ghoſt, as is taught in the firſt article* And then
whether you belieue the *ſecond Article,* wherein is
ſaid:

ſaid : *The Sonne which is the word of the Father, the very
and eternall God of one ſubſtance with the Father, tooke
mans nature in the wombe of the Bleſsed Virgin, of her ſubſtance: So that two whole and perfect natures, that is to ſay,
the Godhead and Manhood were ioyned togeather in one
Perſon neuer to be deuided, whereof is one Chriſt very God,
and very Man.* Thirdly, whether you firmely belieue
the contents of the fifth *Article: The holy Ghoſt procce-
ding from the Father and the ſonne, is of one ſubſtance, Maieſty, and Glory with the Father and the ſonne, very eternall
God.* If theſe demaunds ſeeme harſh, blame your ſelfe
who were forewarned, euen before that which they
call the *Direction* was publiſhed, when it was in your
power to haue freed your ſelfe from this trouble, and
ſecured others from the ſcandall which your Booke
may giue. Neither are theſe queſtions from the matter, but conſequent to principles deliuered in your
Booke.

4. And let no man wonder, that I deſire plaine dealing. For I haue ſeene a *Socinian* Catechiſme in print,
which at firſt grants that Chriſt is God, but then to
the queſtion, whether he haue the *diuine Nature*, it anſwers, No: becauſe (forſooth) that is a thing repugnant both to Scripture and Reaſon. It is apparent
that the *Socinians* agree with the *Manicheans*, that
Fayth is reſolued into *Reaſon,* and that the *Manicheans*
maintained a moſt ſtrict brotherhood with the *Priſ-
cillianiſts,* who taught that it is lawfull to diſſemble a
mans Fayth euen by oath : For their ſaying was, *Iu-
ra, periura, ſecretum prodere noli.* And *Arius,* who denied the Diuinity of our Sauiour Chriſt, made no bo-
nes to forſweare himſelfe by a profeſsion of Fayth,

con-

contrary to his internall beliefe. And whether any one who is eſteemed a *Socinian* do not hold it lawfull to deny, or ſpeake ambiguouſly againſt what he be-lieues, that ſo in a very peruerſe ſenſe he may with the Apoſtle, *become all to all*, it is likely you know better then another can tell you .

5. Howſoeuer, euery one doth now expect, that both for theſe and other manifeſt errours mentioned in that litle Booke of Direction , you openly declare your ſelfe : it being not ſufficient to ſay, as you do, in a generall confuſed manner, (k) *Whoſoeuer teaches , or holdes them, let him be Anathema.*For this vniuerſality or collection of errours, in a confuſed ſort, leaues an euaſion to make good your ſpeach, if you reiect but any one of thoſe errours, though withall you imbrace the reſt. And therefore to acquit your credit, and to take away ſcandal , it were your part to renounce ech one in particular. For if in any occaſion, certain-ly in this, ſilence ought to be interpreted a confeſsion of the ſaid errours. *S.Hierome* is of this mind, when he ſayes, (l) *Nolo in ſuſpicione Hæreſeos quemquam eſse pa-tientem, ne apud eos, qui ignorant innocentiam eius, diſſi-mulatio conſcientia iudicetur, ſi taceat.*If you be not guil-ty , I do you a ſingular fauour , in giuing you this fayre and fit occaſion, to wipe of that publicke ſtaine which report hath caſt on you, and wherof you haue not only giuen too great occaſion by your owne words in frequent Conferences, but now by your writings, which being publiſhed after the *Direction*, demonſtrates how deeply *Socinian* errours are rooted both in your iudgment & affection, which could not be abated, either by priuate aduiſe, or publicke ad-monition. 6. But

(k) *Pref.* *n. 28.*

(l) *Ep.* *75. adu.* *Vigilan-* *tium.*

6. But to returne from this neceſſary digreſsion; This your reſoluing Fayth into naturall Reaſon giues occaſion for others at leaſt, if your ſelfe be guilt-leſſe, to deny the Diuinity of our Sauiour Chriſt, and conſequently to deny that he redeemed mankind by his Death; which if he be not true God, had beene (O blaſphemy!) not a price for our Redemption, but a puniſhment rather of his either vſurping the name of the true Sonne of God, or at leaſt for giuing men cauſe to belieue he did ſo. Theſe I grant are harſh inferences, and yet you cannot auoyd them, ſo long as you limit Chriſtian Fayth to probabilities, and reſolue theſe into naturall diſcourſe, as the *concluſion* into the *premiſes.* And giue me leaue to ſay, you do but diſſemble to circumuent an vnwary Reader, when you ſay, (m) that you ſubmit *all other reaſons to this one. God hath ſaid ſo : Therefore it is true.* For you con- (m) *Pref.* ceale the maine point, which is, that you cannot *n. 12.* know, that *God hath ſaid ſo,* except by motiues of credibility, which can produce only a probable aſſent; and this muſt yield to the contrary, if it ſeeme euident by conuincing arguments, as *Socinians* conceiue their reaſons againſt the Bleſſed Trinity, and the Deity of our Sauiour Chriſt, to be. The like I ſay of other high miſteryes of Chriſtian Fayth; and ſtill muſt conclude, that vnder colour of vpholding your cauſe you ouerthrow Chriſtianity.

The

The ſixth Doctrine.

Deſtructiue of the Theologicall Vertues of Chriſtian Hope, and Charity .

C H A P.   V I I.

1. THe grounds which he hath layd for the o-
uerthrow of *Chriſtian Fayth*, doe by conſequence ouerthrowe alſo Chriſtian *Hope*,
and *Charity*, and bring them downe to the ranke of
ordinary *Morall* vertues. But not content with this,
he hath other paſſages, in which he ſtrikes more neere
the roote, and deliuers doctrines which tend imme·
diatly to the deſtruction of them. *It is*, ſayth he, (n)
*againſt reaſon and experience, that by the commiſsion of any
deadly ſinne, the Habit of Charity is quite extirpated*. Reaſon and experience are his Guides, you ſee, in all the
moſt ſupernaturall buſineſſes of our ſoules. Reaſon
and experience, as it ſeemes, do tell him, that euen
when he is committing a mortall ſinne, that is, in-
fringing the commaundment of God in a matter of
weight and moment, and in effect ſaying, I will not
ſerue him; he is notwithſtanding in Chriſtian *Charity*
with him, and his *humble ſeruant*. Chriſtian *Charity*, as
all Chriſtians are taught, is a ſupernaturall infuſed
Habit, whereby we doe loue and preferre God before
all things, and are habitually inclined to it. When
we do not preferre him before all things, but turne
our ſelues to Creatures by ſome ouerweening affection

(n)*Pag*. 368.

&ion to them, that act of commifsion or omifsion, if
it be as I faid Mortall, is not only to be confidered as
an Act, but as an Act killing the foule, and bereauing
it of the life thereof, that is of *Charity*, whereby only
we liue in God: and confequently the Infufed Habit
of *Charity* ceafeth in vs : howfoeuer we may find by
experience fome inclination ftill to loue God, either
by fome repetition of former acts of our owne, or
rayfed by fome confideration reprefented to vs.

2. This is the doctrine receiued amongft Chriftians,
which I do not now vndertake to difpute, and declare at large, but referue it for a larger worke; my intent in this being only to point out the heades from
whence very ill confequences muft needes follow,
that people may take heed of them, and not be too
greedy of fuch nouelties, leaft togeather with them
they fucke their euerlafting bane. For to goe no further, to what paffe would this one doctrine bring a
Commonwealth or Kingdome if it were receaued?
Certainly to all licentioufneffe and liberty. For if
deadly finne may confift with the Habit of Charity,
much more with the Habit of *Fayth* and *Hope*. And it
being certain amõg Chriftians, that God will damne
no man in whofe foule he beholds the precious gem-
mes of thefe three Theologicall vertues *Fayth, Hope,*
and *Charity*; it will be concluded, that deadly finne
vnrepented cannot exclude a man from Heauen. An
errour moft pernicious, and to be banifhed the
thoughts of euery Chriftian Man.

3. For the vertue of *Hope*, if I vnderftand him right,
he fometimes deftroyes it by *Prefumption* with ouer-
much largeneffe, and fometimes turnes it to *Defpera-*

H   *tion*

tion by denying ſinners a poſſibility to be ſaued, euen with the beſt repentãce that they can haue. In proofe of too much largeneſſe it will be ſufficient to alleadge words, wherin he ſpeakes thus to Catholicks: (o) *This pretenſe of yours, that Contrition will ſerue without actuall Confeſſion, but Attrition will not, is a nicety, or phanſy, or rather, to giue it the true name, a deuiſe of your owne to ſerue ends and purpoſes; God hauing no where declared himſelfe, but that whereſoeuer he will accept of that repentance which you are pleaſed to call Contrition, he will accept of that which you call Attrition. For though he like beſt the bright-flaming Holocauſt of Loue, yet he reiects not the ſmoaking flame of that repentance (if it be true and effectuall) which proceeds from Hope and Feare.* Heere he is very large, and againſt all good Diuinity will needes haue an Act proceeding from *Hope* or Feare, to be a ſufficient and proportionable diſpoſition to the nobleſt of the three Theologicall vertues *Charity.* Among Proteſtant Deuines there want not ſome who are ſo farre from belieuing, that ſorrow ariſing from *Feare* of Hell, is ſufficient for remiſſion of ſinnes, that they hold it rather to be a ſinnefull Act.

(o) *Pag.* 32.

4. But neither in this doe I intend for the preſent to enter into long diſputation, and therefore goe forward to ſhew that in other places of his Booke, he is as ſtrict. For he calls (p) *it a doctrine of Licentiouſneſſe, that though a man liue and dye without the practiſe of Chriſtian vertues, and with the Habits of many damnable ſinnes vnmortified, yet, if he in the laſt moment of his life, haue any ſorrow for his ſinnes, and ioyne confeſſion with it, certainly he ſhall be ſaued.* I ſee not how this agrees with his former doctrine, that *Attrition,* and not only *Contrition*

(p) *Pag.* 292.

trition, is fufficient for remiffion of finnes. It is his part to reconcile and vindicate from contradiction his owne affertions. For me it is fufficient that euery body may be apt inough to inferre from hence, that by this meanes a poore finner muft defpayre, though he haue euen *Contrition* of his finnes. For in thofe cir-cumftances, he hath no tyme *for the practife of Chri-stian vertues,* nor for the mortifying *the habits of many damnable finnes,* if he meane the acquired phyficall ha-bits of vice, produced by former vicious acts, as he muft vnderftand if he meane to fay any thing. For if by Habits of vice he vnderftand Habituall finnes, or finnes remayning not fufficiently retracted by for-row, it is to beg the queftion, as if he fhould fay fuch repentance is infufficient for pardon of our finnes, becaufe it takes not away our finnes.

5. But he does more cleerly declare himfelfe, and caft men vpon defperation, by what he fayes of vs in another place: (q) That although we preted *to be rigid* (q) Pag: *defenders, and flout Champions for the neceffity* of Good 392. *workes,* yet indeed we doe it, *to make our owne fun-ctions neceffary, but obedience to God vnneceffary: which will appeare* (fayth he) *to any man who confiders what strict neceffity the Scripture impofes vpon all men of effe-ctuall mortification of the Habits of all vices, and effectuall conuerfion to newnes of life, and vniuerfall obedience; and withall remembers, that an Act of Attrition, which you fay with Prieftly abfolution is fufficient to faluation, is not mor-tification, which being a worke of difficulty and time, cannot be performed in an instant,* and therefore neither *Attri-tion,* nor *Contrition,* which fignifieth the moft perfect kind of repentance willferue at fuch an exigent. It is

ftrange

ftrange, *Attrition* alone fhould fuffice for pardon of
our finnes, and that it fhould be infufficient when it
is ioyned with abfolution, which I hope you will not
fay, is ill, though you hold it not neceffary. Or if you
meane, that Attrition is fufficient only when there remaines further time for mortification of vicious habits, this anfwere feemes repugnant to your owne
words, where fpeaking of fome kind of men, you fay,
(r) That notwithftanding their errours, *they may dye*
with Contrition, or if not with Cotrition, yet with Attrition,
which, you fay, God will accept. Which fuppofition
of yours feemes either to fpeake of dying men, or at
leaft to comprehend them. And (*pag.* 133.) you teach
that for thofe men that haue meanes to find the Truth
and will not vfe them, though their cafe be daungerous, yet if they dye *with a generall repentance for all*
their finnes knowne and vnknowne, their Saluation is not
defperate. Where you feeme alfo to fpeake of men at
the houre of their Death, when yet they haue not
time to mortify the habits of vice. And indeed it is
repugnant to Reafon, that by Attrition a mans finnes
fhould be forgiuen, and yet this forgiueneffe depend
on the future performance of mortification, which
you fay requires time. Howfoeuer, for my purpofe it
is fufficient, that by denying poffibility of forgiueneffe to a repentant finner, at the laft inftant of his
life, you vncharitably caft men on defperation, and
deftroy the *Hope*, yea and *Fayth* of Chriftians, which
affures vs, that forgiueneffe is neuer denied to any
that repents.

6. But there remaines yet a more daungerours errour, that one may be faued with a generall repentance

(r) *Pag.*
32.

tance for his finnes, euen while he actually continues in them . This, vnleffe I miftake, is implyed in the words which I cited euen now(s),that for thofe who *(s) Pag.* *haue meanes to find the truth and will not vfe them, if they* 133. *dye with a generall repentance for all their finnes knowne and vnknown , their faluation is not defperate.* Where you fuppofe , that a man remaines in a culpable errour, & yet that a generall repentance may obtaine pardon without actuall dereliction of it. For if he forfake his errour, he is out of your cafe, which fpeakes *of men that haue meanes to find the Truth, and will not vfe them .* A very eafy pillow if it could be fowed vnder any vnderftanding eare. For if fuch a generall repentan- ce would fuffice at the houre of death, it would alfo be fufficient at other times , and confequently one might haue pardon of his finnes whilft he is actually committing them . Or if this be not the meaning of that paffage, it wil notwithftanding be true, that ei- ther forrow is fufficient to obtaine pardon for finnes, when there remaines no time to mortify the habits of vice , which is againft your Tenet; or elfe that a finner cannot obtaine pardon at the hower of his Death, euen with repentance.

The

The ſeauenth Doctrine.

Takes away the grounds of rationall diſcourſe.

CHAP. VIII.

1. **I**T may ſeeme ſtrange, that a man ſhould reſolue *Chriſtian Fayth* into *naturall Reaſon* , and yet fall vpon a way which deſtroyes all diſcourſe of *Reaſon* . But to theſe exigents human Vnderſtanding is brought, when it forſakes the ground of *Chriſtianity.* He teacheth, and endeauoureth to prooue *(t)* by no fewer then ſeauen reaſons, that it is poſſible to aſſent to contradictions at the ſelfe ſame time . If a man wil ſpeake in this to the purpoſe, he muſt vnderſtand of formall and direct contradictions; for example, Chriſt is the Sauiour of the world : Chriſt is not the Sauiour of the world. Whereof to haue put thee in mind, good Reader, ſhall ſuffice at this preſent, according to the breuity which in this diſcourſe I haue propoſed to my ſelfe , not doubting but thou wilt vpon this reflection and thyne owne examination find that all his ſeauen arguments, are very weake, and ſo farre from proouing his Aſſertion, that all of them, not one excepted, ſhew directly the contrary of that which he intended, notwithſtāding that as it ſeemes of purpoſe he tooke this ſubiect in taske to ſhew ſome ſtraine of wit , and to purchaſe ſome opinion of knowledge in Metaphyſicke .

2. How it hath thriued in his hand, tyme may ſhew
in

(t) P*ag.* 215. *&* 217. *n.* 47.

in some other treatise.Where also perhaps some other
subtiltyes or quircks will be sifted: to wit, first, Whether *Fayth* be properly *Knowledge* or *Apprehension* (v) , (v) *Pag.*
for he mightily mistakes in Philosophy . Secondly, 325. *n.* 2.
Whether *obscure* and *euident* be *affections not of our af-*
sent, but of the obiect of it (w); which were a strange (w) *Pag.*
kind of Philosophy, as if we should say, *God in him-* 328.
selfe is *obscure* and *euident*, because some vnderstand
him with an *obscure*, and others with a *cleere* or *euident*
assent. Thirdly, his discourse *(pag.* 69. *n.* 48. *)* about
the eye, obiect, and act of Seeing, with the proportion which he would make betweene them , and the
obiect and act of Fayth, which must fall vpon an heresy condemned in the Pelagians, besides some mistakes in Philosophy. Fourthly, another subtilty about
the essence of Habits , and formall motiue, to any
Act &c. whereof he speakes *pag.* 138. *n.* 24. and does
after his manner mistake. Then also it shalbe shewed
with how little reason he despises (x) the distinction (x) *Pag.*
of being obliged not to disbelieue, and of not being 195. *n.* 11.
obliged explicitly to belieue ; and with as litle declai-
mes bitterly *(pag.* 391. *n.* 8. *)* against the doctrine
that some things are necessary because they are commaunded, and others commaunded because they are
necessary. And finally, the Reader must not be depriued at that time of the recreation he will receiue by
a speciall subtilty indeed , about a saying in Charity
maintayned, *That the Creed was an abridgment* (y). Ma- (y) *Pag.*
ny more of the like nature will be then brought to 227. *n.* 65.
the touchstone, and layd as flat, as now perhaps to
some partiall men they may haue seemed lofty and
learned. My purpose here is only to giue the Reader
                                                warning

warning,that there be in the current of his diſcourſe
ſuch ſhelues,as by croſſing the general receiued principles among Chriſtians, deſtroy *Fayth*, and recipro-
cally by the ouerthrow of *Fayth*, come at length to
ouerwhelme Reaſon it ſelfe.

The eight Doctrine.

*Opens a way to deny the B. Trinity , and other
high miſteryes of Chriſtian Fayth .*

CHAP. IX.

1. I Cannot omit notwithſtanding here to ſhew,
that one of the Reaſons which he brings to
prooue, that one may at the ſelfe ſame tyme,
yield aſſent to contradictories , muſt be ranked a-
mongſt the reſt of his Doctrins, which do cleerly tend
to the ouerthrow of Chriſtianity . It is the third reaſon wherin he argues thus :(z) *They which do capti-*
(z) *Pag.* 215. *uate their vnderſtandings to the beliefe of thoſe things ,
which to their vnderſtandings ſeeme irreconciliable contradictions, may as well belieue reall contradictions (for the
difficulty of belieuing ariſes not from their being repugnāt ,
but from their ſeeming to be ſo .) But yen (he ſpeakes to
vs Catholicks)do captiuate your vnderſtandings to the
beliefe of thoſe things, which ſeeme to your vnderſtandings
irreconciliable contradictions. Therefore it is as poſsible, &
eaſy for you to belieue thoſe that indeed are ſo .* Change
but a word , and inſteed of *Catholicks,* put *Chriſtians ,*
and the Concluſion will be : Therefore *it is as poſsi-*
ble

ble, and eaſy for Chriſtians to belieue contradictions *that indeed are ſo,* as to belieue thoſe which to their vn-derſtanding *ſeeme ſo.* And ſeeing it is the common conceit of men, that one cannot at the ſame time be-lieue contradictions; and he himſelfe acknowledges in the ſame place, (a) that men ſhould not do ſo, and (a) *Pag.* that to do ſo, is both *vnreaſonable* and very *difficult;* 217. *n.* what will follow but that to belieue the higheſt my- 47. ſteryes of Chriſtian Fayth, is, if not *impoſsible,* at leaſt *very difficult,* and *vnreaſonable,* and a thing that men ſhould not doe.

2. Now that Chriſtians belieue myſteries which to human reaſon ſeeme to imply contradiction, he him-ſelfe will not deny. For though all the myſteryes of Chriſtian Fayth be in themſelues moſt ſacred & true, yet to the weake eye of human reaſon ſome of them ſeeme to be againſt the Goodneſſe of God : as that, *Many are called,* and *few elected,* it being in his power to haue *elected,* and preuented with congruous & ef-ficacious Grace, as well thoſe many, as theſe few. And our vnderſtäding is apt to be the more ſtaggard with the depth of this myſtery, by conſidering that Chriſt our Lord dyed for the ſaluation of all; and that euery thought, word, or worke of his was ſuperabundant-ly ſufficient for the Redemption of infinite millions of worlds. Other points of Chriſtian Fayth appeare contrary to Gods infinite Mercy, and Iuſtice. Such is our beliefe, that for euery deadly ſinne committed in a moment, and perhaps in a matter ſeeming but a trifle, as the eating of an apple, he ſhould inflict an eternity of torments, if it be not repented. Or, that Infants can be iuſtly depriued of Beatitude in puniſh-

I   ment

ment of Originall ſinne, to which they neuer concurred by any Act properly theirs. And it might haue been to good purpoſe, if this man had declared himſelfe directly in theſe two points, ſeeing he was not without good ground *directed* to doe ſo.

3. But I goe on with the difficulty of Chriſtian verities. For as the former may ſeeme harſh and rigorous, ſo others may ſeeme, as it were, ſilly, & *vnreaſonable* if Fayth be reſolued, as this man will haue it, into human *Reaſon*. Others beare a ſhew of repugnance to the moſt receiued Principles of Philoſophy, and Metaphyſicke, as the Myſtery of the moſt Bleſſed Trinity. Others in appearance derogate from the ſupreme reſpect we owe to God, as the myſtery of the Incarnation and Death of the ſonne of God. Where I cannot but obſerue, that this man ſpeakes ſo irreligiouſly ſometimes, that it may giue iuſt occaſion for men to enquire what he belieues concerning the Diuinity of our Sauiour Chriſt, as when he ſayth; (b)
(b) *Pref.*
n. 8. *that the Doctrine of Tranſubſtantiation may bring a great many others, as well, as himſelfe to Auerroes his reſolution:* *Quandoquidem Chriſtiani adorant quod comedunt, ſit anima mea cum Philoſophis:* *ſeeing Chriſtians adore what they eate, my ſoule be with the Philoſophers.* Is this matter of eating our Sauiour ſuch a pill to your vnderſtanding, that rather then diſgeſt it you will turne Turke or Infidell? If you belieued indeed that our Sauiour Chriſt is truly God, you would not be ſcandalized that Chriſtians adore Him, who would and could be eaten, no more then Him who ſtood in need of *eating*, and whom the Iewes were able to wound and murder, and might *haue eaten* (euen in a Capharnaiticall

eall ſauage manner, farre different from the manner we receiue him in the B. Sacrament) if it had
beene his will to permit it. Perhaps for theſe reaſons,
hauing ſubiected Fayth to Reaſon, you wiſh with
Auerroes, a profeſſed enemy of Chriſtians, *My ſoule
be with the Philoſophers*.

4. He giues another ſuſpicion of it in the paſſage
following. For hauing alleadged diuers ſeeming contradictions in our Doctrine concerning the Bleſſed
Sacrament of the Altar, he concludes, *(c)* that if I (c) *Pag.*
(that is the Author of Charity Maintayned) *cannot* 216.217.
*compoſe the repugnance, and that after an intelligible man-
ner, then I muſt giue him leaue to belieue, that either we do
not belieue Tranſubſtantiation, or els that it is no contradiction, that men ſhould ſubiugate their vnderſtandings to the
beliefe of contradictions*; which yet, as I ſaid before, he
iudgeth either *impoſsible*, or at leaſt *vnreaſonable (*d*)* . (d) *Ibid.*
And who I pray, can vndertake againſt a cauilling
wit, to anſwere all arguments obiected againſt the
Bleſſed Trinity, Incarnation, and other ſublime verityes of Chriſtian Fayth, and *compoſe* all ſeeming *repugnances after an intelligible manner?* Deuines are not
ignorant, what inexplicable difficulties offer themſelues, euen concerning the Deity it ſelfe, for example, his Immutability, Freedom of will, voluntary decrees, knowledge of creatures, and the like. Muſt we
then deny them, becauſe we are not able *to compoſe all
repugnances* after *an intelligible manner?* It may ſeeme
that you are of opinion that we muſt; to which perſuaſion if you adde another Doctrine of yours, That
there is no Chriſtian Church aſſiſted with Infallibility fit to teach any man, euen ſuch articles as are fun-
damen-

damentall, or neceſſary to ſaluation, but that euery one may, and muſt follow the Dictates of his owne reaſon, be he otherwiſe neuer ſo vnlearned: what wil follow, but a miſerable freedome, or rather necefſity for men to reiect the higheſt, and moſt diuine miſteries of Chriſtian Fayth, vnleſſe you can either *compoſe all repugnances after a manner*, euen *intelligible* to euery ignorant and ſimple perſon (which I hope you will confeſſe to be impoſſible) or els ſay, it is *reaſonable* for men to belieue contradictions at the ſame time, which by your confeſſion were very *vnreaſonable*.

5. And here I appeale to your owne Conſcience, whether in true Philoſophy, the obiections which may be made againſt the myſtery of the Bleſſed Trinity, and the Incarnation of the ſonne of God, be not incomparably more difficult, then any which can be brought againſt Traſubſtantiation. Some one whom you know could ſay in ſome company, where there was occaſion of arguing, *Either deny the Trinity, or admit of Tranſubſtantiation*; and it was anſwered, *We will rather admit this, then deny that*. And with good reaſon. For if we reſpect human diſcourſe, there are more difficult obiections againſt that miſtery, then againſt this. And if we regard Reuelation, Scripture is more cleare for the reall preſence, and Tranſubſtantiation, then for the myſtery of the Bleſſed Trinity. But no wonder if they who reduce all certainty of Chriſtian Fayth to the weight of naturall reaſon, are well content vnder the name of Tranſubſtantiation, to vndermine the doctrine of the Bleſſed Trinity, and all the prime verityes proper to Chriſtian Fayth. For which

which cauſe I haue ſome reaſon, as I touched before,
(d) not to be ſatisfyed, that this man for all his brag- (d)*Chap.*
ges of belieuing Scripture, doth make that account *6.n.6.*
of it which Chriſtians doe, and ought to doe, but de-
ludes the Reader with ſpecious words : as for example, when ſpeaking of the holy Scripture he ſayes:(e) (e) *Pag.*
Propoſe me any thing out of this Booke and require whether 376.
*I belieue it or not, and ſeeme it neuer ſo incomprehenſible to
human reaſon, I will ſubſcribe it with hand and hart, as
knowing no demonſtration can be ſtronger then this : God
hath ſaid ſo : Therefore it is true .* Theſe are glorious
words, but contrary to his owne principles. For reſoluing Fayth into Reaſon, he cannot belieue that
which to his reaſon ſeemes contradictory, but muſt
thinke that the Motiues for which he receiues Scripture being but probable, and ſubiect to falſhood, muſt
of neceſſity yield to arguments more then probable,
and demonſtratiue to human reaſon. And how then
can he ſubſcribe to Myſteryes *incomprehenſible to human reaſon,* and capable of obiections which cannot
alwayes be anſwered, *after a manner intelligible,* as he
requires? And conſequently he *muſt,* to vſe his owne
words, *giue me leaue to belieue, that either he doth not belieue* thoſe miſteryes, *or els,* that he *ſubiugates his vnderſtanding to the beliefe of ſeeming contradictions,* which
he acknowledges to be *vnreaſonable,* and a thing
which *men ſhould not doe,* according to his owne
words (f). And the Reader had need to take heed (f)*Pag.*
that he be not taken alſo with that proteſtation of ²¹⁷.
his : (g) *I know no demonſtration can be ſtronger then* (g) *Pag.*
this ; God hath ſaid ſo : Therefore it is true : ſince he tea- *376 ;*
ches, that he knowes not that God hath ſaid ſo, other-

wiſe

wiſe then by probable inducements, and only by a probable aſſent. So that in fine this muſt be his *ſtrong demonſtration :* Whatſoeuer God ſpeakes or reueales, is moſt certainly true *:* But I am not certaine, that God ſpeakes in the Scripture *:* Therefore I am certaine that whatſoeuer is in Scripture is true. Behold his *demonſtration,* that is, a very falſe Syllogiſme, according to his owne diſcourſe in another place where he not only graunts, but endeauours to prooue that the *minor* of this Demonſtration exceedes not probability, and conſequently cannot inferre a concluſion more then probable. Somewhat like to this is another cunning ſpeach of his *:* (h) *That he hartily belieues the Articles of our Fayth be in themſelues Truths, as certaine and infallible, as the very common principles of Geometry, or Metaphyſicke* . Which being vnderſtood of the *Obiects,* or *Truths* of Chriſtian Fayth *in themſelues,* is no priuiledge at all. For euery Truth is in it ſelfe as certaine as the Principles of Geometry, it being abſolutely impoſsible that a Truth can be falſhood. But the point is, that he does not certainely know or belieue theſe Truths, as he does the Principles of Metaphyſicke, but onely with a probable aſſent, and ſo to him the Truths cannot be certaine. The like art alſo he vſes *pag.* 357. ſaying in theſe wordes : *I doe belieue the Goſpell of Chriſt, as verily as that it is now day, that I ſee the light, that I am now writing* ; for all this floriſh ſignifies only, that he is certaine he belieues the Goſpel of Chriſt with probable aſſent. As for the argument, it deſerues no anſwere ; For who knowes not that contradictories inuolue two propoſitions? but he who captiuates his vnderſtanding, aſſents

(h) *Pag.* 225. *n.* 5.

ſents

ſents to one part only, and therefore is ſure inough
not to belieue contradictories at the ſame time, as he
pretends. All which conſidered, the Reader will eaſily
ſee, that his Doctrines vndermine the chiefeſt myſteries of Chriſtian Fayth, and ouerthrow Chriſtianity.

The ninth Doctrine.

Layes grounds to be conſtant in no Religion.

CHAP. X.

1. **I** Said in the beginning, that as we could not
know the way, vnleſſe we firſt be told whither we goe; ſo it could litle auayle vs to be
put in a way, if by following it we might be miſled.
But ſuppoſe the end of our iourney be knowne, and
the right way found, what better ſhall we be, if withall we be continually harkning to ſome ſuggeſtions,
which neuer let vs reſt, till we haue abandoned that
path, by following other croſſe-wayes, as we chance
to fall vpon them. This is the caſe of the man with
whome we haue to deale. I will not build vpon his
deeds, I meane his changes firſt from Proteſtant, to
Catholique, then from Catholique to Proteſtant, &
then about againe to Catholique, till at laſt he be
come to that paſſe, that it is hard to ſay, What he is,
neyther *Preciſian*, nor Subſcriber to the 39. *Articles*,
nor confeſſed *Socinian*, nor right Chriſtian according
to the grounds which he hath layd. If you will belieue himſelfe, for matters of Religion, he is conſtant
in nothing, but in *following that way to heauen which*
for

for the preſent ſeemes to him the moſt probable. He followes that which *at the preſent ſeemes moſt probable*: A
poore comfort in matters of *Fayth*, wherin errour is
of ſo great conſequence. And yet this cold comfort is
vpon the point of being loſt; for the probability is limited to *the preſent.*

2. Would any man thinke that in matters of this
nature, and after ſo much profeſsion that he is
now ſatisfied, he ſhould (i) profeſſe himſelfe, *ſtill
to haue a Trauellers indifferency, moſt willing to be led
by reaſon to any way, or from it?* And accordingly to tell
vs, (k) *That had there been repreſented to his vnderſtanding ſuch Reaſons for our Doctrine, as would haue made our
Religion more credible then the contrary, certainly he ſhould
haue deſpiſed the ſhame of one more alteration, & with both
armes, and all his hart moſt readily haue imbraced it.* Such
*was the preparation which he brought to the reading of that
Booke,* comming with *ſuch a mind to the reading of it, as*
S. *Auſtin before he was a ſetled Catholique, brought to his
conference with Fauſtus the Manichee.* Did S. *Auſtin* after he was a ſetled Catholicke come with the like diſpoſition to conference with any Heretique or misbe-
lieuer? To what purpoſe then doth this man bring S.
Auſtin here, but to ſhew the difference betwixt the
Fayth of one that is a *Catholicke,* and of one that is not;
the difference I ſay in point of *adheſion* to his *Fayth,*
the Catholicke belieuing ſo aſſuredly that he may ſay
with the Apoſtle, *If we, or an Angell from heauen euangelize* (l) *to you beſides that which we haue euangelized to
you, be he Anathema.* Others not being able euer to be
certaine of what they belieue becauſe they build vpon
grounds which by their owne confeſsion are not
ce̶r-

(i) *Pref.*
n. 2.

(k) *Pref.*
n. 1.

(l) *Gal.* 1.
8.

certaine and infallible.

3. In which refpeƈt alfo it may be iuftly wondred with what fenfe this man taking vpon him to be a guide to others, and to leade them a *fafe way* to heauen, profeffeth himfelfe not to be fetled in his way, and ftil to haue not only a (m) *Trauellers*, but an Ig- (m)*Pref.* norant *Trauellers Indifferency*, willing to be *led* to any *n. 2.* way, or from it, becaufe he knowes not whether he be right or wrong; otherwife if he know himfelfe to be right, certainly it were not his part to be fo willing to be led *to any way, or from it*: which giues me hope, that no man of iudgment, and timorous confcience, will aduenture the eternall faluation of his foule, vpon the writings or Doƈtrine of one, who is fo vnfetled, & whom he either knowes not where to find, or how long to keep in any one opinion or profeffion; to whom the words of *S. Bernard (*n) concerning (n) *Ep.* *Petrus Abailardus* (who taught that *Fayth* was but *opi-* 193. *nion)* may be applyed: *Homo fibi difsimilis eft, totus ambiguus. He is a man who difagrees euen from himfelfe, wholely compofed of doubtings.* I leaue out his middle words, *intus Herodes, foris Ioannes.*

4. One thing certainly people would be very glad to know, that whereas he maintaines, that his *Alterations were the moft fatisfaƈtory aƈtions to himfelfe (*o) *that* (o) *Pag.* *euer he did, and the greateft viƈtories that euer he obtained* 303. *ouer himfelfe:* Men, I fay, would be glad to know vpon what new and great Motiues, thefe moft *fatisfaƈtory aƈtions*, & *greateft viƈtoryes* were ouerthrowne againe, and frequent changes grounded. For his firft being Catholicke, we haue Motiues in writing vnder his owne hand, and now in print. But what new reafons

K   mooued

mooued him to forſake vs, this would people willingly know. If he had no better reaſons, then be the anſwers to his owne Motiues, I ſcarcely belieue, that any iudicious Proteſtant will allow the alteration to haue been good, diuers of them being againſt Proteſtants themſelues, and ſome repugnant to all Chriſtianity, as may be well ſeene by the effects, which they haue wrought in him, to wit, ſo much vnſetledneſſe in beliefe and Religion, that he knowes not to this day, what he would be at. But we may well ſuppoſe that as he willingly leaues *all men to their liberty, prouided that they improue it not to a Tyranny ouer others*; ſo he reſerues the like liberty to himſelfe, and is in fine reſolued to belieue *whatſoeuer for the preſent doth ſeeme moſt probable to him:* and ſo liuing in perpetuall Indifferency, be an example to others to be conſtant in no profeſſion, which is as good as to be of no Religion.

The tenth Doctrine.

Prouides for the impunity & preſeruation of whatſoeuer damnable errour againſt Chriſtian Fayth.

CHAP. XI.

1. **H**E is no leſſe prouidēt to conſerue then induſtrious to beget Vnchriſtian errours & Atheiſmes. Suppoſe an Orthodoxe Belieuer fall firſt into damnable Hereſies, then to Turciſme or Iudaiſme, afterward to Paganiſme, and finally to Atheiſme. Let him freely ſpeake his mind to the learned,

ned,and vnlearned,to high and low,to the Laity and
Clergy,to all forts of perfons:Let him haue fwarmes
of followers,let Circumcifion be reduced, the Satur-
day obferued for Sunday with Iewes, or Friday with
the Turkes, and in confirmation of thefe facrileges,
let Bookes be written. What remedy ? Muft thefe
things be tolerated in a Chriftian Commonwealth,or
Kingdome? with refentment of a Chriftian Prince ?
in defpite of Chriftian Prelates? vnder the eyes of
Chriftian Deuines?in the midft of Chriftian people?
They muft be fuffered , if we belieue this mans do-
&rine, *(p)* that no man ought to be punifhed for his
opinions in Religion.*We are willing (* fayth he *) to leaue*
all men to their liberty,prouided they will not improue it to a
Tyrany ouer others (q),a good meanes to preferue euery
one in his liberty without feare of punifhment. *And*
*the contrary perfuafion and praEtife,*what is it ? *It well be-*
comes them who haue their portions in this life,who ferue no
higher ftate then that of England, or Spayne,or France,who
thinke of no other happineffe but the preferuation of their
owne fortunes,and tranquillity in this world, who thinke of
no other meanes to preferue States,but human power & Ma-
chiauillian Policy. How daungerous to Church,& euen
to State this pernicious errour is, and what encoura-
gement it giues for vnquiet perfons to oppofe Authority,and how deepely it taxes England & other Proteftant Churches of *Machiauillian Policy ,* and *to be*
men who haue their portions in this life,who ferue no higher
State then that of England,or Spayne, or France,who thinke
of no other Happines , but the preferuation of their owne
fortunes in this world , for hauing punifhed Heretiques
euen with death, I leaue to be confidered by higher
Powers. K 2 2. I

(p) *Pag.* 297.

(q) *Pag.* 179.*n.*81.

2. I grant he would seeme to mitigate his doctrine, and confine it within certaine limits, but such, that his exception is worse then his generall Rule, vnlesse I mistake his meaning, & therefore present his words as they lye to the Readers iudgment. *There is,* saith he, *no daunger to any State from any mans opinion, vnlesse it be such an opinion, by which disobedience to Authority, or impiety is taught, or licenced; which sort I confesse may iustly be punished, as well as other faults: or vnlesse this sanguinary doctrine be ioyned with it, That its lawful for him by human violence to enforce others to it.* Thus he. As for his first limitation, it either destroyes all that he said before, or els it is but a verball glosse for his owne security. For if he grant that euery Heresy is *impiety,* and brings with it *disobedience* to Authority (as certainly it does, if it be professed against the lawes of the Kingdome, or Decrees and Commaunds of the Church, State, & Prelats where the contrary is maintained:) If, I say, his meaning be this, then his former generall Doctrine vanisheth into nothing; & it will still remaine true, that men may be punished for their opinions & heresyes. But if his meaning be, that no opinion is to be punished, except such as implyes disobedience to Authority, or licenseth Impiety in things which belong meerely to Temporall affayres, and concerne only the ciuill comportment of one man to another, as theft, murther, and the like; then he still leaues a freedome for men to belieue, and professe what they please for matters of Religion. And so, if they iudge a thing to be vnlawfull, which their Superiours affirme to be indifferent, yet they may hold their opinion, and disobey their Prelates, and may be able to

tell

tel them from this mans doctrine, that to enforce any
man in points of this kind, is vnlawfull *Machiauillian Policy.*

3. His second limitation ſeemes to goe further,
telling vs, that a mãs opinion may be puniſhed, if this
*ſanguinary doctrine be ioyned with it, That it is lawfull for
him by human violence to enforce others to it.* Frõ whence, for ought I can perceiue, it cleerly followes, that
if any Church preſcribe ſome forme of Beliefe, and
puniſh others for belieuing and profeſſing the contrary, the Prelats or others of that Church, who cõ-
curre to enforce by puniſhment ſuch contrary belie-
uers, may themſelues be iuſtly puniſhed. As if for
example, an *Arian* be puniſhed with Death in any
Kingdome, the Prelats, or other Perſons of authority in that State, may according to his doctrine be
lawfully puniſhed, as holding it lawfull to enforce
men againſt their conſcience, which he calles a *ſanguinary Doctrine.* How daungerous a poſition this
might prooue, if *Arians,* or *Socinians,* or any other ſect,
or vnquiet ſpirit could preuaile in any Kingdome or
Commonwealth where Hereticks are puniſhed, it is
not fit for me to exaggerate; being ſufficient for my
intention, to haue made it cleere, that the enemy of
mankind could neuer haue inuented a more effectual
meanes then this freedome of opinion, and encou-
ragement by impunity, for theenlarging of his infer-
nall Kingdome by Hereſy, Paganiſme, Atheiſme,
and in a word, by deſtroying whatſoeuer belongs to
Chriſtianity.

4. As for puniſhing Heretiks with Excommunication, in words he grants it may be done; but I haue
K 3 reaſon

reaſon to ſuſpect what his meaning is indeed,&whe-
ther he ſpeake thus only for ſomereſpects.For I know
Iren.Phi-
lal.diſp.
de Pace
*Eccleſ.*that a great *Socinian* hath printed the contrary . And
if no man can be puniſhed with temporall puniſhmēt
for imbracing that which his Conſcienſe perſuades
him to be Truth, how can he be lawfully puniſhed
by Excommunication, for doing that which to his
vnderſtanding he is obliged to do? For not acknow-
ledging any authority of Church, or Prelats indued
with infallibility, he is ſtill left to his owne reaſon.
Beſides one effect of excommunication is to exclude
the Perſon ſo cenſured, from the ciuill conuerſation
with others ; other temporall puniſhments in all
Courts being alſo conſequent to it.Seeing then he denyes that men are to be puniſhed for their opinions
by Temporall puniſhments, he cannot with coherence affirme, that they may lawfully be excommu-
nicated: This certainly being a greater enforcement
then death it ſelfe, to ſuch as vnderſtand the ſpirituall benefits, and aduantages, of which men are depriued by that Cenſure .

The Concluſion.

1. **B**Y *that which hath been ſaid in theſe few prece-*
dent Chapters it euidently appeares; firſt,how fit-
ting it was for the good of our Country in theſe
preſent circuſtances,that people ſhould haue learned by ſome
ſuch Treatiſe as the Direction, *to beware of impious* Do-
ctrines, ſuch as were foreſeene that this mā would vent vn-
der colour of defending the Proteſtant cauſe, and anſwering
Charity maintayned. *And that although nothing could*
be

*be intended more disgracefull to Protestant Religion, then
to see a Champion, & a way chosen to defend it, which openly destroyes all Religion; yet Compassion could not but worke
in a wel-wishing soule, and mooue it to desire, and to endeauour that such a way should not be taken, which might make
people more and more insensible of any Religion, by blurring
the common principles of Christianity, and digging vp the
foundation thereof, to lay insteed of them, the grounds
of Atheisme.*

2. *Secondly though this hath not taken the full effect which
could haue been wished, & that notwithstading the warning
giuen, he hath interlaced his whole booke with such stuffe as
here you haue seene; yet this we haue gotten further, that it
is discouered cleerly to the world, how deeply* Socinianisme
*is rooted in this man, (and, as it is to be feared, in many o-
thers with whome he must needes haue had much conference
since his vndertaking the worke) in regard that no timely
aduise or* Direction, *no force of reason, no feare of shame or
punishment, no former impressions of Christianity could
withdraw him from steeping his thoughts and pen in such
vn-Christian inke; nor the many Corrections endeauoured
by the Approouers of his Booke, blot out his errours, though
in respect of the alterations which haue been by report made
in it by them, it is quite another thing from the first plat-
forme which he drew, and put into their hands; and confequently how iust reason the* Directour *had to suspect, that
his* true intention, was not to defend Protestantisme,
but couertly to vent Socinianisme.

3. *Now, thirdly, whether it be not high time that people
should now at the least open their eyes vpon this second warning, and take that order which may be conuenient to prevent the spreading of so pernicious a Sect, I must leaue to
the*

the conſideration of euery one whome it may concerne . I do only for the preſent wiſh from my hart, that the maintayning of that Bleſſed Title, and State of Chriſtianity *, of which our Countrey hath been for ſo many ages poſſeſſed, may be the effect both of this mans wauering and wandering tra-uells, and of theſe my labours.*

F I N I S.

Errata.

P Ræfat. pag. 10. lin. 25. *toour nation* corrige *of our nation*
   Ibid. pag. *11*. lin. 26. *with* corrige *wish*
   Pag. 32. lin. 3. *is the* corrige *is ſo*
   Ibid. lin. 4. *by ſo* corrige *by the*
   Pag. 53. lin. 21. Chriſt *is God, lege, is the Sonne of God*

   In the margent *pag.* 11. ouer againſt S. Bernard cited *line* 8. put, *Bernard. Epiſt*. 87.

OLIVER ALMOND

*The Life and Gate
of Christianitie*
1614

THE LIFE

AND GATE OF CHRISTIANITIE, EN-TREATING OF THE SA-CRAMENT OF BAPTISME, DE-VIDED INTO FIVE BOOKES.

Contayning the effects, the mater, the forme, the Baptiser, and the partie Baptised: with the reasons and vse of all the auntient rites and Ceremonies.

Wonderful necessarie, duringe these times, to be vnderstood and perused of all sortes of persons.

Composed, gathered, and written by O. A.

Effundam super vos aquam mundam, & munda-bini ab omnibus inquinamentis vestris.
Ezechi. cap. 34.

With permission.
Anno M. DC. XIIII,

THE PREFACE TO
THE CVRTEOVS
READER.

COnfidering with my felfe (Gentle Reader) what should be the principall caufe and moft effectuall motiues, that should vrge the kings maieftie and moft high Court of *Parlament*, to enacte and make that rigorous lawe and penall Statute concerning the *Baptifme* of *Catholikes* Children : *Firft that they should not be Baptifed by their owne Priefts:nor anie Catholike Layman or Mydwife of their Profeßion in Religion : Secondlie that they muft be forced contrarie to their confciences vpon paine of forfeiture of an hundreth pounds,to bring or caufe their Children to be brought to a Minifter of a contrarie Profeßion in Religion, and that Publikely in Church or Chapell there to be Baptifed; vnleffe the Child were in danger of death, then the Minifter to be fent for home to the Catholikes houfe, and ther to minifter this Sacrament.*

The firft reafon or caufe may be; for that perchaunce they thought it could not be fo fufficientlie performed by anie other then of their owne minifterie, pro-

The firft reafon of te Statu- te.

A 2   feſſion

feſſion and Religion. But if they imagined
any ſuch thing ſurely they were mighte-
ly deceaued : and ſome of the learned
amongſt them (I meane the Lords Spirituall) might haue informed them, that
this conceit or opinion inclined to the
practiſe of the old *Heretikes* the *Donatiſts,*

Aug. againſt whom *S. Auguſtine* writte many
lib.1. bookes aboue a thouſand yeares agoe,
con. who were perſwaded that the Children
Donat. *Baptiſed* by anie other then them ſelues,
were not ſufficiently *Baptiſed*: but they
Rebaptiſed againe euen *Catholikes* if any returned or came to be of their profeſſion.
Not much vnlike by reaſon of this ſtatute it is nowe practiſed. For if any *Catholike*
doe preſent his Child at *Church* or Chappell for auoyding the penaltie with proteſtation that the Child is all readie chri-
ſtined: yet not withſtanding, ſay the moſt
part of the vnlearned miniſters, I will
doe my dutie and office, and ſo rebaptiſe
the Child, although this be expreſslie
contrarie to the conſtitutions of the Ca-
De Cō- non Law : and by the ſame Canon Law
ſecra. they incurre by the acte of *Rebaptization*
diſt. 4. *Irregularitie.* Some in deed of the Ciuiller
can. qui and learneder ſort of *Miniſters,* doe not
bis. abſo-

THE PREFACE.

abfolutly *Rebaptife*, but with Condition: *If thou arte not Baptifed, I Baptife thee*. But this will not ferue their turne, but rather betrayeth their ignorance ? For they ought not to *Rebaptife*, vpon Condition, but when there is probable doubt, that the partie prefented vnto them is not *Baptifed.* Here is no fuch matter, but proteftation made by the parents or others that the Child is allready *Baptifed.*

For a fecond reafon I imagine they could not fo much as thinke that the *Baptifme* practifed in the *Roman Catholike Church,* or by a *Roman Catholike Prieft* was no *Baptifme,* was not auaylable, and therfore they made this ftatute and law. For if this doctrine were true, woe then to their *Proteftanticall* congregation. For firft, then many of them were not *Chriftians.* Secondlythey neuer had any head of their *Church a Chriftian.* They haue had but fower heads of their *Church,* and they of diuerfe forts: An old man, a man of middle age, a woman, and a child; and thefe fower all different in age, or fexe, and all fower baptifed *Catholiklie* by a *Catholike Bishop* or *Prieft* according to the *Roman* vfe. But if *Baptifme* acted and done by a

The Second reafon.

A 3   Catholike

Catholike Bishop or *Prieſt* according to the
Roman vſe were not auaylable , why then
no *Baptiſme* no *Chriſtianitie* , and conſequentlie the head of their *Church* no *Chriſtian*. For K. *Henrie* the eight the firſt head
of the *Church* of *England* , was *Catholikly*
Baptiſed before *Proteſtancie* was preached.
King *Edward* the ſixth a Chid a boy , he
alſo was *Baptiſed* according to the *Roman*
vſe by *Henry* his Father. And for the woman Queene *Elizabeth* , she was baptiſed
Catholiklie , & (God ſaue all good tokés) as
the report goeth , she berayed the font.

*Premo-
ſition.* And for our King Iames , who now raigneth , he reporteth him ſelf that he was
Baptiſed by a *Catholike Biſhop*. And for the
Circumſtances, I had rather an other should
examine then my ſelf. But what milke
he ſucked from his nurces breaſt I know
not , but ſure I am his mother , from
whom he had his being and firſt entrance into this world, was a Conſtant *Roman
Catholike* and a worthie Queene and *Martyr*. But to conclud the ſtatute ſure was
not acted vpon conceat that *Catholikes* did
not trulie *Baptiſe* , and that by *Catholike
Baptiſme* they were not true *Chriſtians*.
Some other reaſon they had , and
what

what may that be?

Thirdly their motiue surely might be to *The third reason*. getre monie, and begger and impouerish Catholikes. This in deed hath wrought some effect. For some Gentlemen haue bene brought in question by some Promoters for not bringing their Children W. C. to the Church to be *Baptised*, and so for- R. B. ced to compound, or else by *Publike* Court to haue beene censured for the whole penaltie. The Composition hath cost, some twentie pounds, some ten pounds, some more, some lesse. We know that God doth suffer temptations, tribulations, miseries, wants, pouertie, and some tyme beggerie it self to fall vpon is seruants, yet we are instructed by *1. Cor.* the *Apostle S. Paule* : *Deus autem fidelis est, qui* *10. v.* *non patietur vos tentari vltra id quod, &c. That* *13.* *God is faithfull, and will not suffer vs to be tem-* *pted aboue that which we are able. But Will* *make also with tentation yssue*, that we may be able to sustaine, and withall to take cheere and Comfort. We read that old *Tobi.2.* *Tobie* by reason he did obserue his *Religion*, burie the dead, releeue and comfort the afflicted, who were persecuted for their Consciences (and this he did contrarie to

A 4   the

THE PREFACE.

the lawes and commaundement of the
King Sennach rib) he grewe into miferies,
was ftroken blind by mifchaunce, had
wants,became verie poore:yet afterward
the *Scripture* fayeth: God fent his *Angell*
reftored him to his fight, and he became
againe verie rich. In like manner God
Iob. 1. fuffered Iob to be tryed in the loffe of his
& 2. wealth and goods, in the death of his
Children and fore punifhment of his bo-
die:yet afterward his welth was reftored,
his Children multiplied, and he recoue-
red his former health. Almightie God
commaunded *Abraham* that he should
Gen.22 with his own hand, facrifice his owne
Sonne : yet prefently God fent his *Angell*
who fayd : *Ne extendas manum tuam in Pue-*
rum : Extend not thy hand againft the Child. So
I hope God will one day at his pleafure
put you in a better mind to recall thefe
Cruelties and penall exactions, incline
you to mercie, fend his Comforts to his
afflicted, and giue to euerie one in the
end their right.

In the *Intherim* this muft be our daylie
prayer which the Church vfeth on the
Miffa Sabaothe *of Quatuor Tempora in Lent : Adefto*
Rom. *quæfumus Domine fupplicationibus , &c. Be thou*
Prefent

THE PREFACE.

Prefent ô Lord, we befeech thee to our fupplications, that we may deferue thou being the giuer of all graces in profperitie to be humble, and in aduerfitie fecure and ftêdfaft . *And thou ô Lord our Protector looke vpon vs, that we who are preffed downe with the weight of our miferies,may,being partakers of thy mercie, ferue thee with freedom of mind and courage* . Some enuious or litigatorious fellowe may fay, that by thefe kind of words we should feeme to looke for a day and libertie of *Confcience* . I anfwere . Herein we muft referre our felues to the goodnes and mercie of God. And thus farre we affure our felues, and this Confidence we haue vpon the veritie of our caufe, that if we haue no refti tution, or relaxation of our miferies in this life, we hope to receaue *Centuplum,* *an Hundred fold* in the next, *VVhere neither thiefe can fteale;nor canker corrupt.*

Matth.
6. ver.
20.

Fourthlie I thinke the principall caufe and true motiue and intention of the *Parlament* might be , to with drawe the *Lay Catholike People* from all conuerfation with their *Priefts* and *Cleargie,* in that they should haue no vfe of them in *Sacraments and Ceremonies;* and therfore they intended to forbid them all, and put a great penalltie

The
fourth
reafon.

A 5

THE PREFACE.

naltie euen vpon *Baptifme*, *Mariage* and *Buriall*. For preach they muft not, by rea-fon of the Statute of *Perfuation* : fay *Maffe* they may not,you know the penaltie and daunger:heare *Confeßion* they may not,the Statute of *Abfoluing* forbiddeth : nor bu-rie the *Dead*: nor *Baptife* : *nor marrie*. So that they would haue them caft of as vnpro-fitable feruants. What thinke you of the Counfell of *Iulian* the *Emperour?* Was it not as graue, as wife, as politike as the *Parla-ment* of *England* to fuppreffe *Catholike Reli-gion?* Did they not fhed their bloud and martyr them? Did they not difarme them, take from them all their forces? Did they not by lawes and Statutes fpoyle them of their Lands and goods and begger them? Yet *Chriftianitie* flo-risheth, and *Iulians Counfell* confounded. Was not alfo the *Counfell* of the *Iewes* as politike, wife,carefull,and prouident to fuppreffe the *Apoftles*,and commaund they should not fpeake in the name of *Iefu*,as the *Parlament* is to expell *Catholike Priefts,* and the vfe of their *Religion* and function? I would to God they would hearken to the Counfell of *Gamaliel* a graue *Counfeller,* a doctor of the law , honorable to all people

THE PREFACE.

people, who brought vp and inftructed, *s. Paule* in the lawe, what was his Iudg- *Act.* 5. ment: *Let thefe men alone (fayeth he) for if this Counfell or woi ke they goe about be of men it will be diffolued: but if it be of God, you are not able to diffolue them, leaft perhaps you be found to refift God alfo.*

Finallie and fifthly, It may be I haue *The* miffed my ayme all this while in the rea- *fifth* fons alleadged. For the true meaning and *reafon.* purpofe in deed was to bring the *Catho- likes* to obedience and Conformitie with the *Proteftants* in the Adminiftration of this *Sacrament*, and other publike practi- fes of their Religion. In verie deed there were great reafon in making and ena- cting this lawe, and impofing thefe grie- uous penalties, if the *Catholikes* of *England* were *innouators,* bringers in or deuifers of nouelties; or in adminiftration of this *Sacrament* should derogate or take away any effentiall parte, or should practife any rite or Ceremonie which they had not receaued from their Aunceftours, euen from their firft Conuerfion to *Chri- ftianitie.* But confidering that the *Catholi- kes* are verie refpectiue, and more care- full in the due adminiftration of this

Sacraments,

Sacrament, then *Protestant* or *Puritan*; there
is small or no reason in my opinion for
this seuere penall Statute and lawe, to
vrge and force them to bring to the
Church vpon so great a penaltie, their
Children to be *Baptised* of *Puritan* or *Protestant*. For it is manifest to the whole
world, where *Christianitie* hath bene professed , and may appeare by this small
ensuing treatise, how obseruant and vigilant the *Catholikes* haue euer beene in
the prouision of *Baptisme*, as well in tyme
of necessitie in *Priuate Baptisme*, both concerning the *Minister*, as also touching the
matter & the forme , which are the two
principall partes: and also in publike and
solemne Celebration , in obseruing the
auntient rites and Ceremonies therof.
Farther it is open and plaine to the eyes
of all men, that the *Catholikes* doe not
decline nor swarue one iote from the
Institution of *Christ*, but are guided by the
Ioan. 3. *Canon* of holy *Scripture*, especialy concerning the two essentiall parts, that is : that
by the speciall ordinance of *Christ* the
matter must be true elementall water:
and the forme to be: *In the name of the Father, and of the Sonne , and of the Holy Ghost:*
which

THE PREFACE.

Which was prescribed by no other then *Matth.* Chrift himfelf after his glorious *Refurre-* 28. *&ion*, when he gaue Commiffion to his *Apoftles to Baptife*. And as for the rites & Ceremonies which we *Catholikes* vfe (as shall appeare in the 5. Booke of this trea- tife) they are not idle, nor fuperftitious, as the *Proteftants* would haue them: but moft honorable, fignificant, inftrudiue, profitable, and comfortable to Chriftian people. And for Confirmation of them we haue the practife of the *Apoftles*, the *Tradition* of the auntient *Primatiue Church*, the teftimonie of all ages, with the ap- probation of the Fathers, and holie *Do- &ours* of the *Church*. And it is worth the noting and in particular to be obferued, that the *Catholikes* at this day in *England*, vfe in the *Celebration* of this *Sacrament* no other matter, nor no other forme, nor Ceremonie then that which was deliue- red them by antiquitie euen from the firft founders and Conuerters of this Iland to *Chriftianitie*, either among the *Britons*: partly by thofe who were fent *Beda.* from *Rome* by *Pope Elutherius* at the inftan- *li. 2.* ce of *King Lucius*: or afterwarde by *S. Ger-* *hift.* *manus* and *S. Lupus* appointed by *Pope* *Angl.* *cap. 17.*
Celeftine

THE PREFACE.

Celestine for their *Reformation* concerning the *Pelagian* heresie: or amongst the *Scots* or *Picts* by *S. Palladius* : or finallie amongst vs *English* by *S. Augustine* the monke, sent by *S. Gregorie* the *Great* . All which considered (Gentle *Reader*) I referre to thy owne Iudgement what great necessitie thereshould be so eagerlie and with such penaltie to vrge *Catholikes* to present their Children at *Church* or Chappell, to be *Baptised* of *Puritan* or *Protestant*.

Now hauing diued into the viewe why the *Parlament* enacted so seuerely against *Catholike Baptisme*, by compelling all *Catholikes* vpon such penalties to *Baptize* publikely at their *Church* or *Chappell* by their *Ministers*. I will briefly put downe the motiues that moued me to write this small ensuing treatise .

The motiues to write this treatise.
1.
The reason of the title of the booke.

And first (Good *Reader*) I tooke this matter in hand to let thee vnderstand what *Baptisme* is, and the necessitie thereof to saluation. It is here on earth the first begining of *Christianitie* : the entrance into the *Catholike Church* the house of God: the high-way to all other *Sacraments*, in so much that without this no other *Sacrament* is auaylable: a washing and

THE PREFACE.

and cleanſing our ſoules from all ſinne
Originall and others: a *Satisfaction* for all
paines due for ſinne eterñall or temporall: a deliuerie from the bondage and
power of the *Diuell* : a reſtorer of Innocencie : an incorporation to *Chriſt* as
members of his bodie myſticall: and finallie a reconciliation vnto the grace & fauour of God Almightie, wherby we are
made the adopted Sonñes of God,
Coheyres and inheritors with *Chriſt* of
the kingdome of heauen , Hath it all
theſe effects? Take heed then that thou
lay the foundation ſure of thy *Chriſtiani-*
tie, that is: that thou be truely *Baptiſed*
and Chriſtened.

The ſecond motiue was to lay open
and make plaine vnto thee by way of
queſtions and doubts (which I ſuppoſe
to be the eaſieſt and plaineſt Courſe for
thy better vnderſtanding) the effects, the
matter, the forme, the miniſter as well
in neceſſitie as in publike Celebration,
with the ſolemnitie and Ceremonies of
this *Sacrament*; For that thou being more
fullie herein inſtructed , thou mayeſt
haue a more eſpeciall care to haue it perfectlie effected and trulie performed in
                                        theſe

2.

these daungerous tymes of herefie . For
affuredly this is the gate that openeth to
heauen : which if it should be shutte and
not duely miniftred, there were no hope
of faluation , but all open to hell and
damnation.

3.
*The
daun-
gerous
points
of Do-
ctrine
concer-
ning
Baptif-
me*).
1.

Thirdly to giue thee a Caueat and
warning of the daungerous opinions and
affertions , which are taught and fpread
abroad of this *Sacrament* by the *Sectaries* of
this age . The firft daungerous poynt
of doctrine is , that the *Sacrament* of *Baptifme* was inftitued by *S. Iohn Baptift:* and
that the *Baptifme* of *Chrift*, and *S. Iohns,* is
all one and the felfe fame; which is againft
Scripture and reafon . For then we muft
needs fay, that the firft and chiefe *Sacramēt*
of the new *Teftament* and *Ghospell* of *Chrift,*
should be inftituted by a precedent *prophet* , and not by *Chrift* him felf , which
were abfurde , feing all *Sacraments* of the
New Teftament, haue their inftitution by
Chrift , and their force and vertue from
his death and *Paßion.* Secondly that this
Sacrament doth not conferre grace,
cleanfe the foule from finne as an effi-
cient inftrumentall caufe by *Chrift* inftituted and endued with that vertu; which

2.

THE PREFACE.

were to deftroy *Baptifme*. Thirdlie that it doth not impreffe in the foule a feale, figne, and Character of *Chriftianitie* indelible for euer ; which is to make no diftinction betweene Iewe, Gentill, Pagan and *Chriftian*. Fourthly that he, who is once *Baptifed* , can not be damned; which were to fet all at libertie ; and make men careleffe of all other *Chriftian* life . Fifthly that the only memorie of *Baptifme* doth iuftifie from our finnes, which we shall commit after *Baptifme*, which were to take away all fatisfaction, repentance and penance; and other fuch like abfurdities, and daungerous poynts of *Doctrine* againft *Scripture* , *Councells* , *Fathers*, and all antiquitie.

3.

4.

5.

Finallie I would haue thee to confider with what fubtiltie the *Deuill* hath endeauoured in thefe latter tymes by his inftrumenrs the *Heretikes*, to difgrace the beautie of *Chrifts Spoufe* the *Church* , to depopulate roote vp , and deftroy like wild boares the vineyard of our Lord. And I compare the *Sacrament* of *Baptifme* to the tree of life placed in the middeft of *Paradife*;which the *Heretikes* of this age, fome of them haue hacked and hewed at

The fourth motiue.

B   the

THE PREFACE.

the verie chiefe boughes and branches
therof: fome others haue pilled the barke, and pulled of all the leaues, the
beautie therof: and fome others haue
deftroyed all the fruite and vertu therof,
and put the axe euen to the verie roote
to deftroy all. *Martin Luther* endeauoured
at one blowe to cutte of two of the
effentiall parts of this tree of life; that is:
Luther the *forme* and *mater* of *Baptifme*; For(fayeth
in Sym- he)*no forme of words is neceffarie*. It is fuffi-
pofiati- cient with him: *To Baptife in the name of*
eis collo. *the Lord.* And as for the *matter*, anie li-
sa.17. quor that is apte to washe, as Ale, beere,
or milke, is fufficient. Thus this Impe
and inftrument of *Sathan*, maketh no
fcruple to deftroy the two effentiall
parts of this S*acrament* to appoint anie li-
quor for matter, and no forme of words.
Although this errour of *Luthers* be againft
C*hrifts inftitution*,and expreffe Commaundement, who hath ordayned water to
be the matter: and the forme to be: *In the*
Ioan.3. *name of the Father, and of the Sonne, and of the*
Matth. *Holy Ghoft*: *M. Brentius* will make himfelf
28. fo bould with C*hrift* and his C*hurch*,as to
fet downe an order of his owne, neuer
heard of before: *Let the Minifter* (fayeth
he) *re-*

he) *recite the* Creed, *and say: In this faith I Ea-* ~Bren-~
ptise thee ; and this shall passe for currant ~tius~ ~de~
without anie other forme of words.   ~Baptis.~

  But *M.* Iohn Caluin goeth farther, almost
impudēt and blusheth not to say: *That the*
forme of words in Sacraments are meere Magi- ~Caluin~
call charmes and enchauntments. And thus you ~li.4.in-~
may fee how thefe Agents for *Sathan* doe ~stitu.~
difmember the effentiall parts of this ~cap.17.~
Sacrament of *Baptifme*, and doe cutte of the
principall boughes of this tree of life. ~Prote-~
Then come the *Proteſtants* in parte ioy- ~ſtants.~
ning yſſue with the *Pelagians*, and pull of ~Read S.~
the leaues, and pill of the barke of this ~Aug. li-~
tree of life, that is: they deride, neglect ~2. de~
and contēne the auncient Ceremonies of ~nup. &~
this *Sacrament* of *Baptifme*; as well the pre- ~Concu-~ ~piſc. ca.~
cedent Ceremonies, fuch as goe before ~29.~
the acte of *Baptifme*, as exorcifmes, ex-
fufflations, hallowing of the fonte &c:
as the Subfequent fuch as are after *Ba-*
ptifme, videlicet: holy vnction, with holy
Chrifme, the vfe of the waxe-candle or
taper light, the cloathing with the white
garment commonlie called the *Chrifome*.
All which Ceremonies although they be
auncient, profitable, fignificant, and
deliuered by Tradition as from the

Apoſtles,

THE PREFACE.

Apoſtles, as shall appeare in the ſequell: yet are theſe derided, neglected, and contemned by the *Proteſtants.*

Puritans.

Laſt of all come the *Puritans* withe the axe of M. *Caluin*, laying load at the very roote of this tree of life, to ouerthrow all, to beat downe this gate and entrance to ſaluation. This *Sacrament* ſay they, is not neceſſarie to *Saluation* for all men, becauſe Children borne of faithfull *Parents* may be ſaued without *Baptiſme*; either by *Predeſtination*, or by the fayth of their *Parents*; the elder ſort being of vnderſtanding, may be ſure of their *Saluation* only by faith. Alſo they extinguiſh and condemne the two principall effects of *Baptiſme* that is *Remiſſion* of ſinnes, and infuſion of inherent grace wherby the ſoule is cleanſed and iuſtified. Although this be contrarie to *Chriſts* owne wordes, who expreſſeth the neceſſitie of *Baptiſme*

Ioan.3.

vnto all ſaying: *Niſi quis renatus, &c. Vnleſſe euerie one be borne againe of water and the holy Ghoſt, he can not enter into the Kingdome of heauen*, Alſo that *Baptiſme* doth remit ſinne the ancient Fathers when they compiled and made the *Nycen Creed*, which is one of the three *Creeds* beleeued of all *Proteſtants*, haue theſe wordes *Confiteor vnum Baptiſma*

Baptisma in Remissionem Peccatorum: I *Confesse*
one Baptisme vnto Remission of sinnes. Some will
haue it onlie an externall washing , no internall cleansing . And the *Anabaptists* ex-
clud all *Infants* and Childrē from *Baptisme*,
and onlie will admit such as' haue thē vse
of reason, are aged, & mē of vnderstāding.

Take heed therfore(Curteous Reader)
of this daungerous doctrine , beware of
these wicked brood, who hack and hewe,
pill and poll , yea cut downe euen at the
root this tree of life , planted in *Paradise*
by God himself, instituted by *Christ* in the
Church as the onlie ordinarie meanes, gate, and entrie to saluation, They will haue
it vsed onlie as a Commaunded Ceremonie to incorporate vs as the members of
the *Church*, and as a bare signe and seale of
Iustice : not as the ordinarie meanes for
all to saluation , not as conferring grace
inherent, not as cleasing and washing the
soule internallie , not as remitting sinne;
And so cutting downe by the roote the
efficacie, force, vertue and power of this
Sacrament which is to ayme at the ouerthrowe of all *Christianitie*:For if no *Baptis-*
me, no *Christianitie* : no *Christianitie*, no
Christ Vigila ergo & Vale. *Be watchfull ther-*
fore, and so farewell. This 30 of Iulie, 1614.

Thy true friend and wellwiller in Christ O. A.

The generall Pointes contayned in this treatife are fiue.

1. First of the effects of this Sacrament, and the necessitie therof to Saluation.

2. Of the two essentiall Parts of Baptisme, that is : Concerning the matter and the forme, the water and the word.

3. Of the Baptiser, that is of the ordinarie minister, to whom by office, function, or Commission it belongeth to Baptise: or the Extraordinarie who are allowed to Baptise in case of necessitie, as the layeman, midwife, or any other woman.

4. Of the Parties who are to be Baptised, as Infants, and Children, and such as haue vse of reason, as aged, and men of vnderstanding.

5. Of the reasons, vse, and antiquitie of the Rites and Ceremonies of this Sacrament.

THE

THE FIRST

BOOKE OF THE
LIFE AND GATE
OF CHRISTIANITIE,
ENTREATING OF THE
EFFECTS OF THE SACRA-
MENT OF BAPTISME.

CAP. I.

*VVhat a Sacrament is, and why God would vſe
externall ſenſible things for the Sanctiſication
and Iuſtiſication of man.*

FTER our moſt great, Almightie,
and good God had taken by the
ſingular benefit of our Redemptiõ
mankind into his guardion ſafe-
keeping, and protection, being, corporall and carnall men (I ſay) conſiſting of fleſh
and bloud: would of his ineffable omnipotẽcie,
power, and ſingular goodnes conferre and giue
vs his inuiſible grace, vſing and appoynting

externall elements and creatures, as it were con-
deſcéding to the weakneſſe of our natures, ſtate,
condition, and neceſſitie, where vpon S. *Chry-*

Chryſ- *ſoſtome* ſayeth: *Si incorporeus eſſes, nuda, & incor-*
ko. 60. *porea tibi dediſſet dona: ſed quoniam anima corpo-*
ad po- *ri inſerta eſt, in ſenſibilibus intelligibilia tibi præ-*
pulum. *bet: If thou werte a man incorporeus without bo-*
& 83. *die, fleſh and bone, God had giuen thee gifts bare,*
in mat. *vncouered, and vncorporate: but becauſe thy ſoule*
is inſerted and put to thy bodie in ſenſible things
ſubiect to ſenſe he doth offer vnto thee things of vn-
derſtanding. Wherfore a Sacrament is defined to
be: *A Signe of an holie thing; or. A viſible forme of*
an inuiſible grace. Or â Sacramét is: A matter, or
thing ſubiect to our ſenſes, which hath by the
iuſtitution of God power both to ſign, fie, and
alſo to effect ſanctitie and Iuſtice. Or it is that, by
which the Diuine power vnder the couer of
viſible things doth worke more ſecretly ſaluation, health, and ſanctitie in the ſoule of man.
And ſuch is the wiſdome of God to vſe and
inſtitute theſe inferiour and baſe creatures,
wherby it may clearlie appeare that the grace
which is giuen by theſe *Sacraments,* proceedeth
from God onlie. And for this cauſe Chriſt did

Ioan. 9. giue ſight vnto the borneblind man with myre
and dirte made of ſpittle; and did not vſe anie
precious oyntments, that it might appeare to
come from Chriſt God alone, ad by his inſti-
tit on to worke his effect. This is the power of
God onlie by baſe, and bare externall elements
according to his inſtitution & word to worke

Gen. 1. internall effects: *Ipſe dixit & facta ſunt : He ſayd*
the word, and it was done.

                                    C A P.

CAP. 2.

What Baptisme is, how it is defined, and what are the effects in generall.

IT may be defined briefly out of the third of S. Iohns Ghospell, and out of the fifth of S. *Paule* to the Ephesians, to be the *Sacrament of Regeneration by water in the word of life.* It is called *Regeneration* or second birth, in respect of our naturall and carnall birth. As no man can enter into this world, nor haue his life and being in the same, vnlesse he be borne of his carnall parents: no more can any man enter into life and state of grace, which is in Christ, or attaine to life euerlasting, vnlesse he be borne of water and the holie Ghost. You must vnderstand, that I say it is by water, for it is not the water it self, that is: the element permanent, but the lauer, ablution, washing, or the vse of water. And therfore S. Paule sayeth: *That Christ so loued his Church, that he deliuered him self for it, that he might sanctifie it cleansing it by the lauer of water and making vs safe by the lauer of Regeneration.* And as by the washing of the water the bodie externallie is cleansed : so also by the water and word, by the vertue and power of this Sacrament and operation of the holy Ghost the soule internallie is sanctified, and borne anewe in Christ Iesus. Or we may make a more full definition, or rather an absolute description of *Baptisme,* containyng the matter, forme, institution, effects, and necessitie therof to saluation, saying: *Baptisme is the first and principall Sacrament of the newe*

Ioan. 3.

Ephes. 5.

Ephes. 5.

law

lawe and Gofpell, *confifting* (according to te inftitution of *Chrift*) *in an exteriour ablution and
wafhing of the bodie, with a due and lawfull pro-
nuntiation of the forme of words: which is of neceffitie to Salvation for all fortes of people as well children and Infants, as thofe of riper yeares, aged,
or men of underftanding: and we receyuing by this
Sacrament a full and perfecte remiffion of our
finnes, are fpiritually regenerated and borne againe
a newe creature: alfo we, who were before the children of wrath, nowe are made the Children and
heyres of God, and in deed the Coheyres of Chrift
our Redeemer.* Which defcription shall be particularlie difcuffed and proued hereafter.

*The   Now the effects and prerogatiues of this Sa-
Prero-   crament are great and manie. Firft it is the
gatiues   begining of *Chriftianitie*: the firft entrance into
of Bap-   the *Catholike Church*, and houfe of God here
tifme,   on earth: the verie high-way to all other Sacraments; infomuch that no other are auailable
without this: It is the firft gate that openeth
to the Kingdome of heauen; by this we re-
ceyue fuch fingular grace, that thereby we are
cleanfed from all maner of finne: as Originall,
Actuall, be it mortall or veniall, The Infants
not hauing actuall, are cleanfed from Originall:
and the elder forte, or at mans eftate, young or
old haue by this *Sacrament* their foules cleanfed
and washed of all manner of finnes, as Originall, actuall, mortall, or veniall, and the
paines due for finne either eternall or temporall
fullie fatisfied. Yea we are deliuered from the
bondage and power of the deuill, reftored to in-
nocecie, incorporate to *Chrift* as members of his
bodie,

bodit, reconciled to the grace and fauour of
Almigtie God : made his adopted sonnes, and
coheyres and inheritours with *Christ* of the
Kingdome of heauen. The soule is beautified,
made beloued of God, splendent and shining in
the sight of Angells. Heare what S. Basill, called
the *Greate* for his sanctitie, holinesse, and
learninge, in his exhortation to *Baptisme* sayeth:
It is,Mors peccati, animæ regeneratio, amictus
spendens, Character indelebilis, Cœli iter, Regni
cœlestis conciliatio, adoptionis gratia: The deatb
of sinne, the Regeneration of the Soule, the splen-
dent amise or glorious apparell, the indelible Cha-
racter, or the marke, badge, printe of a Christian
man, the way or iourney to heauen,a winning of the
Cælestiall kingdome, the grace of adoption. And to
this holie Father subscribeth almost in the same
words *S. Cyrill Bishop of Ierusalem saying: Baptis-*
mus est Captiuitatis liberatio, Peccatorum remis-
sio, mors Peccati &c. Baptisme is the deliuerie out
of captiuitie,the remissiõ of sinnes,the death of sinne,
the regeneration of the soule, the white garment
wherwith they are clothed who follow the lambe im-
macu'ate, the holy and indelible seale, the chariote
into heauen, the delight of Paradise,the winning of
the heauenlie kingdome, the Chrisme or vnction of
*the children of adoption.*These priuiledges,graces,
prerogatiues & efects,I haue the rather expressed
that in these daungerous tymes of heresie parêts
may take greater care to haue this sacrament
duely executed,and trulie ministred to their children,considering it so much concerneth the life
and eternall saluation of their soules.

Proto-
catbesi.

CAP.

CAP. 3.

VVhether if by errour or other wayes this Sacrament of baptisme be not dulie adminiſtred, one be capable of the other Sacraments.

To this queſtion it may be anſwered, that it is a chief priuiledge and prerogatiue of this *Sacrament*, that it onelie and by it ſelf without anie other *Sacrament* may be receyued to ſaluation; and all other *Sacraments* ſuppoſe this as the gate and entrance, ſo that without this they can take no effect. For howe can the bodie be ſtrengthned, or take armes and weapons to fight againſt his enemies that hath no life in it. So I ſay of *Confirmation* the next *Sacrament* after
Confir- Baptiſme, which ſtrengthneth and armeth the
matiö. ſoule by the inuocation of the holie Ghoſt to fight againſt the enemies of mankind, that is the world the fleſh and the deuill; and to ſtand conſtantlie in confeſſion of fayth in tyme of perſecution of Pagan, Turke, or Hereticke : to weare the cognizance of a *Chriſtian* : to receaue the ſtandard of *Chriſt*, that is his *Croſſe*, that he be not aſhamed to profeſſe *Chriſt crucified*. But how can this be if the ſoule be dead in ſinne, haue not the life of grace, and neuer entred the gate
Sacra- of *Chriſtianitie?* As for the *Sacramēt* of the *Altar*
ment of S. *Paule* ſaieth : *Qui manducat &c. He that*
the Alt. vnworthily receaueth, doth eate and drinke his owne damnation. And how can he worthilie eat *Chriſts*
1. Cor. *Bodie*, whom Gods grace hath not yet made
11.   worthie,

worthie, and who in deed as yet is no *Christian*? *Confes*
And for the *Sacrament* of *Confession*, if it be as
S. Ierome sayeth: *Secunda tabula post naufragium*:
A second table or planke after shipwracke: it must
needes suppose a first entrance before a recouerie of the shippe. And how can he haue helpe
by the table or planke who neuer entred the
shippe? Also in *Extreme vnction*, how can the *Extre-*
Priest by holie vnction and prayer purge the re- *me vn-*
mainder, before the soule hath euer bene clean- *ction.*
sed? Or obtaine pardon of veniall sinnes,
who hath not as yet Originall sinne remitted? Or offer the soule to the hands of Angells to be presented before the throne of God,
who hath not as yet the character, signe, or seale *Matri-*
of a *Christiane*? And for *Matrimonie* how can it *monie.*,
be a *Sacrament* where *Christianitie* is not professed? *Dico magnum Sacramentum in Christo &*
Ecclesia. I say (sayeth *S. Paule*) it *is a great Sacra-* *Holy*
ment in Christ and his Church. And for holie *Orders.*
Orders certainlie it is generally concluded, that
he can be no *Priest* or minister of *Christ*, who is
no member of his *Church*. Read the decree of *Innoce.*
Innocentius the third, written to the *Bishops* of *de Pres*
Ferrara, where he concludeth: that he who is *bit. non*
not *Baptised* can not be a *Priest*. How can anie *Bapti.*
house be builded, where no foundation is layd? *can. ve.*
wherefore I conclude, he that is not trulie *niens*
Christened, can not be capable of anie other Sa- *Apost.*
ment, for that the effect of *Baptisme* is to giue
life, to open the gate, and giue power to the
receiuing of all the other *Sacraments.*

CAP.

Cap. 4.

VVhether all punishment due for Originall sinne be remitted in baptisme.

There is no doubt, but he that shall die immediatlie after *Baptisme* shall be freed from all manner of punishment temporall or eternall due for sinne, and his soule shall incontinentlie flie to heauen. The difficultie of this question is, for that we see and feele our selues after *Baptisme* to be subiect to hunger, famine, thirst, cold; and *Concupicence* to raigne in our flesh, and we to tremble at death and other calamities, which were inflicted vpon man as punishments of our first parent *Adam*. How then are we freed by *Baptisme* from all manner of punishment and penalties of this life, which were due for Originall sinne, seing these infirmities were inflicted for sinne; and yet remaine in vs after *Baptisme*? I answere; First we must consider the state of man as he is in this world, and also as he shall be in the next: Secódlie we must note that there is temporall paine and punishment and also eternall. The eternall is by *Baptisme* vtterlie abolished in this life and in the next: but part of the temporall punishment, which was inflicted for Originall sinne, onlie doth remaine in this life. As for example death was a punishment imposed for sinne, yet notwithstanding all must die. Also hunger, cold, nakednesse, sicknesse, and other such like molestations and penalties of this life, we

life, we ſuſtaine after *Baptiſme*, and are not thereby taken away, but remaine in this life as the
miſeries of mortalitie. But in the next life they
ſhall be vtterlie extinguished, according to that
of *S.Iohn. Abſterget Deus &c.God ſhall wipe away*
all teares from their eyes, and death ſhall be no mo-
re, nor mourning nor crying, neither ſhall there
be ſorrowe anie more. Alſo the reaſon whie *Con-*
cupiſcence raigneth in our fleſh not vterlie extinguished by *Baptiſme* may be: that man may by
ſtriuing to ſuppreſſe & cóquere it, merit the'more
But if by *Baptiſme* our bodies should be made
impaſſible in this life, that is, not ſubieƈt to
death, hunger, nakednes, and other calamities,
we should flie vnto *Baptiſme* rather for this preſent life; then hope for the life to come, which
were a great inconuenience in *Chriſtian* profeſſion. Therefore I ſay with *S. Thomas* the great *Thom.*
Diuine: that the *Sacrament of Baptiſme hath* 3. *p. q-*
power & vertue to take away all the penalties and 69. *ar.*
puniſhments due for ſinne: yet notwithſtanding it 3.
doth not De faƈto take them away in this preſent
life, but by the vertue thereof in the death and Paſ-
ſion of Chriſt they ſhall be extinguished, and vtter-
lie taken away in the generall reſurreƈtion: when
theſe our mortall bodies shal be endued with immor- 1. *Cor.*
talitie, as it is ſayed. And this not without reaſon 15.
by God ordained; Firſt becauſe by *Baptiſme* man
is incorporate to *Chriſt*, and made his member;
And therefore it is conuenient that the ſame
should be performed in the member incorporate, which was aƈted in the head. But *Chriſt* from
the begining of his *Conception*, being full of grace and veritie notwithſtanding had a paſſible
bodie

bodie which after his death and *Paſſion,* was raiſed to a glorious life. Wherefore although euerie *Chriſtian* in *Baptiſme* doth obtaine grace for the beautifying of his ſoule: yet not withſtã-ding becauſe he hath a paſſible bodie to ſuffer for *Chriſt* and with *Chriſt,* he muſt for the ty-me preſent ſuſtaine the penalties thereof : yet ſhall he be rayſed at the generall reſureÁion to Rom.8. an impaſſible life, which *S. Paul* declareth : *Qui ſuſcitauit Ieſum &c. He that rayſed vp Ieſus from the dead, ſhall quicken alſo your mortall bodies, be-cauſe of his ſpirite dwelling in you.* Wherefore although *Baptiſme* hath power and vertue to take awaye all the penalties of this life, and punishment due for ſinne: yet it is conuenient they remaine temporallie, and for a tyme in this life; and be accomplished and fulfilled in the generall reſurreÁion in the next life, when we all ſhall receaue our bodies againe.

CAP. 5.

VVhether Baptiſme doth remit ſinne and giue grace Ex opere operato, that is: By force of the word and worke done and ſayed in the Sa-crament.

It is a generall cõcluſion amongſt all *Catholike Diuines,* that the *Sacraments* are cauſes of our *Iuſtification,* and that God doth applie the me-rits of *Chriſts Paſſion* vnto our ſoules Where-fore we conclude that in *Baptiſme,* by force and vertue of the word and worke done and ſayed, ſinne finne is remitted, grace giuen and *Iuftification* wrought. Therefore we do not *attribute* the obtaining of grace and *Iuftification* to the merits of the minifter miniftering it, nor to the partie receyuinge but as *Chrift* hath taught vs, to the water and the holy Ghoft working it. And for better vnderftanding of *Iuftification* and grace wrought in *Baptifme*, let vs confider how manie things concurre thereunto. Firft doth concurre Almightie God, who is the principall and chiefe agent, worker and firft caufe of *Iuftification.* Then *Chrifts* death and *Paffion* by which we are redeemed, and he hath meritted this grace for vs. Then the facramentall action that is the concurring and applieing togeather the water and the word in due forme according to the *Inftitution* and ordinance of God. This externall action is this *Sacrament*, which God doth vfe as his inftrument for the iuftification, washing and cleanfing of the foule of man: Then is the *Prieft* ordained the ordinarie minifter of God to execute this facrament or externall action in whome there is required that he haue power, authoritie and comiffion to doe it and intention to effect it. Finalie in the receyuer that is, in him who is to be Baptifed, if he be of age and vnderftanding, there is required a will and defire to receaue it, alfo faith and beleefe in *Chrift*, with a penitent harte. Thefe are not caufes of *Iuftification*, but difpofitions in the foule onelie to make the foule apte to receaue the *Sacrament*, and to remoue obftacles and letts that the *Sacrament* may worke his effect. And this *S. Peter* after his firft fermon in the day of *Pentecoft*

C

infinuated

infinuated & told the people, when they asked
him after the preaching was donne, what they
shoud doe. *Difbofe your felues* fayeth he, *doe Pe-*
nance, and be . ie one of you Baptifed. But for
Infantswhat is required in them, we will entreate afterwards. Wherefore we will conclude
Baptifme to be the inftrument of God, and by
Diuine ordinance to haue as an inftrumentall
caufe, efficacie and efficiencie to remit finne, and
worke faluation and iuftification in the foule
of man.

Act. 2.

CAP. 6.

VVhether Baptifme be reallie and in deed an in-
ftrumentall caufe of iuftification, or onlie
a meanes to excite, ftirre vp or moue to
faith.

IT is an abfurd and vnconfcionable dealing,
yea a great flaunder and calumnie of *Caluin*
and his complices to fay that *Catholikes in their*
Doctrine, doe refigne and tye the vertue and
power of God to externall fimboles and *fignes.*
As though they taught that in *Baptifme* the water & the word without God did remitte finne.
It were a vaine thinge to thinke that when
the carpenter doeth vfe his fawe as an inftrumentall caufe to breake, cut or deuide timber,
to fay that the fawe doth cut, worke, or breake
timber of it felf without the carpenter. So
Almightie God , although he vfe the externall
fignes, that is the word and water in *Baptifme*
to cleanfe

to cleanfe the foule and remit finne as feconda-
rie and inftrumentall caufes: yet not fo that they
should worke of themfelues without God, but
God by them doth effect iuftification and remiffion of finne. Neither doth he refigne his power
fo to thefe externall fignes, that they worke
thefe effects in them felues, and not he in them
and with them: but as in the precedent chapter
I fayed, God doth vfe in *Baptifme* water and
the word as his inftrument, and by force of the
word and worke done grace is giuen, and finne
remitted. Therfore they are not vfed (as fome
heretikes of this tyme auerre) as bare fignes and
fimboles, or onlie meanes to excite, ftirre vp, or
moue to faith; and the afterward by faith onelie
to be iuftified. This were to deftroy the efficiencie and force of the *Sacraments*, and to make no
more of them, then we make of an Iuie garland,
which is onlie fet forth to fignifie that there is
wine to be fold, bought, and drunke. It is manifeft that the Ghofpell, the word of God
preached is a greate motiue, and forceable meanes to moue vs to beleeue and to ftrengthen our
faith: and S. *Paule* fayeth it is: *Virtus Dei in falu-*
tem omni credenti: the power of God vnto faluation Rom. 1.
to euerie one that beleeueth: much more then is
the *Sacrament* of *Baptifme* the power of God,
not mouing onlie to faith, but working in it felf
as his inftrument to faluation. And in deed
faith, becaufe it cometh vnto thofe of age &
vnderftanding by hearing as S. *Paule* fayeth: *Fi-*
des ex auditu: Faith is by hearing: therefore faith Rom.
is in them as a neceffarie difpofitió to *Baptifme.* 10.
Where vpon *Chrift* fayeth : *Qui crediderit &*

C 2   *Baptizatus*

Mar. 16.

Baptizatus fuerit, faluus erit: He that beleeueth and is Baptized shall be faued. So that faith going before *Baptifme* is a caufe difpofitiue and neceffarie vnto *Baptifme*, but not the onlie effecte of *Baptifme*, as fome would haue it. For that the immediate effecte of *Baptifme* by applying the merits of *Chrift Paffion*, is remiffion of finnes to faluation, is a newe regeneration and opening the gate to heauen. And this plainlie *Chrift* fpake

Io. 3.

to *Nicodemus: Nifi quis &c. Vnleffe a man be borne againe of water and the holy Ghoft, he can not enter into the kingdome of heauen.* Where we fee our regeneration and fecond Birth attributed vnto *Baptifme*, which confifteth in an externall element of water and an internall power of the holie Goft, and that no man can enter into heauen without it. Who feeth not then, that it is the inftrument of God working to faluation, and not a bare figne or motiue onelie to faith.

That the effect of *Baptifme* is the remiffion of finne the *Scripture* is plaine. The people of

act. 2.

Ierufalem and *Iurie* at the firft fermon *S. Peter* made, being as it were conuerted: *Et compuncti corde: and compuncte of harte,* fayed. *VVhat shall we doe?* S. *Peter* anfwered: *Be euerie one of you Baptifed in the name of Iefus for remiffion of your finnes.* Note that he fayeth *for remiffion of your finnes,* shewing the effect of *Baptifme* to be remiffion of finne. And *S. Paule* as he reporteth

Act. 22.

himfelf being ftroken blind, and called of *Chrift* to be the veffell of election, for the conuerfion of the Gentiles, *Ananias* came vnto him, reftored him to his fight, and then

fayed

fayed vnto him: *Et nunc quid moraris? Sur-*
ge, Baptizare, ablue peccata tua, inuocato no- *Act.*
mine eius. And now what tarriest thou? Rife 22.
vp, be Baptifed, and wash away thy finnes, *v. 16.*
inuocating his name. S. Paule beleeued before he
was *Baptifed*, but his finnes were washed
away by *Baptifme*. I will therefore conclud
vpon thefe teftimonies of *Chrift* and his
Apoftles, that the *Scripture* is plaine that *Baptif-*
me of it felf as the inftrument of God, doeth
wash away finnes by the force & vertue of the
word and worke done and fayed, and that faith
going before *Baptifme* is but a difpofition to remiffion of finnes.

Auoyd then the doctrine of Heretikes, whoe
affirme and teach that this *Sacrament* of *Baptif-*
me doth not remit finnes, but fignifie remiffion
of finnes, and doth worke of it felfe nothing, but
is as a bare figne and fimbole onlie to excite and
moue to faith: as the Iuie garland is onlie a bare
figne to excite and moue men to buy wine, and
to fignifie that in fuch a place it is to be fold.
Flie this Hereticall doctrine. (I fay) which killeth the life of the *Sacrament*, contrarie to the
Doctrine of *S. Paule*: *Chriftus dilexit Ecclefiam,* *Ephef.*
& tradidit feipfum pro ea, mundans eam lauacro 5.
aqua. Chrift (fayeth he) loued his *Church, and*
deliuered him felf for it cleanfing it by the lauer of
water. Alfo in his epiftle to *Titus: Saluos nos fecit*
per lauacrum regenerationis : he fayeth: *Chrift*
hath faued vs and made vs fafe by the lauer of *Ad Ti-*
regeneration, and renouation of the Holie Ghoft. *tum. 3.*
Can anie man more forceablie, or plainlie
expreffe the working, effecte, and force of
Baptifme

Baptifme, then *S. Paule*, in caling it the *Lauer of regeneration*; and that we are to be *cleanfed, made fafe, and faued by this lauer of water?* And withall let vs confider what *Ezechiell* the *Prophet* prophefied of the effects and force of *Baptifme*: *Effundam fuper vos aquam mundam , & mundabimini ab omnibus inquinamentis veftris: I will powre out* (fayeth the *Prophet* in the perfon of God) *cleane water vpon you, and you fhall be cleanfed from all your filthes, and ftaines.* Baptifme therefore reallie and in deed is an inftrumentall caufe of our Iuftification, and not a bare figne and meanes onlie to excite, ftirre vp, and moue vs to faith; or a *Single feale, or figne* (as *Caluin* would haue it) *of former Iuftice.*

Ezech.
ca. 27.

CAP. 7.

Whether he, who once is Baptifed, can not finne, but fhal be faued.

Bellar.
li. 1. de
Bapt.
ca. 14.

Ioro. li.
2. con-
I ouin.

This controuerfie is excellentlie and compendioullie handled by that moft worthie learned *Prelate Cardinall Bellarmine.* It was the errour of Iouinian the heretike againft whom *S. Ierome* wrote: *That he who was trulie and in deed Baptifed, could not be damned, or become a reprobate or finne after Baptifme.* And for this his errour he brought *Scripture* (as all other Heretikes doe) *Chrifts* owne words, and his *Apoftles S. Iohns*. *Chrift* fayed : *Non poteft arbor bona malos*

malos fructus facere: A good tree can not bring forth
euill fruite. Therefore being made good by *Bap-*
tifme, can not finne and confequentlie can not
be damned. But what if this tree be corrupt, the
roote be withered? either it will bring forth no
fruite or bad fruite; which this Heretike confidered not. And for that he alleadgeth out of *S.*
Iohn : Euerie one that is borne of God committeth *Io.ep.1.*
not finne; becaufe his feede abideth in him, and he *ca.3.&*
can not finne becaufe he is borne of God. By which *5.*
words of the *Apostle* this Heretike would proue
that the *Baptifed* can not finne. But the fenfe of
the *Apostle* is, that no man continuing the fonne
of God , committeth mortall finne; becaufe
mortall finne can not ftand togeather with the
grace of God : therefore fo long as we keep the
Innocencie of *Baptifme,* we can not finne. *S. Iohn*
then would not fay that the *Baptifed* could not
fall from their firft eftate of Innocencie. For *S.*
Paule doth reproue this as an errour , and pro- *Rom.*
ueth that he who now hath faith, may fall and be- *11.ver.*
come incredulous: as the *Iewes* were the faithful *19.20.*
people of God, but by incredulitie are become reprobate, fo alfo may doe the Gentiles And therefore fayeth he : *Tu fide stas : noli altum fapere, fed*
time: thou by faith doest Stand: be not too highlie
wife, but feare. Wherefore beware the vaine prefumption and fecuritie of Heretikes; for he who
ftandeth by faith may fall : and he who hath *Aug.li.*
the Innocencie of *Baptifme* , may loofe it. *S.* *20. de*
Augustine doth reprehend fome *Catholikes* of his *ciuita.*
tyme of groffe errour who held that, *thofe who were* *Dei.ca.*
Baptifed, fhould not be damned, although they liued *25.*
wickedlie, fo that they kepte themfelues in the Catho-
C 4   *like*

18 *A Treatise of*

like Church. Againſt whom he wrote a whole booke intitleing it : *de fide & operibus* : *Of faith and good workes*. Alſo againſt this hereſie ſpake. *S. Paule*, prouing that by the lawe of *Chriſt* by *Baptiſme* we are freed from the ſtate of damnation, vnleſſe we againe willfullie giue our ſelues ouer to the fleſh. And therefore he concludeth: *Si* *ſecundum Carnem vixeritis moriemini. If ye liue according to the fleſh, ye ſhall die*. And he plainlie telleth the *Corinthians*, and willeth them to know : that the vniuſt, the wicked (although they are *Chriſtians* and *Baptiſed*) ſhall not poſſeſſe the kingdome of heauen And biddeth them not erre in their opinion: *Nolite errare: for neither* *fornicatours, nor ſeruers of idolles, adulterous, nor the effeminate, nor theeues, nor the couetous, nor drunkarâs, nor railers, nor extortioners ſhall poſſeſſe the kingdome of God*.

Yet after all this comes M. Iohn Caluin with his Hereticall propoſition : *vera fides ſemel habita non poteſt amitti. True faith once had can not be loſt*. Which is contrarie to the expreſſe words of the *Apoſtle* before cited, and examples in *Scripture*. In the *Acts* of the *Apoſtles* it is written of *Simon Magus*, that at the preaching of *S. Phillippe* the *Deacon* he beleeued, was baptiſed an cleaued to *Phillippe*: Yet it is alſo manifeſt that he became a reprobate. For *S. Peter* ſayed of him that *his parte was not right before God* : and ſawe in him the gall of bitternes, and obligation of ſinne. *S. Paule* exhorteth*Thimothie to be ſtedfaſt in faith*, and haue a good conſience : *Quia quidam naufragauerunt circa fidem : For ſome repelling*
their

Rom. 8.
ver. 13.

1. Cor.
5.

Caluin
lib. 3.
inſt. ca.
22. §.
11.

Act. 8.

1. Timo.
cap. 1.

*their good confcience, haue made alfo shipwracke
about the faith.* And he abfolutlie affirmeth that
there shall be *Apoftatates* in the latter dayes: *In*
nouiffimis diebus difcedent quidam a fide: In the
laft dayes certaine shall departe from the faith.
Alfo *Martin Luther* hath this libertine propofition: *Non poteft homo Baptizatus damnari*: *nifi*
nolit credere: *He that is Baptized can not be dam-*
ned: vnleffe he will not beleeue. Againft which
idle pofition I will fette downe the decree of
the generall councell of *Trent* : *Si quis dixerit*
Bapizatum, non poffe etiamfi velit gratiam amit-
tere , quantumcumque peccet, nifi nolit credere,
anathema fit: If any man shall fay, that he who
is Baptifed, can not loofe grace, if he would, let
him finne neuer fo much, vnleffe he will not beleeue,
*let him be accurfed : Werefore I may well
conclude , that he who hath bene once
Baptized,* may finne, may be damned, may be
a reprobate. It is too frequent to heare of renegate *Chriftians* who becomes Turkes, and *Apoftatates* , and *Chatholikes* alfo, who fall from
their *Church* and faith.

*1.Timo.
cap. 4.*

*Luther
lib. de
Capti.
Babil.
cap. 6.*

CAP. 8.

*VVhether Baptifme hath force to remitte finne
committed after Baptifme.*

THere is no queftion (as hath bene declared
before) but that *Baptifme* hath force te re-

mitte all

mitte all manner of finnes, either contracted in
our firft parents, or committed in acte by our
felues, that is either originall or actuall, be they
mortall, or veniall. The difficultie nowe is, in
that there are finnes befides Originall precedent, that is : finnes paft and going before Baptifme in thofe of perfect age : and there are
finnes fubfequent ; that is committed after
Baptifme. Nowe the queftion is , whether
Baptifme extend it felf to finnes committed
after, or onlie contained it felf within the
bounde of thofe committed before. Itis the
generall doctrine of the Catholike Church,
that if we committe any finne after Baptifme,
we muft feeke to releeue our felues not by
Baptifme, but by other meanes; that is : by
the facrament of Penance. And S. Auguftine
expreffeth faying : *Semel acceptam paruulus
gratiam Chrifti non amittit , nifi propria impie-
tate, fi ætatis acceffu &c. The Infant Baptifed
loofeth not the grace of Chrift, vnleffe it be by his
owne proper impietie and wickedneffe. For if he
become euill , when he cometh to vnderftanding
and vfe of reafon , then properlie fhall he begin to
haue finnes, which finnes may not be taken away
by regeneration and Baptifme, but are to be cured
by fome other medicine.* This S. Auguftine : So
that it is plaine by this auntient Doctour, and
learned Fathers opinion, that finnes committed after Baptifme, are not releeued by Baptifme , but by other meanes. S. Paule exhorteth
men to be perfecte , and warneth them to be
carefull that they fall not from their faith and
grace they receiued once in Baptifme : *Impof-
fibile*

*Aug.
ep. 23.
ad Bo-
nif.*

Heb.6.

ſible eſt eos qui ſunt illuminati, iterum renouare ad Pœnitentiam : It is impoſible (ſaieth the Apoſtle) *for them whom are illuminated and Baptiſed, to be Baptiſed againe, to be renewed again by Baptiſmall Penance* : that is : by that eaſie remedie that Baptiſme affordeth. But if thou ſinne after Baptiſme then muſt thou goe to the Sacrament of Penance, which is open to all ſinners, called the ſecond table after ſhipwracke, a remedie, a medicine more painfull then Baptiſme, requiring much faſting, praying corporall affliction, confeſſion, contrition, ſatisfaction &c. So taught S. Ambroſe entreating of Penance; ſo preached S. Iohn Chryſoſtome in his ninth Homilie vpon the ſixth chapter to the Hebrewes. And there is no doubt to be made, but Chriſt after his reſurrection gaue commiſſion and commaundement to his *Apoſtles to Baptiſe all nations and people in remiſſion of their ſinnes· and thoſe who beleeued, and were Baptiſed ſhould be ſaued.* So it is alſo as plaine as may be in S. Iohns Goſpell, that the ſame day of Chriſts Reſurrection, he inſtituted the Sacrament of Penance, knowing the infirmitie and weakneſſe of man, that after Baptiſme he might looſe his firſt grace, and former eſtate, and fall into mortall ſinne: therefore he prouided a ſecond remedie to reuiue him againe. And as he gaue commiſſion to remitte ſinnes in Baptiſme: ſo alſo after Baptiſme he gaue power, authoritie, and commiſſion to forgiue ſinnes. The words of Chriſt in the Goſpell are theſe. As my Father ſent me, I alſo ſend you When he had ſayed

Ambr. li· 2. de Panitē. cap. 3·

Mat. 28.

Mar. 16.

thus he breathed vpon them and he fayed to
them: *Receaue ye the Holy Ghoft, VVhofe finnes
you shall forgiue, they are forgiuen them: and
whofe you shall retaine, they are retained.* Lo
the inftitution of the Sacrament of Penance.
Wherefore Baptifme is not the remedie for
finnes committed after that Sacrament receaued, but we muft recurre to the Sacrament of Confeffion by Chrifts owne inftitution.

Let therefore no Heretike lull you a fleepe
in this plaufible doctrine and Epicurian practife: that if you fall out of the shippe yon entred
into by Baptifme, and make shipwracke, and
loofe by finne your firft grace receaued in
Baptifme, that you shall not need to take hold
and handfaft of the fecond table, that is the
Sacrament of Penance: but that the memorie
onlie of Baptifme, shall be fufficient to recouer
you without contrition, confeffion, or fatisfaction either to God or man, or anie other punishement due for finne. It was alfo decreed in
the great and generall councell of Lateran, vnder Pope Innocentius the Third, at which councell were our English Embaffadours and ora-
tours amongft the reft of the Princes of Chriftendome the words of the Councell are: *Si poft*

*Concil.
Later.
cap. 1.* *fufceptionem Baptifmi contingat prolabi in peccatum, per veram Penitentiam poteft femper recupe-
rari: If it happen that any man, after he hath receaued the Sacrament of Baptifme, fall downe
into finne, he may alwaies continuallie from
tyme to tyme recouer himfelf by true repentance.*

                                                Wherefore

Wherefore I conclude with the venerable councell of Trent: *Si quis dixerit peccata omnia,* **Con.** *quæ poſt Baptifmum fiunt, ſola recordatione, & fide* **Trid.** *fuſcepti Baptiſmi, vel dimitti, vel venialia fieri,* **ſeſſ. 7.** *anathema ſit: If anie man ſhall ſay; that all ſinnes,* **c anon.** *which are committed and done after Baptiſme, are* **9.** *by the onlie recordation, remembrance and faith of Baptiſme before receaued, either remitted, or become veniall, let him be accurſed.* It can not therefore be, that thoſe ſinnes we shall committe after Baptiſme, by Baptiſme should be relieued : but the Sacrament of Penance muſt be our refuge and thither muſt we flie with an humble and contrite harte. This is Chriſts ordinance and in-ſtitution for the helpe and ſuccour of man.

CAP. 9.

VVhether Baptiſme be neceſſarie to ſaluation.

THere is no doubt in Catholike Doctrine, but ordinarlie it is of neceſſitie to ſalua-tion, and the onlie meanes by Chriſts inſtitu-tion to enter into the kingdome of heauen, ac-cording to that ſaying of Chriſt: *Niſi quis rena-* **Ioan. 3.** *t us &c. vnleſſe a man be borne againe by water & the Holy Ghoſt he can not enter into the kingdome of heauen.* As no man can enter into this world, nor haue life and being, vnleſſe he be borne of his carnall parents, no more can any man enter into life and ſtate of ſaluation, vnleſſe he be bor-ne of ne of water and the Holy Ghoſt. He muſt be, *denuo natus*, : Borne againe: who will ſee the kingdome of God. Therefore they can nǿ way

S. Tho. be ſaued (ſayeth S. Thomas) who receaue not *3. p. q.* this Sacrament: In re, or in voto; that is: In deed, *68. ar-* or: In deſire, vowe and will. For they that re-*ticu.* 4. ceaue it not : are neither in deed, nor in vowe, neither Sacramentallie, nor mentallie incorporated to Chriſt , nor made his members, by whom onlie, ſaluation is obtained. He therefore that shal be preuented by death before he actually obtayne this Sacrament in acte and deed realie, if he haue an ardent deſire to be Baptiſed, may be ſaued for and by the deſire of Baptiſme, which did proceed of faith working by loue , by which God inwardly ſanctifieth him. The reaſon is becauſe God hath not ſo bound himſelfe or his power to theſe externall Sacraments (although he haue made them his ordinarie inſtruments) but that he may and doth in ſome caſes of neceſſitie, accept them as Baptiſed, who either are martired before they could be Baptiſed, or els departe this life with vowe and deſire to haue the Sacrament, when by ſome extreame neceſſitie it could not be obtained. Therefore I conclud that he, who shall

Con. neglect or contemne the Sacrament of Baptiſme *Trid.* as neceſſarie to ſaluation, and ſo commaunded *ſeſſ. 7.* by Chriſt, can not be ſaued. For this cauſe the *ca.non.* generall councell of Trent doth Anathematize *cap. 5.* thoſe who affime Baptiſme to be free at libertie, and not neceſſarie to ſaluation.

CAP.

CAP. 10.

VVhether in the third of S. Iohn Chrift *did treate of Baptifme.*

I moue this queftion in refpect of Caluin, becaufe he willing to maintaine Baptifme not to be neceffarie as the ordinarie meanes by Chrift inftituted to faluation , doth abfolutlie denie, That Chrift here in this Chapter recorded by the Euangelift, doth intreate of the Sacrament of Baptifme: and fo abufe the expreffe words of Chrift , with idle gloffes, and falfe interpretations, contrarie to the vnderftanding of generall Councells , auncient Fathers , and meaning of vniuerfall Church. And therefore by thefe words: *vnleffe a man be borne againe by water and the Holie Ghoft he can not enter into the kingdome of heauen.* Chrift *intendeth* (fayeth he) *onlie iuternall renouation, no externall Sacrament: therefore by this word (water) we muft vnderftand onlie the Holie Ghoft to make cleane and purge as water doth.* But this gloffe is abfurd , & the interpretation fained. For if Chrift did not intend an externall Sacrament confifting of water, but onlie an internall renouation, what need had he to vfe this word (Water) at all, but he might haue fayed abfolutlie: vnleffe a man be borne of the Holie Ghoft onlie he can not enter into the kingdome of heauen. But he plainlie fayed: vnleffe a man be borne of water & the Holie

(margin notes:)
Caluin lib . 4. inft .ca. 16. §. 25.

Anti-do.con. Trident. fef. 6.

the Holie Goſt to ſignifie the Sacrament of Baptiſme externallie to be water, and the Holie
Ghoſt internallie to worke:and therefore he put
them ioyntlie together, that by water and the
holie Ghoſt our entrance to heauen should be
effected. I call it a fained interpretation, becauſe it proceedeth from Caluins owne fancie.
For he can bring no generall councell,no cõſent
of Fathers, no practiſe of the primitiue Church
for his interpretation,becauſe they all ſtand firme in this place of Scripture: and the words of
Chriſt here related are manifeſt for the Sacramẽt
of Baptiſme,as the ordinarie meanes for mans
ſaluation, & that by Chriſts inſtitution; as shall

Ob.   & may appeare by the proceſſe of this treatiſe.

But Caluin may ſay:If I haue no councells nor
Fathers:Yet I haue Scripture for my purpoſe.It
Matth. is ſayed, that Chriſt shall Baptiſe in the Holy
3. 11. Ghoſt and fire: but fire maketh no Sacrament.
Luc. 3. nor is neceſſarie to ſaluation, but onlie expreſ-
ver.16. ſeth the effects of the Holie Ghoſt : ſo why
should the word (water) doe anie more . I an-
Sol.   ſwere: theſe words recited: that Chriſt should
Baptiſe in the holie Ghoſt and fire,were not ſpoken by Chriſt himſelf,but by his Prophet S.Iohn
Baptiſt whereby he might foretell & prophecie
of the the power of Chriſt in ſending the Holie
Ghoſt vpon the Apoſtles in the day of Pentecoſt
viſible in the forme of fierie tongues: Where
vpon the Apoſtles & Diſciples might be ſayed
to be Baptiſed in the Holie Ghoſt and fire. But
this was but once effected and done and that
vpon the Apoſtles onlie, and neuer propoſed
by Chriſt as an ordinarie meanes for all
                                    men: and

men: and therefore as much difference in thefe two places of *Scripture*, as betweene fire and water, two contrarie elements.

Secondly *Caluin* might haue marked, if he **2.** would, and fo may his Complices : that this word(fire)is put after the word (*Holy Ghoft*) as expreffing the effects, that the Holie Ghoft may worke: as to illuminate, enflame, and heate the hart and foule with faith and Charitie, as fire docth the bodie externallie.But the word(*water*) is put before the Holie Ghoft by *Chrift* as in his proper fignification, and concurring togeather with the Holie Ghoft to the fpirituall generation and new birth of man to life in C*hrift:* therefore there is not like reafon in the one as in the other.

Thirdlie *S. Iohn Baptift* fpake thofe words **3.** comparatiulie, that *Chrift*, who was to be after him, should *Baptife* in the *Holy Ghoft*, and fire: and that he was not worthie to carrie his shooes after him : to fignifie that his *Baptifme* was but weake, did not remitte° finne, but mo- ue to *Penance*, had not fo abfolutlie conioy- ned with it the operation & power of the Holie Ghoft: and therefore no way comparable with that of *Chrifts*. How then can that faying of *Caluin* and his partakers be approuable and al- **Ob.** lowed. *That Iohns Baptifme and Chrifts is all one, and that Iohns was as forceible as Chrifts?* I an- fwere:the propofition and faying is moft vntrue; and it was fpoken by *Caluin* not fo much to extoll *Iohns Baptifme*, as to derogate from **Sol.** *Chrifts*.Andtherefore he would that*ChriftsBapti- fme* : should not haue efficacie and force to re- mitte finne to giue grace, to caufe Iuftification,

D   and fo

and fo Confequentlie not neceffarie to faluation:
but onlie an externall figne of admittance to the
Congregation . And thus fhall Chrifts Sacraments be. difgraced , to maintaine Caluins
conceit and idle dreame againft all antiquitie.

CAP. II.

VVhen and at what tyme Chrift inftituted
Baptifme.

Math.
3.
Mar.1.
Luc. 3.
1.

2.

Io. 3.

3.

THere are three diuers opinions concerning
the inftitution of this Sacrament, by reafon
that three feuerall times in holie Scripture
Chrift hath in acte or word made fpeciall mention of this Sacrament. The firft opinion is:
that Chrift inftituted this Sacrament, when he
came himfelf in perfon to Iohn Baptift to be
Baptifed of him. The fecond opinion is : then
Chrift to haue inftituted Baptifme , when he
inftructed Nicodemus, and fhewed the neceffitie
thereof faying: *Nifi quis renatus &c. vnleffe euerie*
one be borne againe of water.and the Holy Ghoft, he
can not enter into the kingdome of heauen. The
third opinion is : that this Sacrament was inftituted after Chrifts Refurrection , when he gaue
Commiffion to his Apoftles to Baptife all nations and people; and withall prefcribed vnto
them the forme thereof faying : *Omnis poteftas*
data &c . All power is giuen me in heauen and in
earth ; Going therefore teach ye all nations,
                                        Baptifing

Baptifing them, *In the name of the Father, and of the Sonne, and of the Holie Ghoſt*. To make as it were a reconciliation of thefe three opinions, I will put downe what I thinke, fubmitting not withſtanding my felf to better iudgment.

In the firſt action I fuppofe that Chriſt decreed the inſtitution of this Sacrament, when perfonallie himfelf was Baptifed. In the fecond action, when he inſtructed Nicodemus, he gaue as is were the precept, fhewing the neceſſitie thereof. Finallie in the third action after his Refurrection, when he gaue Commiſſion to Baptife all nations and people, and withall expreſſed the forme, he declared the obligation thereof, that then it was obligatorie, and began to bind all men to receaue it. For proofe of the firſt that it was decreed and inſtituted in Chriſts Baptifme, is the opinion of S. Thomas, and by common confent the auncient Fathers doe teach: that Chriſt, when he was Baptifed in Iordan, did giue force and vertue of Sanctification to the waters. Read Tertullian, S. Hillarie, S. Ambrofe, S. Ierome and S. Gregórie Nazianzen. And no doubt he determined water to be the matter of Baptifme when he would vouchfafe to confecrate, illuſtrate, and make famous the water by the touch of his moſt holie and pure flefh. The forme alfo was fufficientlie declared (although not in words expreffed, as it was in the laſt action after the Refurrection) for the voyce of God the Father was heard from heauen: the Holy Ghoſt appeared in forme of a doue: and Chriſt IESVS the Sonne of God was there prefent in humayne flefh. So that here

Tho. 3. par. q. 66. a. 2. Tertul. li. con. Iudæos cap. de paſſione Hilla. c. 2. in Math. Amb. li 2. in Luc. Iero. in dialogo con Lucifera Greg. Nazi in orat. in Sancta Lumina.

D 2   was

was the forme and matter declared .

2. For the second : that *Christ* gaue as it were a precept and declared it neceſſarie to ſaluation, it is playne by the words of *Christ* to *Nicodemus*. Yet that men were not bound to receaue *Baptiſme*, nor this precept obligatorie before the *Paſſion* of *Christ*, and promulgation of the newe Lawe, and abrogation of the old , *S. Thomas* proueth in the place before cited . For the third : that the obligation, and neceſſitie to vſe *Baptiſme* was declared and proclaimed vnto all men after the *Paſſion* and *Reſurrection* of *Christ*, it is manifeſt. Becauſe at that tyme , and after the *Paſſion* of *Christ* all the Ceremonies and figures of the old lawe ceaſed, and in place of them ſucceeded *Baptiſme*, and other *Sacraments* of the *Ghoſpell* and newe lawe . And alſo becauſe man by *Baptiſme* is configurated and faſhioned alike to the *Paſſion* and *Reſurrection* of *Christ*. For as *Christ* died for ſinne : ſo alſo man ſhould die to ſinne . And as he roſe to life and glorie : ſo alſo he ſhould begin the newe life of *Iuſtice* . Therefore *Christ* muſt firſt ſuffer his *Paſſion*, and riſe againe to life , before man could of neceſſitie configurate and conforme himſelf.

Wherefore I conclude, that *Baptiſme* might be inſtituted, and commaunded by *Christ* in his life tyme : but not obligatorie , nor of bond neceſſarilie to be obſerued before the death and *Paſſion* of *Christ*. It were no improbable opinion to thinke, that *Christ* might haue inſtituted this *Sacrament* of *Baptiſme*, when he in perſon Baptiſed his *Apoſtles*.

                                        C A P.

CAP. 12.

Whether the Sacrament of Baptifme by Martirdome or Contrition of harte may be fupplied.
And whether the definition of three Baptifmes,
that is : Of Bloud, of Charitie, and water be
in holie Scripture .

THere is no doubt but from the begining in
the *Primitiue Church*, and all ages vnto this
day the threefold diftinction of *Baptifme* that is:
*Säguinis, flaminis, & fluminis : Of Bloud, charitie
and water* , hath bene approued and allowed of
all; and that the *Sacrament* of *Baptifme* might be
fupplied by the other two , that is : a man by
Martirdome may be fayed to be *Baptifed* and
bathed in his owne bloud, cleanfed and wafhed
from finne . Alfo by the flames of Charitie and
loue towards *God*, the Holy Ghoft working with
the teares of *Contrition* and *compunction* of harte, may be fayed to haue his foule purged from
finne; and the ruft and canker thereof confumed.
It is manifeft that *Martirdome* in *Scripture* is *Mar.*
called *Baptifme*. For *Chrift* fayed to *Iohn* and 10.
Iames the fonnes of *Zebede : Poteftis bibere cali-
cem, &c. Can you drinke the Cuppe I drinke : or be
Baptized with the Baptifme, where with I am to be
Baptifed*? And he fayed, they fhould , fignifiyng
that *Martirdome* is *Baptifme* . Alfo it is fayed in
the *Apocalyps : Hi funt qui venerunt ex magna, Apoc.
&c. Thefe are they, who are come out of greate tri- 7.
bulation , and haue washed their ftoles , and haue
made them white in the bloud of the lambe . And*

D 3   for

for *flammis*, no doubt but, when the foule fhall
be enflammed with perfect Charitie, and the
hart by the worke of the Holy Ghoſt be moued
to beleeue in God, to loue him, to be penitent for
his finnes, it is a kind of Baptiſme, and
will fupplie the want of the Sacrament in cafe
of neceſſitie . And it is plaine in Scripture
that Penitencie is called Baptiſme ; for it is

Luc. 3. fayed: *Iohn was preaching the Baptiſme of Pe-*
Mar. 1. *nance vnto remiſſion of finnes* . And thus much
Ezech. Ezechiel the Prophet confirmeth : *If the im-*
18. *pious man shall doe Penance fore his finnes, I*
will remember no more his iniquitie. Wherefore
I conclude, that by Martirdome, and Penance
in neceſſity, the Sacrament of Baptiſme may be
fupplied.

CAP. 13.

How there can be vnitie of Baptiſme, if there
be three in diſtinction.

Ephes. 4 WE make no doubt, but S. Paule fayeth:
Vna fides, vnum Baptiſma, vnus Chriſtus.
There is one faith, one Baptiſme, one Chriſt.
Alfo the Nicene Creed maketh profeſſió of one
Baptiſme : *Credo vnum Baptiſma in remiſſionem*
peccatorum : I beleeue one Baptiſme vnto remiſſion
of finnes. Howe then can there be a diſtinction of
Baptiſmes? Or how can thefe three keepe vnitie
of one Baptiſme ? S. Thomas anfwereth : *That*
Th. 3. p. *the vnitie of Baptiſme is not taken away by this di-*
q 66. a. *ſtinction, becaufe the two firſt of Bloud and Charitie*
11 ad 1. *Sanguinis & flamminis, are included in the third of*
vvater,

water,which hath his efficacie and force from one fountaine the Paffion of Chrift *and the Holy Ghoft.* Alfo they worke all one effect, and by one principall caufe: the effect is Remiffion of finnes, confering of grace, wafhing and cleanfing of the foule; the principall caufe is the Holie Ghoft . For although the meanes be different, that is : By Bloud, by fire. by water : yet the effect and principall Agent being all one, the difference of meanes doth not take away vnitie .

Moreouer the two firft are included in the Sacrament of Baptifme, and onlie take place in cafe of neceffitie, when Baptifme can not be had. As for example: If a man fhould be iuftified, and haue Originall finne blotted out by Penance , by loue towards God , by Contrition and vowe of Baptifme : yet afterwards, although his finne fhould be thus remitted, and he made Iuft , if he fhould contemne the Sacrament , that is Baptifme of water, he fhould for this his contempt be damned, and neuer enter into heauen. And this is proued by the example of Nicodemus ; for although when he came to Chrift he had faith and Charitie and beleeued in him : yet Chrift fayed vnto him. Vnleffe one be borne of water and the Holy Ghoft, he can not enter into the Kingdome of heauen. And S. Auguftine writing againft the Donatifts, fayeth: *Although Cornelius the Italian Centurion , of whom it is written in the Acts of the Apoftles, were a Iuft man , and had receaued the Holy Ghoft : yet if he fhould haue neglected the Sacramet of Baptifme: Contēptus tāt Sacramenti reus fieret : He fhould haue bene guiltie of the contempte of fo greate a Sacrament , which* is the gate to faluation. D 4 C A P.

Ioa. 3.
Aug. li.
4. da
Bap.
ca. 21.
Act.
10.

CAP. 14.

Whether if one *Baptised in his owne bloud should ouerliue, were after of necessitie to be Baptised with water.*

THe cafe is, if one sholud be leaft by his Perfecutour as dead , but yet after reuiue againe (as it happened to *S. Sebaſtian*) *although* he were readie to shed his bloud , and yeald his life for *Chriſtian* faith:yet I make no doubt,if he should thus ouerliue , but that he ought to be baptifed with water; And in no refpect , nor for anie reafon of being ready to fuffer martirdom or other wayes, to côtemne or neglect the *Sacrament.* My reafon is , becaufe this *Sacrament* being ordained and commaunded by *Chriſt* as a neceffarie remedie for the foule of man , is of neceffitie to faluation *In re* , or *In voto*, that is : In *deed*, or In *vowe* : Wherefore he that fhould neglect it , or contemne it , although other wayes iuftified, fhould doe againft the ordinance and commaundement of *Chriſt.* For *Chriſt* fayed vnto *Nicodemus* a beleeuing man , a faithfull man , but not fullie instructed in *Baptifme* : *vnleſſe a man be borne of water and the Holy Ghoſt, he can not enter into the kingdome of heauen.* Alfo the example of *Cornelius* is more apparent, and conuinceth that *Baptifme* is neceffarie,becaufe the *Scripture* doth fay : *That he was a Iuſt* man , in refpect of his morall vertues:*one that feared God,* who alfo had receaued the Holie Ghoft at the preaching of *S. Peter,* yet was he *Baptifed* by *S. Peter.* Although fuch may be the

Ion. 3.

Act. 10.

be the grace of God to fome, that they may haue remiffion of finnes and fanctitie, alfo receaue the HolieGhoft before anie *Sacrament* be miniftred: yet not withftanding they muft of neceffitie be *Baptifed* with water . Wherefore I conclude that although *martyrdome* and Contrition may in neceffitie fupplie the want of this *Sacrament* : yet they are not fufficient to faluation, but in cafe of neceffitie, when the other can not be had: but if euer it come fo to paffe, that they may receaue it, they are bound vnto it. And I am of opinion, that if one fhould be a *Martyr* and die, and after be rayfed miraculouflie againe to life, and ouerliue, that he ought to feeke and receaue the *Sacrament* of *Baptifme*, that he may thereby receaue the indeleble Character of a *Chriftian*.

CAP. 15.

Whether *Baptifme* of *Bloud* be *more worthie* then *Baptifme* (Flaminis) *of Charitie*, *or* then the *Sacrament*.

TO fuffer death for confeffing of *Chrift* to be true God and man , to fhed his bloud for teftimonie of the true *Church* of God , to fuffer perfecution for Gods caufe , to yeeld his life for Religion and Iuftice fake, finallie to be a *Martyr*, hath euer beene accounted the perfecteft acte, and greateft figne of the loue of God that could proceed from man in this mortall life: And this *Chrift* hath confirmed: *Maiorem charitatem &c.* Ion.15 *Greater loue then this no man hath , that a man yeeld his life for his friends.* Wherefore no doubt, but the worthieft, and perfecteft *Baptifme* is , to

D 5   be *Bapti-*

Aug. li. be Baptifed in their owne bloud . And S. Augu-
de ec- ftine comparing them togeather, preferreth
clef. Martirdome : *Baptizatus aqua confitetur fidem*
dogma. *fuam coram Sacerdote: Martyr coram perfequutore,*
cap. 74. *&c. He that is* (fayeth this holie Doctour) *Bapti-*
fed vvith vvater, doth confeffe his faith, but before
the Prieft: but he that is Baptifed in his bloud , doth
confeffe his faith , doth proteſte Chrift and his
Church in the face of the Perfecutour & enemie of
Chriſt and his Church . The firſt is vvaſhed vvith
vvater : the fecond is cleanfed vvith bloud . Thus
S. Auguſtine. And no doubt but Martirdome in-
fufeth more grace, then either Contrition or the
Sacrament . Thus much the Holy Church hath
defined , all ages haue confirmed, and S. Auguſtine maketh it a rule : *Qui orat pro Martyre, in-*
iuriam Martyri facit : It is iniurie to pray for a
Martyr to doubt of the glorie of a Martyr, were but
impious.

Tho. 3.   Wherefore I conclude with S. Thomas, that
p. 1. 67. the worthieft Baptifme is in Bloud : becaufe
ar. 12. therein is expreffed liuelie by imitation the Paffion of Chrift, and the vertue of the Holie Ghoſt
by the feruour of loue : But if we fpeake of the
neceffitie (as we did in the precedent Chapters)
then the Sacrament is to be preferred before
them both, as hath bene fayd.

CAP. 16.

Whether by Baptifme a character , or indeleble
Signe be imprinted in the foule of the Baptifed.

IT is the generall opinion of Catholike Diuines auncient and moderne; that the Sacrament
of Baptifme

of Baptisme doth not onlie giue grace, but imprinteth and sealeth the soule of the Baptised with a spirituall signe, marke and badge indeleble, which can neuer be blotted out, but remayneth for euer, the soule being immortall, as the Cognizance and badge of their Christendome, whereby they shall be knowen as a distinct people from those; who were neuer vnder Christs baner, nor of his fold·Therefore S. Paule sayeth: *That God also hath sealed vs, and giuen the pleadge in our hartes*. And he doth exhorte the Ephesians:*That they doe not contristate the Holie Spirite of God, in vvhich they are signed vnto the day of Redemption* : that is, the day of regeneration by Baptisme. And if by Circumcision, which was but a figure of Baptisme, God would that the iewes should haue a marke and token in their bodies, wherby they should be knowen to be his speciall people; and therby discerned from others, whie then should it be impious or inconuenient to thinke, that Christs Baptisme would haue the soule of euere Baptised man to be marked and sealed with the Character and signe of a Christian, whereby he may be knowen for the souldiour of Christ, and distincte from Iewe, Turke, or infidell? This is not onlie the opinion of Scholasticall Diuines, but conforme to the consent of auncient Fathers, and defined· in the Councell of Florence & Trent. Therefore Anathema to Caluin and his followers, who would seeme to impugne so auncient and consonant doctrine.

2.Cor.
1.

Ephes.4

THE

THE SECOND
BOOKE.

Of the matter and forme of Baptiſme.

CAP. I.

Whether water be by Chriſts inſtitution the matter of the Sacrament of Baptiſme.

HERE is no doubte , the *Scripture* is moſt plaine , that *Chriſt* ordained and inſtituted water for the matter of *Baptiſme* as an eſſentiall parte of this *Sacrament*. And firſt when *Chriſt* our *Sauiour* would vouchſafe to be *Baptiſed* in the waters of *Iordan* by *Iohn* the *Baptiſt* , out of queſtion he decreed, inſtituted and ſanctified the waters to be the matter of this *Sacrament*, euen at that tyme by the touch of his holie bodie . This is the common conſent of the auncient Fathers as I haue before cited. Alſo when *Chriſt* tolde *Nicodemus* that there was no way to heauen but by regeneration, by a newe birth , he expreſſed the water as neceſſarie when he ſayed: *Vnleſſe one be borne ex aqua: of water* . And moreouer by the practiſe of the *Primitiue Church it* is pregnant and plainlie proued; for when S. *Philippe* the deacon had inſtructed in the beleef of *Chriſt* a man of *Æthio-*

Lib. I.
cap. II.

Ioa. 3.

Act. 8.

ia, on

pia, one greate in authoritie vnder Queene *Can-daces*, queene of the *Æthiopiás* her chief and high Treafurer, and as they went by the way, they came to a certaine water, the Treafurer fayed: *Lo water, quis prohibet me Baptizari?* Who *doeth lett me to be Baptifed?* And commaunding the Chariote to ftay, they went both into the water and he was *Baptifed*. And *S. Peter* when he came into *Cæfarea* vnto the houfe of *Cornelius* Aß. the *Italian*, who expecting *S.Peters* coming, ga- 10. thered togeather his kinred and fpeciall friends, *S. Peter* Catechizing and inftructing them of IESVS and *Chriftian* faith, as he was fpeaking, the Holy Ghoft fell on them; Whe-re vpon he fayed to the faithfull of the *Cir-cumcifion*: *Can anie man forbid water that thefe be baptifed*. Whereby it is moft manifeft, that wa-ter is the onlie matter of this *Sacrament*. I need not alleadge *S. Paule* who fayeth: *That the Church* Ephef. *was to be fanctified and cleanfed in the lauer of wa-* 5. *ter.* And *S. Peter* compareth *Baptifme* to the *water of the Deluge*. For as the waters bearing vp the 1.Pet.3 *Arke* from finking, the perfons in it were faued from drowning, that is eight foules were faued by water: fo now *Baptifme* bearing vp our fou-les, we doe fwimme and are faued by water. Aug.li. Whervpon S. *Auguftine* fayeth: *As Noe and his* 2. con. *was deliuered by the water and the wood: So the fa-* Fauft. *milie of Chrift by Baptifme figned with Chrifts* cap.14. *Paffion on the Croffe*. & 17.

That water fhould be the matter of this Sacra-ment the *Prophet Ezechiel* did prophefie, faying in the perfon of God. *Effundam fuper vos aquám* Ezech. *mundam: I will powre out vpon you pure cleane* 37. *water.* Nu.29.

water. Alfo as Moyfes the firſt Redeemer of the
people of Ifraëll out of the Captiuitie of Ægypte
did make the waters of the well to afcend:fo the
fecond Redeemer Chriſt our Sauiour in a higher
degree then to refreſh the bodie , hath exalted
the waters to the cleafing of the foule . And Ioël
the Prophet foretold as much prophefieing of
the Sacrament of Baptifme : *Et fons de domo Dei*

Ioel.3. *egredietur, &c. And a vvell ſhall goe forth of the*
houſe of God, and ſhall vvater the brookes of thor-
nes. By the brookes of thornes is vnderſtood the
multitude of finners , which this water ſhall
waſhe and cleanfe. Zacharias prophefiyng of the

Zacha. Baptifme which was to be inſtituted by Chriſt,
ca. 13. fayth: *In illa die, &c.* In that day there ſhall be a
fountaine opened to the houſe of Dauid , and to all
the Inhabitants of Ierufalem : In ablutionem pec-
catorum & menſtruatæ : For the ablution and
cleanfing of finnes , and diſtayned vvith flovvers.
Wherefore I may conclud' by the foretelling of
the Prophets; by Chriſts inſtitution, by the practife of the Apoſtles, by the vfe of the Primitiue
Church,by the confent of Fathers, and the agreement of all ages,water to be true and onlie matter of this Sacrament.

Cap. 2.

VVhat are the reafons whie water aboue all other
things was chofen and taken for the matter of
this Sacrament .

Principallie becaufe water by operation doth
mundifie , purge , cleanfe and waſhe all filth
away:

away:and being thus significatiue doth expresse
the effects of Baptisme, that is : to mundifie,
purge cleanse and washe the foule from sinne.
And S. Cyrill Bishop of Ierusalem doth yeeld *Cyril-*
aboundant reasons. First, water is one of the *lus Ca-*
chiefest elements of the fower, and no terrene *tech. 3.*
Creature hath a being of life without this element; So of the Sacraments Baptisme is the
first and chiefe Sacrament, and no terrene earthlie man borne into this world hath ordinarilie
his being and birth in Christ, his spirituall life
without the water of Baptisme. Second heauen
is the habitacle of Angells ; but the hea-
uens are from the waters : so man, being borne to be Cittizen with Angells , is to haue *Gen. 1.*
his heauen and habitacle from and by the water
of regeneration. Third , the earth is the place for the waters, but the earth is from the waters : so man, although his place and nature
be earth : yet he hath a spirituall being by the
water of regeneration. Fourth , before the
distinction of all things created , and the diuision of the sixe dayes , the spirite of God
moued ouer the waters : so that as water in
the begining of the world, receaued certaine *Gen. ca.*
virtue of the Holie Ghost to giue life *1. v. 2.*
and produce liuing creatures : so the water of Baptisme receaueth virtue of the same
Holie Ghost , to regenerate man anewe,
and to giue him life in Christ . Fifth. At
the waters of Iordan, when Christ came to *Math. 3*
be Baptised , the distinction of persons in the *Mar. 1.*
Blessed Trinitie shewed it self. God the Father *Luc. 3.*
spake from heauen : This is my Beloued Sonne.

God

God the Holie Ghoſt in the forme of a doue light
vpon the ſhoulders of our *Sauiour* . And God the
Sonne *Chriſt Ieſus* in humane nature came to be
Baptiſed of *Iohn.*So in *Baptiſme Chriſt* commaunded the forme to be in the name of the *Bleſſed
Trinitie* the *Father*, the *Sonne*, and the *HolieGhoſt.*
Sixth.*S. Marke* began his Ghoſpell with the *Baptiſme* of *Iohn* , and the waters of *Iordan* : ſo we
begin to enter into the *Church* of God , to be
members of *Chriſts Bodie* miſticall, and to enioy
the fruites of the Ghoſpell by the waters of *Bap-*

*Gen.*1. *tiſme.* Seauenth. As water was at the firſt the be-
ver. 6. gining of the world : ſo the water of *Baptiſme.* by
Chriſts inſtitution is the begining of ſpirituall life

*Exo.*14 Eight.The deliuerie of *Iſraëlites* from*Pharao* was
effected by the waters of the ſeas: ſo deliuerie of
the world from ſinne was in the lauer of water in
the word of God . Ninth. After the deluge and
ouerflowing of the earth with water , God made

*Gen.*9. a leägue , pacte , and promiſe with *Noe* that he
would neuer deſtroy the world with water
againe;but as water was vſed as a puniſhmēt for
ſinne: ſo ſhould it now be a preſeruatiue againſt
ſinne . Tenth. *Elias* firſt paſſed the waters of Ior-

4, Reg. dan, and then after he was rapte into heauen : ſo
2. we muſt firſt paſſe by *Baptiſme* , before we can
enter into heauen. Eleauenth. *Aaron* and his ſon-

Exod. nes by the commaundement of God, were to be
29. waſhed in water before they could be made
Prieſts . ſo in the lawe of *Chriſt* no man can be
capable of holie Orders', or made *Prieſt,* before
he be waſhed in the water of *Baptiſme.* And the

Exod. braſen lauer or ceſterne of water, which God
38. commaunded *Moyſes* to make in the old Teſta-
              men

ment, was a figure of Baptifme. And it was commaunded to be fet and placed betweene the
Tabernacle of teftimonie , and the Altar
being filled full of water: and that none should *Exo40.*
enter vnder the roofe of the Couenant , no
not Moyfes, nor Arron, nor his fonnes, before
they had washed their hands and feete : to
fignifie, how cleane in all partes the water
of baptifme did make the foule of man.

Thefe are the reafons, which S.Cyrill giueth;
why water efpeciallie was elected and chofen
to be the matter, and one of the principall and
effenfiall partes of Baptifme. And S. Thomas *Tho.3.*
addeth : that *there is no generation of terrene p.q.66.*
and earthlie Creatures , but by humiditie and *u 2.*
water; and therefore as Ariftotle reporteth, *Arift.*
according to the opinion of fome Philofo- *li. 2.*
phers : *Aqua erat principium omnium rerum:* *Phyf.*
water was the begining of all creatures : fo Baptifme is the begining of all Spirituall life : and
we are borne anewe and regenerated by
water and the Holy Ghoft. Water is humide, &
moyft, and therefore apte to washe and cleanfe.
It is frigide and cold : and therefore apte to
refrigerate , coole and temper heate: It is
Diaphanike, and cleare as Criftal : and therefore apte to receaue light ; So Baptifme doth
washe and cleanfe the foule from finne, coole
and temper the heate of Concupifcence,
cleare and illuminate the foule with the
lightof faith and true beleefe in Chrift Iefus.

E   C A P.

CAP. 3.

VVhat kind of Water was inflituted the matter of this Sacrament.

THere is no doubt, and it is generallie concluded of all Diuines, that elementall water is the true wather and matter of this Sacrament. And the elementall water, we call either fountaine water, well water, rayne water, riuer water, running water, poole water, or standing water, and fea water. Concernig fea water, fome there are; who moue fome quefion, and make fome difficultie, becaufe it is not fimple and pure water as the other waters are; but troubled, mixte, muddie and falte : yet all Diuines generallie hold, that fea water is fufficient , and true water for this Sacrament. Becaufe it is elementall, hath the Species and forme of true water, and all other elementall water doth iffue, fpring, and hath his begining from the feas, and neuer refteth, but runneth continually vntill it arriue vnto the fea againe, from whence it had his begining, becaufe the fea is the naturall and proper place for the waters. And no doubt Chrift made choyfe, and inftituted this naturall, elementall , and common water, for the vfe of this Sacrament, becaufe it is vfuall , and ordinarie in all places and countreys, and common to all people, rich and poore . This was moft conuenient, for that this Sacrament is of neceffitie to faluation the

tion, the gate and entrie to life eternall , and wthout this no Chriſtianitie . Therefore it was neceſſarie as S. Thomas and other Doctours ſay , that the matter thereof should be eaſie to be gotten of all, vſuall in all places, & common to all people.

CAP. 4.

VVhether one may be Baptiſed with Ice, Snow, or hayle.

IT is the generall opinion of all Diuines, that Baptiſme can not be miniſtred in anie of theſe three, Snow, Ice , or haile. The reaſon is for that they are, *Corpora denſa, non fluida* : *thicke, not reſolued, liquid* , *not fluent bodies.* Although in the opinion of all Philoſophers (as in deed true it is) that in euerie one of them there is reallie and trulie contained the element of water, and that they are nothing but *aqua Congelata* : *water congealed.* Yet as long as they contayne theſe ſpecies , and want the proprieties of water, they can not be the ſufficient matter of Baptiſme. The proprieties of water are, to be liquide, fluent, and abluent, which neiter Ice, show, nor haile haue, remayning in that forme of Ice, ſnow, and haile. But if they be melted and receaue againe the forme of water, and proprieties thereof, that is to be liquide, fluent , and abluent, there is then no doubte but they may be the true matter of Baptiſme. So alſo if you take a ſponge or

E 2   linnen

linnen cloth, and dippe them in water, no
doubt there is water contained in them both:
but yet with them you can not Baptife, vnleffe you wring or fquiefe out the water, that
there may be apparently the forme and Species with the proprietie of water, as I fayed
before.

CAP. 5.

*VVhether water of the Bath, Brimftone-water,
Allume-water, or wyche-water whereof
Salt is made, may be vfed in Baptifme.*

I Aske this queftion, and make a doubt, for
that we haue here in England in the Cittie
of Bath, the water of bathe, which doth fpring
vp verie hoate, and the water of S. Anne of
Buxtons alfo hoate, but fomewhat more tem-
perate. This calor or heate of thefe waters,
is contrarie to the qualitie and proprietie of
elementall water, which is cold & frigide by
nature. Alfo there be fprings, and wells, where the water of fome of them haue the tafte of
Brimftone, fome of Allume, fome of Salt, as
it is well knowen, and proued by experience.
But the Philofopher fayeth, that the elementall
water ordinarilie is not *Saporofa, Hath no fapor
or tafte at all.* The difficulte doth arife, for that
I fayed in the third Chapter before, that Chrift
inftituted the naturall elementall water for the
matter of this Sacrament? But thefe waters
haue their proprietie and qualities contrarie
to the

Ob.

to the element of water, as to be hoat, to taft
of brimftone, of allume, and of falt. Notwithftanding I fay in neceffitie thefe waters may be   *Sol.*
vfed in Baptifme. For that I make no doubt
but in thefe fprings, wells and waters, there is
the true elementall water, although the Acci-
dentall proprieties or qualities be altered. As
the water of the Bath or Buxtons paffing or
fpringing from fome hoat metall or matter
caufeth this alteration of heat. So alfo the brimftone or allume-water haue thofe taftes and
fapours by fpringing and paffing through or
from fome mine of brimftone or allume: Wherfore for a further refolution, I will put downe
the opinion of S. Thomas the moft worthieft *Th.3.p.*
Schoole-diuine : *In quacunque aqua quomodo-* q. 66.
cunque tranfmutata, dummodo non foluatur fpe- *art.* 4.
cies aqua, poteft fieri Baptifmus: In anie water
howfoeuer it be altered, fo that the fpecies or for-
me of water be not altered, or taken away, Bap-
tipme may be effected and done in it .

The reafon why thefe waters of the Bath,
brimftone, allume & wiche may be vfed in neceffitie for Baptifme is, becaufe they retaine the
nature of elementall water, and only are altered
Accidétallie by fpring or paffage of thofe mines,

CAP. 6.

VVhether one may Baptife in Rofe-water, or
any other diftilled water.

I Anfwere with all Catholike Diuines, that
no water made by arte, as Rofe-water,

E 3   and all

and all diftilled waters are , can be vfed in
Baptifme : but of neceffitie it muft be naturall
elementall water . And thus much I haue po-
ued before by the institution of Chrift , by
the practife of the Apostles , and confent of
.ọ. the vniuerfall Church. I haue heard of one who
was baptifed in Rofe Water; but I dare boldlie
pronounce he neuer had true Baptifme.

CAP. 7.

VVheter one may Baptife in VVine , Ale,
Bere, or Milke in neceſſitie , when water can
not be had.

I Anfwere abfolutlie , that in no cafe , in
no neceffitie there can be Baptifme in wine,
ale,beere or milke. My reafon is , becaufe by
the inftitution of Chrift himfelf this Sacrament muft haue his due matter , which is no
other then naturall elementall water ; Ergo
there can be no Baptifme nor Sacrament miniftred in them. But if you aske me , if there
be no doubt or queftion of it , why then
doe I moue it ? I anfwere onlie to giue you

Luth.
warning to beware of the errour and madneffe
in Col-
of Martin Luther,the prime Apoftle of Protef-
loquijs
tancie. For in his banqueting Communications,
fimpo-
or rather I may fay his drunken Conferences
ſiaticis
being asked the queftion , at firft he ftood
ca. 17.
doubtfull and fayed , it was to be remitted
to the diuine Iudgment : but afterward he
added and refolued himfelf faying . *VVhatfoeuer*
was fitte to be applied for bathing , or to make
a bath

*a bath might be applied to Baptife ; but there is
no doubt, but wine, ale, beere and milke may
be vfed for bathing.* Therfore in his idle conceit vfed alfo in Baptifme. But againft this
errour, and fond imagination of this Heretike
the Councell of Trent hath defined : That true
and naturall water is the onlie matter of Bap- *Cōcill.*
tifme. And therfore : *Si quis dixerit aquam* *Triden-*
veram & naturalem non effe de neceffitate *feff. 7.*
Baptifmi, Anathema fit : *If any man fhall fay* *can. 2.*
that true and naturall water is not of neceffitie
of Baptifme, let him be accurfed.

CAP. 8.

*VVhether it be conuenient the font fhould be
hallowed, and the water bleffed before
Baptifme.*

WE neuer held that it was of the effence
of Baptifme that the font fhould be
hallowed, or the water confecrated
and bleffed; but in cafe of neceffitie we allwayes
allowed Baptifme to be avayleable without
benediction of the water. And it was decreed
as a matter in queftion aboue 1200. Yeares
agoe by S. Victor Pope and Martyre: *Vt quauis
aqua, modo naturali, fi neceffitas cogeret quicunque Baptizari poffet* : *That anie one, if neceffitie
did vrge & cōpell might be Baptifed in any kind of
water.* So it were naturall elementall water whether it were hallowed, or nothallowed, confecrated or not confecrated. Yet you muft vnderftand that this decree doth take place on-

E 4   lie in

lie in cafe of necessitie, as in imminent daunger
of the child, or fome other vrget caufe. Otherwayes no doubt but the font ought to be hallowed, and the water bleffed. And we Catholikes make no queftion but that the confecration
of the font, Exorcifmes and blessing of the
water was inftituted by the Apoftles, or their
immediate Succeffours, and euer vfed as a folemne Ceremonie in the auntient Church of
Chrift Therefore no reafon why it should be
abrogated and abolished by the Sectaries of this
age, and not vfed by the Proteftants of our
Countrey, hauing continued fo many ages and
hundred of yeares both in the vniuerfall Church
and our Church of England. Is it not conuenient, that water being common and triuiall to
all prophane vfes, being affumed and taken to
the vfe of a holy Sacrament, should be confecrated and bleffed? Confidering that water by
Chrift was conftituted for the matter of regeneratio of mankind, for the washing and Cleanfing of finne, to make vs readie for heauen, and
fitte Companions whit Angells, (I fay) to fo
high and holie a vfe : What inconuenience
were it to haue the water confecrated, and
bleffed before Baptifme, that we may learne
to difcerne and diftinguish facred and holie
thinge, from prophane and Common thinge?
By this hallowing and Confecration of the
water fayeth S. Thomas : *Excitatur deuotio*
Tho. 3. *fidelium, & impeditur aftutia Dæmonis ne im-*
p.q. 66. *pediat Baptifmi effectum : The Deuotion of the*
a. 3. ad *faithfull is ftirred vp, and the crafte & fubtiltie*
5. *of the Deuill hindered that he may not with-*
ftand the effects of Baptifme. And S. Paule
his rule

his rule was : *Let all things be, done honeftly,* comely *and according to order among you Al-tough* (fayeth S. Bonauenture) *it be not of necef-fitie, that before Baptifme the water be confe-crated : Yet it is : Congruum : It is conuenient and comely, that the water be confecrated and Sanctified by the prayer of the Prieft.* And Therefore fayeth Siluefter : *that the Prieft finneth mortallie, if he Baptife: Extra neceffita-tem: Except in cafe of neceffitie: If the water be-fore be not confecrated and fanctified.* Dionifius S. Paule his Scholler, aduifed that before Bap-tifme the waters be confecrated and fanctified: *Regenerationis aqua facris inuocationibus prius confecretur: Let the water of Regeneration whit Sacred & holy inuocations and prayers before hand be fanctified and Confecrated.* S. Bafill maketh no doubt conftantlie to affirme:*That the Benediction of the font defcended to them in his tyme from the Apoftles , and was vfed by Apoftolicall Tradition.* S. Ambrofe one of the fower principall Doctors of the Church,fayeth:*That the Prieft before Bap-tifme cometh to the font and maketh his prayers, and inuocateth the name of God ouer the water &c.* And S. Cyprian warneth that before Baptifme there muft be Confecration of the font : *Oportet mundari & confecrari aquam prius a facerdote: The water muft firft* (fayeth he) *be cleanfed and Sanctified by the Prieft.* And finallie S Auguftine in manie places fpeaketh of hallowing the font, and fantifiyng the water .

Bona-uen. in Quar-to: Siluef. ver. Bap. §. 2.num. 10. Dionif. Are op. Ecclef. Hier.p. 2.c.2. Bafil. lib. de Spir.S. ca. 27. Amb. li.2.de Sacra-mentis ca. 15. Cyp. Aug.li. 6. de Baptif. cō. Do-nat. tract. 8. in Ioã. & epif. 118.ad Ianua-rium.

CAP.

CAP. 9.

What is the forme of Baptisme.

Auing sufficientlie entreated and spoken concerning the matter of Baptisme: now followeth to speake of the forme, for these two are essentiall partes of the Sacrament, yf either should be wanting, there could be no Baptisme. There is no doubt but the forme of this Sacrament was instituted and determined by Christ our Sauiour himselfe, after his glorious Resurrection, when he appeared to his eleauen Apostles vpon the mount in Galilie saying: *All power is giuen me in heauen and in earth: Going therfore teach yee all nations, Baptizing them, In the name of the Father, and of the Sonne, and of the Holy Ghost.* This recordeth S. Mathew in his Gospell. The forme then the Church giueth and commaundeth according to the institution of Christ is: N. *Ego Baptizo te, In nomine Patris, & Filij, & Spiritus Sancti. Amen.* Iohn or Thomas, I Baptise thee in the name of the Father, and of the Sonne, and of the Holie Ghost: Amen.

I say these two are essentiall partes of Batisme, for neither the water without the word, nor the word without the water, can worke anie effect; but it is necessarie that the matter & the forme goe ioyntlie

togeath

Mat. 28.

togeather. For if I ſhould ſay theſe wordes ouer the child: I *Baptiſe thee in the name of the Father, and of the Sonne, and of the Holy Ghoſt* , and haue no water it were no Baptiſme. Alſo if I had water and powred it vpon the child, and did not ſay the words, it were nothing. The word then and the water muſt goe togeather ioyntlie that Baptiſme may haue his effecte. And this S. Paule expreſſed when he ſayed: *Mundans eam lauacro aquæ in verbo vitæ. Cleanſing her.* (that is: his Church) *with the lauer of water in the word of life.* *Epheſ. 5.*

In this forme ſayeth S. Thomas, are expreſſed the two cauſes of Baptiſme, that is: the Principall cauſe, and the inſtrumentall: the Principall cauſe in theſe words: *In the name of the Father, and of the Sonne, and of the Holie Ghoſt.* Wherby is ſingnified that this Sacrament hath his efficacie, vertue, power and effect from Almightie God: and that the Bleſſed Trinitie is the principall Agent, and worker of remiſſion of ſinnes, and cleanſing the ſoule of man by this Sacrament. And here note that we are taught in this forme of Baptiſme by Chriſt and his Church to ſay: In the name, and not In the names: to ſignifie that there is but one God in eſſence and ſubſtance; Yet alſo we muſt ſay: the Father, the Sonne, & the Holie Ghoſt; to. vnderſtand and knowe, that there are three perſons and one God, all three concurring to the ſanctifieing of the ſoule of man. The Inſtrumentall cauſe is declared in theſe words : *Ego Baptizo te . I Baptiſe the;* Wherby it is declared that necaſſarilie the Miniſter muſt concurre as the inſtrumentall *Tho. 3. p.q.66. a. 5.*

cauſe

caufe externally, to deliuer and giue this Sacrament to the people, and God internallie to worke the effect of it. Therfore Chrift *Ioan.3.* fayed to Nicodemus: *Vnleffe one be borne againe of water and the Holie Ghoft, he can not enter into the kingdome of heauen .* Wherby Chrift would haue vs to vnderftand that the Sacrament, that is, the water and the word externallie muft be miniftred , deliuered , and giuen vs by the Prieft , and the Holy Ghoft working internallie, and both concurring ioyntlie, the one as the Principall caufe, the other as the Inftrumentall , or elfe no entrance into the *Mat* kingdome of heauen. In the laft of S. Mathew *28.* (as I cited before) Chrift fayeth to his Apoftles: *Goe yee Baptifing in the name of the Father, and of the the Sonne, and of the Holie Ghoft.* Where he appoynted his Apoftles as the Inftrumentall caufe , to minifter and deliuer this Sacrament to all nations : but in the name of the Father , and of the Sonne , and of the Holy Ghoft: to fignifie that the Bleffed Trinitie was the principall caufe. Whevpon fayeth S. Auguftine: *Sacerdos tangit corpus, &* *Aug.co.* *Chriftus interius abluit:The prieft doth externallie* *Petil.* *touch the bodie,powre water on it, or dippe it faying* *li. 3. c.* *the words: but Chrift inwardlie doth wafne and* *49.* *cleanfe the Soule.*

CAP.

CAP. 10.

VVhether it may not Lawfullie be fayed that the Prieſt, or that man by this Sacrament dothe waſhe and cleanſe the Soule of the Infant from Originall Sinne.

I Thinke no man Proteſtant or other can with reaſon denie, but the Baptizer, that is he that Baptiſeth, may lawfullie ſay after Baptiſme, that he hath by this Sacrament waſhed, and cleanſed the foule of the Infant from Originall ſinne as the inſtrumentall cauſe, and that God hath giuen this power vnto him to worke this effect, that is to waſhe away ſinne as the Inſtrument and Miniſter of God. And therfore Chriſt ſayed to his Apoſtles: Goe yee Baptiſing, waſhing and cleanſing of ſinne. The forme alſo of Baptiſme, which the Church preſcribeth importes no leſſe: *Ego Baptizo te:* I Baptize thee, is as much to ſay, I waſhe, I cleanſe thee from thy ſinnes in the name of the Father, and of the Sonne, and of the Holy Ghoſt. And that the Diſciples, nor anie other ſhould thinke this no ſtraunge, nor vnlawfull matter, Chriſt gaue the reaſon ſaying: *All power is giuen me in heauen and in earth*; And this power to this end, I giue vnto you as my Miniſters, and inſtrumentall cauſes. *Therfore goe yee, teach yee all Nations, and Baptiſe them, cleanſe them, and waſhe them, In the name of the Father, and of the Sonne, and of the Holy Ghoſt.*

Mat. 28.

Mat. 28.

Soe I thinke there ought to be no doubt,

E 5   but the

but the Prieſt in the Sacrament of Confeſſion
by the power that Chriſt hath giuen and left in
his Church, may lawfullie and trulie ſay : *Ego te*
abſoluo ab omnibus peccatis tuis, In nomine Patris
& Filij , & Spiritus Sancti. Amen. I abſolue thee
from all thy ſinnes , In the name of the Father,
and of the Sonne , and of the Holy Ghoſt. Amen.
For as Chriſt inſtituted and gaue this power and Commiſſion for the Sacrament of
Baptiſme : ſo alſo did he inſtitute and giue
the like power in the Sacrament of Confeſſion. And thus much S. Iohn as playnly expreſſeth in his Goſpel, as S. Mathewe did for the
Sacrament of Baptiſme. Reade S. Iohn, he recordeth thus : *After the glorious Reſurrection*
the ſame day Ieſus came where the Diſciples were
Ioh.20. gathered togeather, and ſtoode in the middeſt and
ſayd vnto them: Peace be vnto you; as my Father
ſent me, I alſo ſend you (Loe the force of
Commiſſion.) *And when he had thus ſayed, he*
breathed vpon them, and ſaied to them: Receaue
yee the Holy Ghoſt , whoſe ſinnes yee ſhall forgiue,
they are forgiuen them: and whoſe you ſhall retayne,
they are retayned. Marke the Circumſtances of
the Commiſſion for the one Sacrament and for
the other. Firſt as Chriſt gaue his commiſſion
after his gloriours Reſurrection for the Sacrament of Baptiſme: ſo alſo vpon the ſame day
of his Reſurrection did he inſtitute and giue
his commiſſion for the Sacrament of Confeſſió.
Secondlie as in Baptiſme, that there ſhould be
no doubt of his power, he made mention
therof, and told them: All power was giuen
him in heauen and in earth ſo alſo in the inſtitution and commiſſion for the Sacrament of
Confeſ-

Confeffion he fayed to his Difciples: As my Father fent me, fo doe I fend you. If then Chrift as he was man, had power here on earth to remitte finnes (as no Chriftian man can denie) no doubt but the fame power he lefte and gaue his Apoftles, and all Priefts their Succeffours to doe the like.

And for further Confirmation hereof, that men should not mifdeeme of thofe highe functions of his Apoftles and Prieftes, he breathed vpon them and fayed: *Receaue you the Holy Ghoft, whofe finnes you forgiue, are forgiuen* &c. to fignifie that they should doe thofe things, that is: remette finnes, not of them felues, but by the commiffion of Chrift, and by the vertue and power of the Holy Ghoft. Wherfore S Cyrill fayeth: *It is not abfurd that Priefts* Cyr. *forgiue finnes, for when they remitte or retaine* lib. 12. *the holy Ghoft remitteth or retaineth in them: and* ca. 56. *this they doe both in Baptifme and Confeffion.* in Ioã. And no doubt as they are the Inftruments of God in Baptifme to purge and cleanfe Originall finne: fo no doubt they are the Inftruments of the Holy Ghoft after Baptifme to remitte and retayne Actuall finne.

S. Ambrofe contending with the Nouatians S. Amb. old Heretikes, who denied this power in Priefts li. 1. to remitte and retayne finne asked of them 6. 7. de this queftion: *VVhy is fhould be more difhonour* Panité, *to God, or more impoffible or inconuenient for men to haue their finnes forgiuen by Confeffion. then cleanfed by Baptifme: feing it is the power of God, and the Holy Ghoft that doth worke it by the Priefts office and minifterie in them both, as well the one as the other?* I thinke the fame
demaund

demaund may be made to the Proteſtâts of this
age, and I ſuppoſe they will anſwere with as
much ſhame as the old Hereticall Nouations
did: Who can (ſay they)forgiue ſinnes but God
only ? True it is that he is the only Principall
cauſe of releaſing all ſinne: Yet we may not denie but the Prieſt is Gods Inſtrument and vicar
here on earth to miniſter his Sacraments;
Wherby firſt we are receyued to be of the
houshold of God, and made his Children, and
then after, if we offend him, we haue the meanes to be reconciled and vnited to him againe,
the one no doubt as beneficiall, profitable, and
neceſſarie for man, as the other.

—————————————

CAP. II.

*VVhether it be neceſſarie that all the words be
ſpoken, that are of the forme of Baptiſme.*

THe forme of Baptiſme is (as I ſayed before)
        *Iohn, or Francis, I Baptiſe thee in the name
of the Father, and of the Sonne, and of the Holy
Ghoſt. Amen.* which wordes (I ſay) it is necef-
ſarie diſtinctlie and trulie to be ſpoken, or elſe
there can be no Baptiſme. The reaſon is,becauſe
firſt the Miniſter of this Sacramét, muſt expreſſe the facte he intendeth; ſecondly, he muſt declare the perſon for whom he intendeth it; thirdly, he muſt manifeſt in whoſe name ; and by
whoſe vertue and power he effecteth it. The
Miniſter, and the fact intended are declared in
theſe wordx: *I Baptiſe thee* : the perſon vnto
whom this Sacrament is giuen by theſe words:
                                              Iohn or

Iohn or Francis. In whoſe name, and by whoſe power it is done, is ſhewed in theſe worde: *In the name of the Father, and of the Sonne, and of the Holy Ghoſt.* All which three poynts (I ſay) are neceſſarie to be expreſſed. For if one ſhould take or leaue out the firſt words : I Baptiſe thee; and only repeat the words following : In the name of the Father, and of the Sonne, and of the Holy Ghoſt, it were no Baptiſme. Alſo if one ſhould ſay only theſe wordes: I Baptiſe thee: and leaue vnſayd the words that followe, which are: In the name of the Father, and of the Sonne, and of the Holy Ghoſt, it were alſo no Baptiſme. This I ſay for a Caueat, and warning to all middwifes, and other Laye Perſons, that if in neceſſitie, or daunger of death they be vrged to Baptiſe, that they haue a ſpeciall care to ſpeake and pronounce, trulie, and diſtinſtlie, the whole forme of Baptiſme, not leaning anie parte or word out, for yf they doe, nothing is performed. Alſo I would aduiſe them to be carefull, not to inuerte or chaunge the forme of Baptiſme, that is , when one ſayeth that laſt which is to be ſpoken firſt. As for example to ſay : In the name of the Father, & of the Sonne, and of the Holy Ghoſt. Amen. I Baptiſe thee Francis: wheras they ſhould ſay as before is expreſſed: Francis I Baptiſe the: In the name of the Father, and of the Sonne, and of the Holy Ghoſt: Amen.

If you aske me to auoyd ſcruple, whether if the words ſhould be thus inuerted, altered, or chaunged , the Child wert trulie Baptiſed: I dare not ſay that the words thus altered, did take away the forme of Baptiſme, and ſo con-

F   ſequentlie

fequentlie that the child were not Baptifed. For although wordes be altered: yet if the fenfe remaine, Baptifme is effected: yet I muft needes confeffe, that he or shee, who shall willinglie and wittingly inuert,alter, or change the words from the forme prefcribed and ordained by Chrift, and his Church, should finne greatlie. Wherfore let them be carefull, who vndertake a matter of fuch importance, that they know the forme of Baptifme prefcribed,and truly and diftinctlie pronounce it accordinglie.

CAP. 12.

VVhether if one should leaue out to expreffe the partie who were to be Baptifed, it were Baptifme.

THe difficultie of this queftion confifteth in the word (thee) which expreffeth and defigneth the perfon, who is to be Baptifed. I fayed in the precedent Chapter that the denomination, and defignation of the partie prefent to be Baptifed, was neceffarie in the forme of Baptifme particullarlie to be expreffed and declared. Wherfore if anie one should leaue out to expreffe the partie who is to be Baptifed, it were no Baptifme. As for example, yf one should fay: I Baptife: In the name of the Father, and of the Sonne, and of the Holie Ghoft: and leaue out this word (thee) which doth expreffe the perfon to be Baptifed, it were of no valewe. For Chrift infinuated as much when he fayed not onlie: Goe yee Baptifing: but alfo

Mat. 28.

but alfo added: Baptifing them; which word
(them) was particularlie added by Chrift, to
fignifie that the perfon, or partie to be Baptifed, were neceffarie to be expreffed. So alfo if
the Prieft fhould fay, when he abfolueth his
Penitent; I abfolue, In the name of the Father,
and of the Sonne, and of the Holy Ghoft; lea-
uing out this word (thee) and fo fhould not
fay: I obfolue the, defigning and denoting the
Penitent and partie prefent, it were no. Abfolution. Wherfore I conclude , it is neceffarie to
expreffe the partie, who is to be Baptifed, in
faying : Iohn or Francis I Baptife thee.

CAP. 13.

*Wether the forme which the Greeke Church
vfeth, be fufficient for Baptifme.*

THe reafon of this queftion, is, becaufe the
Greeke Church doeth differ fomewhat
from the forme of the Latine Church. Their
forme is: *Baptizetur feruus Chrifti. N. talis. In
In nomine Patris, & Filij, & Spiritus Sancti Amen.
The feruant of Chrift Iohn or Thomas, be he, or let
him be Baptifed: In the name of the Father, and
of the Sonne, and of the Holy Ghoft. Amen.* The
Latine Church, that is , the Roman hath alwayes vfed this forme. *Iohn or Thomas, I Baptife
thee: In the name of the Father, and of the Sonne,
and of the Holy Ghoft.* The difference of and in
thefe two formes of Baptifme is, that the Gree-
kes in their Baptifme doe not attribute the
acte of Baptifme vnto the Prieft, or Minifter,

F 2   who

who Baptizeth, as the Roman Church doth.
For they fay cōmaunding, or in the Imperatiue
Moode: Be he, or let him be Baptifed : butthe
Prieſt in the Roman inſtitution doeth abſoutlie
faye in the prefent Tenfe: I Baptife thee. The
reafon of this difference and alteration in the
Greeke Church, and amongſt the Grecians was,
becaufe at the firſt in the verie begining of
Chriſtianitie amongſt them ; there grewe a
Schifme and errour in that they did attribute
too much vnto the partie, who Baptifed them;
As appeareth by S. Paule, who dehorteth the
Corinthians from their Schifmaticall boaſting
againſt one an other in their Baptifers, telling
them that they muſt boaſt only in Chriſt for
their Baptifme. Some contentiouſly fay : *I certes
am Paules; and I Apolloes. But I take Baptifme of
Cephas, I of Apollo; I of Paule·* So that to auoyd
this errour and Schifme, this alteration of the
forme of Baptifme grewe: Yet not with ſtanding there is no doubt but this their forme is
fufficient and auailable: For although the perfon Baptifing, or the Baptizer, be not particularlie declared: Yet the acte, which is performed by
the Sacrament is expreſſed, which is fufficient.
And the forme in fubſtance really doth not differ from the Latine Church: neither is there
anie eſſentiall parte left out, nor reall alteration
in the forme. And this was defined and decreed
in the Councell of Florence. Wherby it may be
gathered, that by the generall confent of the
Church, for the auoyding of Contention Schifme or Herefie, there may be alteration, in the
verie forme of Sacraments, fo that they doe not
take away or touch anie eſſentiall part thereof.
So teacheth

*1. Cor.
cap. 1.*

*Cō Flo-
ren ſeſſ.
vlt. de
Bap.*

So teacheth S. Thomas, and practise confirmeth.

Tho. 3.
p.q.60.
ar. 8.

CAP. 14.

VVhether the Arrian Heretikes in their forme did trulie Baptise.

THe Church of God alwayes acknowledged the Baptisme of Heretikes to be sufficient, when they haue not altered anie essentiall parte of the forme. Only the Arrian Heretikes, and some of their followers haue bene condemned, for that some of them would alter the forme of Baptisme according to their erroneous and Hereticall conceit and opinion of Christ: in that they would haue Christ not equall, but inferiour to his Father. So that some did Baptise, as reporteth Nicephorus Calixtus in this forme : *In no-* *Niceph.*
mine Patris, per Filium, in Spiritu Sancto: In the *hist.lib.*
name of the Fhather, through the Sonne, in the *16.c.15.*
Holy Ghost. And some otheres: *In nomine Patris*
matoris, & Filij minoris: In the name of the Father
the greater, and the Sonne the lesser : as recordeth S. Thomas. Which formes of Baptisme *Tho. 3.*
doe peruert the essentiall partes of the true for- *p.q.60.*
me, and consequentlie take awaye the effects *art. 8.*
of Baptisme. Therefore there was greate care
taken in the first Arelatense Councell, and *Conc.*
commaundement giuen to examine those of *Aret de*
the Arrian heresie, when they returned to the *Conse.*
Catholike Church, how and in what forme they *dist. 4.*
were Baptised; & if they were not found to be *cap. de*
Baptized in the right forme, then to be Bapti- *Arria.*
sed againe.

fed againe. Not that they allowed Rebaptization, but becaufe Baptifme tooke no effect without the right forme. Wherefore I conclude
that the Arrian Heretikes in this their particular forme did not trulie Baptife.

CAP. 15.

VVhether Baptifme giuen only in the name of
Iefus Chrift be auaylable.

THe diffigultie of this queftió doth arife out
of two difficultes and hard places of Scripture, that is : the tenth and ninth of the Acts of
the Apoftles. In the firft S. Peter commaunded
Cornelius the deuout Italian, with his kinred
and freinds to be Baptifed in the name of our
Lord Iefus Chrift. In the fecond : S. Paule co-
Act.10. ming to Ephefus, finding fome twelue Baptized
v. 48. only with Iohns Baptifme, told them that Iohns
Baptifme, was not fufficient; for that Iohn Baptifed the people with the Baptifme of Penance:
Act.19. faying that they should beleeue in him that was
to come after him, that is to fay : in Iefus. They
hearing thefe things, were Baptifed in the name
of our Lord Iefus. Out of which two places
fome haue gathered, that Baptifme onely miniftred in the name of Iefus without the inuocation of the Bleffed Trinitie, the Father, the
Sonne, the holy Ghofte, was fufficient and
auaylable; alfo fo commaunded and permitted
by the two Chiefe Apoftles S. Peter & S. Paule.

Not withftanding thefe two places of Scrip ture, in myne opinion there ought to be no doubt
(as hath bene proued before) but that the forme of Baptifme was inftituted, determined and
commaunded by Chrift himfelf to be : In the
name

name of the Father, and of the Sonne, and of
the Holy Ghoft. And therfore no way to be altered, becaufe it was Chrifts Inftitution; nor fuf-
ficiét or auaylable without the Inuocatió of the
whole Trinitie, the Father, the Sonne, & the
Holy Ghoft. Wherfore as I fayd, thefe two places of Scripture are hard & difficulte. The generall doctrine of the auncét Fathers, & the practife
of the Church hath euer beene to Baptife: In the
name of the Father, and of the Sonne & of the
Holy Ghoft: and neuer to awarrant or approue
Baptifme miniftred onely in the name of Iefus
Chrift, or onely in the name of the Father, or
onely in the name of the Holy Ghoft. Therfore we are not to thinke that S. Peter, nor S.
Paule commaunded or permitted Baptifme to
be onely in the name of Chrift or Iefus. As
concerning S. Paule it is plaine he asked the
twelue he found at Ephefus, whether they
had receyued the Holie Ghoft? They anfuered: *Act. 19.*
Nay neither haue we heard whether there be
a holy Ghoft. But he fayed: In whom then were
yee Baptifed? As if he should haue fayd: why
then no Baptifme without the Father, the Sonne, and the Holy Ghoft. They anfwered: In
Iohns Baptifme. But that not being fufficient,
he farther inftructed them in Chrift, and the
Holy Ghoft. So that there is no doubt but
Chrifts Baptifme according to S. Paule was:
In the name of the Father, and of the Sonne,
and of the Holie Ghoft.

Werefore we muft vnderftand S. Luke who
writeth the two Apoftles to haue commaunded
Baptifme in the name of our Lord Iefus, not
fo, that it was onlie in the name of Iefus, but

wit all

withall in the name of the Father,and the Holy
Ghoſt., Or we may ſuppoſe that S. Luke named Chriſt Ieſus onlie for the greater honour
of his name : altough the Baptiſme was in the
name of the whole Trinitie. Or we may inter-
prete S. Luke that he would ſay the Apoſtles to
haue Baptized in the name of Chriſt Ieſus·that
is: In the fayth of our Lord Ieſus, or by the authoritie of Chriſt, or with the Baptiſme, vhich
Chriſt had inſtituted ; and ſo for breuities ſake to haue named onlie Chriſt, not denieing
the Trinitie. And Iuſtinus Martyr thinketh that
the Apoſtles might adde the name of Ieſus to
the forme which Chriſt had inſtituted ſaying:
Ego Baptizo te, In nomine Patris, & Filij eius Ieſu
Chriſti, & Spiritus Sancti: I Baptiſe thee, In the
name of the Father, and of his Sonne Ieſus Chriſt,
and of the Holy Ghoſt. And this they might doe
at that tyme for to make more honorable the
name of Ieſus , becauſe his name was in contempte and hatred amengſt the Iewes.
    Wherfore I conclude,if any ſhould vpon mi-
ſtaking or errour of theſe places Baptiſe onlie
in the name Chriſt , or onlie in the name of
Ieſus , not inuocating the Bleſſed Trinitie, it
were no Baptiſe .

THE

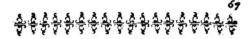

THE THIRD
BOOKE.

Of the Minifter Baptizing, &
the Partie Baptized.

CAP. I.

VVhether Chrift in his owne Perfon with his owne hands did Baptize.

SAINT Chryfoftome was of opinion; as reporteth Dionifius Carthufianus, that Chrift did not Baptize in his owne perfon with his owne hands, becaufe the Scripture fayeth: *Quamquam Iefus non Baptizaret, fed Difcipuli eius: Howbeit Iefus dit not Baptize, but his Difciples.* Secondly if Chrift did Baptize any in his owne perfon with his owne hands, it muft be in moft liklichood his Apoftles and Difciples: but after his refurrection vpon the day of his afcenfion Chrift fayed to his Apoftles: *Vos Baptizabimini Spiritu Sancto &c. After thefe few dayes yea fhall be Baptized with the Holy Ghoft.* Therfore it may feeme Chrift did not Baptize any, for that the Apoftles may be fayed to haue bene Baptifed vpon the day of Pentecoft by the Holy Ghoft.

Dionif. Car. in ca. 3. Ioan.

Ioa. 3.
5.

Act. 1.

F 5   Yet not

Yet not withftanding S. Auguftine is of opinion, that Chrift did in proper perfon with his owne hands Baptize his Apoftles, and fome of his Difciples, which opinion is rather to be approued as more probable. For S. Iohn in his Ghofpell fayed: *That Iefus came and his Difciples into the Countrey of Iewrie, and there he abode with them, and did Baptize.* Secondlie no man can or will denie; but that all the Sacraments were inftituted by Chrift, and the two principall, as Baptifme and the Sacrament of the Altar, or holy Maffe were executed & performed in proper perfon with his owne hands. For as we haue fayed, the firft Sacrament, which is Baptifme, Chrift in proper perfon with his owne hands did Baptife the Apoftles. And for the other Sacrament of the Altar, or holy Maffe, the three Euangelift with the Apoftle S. Paule record; that Chrift after his laft fupper: *Tooke bread in his hands, bleffed it, brake it, gaue it to his Apoftles faying: Hoc eft Corpus meum;* and fo confecrated it. And in like manner tooke the Chalice in his hands faying: *This is the newe Teftament in my bloud, which fhall be fed for you* Wherfore we may coclude, that feing it is plaine that Chrift did Baptize and minifter this Sacrament in his proper perfon with his owne hands, it is likely that it was firft to his Apoftles and Difciples. For if Chrift thaught it good for others, why alfo should it not be profitable for the Apoftles? why should any man thinke that Chrift would be wanting with his own hands to Baptize his Apoftles, who did not difdaine with his owne hands to wash their feete? And furely confidering Chrifte, was to committe this of-

*Ioa. 3.
v. 22.*

*Math.
26.
mar. 14.
Luc. 22.
1. Cor.
11.*

Ioa. 23.

this office and function of Baptizing by speciall commission to his Apostles and Disciples, it is likely he would first Baptize, his seruants, who were to be Baptizers of others. *VVe must take heed* (sayeth S. Augustine) *that we doe not say, that the Apostles were not Baptized with water, but only with the Holy Ghost, least, we giue occasion to others to contenme Baptisme, and that we our selues in so saying, be not found to striue against Apostolicall practise, discipline and order. For Cornelius, and those who were with S. Peter, although they receaued the Holy Ghost: yet notwithstanding they were Baptized with water.* So that the receauing of the holy Ghost did not take away the Baptisme of water. And further sayeth this holy doctour. *VVe ought in no case to doubt, although there be no expresse mention in Scripture made therof, but that the Apostles were Baptised with water in respect of that generall sentence which Christ hath pronounced: Nisi quis renatus &c. Vnlesse a man be borne againe of water and the Holy Ghost, he shall not enter into the kingdome of heauen.* And in particular he proueth S. Peter to haue bene Baptised out of those words of Christ: *Qui lotus est, non indiget nisi vt pedes lauet &c. He that is washed, needeth not but to wash his feete, but is cleane wholie.* As if he should haue sayed; you haue bene washed & Baptised by me alreadie, and therfore you are whollie cleane, now you need no more. Or, my will is no further but to wash your feete only. When. S. Peter vpon humilitie thought himself vnworthie that Christ should wash his feete, Christ sayed: *If I doe not washe thy feete, thou shalt haue no parte withe me.* S. Peter hearing this

Aug.ep. 108.

Ibid.

Ioa. 3.

ring this made this petition: *Non tantum pedes,
ſed caput & manus*: Then o `Lord, *not only my
feet, but my head, and handes*. Chriſt anſwered:
*He that is waſhed, needeth not but to waſhe his
feete*. So that I may conclude that Chriſt with
his owne handes did Baptiſe his Apoſtles or
ſome of them: it remaineth only to accord
thoſe two places of Scripture in S. Iohn, which
ſeeme contrarie.

*Io. 3. &
4.*

  *Chriſtus Baptizabat; &: Chriſtus non Baptiza-
bat, ſed Diſcipuli eius: Chriſt did Baptize; and:
Chriſt did not Baptize, but his Diſciples*. I anſwere they are not contrarie but both true.
Chriſt did Baptize at the firſt inſtitution and
begining of his Baptiſme: and then afterwarde
Chriſt did not Baptiſe himſelf, but committed
this office and function to his Diſciples as proper vnto them; and he himſelf tooke a higher
charge and care vpon him, which was: to
preach, and teach and confirme by miracles.
So did alſo the Apoſtles after Chriſts aſcenſion
in the begining Baptize them ſelues: but afterwards that their preaching might not be hindered, they committed this office and function as
proper to the Prieſt, and betooke them ſelues,

*1. Cor.
1.*

To Euangelize, and not Baptiſe, as S. Paule
ſayeth. So that we may vnderſtand S. Iohn,
when he ſayeth: That Chriſt did not Baptize,
but his Diſciples: that is, he did not ordinarilie
by himſelf with his owne hands Baptize all
ſorts of people, but only ſome of his Apoſtles
and Diſciples. And when he had done thus,
he gaue commiſſion to them as his Miniſters
to Baptize all others. Wherfore when Chriſt
ſayed vpon the day of his aſcenſion, that his
         Apoſtles

Apoftles should be baptized with the Holy
Ghoft vpon the day of Pentecofte, we muft not
fo vnderftand, as though they had not bene
Baptized before with water : but that they
should be cleanfed, Baptized, and inflamed
with a fpeciall internall-infufion of the grace
of the holy Ghoft, vnder the vifible forme of
fierie tongues, as hauing therby no ordinarie
baptifme, but an extraordinarie gift of the
Holy Ghoft to fpeake with tongues, and by
an efpeciall grace of his heauenly fpirit, that
they might Euangelize with courage Chrift
crucified, which was then: *Scandalum Iudæis, &*
ftultitia Gentibus. A Scandall to the Iewes, and
foolishnes to the Gëtiles, & therfore ftood in neede of extraordinarie gift, grace and fortitude.

CAP. 2.

VVhether it doth belong to the Prieſt only, Ex of-
ficio: by Office and frunction to Beptize.

IT is the generall opinion of Catholike Diuines, that ordinarilie by office and function it
appertaineth onlie to Priefts to Baptize. This
word (only) muft not exclude Bishops, for
that they are alfo Priefts, and doe Baptize as
Priefts. Yea in the opinion of fome, although
the Prieft by office and function in his ordination, in that he is made Priefte, hath this power
to Baptize: yet becaufe it is a matter of Iurifdiction, he doeth exercife it with a fubordina-
tion and dependencie of the Bishoppe. As alfo
the Prieft hath by ordination, in that he is made Prieft,

de Prieſt, power to abſolue from ſinne: Yet
becauſe the acte of Abſolution is an acte of
Iuriſdiction, and Iuriſdiction is proper to a
Biſhoppe, he can not vſe and exercife this
power except in caſe of neceſſitie, but
within ſuch limites as the Biſhops ſhall
appoynt. So then ordinarilie by office and
function it appertayneth to the Prieſt only to Baptize, and not to the Biſhop as
Biſhop. Werfore altough the Biſhop may
doe it: yet we can not ſay he doth it: *Ex
officio*, as Biſhop, but as Prieſt. And this
appeareth and may be proued out of S.
Paule, of whom there is no doubt but
he was a Biſhop: yet he ſayeth that Chriſt
1. Cor, ſent him: *To Euangelize, not to Baptize:*
1,   for that it is not by Chriſts Commiſſion
and inſtitution the office of a Biſhop to
Baptize by himſelf as in his owne perſon,
but ordinarilie it is committed by office
and function as belonging to the Prieſt. Yet
in the ſame place S. Paule recordeth that he
Baptized ſome fewe as Criſpus and Caius,
and the houſe of Stephanus, but not as belonging to the office of a Biſhop, but as he
was a Prieſt.

Obiect.   True it is, and may well be obiected,
that, that Chriſt gaue this commiſſion to
his Apoſtles, not only to teach, but
alſo to Baptize ſaying: Going teach yee
Mat.   all nations Baptizing them: but the Bi-
28.   ſhophs are ſucceſſours to the Apoſtles:
Therfore the Biſhops haue by office and
function alſo to Baptize. To this obiection
I anſwe-

I anſwere with that worthie Doctour S.
Thomas: that Chriſt gaue in charge to his *Tho. 3.*
Apoſtles , and ſo conſequently to Biſhops *p.q.67.*
both functions , that is : to teach and to *art. 2.*
Baptize ; The firſt as principall to be exer-
ciſed, and performed by themſelues in their
own perſons ; The ſecond , that is : to Baptize, to be committed by them to the Prieſts
as proper to their office. To manifeſt and
make this plaine S. Iohn in his Ghoſpell ſay- *Ioa. 4.*
eth : That Ieſus himſelf did not Baptize,
but his Diſciples were they, that did Baptize. Wherby it is gathered, that it is ordinarilie the proper office of Prieſts to Baptize ; for that the Prieſts are the Suc-
ceſſours of the Diſciples, as the Biſhops are
to the Apoſtles . Werfore I conclude that
ordinarilie it belongeth *Ex officio* : By office and Function , to the Prieſt to Baptize , although with ſubordination and
dependencie of the Biſhop : and that
alſo the Biſhop may Baptize , becauſe
he is a Prieſt ; for no man can be a Biſhop , vnleſſe firſt he be a Prieſt. Wher
vpon I leaue to your Iudgmentes what
Biſhops we haue now in England conſidering there hath bene no true ordination , Conſecration , or impoſition of
hands of Biſhop , or Biſhops amongſt them,
ſince the begining of Queene Elizabeths raignie , and ſo conſequentlie
neither Bishop nor Prieſt ; for both Bi- *2. Timo-*
ſhop and Prieſt mnſt hiue their ordi- *cap. 1.*
nation by impoſition of hands from
their

74   *A Treatise of*
their Predeceſſours. But no one, but all the
Bishops in England forſookeQueene Elizabeths new-deuiſed Religion,ſo that ſhe remained without Biſhoppe.

CAP. 3.

*VVhether a Deacon may Ex officio, by office mi-
niſter this Sacrament.*

I Anſwere that abſolutlie he hath not by office
and function to baptize; but he may by ſubordination or dependencie of the Prieſt, that
is in abſence of the Prieſt, or in imminent
daunger of the Child, or by commiſſion or
permiſſion of the Prieſt. For properlie his office
and function is to aſſiſt the Prieſt, to read the
Ghoſpell, to miniſter at the Altar, to compoſe,
ſet in order,and prouide althinges neceſſarie for
the adminiſtration of the Sacraments; alſo to
ſerue the widdowes, and other ſuch like offices.
Gelaſ. Therfore Gelaſius the Pope decreed : that *Dea-*
op. ad *cons did vſurpe the office of Prieſtes, if the did pre-*
Epiſco. *ſume to baptize in preſence of prieſtes, they not*
per Lu- *commaunding or permitting of it.* True it is that
caniã. S. Philippe the Deacon baptized the Eunuch
ca. 9. the Queene of Æthiopia her high-treaſurer:
& 10. but it was not Ex officio, but in abſence of the
Act. 8. Apoſtles. Read Gratiam. Diſt. 93

CAP.

CAP. 4.

VVhether a meere Layman, who hath no holy Orders, neither Priest nor Deacon, may lawfully Baptize.

YOu must note and vnderstand that one thing it is to Baptize by function and office, and an other thing to Baptise in necessitie, that is when the Priest can not be had, or in daunger of death. The generall opinion of Catholike Diuines is, and the practise of the Church hath euer bene *A Cunabulis,* From the Cradle, that in absence of the Priest, in case of necessitie a meere Lay-man may lawfullie Baptize. The reasons for proofe of this Conclusion are pregnant and many. First it is not of the essence of Baptisme that the Minister, that is, he that Baptizeth, be in holy Orders: therfore in necessitie it may be lawfull for a meere Layman to minister this Sacrament. Secodly it standeth with the mercie of God, who would haue all men saued, that in those things, which are of necessitie to saluatio, man may easilie find a remedie. But amongst all the Sacraméts Baptisme is most of necessitie to saluation (as hath bene proued) therfore seing Christ our Sauiour would ordaine that cómon water should be the matter of this Sacrament, because it was commó to all & in all places to be had, that it might not be wanting to this Sacrament being of such necessitie to saluation: there is no doubt also

G   but the

but the minifter in cafe of neceffitie fhould and
might be euerie man, not only of the Cleargie,
but alfo of the layety: that for want of a minifter the Infant, or anie other in danger of
death fhould not perifh, or be in way of damnation, or deftitute of the remedies of their
faluation. For Chrift hath fpoken the word:
That vnleffe a man be borne anewe an regenerated
by-water and the holy Ghoft he can not enter in
to the king dome of heauen Therfore fayed Saint
Ierome : *Baptizare, fi neceffitas cogat, fcimus*

Iero.
dial.
cont.
Lucif,
etiam licere laicis : VVe know alfo, if neceffitie
vrge or compell , that it is lawfull for euerie
Layman to Baptize. Thirdlie Ananias in the
firft yeare after Chrifts Paffion Baptized S.
Paule : but Ananias was none of the Apoftles,

Act. 9.
nor Deacon , nor Prieft; therfore in abfence of
the Bifhop , Prieft or Deacon a Lay-man
may lawfully Baptize. And although Ananias
in Scripture be called a difciple : yet that maketh him not a Bifhop, Prieft, or Deacon; For

Act.ca.
9. 36.
Tabitha a widdowe woman is called alfo a
Difciple . Wherfore we haue example in
Scripture that Ananias a Lay-man by vifion and fpeciall commaundement from
God was fent vnto S. Paule, reftored him
to his fight , and in abfence of the Apoftles
in cafe of neceffitie did Baptize him; We
neede not then doubt, but in abfence of
the Prieft a Lay-man may lawfullie Baptize. This confirmeth Saint Ifodorus, and
giueth the reafon why Lay-men may
Baptize : *Ne quifquam fine remedio fa-*
lutari de faculo euocetur : Leaft (fayeth
he) *any*

he) *any should be called out of this world without the sauing helpe and remedie of Saluation.*

Not withstanding these reasons and the necessitie of Baptisme with the generall consent and practise of the Primitiue Church, and all ages sithence; Caluin to crosse all antiquitie, peremptorilie doth denie: *That in anie case of necessitie a Lay-man ought to Baptize: Because Christ sayed onlie to the Apostles: Goe yee and Baptize;* which we graunt, and haue proued in the precedent Chapter that by office ordinarilie it belongeth and appertaineth to the Priest : but extraordinarilie ; and in case of necessitie we allowe it lawfull for all men . And our reason is, because in the same place it was also sayed only to the Apostles : Teach yee all Nations : yet notwithstanding not only the Apostles , but also the Disciples and others did theach ; why may not others also in case of necessitie with the Apostles Baptize ? Yf Caluin should meane , or any other should thinke , that none were trulie Baptized , but those who were Baptized by true Bishops or Priests , and that Lay-mens Baptisme were not auailable or of force, which doth consequently follow in his opinion; Or elfe why should they be denied in case of necessitie , but that he would. make the minister an essentiall poynt for the rightfull administration of this Sacrament ? In what case then were our poore Countrey of England , which hath had no true Bishops , nor Priests since the first of Queene Elizabeth , as hath bene

Cal. li. 4. Inst. cap.

sayed:

fayed. For all the auncient Bifhops of Queene
Maries tyme, ftånding firmlie to the Catholike
fayth,there was by them no impofitiõ of hands,
nor cõfecratiõ vpon any Proteftant Bifhop:but
onlie letters Patents from Queene Elizabeth,&
Confirmation afterward by Parlamēt. But how
auaylable, or of what force the one or the other,
or both ioyntly are to make Bifhops, may eafi-
lie be difcerned,and difcried.Let vs then allow
the Baptifme of Laymē to be auaylable,or elfe
we fhall proue the moft part of England to be
Infidells , and no Chriftians . Idle then and
erroneous muft needs be the opiniõ of Caluin.
And not onlie are the Sectaries of this age
content to approue & allow with Caluin, that
parents rather fhould permitte their Children
to dye without Baptifme,then in any cafe whatfoeuer to feeke or fuffer ther Sacrament to be
giuen or miniftred by any Lay perfon. Not onlie (I fay) doe they mayntaine this wicked pofition and dangerous doctrine concerning children and Infants: but alfo would counfell and
aduife men of age and vnderftanding newlie
conuerted,if they fhould be in danger of death,
not hauing any Prieft or minifter readie, rather
to relie vpon their faith, then to demaund Baptifme at a Lay-mans hand. This is manifeft, for
at the Conference the Sectaries had at mount
Flor: Peglier (as reporteth Florimond de Rœmond
Rœm.   in his Hiftorie of the herefies of this age) where
li.8. ca. Beza beingprefent, asked this queftion of Sme-
11.   deline Brentius Difciple; what he would doe,
or what Counfell he would giue,if a Iewe or Pagan in cafe of neceffitie fhould demaund Baptifme at the hands of a Lay-man, not hauing a
minifter

minifter readie. I would aduife him (fayeth he) to repofe himfelf vpon his faith, and not to require Baptifme at the hands of any lay perfon. But put the cafe (fayed Beza) that the Iewe or Pagan thought with himfelf and were fullie perfuaded, that his fayth were not fufficient to faluation without Baptifme. Then anfwered Smedetine: I would fay vnto him; *Goe then to the Diuells and dwell with them.* Wherupon Beza iefting replied: what M. Doctor, I perceaue you will be a miferable Conforter, in this miferable cafe of neceffitie.

Cap. 5.

VVhether Baptifme may lawfullie be miniſtred priuatly in priuate houfes, by priuate Perfons.

IT is manifeſt and doubted of few or none that in the Primitiue Church in the begining of Chriftianitie this Sacrament was miniſtred in priuate houfes & not in publike places, by reafon at that tyme there were no publike Churches or Chappells builded, neither were the Chriftians fuffered anie publike vfe or exercife of their Religion; but continually purfued by Purfeuants, and other fuch like officers, & extreamly perfecuted by the Pagan Emperours. I may well compare this tyme and ftate now of England with that of the Primitiue Church. For it is euident to the whole world, that Chriftian Catholike people of England, are forced to Baptize priuatlie in their

houfes

houfes, and that with hazarde of great penaltie, they are allowed no publike Church, nor
Chappell, no publike vfe or exercife of their
Religion,but their Priefts,the true Minifters of
this Sacrament, are continuallie purfued by
Purfeuants and other Officers, and extream-
lie perfecuted by Proteftans euen to death.
But after the Church began to be-fetled,
perfecution to ceafe, Chriftianitie to florifh,
the vfe and exercife of Religion permitted,
then were Churches builded, fonts and
Baptifteries publiklie erected, as is euident
and at this day extant in the Mother-Church
of the world in the Cittie of Rome; There
is now ftanding : Baptifterium Conftantini:
The Baptifterie of Conftantine the firft
Chriftian Emperour, And the like you shall
find by the generall vfe and practife of
the whole Church throughout all Catholike countreys publikes fonts and Baptifteries
erected in their Churches, for the publike vfe
of this Sacrament . And in proceffe of tyme-
becaufe, fome began rather to Baptize in their
priuate houfes, then publiklie at the fonts
and Baptifteries of the Church, in the
Councell of Vienna priuate Baptifme was
forbidden in houfes, and publike commun-
ded , as may appeare by the Conftitution
of Clement the Fifth ; except alwayes in

Clem.
tit. de
Baptif. cafe of neceffitie, in danger of death,
or as a prerogatiue for Princes Children.
Wherfore I may conclude that in England,
notwithftanding this . Conftitution , we
may lawfullie Baptize in priuate houfes,
becaufe we are in cafe of neceffitie as in
     the Pri-

the Primitiue Church: no Churches, fonts,
nor Baptifteries allowed, no publike exercife
of Religion, our Priefts purfued, and perfecuted to death. So that our neceffitie compelleth
vs not to be fubieĉt to this Conftitution:
but exempteth vs as the Gloffe doth expreffe : *Neceffitas legi non fubiacet : Neceffitie*
hath no lawe . And thus much for the
place.

Ibid.
lor.cit.

Now concerning the Perfons, whether a priuate Perfon may lawfullie Baptize. Firft we
muft not what we vnderftand by a priuate perfon; A priuate perfon is he, who hath no publike authoritie by impofition of hands, or
holi Orders folemnlie to Baptize, that is : we
call a priuate perfon, a meere Lay-man. And
priuate Baptifme, we call that, which is performed in cafe of neceffitie by a Lay-man or
woman priuatlie without folemnitie or Ceremonies, not in Church, nor Cappell, but
in priuate houfes. I fuppofe in the precedent
chapter I haue fufficientlie proued, that it may
lawfullie be done, and being fo done, to be
fufficient and auaylable. This controuerfie was
particularlie handled betweene the Proeftant
Bishops, and the Puritans, in the prefence of
Kinh Iames at the Conference at Hampton
Court, 1603.

The Bifhop of Worcefter to proue that other *Bilf. of*
befides Bifhops, or Priefts, meere Lay-mē might *worcef.*
alfo lawfullie Baptife, and that their Baptifme
might be fufficient, brought, & vrget the faĉte of
the Apoftlçs, that vpon one day three thoufand
were Baptified: *VVhich was* (fayeth the Bisoppe)
impoffible, or at leaft improbable for the Apoftles to

4 G   *performe*

performe in their owne Perſons. Wherfore in caſe
of neceſſitie in this multitude of people, they
permitted Lay-men (for there were no other
at that tyme) to aſſiſt them, and Baptize, and
approued their Baptiſme as ſufficient and auay-
Bish. of lable. Alſo D. Bilſon Bishop of Wincheſter
winch. earneſtlie vrged, that to denie priuate perſons
in caſe of neceſſitie to Baptiſe, were to croſſe
all antiq uitie, ſeing it had bene the auncient &
common practiſe of the Church , when the
Prieſt or miniſter can not be had, that Lay-men
performe it. Alſo that it was a rule agreed vpon
amongſt Diuines: *That the Miniſter was not of*
Bilſ. fo. *the eſſence of this Sacrament, therfore in caſe of*
18. *neceſſitie it might lawfullie be executed by any other*
then Prieſt or Miniſter. Not withſtanding the
Kings maieſtie being earneſt againſt priuate
Baptiſme by Lay-perſons, anſwered the Bishop
and replyed: *Although* (ſayed the King) *the*
Miniſters be not of the eſſence of the Sacrament:
yet is he of the eſſence and lawfull righ and mini-
ſterie of the Sacrament; But if it be an eſſentiall
point in the adminiſtration of Baptiſme, that the
Baptizer be a lawfull Bishop, Prieſt, or Miniſter,
then it muſt needes followe, if it be acted or admi-
niſtred by any other then a Bishop , Prieſt , or
Miniſter, that it wanteth an eſſentiall parte in ad-
miniſtration, and conſequentlie not auaylable, of
no force, nor perfect. For nothing is perfect that
wanteth his eſſentiall parte. Why then doe they
admitte for baptized thoſe who haue had Lay-
men for their Baptizers , and not Rebaptize
them againe? For either they muſt needes ſay,
that Baptiſme is not abſolutlie neceſſarie to
ſaluation, and therfore not neceſſarie to Rebaptiſe

baptife them againe: or elfe they muft needs
confeffe, that they had the Sacrament fufficiét-
lie and auaylable, being adminiftred by Lay-
men, although there were mortall finne committed in the adminiftration, becaufe fome effentiall parte was not performed. And thus they
caft them felues into manie incumbrances and
inconuéniéces, which might be auoyded by admitting priuate Baptifme by a Lay-man in cafe
of neceffitie, conforme to the Traditions of
the Apoftles, the practife of the Church, and
confent of Fathers.

CAP. 6.

*VVhethe the midwife or any other woman may
in cafe of neceffitie Baptize.*

CAluin detefteth the midwife, and conten-
deth that it were better that the Infant
should die without Baptifme, then to giue
power or allow a woman to Baptize, let the
neceffitie be neuer fo great. And our Puritans
at home following M. Caluin, are verie
peeuifh, froward, and obftinate in this poynt.
For they will by no meanes grant that the midwife, or any other woman may lawfullie in
cafe of neceffitie what foeuer Baptize. This
hath bene a great Controuerfie betweene the
Puritans and the Proteftants: but the Proteftants haue in fome forte yeelded, for they
haue reformed their Communion-booke, and
that libertie which was before for midwifes is
blotted out, & taken away. And by the way
we may note, that the Puritans in this poynt

*Caluin.
Cont.
VVeft.
pa. 157.
128.*

*Booke of
Com.
Pray.
Baptif.*

G 5   difagree

disagree and depart from their first Euangelist
martin Luther, and the Protestants in thus yeel-
ding, from them selues. Also the Puritan partie
in their letters to their friends at Oxford write,
In the that King Iames the first day of their Confe-
end of rence, was so earnest against Priuat Baptisme of
the women, that he should say: *That he had as liefe,*
booke of *& liked as well, that an Ape, as a woman should*
Cöfer. *Baptize.* But of my Conscience I thinke they
misreport his maiestie.

  Let vs but consider that the principall A-
gent in Baptisme is Christ, and that he onlie as
the principall cause, doeth worke the effect
therof; and that man is but the Instrumentall
cause, and minister onlie of Christs. If then in
the absence of the Priest, who was by Christ
appoynted as the ordinarie minister of this Sacrament the Lay-man in case of necessitie may
lawfullie supplie his roome and Baptize,
  (as I haue proued before) why may not
Cap. 3. also in the like case of necessitie the woman
supplie the place of the man in his absence?
The difference of the sexe in this case of
necessitie, whether it be male or female,
is nothing. But because the man is the
1. Cor. head of the woman, and Christ the head
11. of the man, the woman ought not to Baptize in the presence of the man, nor
the Lay-man in presence of the Priest
Christs minister. And for that it is not
conuenient nor decent that men should be
present at the birth of Children, the
Church hath commaunded that the midwife vpon payne of sinne, learne distinctlie the
forme of Baptisme : because she hath speciall li-

ciall licence and commiffion in danger of
death to minifter this Sacrament. It is true
that the fourth councell of Carthage doth
forbid women to Baptize , that is : publi- *Concil.*
kelie or with folemnitie , or in the prefen- *Carth.*
ce of men , or not in cafe of neceffi- *cã.99.*
tie ; and fo all Canonifts vnderftand . Al- *&200.*
fo it is thus at this day obferued , commaunded , and onlie permitted , that women priuatlie in cafe of neceffitie , and
when it is not fitte men to be prefent, to
Baptize.

For Confirmation that women may Baptize,
we haue an example in Scripture of Sephora
Moyfes wife; she circumcifed her fonne in ca- *Exo. 4.*
fe of neceffitie, and although Moyfes was prefent: yet he was fore ficke, vexed with an angell, threatned death that he could not performe it himfelf. For no doubt (although he had
delayed it) at that tyme if he could, he
would haue donne it himfelf , and therfore
fignified to his wife that she should doe it,
which when it was done, Moyfes was deliuered from that fickneffe, or vexation of the angell. But Circumcifiõ was a figure of Baptifme:
Therfore as in circumcifion, fo alfo in Baptifme
in cafe of neceffitie .as Sephora did the one,why
may not the midwife doe theother? It is a world
and wonder to confider, that thefe kind of men
can approue and allow a woman to be head of
the Church, and not permitte in cafe of neceffitie a woman to Baptize. Wheras otherwayes
for want of this Sacrament the Infant were in
danger to perish eternallie, as hath bene
proued.

But againft

Obiect. But againſt this faſt of women Baptizers they alleadge theſe places of S. Paule: That women **1. Cor. 14.** should hold their peace in the Church: And that he would not permitte them to teach, but **1. Tim. cap. 12.** be Silent. Therfore (ſay they) they ought not to Baptize, nor to miniſter anie Sacrament.

Sol. True it is in deed, and they may wnderſtand if they will, that S. Paule doth forbidd women publiklie to preach or teach in Churches or publike aſſemblies, for that it is the proper funſtion & office committed by Chriſt onlie to Bishops and Prieſts: yet I thinke they will not denie, nor no man can miſlike, but women may lawfullie admonish, inſtruſte, and teach priuatlie both women, and men, and children : and olfo deliuer their mind concerning matters of fayth, doſtrine, good life and pietie. And this **Aſt.18.** is confirmed when Priſcilla and Aquila tooke priuatlie Apollo the eloquent Iewe, who preached and taught Ieſus but not ſufficientlie grounded, and they women inſtruſted him, expounded vnto him diligentlie the way of our Lord. Wherfore we doubt not, but that a woman may lawfullie in extreamitie, in danger of **Breden.** eternall ſaluation of the poore Infant priuatlie, **li. 1. c.** Baptize and miniſter this Sacrament. And for **51. Coll.** farther confirmation hereof, you may read a **ſacra.** miracle related by Bredenbacius: In the yeare of our Lorde 1579, it happened in Amſterdame that a Catholike woman being married vnto a Caluiniſt, and deliuered of a child, she cauſed the Infant priuatlie to be Baptized by a Catholike woman of her own profeſſion in Religion, becauſe she would be ſure her child should be trulie Baptized. So it fell out, that the buſ-

the husband being hotte and earneft on the
contrarie, caufed the child to be brought to a
publike preachind, where after the fermon the
minifter being readie in the affemblie of people
to Baptize the Infant, fodenly he became dumbe, not able to fpeake one word. Wherat the
Father being aftonifhed tooke his child in his
armes, came home to his wife, & charged her to
tell him the truth, whether fhe had not caufed
the child before to be Baptized Catholiklie according to her profeffiō. She cōfeffing the truth
fayed, that it was foe. Whervpō he with the reft
of his familie, feing the worke of God, were conuerted frō their herefie, became Catholikes, were
reconciled vnto the Church, & fo liued & died.

This queftion was moued in the Conference
had at Poiffi by a minifter of Mets: whether
the Infant Baptized by the midwife ought
againe to be Baptized by the Minifter. Beza in
the name of all prefent at that Conference anfwered: *That a great number of the Miniflerie*
had alreadie iudged, and that with his confent, that
this Baptifme of the Midwife was of no effect. Yet
forafmuch (fayeth he) that the Contrarie opinion
is not without ground of reafon, it is fitte and verie conuenient, that the matter be remitted to the
Refolution and determination of the Congregation
of Geneua and Zurike. Whervpon worthelie
(fayeth Florimond) the Catholikes of France
iefted at their Conclufion in this their Conference, ane could not but maruell at the madnesfe of thefe kind of people, who could not decide this difficultie by Scripture, by the written
word, wherevpon they would feeme wholie
to relie in decideing matters of Controuerfie,

Bez
cont.
Heff
pag.
533.

Florim.
li. 8. c.
11.

but we-

but were now forced to referre themselues and
the subiect to the Censure and Iudgment of
men, that is : a fewe Ministers of Geneua and
Zurike gathered togeather in a corner of the
world. And in this and the like cases strike not
to skorne and cotemne the decisions, resolu-
tions and indgments of generall Councells law-
Concil. fully gathered of the most vertuous, the wisest,
Later, and best learned throughout the Christiā world
Floren. and no doubt, but according to the promise of
Trid. Christ, they were guided by the Holy Ghost.
As for example : 1. That Children ought to
be Baptized in their infancie. 2. That the Baptisme of Lay-men is allowable and auaylable
in case of necessitie in absence of the Priest. 3.
That the midwife in extreamities in danger of
death may Baptize. The resolution and determination of these cases haue bene decided by
generall Councells, and haue bene deliuered
vnto vs as a Tradition from the Apostles, as a
practise of the primitiue Church, as the sentence of antiquitie, descending in the Church
throughout all ages vntill this day. And nowe
to be condemned and censured by a fewe vnlearned ministers of Zurike and Geneua ? I say no
more but leaue this (Gentle Reader) to thy best
thoughts and considerations.

G   CAP.

CAP. 7.

VVhether an Heretike, an Infidell, or a Iewe may Baptize, and if they doe, VVhether it be auailable.

I Ioyne thefe three togeather, and firft I put an Heretike ; for that herefie is a kind of infidelitie or misbeleefe of Chrift, of his minifteries, his Sacraments, and his Church. Or herefie is: An obftinate refifting or ftriuing againft the true faith of Chrift, his minifters, his Sacraments, or his Church. S. Thomas fayeth: *More grieuous, or greater is the infidelitie of heretikes, then of Pagan or Iewe. For the Heretike, in that he is a Chriftian hath promifed true faith and fidelitie to Chrift, to his Sacraments, and Church, which neither Iewes nor Pagan aid.* It was the opinion of Saint Cyprian, or rather his errour: That Baptifme giuen out of the Church by Heretikes was no Baptifme, nor auaylable. Concerning which point S.Stephen Pope and Martyr writte to S. Cyprian : That there fhould be no Innouation in the Church ; but that the auncient Tradition fhould be obferued, forbidding thofe who were Baptized of Heretikes to be Baptized againe. Whervpon this queftion was much agitated, handled and difputed in his tyme, and by the Church concluded : *That if the Heretikes did Baptize in the name of the moft*
Bleſſed

Tho.2.
2.q.10.
art. 6.

Bleſſed Trinitie, the Father, the Sonne, and the Holy Ghoſt, with intention to doe and effect that which Chriſt inſtituted, that their Baptiſme was auailable, and thoſe by them Baptized, were not to be Baptized againe.

Aug.li. And S. Auguſtine confuted this errour in many
10. de bookes; hisreaſons were; for that Baptiſme was:
Baptiſ. *Vnitas orbis* : One through out the whole world:
eon. Do- And that Heretikes agreed generallie with Ca-
nat .c .1. tholikes in this poynt. And that it was not the
dem. goodnes of the Miniſtres that cauſed this Sacra-
1 . 48. ment, but Chriſt the principall cauſe therfore in
ad Don. neceſſitie auaylable of whom ſoeuer it was gi-
Aug .li. uen. And in his fifth booke of Baptiſme againſt
5. de the Donatiſts, he proueth that God doth giue
Baptiſ. this Sacrament by euill perſons, becauſe they
eon. doe not miniſter this Sacrament : *Sua poteſtate,*
Donat. *ſed virtute Dei :* By their owne power, but by
ea. 20. the vertue of Chriſt. And therfore he conclu-
Aug.li. deth : *Although there be no certaine example*
1. cont. *brought forth out of Scripture to proue that Bap-*
Creſco. *tiſme of Heretikes is true Baptiſme: yet becauſe the*
whole Church hath decreed it, we obſerue (ſayeth
he) *the truth of Scripture; for that the Scripture*
commendeth her authoritie, and telleth vs that
the Church being guided by the Holy Ghoſt can not
erre in her decrees , and deciding of doubtfull
queſtions. Therfore we doubt not of the Baptiſme
of heretikes ſo long as they obſerue the true forme
inſtituted by Chriſt and commended by his Church.

Some difficultie there was in the tyme of the
Arrian hereſie, for that they held Chriſt not to
be equall with his Father and conſequentlie not
God but man. Yet it was concluded that their
Baptiſme was auaylable ſo long as they kepte
the forme

the forme of Baptifme inftituted by Chrift, and commaunded by his Church. Nicephorus Calixtus recordeth in his hiftorie of one Deuttius an Arrian Bifhop Baptizing at Conftantinople one who was called Barbas, and not obferuing the auncient forme of the Church, but altered and changed it according to his hereticall humour faying : *Baptizetur Barbas in nomine Patris , per Filium, in Spiritu fanƈto* : *Barbas be he Baptized In the name of the Fater, through the Sonne, in the holy Ghoƒt* : the water prefentlie dried vp, and vanifhed a way out of the font: At which miracle Barbas being moued, ranne forth, and publifhed the faƈte : where you may fee how God by miracle condemned the Arrian heretike, wen he did not obferue the forme of the Church. Wherfore thofe Heretikes whokeepe not the forme of Baptifme by Chrift inftituted, as the Paulianifts & Cataphrigians, not beleeuing aright of Chrift, nor the Holy Ghoft:the Councell of Nice appoynted that thofe fhould be Baptized againe : *Statutum eſt eos omnino rebaptizari* : *we decree and appoint in any caſe thoſe to Baptized againe.* Yf any of the fore named heretikes flie for helpe vnto the Catholike Church. Read Gratian. And the fame hath S. Gregorie of the Cataphriges and Bonofians, who did not Baptife in the name of the Trinitie, becaufe they thought the Father only to be God, and the Sonne, and the Holy Ghoft to be but men. I will conclude with this Corrolarium or addition;Although in cafe of neceffitie an Heretike may Baptife, and that the Baptifme of Heretikes obferuing the forme of the Church be auaylable, alfo that their ought not

Niceph. lib. 16. *ca.* 15.

Concil. Nicen. can. 19. *Gratiã.* 1. *q.* 1. *can. Si quis cõfugerit. Grego. li.* 9. *epiſtol. epiſter. Idẽ de conſ. diſt.* 4. *cap hi, vero.*

H   to be

to be Rebaptization: Yet notwithſtanding this
can not be no warrant for Catholikes or Schiſmatikes to ſent their children to be Baptized
of Heretikes, or to communicat with them in
this Sacrament, or to permit them to be by
them Baptized. For no penall ſtatute, or Commaundement to the contrarie can free them
from the Cenſure of Commnnicating with Heretikes in Sacraments and Diuine thinges Béſi-
des no man knoweth how farre he may endanger the ſoule of the Infant therby, conſidering that ſome of them maintayne this dangerous opinion: That baptiſme is not neceſſarie
to Saluation. And ſo growe careleſſe whether
they Baptize or not.

    Now concerning the Pagan and Iewe, who
neuer were themſelues Baptized, whether they
could giue an other that they neuer had them-
Nichol. ſelues. It was decreed by Pope Nicholas at the
de conſ. conſultation and petition of theBulgars, what
diſt. 4. was to be done with thoſe, who were Baptized
can. a by Pagan or Iewe; his reſolution was, that if
quodā they were Baptized in the name of the Holie
Iudæo. Trinitie, whether by Iewe or Pagan, they were
not to be Rebaptized againe. Wherfore I will
put the caſe: If two Iewes or Pagans were togeather where no Chriſtians were being in
danger of death, and both deſirous of Baptiſ-
Concil. me: if in that caſe the one ſhould Baptize the
Floren. other, no doubt they both ſhould be ſaued and
can. de their Baptiſme auaylable. Wherfore I conclude
miniſ- with the Councell of Florence: *Miniſter hu-*
triu *ius Sacramenti &c. That the Miniſter of this Sa-*
Baptiſ- *crament is the Prieſt, to whom by office and fun-*
miʒ *ction it appertaineth to Baptize: but in caſe of ne-*
                             ceſſitie

ceffitie not only the Prieſt or Deacon, but alſo the Lay-man and woman yea alſo the Iewe Pagan, and Heretike may Baptiſe, ſo that they obſerue the for-me of the Church, and intend to doe that the Church doth.

CAP. 8.

VVhether Catholike Parents or others may ſend or permitte their Children to he Bapti-zed of Hereticall or Schiſmaticall Mini-ſters, without grieuous mortall ſinne.

ALthough the Baptiſme of Heretikes, as I haue proued in the precedent Chapter, be auailable, and that thoſe children, who are Baptiſed by them, are not to be Rebaptized againe: yet you muſt vnderſtand this not be law-full but in caſe of neceſſitie.

Now the queſtion is: whether it be a grie-uous mortall ſinne for Parents to ſend their children to be Baptized of Hereticall or Schiſ-maticall miniſters. I thinke no man can iuſtlie make any doubt therof. My reaſons are. Firſt if it be a grieuous mortall ſinne for any man to participate or communicate, *In Diuinis* : In Diuine ſeruice or Sacramēts with Heretikes or Schiſmatikes, as generallie all agree it is : but they who ſend their children to be Baptized of, or by Schiſmatikes, doe communicate in Sacra-ments with them. Ergo it is a grieuous mortall ſinne to ſend their Children to be Baptized of ſuch kind of perſons. The Parent can not excu-ſe himſelf ſaying, that he doth not communi-cate, but

cate, but the child, for the Infant is capable of
no fuch action more then is impofed or layed
vpon him: Therfore the acte of communica-
ting is the Parents, and not the Childs. And if
it be a heauier offence to God to communicate
in Sacraments, then to be prefent, at their fer-
uice: then I may lawfully couclude, that they
haue more to anfwere for before God, in fen-
ding their Children to Church to be Baptized,
then in being there prefent them felues. The fecond reafon may be, for that they expofe their
child to greate danger of Irregularitie if he be a
boy. For if he were Baptized at home either by
the midwife or otherwayes, & be rebaptized
againe, he is irregular, that is, not capable of
De Cō- Holy Orders.The Conftitutions and Canons of
fe. diſt. the Church are: that *Rebaptizans , & Rebapti-*
4. Can. zatus: The Rebaptizer , and the Rebaptized are
qui bis. both Irregular. But the Canonifts doe interpret
Sciúter. the lawe, if they doe it willinglie and witinglie.
But you will fay;fome of the minifterie if they
be told the Child is Baptized, will not abfolutlie Rebaptize , but Conditionallie If thou be
not Baptized,I Baptife thee. And fo they auoyd
Irregularitie in them felues, and the Child:Yet
they can not be excufed from finne in this their
doing; becaufe they ought not to doubt of the
Baptifme , and thervpon take occafion to Rebaptize againe, but vpon probable caufe,which
in this cafe is not. The third reafon, Siluefter
Silueſt. a learned Cafuift affirmeth : *That it is a mortall*
verbo finne for any man to require Baptifme at the hands
Baptiſ. of him, whom he knoweth probablie to be either an
cap. 3. *Heretike, Schifmatike , Excommunicate or fufpen-*
*num.*7. *ded perfon, vnleffe it be in extreame neceffitie;* For
in fuch

in fuch a cafe (as hath bene fayed) I may require it at the hands of an Heretike, Iewe or
Pagan. But you will fay: The lawe vrgeth and
compelleth vpon forfeiture of an hundred
pounds; I anfwere: *Iniqua & iniufta eft lex:*
Wicked and vniuft is that Lawe, that vrgeth
and compelleth a man againft his Confcience
to committe a mortall finne, and confequentlie
no lawe. Therefore not to be obeyed. Read
the Conftitutions of Pope Felix the Third in
his firft Epiftle and fecord Chapter. And the
Gloffe hath: *Magis mors eft eligenda, quàm con-
fentire rebaptizari: That one ought rather to fuffer
death, then to confent to Rebaptization.*

*Felix.
de Côfe.
dift. 4.
can.
Eos
quos.*

For a Caueat to Catholike Parents for fen-
ding their Children to Church, to be Baptized
of Proteftant or Puritan, I haue thougt good to
relate what happened here in England in the
Countie of Glocefter about the yeare of our
Lord 1583. as was reported vnto me by an ancient graue man, worthie of credite, who came immediatlie after the fact was done. So it
was that a Catholike gentlewoman being
brought to bed of a Sonne, a Proteftant Ladie
their neighbour, being verie defirous to be
Goffippe to the Child; the parents refufing to
haue it Catholiklie chriftned at home for fatif-
fiyng the Ladies requeft, were content it should
be carried to the Church to be Baptized of a
Proteftant Minifter. But what happened? Prefentlie as the Minifter layed water vpon the
Child, it fell a crying vehementlie, and could in
no cafe be ftilled, but continued crying all that
day and night following, euen fo long as it had
ftrength, and was able to crie, and fo dyed. A

Cafcaf.

H 3   worthie

worthie punishment no doubt for the parents
fault. Alſo I haue read of a child in Flanders,
who being brought by the Father vnto a preaching Miniſter to be Baptized, the Infant ſud-
denlie appeared as dead: but being returned backe vnto the mother being a Catholike, the
Bredē.   child miraculouſlie reuiued againe. Bredenba-
li. 7.   chius relateth the hiſtorie from D. Walter, Ca-
coll.   non at Antwerpe as an eye-witneſſe.
Sacra.   A Catholike woman being married vnto a
ea. 50.   Caluiniſt brought forth a child, whom the Father ſecretlie, his wife being a ſleepe, tooke
away and brought him vnto a preaching miniſter to be Baptized; who being readie to Baptiſe in the preſence of the aſſemblie, perceyued
the child to be dead. Whervpō preſentlie he did
expoſtulate and reaſon with the Father, what
he meant to delude and mocke him, and to
bring a dead child to be Baptized? The father
being ſtroken in a maze with this vnlooked for
miſchance returned home and layd againe the
dead Infant by the mothers ſide; And ſo ſecree-
tlie departing from the chamber, a litle after
returning, called vpon his wife, and asked how
she and the Infant did. She being ignorant what
was done, anſwered all was well, and turning
her ſelf with pleaſing countenance, offered the
child aliue and in good liking to the Father. He
being aſtoniſhed with this miracle reiected his
Caluinian errours and hereſies, embraced the
Catholike faith, became one of his wifes profeſſion, and cauſed the Infant to be Baptiſed
Catholiquelie.
     And for the Miniſter that he be not too haſtie
to Rebaptize the Child alreadie Baptized by a
                                        Catho-

Catholike midwife, let him read what happened at Amfterdame in the yeare of our Lord
1579. as teftifieth Bredenbacius. So it was a *Bredē.*
Catholike woman being married vnto a Calui- *li.7.*
nift, and deliuered of a Child, she caufed the *roll.*
Infant priuatly to be Baptized by a Lay Catho- *Sacra.*
like woman, becaufe she would be fure of Bap- *c. 51.*
tifme. The Father tooke the Child according to
Caluins rule, brought it to the preaching to be
Baptized by the Minifter. So it fell out that the
minifter being readie to baptife in the affemblie
of all the people, fuddenlie he became dumbe
not able to fpeake one word. Wherat the Father being aftonished, tooke his child in his
armes, and came home vnto his wife, charging
her to tell him the truth, whether the Infant had not bene Baptized before according to
the Catholike order. Which shee confeffed to
be true. Wherupon he with the reft of his familie were cōuerted, reconciled to the Church,
and became Catholikes.

CAP. 9.

*VVhetheR one may Baptife many at one
tyme.*

I Say one may vnder this forme faying : *Ego
Baptizo vos: I Baptize yee* : which is as much
to fay : I Baptize thee, and thee, determining
euerie perfon. But you muft vnderftand that
this muft be onlie in cafe of neceffitie, as in
danger of death, or fome extraordinarie caufe,
otherwayes it is not to be done. For this Sacra-
H 4 ment

ment bing of fuch neceffitie; that without it
no faluation it muft and ought carefullie, and
refpe&iuelie to be miniftred. Therfore it is more fecure and better that it be feuerallie done
and a&ed, that the water and the word may
goe togeater, and the intention of the Baptizer
may particulerly be applied to euerie partie
who is to be Baptized.

Aﬅ. 2.   There were three thoufand Baptized vpon
one day by the Apoftles, but the Scriptures doe
not expreffe in what manner they were Baptized. It may be they had helpe of others of the
Difciples: but verie probable they Baptized
many at once. Wherfore I may conclude, that
in cafe of neceffitie, or vppon fome extraordinarie caufe one may Baptize many : at once
otherwife it muft and ought to be done feue-
rally and diftin&lie, that is: one by one.

CAP. 10.

VVhether many at one tyme may togeather Baptize one Child.

Tho. 3.   **S** Aint Thomas is of opinion that manie can
p.q.67.   not well concurre togeather to the Bapti-
art. 6.   zing of one. For when there are multiplicite of
Minifters, there may be many Baptifmes, which
were dangerous. For if the one fhould be before the other, then the firft did Baptize, and the
other Rebaptize, which were a great fault. Alfo
Eph. 4.   S. Paule fayeth: *There is one God, one faith, one
Chrift, and one Baptifme.* So it were fitte there
fhould be but one Minifter to Baptize one
partie.

CAP.

CAP. II.

VVhether one may Baptise himself.

THe generall opinion is that one can not Baptize himself, no not in danger of death, or what other neceffitie foeuer. For better vnderftanding I will propofe the cafe : For example. A Iew or a Pagan hauing heard or read of Baptifme , or liued fometyme amongft the Chriftians, and being defirous of Chriftianitie lying at the poynt of death amongft his owne,neere no Chriftian, and fo confequentlie haueing no meanes to get any other man to Baptize him : taketh water putting himfelf therin faying : *I Baptize thee in the name of the Father , and of the Sonne , and of the Holy Ghoft.* The queftion is,whether in this cafe he be Baptized, and receaue the Sacrament of Baptifme. The refolution is, that he is not Baptifed , nor can of himfelf receaue the Sacremeñt of Baptifme. The reafon is, for that Baptifme is a fpirituall birth or regeneration but no man can be generated or borne of himfelf, but neceffarilie of an other: fo no man can be Baptized of himfelf , but of neceffitie muft be Baptized of an other . Alfo it is gathered out of Chrifts owne words;that the Baptizer muft be a different perfon from the Baptized.For he fayed to his Apofles : *Goe yee and Baptize all nations.* And to fignifie thus much , we may alfo thinke that Chrift would not Baptize himfelf, but be Baptized of Iohn.If you doe aske me what I thinke

H 5   of this

of this Iewe or Pagan, in this cafe, whether he
fhould be faued or not? I anfwere with Pope
Innocentius the Third: that he could not be
faued by the Sacrament of Baptifme, for that
he had it not: but no doubt he might be faued
by the fayth, vowe, and defire of baptifme, and
the zeale, feruour and loue to Chrift, and fo he
might haue it fupplied by Chrift in will and affection. Read *Innocentius libro 4. decretalium. tit.
42. de Baptifmo & eius effectu.*

CAP. 12.

*VVhether the intention of the Minifter be necef-
farie that the Sacrament take effecte.*

ALL Diuines agree, & it is decreed in two
generall Councells of Floréce, and Trent,
and deduced exprefslie out of Scripture, that to
the fubftance of Baptifme as neceffarie are three
thinges; that is: water as the matter, the words
as the forme, and a minifter to doe it and effect
it. For the two firft I haue sufficiently proued
before in my fecond booke, that they are the
two effentiall partes of Baptizme: now that
the minifter muft of neceffitie haue intention to
doe this acte I will briefly fhewe. When Chrift
inftituted this Sacrament, and gaue the forme
he fayed to his Apoftles: *Goe yee Baptizing*: no
man can thinke, but that Chrift meant that they
fhould intend, what he had inftituted. Secondlie, if a man fhould take water, fay the words,
and caft it, and powre it vpon an other, and haue
no intention to Baptize, it were no Sacrament,
no Bap-

no Baptifme, becaufe there was no intention to doe the acte of Baptifme. As alfo if a player vpon a ftage fhould but fhew the acte of Baptifme, no man would fay he Baptized : And why? There was water, the word, the minifter, and all other things. Becaufe there wanted in the player intention to doe the acte of Baptifme. In like manner if a drunken man, who had loft the vfe of reafon, or if a madde man, or if a Prieft fhould rife in his fleepe, and doe all that belongeth to Baptifme : Yet it were no facrament; becaufe in none of thefe thee there were properlie anie humane acte with freedome of will or intention to direct this action, or free mind to worke or not to worke, to Baptize, or not Baptize. So alfo when the nource doth wafh or bath the child, if fhe fhould fay : I bath or wafh thee in the name of the Father, and of the Sonne, and of the holy Ghoft; no man would be fo madde, as to thinke fhe Baptized the child. And why? For no other reafon, but becaufe fhee had no fuch intention as to Baptize. Wherfore I coclude, it is neceffarieto the true effecting of this Sacrament, that the minifter ought to direct this his exteriour acte to this end and purpofe, that is to Baptize, that thereby he intend to performe that which Chrift inftituted and commaunded to be done.

Abfurd then is the opinion of M. Luther and other his followers, who doe not require anie intention in the Minifter of this Sacrament but mayntaine that Baptifme is fufficiently performed, if there be the water & the word, although they doe the acte of Baptifme like a minftrell or player, in ieft or in earneft, idly or
fainedly

Luth.
de cap.
Bab.
cap. de
Bap.

102   *A Treatise of*

fainedly. No man can thinke that the Iewes, when they bowed their knees to Chrift and fayed: *Aue rex Iudeorum: Haile king of the Iewes,* they intended in deed and veritie to adore him, but rather to ieft and fcorne him. Worthely therfore is this opinion condemned as Hereti-

Concil. call by the Councell of Florence againft the Ar-
Floren. menians. And now alfo by the Councell of
Arme. Trent, where Anathema and curffe is layed
Trid. vpon him, who doth not require in the Mini-
feff. 7. fter of this Sacrament intention to doe that,
can,ı ı. which Chrift inftituted when he Baptizeth.Not
without caufe then was Doctor Iohn Rainoldes
Cöfer. one of the agent for the millinarie minifters by
at Häp the Bishops of England reiected, when he mo-
Court. ued the King, that this propofition should be
1603. inferted in their booke of Articles: *That the in-*
Fol.71. *tention of the Minifter was not of the neceffitie of*
Baptifme.

C A P. 13.

What kind of Intention is neceffarie.

THat the minifter of this Sacrament muft of neceffitie haue intention, I haue decla-red in the precedent Chapter. The fchoole-Di-uines difpute what kind of intention may fuffice. For there are three kinds of inten-tion, Actuall, Habituall, and virtuall. The Habituall all Diuines exclude as not fuffi-cient; for that it may be (fay they) in a drunken man, a madde man, or in any man that is aflec-pe, for it extendeth not to the acte, but onlie

to an

to an inclination or promptitude gotten by the
habite. And therfore the Philofopher Arifto- *Arift.*
tle fayed, that *Habitus non eft actus: The Habite Phyf.2.*
cannot be the acte, but a promptnes and power
to the acte.The Actuall intentiō is verie good,
and to be wished to be in all, who Baptife,
which is:De facto,and in deed to haue and produce a mentall intention to execute the acte of
Baptifme,and to doe that the Church doeth, &
Chrift inftituted. But this is not alwaies of neceffitie of the Sacrament; For that men are often fubiect to many diftractions, and hardly it
is in mans power, to be alwayes attentiue vpon
thofe things we haue in hand , although they
be holy.Wherfore, if this actuall intention were alwayes of neceffitie , it would often breed
much trouble and fcruple in the mindes of the
pious Baptizers, and make vncertaine the acte
of Baptifme, Therfore it is geneially holden,
that the virtuall intention is fufficient, that is
when one prouideth and intendeth actually to
Baptife: but yet when he doeth the acte , his
mind may be fo dulled, that he thinke of nothing, or fo diftracted, that he haue quite other
cogitations.Therfore when we purpofe to Baptize, it is fufficient to intend the externall acte
of Baptifme,as inftituted by Chrifte or vfed by
the Church although our mind at the tyme of
the acte, may be wandering vpon other things.
Neither is it neceffarie, that we extend our intention to the effect of Baptifme, that is that
we intend by this actiō to giue grace, to remitte originall finne,and to fanctifie the foule. For
if this were neceffarie , we might iuftly doubt
of the Baptifme of many Heretikes.For the Pelagian,

lagians, and some in thefe dayes, denied that
Baptifme did remitte Originall finne. Alfo it
may be thought, that neither Pagan nor Iew,
do thinke of grace or fanctification of the foule
when they Baptize. And it is probable, that
the Caluinifts and Puritans of England will
not be behind anie of them in this poynt, their
dangerous opinion leading them therunto.
Wherfore to conclude, it is fufficient to haue
internall intention, to doe in deed and veritie
the acte of Baptifmes, in the maner a forefaide
for ther in is included to doe that which the
Church doeth and Chrift inftituted. To take
away all intention in the Baptizer (as Luther
would) were to make a Parrate that can fpeake,
to Baptife.

CAP. 14.

Whether the Deuill can Baptize.

I Moue this queftion, the rather that you may
vnderftand what a friend M. Luther is to the
Deuill. For in his opinion, the Deuill can Baptize, if he obferue the forme. Which Baptifme
of the Deuills, he approueth and alloweth as
auaylable. But to me it is ftrange and vnheard,
to imagine that the Diuell should fanctifie a
foule, being the common defiler and corrupter
of the foule of man. That you may not thinke
this an idle dreame of his, or a fained ftorie of
mine, you muft vnderftand that he goeth about
by argument to proue it Iudas (fayeth he) *The*
betrayer

Luth.
de mif.
pri. v.
painted
1554.

*betrayer of Chriſt, and traitor to his Maiſter did
Baptize: but Iudas was a limme and member of
the Deuill;why then can not the Diuell doe as much
as anie limme or member of his can doe.*M.Luther
might haue conſidered if he would, that Iudas
when he Baptized, he was an Apoſtle, and no
traytor at that tyme. Alſo he might as eaſilie
haue conceaued; that Iudas Baptized as an A-
poſtle and miniſter of Chriſts, and not as a limme and member of the Deuill. Finally it is moſt
manifeſt by Scripture, that Chriſt gaue his commiſſion for miniſtring of this Sacrament, onlie
to men for their good, and not to Diuells the
vtter enemies of mankind. Therfore let vs leaue M. Luther with his Deuills, it is likely he is
amongſt them; take heed & beware of his doctrine leaſt thou be brought were he is.

CAP. 15.

VVhether an Angell may Baptize.

THere is no doubt but the ordinarie commiſſion for the adminiſtring of this Sacrament, was granted and committed only to man; *Heb.* 5.
therfore no angell by ordinary Commiſſion can *Omnis*
Baptize. But if God hath or should ſend an *ponti-*
Angell from heauen, with extraordinarie com- *fex.*
miſſion and warrantiſe to Baptize, I would
make no doubt, but his Baptiſme were auaylable, becauſe it is ordinarie for Angells, to be
aſſiſtants and friends to Gods people here on
earth.

Now

Now hauing spoken of the minister Baptizing: it followeth that we entreate of the parties who are to be Baptized ; that is of Infants
and children, & those who are of riper yeares,
and of vnderstanding , at mans estate, young or
old . And first we will examine concerning
Infants, whether they contracte originall sinne,
and whether the onlie ordinarie remedie for
that sinne be Baptisme. And if they die without
Baptisme, what place & punishement they shall
possesse, and haue after this life. And so forth
as followeth.

THE

THE FOVRTH
BOOKE.

Of the partie to be Baptized, as Infants and others of vnderſtanding and age.

CAP. 1.

VVether Infants doe contraƈte Originall ſinne.

T is manifeſt both in the old and new teſtament, that euerie man borne by man and of woman ſince Adam, are ſubieƈt to Originall ſinne, and in, and by them are con- ceaued, borne, and conſtituted ſinners. There is exception to be made of Chriſt who was not borne by man ; and alſo the bleſſed virgin is to be exempted by ſpeciall priuiledge , becauſe Chriſt was borne of her. That all others are ſubieƈt and borne in Originall ſinne S. Paule proueth ſaying : *Per vnum hominem peccatum &c. By one man ſinne entered into this world, and by ſinne death.and ſo vnto all men death did paſſe, in which all ſinned .* But this ſinne wher with we are infeƈted by Adam can not be Aƈtuall ſinne, becauſe Infants are not capable to doe good or euill ; therfore it muſt needs be Originall ſinne. Rom.5. ver.12.

I   **And**

And holy Iob plainly telleth vs : that no man is cleane from the filth of sinne, no not the Infāt of one day old, *Nemo mundus a sorde, ne Infants. cuius est vnius diei vita super terrā.* And then vpō asked this questiō of Almightie God: *Quis potest &c. who cā make cleane him, who is cōceaued of vncleane seed? Nōne tui qui solus es? Is it not thou Lord, who onlie arte?* So that it is plaine by the testimonie of holy Iob, that Infants are borne in sinne, and by nature vncleane, and that God onlie is to purge theis vncleannes contracted by Conception. And kind Dauid in the Miserere Psalme confesseth of himself, and consequently of others: *Ecce in iniquitatibus conceptus sum, & in peccatis concepit me mater mea* : Behold I was conceaued in *iniquities and my mother conceaued me in sinne.* But no man can imagine anie other sinne, that king Dauid should be conceaued in, then Originall sinne: therfore there is no doubt but Infants in conception contracte Originall sinne. And S. Paule hath this generall proposition: *Omnes peccauerunt, & egent gloria Dei* : *All men haue sinned, and doe stand in neede of the glorie of God.* If all men haue sinned, why then no exception to be made of Infants & Children; But children haue no actuall sinne; therefore it must needes be that they are infected with Originall sinne. And the same Apostle cōfesseth. *Eramus & nos natura Filij ira sicut & cæteri: And were by nature the children of wrath as also the rest:* But they could no way be the children of wrath, but onlie by Originall sinne: therfore euerie one was, and is subiect vnto it. And thus by Scripture it is manifest, that all men are cōceaued in Originall sinne, and borne sinners. The like may be
proued

Iob. 14.

Psal. 50.

Rom. 3. 23.

Ephes. 2. 3.

proued out of the ãunciét Councells & Fathers
of the Primitiue Church, efpecially after the tyme of Pelagius the Arch-heretike, who maintained this herefie: *That Infants & children did not
contract Originall finne; and therfore were not of
neceffitie to be Baptized in remiffion of finne.* Concerning which fubiect, and againft this herefie
S. Auguftine wrote diuerfe bookes: As *De Peccato Originali*, and foure bookes *Contra duas
epiftolas Pelagiani*, three bookes *De Peccatorum
meritis*, and in diuerfe other places of his workes. Wherfore if anie man defire to be farther
fatisfied in this poynt, let him read S. Auguftine.

CAP. 2.

*VVhether it be of neceffitie that Children be Bap-
tized for remiffion of this originall finne.*

IT is neceffarie, and as hath bene proued by
the fentence of Chrift himfelfe. For he hath
made this generall decree without exception
of young or old: *That no man fhall enter into the* Ioa. 3.
*kingdome of heauen, vnleffe he be regenerated and
borne againe by water and the Holy Ghoft.* But
there is no caufe to exclude Infants and children from the kingdome of heauen but Originall finne, therfore it is neceffarie they be Baptized for remiffion therof. Secondly the Church
of Chrift, euen from her cradle and infancie,
hath euer had a Vigilant eye, and carefull folli-
citude grounded vpon the Traditiõ of the Apoftles, continuallie to Baptize Infants and children, efpecially if in that age they were in dan-.

I 2 ger, of

ger of death. But this was principallie that they
should not departe this life without the Sacrament of Baptisme, which is the ordinarie meanes by Christ instituted for remission of Originall sinne, because it is necessarie they be regenerated and borne againe by water and the Holy Ghost. Also they, who are Baptized are sayed
by the Apostle: *To die to sinne, that they may walke*
Rō. 6. ꝑ. *in newnesse of life; And to be cleansed by the lauer of*
Ephes. *regeneratiō.* So it is manifest they haue sinne, frō
5. 26, which they are to be purified and washed; wherfore it is of necessitie that children be Baptized
for remission of this sinne. Thirdlie the Apostle
Rō. 6. S. Paule writeth to the Romans that: *Stipendium*
23. *peccati est mors: The stipend of sinne is death.* Therfore where death is, there is also sinne. But
death is as well amongst children as aged folkes;
Therfore Childrē are also subiect to sinne. Christ
is sayed by the Apostle: To die for all, as well
2. Cor. Infants as aged. But S. Peter sayed: That Christ
5. 15. died for the vniust & wicked. And this doth S.
1. Pet. Paule also proue, asking the questiō: why Christ
3. 18. died for the impious? He yeeldeth the reason,
Rom. and giueth answear: for herin God cōmendeth
5. 8. his Charitie in vs; because when we were Sinners Christ died for vs. But Infants and children
are no way vniust & wicked by anie acte of their
owne; wherfore it must needes be they are
vniust and wiched by Originall sinne. The con-
clusiō thē follweth that they must be cōsepul-
ted & buried againe with Christ in his death &
Passiō by Baptisme, that they may rise with him
to glorie; necessarie thē it is, that childrē be Baptized in remissiō of sinne S. Agustine to proue
that Infants are infected with Originall sinne, &
　　　　　　　　　　　　　　　　　　so con-

ſo côſequentlie vnder the power & might of the Deuill, vſeth this argument: *The Church doth vſe that moſt ancient Ceremonie in Baptiſme, that is, by exorciſmes & Inſufflations to expell the Deuill euen from Infants and children, before they be Baptized, which ſhe would not vſe, but that therby ſhe intendeth to inſtructe & teach, that euē childrē by Originall ſinne were ſubiect to the power of Satha.* The Meleuitane councell vnder S. Innocentius the Firſt of that name, hath decreed & Anathematized thoſe: *Quicunq̃, paruulos recentes ab vteris matrum Baptizandos negat, aut dicit eos in remiſſionem peccatorum Baptizari, ſed nihil ex Adamo trahere originalis peccati, quod lauacro regenerationis expietur, Anathema ſit: VVhoſoeuer do the denie that children newly borne, are not to be Baptized: or doeth affirme that children are to be Baptized vnto remiſſiö of ſinne, but ſo that they cōtracte from Adă nothing of originall ſinne, which is to be purged & cleanſed by the lauer of regeneration, let him be accurſed.* Wherfore to conclude, it is neceſſarie that Infants and Children be Baptized for remiſſion of Originall ſinne.

Aug. li. 1. de pe. meritis ca. 34. & l. 6. in Iulian. c. 2.

CAP. 3.

VVhether Originall ſinne doth appertaine or be to be imputed to Childrē, borne of Chriſtiā Parēts.

I Haue in generall proved in the precedent chapters that all men borne of man and woman ſince Adam (except Chriſt and the B. virgin) are conceaued and borne in Originall ſinne and therby conſtituted and made ſinners : alſo that it is of neceſſitie that Children and Infants be Baptized in

remiſſion

remiſſion of this ſinne, and for the cleanſing and
taking away therof. Now the queſtion is in particular whether to be borne of Chriſtian parents, be a ſufficient meanes to remoue Originall ſinne from their children, that it
may not appertaine, or be imputed vnto
them. I moue this queſtion not that Chriſtian
people ſhoulde make any doubt of the valew,
vertue and force of Baptiſme inſtituted by
Chriſt vnto remiſſion of ſinne, as the ordinarie
meanes for Originall ſiune in children and Infants: but to decypher the dangerous doctrine
Caluin of Caluin, who dares not auouch with the Pela-
li. 4. gian Heretikes, condemned by the Church of
In ſt. c. God aboue ſome twelue or thirteene ages paſt,
16. §. that Children borne of Chriſtian Parents doe
24. not by birth and conception contract Originall
Antid. ſinne.
ad can,
5 ſeſſ.   Yet notwithſtanding hath this newe Ghoſ-
6. peller found out this new deuiſe, that this ſinne ſhall not be imputed, nor layd to the charge
of children borne of Chriſtian Parents, but couered and hidden in the ſight of God. And what
is his intent hereby? Surely no other then. *Iu-
daizare*, *to play the Iewe*, to debilitate and
weaken the vertue, power, and ſtrength of the
Sacrament, and to take away the neceſſitie therof for the ſaluation of Infants and Children, and
withall to make Chriſtian men careleſſe of
Chriſtianitie in their children and poſteritie.
If I ſhould demaund of anie indifferent man,
whether it were not better and a more ſafer
way, to haue Originall ſinne cleane waſhed by
Baptiſme, vtterlie aboliſhed, and taken away
by the Holy Ghoſt, working in, and by that
                                        Sacra-

Sacrament, and so to haue the wound and sore perfectlie cured, then to haue the sinne remaine, although not imputed, but couered, not perfectlie cured, but plaistered? I thinke this would be a sufficient argument to confute this errour, & to make mē beware to endāger their childrēs saluation vpon this slipperie doctrine. For what warrant hath Caluin, or any of his Complices; or partakers our Contreimen out of Scripture; *That children borne of Christian Parents, shall not haue Originall sinne imputed vnto them?* But sure I am, that we haue the testimonie of Christ and his Apostles, that Baptisme doth open the gate to heauen, and regenerate, and cause vs to be borne a new to Christ, And that it is a washing *Ioa. 3.* and cleansing of our soules, in the word of life. *Eph. 5.* And that we therby die to sinne, that we may walke in newnesse of life. Therfore let all Chri- *Rō. 5.* stian Parents of our countrey, with all their Predecessours, and the whole Christian world round about them, seeke the saluation of their children by the Sacrament of Baptisme, and not trust vnto the new deuise of Caluins not imputation, least they be guiltie of their Childrens damnation.

But for further confutation, I will alleadge two or three examples out of Scripture, that to be borne of faithfull parents, is not a sufficiēt meanes to free them from contracting Originall sinne, or being contracted, therfore not to haue it imputed. Dauid was the sonne and child of faithfull parents, and true beleeuers in God, as also of the seed of Abraham: yet he confesseth: That his mother conceaued him in sinne. But *Psal. 50* where can it be found in Scripture, that his Pa-

rents

rents was the cause that this sinne should not be imputed, and not rather Circumcision to be, the true cause which was a figure of Baptisme? And S. Paule when he was borne, his Parents were of the faithfull & true beleeuers: yet sayed he, that he as well as the rest, was by nature the child of wrath. But how became he the child of God, and to be cleared of all sinne? By his Parents, in that they were true beleeuers? No. The Scripture telleth vs no such thing; but rather by the Sacrament of Baptisme. For Ananias bidde him arise, and be Babtized, and so to wash away his sinnes, And the same Apostle proueth the Iewes to be reprobate; although they came of Abrahams flesh; And that to be the sonne of God, goeth not by birth, but by the grace of God. For example Esau, twinne to Iacob, was borne of Isaac the Father, and Rebecca the mother faithfull Parents, and immediatlie from Abraham : yet Esau was a reprobate (sayeth S. Paule) from his birth. Wherfore we may conclude, that it is not the parents that freeth their children from Originall sinne, let them be true beleeuers and faithfull before Christ, or now Christians after Christ.

Act.22.

Ro. 9.

Cyp 11. 3. Epist. ep.8.de Infãt. Bapti- zãdis.

Therfore S. Cyprian writing to fidus the Priest concerning Baptizing of Infants before the eight day, willeth that no man be hindred frõ Baptisme & the grace of God, but especiallie children and Infants newly borne, taken euen from their mothers wombe. For although they haue no actuall sinne: yet becaufe they are borne carnallie according to Adam, they must needs contract Originall sinne. Worthely then we may conclude with S. Augustine: *Quicunque dixe-*
rit & c.

rit &c. VVhofoeuer fhall fay that children alfo fhall   *Aug.*
liue in Chrift, who departe this life without par-   *ep.28,*
ticipation of the Sacrament of Baptifme by him in-   *non lõ-*
ftituted, in verie deed that man doeth oppofe him-   *ge a*
felfe againft the open Apoftolicall declaration,   *finc,*
and condemneth the whole Church, feing that for
that caufe; fhe doth haften the Baptizing of chil-
dren; becaufe without doubt it is beleeued that no
other way at all they can be faued, or haue life life
in Chrift.

Thus S. Auguftine. Idle then is this not
imputation of finne by Caluin maintained, becaufe they are borne of Chriftian Parents.

CAP. 4.

VVhether Infants and children are to be Bap-
tized, before they come to yeares of difcre-
tion.

THe Anabaptift maintaine this herefie,
that children and Infants ought not to be
Baptized, but onlie thofe who are of yeares
and vnderftanding, and doe feeke it and defire
it of themfelues. And fome of this fect doe contend, that they ought to ftay vntill they come
to thirtie yeares of age, becaufe Chrift was at
that age Baptized of Iohn. All men may plainlie fee in this age the worke of the Deuill,
who not only by herefie endeauoureth to deftroy in Chriftédome the foules of a great parte
of the elder fort, but alfo to fend to hell, euen
the poore Infants & children, in taking away frõ

them the vfe of this Sacrament of Baptifme.

The Catholike Church, and all Catholike
Doctours, haue alwaies practifed and taught,
that Infants and children ought to be Baptized.
And firft they proue it by example out of the
old Teftament: Circumcifion fayeth S. Paule
was a figure of Baptifme: but Circumcifion was
commanded to be giuen to children of eight
dayes old. Wherfore then may not Baptifme be
miniftred to children? Secondlie Chrift hath
pronunced, and giuen this fentence generally
without exception, that there can be no faluation without Baptifme. *Vnleffe* (fayeth Chrift)
*a man be borne againe of water and the Holy
Ghoſt he can not enter into the kingdome of heauen.* And that we may not thinke children to be
excluded, Chrift hath recorded by three Euan-
gelifts: *Sinite paruulos &c. Suffer children to come
vnto me for the kindome of heauen is for fuch;* To
fignifie that he would not that children and Infants fhould be left without remedie to faluation. And that children should be members of
the Church of Chrift prophefied Efay: *Ecce le-
uabo ad gentes &c. Behold I will lifte vp my hands
to the Gentiles, and will exalt my figne vnto the
people, and they shall bring their fonnes in their armes, and shall carrie their daughters vpon their
shoulders .* Therfore Children are to be admitted to the Sacrament of Baptifme.

Thirdlie the Church hath euer taught, obferued, and deliuered it as from the Apoftles to
be lawfull, yea neceffarie to Baptize children
and Infants. And no man can denie, but that
Baptifme of children hath bene euer held as
an Apoftolicall tradition. Wherfore although
it be

*Colof.
2.*

Gë.17.

Iſa. 3.

*Mat.
19.
Mar.
10.
Luc.18.
Eſay.
49.22.*

it be not expresfly commaunded in Scripture,
yet it is fufficientlie collected and deducted (as
I haue proued) and no way contradicted, therfore lawfullie to be practifed. We read in the
hiftorie of the Apoftles: that they Baptized whole families. No doubt but their were fome children amongft the familie.

Act.16.

Wherfore we muft nedes conclude that Baptizing of children proceeded from the direction
of the Holy Ghoft, or elfe we muft confeffe,
that the Apoftles fpake and practifed not with
the Spirite of God which were blafphemie. Dionifius Areopagita S. Paules Scholler fayeth:
*Duces diuini noftri, fcilicet Apoftoli probauerunt
Infantes recipi ad Baptifmum:* Our heauëly guides
*the Captaines of our God, the Apoftles haue appro-
ued and allowed Infants to be receaued vnto Baptifme.* Finally no man can doubt, vnleffe he will
become a Pelagian Heretike, but that Infants
are borne in originall finne; therfore it is of neceffitie that children be Baptized, or els that
they be left without remedie for their faluatió,
as the Anabaptifts would haue it. Which were
againft the mercie of God, who would haue all
faued, The difficultie of this queftion is, becaufe there is faith required in the Baptized, and
a will and defire to receaue the fame. How
this can be in children that they may be admitted to Baptifme is the queftion. Wherfore in
the next enfuing Chapter, we will put downe,
what faith is required in children, and how this
may be performed.

*Dionif.
Areop.
Eccle.
Hier.
ca. vl-
timo.*

CAP.

CAP. 5.

VVhat faith is required to the Baptifme of Children and Infants.

Mat. 28.

Mar. 16.

Act. 8.

WE muft vnderftand when Chrift fayed to his Apoftles: *Goe yee firft & teach, & then Baptize.* as S. Matheu reporteth: And: më muft beleeue before they be Baptized, as hath S. Marke. And when the Eunuch asked whether he might not be Baptized, S. Philippe anfwered: *Si credis licet: If thou beleeue thou mayeft,* to fignifie that he muft firft beleeue before he could be Baptized. And S. Paule fayeth: *That faith is by hearing: Fides ex auditu,* and other fuch like places of Scripture we muft vndeftand (I fay) that Chrift fpake of the Conuerfion of nations, of men of vnderftanding, and fuch as had vfe of reafon, who were by preaching, teaching, inftructing, and miracles to be brought to the faith, and beleefe in Chrift. And for thofe, who are at mans eftate, capable of vnderftanding, apte to be taught, readie to heare the word of God preached; I fay it is requifite, yea neceffarie that they haue actuall faith and beleefe in Chrift, and that of themfelues they feeke and defire Baptifme, before it can, or ought to be miniftred vnto them; becaufe the Scripture doth require this actuall faith and beleefe in full age, the elder forte, and thofe at mans eftate, making no mention of Children.

Therfore, fay thefe Anabaptifts, that *Children*

dren are not to be Baptized before they be capable of teaching, & preaching to receaue actuall faith, & to require of them selues Baptesme . So that Infants and children , if they neuer come to age, should perish , and be without remedie of saluation in these mens opinion . But to confound these Heretikes , and satisfie anie reasonable man, in the precedent chapter it hath bene sufficientlie proued, that children may and ought to be Baptized in their childhood and infancie . Now becaufe they are not capable of actuall faith, for that they can not diftinguish betweene good and euill, nor be able to knowe the right hand from the left (as Ionas the Prophet sayeth . Therfore it is sufficient for them to be Baptized : *In fide aliena : In the faith of an other;* that is in the faith of their Parents, or thofe who offer , and bring them to be Baptized , if they be Chriftians ; Or *In fide Ecclefia : In the faith of the Church,* if they be the children of Infidells. This is the doctrine of the Church , and the opinion of Catholike Doctours, both ancient and moderne, and that with reafon. For as thefe Infants contracted Originall finne from their firft parents Adam and Eue and were infected in their foules : *Alieno peccato : with an others finne:* fo now alfo they should be cured, and haue this finne remitted in the faith of an other. Therfore Saint Auguftine writing to Bonifacius fayeth : *In Ecclefia Saluatoris paruuli per alios credunt &c. In the Church of our Sauiour Children beleeue by others , as by others they contracted finne , which is remitted*

Deu.1.
Ionas.
ca. vl.
timo.

Aug.
ep.23.

remitted in Baptifme. And confidering that Baptifme is a fpirituall generation, and hath fome
fimilitude with carnall generation, therfore we
fay; euen as children, when they are in their
mothers wombe, doe not receaue nourishment
from or by themfelues, but are maintained by
foode from their mothers: euen fo we fay as
yet not hauing vfe of reafon, being as it were
placed in the wombe of their mother the
Church, doe not receaue faluation and Baptifme by and from themfelues, but by the faith
and acte of the Church. Therfore S. Auguftine
fayeth: *Our Mother the Church doth offer and lend*
Aug. li. *her mouth to Childrē & Infants, that they may be*
de Peck *indued with holy Mifteries ; for as yet they can not*
meritis. *beleeue with their owne hartes, nor make confef-*
& re- *fion to faluation with their owne mouthes.* Wher-
mess. c. fore we conclude, that children and Infants ha-
33. ue intention to be Baptized, anfwere the Prieft,
& are Baptized by the intention, by the mouth;
by the faith of their mother the Church.

Wherupon the Churche hath inftituted, that
when the child is brougt to the fonte to be
Baptized, the Prieft asketh him: *Quid Petis?*
what intend? what feeke you? what aske you? The
child anfwereth by the mouth of the God-fater
and God-mother, or by the ftanders by : *Peto*
Baptifmum: I intend, and aske Baptifme. Then
the Prieft fayeth: *Vis Baptizari? wilt thou be Bap-*
tized? The child anfwereth as before, or the
Church for him: *Volo: I will.* Then the Prieft
goeth forward: *Credis in Deum Patrem omnipo-*
tentem &c. Doeft thou beleeue in God the Father
Almightie: and in Iefus Chrift his onlie Sonne &c.
The child anfwereth as before: *Credo: I doe*
beleeue.

beleeue. Then the child is Baptized, receaueth the figne and Character of a Chriftian, Originall finne is remitted, and in the foule is infufed the habite of faith, hope, and Charitie, and fo the Child is made. *Vere fidelis: A true faithfull foule.* This is the doctrine & practife of the Catholike Church. Anathema then, and fie vpon thefe Heretikes and herefie, who would leaue the poore Infants remedileffe of faluation, becaufe they are not capable of actuall faith. And Ifidorus fayeth: *Paruuli alio profitente Baptizati funt, quia adhuc loqui vel credere nefciunt &c.* Children are Baptized, an other making profeffion of faith for them; becaufe the know not as yet to fpeake or beleeue. In like manner alfo it is with them, who are ficke, dumbe, or deafe, in whofe fteed and place an other doth make profeffion, that he may make anfwere for them, while they are Baptized.

I thinke M. Luther hath much to anfwere for before God, who gaue occafion of this herefie; for that he would needes maintaine that Infants had actuall faith, which is impoffible, and againft reafon; and not to be content with the generall doctrine of the Church, that habituall faith, & the faith of an other was fufficiet for Baptifme in the Infant. And being dealt for & reafoned with, cocerninge this difficultie, not withftanding did ftifflie defend againft Cocleus: *That Childre haue vfe of reafon, doe actually heare, and beleeue, whileft they are Baptized* And alfo the Lutherans maintained the fame in their Synode held at witenberg, in the yeare of our Lord. 1556.

CAP.

CAP. 6.

VVhether Children if they die before Baptifme can be faued by their fathers faith.

I Haue propofed this queftion, not that there is anie probabilitie in the affirmatiue parte. Becaufe according to S. Paule: *Not only* the children of the vnbeleeuing, but alfo of the faithfull, all are borne the children of wrath, and all conceaued in originall finne.

Eph. 2.

Therfore I abfolutlie anfwere that they can not be faued by the parents faith. For (as I haue fufficientlie proued before) that the ordinarie meanes for the faluation of Children, and remiffion of Originall finne is Baptifme, and therfore not the parents faith. Let this then be a Caueat and warning to all Catholikes and well-minded Chriftians, to beware of the dangerous doctrine, that many of our Countreymen following M. Caluin are not afhamed publiklie to preach; that *Baptifme is not neceffarie to Saluation in Infants; fo that they be borne of Chriftian Parents.* As though the Parents faith could make fafe the child; which is againft Scripture, Councells, Fathers, and all antiquitie. For that the ordinarie meanes (as I haue fayed before) for the faluation of children is Baptifme.

It was decreed by S. Innocencius the firft Pope of that name, who florifhed in the tyme of S. Ierome and S. Auguftine: *That children, althought borne of Chriftian Parents, ought to be borne againe by Baptifme, that in them that which they contracted by birth and genration, fhould be* cleanfed *cleanſed by regeneration and Baptiſme.* True it is (as we haue proued in the precedent chapter) that Infants are Baptized in their parents faith, if the Parents be Chriſtians, or in the faith of the Church, if they be Infidells;but it is the Sacrament that maketh them ſafe, and not the Parents faith, for that is but an introductionto the Sacrament. This priuiledge and ſpeciall helpe children haue being borne of Chriſtian Parents, that they themſelues being Chriſtians, will and ought to haue a ſpeciall care that they be brougt to Baptiſme, and in this reſpect the faith of the Parents, may profitte the Infant, and be a ſecondarie cauſe of his ſanctification. Therfore no doubt it is a deadlie and mortall ſinne in the Parents, if by their negligence the child die vnder their hands without Baptiſme. Surely then I may conclude that this doctrine of Caluins, is but a tricke of Satan to make Parents careleſſe of this Sacrament, that he may bring their Children to vtter danger of ſaluation, and to make themſelues not free from ſinne. I haue heard of ſome greate perſonages, who for pompe at Chriſtening, and to haue ſome honorable perſon for Godfather, haue delayed and neglected Baptiſme, and ſo the Infant dying without it, by the Parents pride and negligence haue beene ſent vnto hell. What griefe this ought to be in Parents iudge you, and what ſinne it was in them, I haue cenſured before. Becauſe this opinion of Caluin is too pregnant in our

K   Countrey

Cal. li. Countrey of England, and some of the best
4. Inst. seeme to incline vnto it, I will solue all his
c∎. 16. arguments.

Obiect.   The first obiection is out of the old Testament, where God made pacte and promise to
Gen.17. Abraham, that he would be a God vnto him;
and this promise was not onlie made vnto him
for his owne person, but to his seed and poste-
ritie after him: but all the Children of the faithfull are of the seed of Abraham. Therfore they
are not so properlie iustified by the acte of Baptisme, as by the promise God made to the seed
Sol.   of Abraham.

Kelliso.   But this argument hath Doctour Kellison
lib. 4. most learnedly answered. First although God
Suruay. made this promise to Abrahams seed, yet after
he instituted Circumcision, and threatened all
those who had it not, that they should perish;
but Circumcisió was a figure of Baptisme; Therfore although we be partakers of the benediction; yet we must be Baptized, or els we perish eternallie. Secondlie this promise and benediction is to be vnderstood either carnally or
spiritually; If carnallie; then it belongeth only
to the Iewes, who where of the seed and flesh
of Abraham, and the carnall children of him;
If spirituallie, then they onlie are partakers,
Rom.9. who, as S. Paule sayeth: *Doe imitate the faith &*
workes of Abraham. For so are they made the
Children of Abraham. But the Children of the
faithfull doe no way imitate Abrahams faith or
workes, vntill they be Baptized, and receaue
the Sacrament of faith, wherby they are in deed:
Verè fideles, and become trulie faithfull. For as
we haue proued before, the Childré cã not haue
faith

faith but by Baptifme. For actuall faith they
are not capable of, and habituall faith they haue infufed in them only by Baptifme. Therfore
that they be the children of Abraham, it is neceffarie they be Baptized to receaue faith. Thirdlie this abfurditie would follow, that children
fhould not contract Originall finne, which were to reuiue the Pelagian herefie. For if children
be iuftified by this that they are of the feed of
Abraham, yf you vnderftand it according to the
flefh, there is no doubt, but in the firft inftance
of their conception, they are of Abrahams feed,
and fo confequentlie iuftified ; Therfore not
borne in Originall finne. Wherfore we muft
needes conclude, that this place of Scripture
no way can proue M. Caluins opinion.

The fecond obiection is out of S. Paule, whe- Ob.
re he fayeth: *That the vnbeleeuing man is fancti-* 1. Cor.
fied by the faithfull woman; and that the Children 7.
of them are cleane and holy. Therfore the children may be borne fanctified by the Fathers
faith. To this I anfwere, that no man will thin- *Sol.*
ke if a Turke fhould marrie a Chriftian woman, and be content to liue with her, and let
her vfe her confcience, that the Turke therby
fhould be fanctified and made Iuft. Or if a Pro-
teftat marrie with a Catholike woma, & be cō-
tent to liue with her, & let her vfe her cōfcien-
ce, that therfore the Proteftant becomes a Pa-
pift. But it may verie well be thought, that by
the prayer of the wife, by her perfwafion, by
her good example of life, the Turke may become a Chriftian, the Proteftant a Catholike,
but the one muft be Baptized, and the other
reconciled, or els the faith of the woman will
K 2   not fuf-

not fuffice . So I fay the faith of the Parents without the Sacraments of Baptifme can not cleanfe or wafh the foule of the Infant from Originall finne contracted. But this benefit the Child may haue being borne of Chriftian Parents, that they will , and are bound to haue care, and feeke the onlie remedie for the foule of their Children , which is Baptifme.

Aug.li. Therfore Saint Auguftine fayeth : *Si vis effe* *3.de a-* *Catholicus, noli dicere , noli docere , noli cre-* *nima.* *dere, Infantes &c. If thou wilt be a Catholi-* *& c.9.* *ke, doe not fay, doe not teach , doenot beleeue, that* *Infants dying before the come to Baptifme,* *can obtaine indulgence , pardon , or remiffion of* *originall finne.*

Secondly I anfwere that the Pelagians vrged this place of Saint Paule againft Saint Auguftine, to proue that Children borne of faithfull Parents did not contract Originall finne; and fo confequentlie were not to be Baptized to take away Originall finne. And Caluin vrgeth the fame place, not daring plainly to fay, that Infants doe not contract from their Parents Originall finne, but to proue by their Fathers faith, that they may be faued without Baptifme , becaufe Originall finne shall , not be imputed. Ther-

Aug.li. fore the fame anfwere Saint Auguftine gaue *2. de* to the Pelagians I thinke may alfo fatisfie *Pect.* the Caluinifts.Firft Saint Auguftine fayeth,that *meritis* the cleanneffe , fanctitie , and holines, that *ca. 26.* the children haue from their parents,the Apo-*& l. 3.* ftle doth not meane to be fanctitie or holines *ca. 12,* to Iuftification , faluation , or to remiffion of finnes . For then it would follow, that the

Turke

Turke or Infidell should be fanctified by the beleeuing woman, and that by the verie coniun-
ction of matrimonie he fhould become Iuft and
faued, which were againft Scripture and reafon, becaufe it is impoffible to pleafe God without faith. *Hab.ii.*

Alfo it is manifeft by Scripture that Chrift
hath layd an other foundation of Iuftification
& faluation then the beleeuing woman for the
husband, and the faith of the Parents for the
Infant, and that is, to be borne againe by water and the Holy Ghoft, and to be incorporate to Chrift by Baptifme. No doubt but the
true fenfe and meaning of the Apoftle was, not
to feperate man and wife, although they were
different in Religion; becaufe who knoweth
whether one may be an occafion of the others
Conuerfion, fayeth the Apoftle.

So alfo the Parent may be a caufe of the
Saluation of the Infant, in feekeing to haue
the Sacrament dulie miniftered. And thus ex-
poundeth S. Chrifoftome vpon this place of
S. Paule the Infidell man to be fanctified *Chry.in*
by the faithfull woman, *Quia fpes eft quod hunc* *there loc.*
a fideli pertrahatur ad fidem, becaufe there loc.
is hope that by the faithfull woman he may be
drawen to true faith and beleefe. And concerning
the Infants of the faithfull : Saint Ieronie
doeth interpret thofe words of Saint Pau- *Iero.li.*
le: *Nunc Sancti, id eft: Fidei Candidati,* *1.cont.*
hoc eft deputati ad Chriftianam fidem: Now *Ioui.c.*
they are holy, that is: now they are cloa- *5. &*
thed in white, endeauoring to obtaine *ep. ad*
faith. That is as much to fay : Now *Paulin.*
they are deputed vnto Chriftian faith and

K 3 fanctitie,

sanctitie, esteemed and admitted as Christians; because there is a great hope that by the industrie and care of the one Parent being faithfull, the children may be brought to Baptisme. This was S. Ieromes opinion, and this I hope may satisfie anie reasonable man.

CAP. 7.

VVhat punishment Children dying without Baptisme shall haue after this life.

HAuing sufficientlie proued in the precedent Chapters, that Infants and Children contract Originall sinne, and are by nature therby become the Children of wrath and in deed constituted sinners, and that the only ordinarie meanes to restore them to grace & Innocencie againe, is by Chrisfs institution the Sacrament of Baptisme, without which if they departe this life, they can not be saued: It must needes consequently follow, that they shall absolutlie be depriued of the Kingdome of heauen, that they shall neuer possesse eternall beatitude and blessednes, which consisteth in the fruition and sight of God, they shall perpetuallie want the blessed vision that is, neuer to see God, and consequentlie they shall be no companions of blessed Angells nor Saintes of Christ in heauen. So that it is the generall opinion of Catholike Diuines, that Children dying without Baptisme, being their ordinarie onely meanes of saluation, shall suffer the paines of damnation. You must vnderstand there are two kinds and

                                                    manners

manners of punifhmentes or paines to be executed vpon finners after this life ; that is : *Pœna damni, & pœna fenfus: The Paine of Damnation and the Paine of fenfe.* The firft doth confift of the perpetuall want of the bleffed vifion and fruition of the fight of God : The other which is *Pœna fenfus: The paine of fenfe,* doeth confift in the eternall torment of hell fier, wherwith the foule for the prefent fhall be torméted, and after the generall refurrection, both foule and bodie eternallie witthout intermiffion. For the firft (as hath beene proued) it is manifeft that childré dying without Baptifme, are fubiect vntodeath eternall, & accounted as damned, who fhall neuer fee God. And the reafon is plaine out of Scripture as hath beene fayed. For by Originall finne, euen children are depriued of, and exiled from the glorious cittie and kingdome of heauen; they are become by nature the children of wrath. Alfo they haue the ire of God hanging ouer them, & continue as Captiues vnder the power of Satan Prince of darkneffe; but thofe who are in this eftate, are in ftate and way of damnation. Therfore childré dying without Baptifme are fubiect to eternall death, and are accounted as damned, and fo confequentlie neuer in poffibilitie to enioy the fruition and fight of God: but incurre *Pœnam damni: The punifhment of damnation.* So that now the queftion is whether Infants dying without Baptifme fhall feele and fuffer the torments of hell fire.

There are fome of opinion as Fulgentius an ancient writer, who feemeth to make no doubt therfore, but that they fhall in fome degree endure

Io. 3.

Eph. 2.

Fulgē. de fide ad Pet. 3. 27,

K 4

dure the verie torments of hell fire. And to
this inclineth Ariminenſis a Scholeman. And
Driedo writing of controuerſies. But the
generall ſentence of Fathers and Diuines is
to the Contrarie : that Infants dying without Baptiſme, ſhall not ſuffer the paines
and torments of hell. The reaſon is, becauſe
Poſitiue actuall puniſhemēt is not inflicted, but
for actuall offence:but Infants neuer did nor can
offend actuallie (for Originall ſinne is in them
but habituall) wherfore it is ſufficient for them
to be reiected from the ſight of God, and baniſhed the kingdome of heauen, and not to be
puniſhed with the torment of hell fire. Wherfore the want of the bleſſed viſion and ſight
of God is attributed the ordinarie penaltie
and paine for Originall : and the torment
of hell fier as the paine due for actuall ſinne. And Saint Iohn heard the voyce from heauen ſpeaking of the ſinnes of Babilon ſaying:
Quantum ſe glorificauit &c. As much as ſhe
hath glorified her ſelfe, and hath beene in delica-
cies; ſoe much giue her torment and mourning.
As if he ſhould haue ſayed; the meaſure of
paines and damnation, is according to the
wicked pleaſures,and vnlawfull delights of this
life, but children and Infants could not
any way be proud, nor giue themſelues to
anie ſenſuall delight or pleaſures of this
world : therfore no way ſenſiblie to be tormented. And Eſay the Prophet ſayeth that
God, *Reddet increpationem &c. will ſhew his*
threatnings in the flame of fire; becauſe our Lord
ſhall indge betweene the good and the badde
in fire. And S. Marke the Euangeliſt deſcri-
beth

Marginal notes (left column):

Arimi.
2. diſt.
33.q.3.
Dried.
de grā.
& lib.
arbit.
tract.
3.c. 2.

Apoc.
18.7.

Eſai.
66,45.

beth the punifhment for them, who committe
fcandall, that is to goe into hell; *Into the fire vn-*
quenchable, where their worme dieth not, and the
fire is not quenched. But there is no action to be
difcerned good or badde in Infants; neither
can they committe anie fcandall, or haue remorfe of confcience, or worme gnawing for
anie euill workes; Therfore the paines of hell
fire are not due or to be executed vpon them
but vpon elder forte, who cõmitte actuall finne.
Wherfore we may cõclude, that Children dying
without Baptifme, fhall haue : *Pœnam damni:*
the punifhment of damnation, that is to be
damned for their Originall finne: but not haue
Pœnam fenfus: The paine of hell fire, becaufe
the haue no actuall finne.

Mar.9. 45.

CAP. 8.

Vhether that Infants shall after this life be
here on earth, and enioy the pleafures as
men doe now, or be in hell, or what place
they shall poffeffe.

SOme there are of opinion, that children
dying without Baptifme, after the generall refurection, fhall haue amiddle place
neither in heauen, nor in hell, but fhall liue here on earth, and enioy a certaine
kind of natuall felicitie and pleafure fuch
as the earth can yeeld. But this opinion, or
rather I may fay this errour, is worthelie confuted by that religious Cardinall Bellarmine.
I call it an errour, becaufe Saint Augu-
K 5

Bellar.
lib. 6.
de fla-
tu pec-
cati. c.
2.
ftine

Aug.li.
de var.
ca.88.
& l. de
Orig.
animæ.
ca. 9.
ftine doth record it as fpeciallie maintained by
the Pelagian Heretikes . And writing of the
origine of the foule fayeth : *Nemo non Baptizatis*
paruulis promittit inter damnationem & regnum
cœlorum locum quietis &c. No man doth giue or
promife to children dying without Baptifme, *as it*
were a middle place of quiet and felicitie betweene
heauen and hell, damnation and faluation . And
why? Becaufe (fayeth S. Auguftine) *Hoc enim*
hæresis Pelagiana eis promifit:thus much the Pela-
Aug.li.
de orig.
animæ.
ca. 14.
gian herefie hath promifed. And intreating of the
fame matter, he fayeth further: *Nouellos Hereti-*
cos Pelagianos iuftiffime &c. Moft iuftlie the late
new-fprong vp Pelagian Heretikes hath the Catho-
like Councells and fea Apoftolike by their authori-
tie worthely condemned , becaufe they prefumed
boldly to appoint and giue to children not Baptized
an other place of quiete and felicitie befides heaue.
Wherfore I doubt not but that it may lawfullie
be called an errour, to affigne to children not
Baptized, a middle and third place of quiete
and felicite, as fhall be proued hereafter by
Scripture and reafon.

Firft S. Iohn in the Apocalyps fayeth: *Bleffed*
and holy is he that hath parte in the firft refurre-
Apoc.
20.3.
ction, for in thofe the fecond death hath no power
Alfo he fayeth: *He that is not found written in*
the booke of life, fhall be caft in ftagnum ignis into
Ibid.36.
the lake or poole of fier. But Children dying without Baptifme are not partakers of the firft
refurrection, that is the wafhing and cleanfing
the foule from Originall finne, that therby they
may haue the grace of God to rife to faluation,
and confequentlie haue not their names written in the booke of life. Whervpon it followeth,

loweth, that the second death, that is damnation must raigne in them, and their place of abode must be the lake of fire, which is hell. And S. Paule doeth tell the Collossians: *That by Chrift we are deliuered from the power of darkenes.* But the onlie meanes by Chrift inftituted to deliuer Infants and children from darkneffe and the power of Satan, is Baptifme; wherfore vntill they be Baptized, they remaine captiue and vnder the power of Satan in darkneffe. But they, who conuerfe with Satan in the dungeon of darkneffe can not be in place of pleafure, nor enioy great felicitie. Ergo it is manifeft they remaine in hell. It is plaine in the Gofpell that in the latter day, when Chrift fhall come to iudge the world, all men muft goe either on the right hand, or on the lefte. There are then but two wayes; but children dying without Baptifme are not for the right hand, then of neceffitie they muft goe on the left hand; but the way on the left hand is damnation and hell: if damnation and hell, then no place of pleafure and felicitie.

Colof. 13.

Mat. 25.23.

Werfore to conclude, what care ought Parents to haue that this Sacrament of Baptifme be duly miniftred to ther Children? And what griefe it ought to be in them, if by their negligence, or by inclining vnto this new deuife of Caluin, they fhould fend their Infants vnto the darke dungeon of hell vnder the power of the deuill, & captiuitie of Satan? There is but one difficultie or obiection of any importance, that may be vrged againft the alleadged reafons, that is: After the generall Iudgment, and deftuction of the world by fire, Almightie

Obiect:

mightie God will make all new: *A new heauen,
and a new earth*; but this new earth fhall not be
vacant without inhabitans : The Angells
and Saints , and feruants of Chrift fhall haue heauen, the deuills and damned fhall haue hell ; It foundeth probablie that the Infants and children dying without Baptifme , who neuer committed actuall finne,
may haue this middle place , inhabite the
earth, and enioy the pleafures therof . To

Sol.

this argument I anfweare : that this earth fhall
not be inhabited neither by man nor beaft.
And that by the heauen is vnderftood
the ayre . Heauen and earth fhall be a
new : that is ; all the fower elementes , the
ayer the water , the earth and the fire fhall
be renewed , made pure without mixture,
and put in their naturall places . The ayre shal
haue no liuing thing in it , the birds and fowles of the ayre shall be gone , the waters shall
enuiron and compaffe about the whole
earth, there shall be no fish in it, the earth
shall haue no cattle, no beafts, no liuing creature in it, no trees, no fruite, no flowres, no
graffe on the ground : *Non erit arida: There
shall be no drie land.* But as I haue fayed,
all shall be enuironed and compaffed about
with the wathers. The reafon is pregnant out

of Saint Iohn. Who fayeth: *Prima terra abijt,
mare iam non eft: The firft earth is gone the feas
now are not.* For the wather shall be without
tearme or limitte. For what are the feas but
waters limitted within fuch a compaffe that
they shall not paffe to enuiron , or ouerwhelme the whole earth . Therfore after the firft
crea-

creation of the elements God fayed: *Congregen-* *Gen.* 1.
tur aquæ in locum vnum, vt appareat arida: Con- 9.
gregationefq, aquarum appellauit maria: Let the
wathers be gathered to geather in one place, that
the drie land may appeare: and the gathering to
geather of the wathers he called the feas. So that
we may conclude that when in the innouation
the feas shall be no more, the waters shall haue
their full courfe ouer the face of the whole
earth. And the reafon in this innouation of the *Tho. in*
deftruction of all things both in the ayre, *fup. a.*
the wathers, and on the earth may be, be- *q.* 91.
caufe all thefe creatures as the fowles of *ar.* 5.
the ayre, the fishes of the feas, the beaft and
fruits of the earth, were ordained of God
only for the vfe, maintenance and comfort
of man : but man being taken away, all the
elements shall be renewed and reftored to
their naturall courfe; So that there can be no
habitatió at all vpon the earth of man or beaft.
Two places there shall remaine only habitable
that is; heauen and hell; heauen for the good
Angells and Saints, and hell for the deuills and
damned foules. Therfore the ordinarie opinion of School diuines is, that the place
for Children dying without Baptifme, shall be *In.* 2:
the horrible prifon and dungeon of hell. And *fenten.*
this onlie reliefe they shall haue (as hath bene *dift.* 33.
fayed) they shal not fuffer anie fenfible pai- *v. in* 4.
ne, nor be tormented with hell fire, nor ha- *dift.* 45.
ue anie worme of confcience grawing on
them, nor remorfe for anie fault they did
vpon earth, becaufe they neuer committed,
anie actuall finne : Wherfore I conclude,
they can

they can haue no middle place betweene heauen and hell: neither can they inhabite or liue
on the earth to enioy anie naturall kind of felicitie or pleasure.

CAP. 9.

VVhether they shall haue anie exceßiue grief in
hell, for that they are depriued of the frui-
tion and sight of God.

Aug. li.
6. in Iu-
li anü
cap. 4.
vltra
mediü.
B. Greg.
lib. 9.
moral.
c. 16.
Fulgë.
de fide
ad Pet.

IT is the opinion of some Doctours , as S.
Augustine, S. Gregorie, and Fulgentius , that
the Infants dying without Baptisme, can not be
exempted, nor freed from all sorrow and grief;
because they know they were created to the
Image and liknesse of God, and that they want
their finall end, for the which they had their begining, which was to prayse God, to see God,
and to haue a certaine beatitude and blessednes,
the want wherof can not but be a certaine great
grief vnto them.

Yet it is the more generall opinion of the
greater part of Diuines that their sorrow and
grief can be but small and litle; because they
haue manie causes to lenifie and mitigate this
their grief and sorrow. Although they had a
knowledge of God, and were not ignorant of
some kind of beatitude and blessednes: yet because they neuer had any acte or habite to execute it, wherby they might attaine vnto it but a
weake, remote, and farre of disposition onlie,
which could effect nothing : therfore their
grief cā not be great for the losse of that, wherof they

of they neuer had perfect knowledge, nor in them selues meanes to attaine.

Againe it was nor by their proper negligéce, but by the fault of an other, that they haue loſt ſo great a good. Alſo theſe Infants neuer taſted of the delights of heauen or earth; but we know by experience, that we neuer grieue ſo much for the want of thoſe things we neuer had, as we doe for the loſſe of thoſe things we haue poſſeſſed, or were in power to enioy. We are eaſely cótent to want toſe things we neuer had vſe of, and neuer looked after neither *in Spe*, nor *In re* : Neither in expectance nor in deed. But ſo it is with the Infants: therfore their grief can not be great. Beſides all this it muſt needes be a great relief and comfort to them, when they ſhall ſee great multitudes farre more vnfortunate, and in more miſerable caſe then themſelues. Becauſe they ſhall ſee others for their owne proper action grieuouſly tormented by the torment of hell fire, and with all the know themſelues freed from it, becauſe they neuer had anie proper vſe of action in themſelues, wherby actuallie they could offend. Wherfore we maie conclud their griefe and ſorrow to be but remiſſe and ſmall, although they are depriued of the ſight of God, and wante of ſome kind of beatitude and bleſſednes, becauſe they had but an vnperfect knowledge therof, and no meanes to obtaine it.

S. Thomas his opinion is, although Children vnbaptized be in hell, and ſuffer *Pœnam damni*: puniſhment of damnation : Yet for all that they ſhall take no ſerrow nor grief at all, neither externall, nor internall; becauſe (ſaieth he) they

T. o. de mal. q. 5. a. 3.

they haue no perfect knowledg that they are
fruſtrate of their beatitude; and vnderſtand full
well, that they neuer had anie naturall meanes
to obtaine it. For what man but a foole would
grieue and ſorrow that he were not a king
or Angell, when he knoweth there is no means
for him to become a King or Angell. And S.

Bon. 2. Bonauenture ſayeth: *That ſo it cometh to paſſe*
Sent. *that the conſideration of the loſe of the kingdome*
diſt. *of heauen is in ſuch manner tempered with the eſ-*
33. *cape of the paines of ſenſe; and the euaſion of the*
torments of hell, that all grief and ſorrowe is auoy-
ded. So that we may conclud that children although damned in hell, yet they haue no excef-
ſiue griefe in reſpect of their depriuation of the
fruition or ſight of almigtie God.

Obiect.   You may obiect that it is a common Maxime
and ſaying amongſt Diuines that : *Dolor amiſſæ*
beatitudinis grauiſſimus eſt: The griefe of the loſ-
ſe of beatitude and the bleſſed viſion of God is the
greateſt and moſt grieuous torment that is in hell;
But children haue loſt beatitude and the bleſſed
viſiõ of God; therfore their grief muſt be great:

Sol.   I anſwere; that the Propoſition and ſaying of
the Diuines is moſt true, that the loſſe of beatitude, and the bleſſed ſight of God is the greateſt grief and torment that can be; But this Propoſition muſt be vnderſtood as proper onlie to
the elder ſort of men and women, who are
damned by their owne fact, and not as apper-
taining to Infants, who haue no fact of their
owne, but are puniſhed for an others, In verie
deed it can not but be an exceſſiue griefe in the
elder ſort of the damned, becauſe t they loſt
heauen and bleſſednes by their owne proper
                                        actuall

actuall offence and finne. And therfore haue
with all conioyned to their damnation, the perpetuall torments of hell without intermiffion;
and their grief the greater by reafon they had by
faith a confident hoppe to haue obtained that
which they haue loft, Wherfore we conclud,
that Infants and children damned may haue fome fmall grief, but no exceffiue forrow for
their loffe of beatitude, and depriuation of the
fight of almightie God.

CAP. 10.

*VVhether the Infant in the mothers wombe may
be Baptized.*

Saint Auguftine folueth this queftion and
fayeth, that the Infant in the mothers wombe can not be Baptized; and yeeldeth the reafon: *Quia nemo renafcitur nifi primò nafcatur:*
No man *is faid to be borne againe, vnleffe he be
first borne carnallie.* Alfo to the fame effect fpeaketh Ifidorus: *Qui adhuc natus non eft fecundum
Adam, non poteft per Chriftum renafci: He that
as yet is not borne according to Adam, can not be
borne againe by Chrift.* And S. Thomas proueth
it by an other reafon. It is of neceffitie and the
effence of Baptifme that the bodie of the Infant
be dipped in water, or haue fome water layed
vpon it; But the bodie of the Infant can not haue wather in the wombe of the mother before
it be Borne. Therfore it cannot be Baptized before it be borne.

*Aug. ep.
57. ad
Dard.*

*Ifidor.
li. 10.
fent de
fummo
bono c.
24.
Tho. 3.
p. q. 68.
art. 11.*

L   CAP.

CAP. II.

VVhether if some parte of the Child appeare,
although the whole bodie be not borne, it may
be Baptized.

THe difficultie of this question ariseth, because the child may be sayed to be borne
totallie, whollie, and perfectlie, also to be borne in parte, that is: when the hand, foote, or
head appeareth out of the wombe of the mother; as happened to Thamar, when she brought
G '.38. forth Phares and Zaram, for Zarams hand first
appeared. The question is, when it so happe-
neth, that parte of the child appeare out of the
wombe of the mother, that then according to
that parte the child may be Baptized. The opinion of some learned Casuists is: That it were
conuenient and good to expect the whole and
perfect birth of the child. But if it be imminent
danger of death, and the principall parte appeare, as the head, and no hope of totall birth (for
the hand and foote there is more difficultie)
then the child may and ought to be baptized.
If thou desire to be better informed concerning
this case, read Siluester a learned Casuist . *In*
Summa, verbo Baptismus. §. 4. *nu.* 2. *And S.*
Thomas. 3. *p. q.* 88. *ar,* 11. *ad* 4.

CAP. 12.

VVhether if the mother being greate with child
being Baptized, the child also in her wombe be
also Baptized.

THe case is, if a Iewish or Turkish woman,
being conuerted to Christianitie, and being
great

great with child defire to be baptized, whether
the Infant in her wombe at the fame tyme, and
by the fame action be alfo Baptized. For if one
parte of the bodie be Baptized, all the members
of the fame bodie be alfo Baptized But the Infant in the mothers wombe is a member of her
bodie. Therfore it is alfo Baptized with the
Baptifme of the mother. S. Thomas refolueth *T*!*o*. 3.
this doubt and fayeth; That the Infant is not *p.q.68.*
Baptized by the Baptifme of the mother, be- *ar. 11.*
caufe properlie the child is not a member of the
bodie of the mother; but hath a diftinct bodie
and foule from hers; onlie vntill it be borne it
is knitte and tyed to the bodie of the mother,
but this doth not make it a member of her
bodie.

There was one Iulianus an Heretike who
liued in S. Auguftines tyme, and he was of opinion, that the Infant was parte of the mother;
and therfore Baptized in the mothers wombe
by the mothers Baptifme. Againft whom S.   *Habe-*
Auguftine wrote manie books. Read him in   *tur de*
his fixth booke and fifth Chapter againft Iulian *Cōfec.*
the Heretike.   *dif. 4.*
                                            C. fi ad
─── *matris.*

CAP. 13.

*VVhether if the mother should be martired, the
Infant in her wombe were alfo a martyr.*

I Thinke in this cafe the Infant fhould be
  Baptized in his owne bloud, and fo confequentlie a martyr with his mother. The Infants
who dyed for Chrift after his birth, the Church
alwayes

alwayes honoured for Martirs, and they Confeſſed Chriſt : *Non loquendo, ſed moriendo : Not by tongue and mouth , but by bloud and death.* Therfore as the mother by conſtant confeſſion and death was a Martyr: ſo alſo the Infant in her wombe being ſlaine in contempt of the mother, and the cauſe ſhe died for, muſt alſo be a Martir by bloud and death. I may put for example that worthie woman miſtris Cleathrow, who was put to death at Yorke in Queene Elizabeths tyme for receauing a reuerent Religious Prieſt into her houſe, and for conſtant confeſſing the Chatholike faith. She was a worthie martyr and true Imitatrix & follower of S. Alban the Protomartyr of England. If ſhe were withe child, & confeſſing as much, but the Iudges not regarding it, I make no doubt, but the child dieyng in her wombe dyed alſo a Martyr.

CAP. 14.

VVhether the Mother may be cut and opened if other wiſe the Child cã not be borne & ſo takē from her aliue that it may be Baptized.

Th. lo-cis ſup. citatis. I anſwere with S. Thomas and learned Silueſter, that the mother, ſo lohg as there is life in her, in no caſe is to be cut and opened. For no man ought to kill the mother for the Baptizing of the child . But if the mother die, and the child be aliue in her wombe, then ſhe ought to be opened & the child Baptized. You *Obiect.* may obiect that tēporall death in the mother is leſſe euill, then the eternall death of the child,

which

which muft needs follow if it die without Baptifme; but of two euills the leffer is to be chofen. Wherfore we fhould rather chufe the temporall death of the mother, then the eternall
damnation of the child. To this obiection we
anfwere with S. Paule: *That no man may doe
euill that good may come of it.* Therfore we may
not murther the mother that the child may liue
fpirituallie or corporallie.

    Sol.
    Rō. 3.

  If it be true (as is reported of King Henrie
the eight, when his Queene Iane Seymer could
not be brought a bed, and deliuered of her Sonne Edward the fixth, he yeelded and gaue confent that fhee fhould be opened & cut, & fayed:
*I may haue an other wife, but I doubt whether I
fhall haue an other child*; and fo the mother dyed
for the life of the child. But what followed?
The child neuer liued to be a man, and by reafon of his noneage, the whole realme was dif-
turbed, Religion contemned, and herefie planted. A plague no doubt for the Fathers iniquitie and finne.

CAP. 15.

*VVhether the children of Iewes or other Infidells,
may lawfullie be Baptized againft their Parents will.*

IT is a hard and difficulte queftion, efpeciallie were Iewes and Infidells are fubiect vnto
a Chriftian Prince, as both Iewes and Indian
Infidells are to the King of Spayne. A man
would thinke it were but Chriftian dutie and
Charitie to take the children of thefe Iewes
and Indian Infidells and Baptize them, educate,

        L 3   inftruct

inſtruct and bring them vp in Chriſtian faith and beleefe whe her the Parents will or nill. For if vpon malice or other diſpleaſure ; the Father ſhould endanger the corporall or temporall life of his child, one might lawfullie by violence reſiſt him. Why not alſo may one for the eternall & ſpirituall life of the ſoule againſt the parents will, or contrarie to their conſent, baptize their children? Notwithſtanding it is the generall opinion of Diuines, and practiſe of the Church , not to Baptize Iewes & Infidells children, without the parents conſent and freewill.

Tho. 3.
p.q.68.
And the reaſon is (as ſayeth S. Thomas) becauſe it is againſt the law of nature. For by the lawe of nature children are vnder the gouernment, tuition and care of their parents vntill they come to the vſe of reaſon , and yeares of vnderſtanding; but the lawe of grace doth not deſtroy the law of nature ; therfore they cannot be Baptized without the parents conſent.

CAP. 16.

VVhether Iewes, Turkes or Infidells being conuerted are preſentlie to be Baptized .

HAuing ſpoken of the Baptiſme of children: now I will entreate of thoſe, who are at mens eſtate adults, & elder ſort, what is required of them before they are Baptized . Firſt concerning Iewes , Turkes and Infidells conuerted, it was the practiſe of the Primitiue Church, and is continued vntill this day in the Catholike Church , that preſentlie after their conuerſion they are not Baptized ; but for a tyme in-

me inftructed and trained vp in the beleefe and
life of a Chriftian, and therfore called, *Cathecu-
meni, Men to be inftructed and Cathechifed.* True
it is in deed, that the Apoftles in the begining
did not vfe this practife : for in the Acts of the
Apoftles we read that on the firft day of S. Peters preaching, there were three thoufand Bap- *Act. 2.*
tized, and afterward on an other day fiue hundred. And S. Philippe the Deacon, prefentlie
the fame day after conference with the Eunuch *Act. 8.*
the Queene Candaces Treafurer, he Baptized
him. Alfo S. Peter at the firft meeting, Baptized
Cornelius the Italiã with his kindred & Friends.
Yet we muft not thinke that the Church immediatlie after the Apoftles, & fo continueth vntill
this day in making Cathecumins, doth anie thing
contrarie to the Apoftles proceedings. For we
muft vnderftand, why the Apoftles did immediatlie vpõ the conuerfiõ of the people Baptize.
Becaufe at thofe tymes the Holie Ghoft fell
vpõ them, and they were fufficientlie inftructed
by the Holy Ghoft himfelf. Yet cã we not fay for
the approuing of this practife of the Church,
but that they were alfo inftructed and Catechifed by the Apoftles, as partly by S. Peters preaching, partlie by priuate conference, as S. Philippe had with the treafurer, and S. Peter with
Cornelius. But to conclud they were all taught
to beleeue before they were Baptized. The reafõ
of this practife of the Church, that they fhould
not prefentlie after theyr Conuerfion be Baptized, but for a tyme inftructed, Catechifed and
made Catecumins, is, becaufe Baptifme is a
certaine profeffion of Chriftian faith, and therfore called the Sacrament of beleefe: but faith
cometh

Rom c.
10.

Mat.
18.
Mar.
16.

cometh by inſtruction: *Quomodo credent &c.*
*How ſhall they beleeue in him whom they haue not
heard? And how shall they heare without a preacher?* Therfore in theſe kind of men it is neceſſarie, that inſtruction and Catechiſing goe before Baptiſme. Wherfore Chriſt in his commiſſion for Baptiſme, ſpake firſt of inſtruction,
then of Baptiſme: *Going yee* (ſayeth he to his
Apoſtles) *teach and preach Baptizing.*

CAP. 17.

*VVhether Iewes and Infidells may be compelled to
Baptiſme.*

TRue it is that Siſebutius King of the Goi-
ths when he entred into Spaine about the
yeare of Chriſt 595. the Iewes, who at that tyme dwelled in Spaine, be compelled by force &
feare of puniſhement to receaue the Chriſtian
faith; which facte of the Kings was not then
approued, but after in the Councell of Toledo decreed and commanded that none ſhould
be forced to the Chriſtian faith. For: *Cui vult
Deus miſeretur: & quem vult indurat: vnto whom
God will he sheweth mercie; and doth indura-
te whom he will .* Thoſe who come of their
owne accord Chriſt accepteth, and not thoſe
who are forced. Therfore ſayeth the Councell:

Con.4.
Toleta.
can.56.

*Non vi, ſed liberi arbitrij voluntate vt conuertan-
tur ſuadendi ſunt: They are not by force to be compelled, but they are to be perſwaded that freelie &
willinglie they may be conuerted.* For it is neceſſitie that the partie, who is to be Baptized,
giue his Conſent and good will to Baptiſme.

tiſme. For if by force without his conſent not hauing faith he be vrged, he hath no Sacrament, no Baptiſme.

In thiſe caſe of Siſebutius, the Iewes being compelled either to make their choyce to be baniſhed & depart the realme, or els to be baptized, they conſenting by this coaction or compulſion rather to be Baptized then to be baniſhed (becauſe it is a conſent although coacte & by compulſion) they receiue Baptiſme, that is the Character and ſigne of a Chriſtian, but not grace, ſaluation or Iuſtification, as ſhall be proued in the ſequent chapter. Read *C. maiores de Baptiſmo & eius effectu lib. 3. decretalium titulo 42.*

CAP. 18.

VVhether he who cometh to this Sacramènt fainedly, not hauing in deed faith in Chriſt, be Baptized.

TRue it is and we can not denie, that he who fainedlie cometh to be Baptized, doth and may receaue the Sacrament of Baptime, that is the character, ſigne and ſeale of a Chriſtian, and therfore not to be rebaptized when he cometh after to beleeue aright. But he that thus fainedlie and without faith doth approche, ſhall neuer be ſaued. for as S. Paule ſayeth: *The Iuſtice of God is by faith of Ieſus Chriſt. He that will come to God muſt beleeue. And it is impoſſible to pleaſe God without faith.* Therfor Chriſt ſayed: *Quicre. diderit &c. He that beleeueth & is Baptized, ſhall be ſaued: and he that beleeueth not ſhall be damned.*

Rom.3.

Hab.11.

Mar. 16.

L 5   Wherfore

Wherfore feeing and confidering, that faith is
fo neceffarie to the obtaining of Baptifme, we
conclud, that euen in children and naturall fooles there muft be faith. And becaufe neither of
them, children nor fooles, are capable of actuall
faith as thofe at mans eftate and vnderftanding,
are therfore we Catholikes fay that: *Aliena fides*:
The fait of an other, that is of the Church is fufficient for them. But for thofe of the elder forte and of vnderftanding, we defend that it is neceffarie they haue actuall faith, or els it will be
with them as it was with Iudas, who receaued
the Sacrament of the Bodie of our Lord at the
hands of Chrift in his laft fupper, but not the
effect of the Sacrament, becaufe he receaued
vnworthelie to his owne damnation. So alfo
he that approcheth to Baptifme fainedly without faith may & doth receaue the Sacrament,
and hath the character and figne of a Chriftian,
but he fhall neuer haue the effect and end of
the Sacrament, that is grace, Iuftification, or
faluation . For example, fome Iewes defire
Baptifme, not for the faith they haue in Iefus
Chrift, but becaufe their flefh and skinne doth
fauour and ftinke: therfore they are called: *Iu-
dai fœtentes: ftinking Iewes.* But as foone as they
are Baptized this filthie fauour of their bodies
is gone , and they fmell as fweet as anie other
Chriftians doe; fo that fome of them may for
this caufe onlie require Baptifme , I fay they
may haue the Sacrament, although they come
with this corrupt intention : but neuer fhall
they haue the effect and end of this Sacrament.

In like manner we read of fome Sarracens &
Turkes, who defire baptifme, not with true faith
in Chrift,

in Chrift, but being fore ficke or troubled and
vexed with an euill fpirit, hauing experience
that by Baptifme they may be deliuered, they
feeke and defire Baptifme, for this caufe onlie
that they may receaue their health, and be deliuered from the vexation of the Deuill. Thefe
kind of men alfo may receaue the Sacrament,
but they fhall not haue faluation and iuftification, if they haue not true faith and beleefe
in Chrift. Wherfore to conclud, one may come
to this Sacrament faineldlie and with a falfe
harte, without faith, with a corrupt intention,
and be Baptized: but he fhall neuer haue faluation and iuftification therby, as hath beene
proued.

CAP. 19.

*VVhether he that is Baptized may be compelled
to liue according to Chriftian Catholike
lawes.*

NO man ought to be compelled to Chriftian
faith, nor forced to receaue Baptifme, as
hath bene proued, but they muft approch and
come voluntarilie and willinglie, and to be
wonne by reafon, perfwafion & preaching. And
therfore the Church hath no authoritie, iurifdiction nor power to force or compell thofe,
who neuer receaued Baptifme, to the obferua-
tion of Chriftian lawes, or Ecclefiafticall Conftitutions. And this S. Paule hath taught, and
practifed, and would not iuge them, who we- 1. *Cor.*
re not Baptized: *Quid mihi de ijs, qui foris funt,* 5.
indicare?

iudicare? what is it to me to iuge of them that are
without? But if once they fubmitted themfelues
vnder the yoake of Iefus Chrift, receaued the
Sacrament of Baptifme, and were incorporate
as members of the bodie of Chrift mifticall:
then no doubt but they are vnder the iurifdiction and power of the Church. And therfore S.
Paule, although he would not iudge the Infidell or vnbaptized: yet it is plaine he excommu-
1. Cor. nicated the publike inceftious Corinthian, and
5.   cómaunded not to keepe companie, or fo much
as to eate with him. Therfore in fo much
as one by Baptifme is incorporate and made a member of the Church, he is fubordinate
to the Iurifdiction of the Church; and fo confequentlie fubiecte to the Cenfures, lawes and
Conftitutions of the fame, and therfore may
be compelled to obferue Chriftian rites and
Conftitutions, and be forced to liue accordinglie.

THE

THE FIFTH
BOOKE
of the Ceremonies.

CAP. I.

VVhat a Ceremonie is.

Ceremonie is an externall acte of Religion, which is exhibited, acted, and done to the honour and worshippe of God.

Considering that man doth cõsist of soule and body, & not of body only nor of soule onlie, but of both ioyntlie: therfore there is internall worship and honour proceeding from the soule, and there is also externall exhibited, acted and done by outward acts and signes. The first honour or adoration, which we call internall, is the chiefe and principall, and that which most pleaseth God, and it is threefold, that is; exercised by three speciall vertues; ffirst by faith & true beleefe in God; secõdly by a firme hope of Gods mercie & grace towards vs, a cõfidence of life eternall, & a trust that God will performe his promises made to his Church; thirdlie by a feruent loue of God Aboue all creatures. These
are the

are the three Theologicall Diuine vertues fayth, hope, and charitie, proceeding from the operation of the soule, working internally by the assistance of the Holy Ghost. Therfore Christ

Ioa. 4. sayed: *God is a Spirite, and they that adore him must adore in spirite and veritie.* Yet there is also externall adoration & worship of God, which is guided and gouerned by the internall, as the Sacrifice and ceremonies were of the old law. And in the new law instituted by Christ are the Sacraments of the Church, the making of the signe of Christ crucified, the crosse, the bowing of the knee at the name of Iesus, praying with our mouth, lifting our eyes and hands towards heauen &c. In Baptisme making the signe of the crosse vpon the Infant, vsing Exvfflations, Exorcismes, holy vnction, Chrisme, and the rest. Therfore the verie wisdome of God in ordaining and instituting this Sacrament, would expresse the state and condition of man and institute and ordaine the Sacrament of Baptisme, to consist of water and the Holy Ghost, externallie signifying what internallie should be wrought; The water washing externallie the bodie, and the Holie Ghost internallie sanctifying the soule, both ioyntlie concurring to the cleansing of man,

---

CAP. 2.

VVhat distinction and diuision there is of the Ceremonies in Baptisme.

THe ceremonies of Baptisme are of three sorts: Some precedent, going before Baptisme

tifme: Some concurring with Baptifme;and fome fubfequent, and following Baptifme.Or we
may make our diuifion : fome before the Baptized come vnto the fonte: fome at the fonte:
and other fome after he is taken out of the fonte. The precedent, or before the Infant come
to the fonte, are fuch as are giuen for the better preparing of the Infant to be Baptized , and
to take away all obftacles, lettes and hinderan-
ces that the Sacrament may haue his full effect. Alfo to weaken the power of Satan, who
would plead pofeffion by reafon of finne in the
foule:The other Ceremonies,fuch as are,when
the partie to be Baptized cometh to the fonte,
are the naming of the child, the Godfathers and
Godmothers, the abrenuntiation of Satan, and
all his pompes and pride,the profeffion of faith,
the Baptizing with the water & word ioyntlie,
with three merfiõs. The ceremonies fubfequēt,
or after the Baptifed is taken out of the fonte,
are the vfe of holie Chrifme , the annoynting
on the crowne of the head, the Godfathers and
Godmothers laying their hands on his head,the
cloathing with the white garment commonlie
called the Chrifome, the giuing him the candle or taper light in his hand ; all which in this
booke and fequent treatife in feuerall Chapters
I will fette downe, and fhew the vfe and reafon
of them. And there is not the leaft rite or ceremonie of this Sacrament of Baptifme now vfed
in the Catholike Church, which either die not
defcend by Tradition from the Apoftles,or were not inftituted by the Holie Church, confirmed by the ancient Fathers, and practifed for
many ages, vntill of late tyme thefe Nouelants
and new-

and new·opſpronge Heretikes began to bay and
barke againſt them.

Cap. 3.

*VVhether theſe Ceremonies are of neceſſitie to
this Sacrament of Baptiſme.*

I anſwere they are neceſſarie : *Ad bene eſſe* , but not *ſimpliciter* , that is they are
no eſſentiall parts of the Sacrament : yet they
are to the Decorum and beautie of the Sacrament. For in caſe of neceſſitie there is no doubt
(as I haue proued before) but this Sacrament
may be miniſtred without theſe Ceremonies,
becauſe they are not of the eſſence and ſubſtance of Baptiſme , Yet no man ſhall or can denie;
but that they are helpes and comforts to the
Baptized, inſtructions, and ſignes to the ſtanders
by, and ornaments for the more ſolemne receauing of this Sacrament, Which is the gate
and firſt entráce to Chriſtianitie. We know full
well, that the leaues of the tree are not the
ſubſtance of the tree: yet no man can denie,
bnt that they are the ornaments and beautie of
the tree. Alſo the hedge is no eſſentiall parte of
the vine : yet all men know it is a protection
and defence to the viueard. Wherfore I hold it a
grieuous mortall ſinne in Catholike Chriſtian
people, negligentlie & careſſely, otherwiſe then
in caſe of neceſſitie, to omitte theſe ceremonies; and ſtatte Schiſme and an open ſigne of an
Heretike proudlie & contemptuouſly to reiect
and contemne them ; hauing bene practiſed in
the Pri-

the Primitiue Church , defcended from antiquitie , and vfed generally in the Church
of God . And why the Church vfeth Ceremonies S. Thomas giueth the reafon: *The
Church (fayeth he) which is guided by the Holy
Ghoſt, vfeth and commaundeth the rites and Ceremonies of Baptifme for three feuerall caufes and
confiderations; although they be no effentiall or
ſubſtantiall parte of the Sacrament : yet are
conuenient for the Decorum and folemnitie of this
Sacrament . Firſt becaufe they are means to ſtir-
re vp and moue the minds of the beleeuing and
faithfull people to greater deuotion and reuerence
vnto this Sacrament , for that there is greater
miſterie in this Sacrament more then the externall waſhing which is ſhewed by water. Secondly
becaufe thefe Ceremonies inſtruƈte and teach many
things more then doe the bare effence and fubſtance as ſhall appeare hereafter in the examination of
euerie rite and ceremonie of this Sacramēt. Thirdly
becaufe by theſe Ceremonies the force and power
of the Deuill is much weakened , that he may not
hinder the effeƈt of Baptifme in the Baptized.*
Thus farre S. Thomas. Not without caufe therfore , the Generall Councell of Trente doth
Anathematize and condemne, whofoeuer ſhall
contemne the approued and receaued rites and
ceremonies of the Catholike Church, which are
accuſtomed to be vfed in folemne celebration
of Sacraments. Maruell not (Good Reader)
that the Heretikes of this age regard not the
Ceremonies of this Sacrament, feing they endeauour to take away all force from the Sacraments themfelues .

*Tho. 3.
p.q.66.
a. 18.*

*Concil.
Trid.
fef.7 ca.
non.13.*

M   C A R.

CAP. 4.

VVhether the child be not to be Signed with the signe of the Crosse in the forehead and breast.

THe Cuſtome of the Catholike Church is, that the Prieſt come to meete the Child at the Church dore, to ſignifie that the Infant as yet is not of the houſhould of the faithfull and congregation of Chriſt, but ſtandeth at the gate readie to enter into the Church of God. And the firſt action he doth is to ſigne the Baptized with the ſigne of the Croſſe firſt in the forehead ſaying : *Signum Saluatoris &c. The ſigne of our Sauiour our Lord Ieſus Chriſt I place or put in thy Forehead* . And then to the breaſt ſaying and doing the like : *The ſigne of our Sauiour our Lord Ieſus Chriſt I put vpon thy breaſt* . This is the practiſe of the Chatholike Church. Concerning this Cheremonie of the Signe of the Croſſe, the Proteſtants Commend highly as a lawfull Ceremonie, and honorable badge , wherby the Infant is dedicated to the ſeruice of Chriſt, who *Confer.* dyed on the Croſſe. Therfore it is Commaun-*fol. 72.* ded in their Communion-Booke , approued by the ſupreame power the King and Cleargie, *Can.* and defended againſt the Puritan, and precifer *30.* ſort of Miniſters in their booke of Conſtituti-ons; and to ſatiſfie thee better, I will put downe *·J·* the reaſons of this Ceremonie . Firſt becauſe amongſt the Iewes the Croſſe was ignominí-ous and hatefull, and the Apoſtles were deri-ded for beleeuing in Chriſt, who was Crucified

                                                                vpon

vpon the Croſſe. Notwithſtanding the Apoſtles and Primitiue Chriſtians therby were not diſmayed, but the rather gloried in the Croſſe of Chriſt, according to that of S. Paule: *God forbid that I ſhould glorie, ſauing in the Croſſe of our Lord Ieſus Chriſt*, And therfore ſayeth S. Auguſtine: *The Croſſe is fixed and faſtened to the forehead of the faithfull, that they being Chriſtians may ſay: God forbid that I ſhould glorie, ſauing in the Croſſe of our Lord Ieſus Chriſt, and not be aſhamed of Chriſt crucified*. Secondly in the Apoſtles tyme the ſigne of the Croſſe was of ſuch honour, dignitie, and eſteeme among Chriſtians, that not onlie the vſed it in all their actions to ſigne themſelues with the ſigne of the Croſſe, but alſo to dicated their children by that ſigne to the ſeruice of Chriſt, when they were to be Baptized; therfore an ancient, honorable and lawfull ceremonie: Thirdlie it began not onlie to be a bage & Cognizance of a Chriſtian, to be diſtinguiſhed from Iewe and Gentill, but alſo a defence and weapon againſt Satan, and the aſſaultes of the diuell. For Satan when he ſawe the ſigne of the Croſſe made, he remembred the victorie Chriſt had ouer him vpon the Croſſe; and therfore abhorreth and flieth from that ſigne, as a ſigne of his deſtruction and Calamitie : And we read that not onlie Chriſtians, who haue faith in Chriſt crucified, haue bene defended from power of Satan by the ſigne of the Croſſe, but ſuch vertue hath God ſhewed by that ſigne, and daylie doth, that euen

Aug.
tract.
in Ioa.
43.
Gal. 6.

3.

M 2   Iewes

Iewes and Pagans haue bene protected by it.
Read the hiſtorie of Iulian the Apoſtata recorded by S. Gregorie Nazianzen, and of Ioſeph
the Iewe as Epiphanius. Iulian being deſirous
to practiſe with Coniurers , and conſult
with diuells that he might knowe whether
he ſhould be Emperour or no , he was
by a Necromancer brought into a Temple
of the Idolls , where the diuells ſolemne-
lie appeared , at whoſe preſence and ſight
being ſore affrighted : *Terrore compellitur in*
fronte ſua Crucis formare ſignaculum : tunc
Dæmones , &c. Was (ſaveth Theodorete)
for feare compelled to make the Signe of the
Croſſe in his forehead : then the diuells loo-
king backe , and ſeing the figure of our Lords
banner , and remembring the fall and ouer-
throwe they had by the Croſſe ſodenlie vani-
ſhed out of ſight. And S. Gregorie Nazianzen recordeth, that after he had bene once
frighted , yet being animated , and encoura-
ged againe the ſecond tyme the diuells appearing , he alſo againe fled to the refuge
of the Croſſe , and ſo put the wicked ſpirits to flight. And S. Gregorie one of the
fower Doctors of the Church , reporteth
the hiſtorie of a Iewe , who had no faith
nor hope in the Paſſion of Chriſt : yet in
trauell being benighted , and ſo forced to
lodge in the temple of Apollo , he made
the ſigne of the Croſſe vpon him ; and as
he thus lay ſigned with the Croſſe , a great
companie of diuells entred . The maiſter diuell ſeeing one ly in the temple , ſent ſome
of the other diuells to ſee who he was that
presumed

Greg.
Naz.
orat. in
Iulian.
Epiph.
hareſ.
30.

Hiſt.
Eccle.
trip. li.
8.ca 1.

Greg.
Naz.
orat. in
Iulian.

Greg.
lib. 3.
dial.
ca. 7.

prefumed to take vp his lodging , in the temple of Apollo . They brought word that he was : *Vas vacuum , fed fignatum : A voyde and emptie veffell , but figned with the figne of the Croffe .* At which words the whole companie vanifhed out of fight . By which examples and authorities, we may gather the figne of the Croffe to be a defence againft diuells , and a putter to flight of euill fpirits , as alfo fpirituall vertue againft the fnares and wiles of Satan . Wherefore worthilie vfed not onlie as a badge of a Chriftian , but alfo as a protection againft all ambufhes and craftie fetches of the enemie of mankind . And this may be effected either by the apprehenfion of the diuell , for then they flie when they fee the Croffe , whereby they were conquered ; or among the Chriftians by him that maketh the figne of the Croffe with deuotion , for that the Croffe is a memorie and a certaine inuocation of the merits of Chrifts paffion ; or amongft the Infidells and Pagans , in whom there is no fayth nor beleefe in Chrift, it doth worke euen by the verie doing and making of the Croffe , as may appeare in the examples alleadged , where the verie making of the figne of the Croffe made the diuells to flie . Wherfore to Conclude laudable , ancient , and profitable is the vfe of the figne of the Croffe in Baptifme .

Although the Proteftants agree and

accord with vs to vfe the figne of the Croffe in
Baptifme: yet becaufe they will be Schifmatikes
from the Catholike Church, and from the firft
founders of Chriftianitie in this land, both a
mong the Brittons and Saxons, they differ in
three poynts. Firft, for that they figne the child
after Baptifme and not before, as we Catholikes doe, as though the Croffe were not a meanes as well to expell Satan the enemie of man,
as to be a badge and Cognizance of Chriftian
profeffion. Secondlie, they omitte to figne the
Child in the breaft, for if it be lawfull and conuenient to vfe the Croffe in the forehead, for
an outward figne of profeffion of Chrift crucified vpon the Croffe, why alfo doe they not
vfe it vpon the breaft, where the harte is, that it
may fignifie that this profeffion of the Croffe,
proceedeth alfo from the harte and inward affection. Thirdlie, the Proteftants feeme to in-
finuate that the Catholikes make the figne of
the Croffe an effentiall and fubftantiall parte of
Baptifme, as though we held that there could
be no, Baptifme without it, which is a flander
and calumnie. For if it be but a ceremonie annexed to this Sacrament (as we haue fayed) it
can be no effentiall parte of Baptifme.

CAP. 5.

*VVhether they Who are of yeares and vnder-
ftanding being conuerted, ought to be Cathecumines before they be Baptized.*

I haue fpoken fomething of this ceremonie
in the precedent booke. It was a laudable
ordinan-

ordinance, rite and ceremonie vfed in the Primitiue Church, and to this day diligentlie obferued in the Catholike Church , that thofe
who being at mans eftate, and were conuerted
and defired Baptifme , fhould before they were
Baptifed be Cathecumines, that is to be inftru-
&ed and trained vp in Chriftian beleefe and
life , and taught the rudiments and principles
of Chriftian Catholike Do&rine , The fecond *Concil.*
Bracharenfe Councell, apointed twentie dayes *Bra-*
before Baptifme , that the newlie conuerted *cha.*
fhould be cathechized, inftru&ed and learne *can.1.*
the Creed &c. And this pra&ife is plainlie proued out of S. Auguftine , for he wrote a booke *Aug. de*
of the expofition of the Creed, and deliuered it *Symb.*
to the Cathecumines, that is, the newlie con- *ad Ca-*
uerted . This ceremonie is moft obferued *the. |li.*
in Italie , Spaine , and the Indians , eaft and *4.ca. 1.*
wefte , in which countreyes daylie are conuerted vnto the Chriftian faith, Ieues, Turkes,
and Pagans ; but in England there is no vfe of
this Cheremonie and that for two caufes- Firft
becaufe there are neither Iewes, nor Turkes,
nor Pagans , who publikely inhabite, or are
permitted in the land , and therfore no dealing
for their conuerfion. I will not fay there are no
Infidells, for that Atheifme and herefie (as hath
bene fayed) is a kind of Infidelitie or misbeleefe;
but how that countrey fwarmeth with fuch
kind of people. *Notum eft omnibus*: It is knowen
to all the world . The fecond caufe why this
ceremonie is not in vfe in England is, becaufe
it was neuer heard of as yet, that euer any Proteftant conuerted to Chriftianitie anie Iewe,
Turke or Pagan , although it be moft manifeft,

M 4   they

they haue had dealing and traffike with all three
and haue of late fought to plant them felues in
fome Pagan partes of the world, as Guiana and
Virginea : yet did we not heare of anie Conuerfion to Chriftianitie in anie parte or place
of the world. And will you haue the reafon
why they can not effect this Conuerfion of Infidells ? Surely Schifmatikes and Heretikes di-
uided from Gods Church, haue alwayes bene
peruerters, no Conuerters, deftroyers, no buil-
ders of Chriftianitie; and therefore we muft not
looke nor expecte that Proteftants fhould con-
uerte Countries, or bring Iewes or Pagans to

Tertul.
li. de
Præf.ad
Hær.
Chriftianitie. And this obferued Tertullian in
his tyme, that Heretikes fcarfe euer endeauoured to conuert Heathens and Pagans, but al-
waye were readie to peruert Catholikes: *Noftra*
fuffodiunt (fayeth he) *vt fua ædificent : They vn-*

Niceph.
de Eccl.
hifto.
dermine and digge vp our foundations, that they
may build their owne. And for confirmation of
this read the hiftorie of Alamundarus, a moft
mightie Prince and potent King of the Sara-
cens, being conuerted to the Chriftian faith by
the Catholikes; and coming to be Baptized, the
Eutychean Heretikes laboured all they could
that he would be Baptized by their Bifhops,

D. An-
toninus
Chron.
p. 2. tit.
11. ca.
2. ſſ. 5.
and profeffe their hereticall doctrine. And the
rather they prefumed to preuaile with him, becaufe at that tyme the Emperour Anaftafius
was alfo an heretike. But fo it fell out by the
prouidence of God, and that the world may
vnderftand and take notice that heretickes can
not preuaile with Infidells, that this great King
vtterlie refufed to communicate with Heretikes in the Sacrament of Baptifme ; and with all
                                        fo con-

ſo confounded their hereticall doctrine, that their Biſhops with ſhame & confuſion departed.

It was my Chance being in Spaine, to haue ſome Conference with one Muſtafan à Mauritanian by birth, a Turke by profeſſion, to become a Chriſtian. His anſwere was, that in deed the new Chriſtians in England, (for ſoe he tearmed them in reſpect of their new opinions and reuolt from the old) came nearer to his Religion then the old Chriſtians in Spayne did. For that they of England had no Images, nor pictures of Chriſt nor his Saintes. Alſo they of England loued them better then they of Spayne did; yet ſayed he, if I ſhould turne Chriſtian, I had rather turne to the old of Spayne, then the newe of England, for the elder the nearer to Chriſt, and ſo the more likelier to be true. Thus this Mauritanian Turke could diſtinguiſh & make his choyſe between new and old Chriſtians, and new and old Chriſtianitie. Therefore I may conclude that the Proteſtants neither haue, nor can haue ordinarilie the vſe of this Ceremonie of the Cathecumines in their Church, nor be Baptizers of Turkes or Pagans, nor Conuerters of Countreyes.

C A P. 6.

Whether the ſolemnitie of Baptization, were eſpeciallie to be reſerued for the feaſts of Eaſter Paſcha, and Pentecoſte.

ALthough in caſe of neceſſitie (as hath bene ſayed) we are not to expect tyme nor ſtand vpō the performāce of ceremonies of Baptiſme, yet it hath bene a laudable cuſtome, and ſolemne ceremonie in the Catholike Church, euen from the tyme of the Apoſtles vnto this day vſed and obſerued, at the feaſts of Paſcha and Pentecoſte that is Eaſter and Whitſontyde to haue honorable Baptization, and ſolemne celebration of this Sacrament. And the reaſon is, firſt for the feaſt of Paſcha or Eaſter, becauſe in the death and Paſſion of Chriſt was giuen the full power to the effects of Baptiſme, *Quicunque Baptizati ſumus*

Rom.6. *&c.* All men (ſayeth S. *Paule*) who are Baptized in *Chriſt Ieſus*, in his death we are Baptized: But at Eaſter is a ſpeciall memorie and recordation of the death and Paſſion of Chriſt, therefore worthelie doeth the Church reſerue a ſolemne Baptization at the feaſt of Eaſter. Secondly becauſe in our Baptiſme is repreſented the death of Chriſt, and his glorious reſurrection. For

Heb.6. as the ſame Apoſtle ſayeth, *we are buried together with Chriſt in Baptiſme vnto death, that as Chriſt is riſen from the dead by the glorie of the Father; ſo we may alſo walke in newneſſe of life*. Therfore true it is that remiſſion of ſinne, new life and ſanctification are giuen by Baptiſme, becauſe it reſembleth in vs, and applieth vnto vs Chriſts death & reſurrection. And Baptiſme doeth repreſent both; For as Chriſt once being dead, doth alwayes liue: ſo we being dead to ſinne, by Baptiſme doe liue againe. And as the death of Chriſt was cauſe of our Purification, and his Reſurrection firſt opened vs the gate of heauen: ſo Baptiſme is the Sacrament that cleanſeth and waſheth

our

our foules and maketh the firft entrance to Chriftiáitie. Thirdly Chrift after his death vpon the day of his Rafurrection gaue commiffion to his Apoftles to Baptize all nations, fet downe and appoynted in what forme they fhould doe it, that is : *In the name of the Father, and of the Sonne and of the Holy Ghoft.* Not without caufe then doth the Catholike Church at the feaft of Pafcha, vfe a folemne hallowing of the fonte, and referue a publike Baptization and celebration of this Sacrament, in memorie of gratitude of this great benefit Chrift lefte in his Church. And for the feaft of Pentecofte or whit funtyde, there is as great reafon as for the other, that on that day there fhould be vfed a publike folemnization of this Sacrament; becaufe on that day the holie Ghoft vifiblie fell vpon the Apoftles and Difciples of Chrift , in fo much that they may be fayed to haue bene Baptized with the Holy Ghoft. Alfo on the fame day was performed by the Apoftles a moft folemne publike Baptization , after S. Peter had fpoken and preached vnto the people, there were Baptized three thoufand. Finally Chrift hath fayed: That our regeneration and new birth muft be by the Holy Ghoft. Worthelie then doth the Catholike Church at this feaft alfo of Pentecofte referue and appoynt a folemne and publike Baptization and celebration of this Sacrament; and Confequentlie with ignominie and fhame doe the Proteftants exile, banifh and reiect this Ceremonie. Read the fourth epiftle of Pope Leo written to all the Bifhops of Sicilie, where he exhorteth to this Ceremonie , and proueth it by Apoftolicall authoritie. And in

Mat. 18

Act. 2.

Ioa. 3.

Leo ep. 4.ca.3.

the

the fixth Chapter of the fame epiftle , he giueth the reafon , why the Romain Catholike
Church doth not vfe anie folemne Baptization
on the Epiphanie day commonlie called the
twelth day , although in the opinion of fome
vpon that day Chrift himfelf was Baptized in
Iordan by Iohn Baprift . Becaufe Iohns Baptifme was inftituted to an other end and purpofe then Chrifts Baptifme , neither had it
that effect as remiffion of finnes or efpeciall
operation of the Holie Ghoft. And therefore no
fuch reafon for folemne Baptization vpon the
Epiphanie day, as vpon the day of Pafcha , and
Pentecofte .

*De Cō-
feera-
dift. 4.
can. Si
quis
Epiph.*

The puritan or precifer fort of Minifters,
would feeme to ayme at this laudable ceremonie and cuftome of the Catholike Church; for
willinglie they would, if anie Child be borne
in the weeke day, differre and put of his Baptization vntill the Sunday. Which if they doe,
becaufe euerie funday is and fo we account it
as the Octaue day of Pafcha or Pentecofte;
then I thinke, if the Child be ftrong and no way
in danger of death, this ceremonie of differing
Baptifme vntill the funday, may be approuable.
But if they doe differre Baptization for an other
end and purpofe, which rather is to be feared,
and that is to broach, approue and allow the
opinion of M. Caluin, that Children may be faued without this Sacrament, and foe to induce
& breed in the mind of the Parēts a carelefnes,
and negligence to fee this Sacrament duelie
performed; and fo confequentlie to endanger
the faluation of the child, then this Ceremonie
is not to be fuffered , but dangerous and intolerable.

lerable. For in doubtfull and dangerous cases, the securer & safer way is euer to be followed. And for côfirmation of this I will recite the historie of Samuel Hubert the minifter, who baptized a chyld on the weake daye, beinge called vp at middinght by the Parents, and vrged ther vnto, in refpect the Infant was in danger of death, Mufculus the fuperintendent hearinge of it, complayned to the counfell of the citie, becaufe he did baptife before the foundaye. Hubert beinge cited to appeare was accufed for this fact of herefie and rebellion: but he pleadinge for himfelfe, fayed, that he did baptife before the foundaye in cafe of neceffitie, which he thought lawfull in refpect of the danger of the chyld, who dyinge without baptifme myght be in danger not only of death of bodie, but alfo of foule. But Mufculus with other minifters replied, yet the wante of baptifme did not hynder the Infant from the fight of God and faluation. But Hubert conftantly auerred befor the counfel and fenat that this propofition was hereticall, becaufe it mayintaned yet children could be faued without baptifme. Vppon this contention Beza in his oldage, (for this was in the yeare of our lord 1595.) was called and confulted with all, alfo other minifters of bafill and Zurike were prefent, the matter being debated among them, Hubert was by them for this fact condemned, and depriued of his minifterie : fo that we may conclud, that this delayinge of baptifme vntill foundaye, is but to pach vp this herefie, and make parents carelefle of Chriftianitie in their pofteritie.

Refcius in A-thifm.

C A P.

CAP. 7.

Whether the Impofition of the *Priefts hands,*
with his benediction and prayer be a Ceremo-
nie allowable.

AFter the Prieft hath figned the Infant with
the figne of the Croffe (as hath bene fayed)
he layeth his right hand vpon the head of the
Child vfing this Benediction or Ceremonie:
Omnipotens, &c. Omnipotent fempiternall God
the Father of our Lord IESVS-CHRIST *vouch-*
fafe to looke backe vpon this thy feruant , whom
thou vouchfafed to call vnto the firft Documents
or inftruction of faith : expell from him all cecitie
and blindnes of harte , breake a funder all the
bands of Satan , with which he hath bene tyed and
bound : open , O Lord , vnto him the gate of thy
pietie, &c. This is the benediction or prayer.
And for the lawfull vfe of this Ceremonie we
haue the example of Chrift himfelf. In the
Ghofpell of S. Mathewe we read, that *the people*
brought, offered, and prefented vnto Chrift Chil-
dren that he might and fhould touch them , impofe
his handes vpon them , and pray ouer them , And
this no doubt Chrift did to leaue an example
for his Apoftles and Difciples to doe the like.
And this the Church doeth efpeciallie before
Baptifme , that the enemie of man may not
hinder the effects of this Sacrament. For the antiquitie of it and that it was practifed in the
Primitiue Church we haue the teftimonie of
Dionifius Areopagita S. Paules fcholler.

Mat.19
Mark.
10.
Luc.18

Dionif-
Areop.
de ec-
clef.
hier.
ca. 7.

CAP.

CAP. 8.

Whether Exorcifmes, adiurations, and ex-vfflations are conuenient to be vfed before Baptifme.

NO man can denie but Chrift gaue to his *Mar.9.* Difciples commiffion and power ouer di- *Luc.10.* uells to exorcife them, to fuppreffe them, to *Aɛt.10.* caft them out of the poffeffed perfons for all which the Scripture is plaine. No man alfo can denie vnles impudent and ignorant of Ecclefia-fticall hiftories, but that the fame power, au-thoritie and practife ouer diuells to exorcife them, to fuppreffe them, to weaken their power by Exorcifmes, Adiurations, Exufflations, prayer and fafting, hath bene continued and practifed in the Catholike Church of God, euen from her cradle and infancie euer to this age 1614. Further alfo no man can denie but that among the holy Orders giuen in the Church, the third of the Minores Ordines is Exorcifta, the Exorcift, and fo called for the power and authoritie he hath giuen him ouer diuells, in fo much as his function and office is by Exorcif-mes, holie prayers, adiurations, infufflations, impofition of hands to expell diuells, to wea-ken his power in Infants and Cathecumines, that the enimie hinder not in them the effects of Baptifme; and for full proofe of this, read *Pet.* *Syntagmata Iuris Petri Gregorij:* And that you *Greg.* may not thinke that this ceremonie is onlie for *lib. 16.* the elder fort, and not for Children, it is mani- *cap. 5.* feft in S. Markes Ghofpell, that not onlie aged *Mar.9.* people

people, but alſo Children and Infants haue bene, and may be moleſted with euill ſpirits euen
from their Infancie, with all conſidering as S.
Paule ſayeth; we are all borne, and by nature
Epheſ.3 are filij iræ : The Children of wrath, and begotten in originall ſinne, and ſo conſequentlie
ſubieƈt to Satan. Therefore worthilie the
Church of God hath ordayned this precedent
Ceremonie of Exorciſmes before Baptiſme, to
debilitate the power of the enemie, that he may
no way hinder the effeƈts of this Sacrament. In
the firſt generall Councell of Conſtantinople
held vnder Damaſus Pope in S. Ieromes tyme
1.Conc. the vſe of Exorciſmes before Baptiſme was
Cõſtāt. enaƈted, commaunded, and the order ſet dow-
can.7. ne : We (ſayeth the Councell) *make them Ca-*
thecumines, we exorciſe and adiure ; Ter ſimul in
faciem eorum inſufflando : Breathing three tymes
one after an other in their faces, and ſo we Cate-
Cele- *chiſe, and then we doe Baptize.* Celeſtinus Pope
ſtin. de the firſt of that name about the yeare of our
Conſec. Lord 423 aboue a thouſand yeares agoe, wri-
diſt. 4. ting to the Biſhops of France, aduiſed that
c. Siue young or old, Infant or aged before they come
paruu- to the fonte of regeneration ſhould haue the
li. vncleane ſpirit caſt out of them by the Exorciſmes, and exufflations of the Prieſt or Cleargie. The ſentence and opinion of S. Auguſtine
is pregnant and manifeſt in many places of his
workes. Firſt in his booke De Symbolo, ſpea-
Aug.li. keing to the Cathecumines : *You know (moſt*
1. de *deare brethren) that not only aged, but alſo In-*
Symb. *fants and Children are exufflated & exorciſed,*
ca.10. *that the aduerſe power of the Diuell may be dri-*
uen from them. Non ergo creatura Dei in Infan-
tibus

tibus exorcizatur, aut exuffatur : sed ille sub quo omnes, qui sub peccato nascuntur : Let therefore no man say, that the Creature of God in the Infants are exorcised or exuffiated, but the enemie of man, who deceaued man, that he might possesse man, and vnder whose power we all are, who are borne vnder sinne. Thus S. Augustine. And the same holy Doctor in an other place, writing against the Pelagian Heretikes, who contemned then, as now our Protestants doe, the Ceremonies of Exorcismes and Exufflations, proued first plainlie that Infants are infected with Originall sinne, and for remedie and remouing therof are to be Baptized with Exorcismes and Exufflations, which Ceremonies the Church doth practise as deliuered vnto her by auncient Tradition as from the Apostles. And they are Exorcised and breathed vpon before Baptisme (sayeth he) that by these meanes they may be transflated from the power of darknesse of the diuell and his Angells, vnto the kingdome of Christ. Wiselie doeth that man order his worke, who first seeketh to take away the impediments that may hinder him; and this is the intention of the Church in the exorcismes to debilitate the power of Satã, that he doe not hinder the effect of Baptisme. You know the the ploughman will tyll his ground againe and againe, and seeke to kill all weeds, and to remoue all impediments, before he will sowe his good seed, according to the aduise of the Prophet Ieremie and Osee: *Nouate vobis nouale, & nolite serere super spinas: Make new your fallow fields, and doe not sowe vpon thornes.*

We read in Eusebius historie that it was

Aug.li. 2. de Nupt. & Cõcup.ca. 29.

Ierem. 4. Ose. 10.

particu-

particularlie noted in Nouatus the Archereti-
ke, who being vexed with an vncleane ſpirite,
and hauing ſpent ſome tyme with the Exorciſts
but falling deſperatlie ſicke , that there was
ſmall hope of his recouerie, they were forced
haſtelie to Baptize him lying in his bed without the Ceremonies . And after neuer hauing
them ſupplied , nor receauing the Sacrament of
Confirmation, was neuer ridde of the vncleane
ſpirite, nor neuer could obtaine the gift of the
holie Ghoſt . And Bredenbachius reporteth,
that a number of children in the lowe Countries neare Delphs beinge chriſtened , without
the exorciſmes and ceremonies of baptiſme
appoynted by the Catholike church , were all
ſtrangly ſtroken ſore ſycke . Their parents be-
thought them ſelues for remedie and humblie
entreated a Catholike prieſt to ſupplie the
wants of the exorciſme and other ceremonies,
which beinge performed, preſently they all re-
couered their healthes. Worthy examples fitly
declaringe the effects of exorciſmes & the force
of the ceremonies, and with all a caueat & war-
ninge that parents be carefull to haue the ceremonies of baptiſme ſupplyed whē in neceſſitie
or otherwayes they are chriſtened without
them. Therfor not without cauſe doth the Catholike prieſt commaund the deuil with theſe
and the lyke exorciſmes. *Maledicte diabole, &c.*
Thou curſed deuil call to mynd with me the ſenten-
ce geuen of thee, and geue honor vnto the true and
lyuing God, geue honor vnto Ieſus Chriſt his ſonne
and to the holly Ghoſt , and departe from this ſer-
uant of God, becauſe God and our lorde Ieſus Chriſt
hath vouchſafed to call him to his holy grace and
                                              gyfte

gyfte of the holy Ghoft. This is the intention of the church, this ceremonie hath bine practifed from the begininge vnto this daye : what then maye be the reafon that the Proteftants of this age fhould contemne and deride this fo auncient and profitable a ceremonie ? I knowe no reafon but on, and that is, becaufe they haue no power nor commiffion ouer diuels , no other I faye then that which dependeth of waxe and parchment, no other holy orders of priefthood then they can deriue from their letters patents of Queene Elizabeth. But how weak that aucthoritie and power is to deale with the diuels, maye eafely be difcryed, therfor maruel not that thefe ceremonies are derided and reiected by them.

CAP. 9.

Whether Salte be to be bleffed and geuen the Infant before baptifme.

Concerning this ceremonie of falt , the prieft after he hath bleffed it, taketh it, and putteth it in the mouth of the chyld fayinge. *Accipe fal fapientia, &c.* Take and receaue the falt of wifdome, that God maye be propitious and merciful vnto thee vnto life eternall , And then maketh this prayer followinge. *Deus patrum noftrorum, &c.* God of our fathers, God the maker of all creaturs. We humble befeeche thee , that thou wilt vouchfafe mercifully to looke backe vppon this thy feruant, and hauinge tafted this firft foode of falt, doe not fuffer him any longer to be hungrie , but that he maye be filled with heauenly fuftenaunce, in fo much O Lord as he maye be feruent in fpirit,

N 2   ioyefull

ioyefull in hope, and bringe him vnto the new la-
uer of regeneration, that he maye deserue to obtay-
ne with the faythfull the eternall reward of thy
promises. This is the ceremonie of the Catholike
church, and this is the prayer. Chrift hath fayed

Mat. 5   that his Apoftles fhould be (*Sal terra*) the falt
of the earth to feafon the world, that is man-
kind with the wifdome vnderftandinge and
doctrine of Chrift. And moreouer Chrift fayed

mar. 9.   to his Apoftles falt is good, haue falt with you.
Coll. 4.   And S. Paule Counfelled the Colloffians that
their mouth and talk fhould be feafoned with
falt. So the prieft doth put falt into the mouth
of the Infant, to fignifie that he fhould and
ought to be feafoned with falt, and make profeffion with his   mouth of Chriftian faith Ca-

lib. 10.   tholick religion and trwe beleife. Salt beinge
inſtit.   bleffed fayeth Rabanus, is put in the mouth of
cleric.   the Infant that therby maye be fygured and fi-
In Ef-   gnified that he beinge feafoned with the falt of
dram.   wifedome, maye be voyde of all fetor and ftin-
lib. 2. c.   ke of fynne and iniquitie, and that hearcafter
9.   he maye not be putrified and corrupted with
Leuit.   the maggotes of fynne, but rather beinge vn-
2.   touched maye be preferued to receaue greater
mar. 9.   grace. S. Bede alludinge to that of the old lawe
Habe-   where god commanded that no facrifice fhould
tur. de   be offered with out falt or not feafoned with
Confec.   falt. And Chrift alfo hath fayed that euerie vi-
diſt. 4.   ctima shalbe falted with falt. where vppon I
Ca. fal   fay, S. Bede fayeth, *Sal calestis* ? The falt of
calestis   heauenly wifedome wherewith the Cathecu-
Hom. 6   mens, or thofe who are to be baptifed were firft
super   inftructed and feafoned we, are commaunded
Ezech.   to offer in all the facrifices of our workes. And
can. 3.   of

of this fyrſt taſt of ſalt ſpeaketh Origen, and the
ſame hath the thyrd Counſel of Carthage. Con-
ſideringe then that this ceremonie of ſalt hath
his ſigni fication and inſtruction , as you haue
heard , alſo of ſuch antiquitie in the church,
what reaſon haue the Proteſtátes of this age tò
còténe and neglecte it? I will tell you the ſalt of
their doctrine is infatuate vnſavorie , without
ſmacke of ſalt, and therfor not ſitt to be putt in
the mouth of the baptiſed. For ſalt that hath
loſte his ſaltneſſe & vertue is profitable nether
for ground nor middinge nor dunghill , but it   *Luc.*14
ſhalbe caſt forth ſayeth Chriſt, he that hath eares to heare , lett him heare.

Cap. 10.

*Whether the vſe of ſpittle before baptiſme , be a
ſuperfluous ceremonie.*

THe order of this ceremonie is that the prieſt
takinge ſpittle to the ears and noſtrels (not
to the mouth as ſome miſtake it, for that ſalt is
proper for that part) and puttinge it fyrſt on the
right eare , ſayeth *Epheta , quod eſt adaperire,
that is be thou opened :* then to the noſtrels, ſayinge , *in odorem ſuauitatis , and be thou opened
vnto the odor of ſweetnes :* and at the leaſte eare
he concludeth. *Tu autem effugare diabole : therfor o thou diuel be thou put to flight and driuen
awaye, for the iudgment of God will drawe nyghe,
and baptiſme now is at hand.* We read in the
ghoſpel that our ſauiour twice vſed this ceremonie of ſpittle, fyrſt when he healed the deafe
and dume man , who was brought vnto him,
then he vſed ſpittle and put his fingers into his   *mar.*7.
ears and lookinge to heauen ſayed theſe wor-
des *Ephata , quod eſt adaperire,* which is as
much to ſaye as , be thou opened. Secondly in

Ioh. 9. the Ghofpel of S. Iohn when he cured the man
who was borne blind, he fpitte on the ground
and made claye of the fpittle and layed it vppon
his eyes and fayed , *Goe Waſhe in Siloe*. The
church of God to the imitation of Chriſt doth
vfe thefe ceremonies of touchinge and fpit le.
And fyrſt for the ears that the deafe deuil doe
not hynder nor ſtopp thofe fences , but that
the ears may be open to heare the worde of
Rom. God, for fayth is by hearinge as fayeth S. Paule .
10. This ceremonie defendeth that worthy Doctor
S. Ambrofe , it hath no worfe a piller to leane
Li.1.de vnto, alfo this waſhinge of the blind borne man
facra in the waters of Siloe was a figure of baptifme,
c. 1. and therfor baptifme is called the facrament of
illuminatiō, for which caufe man beinge borne
in fynne & blindnes, is fent thether for illumination fight and light of fayth and beleife. And
as Chriſt before he fent the blind borne man
to waſhe at the poole of Siloe made a plaſter
with fpittle: fo the church doth vfe this ceremonie of fpittle befor baptifme . To conclud
therfor we maye lawfully and laudablie mayn-
tayne with S. Ambrofe this ceremonie, and that
it is no waye fuperſtitious , feeinge it hath his
imitation from Chriſt , is alfo fignificant and
worketh his effect. Then with out caufe doe the
Caluiniſts and Proteſtants make this ceremo-
nic ridiculous or fuperſtitious . We knowe
Chriſt could haue healed the dume man and
blind borne without touchinge, fpeach, fpittle,
claye, waſhinge or any other ceremonie, & we
affirme that baptifme maye haue his effecte
without thefe ceremonies : but dare any man
faye, that in Chriſt the vfe of fpittle was ridiculous

lous or fuperftitious ? I knowe no man dare
who beareth the face of a chriftian. Beware
therfor in tyme of fuch as M. Caluine who calleth this ceremonie ridiculous, and M. Willet
who tearmeth it an interpretatiue toye, and all
other who deride the ceremonies of the
church , which are done to the imitation of
Chrift, for they may become fcorners of Chrifts
owne actions . The ears and noftrels , fayeth
Rabanus , are touched with fpittle , and thofe
wordes of the ghofpell which Chrift vfed when
he cured the dume man are fpokē, that through
the tipicall and fhaddowed fpittle of the prieft
and his touch , the deuine wifdome and vertue
may worke health to the Cathecumine, that his
noftrels maye be opened to the receauinge of
the fweet fmell of the knowledge of God and
mifteries of chriftian fayth : and that his ears
maye not be fhutt to heare the commaundements of God and found Catholike doctrine . I
haue heard that a parfon of high eftemee, whom
I honor for his parfon and place , and therfor of me not to be named, fhould reporte that
his parents commaunded that this ceremonie
in his baptifme fhould be omitted, becaufe the
prieft fhould not fpit in his mouth. But he was
certaynly mifinformed , for this ceremonie
doth not concerne the mouth but the ears and
noftrels only . And the prieft doth not fpitt vppon any parte of the child , but only out of his
owne hand takinge fpittle , and with touch
therof doth effect this ceremonie . What was
done God he beft knoweth ; but it appeareth
his ears were neuer trwly opened to the Catholike Roman doctrine , nor he neuer tafted nor

*De in-
ftit:cle-
ri. lib. 1
ca. 27.*

N 4 fmelled

of the Roman mother church , nor greatly e-
steemed of the rites and ceremonies of that religion ; It is our parte to hope the best and to
praye hartely , *vt Dominus daret scientiam &
intellectum*, that our lorde would vouchsafe to
geue him knowledge and vnderstanding.

CHAPTER. II.

*VVhether it be a superstitious ceremonie to take
the right hand of the child , and deliuer vnto
him, the signet seale or signe of Christ, wich is
the crosse ; that therby he may learne to blesse
himselfe agaynst the deuil and heresie the
greatest emmies of man and to remayne
Constant in Catholick fayth.*

THe priest taketh the Cathecumine , Infant
or partie who is to be Baptized by the
right hand and doth signe him in the bale or
palme of the hand with the signe of the crosse,
and so deliuer vnto him the signet or seale of
Christ which is the crosse : sayinge. *Trado tibi
signaculū domini nostri Iesu Christi in manu tua
dextra, vt te signes . & te de aduersa parte repellus
& in fide Catholica permanens & habeas vitam
æternam & viuas in sæcula sæculorum Amen.*
Iohn or Thomas I deliuer and geue vnto thee
the signet seale or signe of our lord Iesus Christ
in thy right hand that thou mayest signe thy
selfe and repell thy enimies , defend thee from
the aduerse parte and that thou mayest remayne
steedfast in the Catholick faythe haue life eternal & liue for euer amen. and withall vseth this
benediction *Benedictio* dei &c. The blessing of
god the Father omnipotent and of the sonne ,
and of the holy ghost, let it descēd vpō thee and

continewe with thee for euer. By this Ceremonie the Catholicke Church would enstruct the Baptised in two poynts. Fyrst that he learne to blesse him selfe with the signe of our lord that is the crosse, which is geuen him in his right hand. Secondly that this signe may be a means to protect and defend him agaynst the diuel, all his worckes, heresie or any other misfortune. For the vse of this ceremonie we haue the practise of the Apostles and saynds of the 'primatiue church : who not only blessed the selues with the signe of the crosse as an armor and weapon agaynst any euil that might happen : but also exhorted and counseled all other Christian people to doe the lyke. Abdias who did see Christ in flesh, liuedwiththe Apostles,and was a disciple of theirs,recordeth and wryteth of S. Paule, that when he came to the place of execution, turned himselfe towardes the East, lyfted vp his handes and eyes to heauen *Gentibus flexis Crucisque signo se muniens ceruicem præbuit percussori, kneelinge on his knees fortifinge and blessinge himselfe with the signe of the crosse yelded and offered his necke to the executioner.* Loe the practise and example of the Apostle S. Paule for the vse of blessinge thy selfe with the signe of the crosse. It is wrytten also of S. Andrewe who travelinge vp from Bizantium into Thracia;ther mett him and his companie a multitud of men with drawen swordes and speares in their handes readie to rune vppon them,which when the Apostle perceaued, *Faciens signum crucis contra eos,makinge the signe of the crosse agaynst thë* sayed. *Oro domine nel adã tur sperantes in te. I praye thee o lord ; that they maye not be hurt, who put their trust in thee.* By the synge of the crosse ãd prayer of the Apostle

lib 2.
Apost.
Histo.

Abdias
lib.3.
Hist.
Apost.
nõ lege
a prin-
cipio.

the Angell of God appeared terrified the enimie, and so the Apostle with his companie had
free and safe passage . In lyke manner the same
Ibidem Apostle S. Andrewe beinge at Patras a cittie in
prope Achaia , in the palace of Aegeates the procon-
finem. sul with his wyfe Maximilla and many other
christeans ther gathered together in christean
exercise . Aegeates sodaynly vnlooked for and
vnawars returned from Macedonia , so that
he had like to haue taken them all together:
which the Apostle perceauinge: *Singulis manus
imponens & Consignatis cruce eos abire permisit,
nouissime autem se signans discessit . Layinge his
handes vppon euerie on of them,and withall signinge them with the signe of the crosse , suffered them
to depart , and last of all , also he blessinge himselfe
and signinge himselfe with the signe of the crosse
departed, so that no man was apprehended* . It is
Abdia. reported of S. Iohn the Euangelist when he was
lib. 5 at Ephesus, and had distroyed the temple and
Hist. Idoll of Diana , beinge therfor persecuted by
Apost. Aristodemus the chiefe minister of that Idoll,
the Apostle willinge to haue him satisfyed,
sayed vnto him . *Quid faciam vt tollam indi-
gnationem de animo tuo?* what shall I doe to take
awaye this rancor and malice out of thy hart? He
answered, take and drinke this poyson which I
haue prepared ; which yf thou drinke and dye
not it will appeare , that thy God is the trwe
God . S. Iohn boldly without feare tooke the
cuppe of poyson in his hand,*Et signaculum crucis faciens,and makinge the signe of the crosse ouer
it prayed, and also blessed his mouth and armed
all his bodie with the crosse and drunke vp all that
was in the cvppe, and so passed without any harme
at all*,

at all . Thus you maye fee in the practife and example of S. Iohn the power of prayer and vertue of the croffe . And for this caufe S. Iohn the Euangelift is commonly pictured with a chalice or cuppe in his hand It is wrytten by S. Hierome of S. Anthoine a holly faynt of the primatiue church goinge to vifit S. Paule the fyrft *In vita* Eremite fawe by the waye a monfter, in the vp- *fancti* per parte lyke a man, in the nether parte lyke a *Pauli* horfe , prefently at the fyght therof, *Salutaris Eremi-* *impreffione figni armat frontem . Armed his fore-* *ta.* *head with the figne of the croffe beinge a figne of* *health and comfort.* And incontinently the mon- fter râne awaye and vanifhed out of fyght. Alfo S. Martine Bifshope, a worthy Prelate of the primatiue church a man of great virtue and hol- lines, *fe aduerfus diabolum figno crucis & oratio-* *nis auxilio protegebat ,* protected and defended *himfelfe againft the deuill with the figne of the* *croffe and helpe of prayer.* S. Chrifoftome fetteth *Homil.* a rule for Fathers and mothers to teach their *12. in* children to bleffe themfelues. *A primis annis,* *primâ* *&c.Defend and arme your chyldren, euen from the* *Cor.* *begininge in their tender age with fpirituall armor* *and teach them to make the figne of the croffe in* *their forheades , and before they be able to doe it* *themfelues,doo yee it for them.* Thus S. Chrifofto- *In vita* me, of whom it is alfo wrytten that immediatly *eius.* before his death after he had receaued the fa- crament of the alter, *feq, crucis figno muniens ani-* *mam Deo reddidit,and bleffinge himfelfe with the* *figne of the croffe yealded vp the Ghoft.* And S. Hie- rome exhorteth Demetriades often to make *Epift.* the figne of the croffe , *Crebro fignaculo crucis ad De-* *munias frontem tuam ne exterminator Ægipti meir.* *in te*

in te locum reperiat:thou must often and sundrie tymes fortifie and defend thy Forehead with the signe of the crosse, least the exterminator of Ægipt finde place in thee. The lyke instruction he geeueth to the virgine Eustochium. *Ad omnem actum ad omnem incessum manus pingat crucem: at euerie action, what soeuer you doe, at euerie tyme you goe forth, lett your hand make the signe of the crosse.* And S. Anthonie exhortinge his monkes and followers to take courage to fight agaynst the deuil and shewinge with what weapons they myght ouercome him, amonge the rest putteth the signe of the crosse : *mihi credite fratres vnico Sanctissma crucis signo debilitatus aufugit: beleeue me brethren with one only signe of the crosse the deuil beinge weakned is put to fligh.* Thus you maye see by the example of the Apostles by the practise of the saynts of the primatiue church, by the aduise and instructiō of the auncient fathers, this ceremonie to blesse our selues with the signe of the crosse, and to instruct others to doe the like is not superstitious Idle or vn profitable, as protestants would haue it, vnlesse they will accuse the three Apostles of superstition and condemne the saynctes & Doctors of the primatiue church in their practise doctrine and instructiō thervnto: wherfor to conclud this ceremonie of takinge the right hand of the Infant or partie to be Baptised to deliuer and geue vnto him the signet seale or signe of our lord Iesus Christ therby to protect and defend himselfe from the aduerse part the deuil and heresie and remaine in the Catholick fayth, this ceremonie I saye is ancient profitable and conforme to antiquitie

de custodia virginitatis.

Athenasi, in vita eius.

tie the practife of the the Apoftles and primatiue church. What reafon then haue the proteftants not only to condemne contemne and
blot it out of their bookes, but alfo to forbid
both younge and old to bleffe them felues
with the figne of the croffe? fure I knowe none
but one, and that is to take awaye from Chri-
ftean people their armor of defence, that they
may lye open to Satan and herefie.

CAP. 15.

VVhether the abrenunciation of fathan and his
Worckes and pompes be a Ceremonie appro-
uable.

HAuinge fpoken of the precedent ceremonies fuch as are acted befor the chyld be
brought to the font. Now we are to entreat
of fuch as are done and performed at the font.
The prieft takinge the chyld by the right hand,
bringeth him into the church, fayinge, *Lnter*
thou into the temple of god that thou mayeft haue
eternal life and liue for euer. And fo beinge
brought to the font, the prieft extendeth his
hand ouer him, the god father or godmother
holdinge the chyld ; then fayeth the prieft,
Abrenuncias fathana. Doeft thou renounce fatan?
the godfather and godmother make anfwere
Abrenuneio- I do renounce him ; the prieft proceedeth, *& omnibus operibus eius, and all his*
Workes? I renounce them all. & omnibus
pompis eius, and all his pompes and pride?
I renounce them. For the proofe of this
ceremonie we neede not much to ftand
for

for it is manifeſt that it hath diſcended vnto vs
from the Apoſtles by tradition and ſo continued in the church vntill this daye , and not
contradicted by the Proteſtants. S. Clement the

Lib. 4. fyrſt of that name and the thyrd pope after S.
Conſt. Peter in his conſtitutions ſpeaketh of this ce-
can. 41. remonie of the renunciation of ſatban his wor-
& 42. kes and pompe . And S. Dioniſius Areopagita
conuerted by S. Paule in his eccleſiaſticall Hierarchie in the chapter of baptiſme Tertullian
and others.

C A P. 13.

Whether multiplicitie of God Fathers and God mothers are neceſſarie .

B Y the generall and ordinarie conſtitution
and cuſtome of the church, yf the Infant be
a boye , on God Father is ſufficient without
Godmother, yf it be a wench or girle , on Godmother without Godfather : yet accordinge to
the cuſtome of the countrie we maye admitte
De Cō- both , that is a God Father and a Godmother
ſecr: to on child , but not aboue . So pope Leo de-
diſt. 4. creed: lett no man ſayeth he come to receaue or
Cānon take the Infant from the fonte and baptiſme but
plures. one and that a man or a woman. According to
De re- this order hath the Tridentine Counſell made
for. ſeſ. a reformation agaynſt multiplicitie of God Fa-
24. c.2. thers and God mothers and inſtituted that on
De eccl. was ſufficient or two at the moſt. S. Dioniſius
Hiero. calleth them *ſuſceptores,* that is vndertakers for
c. vlt. them whome they receaue out of the fonte in
Lib. de baptiſme. And Tertullian calleth them *ſponſores,*
baptiſ.   for

for that they doe promise on the behalfe of the *Aug.*
baptized . And some other call them *fideiussores homil.*
that is suerties for that they make themselues 3. *ad*
pleadges for the baptized.   *Neo-*
                                                 phit.

CAP. 14.

VVhether the God Father is to geue the name vnto the child.

I Make no doubt of the question but it hath
allwayes bine a lawdable costome in the
church, that the God Father doth impose or geue the name of the child. And the ancient christeans euer called them after some of the Apostles as Peter , Andrewe, Iames; or some other
of the saynctes, as Frances, Edward and so forth.
It is a prophane custome of late crept into our
countrie to name their children after their sur-
names, as Hatton Dudley, Baggot, Brase, Win-
terTalbot &c. Much more prophane is it to call
them after hethenish names, as some haue vsed,
contrarie to the custome of the ancient christeans , and the constitution of the Counsell *Can. 3.*
of Nice.

CAP. 15.

VVhat God Fathers and God mothers are bound vnto who Christen Children.

S Aynste Augustine exhorteth God Fathers *Sermo*
and God mothers to remember that they *post*
are Suerties and pleadges for their spirituall *pasc.*
children; and sayeth that they are to instruct *hodier.*
                                            them *dies.*

them in good workes and aboue all thinges
that they learne the Apoſtles Creed, the Pater
noſter, and the tenne cōmandementes: and that
they hold conſtantly the Catholike fayth and
beleeue the doctrine of the church. S. Thomas
concluſion is, that euerie on is bound to execut
the office they take vppon them : but the God
Father at the font doth take vppon him to inſtruct and teach the baptized : ergo he is bound
to haue care of their inſtruction, more particularly when there is iuſt cauſe, as yf the baptiſed
were to liue amonge Infidles, or amonge heretikes as nowe at this tyme our countrie ſtan-
dinge as it doth, euerie God Father is bound to
haue a ſpeciall care of his ſpirituall children.
But in chriſtean catholike countries his charge
is not ſo great, becauſe ther is no danger in
education, for the parents and paſtors of their
churches will ſee the children ſufficiently inſtructed, and for this cauſe now there is no exception taken of the God Fathers and God mothers concerninge their ſufficiencie to inſtruct.
But in the primatiue church it was not ſo. For
as Dioniſius ſayeth. *Oportet doctū eſſe in diuinis:*
the God Father ought tobe able to inſtruct in the
rudiments of Chriſtean doctrine and beleife.

3.p.q.
68.a.
8.

eccleſ-
Hiera.
c.7.

CAP. 16.

VVhether the vnction or annoyntinge of the
breaſt and ſhoulders be allowable.

THe prieſt doth exequut this ceremonie in
this manner, he taketh hollie oyle ſayinge,
I doe annoynt the vppon thee breaſt with the
oyle

oyle of health , And between thy shoulders in
Chrift Iefu our lord , that thou mayeft haue
life eternall. The reafon of this ceremonie,
as S. Ambrofe fayethis, becaufe he beinge an- *lib.*1.
noynted vppon the breaft and showelders , he *de Sa-*
is made a champion of almightie god , that he *cramē*
maye be able to wraftel in gods caufe and take *c. 2,*
courage and force agaynft the enimie. And
Innocentius the 3. of that name fayeth,that the
child is annoynted in the breaft , that by the *lib.*1.
gyfte of the holy ghoft he may expell from his *decre.*
harte and caft of error and ignorance that he *tit.*15.
may receaue the trwe Fayth, becaufe the iuft *de fa-*
man doth liue by faith. And he is annoynted *cravn-*
betweene the fhoulders , that by the grace of *ōtione.*
the fame heauenly fpirit , he maye shak of ne- *can. cū*
gligence and Idlenes , and take vppon him the *venif-*
exercife of good workes becaufe fayth with- *fent.*
out good workes is dead. therfor by the mifte-
rie of fayth let cleanenes be in his breaft,and by
the exercife of good worckes,let fortitud of labour be vppon his fhoulders. Yf this ceremonie of annoyntinge the breaft and shoulders
haue this fignification to make vs champions
of Chrift , to encreafe our fayth, to geue cora-
ge for the exercife of good workes. Why doe
the proteftants exile and banishe it out of
their books ? In verie deed maruel not therat,
for of fayth they haue mad shipwrak e , and for
good workes they account them as not neceffarie to faluation. And fo they nether annoynt
nor are annoynted as champions of Chrift to
fight agaynft deuil or enimie, nor yet to make
them felues nimble or fitt for the exercife of
good worckes. And of this vnction of holly

.homil.
6.c.2.
in E-
pist.ad
Collos.

lib.7.
const.
Apost.
c. 23.

188   A Treatise of

oyle speaketh , approueth and alloweth S.
Chrisostome. And S. Cirile Cataches. 2. mista-
gog And to proue it to haue discended by tradition from the Apostles we haue an Apostolicall constitutione recorded by S. Clement.
And for breuitie sake I remite thee to read the
3. Homilie of S. Augustine to the Neophits or
newly baptised.

CAP. 17.

VVether profession of faith be necessarie befor baptisme.

Concerninge this ceremonie I haue spoken
befor in the forth book and sith chapter;
That men of vnderstandinge beinge conuerted
to the Christian fayth are to make profession
of their fayth with their owne mouth at the
interrogotorie of the priest befor they be baptized. But children and Infants becaufe they are
not able to make answere for themselues , nor
as yet haue not vnderstanding, make profession
of their faith by the mouth of the church, or
by the mouth of the godfathers and godmothers or standers by:therfor when the priest af-
keth them and maketh these interrogotories.

*Credis in deum patrem omnipotentem &c. Doest
thou beleeue in god the father almightie, and doest
thou beleeue in Iesus Christ his only sonne our lord
who was borne and sufferd, and doest thou beleeue
in the holy ghost, the holly Catholick church, the
communion of saynctes, the remission of synnes, the
resurrection of the flesh and the lyfe eternal after
death.* Vnto which answere is made by the
mou-

mought of the godfather. *Credo, I doe beleeue*
Therfore Ifidorus fayeth , *paruuli alio profiten-*
te baptizati funt , quia adhuc loqui vel credere
nefciunt. children therfor are baptized a nother
makinge profeffion of faith for them becaufe they
knowe not as yet , neither can they fpeak or beleeue.
Wherfor we conclud that this ceremonie of
profeffion of fayth is neceffarie not only in mē
of vnderftadinge who are conuerted to Chri-
fteanitie and are able in their owne parfons
with harte and mouth to profeffe the fame, but
alfo it is required in Infants and children , and
becaufe they can not performe it with their
owne mouth and hart, the church their mother lendeth them her mouth and tounge to
fpeak and profeffe the fayth for them. For the
Antiquitie of it and that it was an Apoftolicall tradition, I will only note tow authers who
were in the Apoftles tyme as *S.* Clement. lib.
7. conftit. can. 39. 40. & 41. and S. Dionifius.
de eccl. Theologia c. 2.

CAP. 18.

VVether Immerfion or dippinge of the Infant be
neceßarie.

WE muft diftinguifh between cafe of neceffetie and folemne celebration of
the Sacrament. For baptifme beinge
the only fole ordinarie means of faluation, the
Catholike church doth not ftand vppon folem-
nities rites and ceremonies; but in cafe of neceffetie as in danger of death , requireth only
the fubftance and effence of baptifme tobe per-

formed , that is , the matter and forme to b^e
dewly excuted: wherfor feeinge water is the
matter of this Sacrament and affumed to the a-
blution and washinge of the bodie , wherby is
fignified the internal washinge of the foule:ther
is no doubt but incafe of neceffetie, or for fome other refpect , baptifme maye be miniftred
not only by Immerfions or dippinges three or
one , but alfo by afperfion, fprinklinge effufion
or pooringe of water on the head or face of the
child or partie to be baptized. as for example
when ther is little or fmale quantitie of water,
or vrgent neceffetie of baptifme , or the prieft
be fickly or weake, not able to beare the child,
or on the other fyd the Infant be fo feable that
it might be'dager to dippe it. In thefe cafes immerfions or dippings are not neceffarie , but it
shalbe fufficient to poore or laye water vppon
the head or face of the baptifed. So that we
may conclud that immerfions are not abfolutly
neceffarie ; yet without cafe ofneceffetie in folemne ordinarie , or publick baptization,vppo
wilfulnes,negligence or contempt, to omitt or
neglect immerfions were a grieuous mortall
fynne:becaufe it is an auncièt rite and ceremonie comaunded by the church, and alfo becaufe
it is fo fignificant a ceremonie,and fo cofigurat
to the paffion of Chrift as is pregnant and proued by Scriptur and fathers.S.Paule compareth
the baptifedto thofe who are layed in the fepulcher with Chrift and rife withhim to glorie.
All we fayeth he, who are baptized in Chrift
Iefus , in his death we are baptifed , for we
are buried together with him by baptifme vnto
death , that as Chrift is rifen from the dead by
the

the glorie of his father, fo we alfo may walke
in newnes of lyfe. And therfor fayeth S. Chrifoftome, we are as it were layed in a fepulcher *Homil.*
when we are fubmerfed and dipped in the font 24. *in*
& *vetus homo fepelitur*, and the old man is bu- Ioan.
ried fubmerfed and hidden, then after arifeth
and afcendeth the new man moft liuely, then
doth immerfion reprefent the figure of the fepulcher of our lord, wherfor a ceremonie not
to be contemned. Alfo by immerfion the whole bodie is washed and dipped : who feeleth
not but by the effects originall fyne doth work
the whole bodie is infected. What inconuenience then were it, yf the whole bodie be dipped and washed with the water of baptifme.
You will faye the head is the principal part of
mans bodie becaufe therin are moft vigent and
liuely the internal and external fenfes of man,
as vnderftandinge, witte, memorie, fight, hearinge and fmellinge: wherfor it is fufficient that
water be layed vppon the head or face of the
child. Trwe it is in deed in cafe of neceffitie,
or when conueniently immerfion can not be,
but you muft learne to diftinguifh, as I fayed
befor between vrgent caufe, and folemne ordinarie Chrifteninge.

C A P.   X IX.
Wether one or trinall immerfions are to be vfed
in baptifme.

THe church of god ordinarely doth vfe and
cõmaund three immerfions or dippings of
the child. Wherfor although one myght fuffice

yet

yet it were a great synne to infringe and breake the rite and ordinarie custome of the church. By three immersions is signified the trinitie of persons in God, that is, the Father the sonne, and the hollie ghost, and as the forme doth geue so the immersions followe. Also because S.

Rom. 6.

Paule sayeth that by baptisme we are sayed to be buried with Christ, therfor the three immersions are done to signifie the three dayes Christ was in the sepulcher, wherfor S. Augustine in a sermon he made to the new baptised hath these wordes, *recte tertio mersi estis &c.*

Serm. 3. & 4. ad Neophitas.

You who haue receaued baptisme in the name of the trinitie, rightfully you are three tymes dipped, and with reason also bee thrice dipped who haue bine baptised in the name of Iesus Christ who the thyrd daye rose from death, for that thyrd immersion doth expresse the type and figure of our lordes buriall, by which you are consepulted and buried together with Christ in baptisme. thus much S. Augustine. And to the same effect speaketh S. Hierome, *ter mergimur &c.* We are three tymes diped that the mysterie of the trinitie may be shewed and appeare. And we are not baptized in the names, in the plurall number but in the name in the singular number, wherby is signified on God: wherfor although we are thrice dipped to declare the misterie of the trinitie,

lib. Epist. 41.

yet it is but one god on baptisme, *vnus Deus vnum Baptisma*, one god, on baptisme. Also S. Gregorie wrytinge vnto Leander bishope in Spayne doth approue three immersions, and also not disallowe yf there be but one. So that for this ceremonie of three immersions we haue

ue three Doctors of the church S. Hierome S.
Auguſtine and S. Gregorie beſides theſe there
is an Apoſtolicall conſtitution, as recordeth S.
Clement which doth depoſe that prieſt who
ſhall baptize without trinall immerſion : by
reaſon of ſome heretick in the verie begeninge
and infancie of the church , who baptized not
in the name of the trinitie , but only in the
death of Chriſt , and becauſe Chriſt dyed but
once, he would vſe but one immerſion. You
maye obiect that in the forth Counſell of Toledo , baptiſme was commaunded to be effected with one immerſion. I aunſwere , it is
trwe it was ſo commaunded , and this was to
avoyed the ſcandall of ſchiſme and the vſe of
hereticall doctrine, wherfor S. Gregorius ſayeth baptiſme may be effected with one immerſion to ſignifie one deitie in three parſons. And
this was at that tyme done becauſe ſome Ar-
rians began to baptiſe with three immerſions,
not to ſignifie as the Catholikes did the three
parſons in one deitie , but to ſignifie three na-
turs , which was to make the ſonne and the
holly ghoſt not to be of one ſubſtance with the
father ; wherfor one immerſion was permitted
in Spayne by S. Gregorius and alſo commaunded by the counſel of Toledo becauſe theſe
hereticks ſhould not thinck that Catholicks
did vſe the trinall immerſion to cófirme their
doctrine. And therfor all Catholicks of that
countrie at that tyme agreed to vſe but one
immerſion, but now that occaſion of one immerſion being taken awaye all Catholick cou-
tries ordinarely doe returne to the auncient
coſtome of the primatiue church and doe pra-

ctiſe

(margin) Can. 49.

ƣife and commaund three immerſions. and
this power and right the Catholick church hath
and euer had concerning ceremonies & rites to
alter as occaſion by heretickes was geuen to e-
dification. But for any eſſentiall parte of any ſa-
crament, ſhe newer hath nor can alter or per-
mitt to be altered vppon any occaſion what
ſoeuer : for the eſſentiall part Chriſt himſelfe
inſtituted and leafte the rites and ceremonies
to hi: church.

C A P. 20.

*Wether the vnction with holie chriſme on the
crowne of the head after baptiſme be allowable.*

Now being come to our thyrd diuiſion of
ceremonies which are to be done and a-
cted after baptiſme, you ſhall vnderſtand that
they are three in number, which the Catholick
church doth ſpecially practiſe ; The fyrſt is vnction with holy chriſme vppon the topp or
crowne of the head. The ſecond is the chriſo-
me or white garment which is put vppon the
baptiſed. The third is the taper or waxe candle
light and burning beinge geuen and putt in the
right hand of the baptized. All which three the
Proteſtants neglect or contemne as vnprofita-
ble, not honorable nor ſignificant, and haue
quiet blotted them out of theire bookes. Concerninge the fyrſt. Soe ſoone as the child is taken out of the font, the prieſt doth annoynt
him not with holy oyle as before on the breaſt
and ſhoulders : but with holy Chriſme and that
on the crowne of the head; to ſignifie that now
he is become a Chriſtea and ſo called of Chriſt,
which

which is as much as *vnctus*, annoynted; and
therfor an annoynted Christean, and then he
vseth this orison or prayer. *God omnipotent father of our lord Iesus Christ, who hath regenerated thee of water and the holy ghost, and also who
hath geuen thee remission of all thy synnes, he
doth annoynt the with the crisme of oyle of health
into life everlastinge.* S. Ambrose after this ceremonie is perfected sayeth to euerie Christean
man. *vnctus es quasi Athleta Christi.* Now thou
art annoynted as the champion of Christ vnto
life eternall. And Rabanus wryteth to this effect, after sayeth he, the child is taken out of
the font presently he is signed *in cerebro,* in the
crowne of the head with sacred Chrisme together with the prayer of the priest, that
he may be made partaker of the kingdome
of Christ, and of Christ be called a Christean.
S. Ambrose goeth farther and asketh the question. *Quare Caput ?* why hast thou receaued
oyntment and holy Chrisme vppon thy head?
he maketh the answere and geueth the reason
quia sensus sapientis in capite eius. because the
sense and vnderstandinge, the eyes of the wise
are in his head, And thus much to shewe how
significant this ceremonie is. Now for the
antiquitie therof that it was vsed in the primatiue church, we haue amonge the decrees and
rites of the church which were published and
instituted by S. Syluester the fyrst pope of that
name who baptised Constantine the great
and fyrst christean Emperor; *vt presbiter
baptizati Chrismate summum liniret verticem.*
That the priest should annoynt the crowne
of the head of the baptized, with chrisme.
Also

*lib. 30.
de Sa-
cra-
mentis
t. 1.*

*lib. 3.
de sa-
cra. c.
1. &
2.
Eccles.
2.*

in dia- Also S. Hierome reporteth that in his tyme, it
logo waz not lawfull for the priests to baptise with-
contra out chrisme. What reason then haue the pro-
lucife- testants of this age not to allowe, but to ne-
ranos. glect and contemne so significant a ceremonie
I knowe no reason but one because they are
not *vncti domini*, the annoynted of our lord.
And as the Spayniards commonly saye *Christeanos may no veros Christeanos,* Christeans by
name, but not trwe Christeans in dead, but
misbeleeuers of Christian misteries, contem-
ners of the rites and ceremonies of the Christean Catholick church.

Cap. XXI.

Whether the vse of puttinge vppon the baptised the white garment be not significant.

THe vse of this ceremonie of clothinge the
baptised with a white vesture or garment
or with a linnen cloth commonly called the
chrisome, as the manner and custome of our
countrie of England hath bine, is on this forme. The priest after he hath annoynted the baptised vppon the head, taketh the chrisome or
white garment and sayeth, *Accipe vestem
candidam &c. Receaue and take the bright, white
holly and immaculate vesture, which thou mayest
carrie befor the tribuxal of our lord Iesus Christ
and that thou mayest haue life eternall and liue
for euer.* this is the ceremonie with the prayer.
The sacred scripture doth often allude to this

cere-

ceremonie of white vestments and clothinge. And fyrst in Chrifts transfiguration did not his garments turne and become white as snowe? **Matth. 17.** And the Angelicall vesture was it not white when they appeared to the holly women the **Luc. 9.** three Maries at the sepulcher of our lord the **Mar.** daye of his refurrection? alfo when they fpake **vlto.** to the Apostles after the Afcenfion of Chrift **Act.2.** they were all in white. And how often doth S. Iohn in the Apocalips difcribe the fayntes to **Apo.** be clothed in white garmentes, white ftolles, **3.** white robes. In the thyrd chapter it is fayed, that there were fome in the church of Sardis, who had not after baptifme defiled their garmentes with deadly fynne, and thofe are they who shall wa ke with god in whites, *ambula-bunt mecum in albis*, becaufe they are worthie. he that shall ouercome, shall thus be vefted in white garments, and I will not putt his name out of the book of lyfe. Alfo he defcribeth how he fawe the foure and twenty feniors a- **Apo.** bout the throne clothed in white garments. **4.** alfo he declareth that the foules who were vn- **Apoc.** der the alter had white ftolles geué them eue- **6.** rie one had on. And the multitud of faynéts **Apoc.** ftandinge befor the throne in the fight of the **7.** lambe were all clothed in white robes. The white vefture which is geuen immediatly after baptifme to the baptifed hath three or foure fignificatiós deduced out of Scriptur. Fyrft it is geuen in the memorie and figne of the glorious refurrection, for all thofe who are regenerated and borne agayne by baptifme, are capable and may be made partakers of Chrifts glorious re- furrection, and fo to walk with god in whits.

Sç-

Secondly to fignifie what we haue gotten and obtayned by baptifme, that is innocencie, a white foule, cleane washed from all fpottes and ftaynes of fynne. Thyrdly to fignifie and putt vs in mynd, of that puritie of lyfe which euerie one ought to obferue and keepe after baptifme, accordinge to that of S. Paule, that we maye walke in newnes of lyfe; Forthly and laft of all, to putt vs in mynde of the glorie of the next life, for there we muft be ftandinge in the fight of the lambe clothed in white robes, For *nullum coinquinatum* nothinge defiled shall enter into heauen, and thus much for the fignification. Wherfor I doubt not but that I maye conclud this ceremonie to be fignificant to haue his inftruction and fignification. Now for the antiquitie we haue the teftimonie of S. Dionifius in his ecclefiafticall Hierarchie, and the fame confirmeth S. Ambrofe lib. *de ijs qui initian : mifte c. 7.* Alfo of auncient tyme the octaue daye of pafcha or Eafter, is and was called *dominica in albis, the founday in whites,* becaufe after that daye the Neophits, that is to faye thofe who were newly baptifed, ether vppon Eafter euen or vppon the daye, beinge clothed at their baptifme in whits, did vfually on the foundaye after put of thofe white garments. *Ita tamen,* fayeth S. Auguftine, *vt candor qui in habitu deponitur, femper in corde teneatur.* But fo notwithftandinge, that the puritie and whitnes which the garment did fignifie, although layed awaye in the habite, yet allwayes to be kept and repofed in the harte and mynd. The Roman church, the mother church of this part of the world, folemnely
doth

Rom. 6

Sermo de octaua pafchalis.

doth obferue euen vntill this daye this ceremo
nie ; And ther you fhall fee from Eafter daye
vntill the founday after , the Neophits, or new
baptifed Iewes, to walk in their white garmets.
And all other Catholick countries omitt not
this ceremonie : what may we imagin myght
moue the proteftants , to contemne neglect and
deride this ceremonie, fo.fignificant and fo generally practifed throughout Chriftendome. I
can fay nothinge but that they are coinquina-
ted with fchifme from their mother church.
Candidi non funt , they are not white.

Cap. XXII.

Wether the geuing of the waxe candle light into
the hand of the baptized be a ceremonie vn-
profitable.

THe order of this ceremonie is , that the
prieft afterthe white garment geuen he taketh a taper or waxe candle light , and putteth
it into the right hand of the baptifed fayinge.
Accipe lampadem ardentem &c. Take and recea-
ue the burninge and irreprehenfible lampe , keepe
thy baptifme , obferue the commaundements, that
when our lord shall come to the mariage thou ma-
yeft meet him together with the fayncts in the hea-
uenly hall , that fo thou mayeft haue eternall lyfe
and liue for euer. The meaninge of this ceremonie is , and fo the church intendeth to inftruct,
that the baptifed hath geuen him by this facrament the light of fayth , and the light withall of gods grace , that he maye and ought
therby to worke the works of light and virtue, and not of darknes and fynne , accor-
ge to that fayinge of chrift, let your light shine
before

Matth. before men, that they may fee your good works
5.5. and glorifie your father which is in heauen.
And alfo that they haue alwayes their lampes
readie in their hádes, light and full of oyle that
when the bridegrome cometh they may be
readie to enter in with him: alludinge vnto the
parable of the fiue wife virgins. For the lampe
will not ferue the turne without light and oyle,
which is as much to faye, that fayth is dead
without the oyle of charitie and good worcks
Matth. to lighten it. And therfor the gate was shut
25. agaynft the foolishe virgins; fo that they could
not enter, nor would be kno uen, becaufe they
had no oyle nor light in their lampes: wherfor
I conclud that this ceremonie of gevinge a taper light in the right hand of the baptized to be
profitable, comfortable and fignificant. What
is the reafon then that the proteftantes forfake
this ceremonie, blot it out of their books, will
haue no light in their churches? I feare me although they beare the name of Chriftians, yet
they are become darknes, they wilbe lampes
without oyle, or light which is contrarie to
Scriptur and reafon; lett them take heed the
gate be not shut agaynft them, and that in the
latter daye they will not be knowen of Chrift
and to their confufion, they heare not that voice *Nefcio vos.* I knowe you not. I praye god
lightë their parts and geue them vnitie of fayht,
that we may once be all mébers of one Catholik and Apoftolik church, and therin to haue
the trwe vfe of the facraments with the rits and
ceremonies therof Amen.

EPILOGVS.

IN this treatiſe gentle reader, hath binne briefly ſhewed and by queſtions declared vnto thee, what baptiſme is, the effects therof, the matter, the forme, the miniſter, the partie baptized, and finally the reaſons of the rites and ceremonies, and with all howe honorable, ſignificant, profitable, and comfortable they are to chriſtian people.The lyk may be declared of the other ſyxe ſacraments, but not to be expected at my hands. For I will promiſe no more then I meane to performe. The catholik church hath euer mayntayned ſeauen ſacraméts, which chriſt himſelfe and no other could inſtitute. And this was the bountie and goodnes of our ſauiour chriſt,therby to aſſiſt and comfort man to make this his paſſage in this vale of miſerie. So that chriſt would not leaue vs without a remedie all the tyme of our life, euen from the heure of our birth vnto the daye of our death, baptiſme at our birth, Confeſſion, the Euchariſte with the other ſacraments all the middle of our life, and extreame vnction at our death. It is wonderfull to conſider,what eaſieway the proteſtans haue found out, they haue cutt of fiue of theſe ſeaven ſacraments, and would ſeeme to retayne only two. But in verie deed they haue but bare one, And that is baptiſme, which is allowed to be miniſtred by them and of them in caſe only of neceſſetie. And this one which they retayne,god knoweththey haue pilled and pouled, and the puritans iſſuinge from them haue endouered to roote it quit vp,

aſ

as may appeare by this precedēt treatise. As for the lords supper as they call, it it is with them no Sacrament for they haue no cōsecration, no change of bread into the bodie of Christ, bread befor and bread after, you maye make as good a Communion ar home in takinge bread at breakfast, in memorie that christ dyed for you. And as concerninge the rites and ceremonies of the Catholick church, dayly in their pulpits they baye and barke at them; that they are combersome, troblesome, to manie in number, superstitious: what wilbe the end of this? what tēdeth this vnto? surely to extinguish all externall honor of christ, all communication of Sacraments, and all assotiation of christean people in rits and ceremonies of religion. But S. Augustine shall answere these kind of men and so I will end. Some fewe, sayeth he, Sacraments and ceremonies we haue for many in the tyme of moyses law, most easie to be done, most honorable for signification and most cleane and pure to be obserued and kept, and such as our lord him selfe hath instituted, and Apostolicall discipline deliuered.

de do-
ctrina
Cǖri-
stiana.
lib. 3.
c. 9.

LAVS DEO VNI ET TRINO
23. Iunij 1614.

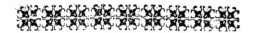

A TABLE OF THE

Chapters.

THE FYRST BOOK

Cap.

A table of th e chapters.

The second book.

with

A table of the chapters.

The thyrd book.

The fourth booke.

and

The fifth book.

Cap.

A table of the chapters.

The errors, thus correct. pag. 50. lin 23.whit, with. pag. 51. lin 15. whit, with. pag. 62. lin. 4. absoutlie, absolutlie pag. 68. lin 32. ba, be. pag. 98. lin. 1. bing, being. & ibid lin. 1. 2. it no, it, is no. pag. 101. lin. 12. thee, three. pag. 108. lin. 7. tui, tu. ibid lin. 12. kind, king. ibid lin 28. And were, and we were. pag. 110. lin 28 wiched wicked. pag. 135. lin 31. rawing, gnavving. pag. 148. lin. 8. fait, faith. pag. 153. lin 30. aie did. pag. 154. lin 32. statte, flatte. pag. 167. lin.19. yet, that. Ibid lin 23. yet, that.

Some other faultes which are of lesser importance, I dout not but thou thyselfe in the reading, wile easilie correct them.

A DOVAY,
par P I E R R E A V R O I , au
Pelican d'or. Anno 1614.

History of Dogma

Τὸ δόγματος ὄνομα τῆς ἀνθρωπίνης ἔχεται βουλῆς
τε καὶ γνώμης. Ὅτι δὲ τοῦθ᾽ οὕτως ἔχει, μαρτυρεῖ
μὲν ἱκανῶς ἡ δογματικὴ τῶν ἰατρῶν τέχνη,
μαρτυρεῖ δὲ καὶ τὰ τῶν φιλοσόφων καλούμενα
δόγματα. Ὅτι δὲ καὶ τὰ συγκλήτῳ δόξαντα
ἔτι καὶ νῦν δόγματα συγκλήτου λέγεται, οὐδένα
ἀγνοεῖν οἶμαι.

MARCELLUS OF ANCYRA.

Die Christliche Religion hat nichts in der Philosophie
zu thun, Sie ist ein mächtiges Wesen für sich, woran
die gesunkene und leidende Menschheit von Zeit zu
Zeit sich immer wieder emporgearbeitet hat; und
indem man ihr diese Wirkung zugesteht, ist sie über
aller Philosophie erhaben und bedarf von ihr keine
Stütze.

Gespräche mit GOETHE von ECKER-
MANN, 2 Th. p. 39.

ADOLPH HARNACK

History of Dogma

VOLUME ONE

New York

RUSSELL AND RUSSELL

The Library of Congress has cataloged
this book as follows:

Harnack, Adolf von, 1851–1930.
　　History of dogma. Translated from the 3d German ed.,
by Neil Buchanan. [New York, Russell & Russell, 1958]

　　　7 v.　23 cm.　(Theological translation library, v. 2, 7–12)

　　　Vols. 3, 5 translated by J. Millar; v. 4, by E. B. Speirs and J. Millar;
v. 6–7, by W. M'Gilchrist.
　　　Translation of Lehrbuch der Dogmengeschichte.

　　　1. Theology, Doctrinal—Hist.　　(Series: Theological translation
library, v. 2 [etc.])
　　　　　　　　　　　　　Full name: Carl Gustav Adolf von Harnack.

　BT21.H33　1958　　　　　　　230　　　　　　　　58–12862

　Library of Congress

Printed in the United States of America by

NOBLE OFFSET PRINTERS, INC.

VORWORT ZUR ENGLISCHEN AUSGABE.

Ein theologisches Buch erhält erst dadurch einen Platz in der Weltlitteratur, dass es Deutsch und Englisch gelesen werden kann. Diese beiden Sprachen zusammen haben auf dem Gebiete der Wissenschaft vom Christenthum das Lateinische abgelöst. Es ist mir daher eine grosse Freude, dass mein Lehrbuch der Dogmengeschichte in das Englische übersetzt worden ist, und ich sage dem Uebersetzer sowie den Verlegern meinen besten Dank. 1343430

Der schwierigste Theil der Dogmengeschichte ist ihr Anfang, nicht nur weil in dem Anfang die Keime für alle späteren Entwickelungen liegen, und daher ein Beobachtungsfehler beim Beginn die Richtigkeit der ganzen folgenden Darstellung bedroht, sondern auch desshalb, weil die Auswahl des wichtigsten Stoffs aus der Geschichte des Urchristenthums und der biblischen Theologie ein schweres Problem ist. Der Eine wird finden, dass ich zu viel in das Buch aufgenommen habe, und der Andere zu wenig—vielleicht haben Beide recht; ich kann dagegen nur anführen, dass sich mir die getroffene Auswahl nach wiederholtem Nachdenken und Experimentiren auf's Neue erprobt hat.

Wer ein theologisches Buch aufschlägt, fragt gewöhnlich zuerst nach dem "Standpunkt" des Verfassers. Bei geschichtlichen Darstellungen sollte man so nicht fragen. Hier handelt es sich darum, ob der Verfasser einen Sinn hat für den Gegenstand den er darstellt, ob er Originales und Abgeleitetes zu unterscheiden versteht, ob er seinen Stoff volkommen kennt, ob er sich der Grenzen des geschichtlichen Wissens bewusst ist, und ob er wahrhaftig ist. Diese Forderungen enthalten den kategorischen Imperativ für den Historiker; aber nur indem man rastlos an sich selber arbeitet, sind sie zu erfüllen, — so ist jede geschichtliche Darstellung eine ethische Aufgabe. Der Historiker soll in jedem Sinn *treu* sein: ob er das gewesen ist, darnach soll mann fragen.

Berlin, am 1. Mai, 1894.

ADOLF HARNACK.

THE AUTHOR'S
PREFACE TO THE ENGLISH EDITION.

No theological book can obtain a place in the literature of the world unless it can be read both in German and in English. These two languages combined have taken the place of Latin in the sphere of Christian Science. I am therefore greatly pleased to learn that my "History of Dogma" has been translated into English, and I offer my warmest thanks both to the translator and to the publishers.

The most difficult part of the history of dogma is the beginning, not only because it contains the germs of all later developments, and therefore an error in observation here endangers the correctness of the whole following account, but also because the selection of the most important material from the history of primitive Christianity and biblical theology is a hard problem. Some will think that I have admitted too much into the book, others too little. Perhaps both are right. I can only reply that after repeated consideration and experiment I continue to be satisfied with my selection.

In taking up a theological book we are in the habit of enquiring first of all as to the "stand-point" of the Author. In a historical work there is no room for such enquiry. The question here is, whether the Author is in sympathy with the subject about which he writes, whether he can distinguish original elements from those that are derived, whether he has a thorough acquaintance with his material, whether he is conscious of the limits of historical knowledge, and whether he is truthful. These requirements constitute the categorical imperative for the historian: but they can only be fulfilled by an unwearied self-discipline. Hence every historical study is an ethical task. The historian ought to be faithful in every sense of the word; whether he has been so or not is the question on which his readers have to decide.

Berlin, 1st May, 1894.

ADOLF HARNACK.

FROM THE
AUTHOR'S PREFACE TO THE FIRST EDITION.

The task of describing the genesis of ecclesiastical dogma which I have attempted to perform in the following pages, has hitherto been proposed by very few scholars, and, properly speaking, undertaken by one only. I must therefore crave the indulgence of those acquainted with the subject for an attempt which no future historian of dogma can avoid.

At first I meant to confine myself to narrower limits, but I was unable to carry out that intention, because the new arrangement of the material required a more detailed justification. Yet no one will find in the book, which presupposes the knowledge of Church history so far as it is given in the ordinary manuals, any repertory of the theological thought of Christian antiquity. The diversity of Christian ideas, or of ideas closely related to Christianity, was very great in the first centuries. For that very reason a selection was necessary; but it was required, above all, by the aim of the work. The history of dogma has to give an account, only of those doctrines of Christian writers which were authoritative in wide circles, or which furthered the advance of the development; otherwise it would become a collection of monographs, and thereby lose its proper value. I have endeavoured to subordinate every-thing to the aim of exhibiting the development which led to the ecclesiastical dogmas, and therefore have neither, for example, communicated the details of the gnostic systems, nor brought forward in detail the theological ideas of Clemens Romanus, Ignatius, etc. Even a history of Paulinism will be sought for in the book in vain. It is a task by itself, to trace the after-effects of the theology of Paul in the post-Apostolic age. The History of Dogma can only furnish fragments here; for it is not consistent with its task to give an accurate account of the history of a theology the effects of which were at first very limited. It is certainly no easy matter to determine what was authoritative in wide circles at the time when dogma was first being developed, and I may confess that I have found the working out of the third chapter of the first book very difficult. But I hope that the severe limitation in the material will be of service to the subject. If the result of this limitation should be to lead students to read connectedly the manual which has grown out of my lectures, my highest wish will be gratified.

There can be no great objection to the appearance of a text-book on the history of dogma at the present time. We now know in what direction we have to work; but we still want a history of Christian theological ideas in their relation to contemporary philosophy. Above all, we have not got an exact knowledge of the Hellenistic philosophical terminologies in their development up to the fourth century. I have keenly felt this want, which can only be remedied by well-directed common labour. I have made a plentiful use of the controversial treatise of Celsus against Christianity, of which little use has hitherto been made for the history of dogma. On the other hand, except in a few cases, I have deemed it inadmissible to adduce parallel passages, easy to be got, from Philo, Seneca, Plutarch, Epictetus, Marcus Aurelius, Porphyry, etc.; for only a comparison strictly carried out would have been of value here. I have been able neither to borrow such from others, nor to furnish it myself. Yet I have ventured to submit my work, because, in my opinion, it is possible to prove the dependence of dogma on the Greek spirit, without being compelled to enter into a discussion of all the details.

The Publishers of the Encyclopædia Britannica have allowed

me to print here, in a form but slightly altered, the articles
on Neoplatonism and Manichæism which I wrote for their
work, and for this I beg to thank them.

It is now eighty-three years since my grandfather, Gustav
Ewers, edited in German the excellent manual on the earliest
history of dogma by Münter, and thereby got his name associated with the history of the founding of the new study. May
the work of the grandson be found not unworthy of the clear
and disciplined mind which presided over the beginnings of
the young science.

Giessen, 1st August, 1885.

AUTHOR'S
PREFACE TO THE SECOND EDITION.

In the two years that have passed since the appearance of the first edition I have steadily kept in view the improvement of this work, and have endeavoured to learn from the reviews of it that have appeared. I owe most to the study of Weizsäcker's work, on the Apostolic Age, and his notice of the first edition of this volume in the Göttinger gelehrte Anzeigen, 1886, No. 21. The latter, in several decisive passages concerning the general conception, drew my attention to the fact that I had emphasised certain points too strongly, but had not given due prominence to others of equal importance, while not entirely overlooking them. I have convinced myself that these hints were, almost throughout, well founded, and have taken pains to meet them in the new edition. I have also learned from Heinrici's commentary on the Second Epistle to the Corinthians, and from Bigg's "Lectures on the Christian Platonists of Alexandria". Apart from these works there has appeared very little that could be of significance for my historical account; but I have once more independently considered the main problems, and in some cases, after repeated reading of the sources, checked my statements, removed mistakes and explained what had been too briefly stated. Thus, in particular, Chapter II. §§ 1-3 of the "Presuppositions", also the Third Chapter of the First Book (especially Section 6), also in the Second Book, Chapter I. and Chapter II. (under B), the Third

Chapter (Supplement 3 and excursus on "Catholic and Romish"),
the Fifth Chapter (under 1 and 3) and the Sixth Chapter (under
2) have been subjected to changes and greater additions.
Finally, a new excursus has been added on the various modes
of conceiving pre-existence, and in other respects many things
have been improved in detail. The size of the book has thereby
been increased by about fifty pages. As I have been misrepre-
sented by some as one who knew not how to appreciate the
uniqueness of the Gospel history and the evangelic faith, while
others have conversely reproached me with making the history
of dogma proceed from an "apostasy" from the Gospel to
Hellenism, I have taken pains to state my opinions on both
these points as clearly as possible. In doing so I have only
wrought out the hints which were given in the first edition,
and which, as I supposed, were sufficient for readers. But it
is surely a reasonable desire when I request the critics in
reading the paragraphs which treat of the "Presuppositions",
not to forget how difficult the questions there dealt with are,
both in themselves and from the nature of the sources, and
how exposed to criticism the historian is who attempts to
unfold his position towards them in a few pages. As is self-
evident, the centre of gravity of the book lies in that which
forms its subject proper, in the account of the origin of dogma
within the Græco-Roman empire. But one should not on that
account, as many have done, pass over the beginning which
lies before the beginning, or arbitrarily adopt a starting-point
of his own; for everything here depends on where and how
one begins. I have not therefore been able to follow the well-
meant counsel to simply strike out the "Presuppositions".

I would gladly have responded to another advice to work
up the notes into the text; but I would then have been
compelled to double the size of some chapters. The form of
this book, in many respects awkward, may continue as it is
so long as it represents the difficulties by which the subject
is still pressed. When they have been removed — and the
smallest number of them lie in the subject matter — I will
gladly break up this form of the book and try to give it

another shape. For the friendly reception given to it I have
to offer my heartiest thanks. But against those who, believing
themselves in possession of a richer view of the history here
related, have called my conception meagre, I appeal to the
beautiful words of Tertullian; "Malumus in scripturis minus,
si forte, sapere quam contra".

Marburg, 24th December, 1887.

AUTHOR'S
PREFACE TO THE THIRD EDITION.

In the six years that have passed since the appearance of the second edition I have continued to work at the book, and have made use of the new sources and investigations that have appeared during this period, as well as corrected and extended my account in many passages. Yet I have not found it necessary to make many changes in the second half of the work. The increase of about sixty pages is almost entirely in the first half.

Berlin, 31st December, 1893.

CONTENTS

SUPPLEMENTARY.

CHAPTER IV. — THE ATTEMPTS OF THE GNOSTICS TO CREATE AN APOSTOLIC DOGMATIC, AND A CHRISTIAN THEOLOGY; OR THE ACUTE SECULARISING OF CHRISTIANITY

CHAPTER V. — THE ATTEMPT OF MARCION TO SET ASIDE THE OLD TESTAMENT FOUNDATION OF CHRISTIANITY, TO PURIFY THE TRADITION AND REFORM CHRISTENDOM ON THE BASIS OF THE PAULINE GOSPEL

I

PROLEGOMENA TO THE DISCIPLINE OF THE HISTORY OF DOGMA.

II

THE PRESUPPOSITIONS OF THE HISTORY OF DOGMA.

CHAPTER I

PROLEGOMENA TO THE DISCIPLINE OF THE HISTORY
OF DOGMA.

§ 1. *The Idea and Task of the History of Dogma.*

1. THE History of Dogma is a discipline of general Church History, which has for its object the dogmas of the Church. These dogmas are the doctrines of the Christian faith logically formulated and expressed for scientific and apologetic purposes, the contents of which are a knowledge of God, of the world, and of the provisions made by God for man's salvation. The Christian Churches teach them as the truths revealed in Holy Scripture, the acknowledgment of which is the condition of the salvation which religion promises. But as the adherents of the Christian religion had not these dogmas from the beginning, so far, at least, as they form a connected system, the business of the history of dogma is, in the first place, to ascertain the origin of Dogmas (of Dogma), and then secondly, to describe their development (their variations).

2. We cannot draw any hard and fast line between the time of the origin and that of the development of dogma; they rather shade off into one another. But we shall have to look for the final point of division at the time when an article of faith logically formulated and scientifically expressed, was first raised to the *articulus constitutivus ecclesiæ*, and as such was universally enforced by the Church. Now that first happened when the doctrine of Christ, as the pre-existent and personal Logos of God, had obtained acceptance everywhere in the confederated Churches as the revealed and

fundamental doctrine of faith, that is, about the end of the
third century or the beginning of the fourth. We must therefore, in our account, take this as the final point of division. [1]
As to the development of dogma, it seems to have closed in
the Eastern Church with the seventh Œcumenical Council (787).
After that time no further dogmas were set up in the East as
revealed truths. As to the Western Catholic, that is, the
Romish Church, a new dogma was promulgated as late as the
year 1870, which claims to be, and in point of form really
is, equal in dignity to the old dogmas. Here, therefore, the
History of Dogma must extend to the present time. Finally,
as regards the Protestant Churches, they are a subject of special difficulty in the sphere of the history of dogma; for at the
present moment there is no agreement within these Churches
as to whether, and in what sense, dogmas (as the word was
used in the ancient Church) are valid. But even if we leave
the present out of account and fix our attention on the Protestant Churches of the 16th century, the decision is difficult.
For, on the one hand, the Protestant faith, the Lutheran as
well as the Reformed (and that of Luther no less), presents
itself as a doctrine of faith which, resting on the Catholic
canon of scripture, is, in point of form, quite analogous to the
Catholic doctrine of faith, has a series of dogmas in common
with it, and only differs in a few. On the other hand, Pro-

1 Weizsäcker, Gött. Gel. Anz. 1886, p. 823 f., says, "It is a question whether
we should limit the account of the genesis of Dogma to the Antenicene period
and designate all else as a development of that. This is undoubtedly correct
so long as our view is limited to the history of dogma of the Greek Church
in the second period, and the development of it by the Œcumenical Synods.
On the other hand, the Latin Church, in its own way and in its own province,
becomes productive from the days of Augustine onwards; the formal signification of dogma in the narrower sense becomes different in the middle ages.
Both are repeated in a much greater measure through the Reformation. We
may therefore, in opposition to that division into genesis and development, regard the whole as a continuous process, in which the contents as well as the
formal authority of dogma are in process of continuous development." This
view is certainly just, and I think is indicated by myself in what follows. We
have to decide here, as so often elsewhere in our account, between rival points
of view. The view favoured by me has the advantage of making the nature
of dogma clearly appear as a product of the mode of thought of the early
church, and that is what it has remained, in spite of all changes both in form
and substance, till the present day.

testantism has taken its stand in principle on the Gospel exclusively, and declared its readiness at all times to test all
doctrines afresh by a true understanding of the Gospel. The
Reformers, however, in addition to this, began to unfold a
conception of Christianity which might be described, in contrast with the Catholic type of religion, as a new conception,
and which indeed draws support from the old dogmas, but
changes their original significance materially and formally.
What this conception was may still be ascertained from those
writings received by the Church, the Protestant symbols of
the 16th century, in which the larger part of the traditionary
dogmas are recognised as the appropriate expression of the
Christian religion, nay, as the Christian religion itself. [1] Accordingly, it can neither be maintained that the expression of
the Christian faith in the form of dogmas is abolished in the
Protestant Churches — the very acceptance of the Catholic
canon as the revealed record of faith is opposed to that view —
nor that its meaning has remained absolutely unchanged. [2]
The history of dogma has simply to recognise this state of
things, and to represent it exactly as it lies before us in the
documents.

But the point to which the historian should advance here
still remains an open question. If we adhere strictly to the
definition of the idea of dogma given above, this much is
certain, that dogmas were no longer set up after the Formula
of Concord, or in the case of the Reformed Church, after the
decrees of the Synod of Dort. It cannot, however, be maintained that they have been set aside in the centuries that

---

1 See Kattenbusch. Luther's Stellung zu den ökumenischen Symbolen, 1883.
2 See Ritschl, Geschichte des Pietismus. I. p. 80 ff.: 93 ff. II. p. 60 f.: 88 f.
"The Lutheran view of life did not remain pure and undefiled, but was
limited and obscured by the preponderance of dogmatic interests. Protestantism was not delivered from the womb of the western Church of the
middle ages in full power and equipment, like Athene from the head of
Jupiter. The incompleteness of its ethical view, the splitting up of its
general conceptions into a series of particular dogmas, the tendency to
express its beliefs as a hard and fast whole; are defects which soon made
Protestantism appear to disadvantage in comparison with the wealth of
Mediæval theology and asceticism... The scholastic form of pure doctrine
is really only the provisional, and not the final form of Protestantism."

have passed since then; for apart from some Protestant National- and independent Churches, which are too insignificant and whose future is too uncertain to be taken into account here, the ecclesiastical tradition of the 16ᵗʰ century, and along with it the tradition of the early Church, have not been abrogated in authoritative form. Of course, changes of the greatest importance with regard to doctrine have appeared everywhere in Protestantism from the 17ᵗʰ century to the present day. But these changes cannot in any sense be taken into account in a history of dogma, because they have not as yet attained a form valid for the Church. However we may judge of these changes, whether we regard them as corruptions or improvements, or explain the want of fixity in which the Protestant Churches find themselves, as a situation that is forced on them, or the situation that is agreeable to them and for which they are adapted, in no sense is there here a development which could be described as history of dogma.

These facts would seem to justify those who, like Thomasius and Schmid, carry the history of dogma in Protestantism to the Formula of Concord, or, in the case of the Reformed Church, to the decrees of the Synod of Dort. But it may be objected to this boundary line; (1) That those symbols have at all times attained only a partial authority in Protestantism; (2) That as noted above, the dogmas, that is, the formulated doctrines of faith have different meanings on different matters in the Protestant and in the Catholic Churches. Accordingly, it seems advisable within the frame-work of the history of dogma, to examine Protestantism only so far as this is necessary for obtaining a knowledge of its deviations from the Catholic dogma materially and formally, that is, to ascertain the original position of the Reformers with regard to the doctrine of the Church, a position which is beset with contradictions. The more accurately we determine the relation of the Reformers to Catholicism, the more intelligible will be the developments which Protestantism has passed through in the course of its history. But these developments themselves (retrocession and advance) do not belong to the sphere of the history of dogma,

because they stand in no comparable relation to the course
of the history of dogma within the Catholic Church. As history of Protestant doctrines they form a peculiar independent
province of Church history.

As to the division of the history of dogma, it consists of
two main parts. The first has to describe the origin of dogma,
that is, of the Apostolic Catholic system of doctrine based on the
foundation of the tradition authoritatively embodied in the
creeds and Holy scripture, and extends to the beginning of
the fourth century. This may be conveniently divided into
two parts, the first of which will treat of the preparation, the
second of the establishment of the ecclesiastical doctrine of
faith. The second main part, which has to portray the development of dogma, comprehends three stages. In the first stage
the doctrine of faith appears as Theology and Christology.
The Eastern Church has never got beyond this stage, although
it has to a large extent enriched dogma ritually and mystically
(see the decrees of the seventh council). We will have to shew
how the doctrines of faith formed in this stage have remained
for all time in the Church dogmas κατ' ἐξοχήν. The second
stage was initiated by Augustine. The doctrine of faith appears
here on the one side completed, and on the other re-expressed
by new dogmas, which treat of the relation of sin and grace,
freedom and grace, grace and the means of grace. The number
and importance of the dogmas that were, in the middle ages,
really fixed after Augustine's time, had no relation to the range
and importance of the questions which they raised, and which
emerged in the course of centuries in consequence of advancing
knowledge, and not less in consequence of the growing power
of the Church. Accordingly, in this second stage which comprehends the whole of the middle ages, the Church as an
institution kept believers together in a larger measure than
was possible to dogmas. These in their accepted form were
too poor to enable them to be the expression of religious
conviction and the regulator of Church life. On the other
hand, the new decisions of Theologians, Councils and Popes,
did not yet possess the authority which could have made them

incontestable truths of faith. The third stage begins with the
Reformation, which compelled the Church to fix its faith on
the basis of the theological work of the middle ages. Thus
arose the Roman Catholic dogma which has found in the Vatican
decrees its provisional settlement. This Roman Catholic dogma,
as it was formulated at Trent, was moulded in express opposition to the Theses of the Reformers. But these Theses
themselves represent a peculiar conception of Christianity, which
has its root in the theology of Paul and Augustine, and includes
either explicitly or implicitly a revision of the whole ecclesiastical tradition, and therefore of dogma also. The History of
Dogma in this last stage, therefore, has a twofold task. It
has, on the one hand, to present the Romish dogma as a product
of the ecclesiastical development of the middle ages under the
influence of the Reformation faith which was to be rejected,
and on the other hand, to portray the conservative new formation which we have in original Protestantism, and determine
its relation to dogma. A closer examination, however, shews
that in none of the great confessions does religion live in
dogma, as of old. Dogma everywhere has fallen into the background; in the Eastern Church it has given place to ritual,
in the Roman Church to ecclesiastical instructions, in the
Protestant Churches, so far as they are mindful of their origin,
to the Gospel. At the same time, however, the paradoxical
fact is unmistakable that dogma as such is nowhere at this
moment so powerful as in the Protestant Churches, though by
their history they are furthest removed from it. Here, however,
it comes into consideration as an object of immediate religious
interest, which, strictly speaking, in the Catholic Church is not
the case.[1] The Council of Trent was simply wrung from the
Romish Church, and she has made the dogmas of that council

---

1 It is very evident how the mediæval and old catholic dogmas were transformed in the view which Luther originally took of them. In this view we must
remember that he did away with all the presuppositions of dogma, the infallible Apostolic Canon of Scripture, the infallible teaching function of the Church,
and the infallible Apostolic doctrine and constitution. On this basis dogmas
can only be utterances which do not support faith, but are supported by it.
But, on the other hand, his opposition to all the Apocryphal saints which the
Church had created, compelled him to emphasise faith alone, and to give it a
firm basis in scripture, in order to free it from the burden of tradition.

in a certain sense innocuous by the Vatican decrees. [1] In this sense, it may be said that the period of development of dogma is altogether closed, and that therefore our discipline requires

Here then, very soon, first by Melanchthon, a summary of *articuli fidei* was substituted for the faith, and the scriptures recovered their place as a rule. Luther himself, however, is responsible for both, and so it came about that very soon the new evangelic standpoint was explained almost exclusively by the "abolition of abuses", and by no means so surely by the transformation of the whole doctrinal tradition. The classic authority for this is the Augsburg confession ("hæc fere summa est doctrina apud suos, in qua cerni potest nihil inesse, quod discrepet a scripturis vel ab ecclesia Catholica vel ab ecclesia Romana .... sed dissensio est de quibusdam abusibus"). The purified catholic doctrine has since then become the palladium of the Reformation Churches. The refuters of the Augustana have justly been unwilling to admit the mere "purifying," but have noted in addition that the Augustana does not say everything that was urged by Luther and the Doctors (see Ficker, Die Konfutation des Augsburgischen Bekenntnisse, 1891). At the same time, however, the Lutheran Church, though not so strongly as the English, retained the consciousness of being the true Catholics. But, as the history of Protestantism proves, the original impulse has not remained inoperative. Though Luther himself all his life measured his personal Christian standing by an entirely different standard than subjection to a law of faith; yet, however presumptuous the words may sound, we might say that in the complicated struggle that was forced on him, he did not always clearly understand his own faith.

1 In the modern Romish Church, Dogma is, above all, a judicial regulation which one has to submit to, and in certain circumstances submission alone is sufficient, *fides implicita*. Dogma is thereby just as much deprived of its original sense and its original authority as by the demand of the Reformers, that every thing should be based upon a clear understanding of the Gospel. Moreover, the changed position of the Romish Church towards dogma is also shewn by the fact that it no longer gives a plain answer to the question as to what dogma is. Instead of a series of dogmas definitely defined, and of equal value, there is presented an infinite multitude of whole and half dogmas, doctrinal directions, pious opinions, probable theological propositions, etc. It is often a very difficult question whether a solemn decision has or has not already been taken on this or that statement, or whether such a decision is still necessary. Everything that must be believed is nowhere stated, and so one sometimes hears in Catholic circles the exemplary piety of a cleric praised with the words that "he believes more than is necessary". The great dogmatic conflicts within the Catholic Church, since the Council of Trent, have been silenced by arbitrary Papal pronouncements and doctrinal directions. Since one has simply to accommodate oneself to these as laws, it once more appears clear that dogma has become a judicial regulation, administered by the Pope, which is carried out in an administrative way and loses itself in an endless casuistry. We do not mean by this to deny that dogma has a decided value for the pious Catholic as a Summary of the faith. But in the Catholic Church it is no longer piety, but obedience that is decisive. The solidarity with the orthodox Protestants may be explained by political reasons, in order from political reasons again, to condemn, where it is necessary, all Protestants as heretics and revolutionaries.

a statement such as belongs to a series of historical phenomena
that has been completed.

3. The church has recognised her faith, that is religion
itself, in her dogmas. Accordingly, one very important business of the History of Dogma is to exhibit the unity that exists
in the dogmas of a definite period, and to shew how the several
dogmas are connected with one another and what leading
ideas they express. But, as a matter of course, this undertaking
has its limits in the degree of unanimity which actually existed
in the dogmas of the particular period. It may be shewn without much difficulty, that a strict though by no means absolute
unanimity is expressed only in the dogmas of the Greek Church.
The peculiar character of the western post-Augustinian ecclesiastical conception of Christianity, no longer finds a clear
expression in dogma, and still less is this the case with the
conception of the Reformers. The reason of this is that
Augustine, as well as Luther, disclosed a new conception of
Christianity, but at the same time appropriated the old
dogmas. [1] But neither Baur's nor Kliefoth's method of writing
the history of dogma has done justice to this fact. Not
Baur's, because, notwithstanding the division into six periods,
it sees a uniform process in the development of dogma, a
process which begins with the origin of Christianity and has
run its course, as is alleged, in a strictly logical way. Not
Kliefoth's, because, in the dogmas of the Catholic Church
which the East has never got beyond, it only ascertains the
establishment of one portion of the Christian faith, to which
the parts still wanting have been successively added in later
times. [2] In contrast with this, we may refer to the fact that
we can clearly distinguish three styles of building in the
history of dogma, but only three; the style of Origen, that of
Augustine, and that of the Reformers. But the dogma of the
post-Augustinian Church, as well as that of Luther, does not

---

1 See the discussions of Biedermann (Christliche Dogmatik. 2 Ed. p. 150
f.) about what he calls the law of stability in the history of religion.

2 See Ritschl's discussion of the methods of the early histories of dogma
in the Jahrb. f. Deutsche Theologie, 1871, p. 181 ff.

in any way represent itself as a new building, not even as the mere extension of an old building, but as a complicated rebuilding, and by no means in harmony with former styles, because neither Augustine nor Luther ever dreamed of building independently. [1] This perception leads us to the most peculiar phenomenon which meets the historian of dogma, and which must determine his method.

Dogmas arise, develop themselves and are made serviceable to new aims; this in all cases takes place through Theology. But Theology is dependent on innumerable factors, above all, on the spirit of the time; for it lies in the nature of theology that it desires to make its object intelligible. Dogmas are the product of theology, not inversely; of a theology of course which, as a rule, was in correspondence with the faith of the time. The critical view of history teaches this: first we have the Apologists and Origen, then the councils of Nice and Chalcedon; first the Scholastics, then the Council of Trent. In consequence of this, dogma bears the mark of all, the factors on which the theology was dependent. That is one point. But the moment in which the product of theology became dogma, the way which led to it must be obscured; for, according to the conception of the Church, dogma can be nothing else than the revealed faith itself. Dogma is regarded not as the exponent, but as the basis of theology, and therefore the product of theology having passed into dogma limits, and criticises the work of theology both past and future.[2] That is the second point. It follows from this that the history of the Christian religion embraces a very complicated relation of ecclesiastical dogma and theology, and that the

1 In Catholicism, the impulse which proceeded from Augustine has finally proved powerless to break the traditional conception of Christianity, as the Council of Trent and the decrees of the Vatican have shewn. For that very reason the development of the Roman Catholic Church doctrine belongs to the history of dogma. Protestantism must, however, under all circumstances be recognised as a new thing, which indeed in none of its phases has been free from contradictions.

2 Here then begins the ecclesiastical theology which takes as its starting-point the finished dogma it strives to prove or harmonise, but very soon, as experience has shewn, loses its firm footing in such efforts and so occasions new crises.

ecclesiastical conception of the significance of theology cannot
at all do justice] to this significance. The ecclesiastical scheme
which is here formed and which denotes the utmost concession
that can be made to history, is to the effect that theology gives
expression only to the form of dogma, while so far as it is
ecclesiastical theology, it presupposes the unchanging dogma,
i.e., the substance of dogma. But this scheme, which must
always leave uncertain what the form really is, and what the
substance, is in no way applicable to the actual circumstances.
So far, however, as it is itself an article of faith it is an object
of the history of dogma. Ecclesiastical dogma when put on
its defence must at all times take up an ambiguous position towards theology, and ecclesiastical theology a corresponding position towards dogma; for they are condemned to
perpetual uncertainty as to what they owe each other, and
what they have to fear from each other. The theological
Fathers of dogma have almost without exception failed to
escape being condemned by dogma, either because it went
beyond them, or lagged behind their theology. The Apologists, Origen and Augustine may be cited in support of this;
and even in Protestantism, *mutatis mutandis*, the same thing
has been repeated, as is proved by the fate of Melanchthon
and Schleiermacher. On the other hand, there have been
few theologians who have not shaken some article of the
traditional dogma. We are wont to get rid of these fundamental facts by hypostatising the ecclesiastical principle or
the common ecclesiastical spirit, and by this normal hypostasis, measuring, approving or condemning the doctrines of
the theologians, unconcerned about the actual conditions and
frequently following a hysteron-proteron. But this is a view
of history which should in justice be left to the Catholic
Church, which indeed cannot dispense with it. The critical
history of dogma has, on the contrary, to shew above all how
an ecclesiastical theology has arisen; for it can only give
account of the origin of dogma in connection with this main
question. The horizon must be taken here as wide as possible; for the question as to the origin of theology can only

be answered by surveying all the relations into which the Christian religion has entered in naturalising itself in the world and subduing it. When ecclesiastical dogma has once been created and recognised as an immediate expression of the Christian religion, the history of dogma has only to take the history of theology into account so far as it has been active in the formation of dogma. Yet it must always keep in view the perculiar claim of dogma to be a criterion and not a product of theology. But it will also be able to shew how, partly by means of theology and partly by other means—for dogma is also dependent on ritual, constitution, and the practical ideals of life, as well as on the letter, whether of Scripture, or of tradition no longer understood — dogma in its development and re-expression has continually changed, according to the conditions under which the Church was placed. If dogma is originally the formulation of Christian faith as Greek culture understood it and justified it to itself, then dogma has never indeed lost this character, though it has been radically modified in later times. It is quite as important to keep in view the tenacity of dogma as its changes, and in this respect the Protestant way of writing history, which, here as elsewhere in the history of the Church, is more disposed to attend to differences than to what is permanent, has much to learn from the Catholic. But as the Protestant historian, as far possible, judges of the progress of development in so far as it agrees with the Gospel in its documentary form, he is still able to shew, with all deference to that tenacity, that dogma has been so modified and used to the best advantage by Augustine and Luther, that its Christian character has in many respects gained, though in other respects it has become further and further alienated from that character. In proportion as the traditional system of dogmas lost its stringency it became richer. In proportion as it was stripped by Augustine and Luther of its apologetic philosophic tendency, it was more and more filled with Biblical ideas, though, on the other hand, it became more full of contradictions and less impressive.

This outlook, however, has already gone beyond the limits fixed for these introductory paragraphs and must not be pursued further. To treat *in abstracto* of the method of the history of dogma in relation to the discovery, grouping and interpretation of the material is not to be recommended; for general rules to preserve the ignorant and half instructed from overlooking the important, and laying hold of what is not important, cannot be laid down. Certainly everything depends on the arrangement of the material; for the understanding of history is to find the rules according to which the phenomena should be grouped, and every advance in the knowledge of history is inseparable from an accurate observance of these rules. We must, above all, be on our guard against preferring one principle at the expense of another in the interpretation of the origin and aim of particular dogmas. The most diverse factors have at [all times been at work in the formation of dogmas. Next to the effort to determine the doctrine of religion according to the *finis religionis*, the blessing of salvation, the following may have been the most important. (1) The conceptions and sayings contained in the canonical scriptures. (2) The doctrinal tradition originating in earlier epochs of the church, and no longer understood. (3) The needs of worship and organisation. (4) The effort to adjust the doctrine of religion to the prevailing doctrinal opinions. (5) Political and social circumstances. (6) The changing moral ideals of life. (7) The so-called logical consistency, that is the abstract analogical treatment of one dogma according to the form of another. (8) The effort to adjust different tendencies and contradictions in the church. (9) The endeavour to reject once for all a doctrine regarded as erroneous. (10) The sanctifying power of blind custom. The method of explaining everything wherever possible by "the impulse of dogma to unfold itself," must be given up as unscientific, just as all empty abstractions whatsoever must be given up as scholastic and mythological. Dogma has had its history in the individual living man and nowhere else. As soon as one adopts this statement in real earnest, that mediæval realism must vanish to which a man so often thinks himself superior while imbedded in it all the time. Instead of investigating the actual conditions in which believing and intelligent men have been placed, a system of Christianity has been constructed from which, as from a Pandora's box, all doctrines which in course of time have been formed, are extracted, and in this way legitimised as Christian. The simple fundamental proposition that that only is Christian which can be established authoritatively by the Gospel, has never yet received justice in the history of dogma. Even the following account will in all probability come short in this point; for in face of a prevailing false tradition the application of a simple principle to every detail can hardly succeed at the first attempt.

Explanation as to the Conception and Task of the History of Dogma.

No agreement as yet prevails with regard to the conception of the history of dogma. Münscher (Handbuch der Christl. D. G. 3rd ed. I. p. 3 f.) declared that the business of the history of dogma is "To represent all the changes which the theoretic part of the Christian doctrine of religion has gone through from its origin up to the present, both in form and substance," and this definition held sway for a long time. Then it came to be noted that the question was not about changes that were accidental, but about those that were historically necessary, that dogma has a relation to the church, and that it represents a rational expression of the faith. Emphasis was put sometimes on one of these elements and sometimes on the other. Baur, in particular, insisted on the first; V. Hofmann, after the example of Schleiermacher, on the second, and indeed exclusively (Encyklop. der theol. p. 257 f.: "The history of dogma is the history of the Church confessing the faith in words"). Nitzsch (Grundriss der Christl. D. G. I. p. 1) insisted on the third: "The history of dogma is the scientific account of the origin and development of the Christian system of doctrine, or that part of historical theology which presents the history of the expression of the Christian faith in notions, doctrines

and doctrinal systems". Thomasius has combined the second
and third by conceiving the history of dogma as the history
of the development of the ecclesiastical system of doctrine.
But even this conception is not sufficiently definite, inasmuch
as it fails to do complete justice to the special peculiarity of
the subject.

Ancient and modern usage does certainly seem to allow the
word dogma to be applied to particular doctrines, or to a
uniform system of doctrine, to fundamental truths, or to opinions, to theoretical propositions or practical rules, to statements of belief that have not been reached by a process of
reasoning, as well as to those that bear the marks of such a
process. But this uncertainty vanishes on closer examination.
We then see that there is always an authority at the basis of
dogma, which gives it to those who recognise that authority the
signification of a fundamental truth *"quæ sine scelere prodi non
poterit"* (Cicero Quæst. Acad. IV. 9). But therewith at the same
time is introduced into the idea of dogma a social element (see
Biedermann, Christl. Dogmatik. 2. Edit. I. p. 2 f.); the confessors of one and the same dogma form a community.

There can be no doubt that these two elements are also
demonstrable in Christian dogma, and therefore we must reject
all definitions of the history of dogma which do not take them
into account. If we define it as the history of the understanding of Christianity by itself, or as the history of the changes
of the theoretic part of the doctrine of religion or the like,
we shall fail to do justice to the idea of dogma in its most
general acceptation. We cannot describe as dogmas, doctrines
such as the Apokatastasis, or the Kenosis of the Son of God,
without coming into conflict with the ordinary usage of language and with ecclesiastical law.

If we start, therefore, from the supposition that Christian
dogma is an ecclesiastical doctrine which presupposes revelation as its authority, and therefore claims to be strictly binding, we shall fail to bring out its real nature with anything
like completeness. That which Protestants and Catholics call
dogmas, are not only ecclesiastical doctrines, but they are

also: (1) theses expressed in abstract terms, forming together a unity, and fixing the contents of the Christian religion as a knowledge of God, of the world, and of the sacred history under the aspect of a proof of the truth. But (2) they have also emerged at a definite stage of the history of the Christian religion; they shew in their conception as such, and in many details, the influence of that stage, viz., the Greek period, and they have preserved this character in spite of all their reconstructions and additions in after periods. This view of dogma cannot be shaken by the fact that particular historical facts, miraculous or not miraculous are described as dogmas; for here they are regarded as such, only in so far as they have got the value of doctrines which have been inserted in the complete structure of doctrines and are, on the other hand, members of a chain of proofs, viz., proofs from prophecy.

But as soon as we perceive this, the parallel between the ecclesiastical dogmas and those of ancient schools of philosophy appears to be in point of form complete. The only difference is that revelation is here put as authority in the place of human knowledge, although the later philosophic schools appealed to revelation also. The theoretical as well as the practical doctrines which embraced the peculiar conception of the world and the ethics of the school, together with their rationale, were described in these schools as dogmas. Now, in so far as the adherents of the Christian religion possess dogmas in this sense, and form a community which has gained an understanding of its religious faith by analysis and by scientific definition and grounding, they appear as a great philosophic school in the ancient sense of the word. But they differ from such a school in so far as they have always eliminated the process of thought which has led to the dogma, looking upon the whole system of dogma as a revelation and therefore, even in respect of the reception of the dogma, at least at first, they have taken account not of the powers of human understanding, but of the Divine enlightenment which is bestowed on all the willing and the virtuous. In later times, indeed, the analogy was far more complete, in so far as the

Church reserved the full possession of dogma to a circle of consecrated and initiated individuals. Dogmatic Christianity is therefore a definite stage in the history of the development of Christianity. It corresponds to the antique mode of thought, but has nevertheless continued to a very great extent in the following epochs, though subject to great transformations. Dogmatic Christianity stands between Christianity as the religion of the Gospel, presupposing a personal experience and dealing with disposition and conduct, and Christianity as a religion of cultus, sacraments, ceremonial and obedience, in short of superstition, and it can be united with either the one or the other. In itself and in spite of all its mysteries it is always intellectual Christianity, and therefore there is always the danger here that as knowledge it may supplant religious faith, or connect it with a doctrine of religion, instead of with God and a living experience.

If then the discipline of the history of dogma is to be what its name purports, its object is the very dogma which is so formed, and its fundamental problem will be to discover how it has arisen. In the history of the canon our method of procedure has for long been to ask first of all, how the canon originated, and then to examine the changes through which it has passed. We must proceed in the same way with the history of dogma, of which the history of the canon is simply a part. Two objections will be raised against this. In the first place, it will be said that from the very first the Christian religion has included a definite religious faith as well as a definite ethic, and that therefore Christian dogma is as original as Christianity itself, so that there can be no question about a genesis, but only as to a development or alteration of dogma within the Church. Again it will be said, in the second place, that dogma as defined above, has validity only for a definite epoch in the history of the Church, and that it is therefore quite impossible to write a comprehensive history of dogma in the sense we have indicated.

As to the first objection, there can of course be no doubt that the Christian religion is founded on a message, the con-

tents of which are a definite belief in God and in Jesus Christ
whom he has sent, and that the promise of salvation is attached to this belief. But faith in the Gospel and the later dogmas of the Church are not related to each other as theme
and the way in which it is worked out, any more than the
dogma of the New Testament canon is only the explication
of the original reliance of Christians on the word of their
Lord and the continuous working of the Spirit; but in these
later dogmas an entirely new element has entered into the
conception of religion. The message of religion appears here
clothed in a knowledge of the world and of the ground of the
world which had already been obtained without any reference
to it, and therefore religion itself has here become a doctrine
which has, indeed, its certainty in the Gospel, but only in part
derives its contents from it, and which can also be appropriated by such as are neither poor in spirit nor weary
and heavy laden. Now, it may of course be shewn that a
philosophic conception of the Christian religion is possible,
and began to make its appearance from the very first, as in
the case of Paul. But the Pauline gnosis has neither been
simply indentified with the Gospel by Paul himself (1 Cor. III.
2 f.: XII. 3: Phil. I. 18) nor is it analogous to the later
dogma, not to speak of being indentical with it. The characteristic of this dogma is that it represents itself in no sense
as foolishness, but as wisdom, and at the same time desires to
be regarded as the contents of revelation itself. Dogma in its
conception and development is a work of the Greek spirit on
the soil of the Gospel. By comprehending in itself and giving
excellent expression to the religious conceptions contained in
Greek philosophy and the Gospel, together with its Old Testament basis; by meeting the search for a revelation as well as
the desire for a universal knowledge; by subordinating itself
to the aim of the Christian religion to bring a Divine life to
humanity as well as to the aim of philosophy to know the
world: it became the instrument by which the Church conquered the ancient world and educated the modern nations.
But this dogma—one cannot but admire its formation or

fail to regard it as a great achievement of the spirit, which
never again in the history of Christianity has made itself at
home with such freedom and boldness in religion—is the
product of a comparatively long history which needs to be
deciphered; for it is obscured by the completed dogma. The
Gospel itself is not dogma, for belief in the Gospel provides
room for knowledge only so far as it is a state of feeling and
course of action, that is a definite form of life. Between
practical faith in the Gospel and the historico-critical account
of the Christian religion and its history, a third element can
no longer be thrust in without its coming into conflict with
faith, or with the historical data—the only thing left is the
practical task of defending the faith. But a third element
has been thrust into the history of this religion, viz., dogma,
that is, the philosophical means which were used in early
times for the purpose of making the Gospel intelligible
have been fused with the contents of the Gospel and raised
to dogma. This dogma, next to the Church, has become a
real world power, the pivot in the history of the Christian
religion. The transformation of the Christian faith into dogma
is indeed no accident, but has its reason in the spiritual character of the Christian religion, which at all times will feel the
need of a scientific apologetic. [1]   But the question here is not
as to something indefinite and general, but as to the definite
dogma formed in the first centuries, and binding even yet.

This already touches on the second objection which was
raised above, that dogma, in the given sense of the word, was
too narrowly conceived, and could not in this conception be

---

[1] Weizsäcker, Apostolic Age, Vol. I. p. 123. "Christianity as religion is
absolutely inconceivable without theology; first of all, for the same
reasons which called forth the Pauline theology. As a religion it cannot
be separated from the religion of its founder, hence not from historical
knowledge. And as Monotheism and belief in a world purpose, it is the
religion of reason with the inextinguishable impulse of thought. The first
gentile Christians therewith gained the proud consciousness of a gnosis."
But of ecclesiastical Christianity which rests on dogma ready made, as
produced by an earlier epoch, this conception holds good only in a very
qualified way; and of the vigorous Christian piety of the earliest and of
every period, it may also be said that it no less feels the impulse to
think against reason than with reason.

applied throughout the whole history of the Church. This objection would only be justified, if our task were to carry the history of the development of dogma through the whole history of the Church. But the question is just whether we are right in proposing such a task. The Greek Church has no history of dogma after the seven great Councils, and it is incomparably more important to recognise this fact than to register the theologoumena which were later on introduced by individual Bishops and scholars in the East, who were partly influenced by the West. Roman Catholicism in its dogmas, though, as noted above, these at present do not very clearly characterise it, is to-day essentially—that is, so far as it is religion—what it was 1500 years ago, viz., Christianity as understood by the ancient world. The changes which dogma has experienced in the course of its development in western Catholicism are certainly deep and radical: they have, in point of fact, as has been indicated in the text above, modified the position of the Church towards Christianity as dogma. But as the Catholic Church herself maintains that she adheres to Christianity in the old dogmatic sense, this claim of hers cannot be contested. She has embraced new things and changed her relations to the old, but still preserved the old. But she has further developed new dogmas according to the scheme of the old. The decrees of Trent and of the Vatican are formally analogous to the old dogmas. Here, then, a history of dogma may really be carried forward to the present day without thereby shewing that the definition of dogma given above is too narrow to embrace the new doctrines. Finally, as to Protestantism, it has been briefly explained above why the changes in Protestant systems of doctrine are not to be taken up into the history of dogma. Strictly speaking, dogma, as dogma, has had no development in Protestantism, inasmuch as a secret note of interrogation has been here associated with it from the very beginning. But the old dogma has continued to be a power in it, because of its tendency to look back and to seek for authorities in the past, and partly in the original unmodified form. The dogmas of

the fourth and fifth centuries have more influence to-day in
wide circles of Protestant Churches than all the doctrines
which are concentrated around justification by faith. Deviations
from the latter are borne comparatively easy, while as a rule,
deviations from the former are followed by notice to quit the
Christian communion, that is, by excommunication. The historian of to-day would have no difficulty in answering the
question whether the power of Protestantism as a Church lies
at present in the elements which it has in common with the
old dogmatic Christianity, or in that by which it is distinguished
from it. Dogma, that is to say, that type of Christianity
which was formed in ecclesiastical antiquity, has not been suppressed even in Protestant Churches, has really not been
modified or replaced by a new conception of the Gospel.
But, on the other hand, who could deny that the Reformation
began to disclose such a conception, and that this new conception was related in a very different way to the traditional
dogma from that of the new propositions of Augustine to the
dogmas handed down to him? Who could further call in
question that, in consequence of the reforming impulse in
Protestantism, the way was opened up for a conception which
does not identify Gospel and dogma, which does not disfigure
the latter by changing or paring down its meaning while
failing to come up to the former? But the historian who has
to describe the formation and changes of dogma can take no
part in these developments. It is a task by itself more
rich and comprehensive than that of the historian of dogma,
to portray the diverse conceptions that have been formed of
the Christian religion, to portray how strong men and weak
men, great and little minds have explained the Gospel outside
and inside the frame-work of dogma, and how under the
cloak, or in the province of dogma, the Gospel has had its
own peculiar history. But the more limited theme must not
be put aside. For it can in no way be conducive to historical
knowledge to regard as indifferent the peculiar character of
the expression of Christian faith as dogma, and allow the
history of dogma to be absorbed in a general history of the

various conceptions of Christianity. Such a "liberal" view would not agree either with the teaching of history or with the actual situation of the Protestant Churches of the present day: for it is, above all, of crucial importance to perceive that it is a peculiar stage in the development of the human spirit which is described by dogma. On this stage, parallel with dogma and inwardly united with it, stands a definite psychology, metaphysic and natural philosophy, as well as a view of history of a definite type. This is the conception of the world obtained by antiquity after almost a thousand years' labour, and it is the same connection of theoretic perceptions and practical ideals which it accomplished. This stage on which the Christian religion has also entered we have in no way as yet transcended, though science has raised itself above it. [1] But the Christian religion, as it was not born of the culture of the ancient world, is not for ever chained to it. The form and the new contents which the Gospel received when it entered into that world have only the same guarantee of endurance as that world itself. And that endurance is limited. We must indeed be on our guard against taking episodes for decisive crises. But every episode carries us forward, and retrogressions are unable to undo that progress. The Gospel since the Reformation, in spite of retrograde movements which have not been wanting, is working itself out of the forms which it was once compelled to assume, and a true comprehension of its history will also contribute to hasten this process.

1. The definition given above, p. 17: "Dogma in its conception and development is a work of the Greek spirit on

---

[1] In this sense it is correct to class dogmatic theology as historical theology, as Schleiermacher has done. If we maintain that for practical reasons it must be taken out of the province of historical theology, then we must make it part of practical theology. By dogmatic theology here, we understand the exposition of Christianity in the form of Church doctrine, as it has been shaped since the second century. As distinguished from it, a branch of theological study must be conceived which harmonises the historical exposition of the Gospel with the general state of knowledge of the time. The Church can as little dispense with such a discipline as there can be a Christianity which does not account to itself for its basis and spiritual contents.

the soil of the Gospel," has frequently been distorted by my
critics, as they have suppressed the words "on the soil of the
Gospel." But these words are decisive. The foolishness of
identifying dogma and Greek philosophy never entered my
mind; on the contrary, the peculiarity of ecclesiastical dogma
seemed to me to lie in the very fact that, on the one hand,
it gave expression to Christian Monotheism and the central
significance of the person of Christ, and, on the other hand,
comprehended this religious faith and the historical knowledge
connected with it in a philosophic system. I have given
quite as little ground for the accusation that I look upon
the whole development of the history of dogma as a patho-
logical process within the history of the Gospel. I do not
even look upon the history of the origin of the Papacy as
such a process, not to speak of the history of dogma. But
the perception that "everything must happen as it has happened"
does not absolve the historian from the task of ascertaining
the powers which have formed the history, and distinguishing
between original and later, permanent and transitory, nor from
the duty of stating his own opinion.

2. Sabatier has published a thoughtful treatise on "Christian
Dogma: its Nature and its Development." I agree with the
author in this, that in dogma—rightly understood—two
elements are to be distinguished, the religious proceeding from
the experience of the individual or from the religious spirit
of the Church, and the intellectual or theoretic. But I regard
as false the statement which he makes, that the intellectual
element in dogma is only the symbolical expression of religious experience. The intellectual element is itself again to
be differentiated. On the one hand, it certainly is the attempt
to give expression to religious feeling, and so far is symbolical; but, on the other hand, within the Christian religion it
belongs to the essence of the thing itself, inasmuch as this
not only awakens feeling, but has a quite definite content
which determines and should determine the feeling. In this
sense Christianity without dogma, that is, without a clear
expression of its content, is inconceivable. But that does not

justify the unchangeable permanent significance of that dogma which has once been formed under definite historical conditions.

3. The word "dogmas" (Christian dogmas) is, if I see correctly, used among us in three different senses, and hence spring all manner of misconceptions and errors. By dogmas are denoted: (1) The historical doctrines of the Church. (2) The historical facts on which the Christian religion is reputedly or actually founded. (3) Every definite exposition of the contents of Christianity is described as dogmatic. In contrast with this the attempt has been made in the following presentation to use dogma only in the sense first stated. When I speak, therefore, of the decomposition of dogma, I mean by that, neither the historical facts which really establish the Christian religion, nor do I call in question the necessity for the Christian and the Church to have a creed. My criticism refers not to the general genus dogma, but to the species, viz., the defined dogma, as it was formed on the soil of the ancient world, and is still a power, though under modifications.

§ 2. History of the History of Dogma.

The history of dogma as a historical and critical discipline had its origin in the last century through the works of Mosheim, C. W. F. Walch, Ernesti, Lessing and Semler. Lange gave to the world in 1796 the first attempt at a history of dogma as a special branch of theological study. The theologians of the Early and Mediæval Churches have only transmitted histories of Heretics and of Literature, regarding dogma as unchangeable. [1] This presupposition is so much a part of the nature of Catholicism that it has been maintained till the present day. It is therefore impossible for a Catholic to make a free, impartial and

---

1 See Eusebius' preface to his Church History. Eusebius in this work set himself a comprehensive task, but in doing so he never in the remotest sense thought of a history of dogma. In place of that we have a history of men "who from generation to generation proclaimed the word of God orally or by writing," and a history of those who by their passion for novelties, plunged themselves into the greatest errors.

scientific investigation of the history of dogma. ¹ There have,
indeed, at almost all times before the Reformation, been critical
efforts in the domain of Christianity, especially of western
Christianity, efforts which in some cases have led to the proof
of the novelty and inadmissibility of particular dogmas. But,
as a rule, these efforts were of the nature of a polemic against
the dominant Church. They scarcely prepared the way for,
far less produced a historical view of, dogmatic tradition.² The
progress of the sciences ³ and the conflict with Protestantism
could here, for the Catholic Church, have no other effect than
that of leading to the collecting, with great learning, of material
for the history of dogma, ⁴ the establishing of the *consensus patrum et doctorum*, the exhibition of the necessity of a continuous
explication of dogma, and the description of the history of
heresies pressing in from without, regarded now as unheard-

1 See for example, B. Schwane, Dogmengesch. d. Vornicänischen Zeit,
1862, where the sense in which dogmas have no historical side is first
expounded, and then it is shewn that dogmas, "notwithstanding, present
a certain side which permits a historical consideration, because in point
of fact they have gone through historical developments." But these historical developments present themselves simply either as solemn pro-
mulgations and explications, or as private theological speculations.

2 If we leave out of account the Marcionite gnostic criticism of ecclesiastical Christianity, Paul of Samosata and Marcellus of Ancyra may be
mentioned as men who, in the earliest period, criticised the apologetic
Alexandrian theology which was being naturalised (see the remarkable
statement of Marcellus in Euseb. C. Marc. 1.4: τὸ τοῦ δόγματος ὄνομα τῆς
ἀνθρωπίνης ἔχεται βουλῆς τε καὶ γνώμης κ.τ.λ., which I have chosen as the
motto of this book). We know too little of Stephen Gobarus (VI. cent.)
to enable us to estimate his review of the doctrine of the Church and
its development (Photius Bibl. 232). With regard to the middle ages
(Abelard "Sic et Non"), see Reuter, Gesch. der relig. Aufklärung im MA.,
1875. Hahn Gesch. der Ketzer, especially in the 11th, 12th and 13th centuries,
3 vols., 1845. Keller, Die Reformation und die alteren Reform-Parteien, 1885.

3 See Voigt, Die Wiederbelebung des classischen Alterthums. 2 vols.,
1881, especially vol. II. p. 1 ff. 363 ff. 494 ff. ("Humanism and the science of
history"). The direct importance of humanism for illuminating the history
of the middle ages is very little, and least of all for the history of the
Church and of dogma. The only prominent works here are those of
Saurentius Valla and Erasmus. The criticism of the scholastic dogmas
of the Church and the Pope began as early as the 12th century. For
the attitude of the Renaissance to religion, see Burckhardt, Die Cultur
der Renaissance. 2 vols., 1877.

4 Baronius, Annals Eccles. XII. vol. 1588-1607. Chief work: Dionysius
Petavius, Opus de theologicis dogmatibus. 4 vols. (incomplete) 1644-1650.
See further Thomassin, Dogmata theologica. 3 vols. 1684-1689.

of novelties, and again as old enemies in new masks. The modern Jesuit-Catholic historian indeed exhibits, in certain circumstances, a manifest indifference to the task of establishing the *semper idem* in the faith of the Church, but this indifference is at present regarded with disfavour, and, besides, is only an apparent one, as the continuous though inscrutable guidance of the Church by the infallible teaching of the Pope is the more emphatically maintained. [1]

It may be maintained that the Reformation opened the way for a critical treatment of the history of dogma. [2] But even

1 See Holtzmann, Kanon und Tradition, 1859. Hase, Handbuch der protest. Polemik, 1878. Joh. Delitzsch, Das Lehrsystem der röm. Kirche, 1875. New revelations, however, are rejected, and bold assumptions leading that way are not favoured: See Schwane, above work p. 11: "The content of revelation is not enlarged by the decisions or teaching of the Church, nor are new revelations added in course of time.... Christian truth cannot therefore in its content be completed by the Church, nor has she ever claimed the right of doing so, but always where new designations or forms of dogma became necessary for the putting down of error or the instruction of the faithful, she would always teach what she had received in Holy scripture or in the oral tradition of the Apostles". Recent Catholic accounts of the history of dogma are Klee. Lehrbuch der D.G. 2 vols., 1837, (Speculative). Schwane, Dogmengesch. der Vornicänischen Zeit, 1862, der patrist. Zeit, 1869; der Mittleren Zeit, 1882. Bach, Die D.G. des MA. 1873. There is a wealth of material for the history of dogma in Kuhn's Dogmatik, as well as in the great controversial writings occasioned by the celebrated work of Bellarmin; Disputationes de controversiis Christianæ fidei adversus hujus temporis hæreticos, 1581-1593. It need not be said that, in spite of their inability to treat the history of dogma historically and critically, much may be learned from these works, and some other striking monographs of Roman Catholic scholars. But everything in history that is fitted to shake the high antiquity and unanimous attestation of the Catholic dogmas, becomes here a problem, the solution of which is demanded, though indeed its carrying out often requires a very exceptional intellectual subtlety.

2 Historical interest in Protestantism has grown up around the questions as to the power of the Pope, the significance of Councils. or the Scripturalness of the doctrines set up by them, and about the meaning of the Lord's supper, of the conception of it by the Church Fathers; (see Œcolampadius and Melanchthon.) Protestants were too sure that the doctrine of justification was taught in the scriptures to feel any need of seeking proofs for it by studies in the history of dogma, and Luther also dispensed with the testimony of history for the dogma of the Lord's supper. The task of shewing how far and in what way Luther and the Reformers compounded with history has not even yet been taken up. And yet there may be found in Luther's writings surprising and excellent critical comments on the history of dogma and the theology of the Fathers, as well as genial conceptions which have certainly remained inoperative; see especially the treatise "Von den Conciliis und Kirchen," and his judgment on different Church Fathers. In the first edition of the *Loci* of Melanchthon we have also critical material for estimating the old systems of dogma. Calvin's

in Protestant Churches, at first, historical investigations remained under the ban of the confessional system of doctrine and were used only for polemics. [1] Church history itself up to the 18th century was not regarded as a theological discipline in the strict sense of the word; and the history of dogma existed only within the sphere of dogmatics as a collection of testimonies to the truth, *theologia patristica.* It was only after the material had been prepared in the course of the 16th and 17th centuries by scholars of the various Church parties, and, above all, by excellent editions of the Fathers, [2] and after Pietism had exhibited the difference between Christianity and Ecclesiasticism, and had begun to treat the traditional confessional structure of doctrine with indifference, [3] that a critical investigation was entered on.

The man who was the Erasmus of the 18th century, neither orthodox nor pietistic, nor rationalistic, but capable of appreciating all these tendencies; familiar with English, French and Italian literature; influenced by the spirit of the new English

depreciatory estimate of the Trinitarian and Christological Formula, which, however, he retracted at a later period is well known.

1 Protestant Church history was brought into being by the Interim, Flacius being its Father; see his Catalogus Testium Veritatis, and the so-called Magdeburg Centuries, 1559-1574; also Jundt., Les Centuries de Magdebourg. Paris, 1883. Von Engelhardt (Christenthum Justin's, p. 9 ff.) has drawn attention to the estimate of Justin in the Centuries, and has justly insisted on the high importance of this first attempt at a criticism of the Church Fathers. Kliefoth (Einl. in d. D.G. 1839) has the merit of pointing out the somewhat striking judgment of A. Hyperius on the history of dogma. Chemnitz, Examen concilii Tridentini, 1565. Forbesius a Corse (a Scotsman). Instructiones historico-theologiæ de doctrina Christiana, 1645.

2 The learning, the diligence in collecting, and the carefulness of the Benedictines and Maurians, as well as of English, Dutch and French theologians, such as Casaubon, Vossius, Pearson, Dalläus, Spanheim, Grabe, Basnage, etc have never since been equalled, far less surpassed. Even in the literary, historical and higher criticism these scholars have done splendid work, so far as the confessional 'dogmas did not come into question.

3 See especially, G. Arnold, Unpartheyische Kirchen- und Ketzerhistorie, 1699: also Baur, Epochen der kirchlichen Geschichtsschreibung, p. 84 ff ; Floring, G. Arnold als Kirchenhistoriker. Darmstadt, 1883. The latter determines correctly the measure of Arnold's importance. His work was the direct preparation for an impartial examination of the history of dogma. however partial it was in itself. Pietism, here and there, after Spener, declared war against scholastic dogmatics as a hindrance to piety, and in doing so broke the ban under which the knowledge of history lay captive.

Science, [1] while avoiding all statements of it that would endanger positive Christianity: John Lorenz Mosheim, treated Church history in the spirit of his great teacher Leibnitz, [2] and by impartial analysis, living reproduction, and methodical artistic form raised it for the first time to the rank of a science. In his monographic works also, he endeavours to examine impartially the history of dogma, and to acquire the historic standpoint between the estimate of the orthodox dogmatists and that of Gottfried Arnold. Mosheim, averse to all fault-finding and polemic, and abhorring theological crudity as much as pietistic narrowness and undevout Illuminism, aimed at an actual correct knowledge of history, in accordance with the principle of Leibnitz, that the valuable elements which are everywhere to be found in history must be sought out and recognised. And the richness and many-sidedness of his mind qualified him for gaining such a knowledge. But his latitudinarian dogmatic stand-point as well as the anxiety to awaken no controversy or endanger the gradual naturalising of a new science and culture, caused him to put aside the most important problems of the history of dogma and devote his attention to political Church history as well as to the more indifferent historical questions. The opposition of two periods which he endeavoured peacefully to reconcile could not in this way be permanently set aside. [3] In Mosheim's sense, but without the

1 The investigations of the so-called English Deists about the Christian religion contain the first, and to some extent a very significant free-spirited attempt at a critical view of the history óf dogma (see Lechler, History of English Deism, 1841). But the criticism is an abstract, rarely a historical one. Some very learned works bearing on the history of dogma were written in England against the position of the Deists, especially by Lardner: see also at an earlier time Bull, Defensio fidei nic.

2 Calixtus of Helmstädt was the forerunner of Leibnitz with regard to Church history. But the merit of having recognised the main problem of the history of dogma does not belong to Calixtus. By pointing out what Protestantism and Catholicism had in common he did not in any way clear up the historico-critical problem. On the other hand, the *Consensus repetitus* of the Wittenberg theologians shews what fundamental questions Calixtus had already stirred.

3 Among the numerous historical writings of Mosheim may be mentioned specially his Dissert. ad hist. Eccles. pertinentes. 2 vols. 1731-1741, as well as the work: "De rebus Christianorum ante Constantinum M. Commentarii," 1753: see also "Institutiones hist Eccl." last Edition, 1755.

spirit of that great man, C. W. F. Walch taught on the subject
and described the religious controversies of the Church with
an effort to be impartial, and has thus made generally accessible the abundant material collected by the diligence of earlier
scholars. [1] Walch, moreover, in the "Gedanken von der Geschichte der Glaubenslehre," 1756, gave the impulse that was
needed to fix attention on the history of dogma as a special
discipline. The stand-point which he took up was still that
of subjection to ecclesiastical dogma, but without confessional
narrowness. Ernesti in his programme of the year 1759. "De
theologiæ historicæ et dogmaticæ conjungendæ necessitate,"
gave eloquent expression to the idea that Dogmatic is a positive science which has to take its material from history, but
that history itself requires a devoted and candid study, on
account of our being separated from the earlier epochs by a
complicated tradition. [2] He has also shewn in his celebrated
"Antimuratorius" that an impartial and critical investigation
of the problems of the history of dogma, might render the
most effectual service to the polemic against the errors of
Romanism. Besides, the greater part of the dogmas were already
unintelligible to Ernesti, and yet during his lifetime the way
was opened up for that tendency in theology, which prepared
in Germany by Chr. Thomasius, supported by English writers,
drew the sure principles of faith and life from what is called
reason, and therefore was not only indifferent to the system

1 Walch, "Entwurf einer vollständigen Historie der Ketzereien, Spal-
tungen und Religionsstreitigkeiten bis auf die Zeiten der Reformation."
11 Thle (incomplete), 1762-1785. See also his "Entwurf einer vollständigen
Historie der Kirchenversammlungen" 1759, as well as numerous monographs
on the history of dogma. Such were already produced by the older
Walch, whose "Histor. theol. Einleitung in die Religionsstreitigkeiten der
Ev. Luth. Kirche," 5 vols. 1730-1739, and "Histor.-theol. Einleit. in die
Religionsstreitigkeiten welche sonderlich ausser der Ev. Luth. Kirche
entstanden sind 5 Thle", 1733-1736, had already put polemics behind the
knowledge of history (see Gass. "Gesch. der protest. Dogmatik," 3rd Vol.
p. 205 ff).

2 Opusc. p. 576 f.: "Ex quo fit, ut nullo modo in theologicis, quæ omnia e
libris antiquis hebraicis, græcis, latinis ducuntur, possit aliquis bene in defin-
iendo versari et a peccatis multis et magnis sibi cavere, nisi litteras et his-
toriam assumat". The title of a programme of Crusius, Ernesti's opponent,
"De dogmatum Christianorum historia cum probatione dogmatum non con-
fundenda," 1770, is significant of the new insight which was steadily
making way.

of dogma, but felt it more and more to be the tradition of unreason and of darkness. Of the three requisites of a historian; knowledge of his subject, candid criticism, and a capacity for finding himself at home in foreign interests and ideas, the Rationalistic Theologians who had outgrown Pietism and passed through the school of the English Deists and of Wolf, no longer possessed the first, a knowledge of the subject, to the same extent as some scholars of the earlier generation. The second, free criticism, they possessed in the high degree guaranteed by the conviction of having a rational religion; the third, the power of comprehension, only in a very limited measure. They had lost the idea of positive religion, and with it a living and just conception of the history of religion.

In the history of thought there is always need for an apparently disproportionate expenditure of power, in order to produce an advance in the development. And it would appear as if a certain self-satisfied narrow-mindedness within the progressing ideas of the present, as well as a great measure of inability even to understand the past and recognise its own dependence on it, must make its appearance, in order that a whole generation may be freed from the burden of the past. It needed the absolute certainty which Rationalism had found in the religious philosophy of the age, to give sufficient courage to subject to historical criticism the central dogmas on which the Protestant system as well as the Catholic finally rests, the dogmas of the canon and inspiration on the one hand, and of the Trinity and Christology on the other. The work of Lessing in this respect had no great results. We to-day see in his theological writings the most important contribution to the understanding of the earliest history of dogma, which that period supplies; but we also understand why its results were then so trifling. This was due, not only to the fact that Lessing was no theologian by profession, or that his historical observations were couched in aphorisms, but because like Leibnitz and Mosheim, he had a capacity for appreciating the history of religion which forbade him to do violence to that history or to sit in judgment on it, and because his philosophy in its bearings on the case allowed him to seek no more from his materials than an assured understanding of them, in a word again, because he was no theologian. The Rationalists, on the other hand, who within certain limits were no less his opponents than the orthodox, derived the strength of their opposition to the systems of dogma, as the Apologists of the second century had already done with regard to polytheism, from their religious belief and their inability to estimate these systems historically. That, however, is only the first impression which one gets here from the history, and it is everywhere modified by other impressions. In the first place, there is no mistaking a certain latitudinarianism in several prominent theologians of the rationalistic tendency. Moreover, the attitude to the canon was still frequently, in virtue of the Protestant principle of scripture, an uncertain one, and it was here chiefly that the different types of rational supernaturalism were developed. Then, with all subjection to the dogmas of Natural religion, the desire for a real true knowledge was unfettered and powerfully excited. Finally, very significant attempts were made by some rationalistic theologians to explain in a real historical way the phenomena of the history of dogma, and to put an authentic and historical view of that history in the place of barren pragmatic or philosophic categories.

The special zeal with which the older rationalism applied itself to the investigation of the canon, either putting aside the history of dogma, or treating it merely in the frame-work of Church history, has only been of advantage for the treatment of our subject. It first began to be treated with thoroughness when the historical and critical interests had become more powerful than the rationalistic. After the important labours of Semler which here, above all, have wrought in the interests of freedom, [1] and after some monographs on the history

1 Semler, Einleitung zu Baumgartens evang. Glaubenslehre, 1759: also Geschichte der Glaubenslehre, zu Baumgartens Untersuch. theol. Streitigkeiten, 1762-1764. Semler paved the way for the view that dogmas have arisen and been gradually developed under definite historical conditions. He was the first to grasp the problem of the relation of Catholicism to early christianity, because he freed the early Christian documents from the fetters of the Canon. Schröckh (Christl. Kirchengesch., 1786,) in

of dogma, [1] S. G. Lange for the first time treated the history of dogma as a special subject. [2] Unfortunately, his comprehensively planned and carefully written work, which shews a real understanding of the early history of dogma, remains incomplete. Consequently, W. Münscher, in his learned manual, which was soon followed by his compendium of the history of dogma, was the first to produce a complete presentation of our subject. [3] Münscher's compendium is a counterpart to Giesler's Church history; it shares with that the merit of drawing from the sources, intelligent criticism and impartiality, but with a thorough knowledge of details it fails to impart a real conception of the development of ecclesiastical dogma. The division of the material into particular *loci*, which, in three sections, is carried through the whole history of the Church, makes insight into the whole Christian conception of the different epochs impossible, and the prefixed "General History of Dogma," is far too sketchily treated to make up for that

the spirit of Semler described with impartiality and care the changes of the dogmas.

1 Rössler, Lehrbegriff der Christlichen Kirche in den 3 ersten Jahrh. 1775; also, Arbeiten by Burscher, Heinrich, Stäudlin, etc., see especially, Löffler's "Abhandlung welche eine kurze Darstellung der Entstehungsart der Dreieinigkeit enthält, 1792, in the translation of Souverain's Le Platonisme devoilé, 1700. The question as to the Platonism of the Fathers, this fundamental question of the history of dogma, was raised even by Luther and Flacius, and was very vigorously debated at the end of the 17th and beginning of the 18th centuries, after the Socinians had already affirmed it strongly. The question once more emerges on German soil in the church history of G. Arnold, but cannot be said to have received the attention it deserves in the 150 years that have followed (see the literature of the controversy in Tzschirner, Fall des Heidenthums, p. 580 f.). Yet the problem was first thrust aside by the speculative view of the history of christianity

2 Lange. Ausführ. Gesch. der Dogmen, oder der Glaubenslehre der Christl. Kirche nach den Kirchenväter ausgearbeitet. 1796.

3 Münscher, Handb. d. Christl. D. G. 4 vols. first 6 Centuries 1797-1809; Lehrbuch, 1st Edit. 1811; 3rd. Edit. edited by v Cölln, Hupfeld and Neudecker, 1832-1838. Planck's epoch-making work: Gesch. der Veränderungen und der Bildung unseres protestantischen Lehrbegriffs. 6 vols. 1791-1800, had already for the most part appeared. Contemporary with Münscher are Wundemann, Gesch. d. Christl. Glaubenslehren vom Zeitalter des Athanasius bis auf Gregor. d. Gr. 2 Thle. 1789-1799; Münter, Handbuch der alteren Christl. D. G. hrsg. von Ewers, 2 vols. 1802-1804; Stäudlin, Lehrbuch der Dogmatik und Dogmengeschichte, 1800. last Edition 1822, and Beck, Comment. hist. decretorum religionis Christianæ, 1801.

defect. Finally, the connection between the development of dogma and the general ideas of the time is not sufficiently attended to. A series of manuals followed the work of Mün-scher, but did not materially advance the study. [1] The compendium of Baumgarten Crusius, [2] and that of F. K. Meier, [3] stand out prominently among them. The work of the former is distinguished by its independent learning as well as by the discernment of the author that the centre of gravity of the subject lies in the so-called general history of dogma. [4] The work of Meier goes still further, and accurately perceives that the division into a general and special history of dogma must be altogether given up, while it is also characterised by an accurate setting and proportional arrangement of the facts. [5]

The great spiritual revolution at the beginning of our century, which must in every respect be regarded as a reaction against the efforts of the rationalistic epoch, changed also the conceptions of the Christian religion and its history. It appears therefore plainly in the treatment of the history of dogma. The advancement and deepening of Christian life, the zealous study of the past, the new philosophy which no longer thrust history aside, but endeavoured to appreciate it in all its phe-

1 Augusti, Lehrb. d. Christl. D. G. 1805. 4 Edit. 1835. Berthold, Handb. der D. G. 2 vols. 1822-1823. Schickedanz, Versuch einer Gesch. d. Christl. Glaubenslehre etc. 1827. Ruperti, Geschichte der Dogmen, 1831. Lenz, Gesch. der Christl. Dogmen. 2 parts. 1834-1835. J. G. V. Engelhardt, Dogmengesch. 1839. See also Giesler, Dogmengesch. 2 vols. edited by Redepenning, 1855: also Illgen, Ueber den Werth der Christl. D. G. 1817.

2 Baumgarten Crusius, Lehrb. d. Christl. D. G. 1852: also compendium d. Christl. D. G. 2 parts 1830-1846, the second part edited by Hase.

3 Meier, Lehrb. d. D. G. 1840. 2nd Edit. revised by G. Baur 1854.

4 The "Special History of Dogma" in Baumgarten Crusius, in which every particular dogma is by itself pursued through the whole history of the Church, is of course entirely unfruitful. But even the opinions which are given in the "General History of Dogma," are frequently very far from the mark :Cf., e. g., § 14 and p. 67), which is the more surprising as no one can deny that he takes a scholarly view of history.

5 Meier's Lehrbuch is formally and materially a very important piece of work, the value of which has not been sufficiently recognised, because the author followed neither the track of Neander nor of Baur. Besides the excellences noted in the text, may be further mentioned, that almost everywhere Meier has distinguished correctly between the history of dogma and the history of theology, and has given an account only of the former.

nomena as the history of the spirit, all these factors co-operated in begetting a new temper, and accordingly, a new
estimate of religion proper and of its history. There were
three tendencies in theology that broke up rationalism; that
which was indentified with the names of Schleiermacher and
Neander, that of the Hegelians, and that of the Confession-
alists. The first two were soon divided into a right and a left,
in so far as they included conservative and critical interests
from their very commencement. The conservative elements
have been used for building up the modern confessionalism,
which in its endeavours to go back to the Reformers has never
actually got beyond the theology of the Formula of Concord,
the stringency of which it has no doubt abolished by new
theologoumena and concessions of all kinds. All these tendencies have in common the effort to gain a real comprehension of history and be taught by it, that is, to allow the idea
of development to obtain its proper place, and to comprehend
the power and sphere of the individual. In this and in the
deeper conception of the nature and significance of positive
religion, lay the advance beyond Rationalism. And yet the
wish to understand history, has in great measure checked the
effort to obtain a true knowledge of it, and the respect for
history as the greatest of teachers, has not resulted in that
supreme regard for facts which distinguished the critical rationalism. The speculative pragmatism, which, in the Hegelian
School, was put against the "lower pragmatism," and was
rigorously carried out with the view of exhibiting the unity
of history, not only neutralised the historical material, in so
far as its concrete definiteness was opposed, as phenomenon,
to the essence of the matter, but also curtailed it in a suspicious way, as may be seen, for example, in the works of
Baur. Moreover, the universal historical suggestions which the
older history of dogma had given were not at all, or only
very little regarded. The history of dogma was, as it were,
shut out by the watchword of the immanent development of
the spirit in Christianity. The disciples of Hegel, both of the
right and of the left, were, and still are, agreed in this watch-

word, [1] the working out of which, including an apology for the
course of the history of dogma, must be for the advancement
of conservative theology. But at the basis of the statement
that the history of Christianity is the history of the spirit,
there lay further a very one-sided conception of the nature
of religion, which confirmed the false idea that religion is
theology. It will always, however, be the imperishable merit
of Hegel's great disciple, F. Chr. Baur, in theology, that he
was the first who attempted to give a uniform general idea
of the history of dogma, and to live through the whole process
in himself, without renouncing the critical acquisitions of the
18th century. [2] His brilliantly written manual of the history of
dogma, in which the history of this branch of theological
science is relatively treated with the utmost detail, is, however,
in material very meagre, and shews in the very first proposition of the historical presentation an abstract view of history. [3]
Neander, whose "Christliche Dogmengeschichte," 1857, is distinguished by the variety of its points of view, and keen apprehension of particular forms of doctrine, shews a far more lively

1 Biedermann (Christl. Dogmatik. 2 Edit. 1 vol. p. 332 f.): says, "The history
of the development of the Dogma of the Person of Christ will bring before
us step by step the ascent of faith in the Gospel of Jesus Christ to its metaphysical basis in the nature of his person. This was the quite normal and necessary way of actual faith, and is not to be reckoned as a confused mixture of
heterogeneous philosophical opinions.... The only thing taken from the ideas
of contemporary philosophy was the special material of consciousnes in
which the doctrine of Christ's Divinity was at any time expressed. The process of this doctrinal development was an inward necessary one."
2 Baur, Lehrbuch der Christl. D. G. 1847. 3rd Edit. 1867: also Vorles.
über die Christl. D. G. edited by F. Baur, 1865-68. Further the Monographs,
"Ueber die Christl. Lehre v.d. Versöhnung in ihrer gesch. Entw." 1838: "Ueber
die Christl. Lehre v. d. Dreieinigkeit u. d. Menschwerdung." 1841. etc. D. F.
Strauss preceded him with his work: Die Christl. Glaubenslehre in ihrer
gesch. Entw. 2 vols. 1840-41. From the stand-point of the Hegelian right we
have: Marheineke, Christl. D. G. edited by Matthias and Vatke, 1849. From the
same stand-point, though at the same time influenced by Schleiermacher,
Dorner wrote "The History of the Person of Christ."
3 See p. 63: "As Christianity appeared in contrast with Judaism and
Heathenism, and could only represent a new and peculiar form of the religious
consciousness in distinction from both, reducing the contrasts of both to a
unity in itself, so also the first difference of tendencies developing themselves
within Christianity, must be determined by the relation in which it stood to
Judaism on the one hand, and to Heathenism on the other." Compare also
the very characteristic introduction to the first volume of the "Vorlesungen".

and therefore a far more just conception of the Christian religion. But the general plan of the work, (General history of dogma—*loci*, and these according to the established scheme), proves that Neander has not succeeded in giving real expression to the historical character of the study, and in attaining a clear insight into the progress of the development. [1]

Kliefoth's thoughtful and instructive, "Einleitung in die Dogmengeschichte," 1839, contains the programme for the conception of the history of dogma characteristic of the modern confessional theology. In this work the Hegelian view of history, not without being influenced by Schleiermacher, is so represented as to legitimise a return to the theology of the Fathers. In the successive great epochs of the Church several circles of dogmas have been successively fixed, so that the respective doctrines have each time been adequately formulated. [2] Disturbances of the development are due to the influence of sin. Apart from this, Kliefoth's conception is in point of form equal to that of Baur and Strauss, in so far as they also have considered the theology represented by themselves as the goal of the whole historical development. The only distinction is that, according to them, the next following stage always cancels the preceding, while according to Kliefoth, who, moreover, has no desire to give effect to mere traditionalism, the new knowledge is added to the old. The new edifice of true historical knowledge, according to Kliefoth, is raised on the ruins of Traditionalism, Scholasticism, Pietism, Rationalism and Mysticism. Thomasius (Das Bekenntniss der evang.-luth. Kirche in der Consequenz seines Princips, 1848) has,

1 Hagenbach's Manual of the history of dogma, might be put alongside of Neander's work. It agrees with it both in plan and spirit. But the material of the history of dogma, which it offers in superabundance, seems far less connectedly worked out than by Neander. In Shedd's history of Christian doctrine the Americans possess a presentation of the history of dogma worth noting. 2 vols. 3 Edit. 1883. The work of Fr. Bonifas. Hist. des Dogmes. 2 vols. 1886. appeared after the death of the author and is not important.

2 No doubt Kliefoth also maintains for each period a stage of the disintegration of dogma, but this is not to be understood in the ordinary sense of the word. Besides, there are ideas in this introduction which would hardly obtain the approval of their author to-day.

after the example of Sartorius, attempted to justify by history the
Lutheran confessional system of doctrine from another side, by
representing it as the true mean between Catholicism and the
Reformed Spiritualism.   This conception has found much approbation in the circles of Theologians related to Thomasius, as
against the Union Theology.   But Thomasius is entitled to the
merit of having produced a Manual of the history of dogma which
represents in the most worthy manner, [1] the Lutheran confessional
view of the history of dogma.   The introduction, as well as
the selection and arrangement of his material, shews that
Thomasius has learned much from Baur.   The way in which
he distinguishes between central and peripheral dogmas is,
accordingly, not very appropriate, especially for the earliest
period.   The question as to the origin of dogma and theology
is scarcely even touched by him.   But he has an impression
that the central dogmas contain for every period the whole of
Christianity, and that they must therefore be apprehended in this
sense. [2]   The presentation is dominated throughout by the idea
of the self-explication of dogma, though a malformation has
to be admitted for the middle ages; [3] and therefore the for-

---

1 Thomasius' Die Christl. Dogmengesch. als Entwickel. Gesch. des
Kirchl. Lehrbegriffs. 2 vols. 1874-76. 2nd Edit. intelligently and carefully
edited by Bonwetsch. and Seeberg, 1887. (Seeberg has produced almost
a new work in vol. II). From the same stand-point is the manual of the
history of dogma by H. Schmid, 1859, (in 4th Ed. revised and transformed
into an excellent collection of passages from the sources by Hauck, 1887),
as well as the Luther. Dogmatik (Vol. II. 1864: Der Kirchenglaube) of
Kahnis, which, however, subjects particular dogmas to a freer criticism.
2 See Vol. I. p. 14.
3 See Vol. I. p. 11. " The first period treats of the development of the
great main dogmas which were to become the basis of the further development (the Patristic age). The problem of the second period was,
partly to work up this material theologically, and partly to develop it.
But this development, under the influence of the Hierarchy, fell into false
paths, and became partly, at least, corrupt (the age of Scholasticism),
and therefore a reformation was necessary. It was reserved for this third
period to carry back the doctrinal formation which had become abnormal,
to the old sound paths, and on the other hand, in virtue of the regeneration of the Church which followed, to deepen it and fashion it according to that form which it got in the doctrinal systems of the Evangelic
Church, while the remaining part fixed its own doctrine in the decrees of
Trent (period of the Reformation)". This view of history, which, from
the Christian stand-point, will allow absolutely nothing to be said against
the doctrinal formation of the early Church, is a retrogression from the

mation of dogma is almost everywhere justified as the testimony of the Church represented as completely hypostatised, and the outlook on the history of the time is put into the background. But narrow and insufficient as the complete view here is, the excellences of the work in details are great, in respect of exemplary clearness of presentation, and the discriminating knowledge and keen comprehension of the author for religious problems. The most important work done by Thomasius is contained in his account of the history of Christology.

In his outlines of the history of Christian dogma (Grundriss der Christl. Dogmengesch. 1870), which unfortunately has not been carried beyond the first part (Patristic period), F. Nitzsch, marks an advance in the history of our subject. The advance lies, on the one hand, in the extensive use he makes of monographs on the history of dogma, and on the other hand, in the arrangement. Nitzsch has advanced a long way on the path that was first entered by F. K. Meier, and has arranged his material in a way that far excels all earlier attempts. The general and special aspects of the history of dogma are here almost completely worked into one,[1] and in the main divisions, "Grounding of the old Catholic Church doctrine," and "Development of the old Catholic Church doctrine," justice is at last done to the most important problem which the history of dogma presents, though in my opinion the division is not made at the right place, and the problem is not so clearly kept in view in the execution as the arrangement would lead one to expect.[2] Nitzsch has freed himself

view of Luther and the writers of the "Centuries," for these were well aware that the corruption did not first begin in the middle ages.

1 This fulfils a requirement urged by Weizsäcker (Jahrb. f. Deutsche Theol. 1866 p 170 ff.)

2 See Ritschl's Essay, "Ueber die Methode der älteren Dogmengeschichte" (Jahrb. f. deutsche Theol. 1871 p 191 ff.) in which the advance made by Nitzsch is estimated, and at the same time, an arrangement proposed for the treatment of the earlier history of dogma which would group the material more clearly and more suitably than has been done by Nitzsch. After having laid the foundation for a correct historical estimate of the development of early Christianity in his work "Entstehung der Alt-Katholischen Kirche", 1857, Ritschl published an epoch-making study in the history of dogma in his "History of the doctrine of justification and reconciliation" 2 edit. 1883. We have no superabundance of good

from that speculative view of the history of dogma which reads ideas into it. No doubt idea and motive on the one hand, form and expression on the other, must be distinguished for every period. But the historian falls into vagueness as soon as he seeks and professes to find behind the demonstrable ideas and aims which have moved a period, others of which, as a matter of fact, that period itself knew nothing at all. Besides, the invariable result of that procedure is to concentrate the attention on the theological and philosophical points of dogma, and either neglect or put a new construction on the most concrete and important, the expression of the religious faith itself. Rationalism has been reproached with "throwing out the child with the bath," but this is really worse, for here the child is thrown out while the bath is retained. Every advance in the future treatment of our sub-

monographs on the history of dogma. There are few that give such exact information regarding the Patristic period as that of Von Engelhardt "Ueber das Christenthum Justin's", 1878, and Zahn's work on Marcellus, 1867. Among the investigators of our age, Renan above all has clearly recognised that there are only two main periods in the history of dogma, and that the changes which Christianity experienced after the establishment of the Catholic Church bear no proportion to the changes which preceded. His words are as follows (Hist. des origin. du Christianisme T. VII. p. 503 f.): — the division about the year 180 is certainly placed too early, regard being had to what was then really authoritative in the Church.—"Si nous comparons maintenant le Christianisme, tel qu'il existait vers l'an 180, au Christianisme du IVe et du Ve, siècle, au Christianisme du moyen âge, au Christianisme de nos jours, nous trouvons qu'en réalité il s'est augmenté des très peu de chose dans les siècles qui ont suivis. En 180, le Nouveau Testament est clos: il ne s'y ajoutera plus un seul livre nouveau(?). Lentement, les Épitres de Paul ont conquis leur place à la suite des Evangiles, dans le code sacré èt dans la liturgie. Quant aux dogmes. rien n'est fixé; mais le germe de tout existe; presque aucune idée n'apparaitra qui ne puisse faire valoir des autorités du 1er et du 2e siècles. Il y a du trop, il y a des contradictions; le travail théologique consistera bien plus à émonder, à écarter des superfluités qu'à inventer du nouveau. L'Église laissera tomber une foule de choses mal commencées, elle sortira de bien des impasses. Elle a encore deux cœurs, pour ainsi dire; elle a plusieurs têtes; ces anomalies tomberont; mais aucun dogme vraiment original ne se formera plus". Also the discussions in chapters 28-34. of the same volume. H. Thiersch (Die Kirche im Apostolischen Zeitalter, 1852) reveals a deep insight into the difference between the spirit of the New Testament writers and the post-Apostolic Fathers, but he has overdone these differences and sought to explain them by the mythological assumption of an Apostasy. A great amount of material for the history of dogma may be found in the great work of Böhringer. Die Kirche Christi und ihre Zeugen, oder die Kirchengeschichte in Biographien. 2 Edit. 1864.

ject will further depend on the effort to comprehend the
history of dogma without reference to the momentary opinions
of the present, and also on keeping it in closest connection
with the history of the Church, from which it can never be
separated without damage. We have something to learn on
this point from rationalistic historians of dogma. [1] But progress
is finally dependent on a true perception of what the Christian
religion originally was, for this perception alone enables us to

---

[1] By the connection with general church history we must, above all, understand, a continuous regard to the world within which the church has been
developed. The most recent works on the history of the church and of
dogma, those of Renan, Overbeck (Anfänge der patristischen Litteratur).Aube,
Von Engelhardt (Justin), Kühn (Minucius Felix). Hatch ("Organization of the
early church," and especially his posthumous work "The influence of Greek
ideas and usages upon the Christian Church," 1890, in which may be found the
most ample proof for the conception of the early history of dogma which is
set forth in the following pages), are in this respect worthy of special note.
Deserving of mention also is R. Rothe, who, in his "Vorlesungen über Kirchengeschichte", edited by Weingarten," 1875. 2 vols, gave most significant suggestions towards a really historical conception of the history of the church
and of dogma. To Rothe belongs the undiminished merit of realising thoroughly the significance of nationality in church history But the theology of our
century is also indebted for the first scientific conception of Catholicism, not
to Marheineke or Winer, but to Rothe. (see Vol II. pp. 1-11 especially p. 7 f.).
"The development of the Christian Church in the Græco-Roman world was not
at the same time a development of that world by the Church and further by
Christianity. There remained, as the result of the process, nothing but the completed Church. The world which had built it had made itself bankrupt in doing
so". With regard to the origin and development of the Catholic cultus and
constitution, nay, even of the Ethic (see Luthardt, Die antike Ethik, 1887,
preface), that has been recognised by Protestant scholars, which one always
hesitates to recognise with regard to catholic dogma: see the excellent remarks
of Schwegler, Nachapostolisches Zeitalter. Vol. 1. p. 3 ff. It may be hoped that
an intelligent consideration of early christian literature will form the bridge to
a broad and intelligent view of the history of dogma The essay of Overbeck
mentioned above (Histor. Zeitschrift. N. F. XII p. 417 ff.) may be most heartily
recommended in this respect. It is very gratifying to find an investigator so
conservative as Sohm, now fully admitting that "Christian theology grew up
in the second and third centuries, when its foundations were laid for all time (?),
the last great production of the Hellenic Spirit". (Kirchengeschichte im
Grundriss. 1888. p. 37). The same scholar in his very important Kirchenrecht.
Bd. I. 1892, has transferred to the history of the origin of Church law and Church
organization, the points of view which I have applied in the following account
to the consideration of dogma He has thereby succeeded in correcting many
old errors and prejudices; but in my opinion he has obscured the truth by
exaggerations connected with a conception, not only of original Christianity,
but also of the Gospel in general, which is partly a narrow legal view, partly
an enthusiastic one. He has arrived *ex errore per veritatem ad errorem;* but
there are few books from which so much may be learned about early church
history as from this paradoxical "Kirchenrecht".

distinguish that which sprang out of the inherent power of
Christianity from that which it has assimilated in the course
of its history. For the historian, however, who does not wish
to serve a party, there are two standards in accordance with
which he may criticise the history of dogma He may either,
as far as this is possible, compare it with the Gospel, or he may
judge it according to the historical conditions of the time and
the result. Both ways can exist side by side, if only they are
not mixed up with one another. Protestantism has in principle
expressly recognised the first, and it will also have the power
to bear its conclusions; for the saying of Tertullian still holds
good in it; "Nihil veritas erubescit nisi solummodo abscondi."
The historian who follows this maxim, and at the same time
has no desire to be wiser than the facts, will, while furthering
science, perform the best service also to every Christian community that desires to build itself upon the Gospel.

After the appearence of the first and second editions of this
Work, Loofs published, "Leitfaden für seine Vorlesungen
über Dogmengeschichte," Halle, 1889, and in the following
year, "Leitfaden zum Studium der Dogmengeschichte, zunächst
für seine Vorlesungen," (second and enlarged edition of the first-
named book). The work in its conception of dogma and its
history comes pretty near that stated above, and it is distinguished by independent investigation and excellent selection of
material. I myself have published a "Grundriss der Dogmengeschichte," 2 Edit. in one vol. 1893. (Outlines of the history
of dogma, English translation. Hodder and Stoughton). That
this has not been written in vain, I have the pleasure of seeing
from not a few notices of professional colleagues. I may
mention the Church history of Herzog in the new revision by
Koffmane, the first vol. of the Church history of Karl Müller,
the first vol. of the Symbolik of Kattenbusch, and Kaftan's
work. "The truth of the Christian religion." Wilhelm Schmidt,
"Der alte Glaube und die Wahrheit des Christenthums," 1891,
has attempted to furnish a refutation in principle of Kaftan's work.

CHAPTER II

THE PRESUPPOSITIONS OF THE HISTORY OF DOGMA

§ 1. *Introductory.*

THE Gospel presents itself as an Apocalyptic message on the soil of the Old Testament, and as the fulfilment of the law and the prophets, and yet is a new thing, the creation of a universal religion on the basis of that of the Old Testament. It appeared when the time was fulfilled, that is, it is not without a connection with the stage of religious and spiritual development which was brought about by the intercourse of Jews and Greeks, and was established in the Roman Empire; but still it is a new religion because it cannot be separated from Jesus Christ. When the traditional religion has become too narrow the new religion usually appears as something of a very abstract nature; philosophy comes upon the scene, and religion withdraws from social life and becomes a private matter. But here an overpowering personality has appeared—the Son of God. Word and deed coincide in that personality, and as it leads men into a new communion with God, it unites them at the same time inseparably with itself, enables them to act on the world as light and leaven, and joins them together in a spiritual unity and an active confederacy.

2. Jesus Christ brought no new doctrine, but he set forth in his own person a holy life with God and before God, and gave himself in virtue of this life to the service of his brethren in order to win them for the Kingdom of God, that is, to lead them out of selfishness and the world to God, out of

the natural connections and contrasts to a union in love, and prepare them for an eternal kingdom and an eternal life. But while working for this Kingdom of God he did not withdraw from the religious and political communion of his people, nor did he induce his disciples to leave that communion. On the contrary, he described the Kingdom of God as the fulfilment of the promises given to the nation, and himself as the Messiah whom that nation expected. By doing so he secured for his new message, and with it his own person, a place in the system of religious ideas and hopes, which by means of the Old Testament were then, in diverse forms, current in the Jewish nation. The origin of a doctrine concerning the Messianic hope, in which the Messiah was no longer an unknown being, but Jesus of Nazareth, along with the new temper and disposition of believers was a direct result of the impression made by the person of Jesus. The conception of the Old Testament in accordance with the *analogia fidei*, that is, in accordance with the conviction that this Jesus of Nazareth is the Christ, was therewith given. Whatever sources of comfort and strength Christianity, even in its New Testament, has possessed or does possess up to the present, is for the most part taken from the Old Testament, viewed from a Christian stand-point, in virtue of the impression of the person of Jesus. Even its dross was changed into gold; its hidden treasures were brought forth, and while the earthly and transitory were recognised as symbols of the heavenly and eternal, there rose up a world of 'blessings, of holy ordinances, and of sure grace prepared by God from eternity. One could joyfully make oneself at home in it; for its long history guaranteed a sure future and a blessed close, while it offered comfort and certainty in all the changes of life to every individual heart that would only raise itself to God. From the positive position which Jesus took up towards the Old Testament, that is, towards the religious traditions of his people, his Gospel gained a footing which, later on, preserved it from dissolving in the glow of enthusiasm, or melting away in the ensnaring dream of antiquity, that dream of the indestructible Divine nature of the human spirit, and the nothingness and baseness of all material things. [1] But from the positive attitude of Jesus to the Jewish tradition, there followed also, for a generation that had long been accustomed to grope after the Divine active in the world, the summons to think out a theory of the media of relevation, and so put an end to the uncertainty with which speculation had hitherto been afflicted. This, like every theory of religion, concealed in itself the danger of crippling the power of faith; for men are ever prone to compound with religion itself by a religious theory.

3. The result of the preaching of Jesus, however, in the case of the believing Jews, was not only the illumination of the Old Testament by the Gospel and the confirmation of the Gospel by the Old Testament, but not less, though indirectly, the detachment of believers from the religious community of the Jews from the Jewish Church. How this came about cannot be discussed here: we may satisfy ourselves with the fact that it was essentially accomplished in the first two generations of believers. The Gospel was a message for humanity even where there was no break with Judaism: but it seemed impossible to bring this message home to men who were not Jews in any other way than by leaving the Jewish Church. But to leave that Church was to declare it to be worthless, and that could only be done by conceiving it as a malformation from its very commencement, or assuming that it had temporarily or completely fulfilled its mission. In either case it was necessary to put another in its place, for, according to the Old Testament, it was unquestionable that God had not only given revelations, but through these revelations had founded a nation, a religious community. The result, also, to which the conduct of the unbelieving Jews and the social union of the disciples of Jesus required by that

---

1 The Old Testament of itself alone could not have convinced the Græco-Roman world. But the converse question might perhaps be raised as to what results the Gospel would have had in that world without its union with the Old Testament. The Gnostic Schools and the Marcionite Church are to some extent the answer. But would they ever have arisen without the presupposition of a christian community which recognised the Old Testament?

conduct, led, was carried home with irresistible power: believers in Christ are the community of God, they are the
true Israel, the ἐκκλησία τοῦ θεοῦ: but the Jewish Church per-
sisting in its unbelief is the Synagogue of Satan. Out of this
consciousness sprang—first as a power in which one believed,
but which immediately began to be operative, though not as
a commonwealth—the christian church, a special communion
of hearts on the basis of a personal union with God, established
by Christ and mediated by the Spirit; a communion whose
essential mark was to claim as its own the Old Testament
and the idea of being the people of God, to sweep aside the
Jewish conception of the Old Testament and the Jewish Church,
and thereby gain the shape and power of a community that
is capable of a mission for the world.

4. This independent Christian community could not have
been formed had not Judaism, in consequence of inner and
outer developments, then reached a point at which it must
either altogether cease to grow or burst its shell. This community is the presupposition of the history of dogma, and the
position which it took up towards the Jewish tradition is,
strictly speaking, the point of departure for all further developments, so far as with the removal of all national and ceremonial peculiarities it proclaimed itself to be what the Jewish
Church wished to be. We find the Christian Church about the
middle of the third century, after severe crisis, in nearly the
same position to the Old Testament and to Judaism as it was
150 or 200 years earlier. [1] It makes the same claim to the
Old Testament, and builds its faith and hope upon its teaching. It is also, as before, strictly anti-national; above all, anti-
judaic, and sentences the Jewish religious community to the
abyss of hell. It might appear, then, as though the basis for
the further development of Christianity as a church was com-

---

1 We here leave out of account learned attempts to expound Paulinism.
Nor do we take any notice of certain truths regarding the relation of
the Old Testament to the New, and regarding the Jewish religion, stated
by the Antignostic church teachers, truths which are certainly very important, but have not been sufficiently utilised.

pletely given from the moment in which the first breach of
believers with the synagogue and the formation of independent Christian communities took place. The problem, the
solution of which will always exercise this church, so far as it
reflects upon its faith, will be to turn the Old Testament
more completely to account in its own sense, so as to condemn the Jewish .Church with its particular and national forms.

5. But the rule even for the Christian use of the Old Testament lay originally in the living connection in which one
stood with the Jewish people and its traditions, and a new
religious community, a religious commonwealth, was not yet
realised, although it existed for faith and thought. If again
we compare the Church about the middle of the third century
with the condition of Christendom 150 or 200 years before,
we shall find that there is now a real religious commonwealth, while at the earlier period there were only communities who believed in a heavenly Church, whose earthly image
they were, endeavoured to give it expression with the simplest means, and lived in the future as strangers and pilgrims
on the earth, hastening to meet the Kingdom of whose existence they had the surest guarantee. We now really find a
new commonwealth, politically formed and equipped with
fixed forms of all kinds. We recognise in these forms few
Jewish, but many Græco-Roman features, and finally, we perceive also in the doctrine of faith on which this commonwealth is based, the philosophic spirit of the Greeks. We find
a Church as a political union and worship institute, a formulated faith and a sacred learning; but one thing we no longer
find, the old enthusiasm and individualism which had not felt
itself fettered by subjection to the authority of the Old Testament. Instead of enthusiastic independent Christians, we
find a new literature of revelation, the New Testament, and
Christian priests. When did these formations begin? How and
by what influence was the living faith transformed into the
creed to be believed, the surrender to Christ into a philosophic Christology, the Holy Church into the *corpus permixtum*,
the glowing hope of the Kingdom of heaven into a doctrine

of immortality and deification, prophecy into a learned exegesis and theological science, the bearers of the spirit into clerics, the brethren into laity held in tutelage, miracles and healings into nothing, or into priestcraft, the fervent prayers into a solemn ritual, renunciation of the world into a jealous dominion over the world, the " spirit" into constraint and law?

There can be no doubt about the answer : these formations are as old in their origin as the detachment of the Gospel from the Jewish Church. A religious faith which seeks to establish a communion of its own in opposition to another, is compelled to borrow from that other what it needs. The religion which is life and feeling of the heart cannot be converted into a knowledge determining the motley multitude of men without deferring to their wishes and opinions. Even the holiest must clothe itself in the same existing earthly forms as the profane if it wishes to found on earth a confederacy which is to take the place of another, and if it does not wish to enslave, but to determine the reason. When the Gospel was rejected by the Jewish nation, and had disengaged itself from all connection with that nation, it was already settled whence it must take the material to form for itself a new body and be transformed into a Church and a theology. National and particular, in the ordinary sense of the word, these forms could not be : the contents of the Gospel were too rich for that; but separated from Judaism, nay, even before that separation, the Christian religion came in contact with the Roman world and with a culture which had already mastered the world, viz., the Greek. The Christian Church and its doctrine were developed within the Roman world and Greek culture in opposition to the Jewish Church. This fact is just as important for the history of dogma as the other stated above, that this Church was continuously nourished on the Old Testament. Christendom was of course conscious of being in opposition to the empire and its culture, as well as to Judaism; but this from the beginning—apart from a few exceptions—was not without reservations. No man can serve two masters'; but in setting up a spiritual power in this world one must serve an earthly master, even when he desires to naturalise the spiritual in the world. As a consequence of the complete break with the Jewish Church there followed not only the strict necessity of quarrying the stones for the building of the Church from the Græco-Roman world, but also the idea that Christianity has a more positive relation to that world than to the synagogue. And, as the Church was being built, the original enthusiasm must needs vanish. The separation from Judaism having taken place, it was necessary that the spirit of another people should be admitted, and should also materially determine the manner of turning the Old Testament to advantage.

6. But an inner necessity was at work here no less than an outer. Judaism and Hellenism in the age of Christ were opposed to each other, not only as dissimilar powers of equal value, but the latter having its origin among a small people, became a universal spiritual power, which, severed from its original nationality, had for that very reason penetrated foreign nations. It had even laid hold of Judaism, and the anxious care of her professional watchmen to hedge round the national possession, is but a proof of the advancing decomposition within the Jewish nation. Israel, no doubt, had a sacred treasure which was of greater value than all the treasures of the Greeks,—the living God—but in what miserable vessels was this treasure preserved, and how much inferior was all else possessed by this nation in comparison with the riches, the power, the delicacy and freedom of the Greek spirit and its intellectual possessions. A movement like that of Christianity, which discovered to the Jew the soul whose dignity was not dependent on its descent from Abraham, but on its responsibility to God, could not continue in the framework of Judaism however expanded, but must soon recognise in that world which the Greek spirit had discovered and prepared, the field which belonged to it : εἰκότως Ἰουδαίοις μὲν νόμος, Ἕλλεσι δὲ φιλοσοφία μέχρις τῆς παρουσίας ἐντεῦθεν δὲ ἡ κλῆσις ἡ καθολική [to the Jews the law, to the Greeks Philosophy, up to the Parousia; from that time the catholic invi-

tation]. But the Gospel at first was preached exclusively to the lost sheep of the house of Israel, and that which inwardly united it with Hellenism did not yet appear in any doctrine or definite form of knowledge.

On the contrary, the Church doctrine of faith, in the preparatory stage, from the Apologists up to the time of Origen, hardly in any point shews the traces, scarcely even the remembrance of a time in which the Gospel was not detached from Judaism. For that very reason it is absolutely impossible to understand this preparation and development solely from the writings that remain to us as monuments of that short earliest period. The attempts at deducing the genesis of the Church's doctrinal system from the theology of Paul, or from compromises between Apostolic doctrinal ideas, will always miscarry; for they fail to note that to the most important premises of the Catholic doctrine of faith belongs an element which we cannot recognise as dominant in the New Testament, [1]

1 There is indeed no single writing of the new Testament which does not betray the influence of the mode of thought and general conditions of the culture of the time which resulted from the Hellenising of the east: even the use of the Greek translation of the Old Testament attests this fact. Nay, we may go further, and say that the Gospel itself is historically unintelligible, so long as we compare it with an exclusive Judaism as yet unaffected by any foreign influence. But on the other hand, it is just as clear that, specifically, Hellenic ideas form the presuppositions neither for the Gospel itself, nor for the most important New Testament writings. It is a question rather as to a general spiritual atmosphere created by Hellenism, which above all strengthened the individual element, and with it the idea of completed personality, in itself living and responsible. On this foundation we meet with a religious mode of thought in the Gospel and the early Christian writings, which so far as it is at all dependent on an earlier mode of thought, is determined by the spirit of the Old Testament (Psalms and Prophets) and of Judaism. But it is already otherwise with the earliest Gentile christian writings. The mode of thought here is so thoroughly determined by the Hellenic spirit that we seem to have entered a new world when we pass from the synoptists, Paul and John, to Clement, Barnabas, Justin or Valentinus. We may therefore say, especially in the frame-work of the history of dogma, that the Hellenic element has exercised an influence on the Gospel first on Gentile Christian soil, and by those who were Greek by birth, if only we reserve the general spiritual atmosphere above referred to. Even Paul is no exception; for in spite of the well-founded statements of Weizsäcker (Apostolic Age, vol. I. Book 11) and Heinrici (Das 2 Sendschreiben an die Korinthier, 1887, p. 578 ff.), as to the Hellenism of Paul, it is certain that the Apostle's mode of religious thought, in the strict sense of the word, and therefore also the doctrinal formation peculiar to him, are but little determined by the Greek spirit.

viz., the Hellenic spirit. [1] As far backwards as we can trace
the history of the propagation of the Church's doctrine of
faith, from the middle of the third century to the end of the
first, we nowhere perceive a leap, or the sudden influx of an
entirely new element. What we perceive is rather the gradual disappearance of an original element, the Enthusiastic
and Apocalyptic, that is, of the sure consciousness of an immediate possession of the Divine Spirit, and the hope of the
future conquering the present; individual piety conscious of
itself and sovereign, living in the future world, recognising no
external authority and no external barriers. This piety became
ever weaker and passed away: the utilising of the Codex of
Revelation, the Old Testament, proportionally increased with
the Hellenic influences which controlled the process, for the
two went always hand in hand. At an earlier period the
Churches made very little use of either, because they had in
individual religious inspiration on the basis of Christ's preaching

But it is to be specially noted that as a missionary and an Apologist he made
use of Greek ideas(Epistles to theRomans and Corinthians). He was not afraid
to put the Gospel into Greek modes of thought. To this extent we can already
observe in him the beginning of the development which we can trace so clearly
in the Gentile Church from Clement to Justin, and from Justin to Irenæus.

1 The complete universalism of salvation is given in the Pauline conception
of Christianity. But this conception is singular. Because: (1) the Pauline
universalism is based on a criticism of the Jewish religion as religion, including the Old Testament, which was not understood and therefore not received
by Christendom in general. (2) Because Paul not only formulated no national
anti-judaism, but always recognised the prerogative of the people of Israel as
a people. (3) Because his idea of the Gospel, with all his Greek culture, is
independent of Hellenism in its deepest grounds. This peculiarity of the
Pauline Gospel is the reason why little more could pass from it into the common consciousness of Christendom than the universalism of salvation, and
why the later development of the Church cannot be explained from Paulinism.
Baur, therefore, was quite right when he recognised that we must exhibit
another and more powerful element in order to comprehend the post-Pauline
formations. In the selection of this element, however, he has made a fundamental mistake, by introducing the narrow national Jewish Christianity, and
he has also given much too great scope to Paulinism by wrongly conceiving
it as Gentile Christian doctrine. One great difficulty for the historian of
the early Church is that he cannot start from Paulinism, the plainest
phenomenon of the Apostolic age, in seeking to explain the following
development, that in fact the premises for this development are not at all
capable of being indicated in the form of outlines, just because they were
too general. But, on the other hand, the Pauline Theology, this theology
of one who had been a Pharisee, is the strongest proof of the independent
and universal power of the impression made by the Person of Jesus.

and the sure hope of his Kingdom which was near at hand, much more than either could bestow. The factors whose co-operation we observe in the second and third centuries, were already operative among the earliest Gentile Christians. We nowhere find a yawning gulf in the great development which lies between the first Epistle of Clement and the work of Origen, Περὶ ἀρχῶν. Even the importance which the "Apostolic" was to obtain, was already foreshadowed by the end of the first century, and enthusiasm always had its limits. [1] The most decisive division, therefore, falls before the end of the first century; or more correctly, the relatively new element, the Greek, which is of importance for the forming of the Church as a commonwealth, and consequently for the formation of its doctrine, is clearly present in the churches even in the Apostolic age. Two hundred years, however, passed before it made itself completely at home in the Gospel, although there were points of connection inherent in the Gospel.

7. The cause of the great historical fact is clear. It is given in the fact that the Gospel, rejected by the majority of the Jews, was very soon proclaimed to those who were not Jews, that after a few decades the greater number of its professors were found among the Greeks, and that, consequently, the development leading to the Catholic dogma took place within Græco-Roman culture. But within this culture there was lacking the power of understanding either the idea of the

---

1 In the main writings of the New Testament itself we have a twofold conception of the Spirit. According to the one he comes upon the believer fitfully, expresses himself in visible signs, deprives men of self-consciousness, and puts them beside themselves. According to the other, the spirit is a constant possession of the Christian, operates in him by enlightening the conscience and strengthening the character, and his fruits are love, joy, peace, patience, gentleness, etc. (Gal. V. 22). Paul above all taught Christians to value these fruits of the spirit higher than all the other effects of his working. But he has not by any means produced a perfectly clear view on this point: for "he himself spoke with more tongues than they all". As yet "Spirit" lay within "Spirit." One felt in the spirit of sonship a completely new gift coming from God and recreating life, a miracle of God; further, this spirit also produced sudden exclamations — "Abba, Father;" and thus shewed himself in a way patent to the senses. For that very reason, the spirit of ecstasy and of miracle appeared identical with the spirit of sonship. (See Gunkel, Die Wirkungen d. h. Geistes nach der populären Anschauung der Apostol. Zeit. Göttingen, 1888).

completed Old Testament theocracy, or the idea of the Messiah. Both of these essential elements of the original proclamation, therefore, must either be neglected or remodelled. [1] But it is hardly allowable to mention details however important, where the whole aggregate of ideas, of religious historical perceptions and presuppositions, which were based on the old Testament, understood in a Christian sense, presented itself as something new and strange. One can easily appropriate words, but not practical ideas. Side by side with the Old Testament religion as the presupposition of the Gospel, and using its forms of thought, the moral and religious views and ideals dominant in the world of Greek culture could not but insinuate themselves into the communities consisting of Gentiles. From the enormous material that was brought home to the hearts of the Greeks, whether formulated by Paul or by any other, only a few rudimentary ideas could at first be appropriated. For that very reason, the Apostolic Catholic doctrine of faith in its preparation and establishment, is no mere continuation of that which, by uniting things that are certainly very dissimilar, is wont to be described as "Biblical Theology of the New Testament." Biblical Theology, even when kept within reasonable limits, is not the presupposition of the history of dogma. The Gentile Christians were little able to comprehend the controversies which stirred the Apostolic age within Jewish Christianity. The presuppositions of the history of dogma are given in certain fundamental ideas, or rather motives of the Gospel, (in the preaching concerning Jesus Christ, in the teaching of Evangelic ethics and the future life, in the Old Testament capable of any interpretation, but to be interpreted with reference to Christ and the Evangelic history), and in the Greek spirit. [2].

---

1 It may even be said here that the ἀθανασία (ζωὴ αἰώνιος), on the one hand, and the ἐκκλησία, on the other, have already appeared in place of the Βασιλεία τοῦ θεοῦ, and that the idea of Messiah has been finally replaced by that of the Divine Teacher and of God manifest in the flesh.

2 It is one of the merits of Bruno Bauer (Christus und die Cäsaren, 1877), that he has appreciated the real significance of the Greek element in the Gentile Christianity which became the Catholic Church and doctrine, and that he

8. The foregoing statements involve that the difference
between the development which led to the Catholic doctrine
of religion and the original condition, was by no means a
total one. By recognising the Old Testament as a book of
Divine revelation, the Gentile Christians received along with
it the religious speech which was used by Jewish Christians,
were made dependent upon the interpretation which had been
used from the very beginning, and even received a great part
of the Jewish literature which accompanied the Old Testament.
But the possession of a common religious speech and literature is never a mere outward bond of union, however strong
the impulse be to introduce the old familiar contents into the
newly acquired speech. The Jewish, that is, the Old Testament element, divested of its national peculiarity, has remained
the basis of Christendom. It has saturated this element with the
Greek spirit, but has always clung to its main idea, faith in

has appreciated the influence of the Judaism of the Diaspora as a preparation
for this Gentile Christianity.   But these valuable contributions have unfortunately been deprived of their convincing power by a baseless criticism of the
early Christian literature, to which Christ and Paul have fallen a sacrifice.
Somewhat more cautious are the investigations of Havet in the fourth volume
of Le Christianisme, 1884 ; Le Nouveau Testament.   He has won great merit
by the correct interpretation of the elements of Gentile Christianity developing themselves to catholicism, but his literary criticism is often unfortunately
entirely abstract, reminding one of the criticism of Voltaire, and therefore his
statements in detail are, as a rule, arbitrary and untenable. There is a school
in Holland at the present time closely related to Bruno Bauer and Havet,
which attempts to banish early Christianity from the world. Christ and Paul
are creations of the second century: the history of Christianity begins with
the passage of the first century into the second—a peculiar phenomenon on
the soil of Hellenised Judaism in quest of a Messiah.   This Judaism created
Jesus Christ just as the later Greek religious philosophers created their Saviour
(Apollonius, for example). The Marcionite Church produced Paul and the
growing Catholic Church completed him. See the numerous treatises of Lo-
man, the Verisimilia of Pierson and Naber (1886), and the anonymous English
work "Antiqua Mater" (1887), also the works of Steck (see especially his Un-
tersuchung über den Galaterbrief). Against these works see P. V. Schmidt's.
"Der Galaterbrief" 1892. It requires a deep knowledge of the problems which
the first two centuries of the Christian Church present, in order not to thrust
aside as simply absurd these attempts, which as yet have failed to deal with
the subject in a connected way.   They have their strength in the difficulties
and riddles which are contained in the history of the formation of the Catholic
tradition in the second century. But the single circumstance that we are
asked to regard as a forgery such a document as the first Epistle of Paul to
the Corinthians, appears to me, of itself, to be an unanswerable argument
against the new hypotheses.

God as the creator and ruler of the world. It has in the course of its development rejected important parts of that Jewish element, and has borrowed others at a later period from the great treasure that was transmitted to it. It has also been able to turn to account the least adaptable features, if only for the external confirmation of its own ideas. The Old Testament applied to Christ and his universal Church has always remained the decisive document, and it was long ere Christian writings received the same authority, long ere individual doctrines and sayings of Apostolic writings obtained an influence on the formation of ecclesiastical doctrine.

9. From yet another side there makes its appearance an agreement between the circles of Palestinian believers in Jesus and the Gentile Christian communities, which endured for more than a century, though it was of course gradually effaced. It is the enthusiastic element which unites them, the consciousness of standing in an immediate union with God through the Spirit, and receiving directly from God's hand miraculous gifts, powers and revelations, granted to the individual that he may turn them to account in the service of the Church. The depotentiation of the Christian religion, where one may believe in the inspiration of another, but no longer feels his own, nay, dare not feel it, is not altogether coincident with its settlement on Greek soil. On the contrary, it was more than two centuries ere weakness and reflection suppressed, or all but suppressed, the forms in which the personal consciousness of God originally expressed itself. [1] Now it certainly lies in the nature of

1 It would be a fruitful task, though as yet it has not been undertaken, to examine how long visions, dreams and apocalypses, on the one hand, and the claim of speaking in the power and name of the Holy Spirit, on the other, played a *rôle* in the early Church; and further to shew how they nearly died out among the laity, but continued to live among the clergy and the monks, and how, even among the laity, there were again and again sporadic outbreaks of them. The material which the first three centuries present is very great. Only a few may be mentioned here: Ignat. ad. Rom. VII. 2: ad. Philad. VII. ad. Eph. XX. 1, etc.: 1 Clem. LXIII. 2: Martyr. Polyc.: Acta Perpet. et Felic: Tertull. de animo XLVII.: "Major pæne vis hominum e visionibus deum discunt." Orig. c. Celsum. I. 46: πολλοὶ ὡσπερεὶ ἄκοντες προσεληλύθασι χριστιανισμῷ, πνεύματός τινος τρέψαντος. . . . καὶ φαντασιώσαντος αὐτοὺς ὕπαρ ἤ ὄναρ (even Arnobius was ostensibly led to Christianity by a dream) Cyprian makes the most extensive use of dreams, visions, etc., in

enthusiasm, that it can assume the most diverse forms of expression, and follow very different impulses, and so far it frequently separates instead of uniting. But so long as criticism and reflection are not yet awakened, and a uniform ideal hovers before one, it does unite, and in this sense there existed an identity of disposition between the earliest Jewish Christians and the still enthusiastic Gentile Christian communities.

10. But, finally, there is a still further uniting element between the beginnings of the development to Catholicism, and the original condition of the Christian religion as a movement within Judaism, the importance of which cannot be overrated, although we have every reason to complain here of the obscurity of the tradition. Between the Græco-Roman world which was in search of a spiritual religion, and the Jewish commonwealth which already possessed such a religion as a national property, though vitiated by exclusiveness, there had long been a Judaism which, penetrated by the Greek spirit, was, *ex professo*, devoting itself to the task of bringing a new religion to the Greek world, the Jewish religion, but that religion in its kernel Greek, that is, philosophically moulded, spiritualised and secularised. Here then was already consummated an intimate union of the Greek spirit with the Old Testament religion, within the Empire and to a less degree in Palestine itself. If everything is not to be dissolved into a grey mist, we must clearly distinguish this union between Judaism and Hellenism and the spiritualising of religion it produced, from the powerful but indeterminable influences which the Greek spirit

his letters, see for example Ep. XI. 3-5 : XVI. 4 ("præter nocturnas visiones per dies quoque impletur apud nos spiritu sancto puerorum innocens ætas, quæ in ecstasi videt," etc.); XXXIX. 1 : LXVI. 10 (very interesting : "quamquam sciam somnia ridicula et visiones ineptas quibusdam videri, sed utique illis, qui malunt contra sacerdotes credere quam sacerdoti, sed nihil mirum, quando de Joseph fratres sui dixerunt: ecce somniator ille," etc.). One who took part in the baptismal controversy in the great Synod of Carthage writes, "secundum motum animi mei et spiritus sancti." The enthusiastic element was always evoked with special power in times of persecution, as the genuine African matyrdoms, from the second half of the third century, specially shew. Cf. especially the passio Jacobi, Mariani, etc. But where the enthusiasm was not convenient it was called, as in the case of the Montanists, dæmonic. Even Constantine operated with dreams and visions of Christ (see his Vita).

exercised on all things Jewish, and which have been a historical condition of the Gospel. The alliance, in my opinion,
was of no significance at all for the *origin* of the Gospel, but
was of the most decided importance, first, for the propagation
of Christianity, and then, for the development of Christianity
to Catholicism, and for the genesis of the Catholic doctrine of
faith. [1] We cannot certainly name any particular personality
who was specially active in this, but we can mention three
facts which prove more than individual references. (1) The
propaganda of Christianity in the Diaspora followed the Jewish
propaganda and partly took its place, that is, the Gospel was
at first preached to those Gentiles who were already acquainted with the general outlines of the Jewish religion, and who
were even frequently viewed as a Judaism of a second order,
in which Jewish and Greek elements had been united in a
peculiar mixture. (2) The conception of the Old Testament,
as we find it even in the earliest Gentile Christian teachers,
the method of spiritualising it, etc., agrees in the most surprising way with the methods which were used by the Alexandrian Jews. (3) There are Christian documents in no small
number and of unknown origin, which completely agree in plan,
in form and contents with Græco-Jewish writings of the Diaspora,
as for example, the Christian Sibylline Oracles, and the pseudo-
Justinian treatise, " de Monarchia." There are numerous trac-
tates of which it is impossible to say with certainty whether
they are of Jewish or of Christian origin.

The Alexandrian and non-Palestinian Judaism is still Judaism. As the Gospel seized and moved the whole of Judaism,

---

1 As to the first, the recently discovered "Teaching of the Apostles"
in its first moral part, shews a great affinity with the moral philosophy
which was set up by Alexandrian Jews and put before the Greek world
as that which had been revealed: see Massebieau, L'enseignement des
XII. Apôtres. Paris. 1884, and in the Journal "Le Témoignage," 7 Febr.
1885. Usener, in his Preface to the Ges. Abhandl. Jacob Bernays', which
he edited, 1885, p. v. f., has, independently of Massebieau, pointed out
the relationship of chapters 1-5 of the "Teaching of the Apostles" with
the Phocylidean poem (see Bernays' above work, p. 192 ff.). Later Taylor
"The teaching of the twelve Apostles", 1886, threw out the conjecture
that the Didache had a Jewish foundation, and I reached the same conclusion independently of him: see my Treatise: Die Apostellehre und die
jüdischen beiden Wege, 1886.

it must also have been operative in the non-Palestinian Judaism.
But that already foreshadowed the transition of the Gospel to
the non-Jewish Greek region, and the fate which it was to
experience there. For that non-Palestinian Judaism formed
the bridge between the Jewish Church and the Roman Empire,
together with its culture. [1] The Gospel passed into the world
chiefly by this bridge. Paul indeed had a large share in this,
but his own Churches did · not understand the way he led
them, and were not able on looking back to find it. [2] He indeed
became a Greek to the Greeks, and even began the undertaking of placing the treasures of Greek knowledge at the ser-

1 It is well known that Judaism at the time of Christ embraced a great
many different tendencies. Beside Pharisaic Judaism as the stem proper,
there was a motley mass of formations which resulted from the contact
of Judaism with foreign ideas, customs and institutions (even with Babylonian and Persian), and which attained importance for the development
of the predominant church, as well as for the formation of the so-called
gnostic Christian communions. Hellenic elements found their way even
into Pharisaic theology. Orthodox Judaism itself has marks which shew
that no spiritual movement was able to escape the influence which proceeded from the victory of the Greeks over the east. Besides, who would
venture to exhibit definitely the origin and causes of that spiritualising
of religions and that limitation of the moral standard of which we can
find so many traces in the Alexandrian age? The nations who inhabited the
eastern shore of the Mediterranean sea, had, from the fourth century B.C., a
common history, and therefore had similar convictions. Who can decide
what each of them acquired by its own exertions, and what it obtained
through interchange of opinions? But in proportion as we see this we
must be on our guard against jumbling the phenomena together and effacing
them. There is little meaning in calling a thing Hellenic, as that really formed
an element in all the phenomena of the age. All our great political and ecclesiastical parties to-day are dependent on the ideas of 1789, and again on
romantic ideas. It is just as easy to verify this as it is difficult to determine
the measure and the manner of the influence for each group. And yet the
understanding of it turns altogether on this point. To call Pharisaism, or the
Gospel, or the old Jewish Christianity Hellenic, is not paradox, but confusion.

2 The Acts of the Apostles is in this respect a most instructive book. It,
as well as the Gospel of Luke, is a document of Gentile christianity developing
itself to Catholicism: Cf. Overbeck in his Commentar z. Apostelgesch But
the comprehensive judgment of Havet (in the work above mentioned, IV. p.
395) is correct. "L'hellénisme tient assez peu de place dans le N. T., du moins
l'hellénisme voulu et réfléchi. Ces livres sont écrits en grec et leurs auteurs
vivaient en pays grec; il y a donc eu chez eux infiltration des idées et des
sentiments helléniques; quelquefois même l'imagination hellénique y à péné-
tré comme dans le 3 évangile et dans les Actes .... Dans son ensemble, le
N. T. garde le caractère d'un livre hébraïque. Le christianisme ne commence
avoir une littérature et des doctrines vraiment helléniques qu'au milieu du
second siècle. Mais il y avait un judaïsme, celui d'Alexandrie, qui avait faite
alliance avec l'hellénisme avant même qu'il y eût des chrétiens"

vice of the Gospel. But the knowledge of Christ crucified, to which he subordinated all other knowledge as only of preparatory value, had nothing in common with Greek philosophy, while the idea of justification and the doctrine of the Spirit (Rom. VIII.), which together formed the peculiar contents of his Christianity, were irreconcilable with the moralism and the religious ideals of Hellenism. But the great mass of the earliest Gentile Christians became Christians because they perceived in the Gospel the sure tidings of the benefits and obligations which they had already sought in the fusion of Jewish and Greek elements. It is only by discerning this that we can grasp the preparation and genesis of the Catholic Church and its dogma.

From the foregoing statements it appears that there fall to be considered as presuppositions of the origin of the Catholic Apostolic doctrine of faith, the following topics, though of unequal importance as regards the extent of their influence.

(a). The Gospel of Jesus Christ.

(b). The common preaching of Jesus Christ in the first generation of believers.

(c). The current exposition of the Old Testament, the Jewish speculations and hopes of the future, in their significance for the earliest types of Christian preaching. [1]

(d). The religious conceptions, and the religious philosophy of the Hellenistic Jews, in their significance for the later restatement of the Gospel.

(e). The religious dispositions of the Greeks and Romans of the first two centuries, and the current Græco-Roman philosophy of religion.

---

1 The right of distinguishing (b) and (c) may be contested. But if we surrender this we therewith surrender the right to distinguish kernel and husk in the original proclamation of the Gospel. The dangers to which the attempt is exposed should not frighten us from it, for it has its justification in the fact that the Gospel is neither doctrine nor law.

§ 2. *The Gospel of Jesus Christ according to His own
testimony concerning Himself.*

I. The Fundamental Features.

The Gospel entered into the world as an apocalyptic eschatological message, apocalyptical and eschatological not only
in its form, but also in its contents. But Jesus announced that
the kingdom of God had already begun with his own work,
and those who received him in faith became sensible of this
beginning; for the "apocalyptical" was not merely the unveil-
ing of the future, but above all the revelation of God as the
Father, and the "eschatological" received its counterpoise in
the view of Jesus' work as Saviour, in the assurance of being
certainly called to the kingdom, and in the conviction that
life and future dominion is hid with God the Lord and preserved for believers by him. Consequently, we are following
not only the indications of the succeeding history, but also
the requirement of the thing itself, when, in the presentation of the Gospel, we place in the foreground, not that which
unites it with the contemporary disposition of Judaism, but
that which raises it above it. Instead of the hope of inherit-
ing the kingdom, Jesus had also spoken simply of preserving
the soul, or the life. In this one substitution lies already a
transformation of universal significance, of political religion
into a religion that is individual and therefore holy; for the
life is nourished by the word of God, but God is the Holy One.

The Gospel is the glad message of the government of the
world and of every individual soul by the almighty and holy
God, the Father and Judge. In this dominion of God, which
frees men from the power of the Devil, makes them rulers in a
heavenly kingdom in contrast with the kingdoms of the world,
and which will also be sensibly realised in the future æon
just about to appear, is secured life for all men who yield
themselves to God, although they should lose the world and
the earthly life. That is, the soul which is pure and holy
in connection with God, and in imitation of the Divine

perfection is eternally preserved with God, while those who would gain the world and preserve their life, fall into the hands of the Judge who sentences them to Hell. This dominion of God imposes on men a law, an old and yet a new law, viz., that of the Divine perfection and therefore of undivided love to God and to our neighbour. In this love, where it sways the inmost feeling, is presented the better righteousness (better not only with respect to the Scribes and Pharisees, but also with respect to Moses, see Matt. V.), which corresponds to the perfection of God. The way to attain it is a change of mind, that is, self-denial, humility before God, and heartfelt trust in him. In this humility and trust in God there is contained a recognition of one's own unworthiness; but the Gospel calls to the kingdom of God those very sinners who are thus minded, by promising the forgiveness of the sins which hitherto have separated them from God. But the Gospel which appears in these three elements, the dominion of God, a better right-eousness embodied in the law of love, and the forgiveness of sin, is inseparably connected with Jesus Christ; for in preach-ing this Gospel Jesus Christ everywhere calls men to himself. In him the Gospel is word and deed; it has become his food, and therefore his personal life, and into this life of his he draws all others. He is the Son who knows the Father. In him men are to perceive the kindness of the Lord; in him they are to feel God's power and government of the world, and to become certain of this consolation; they are to follow him the meek and lowly, and while he, the pure and holy one, calls sinners to himself, they are to receive the assurance that God through him forgiveth sin.

Jesus Christ has by no express statement thrust this con-nection of his Gospel with his Person into the foreground. No words could have certified it unless his life, the overpow-ering impression of his Person, had created it. By living, acting and speaking from the riches of that life which he lived with his Father, he became for others the revelation of the God of whom they formerly had heard, but whom they had not known. He declared his Father to be their Father and

they understood him. But he also declared himself to be
Messiah, and in so doing gave an intelligible expression to his
abiding significance for them and for his people. In a solemn
hour at the close of his life, as well as on special occasions
at an earlier period, he referred to the fact that the surrender
to his Person which induced them to leave all and follow him,
was no passing element in the new position they had gained
towards God the Father. He tells them, on the contrary,
that this surrender corresponds to the service which he will
perform for them and for the many, when he will give his
life a sacrifice for the sins of the world. By teaching them
to think of him and of his death in the breaking of bread
and the drinking of wine, and by saying of his death that
it takes place for the remission of sins, he has claimed as his
due from all future disciples what was a matter of course so
long as he sojourned with them, but what might fade away
after he was parted from them. He who in his preaching of
the kingdom of God raised the strictest self-examination and
humility to a law, and exhibited them to his followers in his
own life, has described with clear consciousness his life crowned
by death as the imperishable service by which men in all ages
will be cleansed from their sin and made joyful in their God.
By so doing he put himself far above all others, although
they were to become his brethren; and claimed a unique and
permanent importance as Redeemer and Judge. This permanent importance as the Lord he secured, not by disclosures
about the mystery of his Person, but by the impression of
his life and the interpretation of his death. He interprets it,
like all his sufferings, as a victory, as the passing over to his
glory, and in spite of the cry of God-forsakenness upon the
cross, he has proved himself able to awaken in his followers
the real conviction that he lives and is Lord and Judge of
the living and the dead.

The religion of the Gospel is based on this belief in Jesus
Christ, that is, by looking to him, this historical person, it
becomes certain to the believer that God rules heaven and
earth, and that God, the Judge, is also Father and Redeemer.

The religion of the Gospel is the religion which makes the highest moral demands, the simplest and the most difficult, and discloses the contradiction in which every man finds himself towards them. But it also procures redemption from such misery, by drawing the life of men into the inexhaustible and blessed life of Jesus Christ, who has overcome the world and called sinners to himself.

In making this attempt to put together the fundamental features of the Gospel, I have allowed myself to be guided by the results of this Gospel in the case of the first disciples. I do not know whether it is permissible to present such fundamental features apart from this guidance. The preaching of Jesus Christ was in the main so plain and simple, and in its application so manifold and rich, that one shrinks from attempting to systematise it, and would much rather merely narrate according to the Gospel. Jesus searches for the point in every man on which he can lay hold of him and lead him to the Kingdom of God. The distinction of good and evil—for God or against God—he would make a life question for every man, in order to shew him for whom it has become this, that he can depend upon the God whom he is to fear. At the same time he did not by any means uniformly fall back upon sin, or even the universal sinfulness, but laid hold of individuals very diversely, and led them to God by different paths. The doctrinal concentration of redemption on sin was certainly not carried out by Paul alone; but, on the other hand, it did not in any way become the prevailing form for the preaching of the Gospel. On the contrary, the antitheses, night, error, dominion of demons, death and light, truth, deliverance, life, proved more telling in the Gentile Churches. The consciousness of universal sinfulness was first made the negative fundamental frame of mind of Christendom by Augustine.

II. Details.

1. Jesus announced the Kingdom of God which stands in opposition to the kingdom of the devil, and therefore also

to the kingdom of the world, as a future Kingdom, and yet
it is presented in his preaching as present; as an invisible,
and yet it was visible — for one actually saw it. He lived
and spoke within the circle of eschatological ideas which Judaism had developed more than two hundred years before:
but he controlled them by giving them a new content and
forcing them into a new direction. Without abrogating the
law and the prophets he, on fitting occasions, broke through
the national, political and sensuous eudæmonistic forms in
which the nation was expecting the realisation of the dominion of God, but turned their attention at the same time to a
future near at hand, in which believers would be delivered
from the oppression of evil and sin, and would enjoy blessedness and dominion. Yet he declared that even now, every
individual who is called into the kingdom may call on God
as his Father, and be sure of the gracious will of God, the
hearing of his prayers, the forgiveness of sin, and the protection of God even in this present life. [1] But everything
in this proclamation is directed to the life beyond: the certainty of that life is the power and earnestness of the Gospel.

2. The conditions of entrance to the kingdom are, in the
first place, a complete change of mind, in which a man renounces the pleasures of this world, denies himself, and is
ready to surrender all that he has in order to save his soul;
then, a believing trust in God's grace which he grants to the
humble and the poor, and therefore hearty confidence in Jesus
as the Messiah chosen and called by God to realise his kingdom on the earth. The announcement is therefore directed
to the poor, the suffering, those hungering and thirsting for
righteousness, not to those who live, but to those who wish
to be healed and redeemed, and finds them prepared for en-

[1] Therewith are, doubtless, heavenly blessings bestowed in the present.
Historical investigation has, notwithstanding, every reason for closely
examining whether, and in how far, we may speak of a present for the
Kingdom of God, in the sense of Jesus But even if the question had to
be answered in the negative, it would make little or no difference for
the correct understanding of Jesus' preaching. The Gospel viewed in its
kernel is independent of this question. It deals with the inner constitution and mood of the soul.

trance into, and reception of the blessings of the kingdom of God, [1] while it brings down upon the self-satisfied, the rich and those proud of their righteousness, the judgment of obduracy and the damnation of Hell.

3. The commandment of undivided love to God and the brethren, as the main commandment, in the observance of which righteousness is realised, and forming the antithesis to the selfish mind, the lust of the world, and every arbitrary impulse, [2] corresponds to the blessings of the Kingdom of God, viz., forgiveness of sin, righteousness, dominion and blessedness. The standard of personal worth for the members of the Kingdom is self-sacrificing labour for others, not any technical mode of worship or legal preciseness. Renunciation of the world together with its goods, even of life itself in certain circumstances, is the proof of a man's sincerity and earnestness in seeking the Kingdom of God; and the meekness which renounces every right, bears wrong patiently, requiting it with kindness, is the practical proof of love to God, the conduct that answers to God's perfection.

4. In the proclamation and founding of this kingdom, Jesus summoned men to attach themselves to him, because he had recognised himself to be the helper called by God, and therefore also the Messiah who was promised. [3] He gradually declared

1 The question whether, and in what degree, a man of himself can earn righteousness before God is one of those theoretic questions to which Jesus gave no answer. He fixed his attention on all the gradations of the moral and religious conduct of his countrymen as they were immediately presented to him, and found some prepared for entrance into the kingdom of God, not by a technical mode of outward preparation, but by hungering and thirsting for it, and at the same time unselfishly serving their brethren. Humility and love unfeigned were always the decisive marks of these prepared ones. They are to be satisfied with righteousness before God, that is, are to receive the blessed feeling that God is gracious to them as sinners, and accepts them as his children. Jesus, however, allows the popular distinction of sinners and righteous to remain, but exhibits its perverseness by calling sinners to himself, and by describing the opposition of the righteous to his Gospel as a mark of their godlessness and hardness of heart.

2 The blessings of the kingdom were frequently represented by Jesus as a reward for work done. But this popular view is again broken through by reference to the fact that all reward is the gift of God's free grace.

3 Some Critics—most recently Havet, Le Christianisme et ses origines, 1884. T. IV. p. 15 ff.—have called in question the fact that Jesus called himself Messiah. But this article of the Evangelic tradition seems to me to stand the

himself to the people as such by the names he assumed, [1] for the names "Anointed," "King," "Lord," "Son of David," "Son of Man," "Son of God," all denote the Messianic office, and were familiar to the greater part of the people. [2] But though, at first, they express only the call, office, and power of the Messiah, yet by means of them and especially by the designation Son of God, Jesus pointed to a relation to God the Father, then and in its immediateness unique, as the basis of the office with which he was entrusted. He has, however, given no further explanation of the mystery of this relation than the declaration that the Son alone knoweth the Father, and that this knowledge of God and Sonship to God are secured for all others by the sending of the Son. [3]   In the

test of the most minute investigation. But, in the case of Jesus, the consciousness of being the Messiah undoubtedly rested on the certainty of being the Son of God, therefore of knowing the Father and being constrained to proclaim that knowledge.

1 We can gather with certainty from the Gospels that Jesus did not enter on his work with the announcement: Believe in me for I am the Messiah. On the contrary, he connected his work with the baptising movement of John, but carried that movement further, and thereby made the Baptist his forerunner (Mark I, 15 : πεπλήρωται ὁ καιρὸς καὶ ἤγγικεν ἡ βασιλεία τοῦ θεοῦ, μετανοεῖτε καὶ πιστεύετε ἐν τῷ εὐαγγελίῳ). He was in no hurry to urge anything that went beyond that message, but gradually prepared, and cautiously required of his followers an advance beyond it. The goal to which he led them was to believe in him as Messiah without putting the usual political construction on the Messianic ideal.

2 Even "Son of Man" probably means Messiah: we do not know whether Jesus had any special reason for favouring this designation which springs from Dan. VII. The objection to interpreting the word as Messiah really resolves itself into this, that the disciples (according to the Gospels) did not at once recognise him as Messiah. But that is explained by the contrast of his own peculiar idea of Messiah with the popular idea. The confession of him as Messiah was the keystone of their confidence in him, inasmuch as by that confession they separated themselves from old ideas.

3 The distinction between the Father and the Son stands out just as plainly in the sayings of Jesus, as the complete obedient subordination of the Son to the Father. Even according to John's Gospel, Jesus finishes the work which the Father has given him, and is obedient in everything even unto death. He declares Matt. XIX. 17 : εἷς ἐστὶν ὁ ἀγαθός. Special notice should be given to Mark XIII. 32, (Matt. XXIV, 36). Behind the only manifested life of Jesus, later speculation has put a life in which he wrought, not in subordination and obedience, but in like independence and dignity with God. That goes beyond the utterances of Jesus even in the fourth Gospel. But it is no advance beyond these, especially in the religious view and speech of the time, when it is announced that the relation of the Father to the Son lies beyond time. It is not even improbable that the sayings in the fourth Gospel referring to this, have a basis in the preaching of Jesus himself.

proclamation of God as Father, [1] as well as in the other proclamation that all the members of the kingdom following
the will of God in love, are to become one with the Son and
through him with the Father, [2] the message of the realised
kingdom of God receives its richest, inexhaustible content: the
Son of the Father will be the first-born among many brethren.

5. Jesus as the Messiah chosen by God has definitely distinguished himself from Moses and all the Prophets: as his
preaching and his work are the fulfilment of the law and the
prophets, so he himself is not a disciple of Moses, but corrects
that law-giver; he is not a Prophet, but Master and Lord. He
proves this Lordship during his earthly ministry in the accomplishment of the mighty deeds given him to do, above all in
withstanding the Devil and his kingdom, [3] and — according
to the law of the Kingdom of God—for that very reason in
the service which he performs. In this service Jesus also

1 Paul knew that the designation of God as the Father of our Lord Jesus
Christ, was the new Evangelic confession. Origen was the first among the
Fathers (though before him Marcion) to recognise that the decisive advance
beyond the Old Testament stage of religion, was given in the preaching of
God as Father; see the exposition of the Lord's prayer in his treatise *De
oratione*. No doubt the Old Testament, and the later Judaism knew the designation of God as Father; but it applied it to the Jewish nation, id dit not
attach the evangelic meaning to the name, and it did not allow itself in
any way to be guided in its religion by this idea.

2 See the farewell discourses in John, the fundamental ideas of which
are, in my opinion, genuine, that is, proceed from Jesus.

3 The historian cannot regard a miracle as a sure given historical event:
for in doing so he destroys the mode of consideration on which all historical
investigation rests. Every individual miracle remains historically quite
doubtful, and a summation of things doubtful never leads to certainty. But
should the historian, notwithstanding, be convinced that Jesus Christ did
extraordinary things, in the strict sense miraculous things, then, from the
unique impression he has obtained of this person, he infers the possession
by him of supernatural power. This conclusion itself belongs to the province
of religious faith: though there has seldom been a strong faith which
would not have drawn it. Moreover, the healing miracles of Jesus are the
only ones that come into consideration in a strict historical examination.
These certainly cannot be eliminated from the historical accounts without
utterly destroying them. But how unfit are they of themselves, after 1800
years, to secure any special importance to him to whom they are attributed,
unless that importance was already established apart from them. That
he could do with himself what he would, that he created a new thing
without overturning the old, that he won men to himself by announcing
the Father, that he inspired without fanaticism, set up a kingdom without politics, set men free from the world without asceticism, was a teacher without
theology, at a time of fanaticism and politics, asceticism and theology, is the

reckoned the sacrifice of his life, designating it as a
" λύτρον" which he offered for the redemption of man. [1] But
he declared at the same time that his Messianic work
was not yet fulfilled in his subjection to death. On the contrary, the close is merely initiated by his death; for the completion of the kingdom will only appear when he returns in
glory in the clouds of heaven to judgment. Jesus seems to
have announced this speedy return a short time before his
death, and to have comforted his disciples at his departure,
with the assurance that he would immediately enter into a
supramundane position with God. [2]

6. The instructions of Jesus to his disciples are accordingly
dominated by the thought that the end, the day and hour

great miracle of his person, and that he who preached the Sermon on the
Mount declared himself in respect of his life and death, to be the Redeemer
and Judge of the world, is the offence and foolishness which mock all reason

[1] See Mark X. 45. --That Jesus at the celebration of the first Lord's supper
described his death as a sacrifice which he should offer for the forgiveness of
sin, is clear from the account of Paul. From that account it appears to be certain, that Jesus gave expression to the idea of the necessity and saving
significance of his death for the forgiveness of sins, in a symbolical ordinance (based on the conclusion of the covenant, Exod. XXIV. 3 ff., perhaps,
as Paul presupposes, .on the Passover), in order that his disciples by
repeating it in accordance with the will of Jesus, might be the more deeply
impressed by it. Certain observations based on John VI., on the supper
prayer in the Didache, nay, even on the report of Mark, and supported
at the same time by features of the earliest practice in which it had the
character of a real meal, and the earliest theory of the supper, which
viewed it as a communication of eternal life and an anticipation of the
future existence, have for years made me doubt very much whether the
Pauline account and the Pauline conception of it, were really either the
oldest, or the universal and therefore only one. I have been strengthened
in this suspicion by the profound and remarkable investigation of Spitta
(z. Gesch. u. Litt. d. Urchristenthums: Die urchristl. Traditionen ü. den
Urspr. u. Sinnd. Abendmahls, 1893). He sees in the supper as not instituted,
but celebrated by Jesus, the festival of the Messianic meal, the anticipated
triumph over death, the expression of the perfection of the Messianic
work, the symbolic representation of the filling of believers with the powers of the Messianic kingdom and life. The reference to the Passover
and the death of Christ was attached to it later, though it is true very
soon. How much is thereby explained that was hitherto obscure—critical,
historical, and dogmatico-historical questions—cannot at all be stated
briefly. And yet I hesitate to give a full recognition to Spitta's exposition:
the words I. Cor. XI. 23 : ἐγὼ γὰρ παρέλαβον ἀπὸ τοῦ κυρίου, ὃ καὶ παρέδωκα
ὑμῖν κ.τ.λ., are too strong for me. Cf. besides, Weizsäcker's investigation
in "The Apostolic Age." Lobstein, La doctrine de la s. cène. 1889. A.
Harnack i. d. Texten u. Unters. VII. 2. p. 139 ff. Schürer, Theol. Lit. Ztg.
1891, p. 29 ff. Jülicher Abhandl. f. Weizsäcker, 1892, p. 215 ff.

[2] With regard to the eschatology, no one can say in detail what proceeds

of which, however, no one knows, is at hand. In consequence of this, also, the exhortation to renounce all earthly good takes a prominent place. But Jesus does not impose ascetic commandments as a new law, far less does he see in asceticism as such, sanctification [1]—he himself did not live as an ascetic, but was reproached as a wine-bibber—but he prescribed a perfect simplicity and purity of disposition, and a singleness of heart which remains invariably the same in trouble and renunciation, in possession and use of earthly good. A uniform equality of all in the conduct of life is not commanded: "To whom much is given, of him much shall be required." The disciples are kept as far from fanaticism and overrating of spiritual results as from asceticism. "Rejoice not that the spirits are subject to you, but rejoice that your names are written in heaven." When they besought him to teach them to pray, he taught them the "Lord's prayer", a prayer which demands such a collected mind, and such a tranquil, childlike elevation of the heart to God, that it cannot be offered at all by minds subject to passion or preoccupied by any daily cares.

7. Jesus himself did not found a new religious community, but gathered round him a circle of disciples, and chose Apostles whom he commanded to preach the Gospel. His preaching was universalistic inasmuch as it attributed no value to ceremonialism as such, and placed the fulfilment of the Mosaic law in the exhibition of its moral contents, partly against or beyond the letter. He made the law perfect by harmonising its particular requirements with the fundamental moral requirements which were also expressed in the Mosaic law. He emphasised the fundamental requirements more decidedly

from Jesus, and what from the disciples. What has been said in the text does not claim to be certain, but only probable. The most important, and at the same time the most certain point, is that Jesus made the definitive fate of the individual depend on faith, humility and love. There are no passages in the Gospel which conflict with the impression that Jesus reserved day and hour to God, and wrought in faith and patience as long as for him it was day.

1 He did not impose on every one, or desire from every one even the outward following of himself: see Mark V. 18-19. The "imitation of Jesus", in the strict sense of the word, did not play any noteworthy rôle either in the Apostolic or in the old Catholic period.

than was done by the law itself, and taught that all details should be referred to them and deduced from them. The external righteousness of Pharisaism was thereby declared to be not only an outer covering, but also a fraud, and the bond which still united religion and nationality in Judaism was sundered. [1] Political and national elements may probably have

---

[1] It is asserted by well-informed investigators, and may be inferred from the Gospels (Mark XII. 32-34 : Luke X. 27, 28), perhaps also from the Jewish original of the Didache, that some representatives of Pharisaism, beside the pedantic treatment of the law, attempted to concentrate it on the fundamental moral commandments. Consequently, in Palestinian and Alexandrian Judaism at the time of Christ, in virtue of the prophetic word and the Thora, influenced also, perhaps, by the Greek spirit which everywhere gave the stimulus to inwardness, the path was indicated in which the future development of religion was to follow. Jesus entered fully into the view of the law thus attempted, which comprehended it as a whole and traced it back to the disposition. But he freed it from the contradiction that adhered to it, (because, in spite of and alongside the tendency to a deeper perception, men still persisted in deducing righteousness from a punctilious observance of numerous particular commandments, because in so doing they became self-satisfied, that is, irreligious, and because in belonging to Abraham they thought they had a claim of right on God). For all that, so far as a historical understanding of the activity of Jesus is at all possible, it is to be obtained from the soil of Pharisaism, as the Pharisees were those who cherished and developed the Messianic expectations, and because, along with their care for the Thora, they sought also to preserve, in their own way, the prophetic inheritance. If everything does not deceive us, there were already contained in the Pharisaic theology of the age, speculations which were fitted to modify considerably the narrow view of history, and to prepare for universalism. The very men who tithed mint, anise and cummin, who kept their cups and dishes outwardly clean, who, hedging round the Thora, attempted to hedge round the people, spoke also of the sum total of the law. They made room in their theology for new ideas which are partly to be described as advances, and on the other hand, they have already pondered the question even in relation to the law, whether submission to its main contents was not sufficient for being numbered among the people of the covenant (see Renan: *Paul*). In particular the whole sacrificial system, which Jesus also essentially ignored, was therewith thrust into the background. Baldensperger (Selbstbewusstsein Jesu. p. 46) justly says, "There lie before us definite marks that the certainty of the nearness of God in the Temple (from the time of the Maccabees) begins to waver, and the efficacy of the temple institutions to be called in question. Its recent desecration by the Romans, appears to the author of the Psalms of Solomon (II. 2) as a kind of Divine requital for the sons of Israel, themselves having been guilty of so grossly profaning the sacrificial gifts. Enoch calls the shewbread of the second Temple polluted and unclean... There had crept in among the pious a feeling of the insufficiency of their worship, and from this side the Essenic schism will certainly represent only the open outbreak of a disease which had already begun to gnaw secretly at the religious life of the nation": see here the excellent explanations of the origin of Essenism in Lucius (Essenism 75 ff. 109 ff.) The spread of Judaism in the world, the secularization and apos-

been made prominent in the hopes of the future, as Jesus ap-

tacy of the priestly caste, the desecration of the Temple, the building of the
Temple at Leontopolis, the perception brought about by the spiritualising of
religion in the empire of Alexander the Great, that no blood of beast can be a
means of reconciling God—all these circumstances must have been absolutely dangerous and fatal, both to the local centralisation of worship, and to the
statutory sacrificial system. The proclamation of Jesus (and of Stephen) as to
the overthrow of the Temple, is therefore no absolutely new thing, nor is the
fact that Judaism fell back upon the law and the Messianic hope, a mere result
of the destruction of the Temple. This change was rather prepared by the
inner development. Whatever point in the preaching of Jesus we may fix on,
we shall find, that—apart from the writings of the Prophets and the Psalms,
which originated in the Greek Maccabean periods—parallels can be found
only in Pharisaism, but at the same time that the sharpest contrasts must
issue from it. Talmudic Judaism is not in every respect the genuine continuance of Pharisaic Judaism, but a product of the decay which attests that the
rejection of Jesus by the spiritual leaders of the people had deprived the
nation, and even the Virtuosi of Religion of their best part: (see for this the
expositions of Kuenen " Judaismus und Christenthum", in his (Hibbert) lectures on national religions and world religions.) The ever recurring attempts
to deduce the origin of Christianity from Hellenism, or even from the Roman
Greek culture, are there also rightly, briefly and tersely rejected. Also the
hypotheses, which either entirely eliminate the person of Jesus or make him
an Essene, or subordinate him to the person of Paul, may be regarded as
definitively settled. Those who think they can ascertain the origin of Christian
religion from the origin of Christian Theology will, indeed, always think of
Hellenism: Paul will eclipse the person of Jesus with those who believe that
a religion for the world must be born with a universalistic doctrine. Finally,
Essenism will continue in authority with those who see in the position of indifference which Jesus took to the Temple worship, the main thing, and who,
besides, create for themselves an "Essenism of their own finding". Hellenism,
and also Essenism, can of course indicate to the historian some of the conditions by which the appearance of Jesus was prepared and rendered possible;
but they explain only the possibility, not the reality of the appearance. But
this with its historically not deducible power is the decisive thing. If some one
has recently said that " the historical speciality of the person of Jesus " is not
the main thing in Christianity, he has thereby betrayed that he does not know
how a religion that is worthy of the name is founded, propagated, and maintained. For the latest attempt to put the Gospel in a historical connection
with Buddhism (Seydel. Das Ev. von Jesus in seinen Verhältnissen zur
Buddha-Sage, 1882: likewise, Die Buddha-Legende und das Leben Jesu, 1884),
see, Oldenburg, Theol. Lit.-Z'g 1882. Col. 415 f. 1884. 185 f. However much
necessarily remains obscure to us in the ministry of Jesus when we seek
to place it in a historical connection,—what is known is sufficient to
confirm the judgment that his preaching developed a germ in the religion
of Israel (see the Psalms) which was finally guarded and in many respects
developed by the Pharisees, but which languished and died under their
guardianship. The power of development which Jesus imported to it was
not a power which he himself had to borrow from without ; but doctrine
and speculation were as far from him as ecstasy and visions. On the
other hand, we must remember we do not know the history of Jesus up
to his public entrance on his ministry, and that therefore we do not know
whether in his native province he had any connection with Greeks.

propriated them for his preaching. But from the conditions
to which the realising of the hopes for the individual was
attached, there already shone the clearer ray which was to
eclipse those elements, and one saying such as Matt. XXII. 21.,
annulled at once political religion and religious politics.

Supplement 1.—The idea of the inestimable inherent value
of every individual human soul, already dimly appearing in
several psalms, and discerned by Greek Philosophers, though
as a rule developed in contradiction to religion, stands out
plainly in the preaching of Jesus. It is united with the idea
of God as Father, and is the complement to the message of
the communion of brethren realising itself in love. In this
sense the Gospel is at once profoundly individualistic and
Socialistic. The prospect of gaining life, and preserving it
for ever, is therefore also the highest which Jesus has set
forth, it is not, however, to be a motive, but a reward of
grace. In the certainty of this prospect, which is the converse of renouncing the world, he has proclaimed the sure
hope of the resurrection, and consequently the most abundant
compensation for the loss of the natural life. Jesus put an
end to the vacillation and uncertainty which in this respect
still prevailed among the Jewish people of his day. The
confession of the Psalmist, "Whom have I in heaven but thee,
and there is none upon the earth that I desire beside thee",
and the fulfilling of the Old Testament commandment, "Love
thy neighbour as thyself", were for the first time presented
in their connection in the person of Jesus. He himself therefore is Christianity, for the "impression of his person convinced
the disciples of the facts of forgiveness of sin and the second
birth, and gave them courage to believe in and to lead a
new life". We cannot therefore state the "doctrine" of Jesus;
for it appears as a supramundane life which must be felt in
the person of Jesus, and its truth is guaranteed by the fact
that such a life can be lived.

Supplement 2.—The history of the Gospel contains two
great transitions, both of which, however, fall within the first
century; from Christ to the first generation of believers, in-

cluding Paul, and from the first, Jewish Christian, generation of these believers to the Gentile Christians, in other words: from Christ to the brotherhood of believers in Christ, and from this to the incipient Catholic Church. No later transitions in the Church can be compared with these in importance. As to the first, the question has frequently been asked, Is the Gospel of Christ to be the authority or the Gospel concerning Christ? But the strict dilemma here is false. The Gospel certainly is the Gospel of Christ. For it has only, in the sense of Jesus, fulfilled its Mission when the Father has been declared to men as he was known by the Son, and where the life is swayed by the realities and principles which ruled the life of Jesus Christ. But it is in accordance with the mind of Jesus and at the same time a fact of history, that this Gospel can only be appropriated and adhered to in connection with a believing surrender to the person of Jesus Christ. Yet every dogmatic formula is suspicious, because it is fitted to wound the spirit of religion; it should not at least be put before the living experience in order to evoke it; for such a procedure is really the admission of the half belief which thinks it necessary that the impression made by the person must be supplemented. The essence of the matter is a personal life which awakens life around it as the fire of one torch kindles another. Early as weakness of faith is in the Church of Christ, it is no earlier than the procedure of making a formulated and ostensibly proved confession the foundation of faith, and therefore demanding, above all, subjection to this confession. Faith assuredly is propagated by the testimony of faith, but dogma is not in itself that testimony·

The peculiar character of the Christian religion is conditioned by the fact that every reference to God is at the same time a reference to Jesus Christ, and *vice versa*. In this sense the Person of Christ is the central point of the religion, and inseparably united with the substance of piety as a sure reliance on God. Such a union does not, as is supposed, bring a foreign element into the pure essence of religion. The pure essence of religion rather demands such a union; for "the

reverence for persons, the inner bowing before the manifestation of moral power and goodness is the root of all true
religion" (W. Herrmann). But the Christian religion knows
and names only one name before which it bows. In this
rests its positive character, in all else, as piety, it is by its
strictly spiritual and inward attitude, not a positive religion
alongside of others, but religion itself. But just because
the Person of Christ has this significance is the knowledge
and understanding of the "historical Christ" required: for no
other comes within the sphere of our knowledge. "The historical Christ" that, to be sure, is not the powerless Christ of
contemporary history shewn to us through a coloured biograph-
ical medium, or dissipated in all sorts of controversies, but
Christ as a power and as a life which towers above our own
life, and enters into our life as God's Spirit and God's Word,
(see Herrmann, Der Verkehr des Christen mit Gott. 2. Edit.
1892, [i. e., "The Fellowship of the Christian with God", an
important work included in the present series of translations.
Ed.] Kähler, Der sog. historische Jesus und der geschichtliche
biblische Christus, 1892). But historical labour and investigation are needed in order to grasp this Jesus Christ ever more
firmly and surely.

As to the second transition, it brought with it the most
important changes, which, however, became clearly manifest
only after the lapse of some generations. They appear, first,
in the belief in holy consecrations, efficacious in themselves,
and administered by chosen persons; further, in the conviction,
that the relation of the individual to God and Christ is, above
all, conditioned on the acceptance of a definite divinely attested
law of faith and holy writings; further, in the opinion that
God has established Church arrangements, observance of which
is necessary and meritorious, as well as in the opinion that
a visible earthly community is the people of a new covenant.
These assumptions, which formally constitute the essence of
Catholicism as a religion, have no support in the teaching of
Jesus, nay, offend against that teaching.

Supplement 3.—The question as to what new thing Christ

has brought, answered by Paul in the words, "If any man be in Christ he is a new creature, old things are passed away, behold all things are become new", has again and again been pointedly put since the middle of the second century by Apologists, Theologians and religious Philosophers, within and without the Church, and has received the most varied answers. Few of the answers have reached the height of the Pauline confession. But where one cannot attain to this confession, one ought to make clear to oneself that every answer which does not lie in the line of it is altogether unsatisfactory; for it is not difficult to set over against every article from the preaching of Jesus an observation which deprives it of its originality. It is the Person, it is the fact of his life that is new and creates the new. The way in which he called forth and established a people of God on earth, which has become sure of God and of eternal life; the way in which he set up a new thing in the midst of the old and transformed the religion of Israel into *the religion*: that is the mystery of his Person, in which lies his unique and permanent position in the history of humanity.

Supplement 4.—The conservative position of Jesus towards the religious traditions of his people had the necessary result that his preaching and his Person were placed by believers in the frame-work of this tradition, which was thereby very soon greatly expanded. But, though this way of understanding the Gospel was certainly at first the only possible way, and though the Gospel itself could only be preserved by such means (see § 1), yet it cannot be mistaken that a displacement in the conception of the Person and preaching of Jesus, and a burdening of religious faith, could not but forthwith set in, from which developments followed, the premises of which would be vainly sought for in the words of the Lord (see §§ 3, 4). But here the question arises as to whether the Gospel is not inseparably connected with the eschatological world-renouncing element with which it entered into the world, so that its being is destroyed where this is omitted. A few words may be devoted to this question. The Gospel possesses properties which oppose every positive religion, because they depreciate it, and these properties form the kernel of the Gospel. The disposition which is devoted to God, humble, ardent and sincere in its love to God and to the brethren, is, as an abiding habit, law, and at the same time, a gift of the Gospel, and also finally exhausts it. This quiet, peaceful element was at the beginning strong and vigorous, even in those who lived in the world of ecstasy and expected the world to come. One may be named for all, Paul. He who wrote I. Cor. XIII. and Rom. VIII. should not, in spite of all that he has said elsewhere, be called upon to witness that the nature of the Gospel is exhausted in its world-renouncing, ecstatic and eschatological elements, or at least. that it is so inseparably united with these as to fall along with them. He who wrote those chapters, and the greater than he who promised the kingdom of heaven to children, and to those who were hungering and thirsting for righteousness, he to whom tradition ascribes the words: "Rejoice not that the spirits are subject to you, but rather rejoice that your names are written in heaven" — both attest that the Gospel lies above the antagonisms between this world and the next, work and retirement from the world, reason and ecstasy, Judaism and Hellenism. And because it lies above them it may be united with either, as it originally unfolded its powers under the ruins of the Jewish religion. But still more; it not only can enter into union with them, it must do so if it is otherwise the religion of the living and is itself living. It has only one aim; that man may find God and have him as his own God, in order to gain in him humility and patience, peace, joy and love. How it reaches this goal through the advancing centuries, whether with the co-efficients of Judaism or Hellenism, of renunciation of the world or of culture, of mysticism or the doctrine of predestination, of Gnosticism or Agnosticism, and whatever other incrustations there may yet be which can defend the kernel, and under which alone living elements can grow — all that belongs to the centuries. However each individual Christian may reckon to the treasure

itself the earthly vessel in which he hides his treasure; it is
the duty and the right, not only of the religious, but also of
the historical estimate to distinguish between the vessel and
the treasure; for the Gospel did not enter into the world as
a positive statutory religion, and cannot therefore have its classic
manifestation in any form of its intellectual or social types,
not even in the first. It is therefore the duty of the historian of the first century of the Church, as well as that of
those which follow, not to be content with fixing the changes
of the Christian religion, but to examine how far the new forms
were capable of defending, propagating and impressing the
Gospel itself. It would probably have perished if the forms
of primitive Christianity had been scrupulously maintained in
the Church; but now primitive Christianity has perished in
order that the Gospel might be preserved. To study this progress of the development, and fix the significance of the newly received forms for the kernel of the matter, is the last
and highest task of the historian who himself lives in his subject. He who approaches from without must be satisfied with
the general view that in the history of the Church some things
have always remained, and other things have always been
changing.

Literature.—Weiss. Biblical Theology of the New Testament.
T. and T. Clark. Wittichen. Beitr. z. bibl. Theol. 3. Thle.
1864-72.

Schürer. Die Predigt Jesu in ihrem Verhaltniss z. A. T. u.
z. Judenthum, 1882.

Wellhausen. Abriss der Gesch. Israels u. Juda's (Skizzen u.
Vorarbeiten) 1. Heft. 1884.

Baldensperger. Das Selbstbewusstsein Jesu im Licht der Mes-
sianischen Hoffnungen seiner Zeit, 1888, (2 Aufl. 1891). The
prize essays of Schmoller and Issel, Ueber die Lehre vom Reiche
Gottes im N. Test. 1891 (besides Gunkel in d. Theol. Lit.
Ztg. 1893. N°. 2).

Wendt. Die Lehre Jesu. (The teaching of Jesus. T. and
T. Clark. English translation.)

Joh. Weiss. Die Predigt Jesu vom Reiche Gottes, 1892.

Bousset. Jesu Predigt in ihrem Gegensatz zum Judenthum, 1892.

C. Holtzman. Die Offenbarung durch Christus und das Neue Testament (Zeitschr. f. Theol. und Kirche I. p. 367 ff.) The special literature in the above work of Weiss, and in the recent works on the life of Jesus, and the Biblical Theology of the New Testament by Beyschlag. [T. T. Clark]

§ 3. *The Common Preaching concerning Jesus Christ in the First Generation of Believers.*

Men had met with Jesus Christ and in him had found the Messiah. They were convinced that God had made him to be wisdom and righteousness, sanctification and redemption. There was no hope that did not seem to be certified in him, no lofty idea which had not become in him a living reality. Everything that one possessed was offered to him. He was everything lofty that could be imagined. Everything that can be said of him was already said in the first two generations after his appearance. Nay, more: he was felt and known to be the ever living one, Lord of the world and operative principle of one's own life. "To me to live is Christ and to die is gain;" "He is the way, the truth and the life." One could now for the first time be certain of the resurrection and eternal life, and with that certainty the sorrows of the world melted away like mist before the sun, and the residue of this present time became as a day. This group of facts which the history of the Gospel discloses in the world, is at the same time the highest and most unique of all that we meet in that history: it is its seal and distinguishes it from all other universal religions. Where in the history of mankind can we find anything resembling this, that men who had eaten and drunk with their Master should glorify him, not only as the revealer of God, but as the Prince of life, as the Redeemer and Judge of the world, as the living power of its existence, and that a choir of Jews and Gentiles, Greeks and Barbarians, wise and foolish, should along with them immediately confess that out of the fulness of this one man they have received grace for grace?

It has been said that Islam furnishes the unique example of
a religion born in broad daylight, but the community of
Jesus was also born in the clear light of day. The darkness
connected with its birth is occasioned not only by the imper-
fection of the records, but by the uniqueness of the fact,
which refers us back to the uniqueness of the Person of Jesus.

But though it certainly is the first duty of the historian to
signalise the overpowering impression made by the Person of
Jesus on the disciples, which is the basis of all further developments, it would little become him to renounce the critical
examination of all the utterances which have been connected
with that Person with the view of elucidating and glorifying
it; unless he were with Origen to conclude that Jesus was to
each and all whatever they fancied him to be for their edification. But this would destroy the personality. Others are of
opinion that we should conceive him, in the sense of the early
communities, as the second God who is one in essence with
the Father, in order to understand from this point of view
all the declarations and judgments of these communities. But
this hypothesis leads to the most violent distortion of the
original declarations, and the suppression or concealment of
their most obvious features. The duty of the historian rather
consists in fixing the common features of the faith of the first
two generations, in explaining them as far as possible from
the belief that Jesus is Messiah, and in seeking analogies for
the several assertions. Only a very meagre sketch can be
given in what follows. The presentation of the matter in the
frame-work of the history of dogma does not permit of more,
because as noted above, § 1, the presupposition of dogma
forming itself in the Gentile Church is not the whole infinitely
rich abundance of early Christian views and perceptions. That
presupposition is simply a proclamation of the one God and
of Christ transferred to Greek soil, fixed merely in its leading
features and otherwise very plastic, accompanied by a message
regarding the future, and demands for a holy life. At the
same time the Old Testament and the early Christian Palestinian writings with the rich abundance of their contents, did

certainly exercise a silent mission in the earliest communities, till
by the creation of the canon they became a power in the Church.

1. The contents of the faith of the disciples, [1] and the
common proclamation which united them, may be comprised
in the following propositions. Jesus of Nazareth is the Messiah promised by the prophets. Jesus after his death is by
the Divine awakening raised to the right hand of God, and
will soon return to set up his kingdom visibly upon the earth.
He who believes in Jesus, and has been received into the
community of the disciples of Jesus, who, in virtue of a sincere
change of mind, calls on God as Father, and lives according
to the commandments of Jesus, is a saint of God, and as such
can be certain of the sin-forgiving grace of God, and of a
share in the future glory, that is, of redemption. [2]

A community of Christian believers was formed within
the Jewish national community. By its organisation, the close
brotherly union of its members, it bore witness to the
impression which the Person of Jesus had made on it, and
drew from faith in Jesus and hope of his return, the assurance
of eternal life, the power of believing in God the Father and
of fulfilling the lofty moral and social commands which Jesus
had set forth. They knew themselves to be the true Israel of
the Messianic time (see § 1), and for that very reason lived
with all their thoughts and feelings in the future. Hence the
Apocalyptic hopes which in manifold types were current in
the Judaism of the time, and which Jesus had not demolished,
continued to a great extent in force (see § 4). One guarantee
for their fulfilment was supposed to be possessed in the various
manifestations of the Spirit, [3] which were displayed in the

1 See the brilliant investigations of Weizsäcker (Apost. Zeitalter. p. 36)
as to the earliest significant names, self-designations, of the disciples.
The twelve were in the first place "μαθηταί," (disciples and family-circle
of Jesus, see also the significance of James and the brethren of Jesus),
then witnesses of the resurrection and therefore Apostles; very soon
there appeared beside them, even in Jerusalem, Prophets and Teachers.

2 The christian preaching is very pregnantly described in Acts XXVIII.
31. as κηρύσσειν τὴν Βασιλείαν τοῦ θεοῦ, καὶ διδάσκειν τὰ περὶ τοῦ κυρίου Ἰησοῦ Χριστοῦ.

3 On the spirit of God (of Christ) see note, p. 50. The earliest christians
felt the influence of the spirit as one coming on them from without.

members of the new communities at their entrance, with which
an act of baptism seems to have been united from the very first, [1]
and in their gatherings. They were a guarantee that believers
really were the ἐκκλησία τοῦ θεοῦ, those called to be saints, and,
as such, kings and priests unto God [2] for whom the world, death
and devil are overcome, although they still rule the course of the
world. The confession of the God of Israel as the Father of Jesus,
and of Jesus as Christ and Lord [3] was sealed by the testimony

---

1. It cannot be directly proved that Jesus instituted baptism, for Matth.
XXVIII. 19, is not a saying of the Lord. The reasons for this assertion are :
(1) It is only a later stage of the tradition that represents the risen Christ
as delivering speeches and giving commandments. Paul knows nothing of it.
(2) The Trinitarian formula is foreign to the mouth of Jesus and has not
the authority in the Apostolic age which it must have had if it had descended from Jesus himself. On the other hand, Paul knows of no other way
of receiving the Gentiles into the Christian communities than by baptism,
and it is highly probable that in the time of Paul all Jewish Christians were
also baptised. We may perhaps assume that the practice of baptism was
continued in consequence of Jesus' recognition of John the Baptist and his
baptism, even after John himself had been removed. According to John
IV. 2, Jesus himself baptised not, but his disciples under his superinten-
dence. It is possible only with the help of tradition to trace back to Jesus a
"Sacrament of Baptism," or an obligation to it *ex necessitate salutis*, though
it is credible that tradition is correct here. Baptism in the Apostolic age
was εἰς ἄφεσιν ἁμαρτιῶν, and indeed εἰς τὸ ὄνομα χριστοῦ (1. Cor. I. 13: Acts
XIX. 5). We cannot make out when the formula, εις τὸ ὄνομα τοῦ πατρὸς, καὶ
τοῦ υἱοῦ, καὶ τοῦ ἁγίου πνεύματος, emerged. The formula εἰς τὸ ὄνομα expresses
that the person baptised is put into a relation of dependence on him into
whose name he is baptised. Paul has given baptism a relation to the death
of Christ, or justly inferred it from the εἰς ἄφεσιν ἁμαρτιῶν. The descent of
the spirit on the baptised very soon ceased to be regarded as the necessary and immediate result of baptism; yet Paul, and probably his contemporaries also, considered the grace of baptism and the communication
of the spirit to be inseparably united. See Scholten. Die Taufformel. 1885.
Holtzman, Die Taufe im N. T. Ztsch. f. wiss. Theol. 1879
2 The designation of the Christian community as ἐκκλησία, originates
perhaps with Paul, though that is by no means certain; see as to this
"name of honour," Sohm, Kirchenrecht, Vol. I. p 16 ff The words of the
Lord, Matt. XVI 18 : XVIII. 17, belong to a later period. According to
Gal. I. 22, ταῖς ἐν Χριστῷ is added to the ταῖς ἐκκλησίαις τῆς Ἰουδαίας. The
independence of every individual Christian in, and before God is strongly
insisted on in the Epistles of Paul, and in the Epistle of Peter, and in
the Christian portions of Revelations: ἐποίησεν ἡμᾶς βασιλείαν, ἱερεῖς τῷ θεῷ
καὶ πατρὶ αὐτοῦ.
3 Jesus is regarded with adoring reverence as Messiah and Lord, that
is, these are regarded as the names which his Father has given him.
Christians are those who call on the name of the Lord Jesus Christ (1. Cor.
I. 2): every creature must bow before him and confess him as Lord
Phil. II. 9): see Deissmann on the N. T. formula "in Christo Jesu."

of the possession of the Spirit, which as Spirit of God assured
every individual of his call to the kingdom, united him personally
with God himself and became to him the pledge of future glory. [1]

2. As the Kingdom of God which was announced had not
yet visibly appeared, as the appeal to the Spirit could not
be separated from the appeal to Jesus as Messiah, and as
there was actually nothing possessed but the reality of the
Person of Jesus, so in preaching all stress must necessarily
fall on this Person. To believe in him was the decisive fundamental requirement, and, at first, under the presupposition
of the religion of Abraham and the Prophets, the sure guarantee of salvation. It is not surprising then to find that in
the earliest Christian preaching Jesus Christ comes before us
as frequently as the Kingdom of God in the preaching of
Jesus himself. The image of Jesus, and the power which proceeded from it, were the things which were really possessed.
Whatever was expected was expected only from Jesus the
exalted and returning one. The proclamation that the Kingdom of heaven is at hand must therefore become the proclamation that Jesus is the Christ, and that in him the revelation of God is complete. He who lays hold of Jesus lays hold
in him of the grace of God, and of a full salvation. We
cannot, however, call this in itself a displacement: but as soon
as the proclamation that Jesus is the Christ ceased to be
made with the same emphasis and the same meaning that it
had in his own preaching, and what sort of blessings they
were which he brought, not only was a displacement inevitable, but even a dispossession. But every dispossession requires the given forms to be filled with new contents. Simple
as was the pure tradition of the confession: "Jesus is the Christ,"

---

1 The confession of Father, Son and Spirit is therefore the unfolding
of the belief that Jesus is the Christ: but there was no intention of expressing by this confession the essential equality of the three persons, or
even the similar relation of the Christian to them. On the contrary, the
Father, in it, is regarded as the God and Father over all, the Son as
revealer, redeemer and Lord, the Spirit as a possession, principle of the
new supernatural life and of holiness. From the Epistles of Paul we perceive
that the Formula Father, Son and Spirit could not yet have been customary,
especially in Baptism. But it was approaching (2 Cor. XIII. 13).

the task of rightly appropriating and handing down entire
the peculiar contents which Jesus had given to his self-wit-
nessing and preaching was nevertheless great, and in its limit
uncertain. Even the Jewish Christian could perform this task only
according to the measure of his spiritual understanding and
the strength of his religious life. Moreover, the external position of the first communities in the midst of contemporaries
who had crucified and rejected Jesus, compelled them to
prove, as their main duty, that Jesus really was the Messiah
who was promised. Consequently, everything united to bring
the first communities to the conviction that the proclamation
of the Gospel with which they were entrusted, resolved itself
into the proclamation that Jesus is the Christ. The διδάσκειν
τηρεῖν πάντα ὅσα ἐνετείλατο ὁ Ἰησοῦς (teaching to observe all
that Jesus had commanded), a thing of heart and life, could
not lead to reflection in the same degree, as the διδάσκειν ὅτι
οὗτὸς ἐστιν ὁ χριστὸς τοῦ θεοῦ (teaching that this is the Christ
of God): for a community which possesses the Spirit does not
reflect on whether its conception is right, but, especially a
missionary community, on what the certainty of its faith rests.

The proclamation of Jesus as the Christ, though rooted entirely in the Old Testament, took its start from the exaltation
of Jesus, which again resulted from his suffering and death.
The proof that the entire Old Testament points to him, and
that his person, his deeds and his destiny are the actual and
precise fulfilment of the Old Testament predictions, was the
foremost interest of believers, so far as they at all looked
backwards. This proof was not used in the first place for the
purpose of making the meaning and value of the Messianic
work of Jesus more intelligible, of which it did not seem to
be in much need, but to confirm the Messiahship of Jesus.
Still, points of view for contemplating the Person and work
of Jesus could not fail to be got from the words of the Prophets. The fundamental conception of Jesus dominating everything was, according to the Old Testament, that God had
chosen him and through him the Church. God had chosen
him and made him to be both Lord and Christ. He had

made over to him the work of setting up the Kingdom, and had led him through death and resurrection to a supramundane position of sovereignty, in which he would soon visibly appear and bring about the end. The hope of Christ's speedy return was the most important article in the "Christology," inasmuch as his work was regarded as only reaching its conclusion by that return. It was the most difficult, inasmuch as the Old Testament contained nothing of a second advent of Messiah. Belief in the second advent became the specific Christian belief.

But the searching in the scriptures of the Old Testament, that is, in the prophetic texts, had already, in estimating the Person and dignity of Christ, given an important impulse towards transcending the frame-work of the idea of the theocracy completed solely in and for Israel. Moreover, belief in the exaltation of Christ to the right hand of God, caused men to form a corresponding idea of the beginning of his existence. The missionary work among the Gentiles, so soon begun and so rich in results, threw a new light on the range of Christ's purpose and work, and led to the consideration of its significance for the whole human race. Finally, the self-testimony of Jesus summoned them to ponder his relation to God the Father, with the presuppositions of that relation, and to give it expression in intelligible statements. Speculation had already begun on these four points in the Apostolic age, and had resulted in very different utterances as to the Person and dignity of Jesus (§ 4). [1]

1 The Christological utterances which are found in the New Testament writings, so far as they explain and paraphrase the confession of Jesus as the Christ and the Lord, may be almost entirely deduced from one or other of the four points mentioned in the text. But we must at the same time insist that these declarations were meant to be explanations of the confession that "Jesus is the Lord," which of course included the recognition that Jesus by the resurrection became a heavenly being (see Weizsäcker in above mentioned work, p. 110). The solemn protestation of Paul. 1 Cor. XII. 3 ; διὸ γνωρίζω ὑμῖν ὅτι οὐδεὶς ἐν πνεύματι θεοῦ λαλῶν λέγει ΑΝΑΘΕΜΑ ΙΗΣΟΥΣ, καὶ οὐδεὶς δύναται εἰπεῖν ΚΥΡΙΟΣ ΙΗΣΟΥΣ εἰ μὴ ἐν πνεύματι ἁγίῳ (cf. Rom. X. 9), shews that he who acknowledged Jesus as the Lord, and accordingly believed in the resurrection of Jesus, was regarded as a full-born Christian. It undoubtedly excludes from the Apostolic age the independent authority of any christological dogma besides that confession and the worship of Christ connected with it. It is

3. Since Jesus had appeared and was believed on as the Messiah promised by the Prophets, the aim and contents of his mission seemed already to be therewith stated with sufficient clearness. Further, as the work of Christ was not yet completed, the view of those contemplating it was, above all, turned to the future. But in virtue of express words of Jesus, and in the consciousness of having received the Spirit of God, one was already certain of the forgiveness of sin dispensed by God, of righteousness before him, of the full knowledge of the Divine will, and of the call to the future Kingdom as a present possession. In the procuring of these blessings not a few perceived with certainty the results of the first advent of Messiah, that is, his work. This work might be seen in the whole activity of Christ. But as the forgiveness of sins might be conceived as *the* blessing of salvation which included with certainty every other blessing, as Jesus had put his death in express relation with this blessing, and as the fact of this death so mysterious and offensive required a special explanation, there appeared in the foreground from the very beginning the confession, in 1 Cor. XV. 3: παρέδωκα ὑμῖν ἐν πρώτοις, ὁ καὶ παρέλαβον, ὅτι χριστὸς ἀπέθανεν ὑπὲρ τῶν ἁμαρτιῶν ἡμῶν. "I delivered unto you first of all that which I also received, that *Christ died for our sins.*" Not only Paul, for whom, in virtue of his special reflections and experiences, the cross of Christ had become the central point of all knowledge, but also the majority of believers, must have regarded the preaching of the death of the Lord as an essential article in the preaching of Christ, [1] seeing that, as a rule, they placed

worth notice, however, that those early Christian men who recognised Christianity as the vanquishing of the Old Testament religion (Paul, the Author of the Epistle to the Hebrews, John) all held that Christ was a being who had come down from heaven.

[1] Compare in their fundamental features the common declarations about the saving value of the death of Christ in Paul, in the Johannine writings, in 1st Peter, in the Epistle to the Hebrews, and in the Christian portions of the book of Revelation: τῷ ἀγαπῶντί ἡμᾶς καὶ λύσαντι ἡμᾶς ἐκ τῶν ἁμαρτιῶν ἐν τῷ αἵματι αὐτοῦ, αὐτῷ ἡ δόξα: Compare the reference to Isaiah LIII. and the Passover lamb: the utterances about the "lamb" generally in the early writings: see Westcott, The Epistles of John, p. 34 f: The idea of the blood of Christ in the New Testament.

it somehow under the aspect of a sacrifice offered to God.
Still, there were very different conceptions of the value of the
death as a means of procuring salvation, and there may have
been many who were satisfied with basing its necessity on the
fact that it had been predicted, (ἀπέθανεν κατὰ τὰς γραφάς:
"he died for our sins *according to the scriptures*"), while their
real religious interests were entirely centered in the future
glory to be procured by Christ. But it must have been of
greater significance for the following period that, from the
first, a short account of the destiny of Jesus lay at the basis
of all preaching about him (see a part of this in 1. Cor. XV.
1-11). Those articles in which the identity of the Christ
who had appeared with the Christ who had been promised
stood out with special clearness, must have been taken up
into this report, as well as those which transcended the common expectations of Messiah, which for that very reason appeared of special importance, viz., his death and resurrection.
In putting together this report, there was no intention of
describing the "work" of Christ. But after the interest which
occasioned it had been obscured, and had given place to other
interests, the customary preaching of those articles must have
led men to see in them Christ's real performance, his "work". [1]

4. The firm confidence of the disciples in Jesus was
rooted in the belief that he did not abide in death, but was
raised by God. That Christ had risen was, in virtue of what
they had experienced in him, certainly only after they had
seen him, just as sure as the fact of his death, and became
the main article of their preaching about him. [2] But in the
message of the risen Lord was contained not only the con-

---

1 This of course could not take place otherwise than by reflecting on its
significance. But a dislocation was already completed as soon as it was
isolated and separated from the whole of Jesus, or even from his future
activity. Reflection on the meaning or the causes of particular facts might
easily, in virtue of that isolation, issue in entirely new conceptions.

2 See the discriminating statements of Weizsäcker, "Apostolic Age",
p. 1 f., especially as to the significance of Peter as first witness of the
resurrection. Cf. 1 Cor. XV. 5 with Luke XXIV. 34: also the fragment of
the "Gospel of Peter" which unfortunately breaks off at the point where
one expects the appearance of the Lord to Peter.

viction that he lives again, and now lives for ever, but also
the assurance that his people will rise in like manner and
live eternally. Consequently, the resurrection of Jesus became
the sure pledge of the resurrection of all believers, that is of
their real personal resurrection. No one at the beginning
thought of a mere immortality of the spirit, not even those
who assumed the perishableness of man's sensuous nature. In
conformity with the uncertainty which yet adhered to the
idea of resurrection in Jewish hopes and speculations, the
concrete notions of it in the Christian communities were also
fluctuating. But this could not affect the certainty of the
conviction that the Lord would raise his people from death.
This conviction, whose reverse side is the fear of that God
who casts into hell, has become the mightiest power through
which the Gospel has won humanity. ¹

1 It is often said that Christianity rests on the belief in the resurrection of
Christ. This may be correct, if it is first declared who this Jesus Christ is, and
what his life signifies. But when it appears as a naked report to which one
must above all submit, and when in addition, as often happens, it is supplemented by the assertion that the resurrection of Christ is the most certain fact
in the history of the world, one does not know whether he should marvel
more at its thoughtlessness or its unbelief. We do not need to have faith in a
fact, and that which requires religious belief, that is, trust in God, can never
be a fact which would hold good apart from that belief. The historical question
and the question of faith must therefore be clearly distinguished here. The
following points are historically certain. (1) That none of Christ's opponents
saw him after his death. (2) That the disciples were convinced that they had
seen him soon after his death. (3) That the succession and number of those
appearances can no longer be ascertained with certainty (4) That the
disciples and Paul were conscious of having seen Christ not in the crucified
earthly body, but in heavenly glory—even the later incredible accounts of
the appearances of Christ, which strongly emphasise the reality of the body,
speak at the same time of such a body as can pass through closed doors,
which certainly is not an earthly body. (5) That Paul does not compare the
manifestation of Christ given to him with any of his later visions, but, on the
other hand, describes it in the words (Gal. I. 15: ὅτε εὐδόκησεν ὁ θεὸς ἀποκαλύψαι τὸν υἱὸν αὐτοῦ ἐν ἐμοί, and yet puts it on a level with the appearances
which the earlier Apostles had seen. But, as even the empty grave on the
third day can by no means be regarded as a certain historical fact, because it appears united in the accounts with manifest legendary features,
and further because it is directly excluded by the way in which Paul has
portrayed the resurrection 1 Cor. XV. it follows: (1) That every conception
which represents the resurrection of Christ as a simple reanimation of his
mortal body, is far from the original conception, and (2) that the question
generally as to whether Jesus has risen, can have no existence for any one
who looks at it apart from the contents and worth of the Person of Jesus.
For the mere fact that friends and adherents of Jesus were convinced that they

5. After the appearance of Paul, the earliest communities
were greatly exercised by the question as to how believers

had seen him, especially when they themselves explain that he appeared to
them in heavenly glory, gives, to those who are in earnest about fixing historical facts, not the least cause for the assumption that Jesus did not continue
in the grave.

History is therefore at first unable to bring any succour to faith here. However firm may have been the faith of the disciples in the appearances of Jesus
in their midst, and it was firm, to believe in appearances which others have
had is a frivolity which is always revenged by rising doubts. But history is
still of service to faith: it limits its scope and therewith shews the province to
which it belongs. The question which history leaves to faith is this: Was Jesus
Christ swallowed up of death, or did he pass through suffering and the cross
to glory, that is, to life, power and honour. The disciples would have been
convinced of that in the sense in which Jesus meant them to understand it,
though they had not seen him in glory (a consciousness of this is found in Luke
XXIV. 26: οὐχὶ ταῦτα ἔδει παθεῖν τὸν χριστὸν καὶ εἰσελθεῖν εἰς τὴν δόξαν αὐτοῦ;
and Joh. XX. 29: ὅτι εώρακας με πεπίστευκας, μακαριοι οἱ μὴ ἰδοντες καὶ πιστεύσαντας
and we might probably add, that no appearances of the Lord could permanently have convinced them of his life, if they had not possessed in their hearts
the impression of his Person. Faith in the eternal life of Christ and in our own
eternal life is not the condition of becoming a disciple of Jesus, but is the final
confession of discipleship. Faith has by no means to do with the knowledge
of the form in which Jesus lives, but only with the conviction that he is the
living Lord. The determination of the form was immediately dependent on the
most varied general ideas of the future life, resurrection, restoration, and glorification of the body, which were current at the time The idea of the rising
again of the body of Jesus appeared comparatively early, because it was this
hope which animated wide circles of pious people for their own future. Faith
in Jesus, the living Lord, in spite of the death on the cross, cannot be generated by proofs of reason or authority, but only to-day in the same way as Paul
has confessed of himself: ὅτε εὐδόκησεν ὁ θεὸς ἀποκαλύψαι τὸν υἱὸν αὐτοῦ ἐν ἐμοί. The
conviction of having seen the Lord was no doubt of the greatest importance
for the disciples and made them Evangelists: but what they saw cannot at
first help us. It can only then obtain significance for us when we have gained
that confidence in the Lord which Peter has expressed in Mark VIII. 29. The
Christian even to-day confesses with Paul: εἰ ἐν τῇ ζωῇ ταύτῃ ἐν χριστῷ ἠλπικότες
ἐσμὲν μόνον, ἐλεεινότεροι πάντων ἀνθρώπων ἐσμέν. He believes in a future life for himself with God because he believes that Christ lives. That is the peculiarity
and paradox of Christian faith. But these are not convictions that can be
common and matter of course to a deep feeling and earnest thinking being
standing amid nature and death, but can only be possessed by those who live
with their whole hearts and minds in God, and even they need the prayer: "I
believe, help thou mine unbelief." To act as if faith in eternal life and in the
living Christ was the simplest thing in the world, or a dogma to which one
has just to submit, is irreligious. The whole question about the resurrection
of Christ, its mode and its significance, has thereby been so thoroughly confused in later Christendom, that we are in the habit of considering eternal life
as certain, even apart from Christ. That, at any rate, is not Christian. It is
Christian to pray that God would give the Spirit to make us strong to overcome the feelings and the doubts of nature, and create belief in an eternal life
through the experience of "dying to live." Where this faith, obtained
in this way, exists, it has always been supported by the conviction

obtain the righteousness which they possess, and what significance a precise observance of the law of the Fathers may
have in connection with it. While some would hear of no
change in the regulations and conceptions which had hitherto
existed, and regarded the bestowal of righteousness by God
as possible only on condition of a strict observance of the
law, others taught that Jesus as Messiah had procured righteousness for his people, had fulfilled the law once for all, and
had founded a new covenant, either in opposition to the old,
or as a stage above it. Paul especially saw in the death of Christ
the end of the law, and deduced righteousness solely from faith
in Christ, and sought to prove from the Old Testament itself,
by means of historical speculation, the merely temporary
validity of the law and therewith the abrogation of the Old
Testament religion. Others, and this view, which is not everywhere to be explained by Alexandrian influences (see above
p. 72 f.), is not foreign to Paul, distinguished between spirit and
letter in the Mosaic law, giving to everything a spiritual significance, and in this sense holding that the whole law as
νόμος πνευματικός was binding. The question whether righteousness comes from the works of the law or from faith, was
displaced by this conception, and therefore remained in its
deepest grounds unsolved, or was decided in the sense of a
spiritualised legalism. But the detachment of Christianity from
the political forms of the Jewish religion, and from sacrificial
worship, was also completed by this conception, although it
was regarded as identical with the Old Testament religion
rightly understood. The surprising results of the direct mission to the Gentiles would seem to have first called forth
those controversies (but see Stephen) and given them the
highest significance. The fact that one section of Jewish
Christians, and even some of the Apostles at length recognised
the right of the Gentile Christians to be Christians without

that the Man lives who brought life and immortality to light. To
hold fast this faith is the goal of life, for only what we consciously
strive for is in this matter our own. What we think we possess is very
soon lost.

first becoming Jews, is the clearest proof that what was above all prized was faith in Christ and surrender to him as the saviour. In agreeing to the direct mission to the Gentiles the earliest Christians, while they themselves observed the law, broke up the national religion of Israel, and gave expression to the conviction that Jesus was not only the Messiah of his people, but the redeemer of humanity.[1] The establishment of the universal character of the Gospel, that is, of Christianity as a religion for the world, became now, however, a problem, the solution of which, as given by Paul, but few were able to understand or make their own.

6. In the conviction that salvation is entirely bound up with faith in Jesus Christ, Christendom gained the consciousness of being a new creation of God. But while the sense of being the true Israel was thereby, at the same time, held fast, there followed, on the one hand, entirely new historical perspectives, and on the other, deep problems which demanded solution. As a new creation of God, ἡ ἐκκλησία τοῦ θεοῦ, the community was conscious of having been chosen by God in Jesus before the foundation of the world. In the conviction of being the true Israel, it claimed for itself the whole historical development recorded in the Old Testament, convinced that all the divine activity there recorded had the

---

[1] Weizsäcker (Apostolic Age, p. 73) says very justly: "The rising of Judaism against believers put them on their own feet. They saw themselves for the first time persecuted in the name of the law, and therewith for the first time it must have become clear to them, that in reality the law was no longer the same to them as to the others. Their hope is the coming kingdom of heaven, in which it is not the law, but their Master from whom they expect salvation. Everything connected with salvation is in him. But we should not investigate the conditions of the faith of that early period, as though the question had been laid before the Apostles whether they could have part in the Kingdom of heaven without circumcision, or whether it could be obtained by faith in Jesus, with or without the observance of the law. Such questions had no existence for them either practically or as questions of the school. But though they were Jews, and the law which even their Master had not abolished, was for them a matter of course, that did not exclude a change of inner position towards it, through faith in their Master and hope of the Kingdom. There is an inner freedom which can grow up alongside of all the constraints of birth, custom, prejudice, and piety. But this only comes into consciousness, when a demand is made on it which wounds it, or when it is assailed on account of an inference drawn not by its own consciousness, but only by its opponents".

new community in view. The great question which was to
find very different answers, was how, in accordance with this
view, the Jewish nation, so far as it had not recognised Jesus
as Messiah, should be judged. The detachment of Christianity
from Judaism was the most important preliminary condition,
and therefore the most important preparation, for the Mission
among the Gentile nations, and for union with the Greek spirit.

Supplement 1.—Renan and others go too far when they
say that Paul alone has the glory of freeing Christianity from
the fetters of Judaism. Certainly the great Apostle could say
in this connection also: περισσότερον αὐτῶν πάντων ἐκοπίασα, but
there were others beside him who, in the power of the Gospel,
transcended the limits of Judaism. Christian communities, it
may now be considered certain, had arisen in the empire, in
Rome for example, which were essentially free from the law
without being in any way determined by Paul's preaching.
It was Paul's merit that he clearly formulated the great question,
established the universalism of Christianity in a peculiar manner, and yet in doing so held fast the character of Christianity
as a positive religion, as distinguished from Philosophy and
Moralism. But the later development presupposes neither his
clear formulation nor his peculiar establishment of universalism,
but only the universalism itself.

Supplement 2.— The dependence of the Pauline Theology
on the Old Testament or on Judaism is overlooked in the traditional contrasting of Paulinism and Jewish Christianity, in
which Paulinism is made equivalent to Gentile Christianity.
This theology, as we might *a priori* suppose, could, apart from
individual exceptions, be intelligible as a whole to born Jews,
if to any, for its doctrinal presuppositions were strictly Pharisaic, and its boldness in criticising the Old Testament, rejecting and asserting the law in its historical sense, could be as
little congenial to the Gentile Christians as its piety towards
the Jewish people. This judgment is confirmed by a glance at
the fate of Pauline Theology in the 120 years that followed.
Marcion was the only Gentile Christian who understood Paul,
and even he misunderstood him: the rest never got beyond

the appropriation of particular Pauline sayings, and exhibited no comprehension especially of the theology of the Apostle, so far as in it the universalism of Christianity as a religion is proved, even without recourse to Moralism and without putting a new construction on the Old Testament religion. It follows from this, however, that the scheme "Jewish Christianity"—"Gentile Christianity" is insufficient. We must rather, in the Apostolic age, at least at its close, distinguish four main tendencies that may have crossed each other here and there,[1] (within which again different shades appear). (1) The Gospel has to do with the people of Israel, and with the Gentile world only on the condition that believers attach themselves to the people of Israel. The punctilious observance of the law is still necessary and the condition on which the messianic salvation is bestowed (particularism and legalism, in practice and in principle, which, however, was not to cripple the obligation to prosecute the work of the Mission). (2) The Gospel has to do with Jews and Gentiles: the first, as believers in Christ, are under obligation as before to observe the law, the latter are not; but for that reason they cannot on earth fuse into one community with the believing Jews. Very different judgments in details were possible on this stand-point; but the bestowal of salvation could no longer be thought of as depending simply on the keeping of the ceremonial commandments of the law[2] (universalism in principle, particularism in practice; the prerogative of Israel being to some extent clung to). (3) The Gospel has to do with both Jews and Gentiles; no one is any longer under obligation to observe

---

1 Only one of these four tendencies—the Pauline, with the Epistle to the Hebrews and the Johannine writings which are related to Paulinism—has seen in the Gospel the establishment of a new religion. The rest identified it with Judaism made perfect, or with the Old Testament religion rightly understood. But Paul, in connecting Christianity with the promise given to Abraham, passing thus beyond the law, that is, beyond the actual Old Testament religion, has not only given it a historical foundation, but also claimed for the Father of the Jewish nation a unique significance for Christianity. As to the tendencies named 1 and 2, see Book I. chap. 6.
2 It is clear from Gal. II. 11 ff. that Peter then and for long before occupied in principle the stand-point of Paul: see the judicious remarks of Weizsäcker in the book mentioned above, p. 75 f.

the law; for the law is abolished (or fulfilled), and the salvation which Christ's death has procured is appropriated by faith. The law (that is the Old Testament religion) in its literal sense is of divine origin, but was intended from the first only for a definite epoch of history. The prerogative of Israel remains, and is shewn in the fact that salvation was first offered to the Jews, and it will be shewn again at the end of all history. That prerogative refers to the nation as a whole, and has nothing to do with the question of the salvation of individuals (Paulinism: universalism in principle and in prac- tice, and Antinomianism in virtue of the recognition of a merely temporary validity of the whole law; breach with the tradi- tional religion of Israel; recognition of the prerogative of the people of Israel; the clinging to the prerogative of the people of Israel was not, however, necessary on this stand-point: see the epistle to the Hebrews and the Gospel of John). (4) The Gospel has to do with Jews and Gentiles: no one need therefore be under obligation to observe the ceremonial com- mandments and sacrificial worship, because these command- ments themselves are only the wrappings of moral and spiritual commandments which the Gospel has set forth as fulfilled in a more perfect form (universalism in principle and in practice in virtue of a neutralising of the distinction between law and Gospel, old and new; spiritualising and universalising of the law). [1]

1 These four tendencies were represented in the Apostolic age by those who had been born and trained in Judaism, and they were collectively trans- planted into Greek territory. But we cannot be sure that the third of the above tendencies found intelligent and independent representatives in this domain, as there is no certain evidence of it. Only one who had really been subject to it, and therefore understood it, could venture on a criticism of the Old Testament religion Still, it may be noted that the majority of non- Jewish converts in the Apostolic age, had probably come to know the Old Testament beforehand—not always the Jewish religion, (see Havet, Le Christianisme, T. IV. p. 120: "Je ne sais s'il y est entré, du vivant de Paul, un seul païen: je veux dire un homme, qui ne connût pas déjà, avant d'y entrer, le judaîsme et la Bible "). These indications will shew how mistaken and misleading it is to express the different tendencies in the Apostolic age and the period closely following by the designations "Jewish Christianity— Gentile Christianity." Short watchwords are so little appropriate here that one might even with some justice reverse the usual conception, and maintain that what is usually understood by Gentile Christianity (criticism of the Old Testament religion) was possible only within Judaism, while that which is frequently called Jewish Christianity is rather a conception which must have

Supplement 3.—The appearance of Paul is the most important fact in the history of the Apostolic age. It is impossible
to give in a few sentences an abstract of his theology and
work; and the insertion here of a detailed account is forbidden,
not only by the external limits, but by the aim of this investigation. For, as already indicated (§ 1), the doctrinal formation in the Gentile Church is not connected with the
whole phenomenon of the Pauline theology, but only with
certain leading thoughts which were only in part peculiar
to the Apostle. His most peculiar thoughts acted on the development of Ecclesiastical doctrine only by way of occasional
stimulus. We can find room here only for a few general
outlines. [1]

(1) The inner conviction that Christ had revealed himself
to him, that the Gospel was the message of the crucified and
risen Christ, and that God had called him to proclaim that
message to the world, was the power and the secret of his
personality and his activity. These three elements were a
unity in the consciousness of Paul, constituting his conversion and determining his after-life. (2) In this conviction he
knew himself to be a new creature, and so vivid was this
knowledge that he was constrained to become a Jew to the
Jews, and a Greek to the Greeks in order to gain them. (3)
The crucified and risen Christ became the central point of
his theology, and not only the central point, but the one
source and ruling principle. The Christ was not in his
estimation Jesus of Nazareth now exalted, but the mighty

readily suggested itself to born Gentiles superficially acquainted with the Old
Testament.
    1 The first edition of this volume could not appeal to Weizsäcker's work,
Das Apostolische Zeitalter der Christlichen Kirche, 1886,[second edition translated in this series]. The author is now in the happy position of being able to
refer the readers of his imperfect sketch to this excellent presentation, the
strength of which lies in the delineation of Paulinism in its relation to the
early Church, and to early Christian theology (p. 79-172). The truth of
Weizsäcker's expositions of the inner relations (p. 85 f.), is but little affected
by his assumptions concerning the outer relations, which I cannot everywhere regard as just. (The work of Weizsäcker as a whole is, in my opinion,
the most important work on Church history we have received since Ritschl's
"Entstehung der alt-katholischen Kirche." (2 Aufl. 1857.)

personal spiritual being in divine form who had for a time humbled himself, and who as Spirit has broken up the world of law, sin, and death, and continues to overcome them in believers. (4) Theology therefore was to him, looking forwards, the doctrine of the liberating power of the Spirit (of Christ) in all the concrete relations of human life and need. The Christ who has already overcome law, sin and death, lives as Spirit, and through his Spirit lives in believers, who for that very reason know him not after the flesh. He is a creative power of life to those who receive him in faith in his re- deeming death upon the cross, that is to say, to those who are justified. The life in the Spirit, which results from union with Christ, will at last reveal itself also in the body (not in the flesh). (5) Looking backwards, theology was to Paul a doctrine of the law and of its abrogation; or more accurately, a description of the old system before Christ in the light of the Gospel, and the proof that it was destroyed by Christ. The scriptural proof, even here, is only a superadded support to inner considerations which move entirely within the thought that that which is abrogated has already had its due, by having its whole strength made manifest that it might then be an- nulled,—the law, the flesh of sin, death: by the law the law is destroyed, sin is abolished in sinful flesh, death is de- stroyed by death. (6) The historical view which followed from this begins, as regards Christ, with Adam and Abraham; as regards the law, with Moses. It closes, as regards Christ, with the prospect of a time when he shall have put all ene- mies beneath his feet, when God will be all in all; as regards Moses and the promises given to the Jewish nation, with the prospect of a time when all Israel will be saved. (7) Paul's doctrine of Christ starts from the final confession of the prim- itive Church, that Christ is with the Father as a heavenly being and as Lord of the living and the dead. Though Paul must have accurately known the proclamation concerning the historical Christ, his theology in the strict sense of the word does not revert to it: but springing over the historical, it begins with the pre-existent Christ (the Man from heaven), whose moral deed it was to assume the flesh in self-denying love, in order to break for all men the powers of nature and the doom of death. But he has pointed to the words and example of the historical Christ in order to rule the life in the Spirit. (8) Deductions, proofs, and perhaps also conceptions, which in point of form betray the theology of the Pharisaic schools, were forced from the Apostle by Christian opponents, who would only grant a place to the message of the crucified Christ beside the διχαιοσύνη ἐξ ἔργων. Both as an exegete and as a typologist he appears as a disciple of the Pharisees. But his dialectic about law, circumcision and sacrifice, does not form the kernel of his religious mode of thought, though, on the other hand, it was unquestionably his very Pharisaism which qualified him for becoming what he was. Pharisaism embraced nearly everything lofty which Judaism apart from Christ at all possessed, and its doctrine of providence, its energetic insistance on making manifest the religious contrasts, its Messianic expectations, its doctrines of sin and predestination, were conditions for the genesis of a religious and Christian character such as Paul. [1] This first Christian of the second generation is the highest product of the Jewish spirit under the creative power of the Spirit of Christ. Pharisaism had fulfilled its mission for the world when it produced this man. (9) But Hellenism also had a share in the making of Paul, a fact which does not conflict with his Pharisaic origin, but is partly given with it. In spite of all its exclusiveness the desire for making proselytes, especially in the Diaspora, was in the blood of Pharisaism. Paul continued the old movement in a new way, and he was qualified for his work among the Greeks by an accurate knowledge of the Greek translation of the Old Testament, by considerable dexterity in the use of the Greek language, and by a growing insight into the spiritual life of the Greeks.

---

[1] Kabisch, *Die Eschatologie des Paulus*, 1893, has shewn how strongly the eschatology of Paul was influenced by the later Pharisaic Judaism. He has also called attention to the close connection between Paul's doctrine of sin and the fall, and that of the Rabbis.

But the peculiarity of his Gospel as a message from the Spirit of Christ, which was equally near to and equally distant from every religious and moral mode of thought among the nations of the world, signified much more than all this. This Gospel—who can say whether Hellenism had already a share in its conception—required that the missionary to the Greeks should become a Greek and that believers should come to know, " all things are yours, and ye are Christ's ". Paul, as no doubt other missionaries besides him, connected the preaching of Christ with the Greek mode of thought; he even employed philosophic doctrines of the Greeks as presuppositions in his apologetic, [1] and therewith prepared the way for the introduction of the Gospel to the Græco-Roman world of thought. But, in my opinion, he has nowhere allowed that world of thought to influence his doctrine of salvation. This doctrine, however, was so fashioned in its practical aims that it was not necessary to become a Jew in order to appropriate it. (10) Yet we cannot speak of any total effect of Paulinism, as there was no such thing. The abundance of its details was too great and the greatness of its simplicity too powerful, its hope of the future too vivid, its doctrine of the law too difficult, its summons to a new life in the spirit too mighty to be comprehended and adhered to even by those communities which Paul himself had founded. What they did comprehend was its Monotheism, its universalism, its redemption, its eternal life, its asceticism; but all this was otherwise combined than by Paul. The style became Hellenic, and the element of a new kind of knowledge from the very first, as in the Church of Corinth, seems to have been the ruling one. The Pauline doctrine of the incarnate heavenly Man was indeed apprehended; it fell in with Greek

---

1 Some of the Church Fathers (see Socr. H. E. III. 16) have attributed to Paul an accurate knowledge of Greek literature and philosophy: but that cannot be proved. The references of Heinrici (2 Kor.-Brief. p. 537-604) are worthy of our best thanks; but no certain judgment can be formed about the measure of the Apostles' Greek culture, so long as we do not know how great was the extent of spiritual ideas which were already precipitated in the speech of the time.

notions, although it meant something very different from the notions which Greeks had been able to form of it.

Supplement 4.—What we justly prize above all else in the New Testament is that it is a union of the three groups, Synoptic Gospels, Pauline Epistles, [1] and Johannine writings, in which are expressed the richest contents of the earliest history of the Gospel. In the Synoptic Gospels and the epistles of Paul are represented two types of preaching the Gospel which mutually supplement each other. The subsequent history is dependent on both, and would have been other than it is had not both existed alongside of each other. On the other hand, the peculiar and lofty conception of Christ and of the Gospel, which stands out in the writings of John, has directly exercised no demonstrable influence on the succeeding development— with the exception of one peculiar movement, the Montanistic, which, however, does not rest on a true understanding of these writings—and indeed partly for the same reason that has prevented the Pauline theology as a whole from having such an influence. What is given in these writings is a criticism of the Old Testament as religion, or the independence of the Christian religion, in virtue of an accurate knowledge of the Old Testament through development of its hidden germs. The Old Testament stage of religion is really transcended and over-come in the Johannine Christianity, just as in Paulinism, and in the theology of the epistle to the Hebrews. "The circle of disciples who appropriated this characterisation of Jesus is," says Weizsäcker, "a revived Christ-party in the higher sense." But this transcending of the Old Testament religion was the very thing that was unintelligible, because there were few ripe for such a conception. Moreover, the origin of the Johannine writings is, from the stand-point of a history of literature and

---

[1] The epistle to the Hebrews and the first epistle of Peter, as well as the Pastoral epistles belong to the Pauline circle; they are of the greatest value because they shew that certain fundamental features of Pauline theology took effect afterwards in an original way, or received independent parallels, and because they prove that the cosmic Christology of Paul made the greatest impression and was continued. In Christology, the epistle to the Ephesians in particular, leads directly from Paul to the pneumatic Christology of the post-apostolic period. Its non-genuineness is by no means certain to me.

dogma, the most marvellous enigma which the early history
of Christianity presents: Here we have portrayed a Christ
who clothes the indescribable with words, and proclaims as
his own self-testimony what his disciples have experienced
in him, a speaking, acting, Pauline Christ, walking on the
earth, far more human than the Christ of Paul and yet
far more Divine, an abundance of allusions to the historical
Jesus, and at the same time the most sovereign treatment of
the history. One divines that the Gospel can find no loftier
expression than John XVII.: one feels that Christ himself put
these words into the mouth of the disciple, who gives them
back to him, but word and thing, history and doctrine are
surrounded by a bright cloud of the suprahistorical. It is
easy to shew that this Gospel could as little have been written without Hellenism, as Luther's treatise on the freedom of
a Christian man could have been written without the "Deutsche Theologie." But the reference to Philo and Hellenism
is by no means sufficient here, as it does not satisfactorily
explain even one of the external aspects of the problem. The
elements operative in the Johannine theology were not Greek
Theologoumena—even the Logos has little more in common
with that of Philo than the name, and its mention at the beginning of the book is a mystery, not the solution of one [1]—

---

1 In the Ztschr. für Theol und Kirche, II. p. 189 ff. I have discussed the
relation of the prologue of the fourth Gospel to the whole work and endeavoured to prove the following: "The prologue of the Gospel is not the key to
its comprehension. It begins with a well-known great object, the Logos, re-
adapts and transforms it—implicitly opposing false Christologies—in order
to substitute for it Jesus Christ, the μονογενὴς θέος, or in order to unveil it as this
Jesus Christ. The idea of the Logos is allowed to fall from the moment that
this takes place". The author continues to narrate of Jesus only with the view
of establishing the belief that he is the Messiah, the son of God. This faith has
for its main article the recognition that Jesus is descended from God and from
heaven; but the author is far from endeavouring to work out this recognition
from cosmological, philosophical considerations. According to the Evangelist,
Jesus proves himself to be the Messiah, the Son of God, in virtue of his self-
testimony, and because he has brought a full knowledge of God and of life—
purely supernatural divine blessings (Cf. besides, and partly in opposition,
Holtzmann, i. d. Ztschr. f. wissensch. Theol. 1893). The author's peculiar world
of theological ideas, is not, however, so entirely isolated in the early Christian
literature as appears on the first impression. If, as is probable, the Ignatian
Epistles are independent of the Gospel of John, further, the Supper prayer in

but the Apostolic testimony concerning Christ has created from the old faith of Psalmists and Prophets, a new faith in a man who lived with the disciples of Jesus among the Greeks. For that very reason, in spite of his abrupt Anti-judaism, we must without doubt regard the Author as a born Jew.

Supplement 5.—The authorities to which the Christian communities were subjected in faith and life, were these: (1) The Old Testament interpreted in the Christian sense. (2) The tradition of the Messianic history of Jesus. (3) The words of the Lord: see the espistles of Paul, especially 1 Corinthians. But every writing which was proved to have been given by the Spirit had also to be regarded as an authority, and every tested Christian Prophet and Teacher inspired by the Spirit could claim that his words be received and regarded as the words of God. Moreover, the twelve whom Jesus had chosen had a special authority, and Paul claimed a similar authority for himself (διατάξεις τῶν ἀποστόλων). Consequently, there were numerous courts of appeal in the earliest period of Christendom, of diverse kinds and by no means strictly defined. In the manifold gifts of the spirit was given a fluid element indefinable in its range and scope, an element which guaranteed freedom of development, but which also threatened to lead the enthusiastic communities to extravagance.

Literature.—Weiss, Biblical Theology of the New Testament, 1884. Beyschlag, New Testament Theology, 1892. Ritschl, Entstehung der Alt-Katholischen Kirche, 2 Edit. 1857. Reuss, History of Christian Theology in the Apostolic Age, 1864. Baur, The Apostle Paul, 1866. Holsten, Zum Evangelium des Paulus und Petrus, 1868. Pfleiderer, Paulinism, 1873: also, Das Urchristenthum, 1887. Schenkel, Das Christusbild der Apostel, 1879. Renan, Origins of Christianity Vols. II.—IV. Havet, Le Christianisme et ses orig. T. IV. 1884. Lechler, The

---

the Didache, finally, certain mystic theological phrases in the Epistle of Barnabas, in the second epistle of Clement, and in Hermas: a complex of Theologoumena may be put together, which reaches back to the primitive period of the Church, and may be conceived as the general ground for the theology of John. This complex has on its side a close connection with the final development of the Jewish Hagiographic literature under Greek influence.

Apostolic and Post-Apostolic Age, 1885. Weizsäcker, The
Apostolic Age, 1892. Hatch, Article "Paul" in the Encyclo-
pædia Britannica. Everett, The Gospel of Paul. Boston, 1893.
On the origin and earliest history of the Christian proofs from
prophecy, see my "Texte und Unters. z. Gesch. der Alt-Christl."
Lit. I. 3, p. 56 f.

§ 4. *The Current Exposition of the Old Testament, and the
Jewish hopes of the future, in their significance for
the earliest types of Christian preaching.*

Instead of the frequently very fruitless investigations about
"Jewish-Christian", and "Gentile-Christian", it should be asked,
What Jewish elements have been naturalised in the Christian
Church, which were in no way demanded by the contents of
the Gospel? have these elements been simply weakened in
course of the development, or have some of them been strengthened by a peculiar combination with the Greek? We have
to do here, in the first instance, with the doctrine of Demons
and Angels, the view of history, the growing exclusiveness,
the fanaticism; and on the other hand, with the cultus, and
the Theocracy, expressing itself in forms of law.

1. Although Jesus had in principle abolished the methods
of pedantry, the casuistic treatment of the law, and the sub-
tleties of prophetic interpretation, yet the old Scholastic exegesis remained active in the Christian communities above all
the unhistorical local method in the exposition of the Old
Testament, both allegoristic and Haggadic; for in the exposition of a sacred text—and the Old Testament was regarded
as such—one is always required to look away from its historical limitations and to expound it according to the needs
of the present. [1] The traditional view exercised its influence
on the exposition of the Old Testament, as well as on the
representations of the person, fate and deeds of Jesus, especially in those cases where the question was about the proof

1 The Jewish religion, specially since the (relative) close of the canon,
had become more and more a religion of the Book.

of the fulfilment of prophecy, that is, of the Messiahship of Jesus. (See above § 3, 2). Under the impression made by the history of Jesus it gave to many Old Testament passages a sense that was foreign to them, and, on the other hand, enriched the life of Jesus with new facts, turning the interest at the same time to details which were frequently unreal and seldom of striking importance. [1]

2. The Jewish Apocalyptic literature, especially as it flourished since the time of Antiochus Epiphanes, and was impregnated with new elements borrowed from an ethico-religious philosophy, as well as with Babylonian and Persian myths (Greek myths can only be detected in very small number), was not banished from the circles of the first professors of the Gospel, but was rather held fast, eagerly read, and even extended with the view of elucidating the promises of Jesus. [2]

---

1 Examples of both in the New Testament are numerous. See, above all, Matt. I. II. Even the belief that Jesus was born of a Virgin sprang from Isaiah VII. 14. It cannot, however, be proved to be in the writings of Paul (the two genealogies in Matt. and Luke directly exclude it: according to Dillmann, Jahrb. f. protest. Theol. p. 192 ff. Luke I. 34, 35 would be the addition of a redactor); but it must have arisen very early, as the Gentile Christians of the second century would seem to have unanimously confessed it (see the Romish Symbol. Ignatius, Aristides, Justin, etc.). For the rest, it was long before theologians recognised in the Virgin birth of Jesus more than fulfilment of a prophecy, viz., a fact of salvation. The conjecture of Usener, that the idea of the birth from a Virgin is a heathen myth which was received by the Christians, contradicts the entire earliest development of Christian tradition which is free from heathen myths, so far as these had not already been received by wide circles of Jews, (above all, certain Babylonian and Persian Myths), which in the case of that idea is not demonstrable. Besides, it is in point of method not permissible to stray so far when we have near at hand such a complete explanation as Isaiah VII. 14. Those who suppose that the reality of the Virgin birth must be held fast, must assume that a misunderstood prophecy has been here fulfilled (on the true meaning of the passage see Dillmann[Jesajas, 5 Aufl.] p. 69]: "of the birth by a Virgin[i. e., of one who at the birth was still a Virgin.] the Hebrew text says nothing ... Immanuel as beginning and representative of the new generation, from which one should finally take possession of the king's throne"). The application of an unhistorical local method in the exposition of the Old Testament—Haggada and Rabbinic allegorism—may be found in many passages of Paul (see, e. g., Gal. III. 16, 19; IV. 22-31; 1 Cor. IX. 9; X. 4; XI. 10; Rom. IV. etc.).

2 The proof of this may be found in the quotations in early Christian writings from the Apocalypses of Enoch, Ezra, Eldad and Modad, the assumption of Moses and other Jewish Apocalypses unknown to us. They were regarded as Divine revelations beside the Old Testament; see the proofs of their frequent and long continued use in Schürer's "History of the Jewish people in the time

Though their contents seem to have been modified on Christian soil, and especially the uncertainty about the person of the Messiah exalted to victory and coming to judgment, [1] yet the sensuous earthly hopes were in no way repressed. Green fat meadows and sulphurous abysses, white horses and frightful beasts, trees of life, splendid cities, war and bloodshed filled the fancy, [2] and threatened to obscure the simple and yet, at bottom, much more affecting maxims about the judgment which is certain to every individual soul, and drew the confessors of the Gospel into a restless activity, into politics, and abhorrence of the State. It was an evil inheritance which the Christians took over from the Jews, [3] an inheritance which makes it impossible to reproduce with certainty the eschatological sayings of Jesus. Things directly foreign were mixed up with them, and, what was most serious, delineations of the hopes of the future could easily lead to the undervaluing of the most important gifts and duties of the Gospel. [4]

---

of our Lord." But the Christians in receiving these Jewish Apocalypses did not leave them intact, but adapted them with greater or less Christian additions (see Ezra, Enoch. Ascension of Isaiah). Even the Apocalypse of John is, as Vischer (Texte u. Unters. 3 altchristl. lit. Gesch. Bd. II. H. 4) has shown, a Jewish Apocalypse adapted to a Christian meaning. But in this activity, and in the production of little Apocalyptic prophetic sayings and articles (see in the Epistle to the Ephesians, and in those of Barnabas and Clement) the Christian labour here in the earliest period seems to have exhausted itself. At least we do not know with certainty of any great Apocalyptic writing of an original kind proceeding from Christian circles. Even the Apocalypse of Peter which, thanks to the discovery of Bouriant, we now know better, is not a completely original work as contrasted with the Jewish Apocalypses.

1 The Gospel, reliance on the Lamb who was slain, very significantly pervades the Revelation of John, that is, its Christian parts. Even the Apocalypse of Peter shews Jesus Christ as the comfort of believers and as the Revealer of the future. In it (v. 3,) Christ says; "Then will God come to those who believe on me, those who hunger and thirst and mourn, etc."

2 These words were written before the Apocalypse of Peter was discovered. That Apocalypse confirms what is said in the text. Moreover, its delineation of Paradise and blessedness are not wanting in poetic charm and power. In its delineation of Hell, which prepares the way for Dante's Hell, the author is scared by no terror.

3 These ideas, however, encircled the earliest Christendom as with a wall of fire, and preserved it from a too early contact with the world.

4 An accurate examination of the eschatological sayings of Jesus in the synoptists shews that much foreign matter is mixed with them (see Weiffenbach, Der Wiederkunftsgedanke Jesu, 1875). That the tradition here was very uncertain, because influenced by the Jewish Apocalyptic, is shewn by the one fact

3. A wealth of mythologies and poetic ideas was naturalised and legitimised [1] in the Christian communities, chiefly by
the reception of the Apocalyptic literature, but also by the
reception of artificial exegesis and Haggada. Most important for the following period were the speculations about
Messiah, which were partly borrowed from expositions of the
Old Testament and from the Apocalypses, partly formed independently, according to methods the justice of which no
one contested, and the application of which seemed to give
a firm basis to religious faith.

Some of the Jewish Apocalyptists had already attributed
pre-existence to the expected Messiah, as to other precious
things in the Old Testament history and worship, and, without
any thought of denying his human nature, placed him as already existing before his appearing in a series of angelic
beings. [2] This took place in accordance with an established

that Papias (in Iren. V. 33) quotes as words of the Lord which had been
handed down by the disciples, a group of sayings which we find in the
Apocalypse of Baruch, about the amazing fruitfulness of the earth during
the time of the Messianic Kingdom.

1 We may here call attention to an interesting remark of Goethe.
Among his Apophthegms (no. 537) is the following: "Apocrypha: It would
be important to collect what is historically known about these books,
and to shew that these very Apocryphal writings with which the communities of the first centuries of our era were flooded, were the real cause why
Christianity at no moment of political or Church history could stand forth in
all her beauty and purity." A historian would not express himself in this
way, but yet there lies at the root of this remark a true historical insight.

2 See Schürer, History of the Jewish people. Div. II. vol. II. p. 160 f. yet
the remarks of the Jew Trypho in the dialogue of Justin shew that the notions of a pre-existent Messiah were by no means very widely spread in Judaism. (See also Orig. c. Cels. 1.49: "A Jew would not at all admit that
any Prophet had said, the Son of God will come: they avoided this
designation and used instead the saying: the anointed of God will come").
The Apocalyptists and Rabbis attributed pre-existence, that is, a heavenly
origin to many sacred things and persons, such as the Patriarchs, Moses, the
Tabernacle, the Temple vessels, the city of Jerusalem. That the true Temple
and the real Jerusalem were with God in heaven and would come down from
heaven at the appointed time, must have been a very wide-spread idea, especially at the time of the destruction of Jerusalem, and even earlier than that
(see Gal. IV. 26: Rev. XXI. 2: Heb. XII. 22). In the Assumption of Moses (c. 1)
Moses says of himself: Dominus invenit me, qui ab initio orbis terrarum præ-
paratus sum, ut sim arbiter (μεσίτης) testamenti illius (τῆς διαθήκης αὐτοῦ). In
the Midrasch Bereschith rabba VIII. 2. we read, "R. simeon ben Lakisch
says, 'The law was in existence 2000 years before the creation of
the world.'" In the Jewish treatise Προσευχὴ Ἰωσήφ, which Origen has
several times quoted, Jacob says of himself (ap. Orig. tom. II. in

method of speculation, so far as an attempt was made thereby
to express the special value of an empiric object, by distinguishing between the essence and the inadequate form of appearance, hypostatising the essence, and exalting it above
time and space. But when a later appearance was conceived
as the aim of a series of preparations, it was frequently hypostatised and placed above these preparations even in time.
The supposed aim was, in a kind of real existence, placed,
as first cause, before the means which were destined to realise it on earth. [1]

Joann. c. 25. Opp. IV. 84: "ὁ γὰρ λαλῶν πρὸς ὑμᾶς, ἐγὼ Ἰακὼβ καὶ Ἰσραήλ, ἄγγελος θεοῦ
εἰμὶ ἐγὼ καὶ πνεῦμα ἀρχικὸν καὶ Ἀβραὰμ καὶ Ἰσαὰκ προεκτίσθησαν προ παντος ἔργου, ἐγὼ
δὲ Ἰακὼβ.... ἐγὼ πρωτογονος παντὸς ζώος ζωουμένου ὑπὸ θεοῦ." These examples could
easily be increased. The Jewish speculations about Angels and Mediators,
which at the time of Christ grew very luxuriantly among the Scribes and
Apocalyptists, and endangered the purity and vitality of the Old Testament
idea of God, were also very important for the development of Christian dogmatics. But neither these speculations, nor the notions of heavenly Archetypes, nor of pre-existence, are to be referred to Hellenic influence. This
may have co-operated here and there, but the rise of these speculations in
Judaism is not to be explained by it; they rather exhibit the Oriental stamp.
But, of course, the stage in the development of the nations had now been
reached, in which the creations of Oriental fancy and Mythology could be
fused with the ideal conceptions of Hellenic philosophy.
    1 The conception of heavenly ideals of precious earthly things followed
from the first naive method of speculation we have mentioned, that of a
pre-existence of persons from the last. If the world was created for the
sake of the people of Israel, and the Apocalyptists expressly taught that,
then it follows, that in the thought of God Israel was older than the world.
The idea of a kind of pre-existence of the people of Israel follows from this.
We can still see this process of thought very plainly in the shepherd of Hermas, who expressly declares that the world was created for the sake of the
Church. In consequence of this he maintains that the Church was very old,
and was created before the foundation of the world. See Vis. I. 2. 4 : II. 4. 1 :
Διατί οὖν πρεσβυτέρα (scil. ἡ ἐκκλησία): "Οτι, φησίν, πάντων πρώτη ἐκτίσθη διὰ τοῦτο πρεσβυτέρα, καὶ διὰ ταύτην ὁ κόσμος κατηρτίσθη. But in order to estimate aright the
bearing of these speculations, we must observe that, according to them, the
precious things and persons, so far as they are now really manifested, were
never conceived as endowed with a double nature. No hint is given of such
an assumption; the sensible appearance was rather conceived as a mere
wrapping which was necessary only to its becoming visible, or, conversely,
the pre-existence or the archetype was no longer thought of in presence
of the historical appearance of the object. That pneumatic form of existence was not set forth in accordance with the analogy of existence verified
by sense, but was left in suspense. The idea of "existence" here could
run through all the stages which, according to the Mythology and Metaphysic of the time, lay between what we now call "valid," and the most
concrete being. He who nowadays undertakes to justify the notion of pre-
existence, will find himself in a very different situation from these earlier

Some of the first confessors of the Gospel, though not all
the writers of the New Testament, in accordance with the
same method, went beyond the declarations which Jesus himself had made about his person, and endeavoured to conceive
its value and absolute significance abstractly and speculatively.
The religious convictions (see § 3. 2): (1) That the founding
of the Kingdom of God on earth, and the mission of Jesus
as the perfect mediator, were from eternity based on God's
plan of Salvation, as his main purpose; (2) that the exalted
Christ was called into a position of Godlike Sovereignty belonging to him of right; (3) that God himself was manifested in Jesus, and that he therefore surpasses all mediators
of the Old Testament, nay, even all angelic powers,—these
convictions with some took the form that Jesus pre-existed, and
that in him has appeared and taken flesh a heavenly being
fashioned like God, who is older than the world, nay, its creative principle. [1] The conceptions of the old Teachers, Paul,
the author of the Epistle to the Hebrews, the Apocalypse,
the author of the first Epistle of Peter, the fourth Evangelist, differ in many ways when they attempt to define these
convictions more closely. The latter is the only one who has
recognised with perfect clearness that the premundane Christ
must be assumed to be θεὸς ὢν ἐν ἀρχῇ πρὸς τὸν θεόν, so as not
to endanger by this speculation the contents and significance
of the revelation of God which was given in Christ. This, in
the earliest period, was essentially a religious problem, that
is, it was not introduced for the explanation of cosmological
problems, (see, especially, Epistle to the Ephesians, 1 Peter;
but also the Gospel of John), and there stood peacefully be-

times, as he will no longer be able to count on shifting conceptions
of existence. See Appendix I. at the end of this Vol. for a fuller discussion of the idea of pre-existence.

1 It must be observed here that Palestinian Judaism, without any
apparent influence from Alexandria, though not independently of the
Greek spirit, had already created a multitude of intermediate beings
between God and the world, avowing thereby that the idea of God had
become stiff and rigid. "Its original aim was simply to help the God
of Judaism in his need." Among these intermediate beings should be
specially mentioned the Memra of God (see also the Shechina and the
Metatron).

side it, such conceptions as recognised the equipment of the
man Jesus for his office in a communication of the Spirit at
his baptism, [1] or in virtue of Isaiah VII., found the germ of
his unique nature in his miraculous origin. [2] But as soon as that
speculation was detached from its original foundation, it necessarily withdrew the minds of believers from the consideration of the work of Christ, and from the comtemplation of
the revelation of God which was given in the ministry of the
historical person Jesus. The mystery of the person of Jesus
in itself, would then necessarily appear as the true revelation. [3]

A series of theologoumena and religious problems for the
future doctrine of Christianity lay ready in the teaching of
the Pharisees and in the Apocalypses (see especially the fourth
book of Ezra), and was really fitted for being of service to
it; e.g., doctrines about Adam, universal sinfulness, the fall,
predestination, Theodocy, etc., besides all kinds of ideas about
redemption. Besides these spiritual doctrines there were not
a few spiritualised myths which were variously made use of
in the Apocalypses. A rich, spiritual, figurative style, only too
rich and therefore confused, waited for the theological artist
to purify, reduce and vigorously fashion. There really remained
very little of the Cosmico-Mythological in the doctrine of the
great Church.

Supplement.—The reference to the proof from prophecy, to
the current exposition of the Old Testament, the Apocalyptic and the prevailing methods of speculation, does not suffice to

---

1 See Justin. Dial. 48. fin: Justin certainly is not favourably disposed towards those who regard Christ as a "man among men," but he knows that
there are such people.

2 The miraculous genesis of Christ in the Virgin by the Holy Spirit and the
real pre-existence are of course mutually exclusive. At a later period, it is
true, it became necessary to unite them in thought.

3 There is the less need for treating this more fully here, as no New Testament Christology has become the direct starting-point of later doctrinal developments. The Gentile Christians had transmitted to them, as a unanimous
doctrine, the message that Christ is the Lord who is to be worshipped, and
that one must think of him as the Judge of the living and the dead, that is,
ὡς περὶ θεοῦ. But it certainly could not fail to be of importance for the result
that already many of the earliest Christian writers, and therefore even Paul,
perceived in Jesus a spiritual being come down from heaven (πνεῦμα) who was
ἐν μορφῇ θεοῦ, and whose real act of love consisted in his very descent.

explain all the elements which are found in the different types
of Christian preaching. We must rather bear in mind here
that the earliest communities were enthusiastic, and had yet
among them prophets and ecstatic persons. Such circumstances will always directly produce facts in the history. But, in
the majority of cases, it is absolutely impossible to account
subsequently for the causes of such productions, because their
formation is subject to no law accessible to the understanding.
It is therefore inadmissible to regard as proved the reality of
what is recorded and believed to be a fact, when the motive
and interest which led to its acceptance can no longer be
ascertained. [1]

Moreover, if we consider the conditions, outer and inner,
in which the preaching of Christ in the first decades was
placed, conditions which in every way threatened the Gospel
with extravagance, we shall only see cause to wonder that it
continued to shine forth amid all its wrappings. We can still,

---

[1] The creation of the New Testament canon first paved the way for putting
an end, though only in part, to the production of Evangelic "facts" within the
Church. For Hermas (Sim. IX. 16) can relate that the Apostles also descended
to the under world and there preached. Others report the same of John the
Baptist. Origen in his homily on 1. Kings XXVII. says that Moses, Samuel
and all the Prophets descended to Hades and there preached. A series of facts
of Evangelic history which have no parallel in the accounts of our Synoptists,
and are certainly legendary, may be but together from the epistle of Barnabas,
Justin, the second epistle of Clement, Papias, the Gospel to the Hebrews, and
the Gospel to the Egyptians. But the synoptic reports themselves, especially
in the articles for which we have only a solitary witness, shew an extensive
legendary material, and even in the Gospel of John, the free production of facts
cannot be mistaken. Of what a curious nature some of these were, and that
they are by no means to be entirely explained from the Old Testament, as for
example, Justin's account of the ass on which Christ rode into Jerusalem, having been bound to a vine, is shewn by the very old fragment in one source
of the Apostolic constitutions (Texte u. Unters II. 5. p. 28 ff.); ὅτε ἤτησεν ὁ
διδάσκαλος τὸν ἄρτον καὶ τὸ ποτήριον καὶ ηὐλόγησεν αὐτὰ λέγων· τοῦτο ἐστι τὸ σῶμά
μου καὶ τὸ αἷμα, οὐκ ἐπέτρεψε ταύταις (the women) συστῆναι ἡμῖν .... Μάρθα εἶπεν διὰ
Μαριάμ, ὅτι εἶδεν αὐτὴν μειδιῶσαν. Μαρία εἶπεν οὐκέτι ἐγέλασα. Narratives such as those
of Christ's descent to Hell and ascent to heaven, which arose comparatively
late, though still at the close of the first century (see Book I. Chap 3) sprang
out of short formulæ containing an antithesis (death and resurrection, first
advent in lowliness, second advent in glory: descensus de cœlo, ascensus in
cœlum; ascensus in cœlum, descensus ad inferna) which appeared to be required by Old Testament predictions, and were commended by their natural-
ness. Just as it is still, in the same way naively inferred: if Christ rose bodily
he must also have ascended bodily (visibly ?) into heaven.

out of the strangest "fulfilments", legends and mythological ideas, read the religious conviction that the aim and goal of history is disclosed in the history of Christ, and that the Divine has now entered into history in a pure form.

Literature.—The Apocalypses of Daniel, Enoch, Moses, Baruch, Ezra; Schürer, History of the Jewish People in the time of Christ; Baldensperger, in the work already mentioned. Weber, System der Altsynagogalen palästinischen Theologie, 1880, Kuenen, Hibbert Lectures, 1883. Hilgenfeld, Die jüdische Apokalyptik, 1857. Wellhausen, Sketch of the History of Israel and Judah, 1887. Diestel, Gesch. des A. T. in der Christl. Kirche, 1869. Other literature in Schürer. The essay of Hellwag in the Theol. Jahrb. von Baur and Zeller, 1848, "Die Vorstellung von der Präexistenz Christi in der ältesten Kirche", is worth noting; also Joël, Blicke in die Religionsgeschichte zu Anfang des 2 Christl. Jahrhunderts, 1880—1883.

§ 5. *The Religious Conceptions and the Religious Philosophy of the Hellenistic Jews, in their significance for the later formulation of the Gospel.*

1. From the remains of the Jewish Alexandrian literature and the Jewish Sibylline writings, also from the work of Josephus, and especially from the great propaganda of Judaism in the Græco-Roman world, we may gather that there was a Judaism in the Diaspora, for the consciousness of which the cultus and ceremonial law were of comparatively subordinate importance; while the monotheistic worship of God, apart from images, the doctrines of virtue and belief in a future reward beyond the grave, stood in the foreground as its really essential marks. Converted Gentiles were no longer everywhere required to be even circumcised; the bath of purification was deemed sufficient. The Jewish religion here appears transformed into a universal human ethic and a monotheistic cosmology. For that reason, the idea of the Theocracy as well as the Messianic hopes of the future faded away or were uprooted. The latter, indeed, did not altogether pass away; but as the oracles

of the Prophets were made use of mainly for the purpose of proving the antiquity and certainty of monotheistic belief, the thought of the future was essentially exhausted in the expectation of the dissolution of the Roman empire, the burning of the world, and the eternal recompense. The specific Jewish element, however, stood out plainly in the assertion that the Old Testament, and especially the books of Moses, were the source of all true knowledge of God, and the sum total of all doctrines of virtue for the nations, as well as in the connected assertion that the religious and moral culture of the Greeks was derived from the Old Testament, as the source from which the Greek Poets and Philosophers had drawn their inspiration. [1]

These Jews and the Greeks converted by them formed, as it were, a Judaism of a second order without law, *i.e.*, ceremonial law, and with a minimum of statutory regulations. This Judaism prepared the soil for the Christianising of the Greeks, as well as for the genesis of a great Gentile Church in the empire, free from the law; and this the more that, as it seems, after the second destruction of Jerusalem, the punctilious observance of the law [2] was imposed more strictly than before on all who worshipped the God of the Jews. [3]

[1] The Sibylline Oracles, composed by Jews, from 160 B.C. to 189 A.D. are specially instructive here: See the Editions of Friedlieb. 1852; Alexandre, 1869; Rzach, 1891. Delaunay, Moines et Sibylles dans l'antiquité judéo-grecque, 1874. Schürer in the work mentioned above. The writings of Josephus also yield rich booty, especially his apology for Judaism in the two books against Apion. But it must be noted that there were Jews, enlightened by Hellenism, who were still very zealous in their observance of the law. "Philo urges most earnestly to the observance of the law in opposition to that party which drew the extreme inferences of the allegoristic method, and put aside the outer legality as something not essential for the spiritual life. Philo thinks that by an exact observance of these ceremonies on their material side, one will also come to know better their symbolical meaning" (Siegfried, Philo, p. 157).

[2] Direct evidence is certainly almost entirely wanting here, but the indirect speaks all the more emphatically: see § 3, Supplements 1, 2.

[3] The Jewish propaganda, though by no means effaced, gave way very distinctly to the Christian from the middle of the second century. But from this time we find few more traces of an enlightened Hellenistic Judaism. Moreover, the Messianic expectation also seems to have somewhat given way to occupation with the law. But the God of Abraham, Isaac and Jacob, as well as other Jewish terms certainly played a great rôle in Gentile and Gnostic magical formulæ of the third century, as may be seen, *e.g.*, from many passages in Origen c. Celsum.

The Judaism just portrayed, developed itself, under the influence of the Greek culture with which it came in contact, into a kind of Cosmopolitanism. It divested itself, as religion, of all national forms, and exhibited itself as the most perfect expression of that "natural" religion which the stoics had disclosed. But in proportion as it was enlarged and spiritualised to a universal religion for humanity, it abandoned what was most peculiar to it, and could not compensate for that loss by the assertion of the thesis that the Old Testament is the oldest and most reliable source of that natural religion, which in the traditions of the Greeks had only witnesses of the second rank. The vigour and immediateness of the religious feeling was flattened down to a moralism, the barrenness of which drove some Jews even into Gnosis, mysticism and asceticism. [1]

2. The Jewish Alexandrian philosophy of religion, of which Philo gives us the clearest conception, [2] is the scientific theory which corresponded to this religious conception. The theological system which Philo, in accordance with the example of others, gave out as the Mosaic system revealed by God, and

[1] The prerogative of Israel was for all that clung to; Israel remains the chosen people.

[2] The brilliant investigations of Bernays, however, have shewn how many-sided that philosophy of religion was. The proofs of asceticism in this Hellenistic Judaism are especially of great interest for the history of dogma (See Theophrastus' treatise on piety). In the eighth Epistle of Heraclitus, composed by a Hellenistic Jew in the first century, it is said (Bernays, p. 182). " So long a time before, O Hermodorus, saw thee that Sibyl, and even then thou wert " (εἶδε σε πρὸ τοσούτου αἰῶνος, Ἑρμόδωρε ἡ Σίβυλλα ἐκείνη, καὶ τότε ἦσθα). Even here then the notion is expressed that foreknowledge and predestination invest the known and the determined with a kind of existence. Of great importance is the fact that even before Philo, the idea of the wisdom of God creating the world and passing over to men had been hypostatised in Alexandrian Judaism (see Sirach, Baruch, the wisdom of Solomon, Enoch, nay, even the book of Proverbs). But so long as the deutero-canonical Old Testament, and also the Alexandrine and Apocalyptic literature continue in the sad condition in which they are at present, we can form no certain judgment and draw no decided conclusions on the subject. When will the scholar appear who will at length throw light on these writings, and therewith on the section of inner Jewish history most interesting to the Christian theologian? As yet we have only a most thankworthy preliminary study in Schürer's great work, and beside it particular or dilettante attempts which hardly shew what the problem really is, far less solve it. What disclosures even the fourth book of the Maccabees alone yields for the connection of the Old Testament with Hellenism!

proved from the Old Testament by means of the allegoric exegetic method, is essentially identical with the system of Stoicism, which had been mixed with Platonic elements and had lost its Pantheistic materialistic impress. The fundamental idea from which Philo starts is a Platonic one; the dualism of God and the world, spirit and matter. The idea of God itself is therefore abstractly and negatively conceived (God, the real substance which is not finite), and has nothing more in common with the Old Testament conception. The possibility, however, of being able to represent God as acting on matter, which as the finite is the non-existent, and therefore the evil, is reached, with the help of the Stoic λόγοι as working powers and of the Platonic doctrine of archetypal ideas, and in outward connection with the Jewish doctrine of angels and the Greek doctrine of demons, by the introduction of intermediate spiritual beings which, as personal and impersonal powers proceeding from God, are to be thought of as operative causes and as Archetypes. All these beings are, as it were, comprehended in the Logos. By the Logos Philo understands the operative reason of God, and consequently also the power of God. The Logos is to him the thought of God and at the same time the product of his thought, therefore both idea and power. But further, the Logos is God himself on that side of him which is turned to the world, as also the ideal of the world and the unity of the spiritual forces which produce the world and rule in it. He can therefore be put beside God and in opposition to the world; but he can also, so far as the spiritual contents of the world are comprehended in him, be put with the world in contrast with God. The Logos accordingly appears as the Son of God, the foremost creature, the representative, Viceroy, High Priest, and Messenger of God; and again as principle of the world, spirit of the world, nay, as the world itself. He appears as a power and as a person, as a function of God and as an active divine being. Had Philo cancelled the contradiction which lies in this whole conception of the Logos, his system would have been demolished; for that system with its hard antithesis of

God and the world, needed a mediator who was, and yet was not God, as well as world. From this contrast, however, it further followed that we can only think of a world-formation by the Logos, not of a world-creation. [1] Within this world man is regarded as a microcosm, that is, as a being of Divine nature according to his spirit, who belongs to the heavenly world, while the adhering body is a prison which holds men captive in the fetters of sense, that is, of sin.

The Stoic and Platonic ideals and rules of conduct (also the Neo-pythagorean) were united by Philo in the religious Ethic as well as in the Cosmology. Rationalistic moralism is surmounted by the injunction to strive after a higher good lying above virtue. But here, at the same time, is the point at which Philo decidedly goes beyond Platonism, and introduces a new thought into Greek Ethics, and also in correspondence therewith into theoretic philosophy. This thought, which indeed lay altogether in the line of the development of Greek philosophy, was not, however, pursued by Philo into all its consequences, though it was the expression of a new frame of mind. While the highest good is resolved by Plato and his successors into knowledge of truth, which truth, together with the idea of God, lies in a sphere really accessible to the intellectual powers of the human spirit, the highest good, the Divine original being, is considered by Philo, though not invariably, to be above reason, and the power of comprehending it is denied to the human intellect. This assumption, a concession which Greek speculation was compelled to make to positive religion for the supremacy which was yielded to it, was to have far-reaching consequences in the future. *A place was now for the first time provided in philosophy for a*

---

1 "So far as the sensible world is a work of the Logos, it is called νεώτερος υἱός (quod deus immut. 6. 1. 277), or according to Prov. VIII. 22, an offspring of God and wisdom: ἡ δὲ παραδεξαμένη τὸ τοῦ θεοῦ σπέρμα τελεσφόροις ὠδῖσι τὸν μόνον καὶ ἀγαπητὸν αἰσθητὸν υἱὸν ἀπεκύησε τόνδε τὸν κόσμον (de ebriet. 8. I. 361 f.). So far as the Logos is High Priest his relation to the world is symbolically expressed by the garment of the High Priest, to which exegesis the play on the word κόσμος, as meaning both ornament and world, lent its aid." This speculation (see Siegfried. Philo, 235) is of special importance; for it shews how closely the ideas κόσμος and λόγος were connected

mythology to be regarded as revelation. The highest truths which could not otherwise be reached, might be sought for in the oracles of the Deity; for knowledge resting on itself had learnt by experience its inability to attain to the truth in which blessedness consists. *In this very experience the intellectualism of Greek Ethics was, not indeed cancelled, but surmounted.* The injunction to free oneself from sense and strive upwards by means of knowledge, remained; but the wings of the thinking mind bore it only to the entrance of the sanctuary. Only ecstasy produced by God himself was able to lead to the reality above reason. The great novelties in the system of Philo, though in a certain sense the way had already been prepared for them, are the introduction of the idea of a philosophy of revelation and the advance beyond the absolute intellectualism of Greek philosophy, an advance based on scepticism, but also on the deep-felt needs of life. Only the germs of these are found in Philo, but they are already operative. They are innovations of world-wide importance: for in them the covenant between the thoughts of reason on the one hand, and the belief in revelation and mysticism on the other, is already so completed that neither by itself could permanently maintain the supremacy. Thought about the world was henceforth dependent, not only on practical motives, it is always that, but on the need of a blessedness and peace which is higher than all reason. It might, perhaps, be allowable to say that Philo was the first who, as a philosopher, plainly expressed that need, just because he was not only a Greek, but also a Jew. [1]

Apart from the extremes into which the ethical counsels of Philo run, they contain nothing that had not been demanded by philosophers before him. The purifying of the affections, the renunciation of sensuality, the acquisition of the four cardinal virtues, the greatest possible simplicity of life, as well

[1] Of all the Greek Philosophers of the second century, Plutarch of Chäronea, died c. 125 A. D, and Numenius of Apamea, second half of the second century, approach nearest to Philo; but the latter of the two was undoubtedly familiar with Jewish philosophy, specially with Philo, and probably also with Christian writings.

as a cosmopolitan disposition are enjoined. [1]   But the attainment of the highest morality by our own strength is despaired of, and man is directed beyond himself to God's assistance. Redemption begins with the spirit reflecting on its own condition; it advances by a knowledge of the world and of the Logos, and it is perfected, after complete asceticism, by mystic ecstatic contemplation in which a man loses himself, but in return is entirely filled and moved by God. [2]   In this condition man has a foretaste of the blessedness which shall be given him when the soul, freed from the body, will be restored to its true existence as a heavenly being.

This system, notwithstanding its appeal to revelation, has, in the strict sense of the word, no place for Messianic hopes, of which nothing but very insignificant rudiments are found in Philo. But he was really animated by the hope of a glorious time to come for Judaism. The synthesis of the Messiah and the Logos did not lie within his horizon. [3]

3. Neither Philo's philosophy of religion, nor the mode of thought from which it springs, exercised any appreciable influence on the first generation of believers in Christ. [4]   But its practical ground-thoughts, though in different degrees, must have found admission very early into the Jewish Christian circles of the Diaspora, and through them to Gentile Christian circles also. Philo's philosophy of religion became

1 As to the way in which Philo (see also 4 Maccab. V. 24) learned to connect the Stoic ethics with the authority of the Torah, as was also done by the Palestinian Midrash, and represented the Torah as the foundation of the world, and therewith as the law of nature : see Siegfried, Philo, p. 156.

2 Philo by his exhortations to seek the blessed life, has by no means broken with the intellectualism of the Greek philosophy, he has only gone beyond it. The way of knowledge and speculation is to him also the way of religion and morality. But his formal principle is supernatural and leads to a supernatural knowledge which finally passes over into sight.

3 But everything was now ready for this synthesis so that it could be, and immediately was, completed by Christian philosophers.

4 We cannot discover Philo's influence in the writings of Paul. But here again we must remember that the scripture learning of Palestinian teachers developed speculations which appear closely related to the Alexandrian, and partly are so, but yet cannot be deduced from them. The element common to them must, for the present at least, be deduced from the harmony of conditions in which the different nations of the East were at that time placed, a harmony which we cannot exactly measure.

operative among Christian teachers from the beginning of
the second century, [1] and at a later period actually obtained
the significance of a standard of Christian theology, Philo
gaining a place among Christian writers. The systems of
Valentinus and Origen presuppose that of Philo. It can no
longer, however, be shewn with certainty how far the direct
influence of Philo reached, as the development of religious
ideas in the second century took a direction which necessarily
led to views similar to those which Philo had anticipated (see
§ 6, and the whole following account).

Supplement. — The hermeneutic principles (the "Biblicalal-
chemy"), above all, became of the utmost importance for the
following period. These were partly invented by Philo himself, partly traditional,—the Haggadic rules of exposition
and the hermeneutic principles of the Stoics having already
at an earlier period been united in Alexandria. They fall
into two main classes; "first, those according to which the
literal sense is excluded, and the allegoric proved to be the
only possible one, and then, those according to which the
allegoric sense is discovered as standing beside and above the
literal sense." [2] That these rules permitted the discovery of
a new sense by minute changes within a word, was a point
of special importance. [3] Christian teachers went still further
in this direction, and, as can be proved, altered the text of
the Septuagint in order to make more definite what suggested
itself to them as the meaning of a passage, or in order to
give a satisfactory meaning to a sentence which appeared to
them unmeaning or offensive. [4] Nay, attempts were not want-

---

1 The conception of God's relation to the world as given in the fourth
Gospel is not Philonic. The Logos doctrine there is therefore essentially
not that of Philo (against Kuenen and others, See p. 93).

2 Siegfried (Philo. p. 160-197) has presented in detail Philo's allegorical
interpretation of scripture, his hermeneutic principles and their application.
Without an exact knowledge of these principles we cannot understand the
Scripture expositions of the Fathers, and therefore also cannot do them justice.

3 See Siegfried, Philo, p. 176. Yet, as a rule, the method of isolating and
adapting passages of scripture, and the method of unlimited combination
were sufficient.

4 Numerous examples of this may be found in the epistle of Barnabas (see
c. 4-9), and in the dialogue of Justin with Trypho (here they are objects of
controversy, see cc. 71-73, 120), but also in many other Christian writings, (*e. g.*,

ing among Christians in the second century—they were
aided by the uncertainty that existed about the extent of
the Septuagint, and by the want of plain predictions about
the death upon the cross — to determine the Old Testament
canon in accordance with new principles; that is, to alter
the text on the plea that the Jews had corrupted it, and to
insert new books into the Old Testament, above all, Jewish
Apocalypses revised in a Christian sense. Tertullian (de cultu
fem. 1. 3,) furnishes a good example of the latter. "Scio
scripturam Enoch, quæ hunc ordinem angelis dedit, non recipi
a quibusdam, quia nec in armorium Judaicum admittitur . . .
sed cum Enoch eadem scriptura etiam de domino prædicarit,
a nobis quidem nihil omnino reiciendum est quod pertinet ad
nos. Et legimus omnem scripturam ædificationi habilem
divinitus inspirari. A Judæis potest jam videri propterea
reiecta, sicut et cetera fere quæ Christum sonant. . . . . Eo
accedit quod Enoch apud Judam apostolum testimonium pos-
sidet." Compare also the history of the Apocalypse of Ezra in
the Latin Bible (Old Testament). Not only the genuine Greek
portions of the Septuagint, but also many Apocalypses were
quoted by Christians in the second century as of equal value
with the Old Testament. It was the New Testament that
slowly put an end to these tendencies towards the formation
of a Christian Old Testament.

1 Clem. ad. Cor. VIII. 3: XVII. 6: XXIII. 3, 4: XXVI. 5: XLVI. 2 : 2, Clem.
XIII. 2). These Christian additions were long retained in the Latin Bible,
(see also Lactantius and other Latins: Pseudo-Cyprian de aleat. 2 etc.), the
most celebrated of them is the addition "a ligno" to "dominus regnavit" in
Psalm XCVI., see Credner, Beiträge II. The treatment of the Old Testament
in the epistle of Barnabas is specially instructive, and exhibits the greatest
formal agreement with that of Philo. We may close here with the words in
which Siegfried sums up his judgment on Philo. "No Jewish writer has contributed so much as Philo to the breaking up of paticularism, and the dissolution of Judaism. The history of his people, though he believed in it literally,
was in its main points a didactic allegoric poem for enabling him to inculcate
the doctrine that man attains the vision of God by mortification of the flesh.
The law was regarded by him as the best guide to this, but it had lost its
exclusive value, as it was admitted to be possible to reach the goal without it,
and it had, besides, its aim outside itself. The God of Philo was no longer the
old living God of Israel, but an imaginary being who, to obtain power over the
world, needed a Logos by whom the palladium of Israel, the unity of God, was
taken a prey. So Israel lost everything which had hitherto characterised her."

To find the spiritual meaning of the sacred text, partly beside the literal, partly by excluding it, became the watchword for the "scientific" Christian theology which was possible only on this basis, as it endeavoured to reduce the immense and dissimilar material of the Old Testament to unity with the Gospel, and both with the religious and scientific culture of the Greeks,—yet without knowing a relative standard, the application of which would alone have rendered possible in a loyal way the solution of the task. Here, Philo was the master; for he first to a great extent poured the new wine into old bottles. Such a procedure is warranted by its final purpose; for history is a unity. But applied in a pedantic and stringently dogmatic way it is a source of deception, of untruthfulness, and finally of total blindness.

Literature.—Gefrörer, Das Jahr des Heils, 1838. Parthey, Das Alexandr. Museum, 1838. Matter, Hist. de l'école d'Alex. 1840. Dähne, Gesch. Darstellung der jüd.-alex. Religionsphilos. 1834. Zeller, Die Philosophie der Griechen, III. 2. 3rd Edition. Mommsen, History of Rome. Vol. V. Siegfried, Philo von Alex. 1875. Massebieau, Le Classement des Œuvres de Philon. 1889. Hatch, Essays in Biblical Greek, 1889. Drummond, Philo Judæus, 1888. Bigg, The Christian Platonists of Alexandria, 1886. Schürer, History of the Jewish People. The investigations of Freudenthal (Hellenistische Studien), and Bernays (Ueber das phokylideische Gedicht; Theophrastos' Schrift über Frömmigkeit; Die heraklitischen Briefe). Kuenen, Hibbert Lectures: "Christian Theology could have made and has made much use of Hellenism. But the Christian religion cannot have sprung from this source." Havet thinks otherwise, though in the fourth volume of his "Origines" he has made unexpected admissions.

§ 6. *The Religious Dispositions of the Greeks and Romans in the first two centuries, and the current Græco-Roman Philosophy of Religion.*

1. After the national religion and the religious sense generally in cultured circles had been all but lost in the age of

Cicero and Augustus, there is noticeable in the Græco-Roman world from the beginning of the second century a revival of religious feeling which embraced all classes of society, and appears, especially from the middle of that century, to have increased from decennium to decennium.[1] Parallel with it went the not altogether unsuccessful attempt to restore the old national worship, religious usages, oracles, etc. In these attempts, however, which were partly superficial and artificial, the new religious needs found neither vigorous nor clear expression. These needs rather sought new forms of satisfaction corresponding to the wholly changed conditions of the time, including intercourse and mixing of the nations; decay of the old republican orders, divisions and ranks; monarchy and absolutism and social crises; pauperism; influence of philosophy on the domain of public morality and law; cosmopolitanism and the rights of man; influx of Oriental cults into the West; knowledge of the world and disgust with it. The decay of the old political cults and syncretism produced a disposition in favour of monotheism both among the cultured classes who had been prepared for it by philosophy, and also gradually among the masses. Religion and individual morality became more closely connected. There was developed a corresponding attempt at spiritualising the worship alongside of and within the ceremonial forms, and at giving it a direction towards the moral elevation of man through the ideas of moral personality, conscience, and purity. The ideas of repentance and of expiation and healing of the soul became of special importance, and consequently such Oriental cults came to the front as required the former and guaranteed the latter. But what was sought above all, was to enter into an inner union with the Deity, to be saved by him and become a partaker in the possession and enjoyment of his life. The worshipper consequently longed to find a " præsens numen " and the revelation of him in the cultus, and hoped to put himself in possession of the Deity by asceticism and mysterious rites. This new

---

1 Proofs in Friedländer, Sittengeschichte, vol. 3.

piety longed for health and purity of soul, and elevation above earthly things, and in connection with these a divine, that is, a painless and eternal life beyond the grave ("renatus in æternum taurobolio"). A world beyond was desired, sought for and viewed with an uncertain eye. By detachment from earthly things and the healing of its diseases (the passions) the freed, new born soul should return to its divine nature and existence. It is not a hope of immortality such as the ancients had dreamed of for their heroes, were they continue, as it were, their earthly existence in blessed enjoyment. To the more highly pitched self-consciousness this life had become a burden, and in the miseries of the present, one hoped for a future life in which the pain and vulgarity of the unreal life of earth would be completely laid aside (Ἐγκράτεια and ἀνάστασις). If the new moralistic feature stood out still more emphatically in the piety of the second century, it vanished more and more behind the religious feature, the longing after life [1] and after a Redeemer God. No one could any longer be a God who was not also a saviour. [2]

With all this Polytheism was not suppressed, but only put into a subordinate place. On the contrary, it was as lively and active as ever. For the idea of a *numen supremum* did not exclude belief in the existence and manifestation of subordinate deities. Apotheosis came into currency. The old state religion first attained its highest and most powerful expression in the worship of the emperor, (the emperor glorified

[1] See the chapter on belief in immortality in Friedländer. Sittengesch. Roms. Bde. 3. Among the numerous mysteries known to us, that of Mythras deserves special consideration. From the middle of the second century the Church Fathers saw in it, above all, the caricature of the Church. The worship of Mithras had its redeemer, its mediator, hierarchy, sacrifice, baptism and sacred meal. The ideas of expiation, immortality, and the Redeemer God, were very vividly present in this cult, which of course, in later times, borrowed much from Christianity: see the accounts of Marquardt, Réville, and the Essay of Sayous, Le Taurobole in the Rev. de l'Hist. des Religions, 1887, where the earliest literature is also utilised. The worship of Mithras in the third century became the most powerful rival of Christianity. In connection with this should be specially noted the cult of Æsculapius, the God who helps the body and the soul; see my essay "Medicinisches aus der ältesten Kirchengeschichte," 1892. p. 93 ff.

[2] Hence the wide prevalence of the cult of Æsculapius.

as "dominus ac deus noster ", [1] as "præsens et corporalis deus ", the Antinous cult, etc.), and in many circles an incarnate ideal in the present or the past was sought, which might be worshipped as revealer of God and as God, and which might be an example of life and an assurance of religious hope. Apotheosis became less offensive in proportion as, in connection with the fuller recognition of the spiritual dignity of man, the estimate of the soul, the spirit, as of supramundane nature, and the hope of its eternal continuance in a form of existence befitting it, became more general. That was the import of the message preached by the Cynics and the Stoics, that the truly wise man is Lord, Messenger of God, and God upon the earth. On the other hand, the popular belief clung to the idea that the gods could appear and be visible in human form, and this faith, though mocked by the cultured, gained numerous adherents, even among them, in the age of the Antonines. [2]

1 Dominus in certain circumstances means more than deus; see Tertull. Apol. It signifies more than Soter: see Irenæus I. 1. 3: ..... τὸν σωτῆρα λέγουσιν, οὐδὲ γὰρ κύριον ὀνομάζειν αὐτὸν θέλουσιν—κύριος and δεσπότης are almost synonymous. See Philo. Quis. rer. div. heres. 6: συνώνυμα ταῦτα εἶναι λέγεται.

2 We must give special attention here to the variability and elasticity of the concept "θεός", and indeed among the cultured as well as the uncultured (Orig. prolegg. in Psalm. in Pitra, Anal. T. II. p. 437, according to a Stoic source; κατ᾽ ἄλλον δέ τρόπον λέγεσθαι θεὸν ζῷον ἀθάνατον λογικὸν σπουδαῖον, ὥστε πᾶσαν ἀστείαν ψυχήν θεὸν ὑπάρχειν, κἂν περιέχηται, ἄλλως δὲ λέγεσθαι θεὸν τὸ καθ᾽ αὑτὸ ὂν ζῷον ἀθάνατον ὡς τὰ ἐν ἀνθρώποις σοφοῖς περιεχομένας ψυχὰς μὴ ὑπάρχειν θεούς). They still regarded the Gods as passionless, blessed men living for ever. The idea therefore of a θεοποίησις, and on the other hand, the idea of the appearance of the Gods in human form presented no difficulty (see Acts XIV. 11 : XXVIII. 6). But philosophic speculation—the Platonic, as well as in yet greater measure the Stoic, and in the greatest measure of all the Cynic— had led to the recognition of something divine in man's spirit (πνεῦμα, νοῦς). Marcus Aurelius in his Meditations frequently speaks of the God who dwells in us. Clement of Alexandria (Strom. VI. 14. 113) says: οὕτως δύναμιν λαβοῦσα κυριακὴν ἡ ψυχὴ μελετᾷ εἶναι θεός, κακὸν μὲν οὐδὲν ἄλλο πλὴν ἀγνοίας εἶναι νομίζουσα. In Bernays' Heraclitian Epistles, pp. 37 f. 135 f., will be found a valuable exposition of the Stoic [Heraclitian] thesis and its history, that men are Gods. See Norden, Beiträge zur Gesch. d. griech. Philos. Jahrb. f. klass Philol. XIX. Suppl. Bd. p. 373 ff., about the Cynic Philosopher who, contemplating the life and activity of man [κατάσκοπος], becomes its ἐπίσκοπος, and further κύριός, ἄγγελος θεοῦ, θεὸς ἐν ἀνθρώποις. The passages which he adduces are of importance for the history of dogma in a twofold respect. (1) They present remarkable parallels to Christology [one even finds the designations, κύριος, ἄγγελός, κατάσκοπος, ἐπίσκοπος, θεὸς associated with the philosophers as with Christ, e.g., in Justin; nay, the Cynics and Neoplatonics speak of

The new thing which was here developed, continued to be

ἐπίσκοποι δαίμονες; cf. also the remarkable narrative in Laertius VI. 102, concerning the Cynic Menedemus; οὗτος, καθά φησιν Ἱππόβοτος, εἰς τοσοςτον τερατείας ἥλασεν, ὥστε Ἐρινύος ἀναλαβὼν σχῆμα περιήει, λέγων ἐπισκοπος ἀφῖχθαι ἐξ Ἅιδου τῶν ἁμαρτόμενων, ὅπως πάλιν κατιὼν ταςτα ἀπαγγέλλοι τοῖς ἐκεῖ, δαίμοσιν]. (2) They also explain how the ecclesiastical ἐπίσκοποι came to be so highly prized, inasmuch as these also were from a very early period regarded as mediators between God and man, and considered as ἐν ἀνθρώποις θεοί). There were not a few who in the first and second centuries, appeared with the claim to be regarded as a God or an organ inspired and chosen by God (Simon Magus [cf. the manner of his treatment in Hippol. Philos. VI. 8 : see also Clem. Hom. II. 27], Apollonius of Tyana (?), see further Tacitus Hist. II. 51 : "Mariccus. . . . iamque adsertor Galliarum et deus, nomen id sibi indiderat"; here belongs also the gradually developing worship of the Emperor: "dominus ac deus noster." cf. Augustus, Inscription of the year 25/24 B.C. in Egypt [where the Ptolemies were for long described as Gods] Ὑπὲρ Καίσαρος Αὐτοκράτορος θεοῦ (Zeitschrift für Ægypt. Sprache. XXXI. Bd. p 3). Domitian : θεὸς Ἀδριανός, Kaibel Inscr. Gr. 829. 1053. θεός Σεουῆρος Εὐσεβής, 1061 — the Antinouscult with its prophets. See also Josephus on Herod Agrippa. Antiq. XIX 8. 2. (Euseb. H. E. II. 10) The flatterers said to him, θεὸν προσαγορεύοντες· εἰ καὶ μέχρι νῦν ὡς ἄνθρωπον ἐφοβήθημεν, ἀλλὰ τούντεῦθεν κρείττονα σε θνητῆς τῆς φύσεως ὁμολογοῦμεν. Herod himself, § 7, says to his friends in his sickness ; ὁ θεὸς ὑμῖν ἐγὼ ἤδη καταστρέφειν ἐπιτάττομαι τὸν βίον .... ὁ κληθεις ἀθάνατος ὑφ᾽ ἡμῶν ἤδη θανεῖν ἀπάγομαι). On the other hand, we must mention the worship of the founder in some philosophic schools, especially among the Epicureans. Epictetus says (Moral. 15), Diogenes and Heraclitus and those like them are justly called Gods. Very instructive in this connection are the reproaches of the heathen against the Christians, and of Christian partisans against one another with regard to the almost divine veneration of their teachers. Lucian (Peregr. 11) reproaches the Christians in Syria for having regarded Peregrinus as a God and a new Socrates. The heathen in Smyrna, after the burning of Polycarp, feared that the Christians would begin to pay him divine honours (Euseb. H E. IV. 15 41). Cæcilius in Minucius Felix speaks of divine honours being paid by Christians to priests. (Octav. IX. 10). The Antimontanist (Euseb. H. E. V. 18. 6) asserts that the Montanists worship their prophet and Alexander the Confessor as divine. The opponents of the Roman Adoptians (Euseb. H. E. V. 28) reproach them with praying to Galen.There are many passages in which the Gnostics are reproached with paying Divine honours to the heads of their schools, and for many Gnostic schools (the Carpocratians, for example the reproach seems to have been just. All this is extremely instructive. The genius, the hero, the founder of a new school who promises to shew the certain way to the *vita beata*, the emperor, the philosopher (numerous Stoic passages might be noted here) finally, man, in so far as he is inhabited by νοῦς — could all somehow be considered as θεοί, so elastic was this concept. All these instances of Apotheosis in no way endangered the Monotheism which had been developed from the mixture of Gods and from philosophy; for the one supreme Godhead can unfold his inexhaustible essence in a variety of existences, which, while his creatures as to their origin, are parts of his essence as to their contents. This Monotheism does not yet exactly disclaim its Polytheistic origin. The Christian, Hermas, says to his Mistress (Vis. I. 1. 7) οὐ πάντοτέ σε ὡς θεάν ἡγησάμην, and the author of the Epistle of Diognetus writes (X. 6), ταῦτα τοις ἐπιδεομένοις χορηγῶν, (*i. e.*, the rich man)θεὸς γίνεται τῶν λαμβανόντων,That the concept θεὸς was again used only of

greatly obscured by the old forms of worship which reasons of state and pious custom maintained. And the new piety, dispensing with a fixed foundation, groped uncertainly around, adapting the old rather than rejecting it. The old religious practices of the Fathers asserted themselves in public life generally, and the reception of new cults by the state, which was certainly effected, though with many checks, did not disturb them. The old religious customs stood out especially on state holidays, in the games in honour of the Gods, frequently degenerating into shameless immorality, but yet protecting the institutions of the state. The patriot, the wise man, the sceptic, and the pious man compounded with them, for they had not really at bottom outgrown them, and they knew of nothing better to substitute for the services they still rendered to society (see the λόγος αληθής of Celsus).

2. The system of associations, naturalised centuries before among the Greeks, was developed under the social and political pressure of the empire, and was greatly extended by the change of moral and religious ideas. The free unions, which, as a rule, had a religious element and were established for mutual help, support, or edification, balanced to some extent the prevailing social cleavage, by a free democratic organisation. They gave to many individuals in their small circle the rights which they did not possess in the great world, and were frequently of service in obtaining admission for new cults. Even the new piety and cosmopolitan disposition seem to have turned to them in order to find within them forms of expression. But the time had not come for the greater corporate unions, and of an organised connection of societies in one city with those of another we know nothing. The state kept these associations under strict control. It granted them only to the

one God, was due to the fact that one now started from the definition "qui vitam æternam habet," and again from the definition "qui est super omnia et originem nescit." From the latter followed the absolute unity of God, from the former a plurality of Gods. Both could be so harmonised (see Tertull. adv. Prax. and Novat. de Trinit.) that one could assume that the God, *qui est super omnia*, might allow his monarchy to be administered by several persons, and might dispense the gift of immortality and with it a relative divinity.

poorest classes (*collegia tenuiorum*) and had the strictest laws
in readiness for them. These free unions, however, did not
in their historical importance approach the fabric of the Roman
state in which they stood. That represented the union of the
greater part of humanity under one head, and also more and
more under one law. Its capital was the capital of the world,
and also, from the beginning of the third century, of religious
syncretism. Hither migrated all who desired to exercise an
influence on the great scale: Jew, Chaldean, Syrian priest,
and Neoplatonic teacher. Law and Justice radiated from Rome
to the provinces, and in their light nationalities faded away,
and a cosmopolitanism was developed which pointed beyond
itself, because the moral spirit can never find its satisfaction
in that which is realised. When that spirit finally turned
away from all political life, and after having laboured for the
ennobling of the empire, applied itself, in Neoplatonism, to
the idea of a new and free union of men, this certainly was
the result of the felt failure of the great creation, but it
nevertheless had that creation for its presupposition. The Church
appropriated piecemeal the great apparatus of the Roman
state, and gave new powers, new significance and respect to
every article that had been depreciated. But what is of greatest
importance is that the Church by her preaching would never
have gained whole circles, but only individuals, had not the
universal state already produced a neutralising of nationalities
and brought men nearer each other in temper and disposition.

3. Perhaps the most decisive factor in bringing about the
revolution of religious and moral convictions and moods, was
philosophy, which in almost all its schools and representatives,
had deepened ethics, and set it more and more in the foreground. After Possidonius, Seneca, Epictetus, and Marcus
Aurelius of the Stoical school, and men like Plutarch of the
Platonic, attained to an ethical view, which, though not very
clear in principle (knowledge, resignation, trust in God), is
hardly capable of improvement in details. Common to them
all, as distinguished from the early Stoics, is the value put
upon the soul, (not the entire human nature), while in some

of them there comes clearly to the front a religious mood, a
longing for divine help, for redemption and a blessed life
beyond the grave, the effort to obtain and communicate a
religious philosophical therapeutic of the soul.[1] From the beginning of the second century, however, already announced
itself that eclectic philosophy based on Platonism which after
two or three generations appeared in the form of a school,
and after three generations more was to triumph over all other
schools. The several elements of the Neoplatonic philosophy,
as they were already foreshadowed in Philo, are clearly seen
in the second century, viz., the dualistic opposition of the
divine and the earthly, the abstract conception of God, the
assertion of the unknowableness of God, scepticism with regard
to sensuous experience, and distrust with regard to the powers
of the understanding, with a greater readiness to examine
things and turn to account the result of former scientific
labour; further, the demand of emancipation from sensuality
by means of asceticism, the need of authority, belief in a
higher revelation, and the fusion of science and religion. The
legitimising of religious fancy in the province of philosophy was
already begun. The myth was no longer merely tolerated
and re-interpreted as formerly, but precisely the mythic form
with the meaning imported into it was the precious element.[2]
There were, however, in the second century numerous representatives of every possible philosophic view. To pass over
the frivolous writers of the day, the Cynics criticised the tra-

---

1 The longing for redemption and divine help is, for example, clearer in
Seneca than in the Christian philosopher, Minucius Felix: see Kühn, Der
Octavius des M. F. 1882, and Theol. Lit. Ztg. 1883. No 6.

2 See the so-called Neopythagorean philosophers and the so-called forerunners of Neoplatonism (Cf. Bigg, The Platonists of Alexandria, p. 250, as to
Numenius). Unfortunately, we have as yet no sufficient investigation of the
question what influence, if any, the Jewish Alexandrian Philosophy of
religion had on the development of Greek philosophy in the second and
third centuries. The answering of the question would be of the greatest
importance. But at present it cannot even be said whether the Jewish
philosophy of religion had any influence on the genesis of Neoplatonism.
On the relation of Neoplatonism to Christianity and their mutual approximation, see the excellent account in Tzschirner, Fall des Heidenthums,
pp. 574-618. Cf. also Réville, La Religion à Rome. 1886.

ditional mythology in the interests of morality and religion.[1] But there were also men who opposed the "ne quid nimis" to every form of practical scepticism, and to religion at the same time, and were above all intent on preserving the state and society, and on fostering the existing arrangements which appeared to be threatened far more by an intrusive religious than by a nihilistic philosophy.[2] Yet men whose interest was ultimately practical and political, became ever more rare, especially as from the death of Marcus Aurelius, the maintenance of the state had to be left more and more to the sword of the Generals. The general conditions from the end of the second century were favourable to a philosophy which no longer in any respect took into real consideration the old forms of the state.

The theosophic philosophy which was prepared for in the second century,[3] was, from the stand-point of enlightenment and knowledge of nature, a relapse: but it was the expression of a deeper religious need, and of a self-knowledge such as had not been in existence at an earlier period. The final consequences of that revolution in philosophy which made consideration of the inner life the starting-point of thought about the world, only now began to be developed. The ideas of a divine, gracious providence, of the relationship of all men, of universal brotherly love, of a ready forgiveness of wrong, of forbearing patience, of insight into one's own weakness—affected no doubt with many shadows—became, for

1 The Christians, that is the Christian preachers, were most in agreement with the Cynics (see Lucian's Peregrinus Proteus), both on the negative and on the positive side; but for that very reason they were hard on one another (Justin and Tatian against Crescens)—not only because the Christians gave a different basis for the right mode of life from the Cynics, but above all, because they did not approve of the self-conscious, contemptuous, proud disposition which Cynicism produced in many of its adherents. Morality frequently underwent change for the worse in the hands of Cynics, and became the morality of a "Gentleman," such as we have also experience of in modern Cynicism.

2 The attitude of Celsus, the opponent of the Christians, is specially instructive here.

3 For the knowledge of the spread of the idealistic philosophy the statement of Origen (c. Celsum VI. 2) that Epictetus was admired not only by scholars, but also by ordinary people who felt in themselves the impulse to be raised to something higher, is well worthy of notice.

wide circles, a result of the practical philosophy of the Greeks as well as, the conviction of inherent sinfulness, the need of redemption, and the eternal value and dignity of a human soul which finds rest only in God. These ideas, convictions and rules, had been picked up in the long journey from Socrates to Ammonius Saccas: at first, and for long afterwards, they crippled the interest in a rational knowledge of the world; but they deepened and enriched the inner life, and therewith the source of all knowledge. Those ideas, however, lacked as yet the certain coherence, but, above all, the authority which could have raised them above the region of wishes, presentiments, and strivings, and have given them normative authority in a community of men. There was no sure revelation, and no view of history which could be put in the place of the no longer prized political history of the nation or state to which one belonged. [1] There was, in fact, no such thing as certainty. In like manner, there was no power which might overturn idolatry and abolish the old, and therefore one did not get beyond the wavering between self-deification, fear of God, and deification of nature. The glory is all the greater of those statesmen and jurists who, in the second and third centuries, introduced human ideas of the Stoics into the legal arrangements of the empire, and raised them to standards. And we must value all the more the numerous undertakings and performances, in which it appeared that the new view of life was powerful enough in individuals to beget a corresponding practice even without a sure belief in revelation. [2]

Supplement.—For the correct understanding of the beginning

1 This point was of importance for the propaganda of Christianity among the cultured. There seemed to be given here a reliable, because revealed, Cosmology and history of the world—which already contained the foundation of everything worth knowing. Both were needed and both were here set forth in closest union.

2 The universalism as reached by the Stoics is certainly again threatened by the self-righteous and self-complacent distinction between men of virtue, and men of pleasure, who, properly speaking, are not men. Aristotle had already dealt with the virtuous élite in a notable way. He says (Polit. 3. 13. p. 1284), that men who are distinguished by perfect virtue should not be put on a level with the ordinary mass, and should not be subjected to the constraints of a law adapted to the average man. "There is no law for these elect, who are a law to themselves."

of Christian theology, that is, for the Apologetic and Gnosis, it is important to note where they are dependent on Stoic, and where on Platonic lines of thought. Platonism and Stoicism, in the second century, appeared in union with each other: but up to a certain point they may be distinguished in the common channel in which they flow. Wherever Stoicism prevailed in religious thought and feeling, as for example, in Marcus Aurelius, religion gains currency as *natural* religion in the most comprehensive sense of the word. The idea of revelation or redemption scarcely emerges. To this rationalism, the objects of knowledge are unvarying, ever the same: even cosmology attracts interest only in a very small degree. Myth and history are pageantry and masks. Moral ideas (virtues and duties) dominate even the religious sphere, which in its final basis has no independent authority. The interest in psychology and apologetic is very pronounced. On the other hand, the emphasis, which, in principle, is put on the contrast of spirit and matter, God and the world, had for results: inability to rest in the actual realities of the cosmos, efforts to unriddle the history of the universe backwards and forwards, recognition of this process as the essential task of theoretic philosophy, and a deep, yearning conviction that the course of the world needs assistance. Here were given the conditions for the ideas of revelation, redemption, etc., and the restless search for powers from whom help might come, received here also a scientific justification. The rationalistic apologetic interests thereby fell into the background: contemplation and historical description predominated. [1]

The stages in the ecclesiastical history of dogma, from the middle of the first to the middle of the fifth century, correspond to the stages in the history of the ancient religion during the same period. The Apologists, Irenæus, Tertullian, Hippolytus; the Alexandrians; Methodius, and the Cappado-

---

[1] Notions of pre-existence were readily suggested by the Platonic philosophy; yet this whole philosophy rests on the fact that one again posits the thing (after stripping it of certain marks as accidental, or worthless, or ostensibly foreign to it) in order to express its value in this form, and hold fast the permanent in the change of the phenomena.

cians; Dionysius, the Areopagite, have their parallels in Seneca, Marcus Aurelius; Plutarch, Epictetus, Numenius; Plotinus, Porphyry; Iamblichus and Proclus.

But it is not only Greek philosophy that comes into question for the history of Christian dogma. The whole of Greek culture must be taken into account. In his posthumous work, Hatch has shewn in a masterly way how that is to be done. He describes the Grammar, the Rhetoric, the learned Profession, the Schools, the Exegesis, the Homilies, etc., of the Greeks, and everywhere shews how they passed over into the Church, thus exhibiting the Philosophy, the Ethic, the speculative Theology, the Mysteries, etc., of the Greeks, as the main factors in the process of forming the ecclesiastical mode of thought.

But, besides the Greek, there is no mistaking the special influence of Romish ideas and customs upon the Christian Church. The following points specially claim attention: (1) The conception of the contents of the Gospel and its application as "salus legitima," with the results which followed from the naturalising of this idea. (2) The conception of the word of Revelation, the Bible, etc., as "lex." (3) The idea of tradition in its relation to the Romish idea. (4) The Episcopal constitution of the Church, including the idea of succession, of the Primateship and universal Episcopate, in their dependence on Romish ideas and institutions (the Ecclesiastical organisation in its dependence on the Roman Empire). (5) The separation of the idea of the "sacrament" from that of the "mystery", and the development of the forensic discipline of penance. The investigation has to proceed in a historical line, described by the following series of chapters: Rome and Tertullian; Rome and Cyprian; Rome, Optatus and Augustine; Rome and the Popes of the fifth century. We have to shew how, by the power of her constitution and the earnestness and consistency of her policy, Rome a second time, step by step, conquered the world, but this time the Christian world. [1]

---

1 See Tzschirn. i. d. Ztschr. f. K.-Gesch. XII. p. 215 ff. "The genesis of the Romish Church in the second century." What he presents is no doubt partly incomplete, partly overdone and not proved: yet much of what he states is useful.

Greek philosophy exercised the greatest influence not only on the Christian mode of thought, but also through that, on the institutions of the Church. The Church never indeed became a philosophic school: but yet in her was realised in a peculiar way, that which the Stoics and the Cynics had aimed at. The Stoic (Cynic) Philosopher also belonged to the factors from which the Christian Priests or Bishops were formed. That the old bearers of the Spirit—Apostles, Prophets, Teachers—have been changed into a class of professional moralists and preachers, who bridle the people by counsel and reproof (νουθετεῖν καὶ ἐλέγχειν), that this class considers itself and desires to be considered as a mediating Kingly Divine class, that its representatives became "Lords" and let themselves be called "Lords", all this was prefigured in the Stoic wise man and in the Cynic Missionary. But so far as these several "Kings and Lords" are united in the idea and reality of the Church and are subject to it, the Platonic idea of the republic goes beyond the Stoic and Cynic ideals, and subordinates them to it. But this Platonic ideal has again obtained its political realisation in the Church through the very concrete laws of the Roman Empire, which were more and more adopted, or taken possession of. Consequently, in the completed Church we find again the philosophic schools and the Roman Empire.

Literature.—Besides the older works of Tzschirner, Döllinger, Burckhardt, Preller, see Friedländer, Darstellungen aus der Sittengesch. Roms. in der Zeit von August bis zum Ausgang der Antonine, 3 Bd. Aufl. Boissier, La Religion Romaine d'Auguste aux Antonins, 2 Bd. 1874. Ramsay, The Church in the Roman Empire before 170. London, 1893. Réville, La Religion à Rome sous les Sévères, 1886. Schiller, Geschichte der Röm. Kaiserzeit, 1883. Marquardt, Römische Staatsverwaltung, 3 Bde. 1878. Foucart, Les Associations Relig. chez les Grecs, 1873. Liebeman, Z. Gesch. u. Organisation d. Röm. Vereinswesen, 1890. K. J. Neumann, Der Röm. Staat und die allg. Kirche, Bd. I. 1890. Leopold Schmidt, Die Ethik der alten Griechen, 2 Bd. 1882. Heinrici, Die Christengemeinde Korinth's und die religiösen Genossenschaften der Griechen, in der Ztschr. f. wissensch. Theol. 1876-77. Hatch, The Influence of Greek Ideas and Usages upon the Christian Church. Buechner, De neocoria, 1888. Hirschfeld, Z. Gesch. d. röm. Kaisercultus. The Histories of Philosophy by Zeller, Erdmann, Ueberweg, Strümpell, Windelband, etc. Heinze, Die Lehre vom Logos in der Griech. Philosophie, 1872. By same Author, Der Eudämonismus in der Griech. Philosophie, 1883. Hirzel, Untersuchungen zu Cicero's philos. Schriften, 3 Thle. 1877-1883. These investigations are of special value for the history of dogma, because they set forth with the greatest accuracy and care, the later developments of the great Greek philosophic schools, especially on Roman soil. We must refer specially to the discussions on the influence of the Roman on the Greek Philosophy. Volkmann, Die Rhetorik der Griechen und Römer, 1872.

SUPPLEMENTARY.

Perhaps the most important fact for the following development of the history of Dogma, the way for which had already been prepared in the Apostolic age, is the twofold conception of the aim of Christ's appearing, or of the religious blessing of salvation. The two conceptions were indeed as yet mutually dependent on each other, and were twined together in the closest way, just as they are presented in the teaching of Jesus himself; but they began even at this early period to be differentiated. Salvation, that is to say, was conceived, on the one hand, as sharing in the glorious kingdom of Christ soon to appear, and everything else was regarded as preparatory to this sure prospect; on the other hand, however, attention was turned to the conditions and to the provisions of God wrought by Christ, which first made men capable of attaining that portion, that is, of becoming sure of it. Forgiveness of sin, righteousness, faith, knowledge, etc., are the things which come into consideration here, and these blessings themselves, so far as they have as their sure result life in the

kingdom of Christ, or more accurately eternal life, may be
regarded as salvation. It is manifest that these two conceptions need not be exclusive. The first regards the final effect
as the goal and all else as a preparation, the other regards
the preparation, the facts already accomplished by Christ and
the inner transformation of men as the main thing, and all
else as the natural and necessary result. Paul, above all, as
may be seen especially from the arguments in the epistle to
the Romans, unquestionably favoured the latter conception and
gave it vigorous expression. The peculiar conflicts with which
he saw himself confronted, and, above all, the great controversy about the relation of the Gospel and the new communities to Judaism, necessarily concentrated the attention on
questions as to the arrangements on which the community of
those sanctified in Christ should rest, and the conditions of
admission to this community. But the centre of gravity of
Christian faith might also for the moment be removed from
the hope of Christ's second advent, and would then necessarily be found in the first advent, in virtue of which salvation was already prepared for man, and man for salvation
(Rom. III.—VIII.). The dual development of the conception
of Christianity which followed from this, rules the whole
history of the Gospel to the present day. The eschatological
view is certainly very severely repressed, but it always
breaks out here and there, and still guards the spiritual from
the secularisation which threatens it. But the possibility of
uniting the two conceptions in complete harmony with each
other, and on the other hand, of expressing them antithetically, has been the very circumstance that has complicated in
an extraordinary degree the progress of the development of
the history of dogma. From this follows the antithesis, that
from that conception which somehow recognises salvation itself
in a present spiritual possession, eternal life in the sense of
immortality may be postulated as final result, though not a
glorious kingdom of Christ on earth; while, conversely, the
eschatological · view must logically depreciate every blessing
which can be possessed in the present life.

It is now evident that the theology, and, further, the Hellenising, of Christianity, could arise and has arisen in connection,
not with the eschatological, but only with the other conception.
Just because the matters here in question were present spiritual blessings, and because, from the nature of the case, the
ideas of forgiveness of sin, righteousness, knowledge, etc., were
not so definitely outlined in the early tradition, as the hopes
of the future, conceptions entirely new and very different,
could, as it were, be secretly naturalised. The spiritual view
left room especially for the great contrast of a religious and
a moralistic conception, as well as for a frame of mind which
was like the eschatological in so far as, according to it, faith
and knowledge were to be only preparatory blessings in contrast with the peculiar blessing of immortality, which of course
was contained in them. In this frame of mind the illusion
might easily arise that this hope of immortality was the very
kernel of those hopes of the future for which old concrete forms
of expression were only a temporary shell. But it might
further be assumed that contempt for the transitory and finite
as such, was identical with contempt for the kingdom of the
world which the returning Christ would destroy.

The history of dogma has to shew how the old eschatological view was gradually repressed and transformed in the Gentile Christian communities, and how there was finally developed and carried out a spiritual conception in which a strict
moralism counterbalanced a luxurious ¦mysticism, and wherein
the results of Greek practical philosophy could find a place.
But we must here refer to the fact, which is already taught
by the development in the Apostolic age, that Christian
dogmatic did not spring from the eschatological, but from the
spiritual mode of thought. The former had nothing but sure
hopes and the guarantee of these hopes by the Spirit, by the
words of prophecy and by the apocalyptic writings. One does
not think, he lives and dreams, in the eschatological mode of
thought; and such a life was vigorous and powerful till beyond
the middle of the second century. There can be no external
authorities here; for one has at every moment the highest

authority in living operation in the Spirit. On the other hand, not only does the ecclesiastical christology essentially spring from the spiritual way of thinking, but very specially also the system of dogmatic guarantees. The co-ordination of λόγος θεοῦ, διδαχή κυρίου, κήρυγμα τῶν δώδεκα ἀποστόλων [word of God, teaching of the Lord, preaching of the twelve Apostles], which lay at the basis of all Gentile Christian speculation almost from the very beginning, and which was soon directed against the enthusiasts, originated in a conception which regarded as the essential thing in Christianity, the sure knowledge which is the condition of immortality. If, however, in the following sections of this historical presentation, the pervading and continuous opposition of the two conceptions is not everywhere clearly and definitely brought into prominence, that is due to the conviction that the historian has no right to place the factors and impelling ideas of a development in a clearer light than they appear in the development itself. He must respect the obscurities and complications as they come in his way. A clear discernment of the difference of the two conceptions was very seldom attained to in ecclesiastical antiquity, because they did not look beyond their points of contact, and because certain articles of the eschatological conception could never be suppressed or remodelled in the Church. Goethe (Dichtung und Wahrheit, II. 8,) has seen this very clearly. "The Christian religion wavers between its own historic positive element and a pure Deism, which, based on morality, in its turn offers itself as the foundation of morality. The difference of character and mode of thought shew themselves here in infinite gradations, especially as another main distinction co-operates with them, since the question arises, what share the reason, and what the feelings, can and should have in such convictions." See, also, what immediately follows.

2. The origin of a series of the most important Christian customs and ideas is involved in an obscurity which in all probability will never be cleared up. Though one part of those ideas may be pointed out in the epistles of Paul, yet the question must frequently remain unanswered, whether he

found them in existence or formed them independently, and accordingly the other question, whether they are exclusively indebted to the activity of Paul for their spread and naturalisation in Christendom. What was the original conception of baptism? Did Paul develop independently his own conception? What significance had it in the following period? When and where did baptism in the name of the Father, Son and Holy Spirit arise, and how did it make its way in Christendom? In what way were views about the saving value of Christ's death developed alongside of Paul's system? When and how did belief in the birth of Jesus from a Virgin gain acceptance in Christendom? Who first distinguished Christendom, as ἐκκλησία τοῦ θεοῦ, from Judaism, and how did the concept ἐκκλησία become current? How old is the triad: Apostles, Prophets and Teachers? When were Baptism and the Lord's Supper grouped together? How old are our first three Gospels? To all these questions and many more of equal importance there is no sure answer. But the greatest problem is presented by Christology, not indeed in its particular features doctrinally expressed, these almost everywhere may be explained historically, but in its deepest roots as it was preached by Paul as the principle of a new life (2 Cor. V. 17), and as it was to many besides him the expression of a personal union with the exalted Christ (Rev. II. 3). But this problem exists only for the historian who considers things only from the outside, or seeks for objective proofs. Behind and in the Gospel stands the Person of Jesus Christ who mastered men's hearts, and constrained them to yield themselves to him as his own, and in whom they found their God. Theology attempted to describe in very uncertain and feeble outline what the mind and heart had grasped. Yet it testifies of a new life which, like all higher life, was kindled by a Person, and could only be maintained by connection with that Person. "I can do all things through Christ who strengtheneth me." "I live, yet not I, but Christ liveth in me." These convictions are not dogmas and have no history, and they can only be propagated in the manner described by Paul, Gal. I. 15, 16.

3. It was of the utmost importance for the legitimising of the later development of Christianity as a system of doctrine. that early Christianity had an Apostle who was a theologian, and that his Epistles were received into the canon. That the doctrine about Christ has become the main article in Christianity is not of course the result of Paul's preaching, but is based on the confession that Jesus is the Christ. The theology of Paul was not even the most prominent ruling factor in the transformation of the Gospel to the Catholic doctrine of faith, although an earnest study of the Pauline Epistles by the earliest Gentile Christian theologians, the Gnostics, and their later opponents, is unmistakable. But the decisive importance of this theology lies in the fact that, as a rule, it formed the boundary and the foundation — just as the words of the Lord himself — for those who in the following period endeavoured to ascertain original Christianity, because the Epistles attesting it stood in the canon of the New Testament. Now, as this theology comprised both speculative and apologetic elements, as it can be thought of as a system, as it contained a theory of history and a definite conception of the Old Testament, finally, as it was composed of objective and subjective ethical considerations and included the realistic elements of a national religion (wrath of God, sacrifice, reconciliation, Kingdom of glory), as well as profound psychological perceptions and the highest appreciation of spiritual blessings, the Catholic doctrine of faith as it was formed in the course of time, seemed, at least in its leading features, to be related to it, nay, demanded by it. For the ascertaining of the deep-lying distinctions, above all for the perception that the question in the two cases is about elements quite differently conditioned, that even the method is different, in short, that the Pauline Gospel is not identical with the original Gospel and much less with any later doctrine of faith, there is required such historical judgment and such honesty of purpose not to be led astray in the investigation by the canon of the New Testament, [1] that no change in the prevailing ideas can be

1 What is meant here is the imminent danger of taking the several constituent

hoped for for long years to come. Besides, critical theology has made it difficult to gain an insight into the great difference that lies between the Pauline and the Catholic theology, by the one-sided prominence it has hitherto given to the antagonism between Paulinism and Judaistic Christianity. In contrast with this view the remark of Havet, though also very one-sided, is instructive, " Quand on vient de relire Paul, on ne peut méconnaître le caractère élevé de son œuvre. Je dirai en un mot, qu'il a agrandi dans une proportion extraordinaire l'attrait que le judaïsme exerçait sur le monde ancien" (Le Christianisme, T. IV. p. 216). That, however, was only very gradually the case and within narrow limits. The deepest and most important writings of the New Testament are incontestably those in which Judaism is understood as religion, but spiritually overcome and subordinated to the Gospel as a new religion,—the Pauline Epistles, the Epistle to the Hebrews, and the Gospel and Epistle of John. There is set forth in these writings a new and exalted world of religious feelings, views and judgments, into which the Christians of succeeding centuries got only meagre glimpses. Strictly speaking, the opinion that the New Testament in its whole extent comprehends a unique literature is not tenable; but it is correct to say that between its most important constituent parts and the literature of the period immediately following there is a great gulf fixed.

But Paulinism especially has had an immeasurable and blessed influence on the whole course of the history of dogma, an influence it could not have had, if the Pauline Epistles had not been received into the canon. Paulinism is a religious and Christocentric doctrine, more inward and more powerful than any other which has ever appeared in the Church. It stands in the clearest opposition to all merely natural moralism,

parts of the canon, even for historical investigation, as constituent parts, that is, of explaining one writing by the standard of another and so creating an artificial unity. The contents of any of Paul's epistles, for example, will be presented very differently if it is considered by itself and in the circumstances in which it was written, or if attention is fixed on it as part of a collection whose unity is presupposed.

all righteousness of works, all religious ceremonialism, all
Christianity without Christ. It has therefore become the conscience of the Church, until the Catholic Church in Jansenism
killed this her conscience. "The Pauline reactions describe
the critical epochs of theology and the Church." [1] One might
write a history of dogma as a history of the Pauline reactions
in the Church, and in doing so would touch on all the turning points of the history. Marcion after the Apostolic Fathers:
Irenæus, Clement and Origen after the Apologists; Augustine
after the Fathers of the Greek Church; [2] the great Reformers
of the middle ages from Agobard to Wessel in the bosom
of the mediæval Church; Luther after the Scholastics; Jansenism after the council of Trent:—Everywhere it has been
Paul, in these men, who produced the Reformation. Paulinism
has proved to be a ferment in the history of dogma, a basis
it has never been. [3] Just as it had that significance in Paul
himself, with reference to Jewish Christianity, so it has continued to work through the history of the Church.

1 See Bigg, The Christian Platonist of Alexandria, pp. 53, 283 ff:
2 Reuter (August. Studien, p. 492) has drawn a valuable parallel between
Marcion and Augustine with regard to Paul
3 Marcion of course wished to raise it to the exclusive basis, but he
entirely misunderstood it.

DIVISION I.

THE GENESIS OF THE ECCLESIASTICAL DOGMA,

OR

THE GENESIS OF

THE CATHOLIC APOSTOLIC DOGMATIC THEOLOGY,

AND

THE FIRST SCIENTIFIC ECCLESIASTICAL

SYSTEM OF DOCTRINE.

BOOK I.
THE PREPARATION.

ʼΕάν μυρίους παιδαγωγούς ἔχητε ἐν χριστῷ ἀλλ᾽ οὐ
πολλοὺς πατέρας.

1 Cor. IV. 15.

Eine jede Idee tritt als ein fremder Gast in
die Erscheinung, und wie sie sich zu reali-
siren beginnt, ist sie kaum von Phantasie
und Phantasterei zu unterscheiden.

GOETHE, Sprüche in Prosa, 566

BOOK I

THE PREPARATION

CHAPTER I

HISTORICAL SURVEY

THE first century of the existence of Gentile Christian communities is particularly characterised by the following features:

I. The rapid disappearance of Jewish Christianity. [1]

I I. The enthusiastic character of the reitgious temper: the Charismatic teachers and the appeal to the Spirit. [2]

I I I. The strength of the hopes for the future, Chiliasm. [3]

IV. The rigorous endeavour to fulfil the moral precepts of Christ, and truly represent the holy and heavenly community of God in abstinence from everything unclean, and in love to God and the brethren here on earth "in these last days". [4]

---

1 This fact must have been apparent as early as the year 100. The first direct evidence of it is in Justin (Apol I. 53).

2 Every individual was, or at least should have been conscious, as a Christian, of having received the πνεῦμα θεοῦ, though that does not exclude spiritual grades. A special peculiarity of the enthusiastic nature of the religious temper is that it does not allow reflection as to the authenticity of the faith in which a man lives. As to the Charismatic teaching, see my edition of the Didache (Texte u. Unters. II. 1. 2. p. 93 ff.).

3 The hope of the approaching end of the world and the glorious kingdom of Christ still determined men's hearts; though exhortations against theoretical and practical scepticism became more and more necessary. On the other hand, after the Epistles to the Thessalonians, there were not wanting exhortations to continue sober and diligent.

4 There was a strong consciousness that the Christian Church is, above all, a union for a holy life, as well as a consciousness of the obligation to help

V. The want of a fixed doctrinal form in relation to the abstract statement of the faith, and the corresponding variety and freedom of Christian preaching on the basis of clear formulæ and an increasingly rich tradition.

VI. The want of a clearly defined external authority in the communities, sure in its application, and the corresponding independence and freedom of the individual Christian in relation to the expression of the ideas, beliefs and hopes of faith. [1]

VII. The want of a fixed political union of the several communities with each other—every *ecclesia* is an image complete in itself, and an embodiment of the whole heavenly Church—while the consciousness of the unity of the holy Church of Christ which has the spirit in its midst, found strong expression. [2]

VIII. A quite unique literature in which were manufactured facts for the past and for the future, and which did not submit to the usual literary rules and forms, but came forward with the loftiest pretensions. [3]

one another, and use all the blessings bestowed by God in the service of our neighbours. Justin (2 Apol. in Euseb. H. E. IV. 17. 10) calls Christianity τὸ διδασκάλιον τῆς θείας ἀρετῆς.

1 The existing authorities (Old Testament, sayings of the Lord, words of Apostles) did not necessarily require to be taken into account; for the living acting Spirit, partly attesting himself also to the senses, gave new revelations. The validity of these authorities therefore held good only in theory, and might in practice be completely set aside (cf. above all, the Shepherd of Hermas).

2 Zahn remarks (Ignatius, v. A. p. VII.): "I do not believe it to be the business of that province of historical investigation which is dependent on the writings of the so-called Apostolic Fathers as main sources, to explain the origin of the universal Church in any sense of the term; for that Church existed before Clement and Hermas, before Ignatius and Polycarp. But an explanatory answer is needed for the question, by what means did the consciousness of the "universal Church," so little favoured by outer circumstances, maintain itself unbroken in the post-Apostolic communities?" This way of stating it obscures, at least, the problem which here lies before us, for it does not take account of the changes which the idea "universal Church" underwent up to the middle of the third century—besides, we do not find the title before Ignatius. In so far as the "universal Church" is set forth as an earthly power recognisable in a doctrine or in political forms, the question as to the origin of the idea is not only allowable, but must be regarded as one of the most important. On the earliest conception of the "Ecclesia" and its realisation, see the fine investigations of Sohm "Kirchenrecht," I. p. 1 ff., which, however, suffer from being a little overdriven.

3 See the important essay of Overbeck: Ueber die Anfänge d. patrist. Litteratur (Hist. Ztschr. N. F. Bd. XII. pp. 417-472). Early Christian literature, as a rule, claims to.be inspired writing. One can see, for example, in the history

IX. The reproduction of particular sayings and arguments of Apostolic Teachers with an uncertain understanding of them. [1]

X. The rise of tendencies which endeavoured to hasten in every respect the inevitable process of fusing the Gospel with the spiritual and religious interests of the time, viz., the Hellenic, as well as attempts to separate the Gospel from its origins and provide for it quite foreign presuppositions. To the latter belongs, above all, the Hellenic idea that knowledge is not a charismatic supplement to the faith, or an outgrowth of faith alongside of others, but that it coincides with the essence of faith itself. [2]

The sources for this period are few, as there was not much written, and the following period did not lay itself out for preserving a great part of the literary monuments of that epoch. Still we do possess a considerable number of writings and important fragments, [3] and further important inferences here are rendered possible by the monuments of the following period, since the conditions of the first century were not changed in a moment, but were partly, at least, long preserved, especially in certain national Churches and in remote communities. [4]

of the resurrection in the recently discovered Gospel of Peter (fragment) how facts were remodelled or created.

1 The writings of men of the Apostolic period, and that immediately succeeding, attained in part a wide circulation, and in some portions of them, often of course incorrectly understood, very great influence. How rapidly this literature was diffused, even the letters, may be studied in the history of the Epistles of Paul, the first Epistle of Clement, and other writings.

2 That which is here mentioned is of the greatest importance ; it is not a mere reference to the so-called Gnostics. The foundations for the Hellenising of the Gospel in the Church were already laid in the first century (50-150).

3 We should not over-estimate the extent of early Christian literature. It is very probable that we know, so far as the titles of books are concerned, nearly all that was effective, and the greater part, by very diverse means, has also been preserved to us. We except, of course, the so-called Gnostic literature of which we have only a few fragments. Only from the time of Commodus, as Eusebius, H. E. V. 21. 27, has remarked, did the great Church preserve an extensive literature.

4 It is therefore important to note the locality in which a document originates, and the more so the earlier the document is. In the earliest period, in which the history of the Church was more uniform, and the influence from without relatively less, the differences are still in the background. Yet the spirit of Rome already announces itself in the Epistle of Clement, that of Alexandria in the Epistle of Barnabas, that of the East in the Epistles of Ignatius.

Supplement.—The main features of the message concerning
Christ, of the matter of the Evangelic history, were fixed in
the first and second generations of believers, and on Palestinian
soil. But yet, up to the middle of the second century, this
matter was in many ways increased in Gentile Christian regions,
revised from new points of view, handed down in very
diverse forms, and systematically allegorised by individual
teachers. As a whole, the Evangelic history certainly appears
to have been completed at the beginning of the second century. But in detail, much that was new was produced at a
later period—and not only in Gnostic circles—and the old
tradition was recast or rejected. [1]

1 The history of the genesis of the four Canonical Gospels, or the
comparison of them, is instructive on this point. Then we must bear in
mind the old Apocryphal Gospels, and the way in which the so-called
Apostolic Fathers and Justin attest the Evangelic history, and in part
reproduce it independently, the Gospels of Peter, of the Egyptians, and
of Marcion; the Diatesseron of Tatian; the Gnostic Gospels and Acts of
the Apostles, etc. The greatest gap in our knowledge consists in the
fact, that we know so little about the course of things from about the
year 61 to the beginning of the reign of Trajan. The consolidating and
remodelling process must, for the most part, have taken place in this
period. We possess probably not a few writings which belong to that
period; but how are we to prove this, how are they to be arranged?
Here lies the cause of most of the differences, combinations and uncer-
tainties; many scholars, therefore, actually leave these 40 years out of
account, and seek to place everything in the first three decennia of the
second century.

CHAPTER II.

THE ELEMENT COMMON TO ALL CHRISTIANS AND
THE BREACH WITH JUDAISM

On account of the great differences among those who, in the first century, reckoned themselves in the Church of God, and called themselves by the name of Christ, [1] it seems at first sight scarcely possible to set up marks which would hold good for all, or even for nearly all, the groups. Yet the great majority had one thing in common, as is proved, among other things, by the gradual expulsion of Gnosticism. The conviction that they knew the supreme God, the consciousness of being responsible to him (Heaven and Hell), reliance on Jesus Christ, the hope of an eternal life, the vigorous elevation above the world—these are the elements that formed the fundamental mood. The author of the Acts of Thecla expresses the general view when he (c. 5.7) co-ordinates τὸν τοῦ χριστοῦ λόγον, with λόγος θεοῦ περὶ ἐγκατείας, καὶ ἀναστάσεως. The following particulars may here be specified. [2]

I. The Gospel, because it rests on revelation, is the sure manifestation of the supreme God, and its believing acceptance guarantees salvation (σωτερία).

II. The essential content of this manifestation (besides the revelation and the verification of the oneness and spirituality of God), [3] is, first of all, the message of the resurrection and

---

1 See, as to this, Celsus in Orig. III. 10 ff. and V. 59 ff.

2 The marks adduced in the text do not certainly hold good for some comparatively unimportant Gnostic groups, but they do apply to the great majority of them, and in the main to Marcion also.

3 Most of the Gnostic schools know only one God, and put all emphasis on the knowledge of the oneness, supramundaneness, and spirituality of this God.

eternal life (ἀνάστασις, ζωὴ αἰώνιος), then the preaching of moral purity and continence (ἐγκράτεια), on the basis of repentance toward God (μετάνοια), and of an expiation once assured by baptism, with eye ever fixed on the requital of good and evil.[1]

III. This manifestation is mediated by Jesus Christ, who is the Saviour (σωτήρ) sent by God "in these last days," and who stands with God himself in a union special and unique, (cf. the ambiguous παῖς θεοῦ, which was much used in the earliest period). He has brought the true and full knowledge of God, as well as the gift of immortality (γνῶσις καὶ ζωή, or γνῶσις τῆς ζωῆς, as an expression for the sum of the Gospel. See the supper prayer in the Didache, c. IX. an X.; εὐχαριστοῦμέν σοι, πάτερ ἡμῶν ὑπερ τῆς ζωῆς καὶ γνώσεως ἧς ἐγνώρισας ἡμῖν διὰ Ἰησοῦ τοῦ παιδός σου), and is for that very reason the redeemer (σώτηρ and victor over the demons) on whom we are to place believing trust. But he is, further, in word and walk the highest example of all moral virtue, and therefore in his own person the law for the perfect life, and at the same time the God-appointed lawgiver and judge.[2]

IV. Virtue as continence, embraces as its highest task, renunciation of temporal goods and separation from the common world; for the Christian is not a citizen, but a stranger on the earth, and expects its approaching destruction.[3]

The Æons, the Demiurgus, the God of matter, do not come near this God though they are called Gods. See the testimony of Hippolytus c. Noet. 11; καὶ γὰρ πάντες ἀπεκλείσθησαν εἰς τοῦτο ἄκοντες εἰπεῖν, ὅτι τὸ πᾶν εἰς ἕνα ἀνατρέχει. εἰ οὖν τὰ πάντα εἰς ἕνα ἀνατρέχει καὶ κατὰ θὐαλεντῖνον καὶ κατὰ Μαρκίωνα. Κήρινθόν τὲ καὶ πᾶσαν τὴν ἐκείνων φλυαρίαν, καὶ ἄκοντες εἰς τοῦτο περιέπεσαν, ἵνα τὸν ἕνα ὁμολογήσωσιν αἴτιον τῶν πάντων οὕτως οὖν συντρέχουσιν καὶ αὐτοὶ μὴ θέλοντες τῇ ἀληθείᾳ ἕνα θεὸν λέγειν ποιήσαντα ὡς ἠθέλησεν.

1 Continence was regarded as the condition laid down by God for the resurrection and eternal life. The sure hope of this was for many, if not for the majority, the whole sum of religion, in connection with the idea of the requital of good and evil which was now firmly established. See the testimony of the heathen Lucian, in Peregrinus Proteus.

2 Even where the judicial attributes were separated from God (Christ) as not suitable, Christ was still comprehended as the critical appearance by which every man is placed in the condition which belongs to him. The Apocalypse of Peter expects that God himself will come as Judge (see the Messianic expectations of Judaism, in which it was always uncertain whether God or the Messiah would hold the judgment).

3 Celsus (Orig. c. Celsum, V. 59) after referring to the many Christian parties mutually provoking and fighting with each other, remarks (V. 64) that

V. Christ has committed to chosen men, the Apostles (or
to one Apostle), the proclamation of the message he received
from God; consequently, their preaching represents that of
Christ himself. But, besides, the Spirit of God rules in Christians, "the Saints." He bestows upon them special gifts, and,
above all, continually raises up among them Prophets and spiritual Teachers who receive revelations and communications
for the edification of others, and whose injunctions are to be
obeyed.

VI. Christian Worship is a service of God in spirit and in
truth (a spiritual sacrifice), and therefore has no legal ceremonial and statutory rules. The value of the sacred acts and
consecrations which are connected with the cultus, consists in
the communication of spiritual blessings. (Didache X., ἡμῖν δὲ
ἐχαρίσω, δέσποτα, πνευματικὴν τροφήν καὶ ποτὸν καὶ ζωὴν αἰώνιον
διὰ τοῦ παιδός σου).

VII. Everything that Jesus Christ brought with him, may
be summed up in γνῶσις καὶ ζωή, or in the knowledge of im-
mortal life. [1] To possess the perfect knowledge was, in wide
circles, an expression for the sum total of the Gospel. [2]

though they differ much from each other, and quarrel with each other,
you can yet hear from them all the protestation, "The world is crucified
to me and I to the world". In the earliest Gentile Christian communities
brotherly love for reflective thought falls into the background behind
ascetic exercises of virtue, in unquestionable deviation from the sayings
of Christ, but in fact it was powerful. See the testimony of Pliny and Lucian,
Aristides, Apol. 15, Tertull. Apol. 39.

1 The word "life" comes into consideration in a double sense, viz., as
soundness of the soul, and as immortality. Neither, of course, is to be separated from the other. But I have attempted to shew in my essay, "Medicinisches aus der ältesten Kirchengesch." (1892), the extent to which the Gospel in the earliest Christendom was preached as medicine and Jesus as a
Physician, and how the Christian Message was really comprehended by the
Gentiles as a medicinal religion. Even the Stoic philosophy gave itself out as
a soul therapeutic, and Æsculapius was worshipped as a Saviour-God; but
Christianity alone was a religion of healing.

2 Heinrici, in his commentary on the epistles to the Corinthians, has dealt
very clearly with this matter; see especially (Bd. II. p. 557 ff.) the description
of the Christianity of the Corinthians: "On what did the community base its
Christian character? It believed in one God who had revealed himself to it
through Christ, without denying the reality of the hosts of gods in the heathen
world (1. VIII. 6) It hoped in immortality without being clear as to the nature
of the Christian belief in the resurrection (I. XV.) It had no doubt as to the
requital of good and evil (I. IV. 5: 2 V. 10: XI. 15: Rom. II. 4), without understanding the value of self-denial, claiming no merit, for the sake of im-

VIII. Christians, as such, no longer take into account the distinctions of race, age, rank, nationality and worldly culture, but the Christian community must be conceived as a communion resting on a divine election. Opinions were divided about the ground of that election.

IX. As Christianity is the only true religion, and as it is no national religion, but somehow concerns the whole of humanity, or its best part, it follows that it can have nothing in common with the Jewish nation and its contemporary cultus. The Jewish nation in which Jesus Christ appeared, has, for the time at least, no special relation to the God whom Jesus revealed. Whether it had such a relation at an earlier period is doubtful (cf. here, *e. g.*, the attitude of Marcion, Ptolemæus the disciple of Valentinus, the author of the Epistle of Barnabas, Aristides and Justin); but certain it is that God has now cast it off, and that all revelations of God, so far as they took place at all before Christ, (the majority assumed that there had been such revelations and considered the Old Testament as a holy record), must have aimed solely at the call of the "new people", and in some way prepared for the revelation of God through his Son. [1]

portant ends. It was striving to make use of the Gospel as a new doctrine of wisdom about earthly and super-earthly things, which led to the perfect and best established knowledge (1 I. 21: VIII. 1). It boasted of special operations of the Divine Spirit, which in themselves remained obscure and non-transparent, and therefore unfruitful (1. XIV), while it was prompt to put aside as obscure, the word of the Cross as preached by Paul (2. IV. 1 f.). The hope of the near Parousia, however, and the completion of all things, evinced no power to effect a moral transformation of society We herewith obtain the outline of a conviction that was spread over the widest circles of the Roman Empire." Naturam si expellas furca, tamen usque recurret.

1 Nearly all Gentile Christian groups that we know, are at one in the detachment of Christianity from empiric Judaism; the "Gnostics," however, included the Old Testament in Judaism, while the greater part of Christians did not. That detachment seemed to be demanded by the claims of Christianity to be the one, true, absolute and therefore oldest religion, foreseen from the beginning. The different estimates of the Old Testament in Gnostic circles have their exact parallels in the different estimates of Judaism among the other Christians; cf. for example, in this respect, the conception stated in the Epistle of Barnabas with the views of Marcion, and Justin with Valentinus. The particulars about the detachment of the Gentile Christians from the Synagogue, which was prepared for by the inner development of Judaism itself, and was required by the fundamental fact that the Messiah, crucified and rejected by his own people, was

recognised as Saviour by those who were not Jews, cannot be given in the frame-work of a history of dogma; though, see Chaps. III. IV. VI. On the other hand, the turning away from Judaism is also the result of the mass of things which were held in common with it, even in Gnostic circles. Christianity made its appearance in the Empire in the Jewish propaganda. By the preaching of Jesus Christ who brought the gift of eternal life, mediated the full knowledge of God, and assembled round him in these last days a community, the imperfect and hybrid creations of the Jewish propaganda in the empire were converted into independent formations. These formations were far superior to the synagogue in power of attraction, and from the nature of the case would very soon be directed with the utmost vigour against the synagogue.

CHAPTER III

THE COMMON FAITH AND THE BEGINNINGS OF KNOWLEDGE IN GENTILE CHRISTIANITY AS IT WAS BEING DEVELOPED INTO CATHOLICISM [1]

§ 1. *The Communities and the Church.*

THE confessors of the Gospels, belonging to organised communities who recognised the Old Testament as the Divine record of revelation, and prized the Evangelic tradition as a public message for all, to which, in its undiluted form, they

[1] The statements made in this chapter need special forbearance, especially as the selection from the rich and motley material—cf. only the so-called Apostolic Fathers—the emphasising of this, the throwing into the background of that element, cannot here be vindicated. It is not possible, in the compass of a brief account, to give expression to that elasticity and those oscillations of ideas and thoughts which were peculiar to the Christians of the earliest period. There was indeed, as will be shewn, a complex of tradition in many respects fixed, but this complex was still under the dominance of an enthusiastic fancy, so that what at one moment seemed fixed, in the next had disappeared. Finally, attention must be given to the fact that when we speak of the beginnings of knowledge, the members of the Christian community in their totality are no longer in question, but only individuals who of course were the leaders of the others. If we had no other writings from the times of the Apostolic Fathers than the first Epistle of Clement and the Epistle of Polycarp, it would be comparatively easy to sketch a clear history of the development connecting Paulinism with the old-Catholic Theology as represented by Irenæus, and so to justify the traditional ideas. But besides these two Epistles which are the classic monuments of the mediating tradition, we have a great number of documents which shew us how manifold and complicated the development was. They also teach us how careful we should be in the interpretation of the post-Apostolic documents that immediately followed the Pauline Epistles, and that we must give special heed to the paragraphs and ideas in them, which distinguish them from Paulinism. Besides, it is of the greatest importance that those two Epistles originated in Rome and Asia Minor, as these are the places where we must seek the embryonic stage of old-Catholic doctrine. Numerous fine threads, in the form of fundamental ideas and particular views, pass over from the Asia Minor theology of the post-Apostolic period into the old-Catholic theology.

wished to adhere truly and sincerely, formed the stem of Christendom both as to extent and importance. [1] The communities stood to each other in an outwardly loose, but inwardly firm connection, and every community by the vigour of its faith, the certainty of its hope, the holy character of its life, as well as by unfeigned love, unity and peace, was to be an image of the holy Church of God which is in heaven, and whose members are scattered over the earth. They were further, by the purity of their walk and an active brotherly disposition, to prove to those without, that is to the world, the excellence and truth of the Christian faith. [2] The hope

[1] The Epistle to the Hebrews (X. 25), the Epistle of Barnabas (IV. 10), the Shepherd of Hermas (Sim. IX. 26. 3), but especially the Epistles of Ignatius and still later documents, shew that up to the middle of the second century and even later, there were Christians who, for various reasons, stood outside the union of communities, or wished to have only a loose and temporary relation to them. The exhortation: ἐπὶ τὸ αὐτὸ συνερχόμενοι συνζητεῖτε περὶ τοῦ κοινῇ συμφέροντος (see my note on Didache, XVI. 2, and cf. for the expression the interesting State Inscription which was found at Magnesia on the Meander. Bull, Corresp. Hellén. 1883, p. 506: ἀπαγορεύω μήτε συνέρχεσθαι τοὺς ἀρτοκόπους κατ᾽ ἑταιρίαν μήτε παρεστηκότας θρασύνεσθαι, πειθάρχιιν δὲ πάντως τοῖς ὑπὲρ τοῦ κοινῇ συμφέροντος ἐπιταττομένοις κ.τ.λ. or the exhortation: κολλᾶσθε τοῖς ἁγίοις, ὅτι οἱ κολλώμενοι αὐτοῖς ἁγιασθήσονται (1. Clem. 46. 2, introduced as γραφή) runs through most of the writings of the post-Apostolic and pre-catholic period New doctrines were imported by wandering Christians who, in many cases, may not themselves have belonged to a community, and did not respect the arrangements of those they found in existence, but sought to form conventicles. If we remember how the Greeks and Romans were wont to get themselves initiated into a mystery cult, and took part for a long time in the religious exercises, and then, when they thought they had got the good of it, for the most part or wholly to give up attending, we shall not wonder that the demand to become a permanent member of a Christian community was opposed by many. The statements of Hermas are specially instructive here.

[2] "Corpus sumus," says Tertullian at a time when this description had already become an anachronism, "de conscientia religionis et disciplinæ unitate et spei foedere." (Apol. 39: cf. Ep. Petri ad Jacob. I.; εἷς θεός, εἷς νόμος, μία ἐλπίς). The description was applicable to the earlier period, when there was no such thing as a federation with political forms, but when the consciousness of belonging to a community and of forming a brotherhood (ἀδελφότης) was all the more deeply felt: See, above all, 1 Clem ad Corinth., the Didache (9-15), Aristides, Apol 15: "and when they have become Christians they call them (the slaves) brethren without hesitation..... for they do not call them brethren according to the flesh, but according to the spirit and in God;" cf. also the statements on brotherhood in Tertullian and Minucius Felix (also Lucian). We have in 1. Clem. 1. 2, the delineation of a perfect Christian Church. The Epistles of Ignatius are specially instructive as to the independence of each individual community: 1 Clem. and Didache, as to the obligation to assist stranger communities by counsel and action, and to support the travelling brethren.

that the Lord would speedily appear to gather into his Kingdom the believers who were scattered abroad, punishing the
evil and rewarding the good, guided these communities in
faith and life. In the recently discovered "Teaching of the
Apostles" we are confronted very distinctly with ideas and
aspirations of communities that are not influenced by Philosophy.

The Church, that is the totality of all believers destined to
be received into the kingdom of God (Didache, 9. 10), is the
holy Church, (Hermas) because it is brought together and preserved by the Holy Spirit. It is the one Church, not because
it presents this unity outwardly, on earth the members of the
Church are rather scattered abroad, but because it will be
brought to unity in the kingdom of Christ, because it is ruled
by the same spirit and inwardly united in a common relation
to a common hope and ideal. The Church, considered in its
origin, is the number of those chosen by God, [1] the true Israel, [2] nay, still more, the final purpose of God, for the world
was created for its sake. [3] There were in connection with
these doctrines in the earliest period, various speculations about
the Church: it is a heavenly Æon, is older than the world,
was created by God at the beginning of things as a companion of the heavenly Christ; [4] its members form the new na-

---

As every Christian is a πάροικος, so every community is a παροικοῦσα τὴν πόλιν
but it is under obligation to give an example to the world, and must watch
that "the name be not blasphemed". The importance of the social element
in the oldest Christian communities, has been very justly brought into
prominence in the latest works on the subject (Renan, Heinrici, Hatch).
The historian of dogma must also emphasise it, and put the fluid notions
of the faith in contrast with the definite consciousness of moral tasks.
See 1. Clem. 47-50; Polyc. Ep. 3; Didache 1 ff.; Ignat. ad Eph. 14, on
ἀγάπη as the main requirement. Love demands that everyone "ζητεῖ τὸ
κοινωφελὲς πᾶσιν καὶ μὴ τὸ ἑαυτοῦ" (1. Clem. 48. 6. with parallels; Didache
16. 3; Barn. 4. 10; Ignatius).

1 1 Clem. 59. 2. in the Church prayer; ὅπως τον ἀριθμὸν τὸν κατηριθμημένον
τῶν ἐκλεκτῶν αὐτοῦ ἐν ὅλῳ τῷ κόσμῳ διαφυλάξῃ ἄθραυστον ὁ δημιουργὸς τῶν ἀπάν-
των διὰ τοῦ ἠγαπημένου παιδὸς αὐτοῦ Ἰησοῦ Χριστοῦ

2 See 1 Clem., 2 Clem., Ignatius (on the basis of the Pauline view;
but see also Rev. II. 9).

3 See Hermas (the passage is given above, p. 103, note.)

4 See Hermas. Vis. I.-III. Papias. Fragm. VI. and VII. of my edition. 2 Clem.
14: ποιοῦντες τὸ θέλημα τοῦ πατρὸς ἡμῶν ἐσόμεθα ἐκ τῆς ἐκκλησίας τῆς πρώτης τῆς
πνευματικῆς, τῆς πρὸ ἡλίου καὶ σελήνης ἐκτισμένης. . . . ἐκκλησία ζῶσα σῶμά ἐστι
Χριστοῦ· λέγει γάρ ἡ γραφή· ἐποίησεν ὁ θεὸς τὸν ἄνθρωπον ἄρσεν καὶ θῆλυ. τὸ ἄρσεν
ἐστιν ὁ Χριστός, τὸ θῆλυ ἡ ἐκκλησία.

tion which is really the oldest nation, [1] it is the λαὸς ὁ τοῦ
ἠγαπημένου ὁ φιλούμενος καὶ φιλῶν αὐτόν, [2] the people whom God
has prepared "in the Beloved," [3] etc. The creation of God,
the Church, as it is of an antemundane and heavenly nature,
will also attain its true existence only in the Æon of the
future, the Æon of the kingdom of Christ. The idea of a
heavenly origin, and of a heavenly goal of the Church, was
therefore an essential one, various and fluctuating as these
speculations were. Accordingly, the exhortations, so far as
they have in view the Church, are always dominated by the
idea of the contrast of the kingdom of Christ with the kingdom of the world. On the other hand, he who communicated
knowledge for the present time, prescribed rules of life, endeavoured to remove conflicts, did not appeal to the peculiar
character of the Church. The mere fact, however, that from
nearly the beginning of Christendom, there were reflections
and speculations not only about God and Christ, but also
about the Church, teaches us how profoundly the Christian
consciousness was impressed with being a new people, viz.,
the people of God. [4] These speculations of the earliest Gentile
Christian time about Christ and the Church, as inseparable
correlative ideas, are of the greatest importance, for they
have absolutely nothing Hellenic in them, but rather have
their origin in the Apostolic tradition. But for that very reason the combination very soon, comparatively speaking, became obsolete or lost its power to influence. Even the Apologists made no use of it, though Clement of Alexandria and
other Greeks held it fast, and the Gnostics by their Æon
"Church" brought it into discredit. Augustine was the first to
return to it.

The importance attached to morality is shewn in *Didache*

1 See Barn. 13 (2 Clem. 2).
2 See Valentinus in Clem. Strom. VI. 6. 52. "Holy Church", perhaps also in
Marcion, if his text (Zahn. Gesch. des N.T.lichen Kanons, II p. 502) in Gal. IV.
21, read; ἥτις ἐστὶν μήτηρ ἡμῶν, γεννῶσα εἰς ἣν ἐπηγγειλάμεθα ἁγίαν ἐκκλησίαν.
3 Barn. 3. 6.
4 We are also reminded here of the "tertium genus." The nickname
of the heathen corresponded to the self-consciousness of the Christians
(see Aristides, Apol.).

cc. 1-6, with parallels. [1] But this section and the statements
so closely related to it in the pseudo-phocylidean poem, which
is probably of Christian origin, as well as in Sibyl, II. v.
56-148, which is likewise to be regarded as Christian, and
in many other Gnomic paragraphs, shews at the same time,
that in the memorable expression and summary statement of
higher moral commandments, the Christian propaganda had
been preceded by the Judaism of the Diaspora, and had entered into its labours. These statements are throughout dependent on the Old Testament wisdom, and have the closest
relationship with the genuine Greek parts of the Alexandrian
Canon, as well as with Philonic exhortations. Consequently,
these moral rules, " the two ways ", so aptly compiled and filled
with such an elevated spirit, represent the ripest fruit of Jewish as well as of Greek development. The Christian spirit
found here a disposition which it could recognise as its own.
It was of the utmost importance, however, that this disposition was already expressed in fixed forms suitable for didactic purposes. The young Christianity therewith received a gift of
first importance. It was spared a labour in a region, the
moral, which experience shews, can only be performed in generations, viz., the creation of simple fixed impressive rules,
the labour of the Catechist. The sayings of the Sermon on
the Mount were not of themselves sufficient here. Those who
in the second century attempted to rest in these alone, and
turned aside from the Judæo-Greek inheritance, landed in
Marcionite or Encratite doctrines. [3] We can see, especially

---

1 See also the letter of Pliny, the paragraphs about Christian morality in the
first third-part of Justin's apology, and especially the apology of Aristides, c.
15. Aristides portrays Christianity by portraying Christian morality. " The
Christians know and believe in God, the creator of heaven and of earth, the
God by whom all things consist, *i. e.*, in him from whom they have received
the commandments which they have written in their hearts, commandments
which they observe in faith and in the expectation of the world to come. For
this reason they do not commit adultery, nor practise unchastity, nor bear
false witness, nor covet that with which they are entrusted, or what does not
belong to them, etc." Compare, how in the Apocalypse of Peter definite penalties in hell are portrayed for the several forms of immorality.
2 An investigation of the Græco-Jewish, Christian literature of gnomes and
moral rules, commencing with the Old Testament doctrine of wisdom on the

from the Apologies of Aristides (c. 15), Justin and Tatian (see also Lucian), that the earnest men of the Græco-Roman world were won by the morality and active love of the Christians.

§ 2. *The Foundations of the Faith.*

The foundations of the faith—whose abridged form was, on the one hand, the confession of the one true God, μόνος ἀλη- θινὸς θεός,[1] and of Jesus, the Lord, the Son of God, the Saviour,[2] and also of the Holy Spirit; and on the other hand, the confident hope of Christ's kingdom and the resurrection—were laid on the Old Testament interpreted in a Christian sense together with the Apocalypses,[3] and the progressively enriched traditions about Jesus Christ. (ἡ παράδοσις — ὁ παραδοθεὶς λόγος — ὁ κανὼν τῆς ἀληθείας or τῆς παραδόσεως — ἡ πίστις — ὁ κανὼν τῆς πίστεως — ὁ δοθεῖσα πίστις — τὸ κήρυγμα — τὰ διδάγματα τοῦ χριστοῦ — ἡ

one hand, and the Stoic collections on the other, then passing beyond the Alexandrian and Evangelic gnomes up to the Didache, the Pauline tables of domestic duties, the Sibylline sayings, Phocylides, the Neopythagorean rules, and to the gnomes of the enigmatic Sextus, is still an unfulfilled task. The moral rules of the Pharisaic Rabbis should also be included.

1 Herm. Mand. I. has merely fixed the Monotheistic confession: πρῶτον πάντων πίστευσον, ὅτι εἷς ἐστιν ὁ θεὸς. ὁ τὰ πάντα κτίσας καὶ καταρτίσας, κ.τ.λ See Praed. Petri in Clem. Strom. VI. 6. 48: VI. 5. 39: Aristides gives in c. 2. of his Apology the preaching of Jesus Christ: but where he wishes to give a short expression of Christianity he is satisfied with saying that Christians are those who have found the one true God. See, *e g.*, c. 15 "Christians have.... found the truth.... They know and believe in God, the creator of heaven and of earth, by whom all things consist, and from whom all things come. who has no other god beside him. and from whom they have received commandments which they have written on their hearts, commandments which they observe in faith and in expectation of the world to come." It is interesting to note how Origen, Comm. in Joh. XXXII 9, has brought the Christological Confession into approximate harmony with that of Hermas First, Mand I. is verbally repeated and then it is said: χρὴ δὲ καὶ πιστεύειν, ὅτι κύριος Ἰησοῦς Χριστὸς καὶ πάσῃ τῇ περὶ αὐτοῦ κατὰ τὴν θεότητα καὶ τὴν ἀνθρωπότητα· ἀληθείᾳ δεῖ δὲ καὶ εἰς τὸ ἅγιον πιστεύειν πνεῦμα, καὶ ὅτι αὐτεξούσιοι ὄντες κολαζόμεθα μὲν ἐφ' οἷς ἁμαρτάνομεν, τιμώμεθα δὲ ἐφ' οἷς εὖ πράττομεν.
2 Very instructive here is 2 Clem ad Corinth. 20. 5: τῷ μόνῳ θεῷ ἀοράτῳ, πατρὶ τῆς ἀληθείας, τῷ ἐξαποστείλαντι ἡμῖν τὸν σωτῆρα καὶ ἀρχηγὸν τῆς ἀφθαρσίας, δι' οὗ καὶ ἐφανέρωσεν ἡμῖν τὴν ἀλήθειαν καὶ τὴν ἐπουράνιον ζωήν, αὐτῷ ἡ δόξα. On the Holy Spirit see previous note.
3 They were quoted as ἡ γραφή, τὰ βιβλία. or with the formula ὁ θεὸς (κύριος) λέγει, γέγραπται. Also "Law and Prophets," "Law Prophets and Psalms." See the original of the first six books of the Apostolic Constitutions.

διδαχὴ — τὰ μαθήματα, or τὸ μάθημα).[1] The Old Testament revelations and oracles were regarded as pointing to Christ; the Old Testament itself, the words of God spoken by the Prophets, as the primitive Gospel of salvation, having in view the new people, which is, however, the oldest, and belonging to it alone.[2] The exposition of the Old Testament, which, as a rule, was of course read in the Alexandrian Canon of the Bible, turned it into a Christian book. A historical view of it, which no born Jew could in some measure fail to take, did not come into fashion, and the freedom that was used in interpreting the Old Testament,—so far as there was a method, it was the Alexandrian Jewish—went the length of even correcting the letter and enriching the contents. [3]

The traditions concerning Christ on which the communities were based, were of a twofold character. First, there were words of the Lord, mostly ethical, but also of eschatological content, which were regarded as rules, though their expression was uncertain, ever changing, and only gradually assuming a fixed form. The διδάγματα τοῦ χριστοῦ are often just the moral commandments. [4] Second, the foundation of the faith, that is, the assurance of the blessing of salvation, was formed by a proclamation of the history of Jesus concisely expressed, and

---

1 See the collection of passages in Patr. App. Opp. edit. Gebhardt. I. 2 p. 133, and the formula, Diogn. 11 : ἀποστόλων γένομενος μαθητὴς γίνομαι διδάσκαλος ἐθνῶν, τὰ παραδοθέντα ἀξίως ὑπηρετῶν γινομένοις ἀληθείας μαθηταῖς. Besides the Old Testament and the traditions about Jesus (Gospels), the Apocalyptic writings of the Jews, which were regarded as writings of the Spirit, were also drawn upon. Moreover, Christian letters and manifestoes proceeding from Apostles, prophets, or teachers, were read. The Epistles of Paul were early collected and obtained wide circulation in the first half of the second century; but they were not Holy Scripture in the specific sense, and therefore their authority was not unqualified.

2 Barn. 5. 6, οἱ προφηται, ἀπὸ τοῦ κύριου ἐχοντες τὴν χάριν, εἰς αὐτὸν ἐπροφήτευσαν. Ignat. ad Magn. 8. 2. cf. also Clem. Paedag. l. 7. 59 : ὁ γὰρ αὐτὸς οὗτος παιδαγωγὸς τότε μὲν "φοβηθήσῃ κύριον τὸν θεὸν ἔλεγεν, ἡμῖν δὲ "ἀγαπήσεις κύριον τὸν θεὸν σου" παρήνεσεν. διὰ τοῦτο καὶ ἐντέλλεται ἡμῖν "παύσασθε ἀπὸ τῶν ἔργων ὑμῶν" τῶν παλαιῶν ἁμαρτιῶν, "μάθετε καλὸν ποιεῖν, ἔκκλινον ἀπὸ κακοῦ καὶ ποίησον ἀγαθόν, ἠγάπησας δικαιοσύνην, ἐμίσησας ἀνομίαν" αὕτη μου ἡ νέα διαθήκη παλαιῷ κεχαραγμένη γράμματι.

3 See above § 5, p. 114 f

4 See my edition of the Didache. Prolegg. p. 32 ff.; Rothe, "De disciplina arcani origine," 1841.

composed with reference to prophecy. [1] The confession of God
the Father Almighty, of Christ as the Lord and Son of God,
and of the Holy Spirit, [2] was at a very early period in the
communities, united with the short proclamation of the history
of Jesus, and at the same time, in certain cases, referred expressly to the revelation of God (the Spirit) through the prophets. [3] The confession thus conceived had not everywhere
obtained a fixed definite expression in the first century (c.
50-150). It would rather seem that, in most of the communities, there was no exact formulation beyond a confession of
Father, Son and Spirit, accompanied in a free way by the historical
proclamation. [4] It is highly probable, however, that a short confession was strictly formulated in the Roman community before the middle of the second century, [5] expressing belief in the
Father, Son and Spirit, embracing also the most important facts in
the history of Jesus, and mentioning the Holy Church, as well
as the two great blessings of Christianity, the forgiveness of
sin, and the resurrection of the dead ($\mathring{\alpha}\varphi\epsilon\sigma\iota\varsigma$ $\mathring{\alpha}\mu\alpha\rho\tau\iota\tilde{\omega}\nu$, $\sigma\alpha\rho\kappa\grave{o}\varsigma$
$\mathring{\alpha}\nu\mathring{\alpha}\sigma\tau\alpha\sigma\iota\varsigma$ [6]).   But, however the proclamation might be handed

1 The earliest example is 1. Cor. XI. 1 f. It is different in 1 Tim. III.
16, where already the question is about $\tau\grave{o}$ $\tau\tilde{\eta}\varsigma$ $\epsilon\mathring{v}\sigma\epsilon\beta\epsilon\acute{\iota}\alpha\varsigma$ $\mu\nu\sigma\tau\acute{\eta}\rho\iota\nu$: See Patr.
App. Opp. 1. 2. p. 134.
2 Father, son, and spirit: Paul; Matt XXVIII. 19; 1 Clem. ad. Cor. 58. 2
(see 2. 1. f.: 42. 3: 46. 6); Didache 7; Ignat. Eph. 9. 1; Magn. 13. 1. 2.;
Philad. inscr.; Mart. Polyc. 14. 1. 2; Ascens. Isai. 8. 18: 9. 27: 10. 4: 11. 32 ff;
Justin *passim*; Montan. ap. Didym. de trinit. 411; Excerpta ex Theodot. 80;
Pseudo Clem. de virg. 1 13. Yet the omission of the Holy Spirit is frequent, as
in Paul, or the Holy Spirit is identified with the Spirit of Christ. The latter
takes place even with such writers as are familiar with the baptismal formula.
Ignat ad Magn. 15; $\kappa\epsilon\kappa\tau\eta\mu\acute{\epsilon}\nu\iota\iota$ $\mathring{\alpha}\delta\iota\acute{\alpha}\kappa\rho\iota\tau\nu\nu$ $\pi\nu\epsilon\tilde{\nu}\mu\alpha$, $\mathring{o}\varsigma$ $\mathring{\epsilon}\sigma\tau\iota\nu$ $^{\prime}I\eta\sigma\nu\tilde{\nu}\varsigma$ $X\rho\iota\sigma\tau\grave{o}\varsigma$.
3 The formulæ run: "God who has spoken through the Prophets," or
the "Prophetic Spirit," etc.
4 That should be assumed as certain in the case of the Egyptian
Church, yet Caspari thinks he can shew that already Clement of Alexandria
presupposes a symbol.
5 Also in the communities of Asia Minor (Smyrna); for a combination of
Polyc. Ep. c. 2 with c. 7, proves that in Smyrna the $\pi\alpha\rho\alpha\delta\nu\theta\epsilon\grave{\iota}\varsigma$ $\lambda\acute{o}\gamma\nu\varsigma$ must have
been something like the Roman Symbol, see Lightfoot on the passage; it can-
not be proved that it was indentical with it. See, further, how in the case of
Polycarp the moral element is joined on to the dogmatic. This reminds us of
the Didache and has its parallel even in the first homily of Aphraates
6 See Caspari, Quellen z. Gesch. des Taufsymbols, III. p. 3 ff. and Patr.
App. Opp. 1. 2. p 115-142 The old Roman Symbol reads: $\Pi\iota\sigma\tau\epsilon\acute{v}\omega$ $\epsilon\mathring{\iota}\varsigma$ $\theta\epsilon\grave{o}\nu$
$\pi\alpha\tau\acute{\epsilon}\rho\alpha$ $\pi\alpha\nu\tau\nu\kappa\rho\acute{\alpha}\tau\nu\rho\alpha$, $\kappa\alpha\grave{\iota}$ $\epsilon\mathring{\iota}\varsigma$ $X\rho\iota\sigma\tau\grave{o}\nu$ $^{\prime}I\eta\sigma\nu\tilde{\nu}\nu$ $(\tau\grave{o}\nu)$ $\nu\mathring{\iota}\grave{o}\nu$ $\alpha\mathring{v}\tau\nu\tilde{\nu}$ $\tau\grave{o}\nu$ $\mu\nu\nu\nu\gamma\epsilon\nu\tilde{\eta}$, (on
this word see Westcott's Excursus in his commentary on 1st John) $\tau\grave{o}\nu$ $\kappa\acute{v}\rho\iota\nu\nu$

down, in a form somehow fixed, or in a free form, the disciples
of Jesus, the (twelve) Apostles, were regarded as the authori-

ἡμῶν τὸν γεννηθέντα ἐκ πνεύματος ἁγίου καὶ Μαρίας τῆς παρθένου, τὸν ἐπὶ Ποντίου
Πιλάτου σταυρωθέντα καὶ ταφέντα; τῇ τρίτῃ ἡμέρᾳ ἀναστάντα ἐκ νεκρῶν, ἀναβάντα
εἰς τοὺς οὐρανούς, καθήμενον ἐν δεξιᾷ τοῦ πατρός, ὅθεν ἔρχεται κρῖναι ζῶντας καὶ
νεκρούς· καὶ εἰς πνεῦμα ἅγιον, ἁγίαν ἐκκλησίαν. ἄφεσιν ἁμαρτιῶν σαρκὸς ἀνάστασιν,
ἀμήν. To estimate this very important article aright we must note the following: (1) It is not a formula of doctrine, but of confession. (2) It has a
liturgical form which is shewn in the rhythm and in the disconnected
succession of its several members, and is free from everything of the nature of polemic. (3) It tapers off into the three blessings, Holy Church,
forgiveness of sin, resurrection of the body, and in this as well as in the
fact that there is no mention of γνῶσις (ἀλήθεια) καὶ ζωὴ αἰώνος, is revealed an early Christian untheological attitude. (4) It is worthy of note,
on the other hand, that the birth from the Virgin occupies the first place,
and all reference to the baptism of Jesus, also to the Davidic Sonship,
is wanting. (5) It is further worthy of note, that there is no express mention of the death of Jesus, and that the Ascension already forms a special
member (that is also found elsewhere, Ascens. Isaiah, c 3. 13. ed. Dillmann.
p. 13. Murator. Fragment, etc.). Finally. we should consider the want of
the earthly Kingdom of Christ and the mission of the twelve Apostles,
as well as, on the other hand, the purely religious attitude, no notice
being taken of the new law. Zahn (Das Apostol. Symbolum, 1893) assumes,
"That in all essential respects the indentical baptismal confession which
Justin learned in Ephesus about 130, and Marcion confessed in Rome
about 145, originated at latest somewhere about 120". In some "unpre-
tending notes" (p. 37 ff.) he traces this confession back to a baptismal
confession of the Pauline period ("it had already assumed a more or less
stereotyped form in the earlier Apostolic period"), which, however, was
somewhat revised. so far as it contained, for example, "of the house of
David", with reference to Christ. "The original formula, reminding us of
the Jewish soil of Christianity, was thus remodelled, perhaps about 70-120,
with retention of the fundamental features, so that it might appear to
answer better to the need of candidates for baptism, proceeding more
and more from the Gentiles .... This changed formula soon spread on
all sides. It lies at the basis of all the later baptismal confessions of the
Church, even of the East. The first article was slightly changed in Rome
about 200-220". While up till then. in Rome as everywhere else. it had
read πιστεύω εἰς ἕνα θεὸν παντοκράτορα, it was now changed in πιστεύω εἰς
θεὸν πατέρα παντοκράτορα. This hypothesis, with regard to the early history
of the Roman Symbol, presupposes that the history of the formation of
the baptismal confession in the Church, in east and west. was originally a
uniform one. This cannot be proved; besides, it is refuted by the facts of the
following period. It presupposes secondly, that there was a strictly formulated
baptismal confession outside Rome before the middle of the second century, which likewise cannot be proved; (the converse rather is probable,
that the fixed formulation proceeded from Rome). Moreover, Zahn himself retracts everything again by the expression "more or less stereotyped
form;" for what is of decisive interest here is the question, when and
where the fixed sacred form was produced. Zahn here has set up
the radical thesis that it can only have taken place in Rome between 200
and 220. But neither his negative nor his positive proof for a change of the
Symbol in Rome at so late a period is sufficient. No sure conclusion as to
the Symbol can be drawn from the wavering *regulæ fidei* of Irenæus and Ter-

ties who mediated and guaranteed it. To them was traced
back in the same way everything that was narrated of the
history of Jesus, and everything that was inculcated from his
sayings.[1] Consequently, it may be said, that beside the Old
Testament, the chief court of appeal in the communities was
formed by an aggregate of words and deeds of the Lord; —
for the history and the suffering of Jesus are his deed: ὁ Ἰησοῦς

tullian which contain the "unum"; further, the "unum" is not found in the
western provincial Symbols, which, however, are in part earlier than the year
200. The Romish correction must therefore have been subsequently taken
over in the provinces (Africa?). Finally, the formula θεὸν πάτερα παντοκράτορα
beside the more frequent θεὸν παντοκράτορα, is attested by Irenæus, I. 10. 1,
a decisive passage. With our present means we cannot attain to any direct
knowledge of Symbol formation before the Romish Symbol. But the following hypotheses, which I am not able to establish here, appear to
me to correspond to the facts of the case and to be fruitful. (1) There
were, even in the earliest period, separate *Kerygmata* about God and
Christ: see the Apostolic writings, Hermas, Ignatius, etc. (2) The
Kerygma about God was the confession of the one God of creation,
the almighty God. (3) The *Kerygma* about Christ had essentially the
same historical contents everywhere, but was expressed in diverse
forms: (a) in the form of the fulfilment of prophecy, (b) in the form
κατὰ σάκρα, κατὰ πνεῦμα, (c) in the form of the first and second advent, (d) in
the form, καταβάς-ἀναβάς; these forms were also partly combined. (4) The
designations "Christ", "Son of God" and "Lord"; further, the birth from
the Holy Spirit, or κατὰ πνεῦμα, the sufferings (the practice of exorcism
contributed also to the fixing and naturalising of the formula "crucified
under Pontius Pilate"), the death, the resurrection, the coming again to
judgment, formed the stereotyped content of the *Kerygma* about Jesus.
The mention of the Davidic Sonship, of the Virgin Mary, of the baptism
by John, of the third day, of the descent into Hades, of the *demonstratio
veræ carnis post resurrectionem*, of the ascension into heaven and the sending
out of the disciples, were additional articles which appeared here and there.
The σάκρα λαβών, and the like, were very early developed out of the forms
(b) and (d). All this was already in existence at the transition of the first
century to the second. (5) The proper contribution of the Roman community
consisted in this, that it inserted the *Kerygma* about God and that about
Jesus into the baptismal formula, widened the clause referring to the Holy
Spirit, into one embracing Holy Church, forgiveness of sin, resurrection of
the body, excluded theological theories in other respects, undertook a
reduction all round, and accurately defined everything up to the last world.
(6) The western *regulæ fidei* do not fall back exclusively on the old Roman
Symbol, but also on the earlier freer *Kerygmata* about God and about Jesus
which were common to the east and west; not otherwise can the *regulæ
fidei* of Irenæus and Tertullian, for example, be explained. But the symbol
became more and more the support of the *regula*. (7) The eastern confessions (baptismal symbols) do not fall back directly on the Roman Symbol,
but were probably on the model of this symbol, made up from the provincial *Kerygmata*, rich in contents and growing ever richer, hardly, however,
before the third century. (8) It cannot be proved, and it is not probable, that
the Roman Symbol was in existence before Hermas, that is, about 135.

1 See the fragment in Euseb. H. E. III. 39, from the work of Papias.

ὑπέμεινεν παθεῖν, κ.τ.λ.,—fixed in certain fundamental features, though constantly enriched, and traced back to apostolic testimony. [1]

The authority which the Apostles in this way enjoyed, did not, in any great measure, rest on the remembrance of direct services which the twelve had rendered to the Gentile Churches: for, as the want of reliable concrete traditions proves, no such services had been rendered, at least not by the *twelve*. On the contrary, there was a theory operative here regarding the special authority which the twelve enjoyed in the Church at Jerusalem, a theory which was spread by the early missionaries, including Paul, and sprang from the *a priori* consi-

---

1 Διδαχὴ κύριον διὰ τῶν ιβ' ἀποστόλων (Διδ. inscr.) is the most accurate expression (similarly 2. Pet. III. 2). Instead of this might be said simply ὁ κύριος (Hegesipp.). Hegesippus (Euseb. H. E.. IV. 22. 3 : See also Steph. Gob.) comprehends the ultimate authorities under the formula: ὡς ὁ νομος κηρύσσει καὶ οἱ προφῆται καὶ ὁ κύριος; just as even Pseudo Clem de Virg. 1. 2: "Sicut ex lege ac prophetis ac a domino nostro Jesu Christo didicimus." Polycarp (6. 3) says: καθὼς αὐτὸς ἐνετείλατο καὶ οἱ εὐαγγελισάμενοι ἡμᾶς ἀπόστολοι καὶ οἱ προφῆται οἱ προκηρύξαντες τὴν ἔλευσιν τοῦ κυρίου ἡμῶν. In the second Epistle of Clement (14. 2) we read : τὰ βιβλία (O. T.) καὶ οἱ ἀπόστολοι; τὸ εὐαγγέλιον may also stand for ὁ κύριος (Ignat., Didache. 2 Clem. etc.). The Gospel, so far as it is described, is quoted as τὰ ἀπομνημονεύματα τ. ἀποστόλων (Justin, Tatian), or on the other hand, as αἱ κυριακαὶ γραφαί, (Dionys. Cor. in Euseb. H. E. IV. 23. 12: at a later period in Tertull. and Clem. Alex.). The words of the Lord, in the same way as the words of God, are called simply τὰ λόγια (κυριακά). The declaration of Serapion at the beginning of the third century (Euseb., H. E. VI. 12. 3): ἡμεῖς καὶ Πέτρον καὶ τοὺς ἄλλους ἀποστόλους ἀποδεχόμεθα ὡς Χριστόν, is an innovation in so far as it puts the words of the Apostles fixed in writing and as distinct from the words of the Lord, on a level with the latter. That is, while differentiating the one from the other, Serapion ascribes to the words of the apostles and those of the Lord equal authority. But the development which led to this position, had already begun in the first century. At a very early period there were read in the communities, beside the Old Testament, Gospels, that is collections of words of the Lord, which at the same time contained the main facts of the history of Jesus. Such notes were a necessity (Luke 1. 4: ἵνα ἐπιγνῷς περὶ ὧν κατηχήθης λόγων τὴν ἀσφάλειαν), and though still indefinite and in many ways unlike, they formed the germ for the genesis of the New Testament. (See. Weiss. Lehrb. d. Einleit in d. N. T. p. 21 ff.). Further there were read Epistles and Manifestoes by apostles, prophets and teachers, but, above all, Epistles of Paul. The Gospels at first stood in no connection with these Epistles, however high they might be prized. But there did exist a connection between the Gospels and the ἀπ' ἀρχῆς αὐτόπταις καὶ ὑπηρέταις τοῦ λόγου, so far as these mediated the tradition of the Evangelic material, and on their testimony rests the *Kerygma* of the Church about the Lord as the Teacher, the crucified and risen One. Here lies the germ for the genesis of a canon which will comprehend the Lord and the Apostles, and will also draw in the Pauline Epistles. Finally, Apocalypses were read as Holy Scriptures.

deration that the tradition about Christ, just because it grew up so quickly,[1] must have been entrusted to eye-witnesses who were commissioned to proclaim the Gospel to the whole world, and who fulfilled that commission. The *a priori* character of this assumption is shewn by the fact that—with the exception of reminiscences of an activity of Peter and John among the ἔθνη, not sufficiently clear to us [2]—the twelve, as a rule, are regarded as a *college*, to which the mission and the tradition are traced back. [3] That such a theory, based on a dogmatic construction of history, could have at all arisen, proves that either the Gentile Churches never had a living relation to the twelve, or that they had very soon lost it in the rapid disappearance of Jewish Christianity, while they had been referred to the twelve from the beginning. But even in the communities which Paul had founded and for a long time guided, the remembrance of the controversies of the Apostolic age must have been very soon effaced, and the vacuum thus produced filled by a theory which directly traced back the *status quo* of the Gentile Christian communities to a tradition of the twelve as its foundation. This fact is extremely paradoxical, and is not altogether explained by the assumptions that the Pauline-Judaistic controversy had not made a great impression on the Gentile Christians, that the way in which Paul, while fully recognising the twelve, had insisted on his own independent importance, had long ceased to be really understood, and that Peter and John had also really been missionaries to the Gentiles. The guarantee that was needed for the "teaching of the Lord" must, finally, be given not by Paul, but only by chosen eye-witnesses. The less that was known

1 Read, apart from all others, the canonical Gospels, the remains of the so-called Apocryphal Gospels, and perhaps the Shepherd of Hermas : see also the statements of Papias.

2 That Peter was in Antioch follows from Gal. II. ; that he laboured in Corinth, perhaps before the composition of the first epistle to the Corinthians, is not so improbable as is usually maintained (1 Cor.; Dionys. of Corinth); that he was at Rome even is very credible. The sojourn of John in Asia Minor cannot, I think, be contested.

3 See how in the three early "writings of Peter" (Gospel, Apocalypse, *Kerygma*) the twelve are embraced in a perfect unity. Peter is the head and spokesman for them all.

about them, the easier it was to claim them. The conviction as to the unanimity of the twelve, and as to their activity in founding the Gentile Churches, appeared in these Churches as early as the urgent need of protection against the serious consequences of unfettered religious enthusiasm and unrestrained religious fancy. This urgency cannot be dated too far back. In correspondence therewith, the principle of tradition in the Church (Christ, the twelve Apostles) in the case of those who were intent on the unity and completeness of Christendom, is also very old. But one passed logically from the Apostles to the disciples of the Apostles, "the Elders," without at first claiming for them any other significance than that of reliable hearers (Apostoli et discentes ipsorum). In coming down to them, one here and there betook oneself again to real historical ground, disciples of Paul, of Peter, of John. [1] Yet even here legends with a tendency speedily got mixed with facts, and because, in consequence of this theory of tradition, the Apostle Paul must needs fall into the background, his disciples also were more or less forgotten. The attempt which we have in the Pastoral Epistles remained without effect, as regards those to whom these epistles were addressed. Timothy and Titus obtained no authority outside these epistles. But so far as the epistles of Paul were collected, diffused, and read, there was created a complex of writings which at first stood beside the "Teaching of the Lord by the twelve Apostles", without being connected with it, and only obtained such connection by the creation of the New Testament, that is, by the interpolation of the Acts of the Apostles, between Gospels and Epistles. [2]

§ 3. *The Main Articles of Christianity and the Conceptions of Salvation. Eschatology.*

1. The main articles of Christianity were (1) belief in God the δεσπότης, and in the Son in virtue of proofs from prophecy, and the

1 See Papias and the Reliq. Presbyter. ap. Iren., collecta in Patr. Opp. I. 2, p. 105 : see also Zahn, Forschungen. III., p. 156 f.

2 The Gentile-Christian conception of the significance of the twelve—a fact to be specially noted—was all but unanimous (see above Chap. II.): the only one who broke through it was Marcion. The writers of Asia Minor,

teaching of the Lord as attested by the Apostles; (2) discipline
according to the standard of the words of the Lord; (3) baptism;

Rome and Egypt coincide in this point. Beside the Acts of the Apostles,
which is specially instructive, see 1 Clem. 42; Barn. 5. 9, 8. 3: Didache
inscr.; Hermas, Vis. III. 5, 11; Sim. IX. 15, 16, 17, 25; Petrusev-Petrusapok.
Præd. Petr. ap. Clem. Strom. VI. 6, 48; Ignat. ad Trall. 3; ad Rom 4; ad
Philad. 5; Papias; Polyc.; Aristides; Justin *passim*; inferences from the
great work of Irenæus, the works of Tertull. and Clem. Alex.; the Valentinians. The inference that follows from the eschatological hope, that the
Gospel has already been preached to the world, and the growing need of
having a tradition mediated by eye-witnesses co-operated here, and out of
the twelve who were in great part obscure, but who had once been authoritative in Jerusalem and Palestine, and highly esteemed in the Christian
Diaspora from the beginning, though unknown, created a court of appeal,
which presented itself as not only taking a second rank after the Lord
himself, but as the medium through which alone the words of the Lord
became the possession of Christendom, as he neither preached to the nations
nor left writings. The importance of the twelve in the main body of the
Church may at any rate be measured by the facts, that the personal activity
of Jesus was confined to Palestine, that he left behind him neither a confession nor a doctrine, and that in this respect the tradition tolerated no
more corrections. Attempts which were made in this direction, the fiction
of a semi-Gentile origin of Christ, the denial of the Davidic Sonship, the
invention of a correspondence between Jesus and Abgarus, meetings of
Jesus with Greeks, and much else, belong only in part to the earliest
period, and remained as really inoperative as they were uncertain (according
to Clem. Alex., Jesus himself is the Apostle to the Jews; the twelve are the
Apostles to the Gentiles in Euseb. H. E. VI. 14). The notion about the twelve
Apostles evangelising the world in accordance with the commission of Jesus,
is consequently to be considered as the means by which the Gentile Christians got rid of the inconvenient fact of the merely local activity of Jesus
(compare how Justin expresses himself about the Apostles: their going out
into all the world is to him one of the main articles predicted in the Old
Testament, Apol. 1. 39; compare also the Apology of Aristides, c. 2, and
the passage of similar tenor in the Ascension of Isaiah, where the "adventus
XII. discipulorum" is regarded as one of the fundamental facts of salvation,
c. 3 13, ed. Dillmann, p. 13, and a passage such as Iren. fragm. XXIX. in Har-
vey II, p. 494, where the parable about the grain of mustard seed is applied
to the λόγος ἐπουράνιος, and the twelve Apostles; the Apostles are the branches
ὑφ' ὧν κλάδων σκεπασθέντες οἱ πάντες ὡς ὄρνεα ὑπὸ καλιὰν συνελθόντα μετέλαβον τῆς ἐξ
αὐτῶν προερχομένης ἐδωδίμου καὶ ἐπουρανίου τροφῆς Hippol, de Antichr. 61. Orig.
c. Cels. III. 28). This means, as it was empty of contents, was very soon to
prove the most convenient instrument for establishing ever new historical
connections, and legitimising the *status quo* in the communities. Finally, the
whole catholic idea of tradition was rooted in that statement which was
already, at the close of the first century, formulated by Clement of Rome
(c. 42): οἱ ἀπόστολοι ἡμῖν εὐηγγελίσθησαν ἀπὸ τοῦ κυρίου Ἰησοῦ Χριστοῦ, Ἰησοῦς ὁ
χριστὸς ἀπὸ τοῦ θεοῦ ἐξεπέμφθη. ὁ χριστὸς οὖν ἀπὸ τοῦ θεοῦ, καὶ οἱ ἀπόστολοι ἀπὸ
τοῦ Χριστοῦ· ἐγένοντο οὖν ἀμφότερα εὐτάκτως ἐκ θελήματος θεοῦ, κ.τ.λ. Here, as in
all similar statements which elevate the Apostles into the history of revelation, the unanimity of all the Apostles is always presupposed, so that the
statement of Clem Alex. (Strom. VII., 17, 108: μία ἡ πάντων γέγονε τῶν ἀποστόλων
ὥσπερ διδασκαλία οὕτως δὲ καὶ ἡ παράδοσις; see Tertull., de præscr. 32: "Apostoli
non diversa inter se docuerent," Iren alii). contains no innovation, but gives

(4) the common offering of prayer, culminating in the Lord's Supper and the holy meal; (5) the sure hope of the nearness expression to an old idea. That the twelve unitedly proclaimed one and the same message, that they proclaimed it to the world, that they were chosen to this vocation by Christ, that the communities possess the witness of the Apostles as their rule of conduct (Excerp. ex Theod 25. ὥσπερ ὑπὸ τῶν ζωδίων ἡ γένεσις διοικεῖται, οὕτως ὑπὸ τῶν ἀποστόλων ἡ ἀναγέννησις), are authoritative theses which can be traced back as far as we have any remains of Gentile-Christian literature. It was thereby presupposed that the unanimous *kerygma* of the twelve Apostles, which the communities possess as κανὼν τῆς παραδόσεως (1 Clem. 7), was public and accessible to all Yet the idea does not seem to have been everywhere kept at a distance, that besides the *kerygma* a still deeper knowledge was transmitted by the Apostles, or by certain Apostles, to particular Christians who were specially gifted. Of course we have no direct evidence of this; but the connection in which certain Gnostic unions stood at the beginning with the communities developing themselves to Catholicism, and inferences from utterances of later writers (Clem. Alex., Tertull), make it probable that this conception was present in the communities here and there even in the age of the so-called Apostolic Fathers. It may be definitely said that the peculiar idea of tradition (θεός—χριστος—οἱ δώδεκα ἀπόστολοι – ἐκκλησία) in the Gentile Churches is very old, but that it was still limited in its significance at the beginning, and was threatened (1) by a wider conception of the idea "Apostle" (besides, the fact is important, that Asia Minor and Rome were the very places where a stricter idea of "Apostle" made its appearance: See my Edition of the Didache, p. 117); (2) by free prophets and teachers moved by the Spirit, who introduced new conceptions and rules, and whose word was regarded as the word of God; (3) by the assumption, not always definitely rejected, that besides the public tradition of the *kerygma* there was a secret tradition. That Paul, as a rule, was not included in this high estimate of the Apostles is shewn by this fact, among others, that the earlier Apocryphal Acts of the Apostles are much less occupied with his person than with the rest of the Apostles. The features of the old legends which make the Apostles in their deeds, their fate, nay, even in appearance as far as possible equal to the person of Jesus himself, deserve special consideration, (see, for example, the descent of the Apostles into hell in Herm. Sim. IX 16); for it is just here that the fact above established. that the activity of the Apostles was to make up for the want of the activity of Jesus himself among the nations, stands clearly out. (See Acta Johannis ed. Zahn, p. 246: ὁ ἐκλεξάμενος ἡμᾶς εἰς ἀποστολὴν ἐθνῶν, ὁ ἐκπέμψας ἡμας εἰς τὴν οἰκουμένην θεος, ὁ δείξας ἑαυτὸν διὰ τῶν ἀποστολῶν, also the remarkable declaration of Origen about the Chronicle of Phlegon [Hadrian], that what holds good of Christ, is in that Chronicle transferred to Peter; finally we may recall to mind the visions in which an Apostle suddenly appears as Christ). Between the judgment of value : ἡμεῖς τούς ἀποστόλους ἀποδεχόμεθα ὡς Χριστὸν, and those creations of fancy in which the Apostles appear as gods and demigods, there is certainly a great interval; but it can be proved that there are stages lying between these extreme points. It is therefore permissible to call to mind here the oldest Apocryphal Acts of the Apostles, although they may have originated almost completely in Gnostic circles (see also the Pistis Sophia which brings a metaphysical theory to the establishment of the authority of the Apostles, p. 11. 14, see Texte u. Unters. VII. 2, p. 61 ff.) Gnosticism here, as frequently elsewhere, is related to common Christianity, as excess progressing to the invention of a myth with a tendency, to a historical theorem determ-

of Christ's glorious kingdom. In these appears the unity of Christendom, that is, of the Church which possesses the Holy Spirit. [1] On the basis of this unity Christian knowledge was free and manifold. It was distinguished as σοφία, σύνεσις, ἐπισ-τήμη, γνῶσις (τῶν δικαιωμάτων), from the λόγος θεοῦ τῆς πίστεως, the κλῆσις τῆς ἐπαγγελίας, and the ἐντολαὶ τῆς διδαχῆς (Barn. 16. 9, similarly Hermas). Perception and knowledge of Divine things was a Charism possessed only by individuals, but like all Charisms it was to be used for the good of the whole. In so far as every actual perception was a perception produced by the Spirit, it was regarded as important and indubitable truth, even though some Christians were unable to understand it. While attention was given to the firm inculcation

ined by the effort to maintain one's own position (cf. the article from the *kerygma* of Peter in Clem. Strom. VI. 6. 48: Ἐξελεξάμην ὑμᾶς δώδεκα μαθητὰς, κ.τ.λ., the introduction to the basal writing of the first 6 books of the Apostolic Constitutions, and the introduction to the Egyptian ritual, κατὰ κέλευσιν τοῦ κυρίου ὑμῶν, κ.τ.λ.). Besides, it must be admitted that the origin of the idea of tradition and its connection with the twelve, is obscure: what is historically reliable here has still to be investigated; even the work of Seufert (Der Urspr. u. d. Bedeutung des Apostolats in der christl. Kirche der ersten zwei Jahrhunderte, 1887) has not cleared up the dark points. We will, perhaps, get more light by following the important hint given by Weizsäcker (Apost. Age. p. 13 ff.), that Peter was the first witness of the resurrection, and was called such in the *kerygma* of the communities (see 1 Cor. XV. 5: Luke XXIV. 34). The twelve Apostles are also further called οἱ περὶ τὸν Πέτρον (Mrc. fin in L. Ign. ad Smyrn. 3; cf. Luke VIII. 45; Acts II. 14; Gal. I. 18 f; 1 Cor. XV. 5), and it is a correct historical reminiscence when Chrysostom says (Hom. in Joh. 88), ὁ Πέτρος ἔκκριτος ἦν τῶν ἀποστόλων καὶ στόμα τῶν μαθητῶν καὶ κορυφὴ τοῦ χόρου. Now, as Peter was really in personal relation with important Gentile-Christian communities, that which held good of him, the recognized head and spokesman of the twelve, was perhaps transferred to these. One has finally to remember that besides the appeal to the twelve there was in the Gentile Churches an appeal to Peter and Paul (but not for the evangelic *kerygma*), which has a certain historical justification; cf Gal. II. 8; 1 Cor. I. 12 f., IX. 5; 1. Clem Ign ad Rom. 4, and the numerous later passages. Paul in claiming equality with Peter, though Peter was the head and mouth of the twelve and had himself been active in mission work, has perhaps contributed most towards spreading the authority of the twelve. It is notable how rarely we find any special appeal to John in the tradition of the main body of the Church. For the middle of the 2nd century, the authority of the twelve Apostles may be expressed in the following statements: (1) They were missionaries for the world; (2) They ruled the Church and established Church Offices; (3) They guaranteed the true doctrine, (a) by the tradition going back to them, (b) by writings; (4) They are the ideals of Christian life; (5) They are also directly mediators of salvation—though this point is uncertain.

1 See Διδαχὴ, c. 1-10, with parallel passages.

and observance of the moral precepts of Christ, as well as to
the awakening of sure faith in Christ, and while all waverings
and differences were excluded in respect of these, there was
absolutely no current doctrine of faith in the communities, in
the sense of a completed theory, and the theological speculations of even closely related Christian writers of this epoch,
exhibit the greatest differences. [1] The productions of fancy,
the terrible or consoling pictures of the future pass for sacred
knowledge, just as much as intelligent and sober reflections,
and edifying interpretation of Old Testament sayings. Even
that which was afterwards separated as Dogmatic and Ethics
was then in no way distinguished. [2] The communities gave
expression in the cultus, chiefly in the hymns and prayers,
to what they possessed in their God and their Christ; here
sacred formulæ were fashioned and delivered to the members. [3]
The problem of surrendering the world in the hope of a life
beyond was regarded as the practical side of the faith, and
the unity in temper and disposition resting on faith in the
saving revelation of God in Christ, permitted the highest degree
of freedom in knowledge, the results of which were absolutely
without control as soon as the preacher or the writer was
recognised as a true teacher, that is, inspired by the Spirit
of God. [4] There was also in wide circles a conviction that

---

1 Cf., for example, the first epistle of Clement to the Corinthians with
the Shepherd of Hermas. Both documents originated in Rome.

2 Compare how dogmatic and ethical elements are inseparably united in the
Shepherd, in first and second Clement, as well as in Polycarp and Justin.

3 Note the hymnal parts of the Revelation of John, the great prayer with
which the first epistle of Clement closes, the "carmen dicere Christo quasi
deo," reported by Pliny, the eucharist prayer in the Διδαχὴ, the hymn 1 Tim.
III. 16: the fragments from the prayers which Justin quotes, and compare
with these the declaration of the anonymous writer in Euseb. H. E. V. 28. 5,
that the belief of the earliest Christians in the Deity of Christ might be proved
from the old Christian hymns and odes. In the epistles of Ignatius the theology frequently consists of an aimless stringing together of articles manifestly
originating in hymns and the cultus.

4 The prophet and teacher express what the Spirit of God suggests to them.
Their word is therefore God's word, and their writings, in so far as they apply
to the whole of Christendom, are inspired, holy writings. Further, not only
does Acts XV. 22 f. exhibit the formula; ἔδοξεν τῷ πνεύματι τῷ ἁγίῳ καὶ ὑμῖν
(see similar passages in the Acts), but the Roman writings also appeal to
the Holy Spirit (1 Clem. 63. 2): likewise Barnabas, Ignatius, etc. Even in the

the Christian faith, after the night of error, included the full knowledge of everything worth knowing, that precisely in its most important articles it is accessible to men of every degree of culture, and that in it, in the now attained truth, is contained one of the most essential blessings of Christianity. When it is said in the Epistle of Barnabas (II. 2. 3); τῆς πίστεως ἡμῶν εἰσὶν βοηθοὶ φόβος καὶ ὑπομονή, τὰ δὲ συμμαχοῦντα ἡμῖν μακροθυμία καὶ ἐγκράτεια· τούτων μενόντων τὰ πρὸς κύριον ἁγνῶς, συνευφραίνονταί αὐτοῖς σοφία, σύνεσις, ἐπιστήμη, γνῶσις, knowledge appears in this classic formula to be an essential element in Christianity, conditioned by faith and the practical virtues, and dependent on them. Faith takes the lead, knowledge follows it: but of course in concrete cases it could not always be decided what was λόγος τῆς πίστεως, which implicitly contained the highest knowledge, and what the special γνῶσις; for in the last resort the nature of the two was regarded as identical, both being represented as produced by the Spirit of God.

2. The conceptions of Christian salvation, or of redemption, were grouped around two ideas, which were themselves but loosely connected with each other, and of which the one influenced more the temper and the imagination, the other the intellectual faculty. On the one hand, salvation, in accordance with the earliest preaching, was regarded as the glorious kingdom which was soon to appear on earth with the visible return of Christ, which will bring the present course of the world to an end, and introduce for a definite series of centuries, before the final judgment, a new order of all things to the joy and blessedness of the saints. [1] In connection with this

controversy about the baptism of heretics a Bishop gave his vote with the formula: "secundum motum animi mei et spiritus sancti" (Cypr. Opp. ed. Hartel, I. p. 457)

1 The so-called Chiliasm—the designation is unsuitable and misleading—is found wherever the Gospel is not yet Hellenised (see, for example, Barn. 4. 15; Hermas; 2 Clem.; Papias [Euseb. III. 39]; Διδαχή, 10. 16; Apoc. Petri; Justin, Dial. 32, 51, 80, 82, 110, 139; Cerinthus), and must be regarded as a main element of the Christian preaching (see my article " Millenium " in the Encycl. Brit.). In it lay not the least of the power of Christianity in the first century, and the means whereby it entered the Jewish propaganda in the Empire and surpassed it. The hopes springing out of Judaism were at first but

the hope of the resurrection of the body occupied the fore-

little modified, that is, only so far as the substitution of the Christian communities for the nation of Israel made modification necessary. In all else, even the details of the Jewish hopes of the future were retained, and the extra-canonical Jewish Apocalypses (Esra, Enoch, Baruch, Moses, etc.) were diligently read alongside of Daniel. Their contents were in part joined on to sayings of Jesus, and they served as models for similar productions (here, therefore, an enduring connection with the Jewish religion is very plain). In the Christian hopes of the future, as in the Jewish eschatology, may be distinguished essential and accidental, fixed and fluid elements. To the former belong (1) the notion of a final fearful conflict with the powers of the world which is just about to break out τὸ τέλειον σκάνδαλον ἤγγικεν), (2) belief in the speedy return of Christ, (3) the conviction that after conquering the secular power (this was variously conceived, as God's Ministers, as "that which restrains"—2 Thess. II. 6, as a pure kingdom of Satan; see the various estimates in Justin, Melito, Irenæus and Hyppolytus), Christ will establish a glorious kingdom on the earth, and will raise the saints to share in that kingdom, and (4) that he will finally judge all men. To the fluid elements belong the notions of the Antichrist, or of the secular power culminating in the Antichrist, as well as notions about the place, the extent, and the duration of Christ's glorious kingdom. But it is worthy of special note, that Justin regarded the belief that Christ will set up his kingdom in Jerusalem, and that it will endure for 1000 years, as a necessary element of orthodoxy, though he confesses he knew Christians who did not share this belief, while they did not, like the pseudo-Christians, reject also the resurrection of the body (the promise of Montanus that Christ's kingdom would be let down at Pepuza and Tymion is a thing by itself, and answers to the other promises and pretensions of Montanus). The resurrection of the body is expressed in the Roman Symbol, while, very notably, the hope of Christ's earthly kingdom is not there mentioned, (see above, p. 157.) The great inheritance which the Gentile Christian communities received from Judaism, is the eschatological hopes, along with the Monotheism assured by revelation and belief in providence. The law as a national law was abolished. The Old Testament became a new book in the hands of the Gentile Christians. On the contrary, the eschatological hopes in all their details, and with all the deep shadows which they threw on the state and public life, were at first received, and maintained themselves in wide circles pretty much unchanged, and only succumbed in some of their details—just as in Judaism—to the changes which resulted from the constant change of the political situation. But these hopes were also destined in great measure to pass away after the settlement of Christianity on Græco-Roman soil. We may set aside the fact that they did not occupy the foreground in Paul, for we do not know whether this was of importance for the period that followed. But that Christ would set up the kingdom in Jerusalem, and that it would be an earthly kingdom with sensuous enjoyments—these and other notions contend, on the one hand, with the vigorous antijudaism of the communities, and on the other, with the moralistic spiritualism, in the pure carrying out of which the Gentile Christians, in the East at least, increasingly recognised the essence of Christianity. Only the vigorous world-renouncing enthusiasm which did not permit the rise of moralistic spiritualism and mysticism, and the longing for a time of joy and dominion that was born of it, protected for a long time a series of ideas which corresponded to the spiritual disposition of the great multitude of converts, only at times of special oppres-

ground. [1]   On the other hand, salvation appeared to be given
in the truth, that is, in the complete and certain knowledge
of God, as contrasted with the error of heathendom and the
night of sin, and this truth included the certainty of the gift

sion. Moreover, the Christians, in opposition to Judaism, were, as a rule, instructed to obey magistrates, whose establishment directly contradicted
the judgment of the state contained in the Apocalypses. In such a conflict,
however, that judgment necessarily conquers at last, which makes as little
change as possible in the existing forms of life. A history of the gradual
attenuation and subsidence of eschatological hopes in the II.-IV. centuries
can only be written in fragments. They have rarely — at best, by fits
and starts — marked out the course. On the contrary, if I may say so,
they only gave the smoke: for the course was pointed out by the abiding
elements of the Gospel, trust in God and the Lord Christ, the resolution
to a holy life, and a firm bond of brotherhood. The quiet, gradual change in
which the eschatological hopes passed away, fell into the background, or lost
important parts, was, on the other hand, a result of deep-reaching changes in
the faith and life of Christendom. Chiliasm as a power was broken up by speculative mysticism, and on that account very much later in the West than in
the East. But speculative mysticism has its centre in christology. In the earliest period, this, as a theory, belonged more to the defence of religion than to
religon itself. Ignatius alone was able to reflect on that transference of power
from Christ which Paul had experienced The disguises in which the apocalyptic eschatological prophecies were set forth, belonged in part to the form
of this literature, (in so far as one could easily be given the lie if he became
too plain, or in so far as the prophet really saw the future only in large outline),
partly it had to be chosen in order not to give political offence. See Hippol,
comm. in Daniel (Georgiades, p. 49, 51 : νοεῖν ὀφείλομεν τὰ κατὰ καιρὸν συμβαίνοντα
καὶ εἰδότας σιωπᾶν); but, above all, Constantine, orat ad s. coetum 19, on some
verses of Virgil which are interpreted in a Christian sense, " but that none of
the rulers in the capital might be able to accuse their author of violating the
laws of the state with his poetry, or of destroying the traditional ideas of the
procedure about the gods, he concealed the truth under a veil." That holds
good also of the Apocalyptists and the poets of the Christian Sibylline sayings.

1 The hope of the resurrection of the body (1 Clem. 26. 3 : ἀναστήσεις τὴν
σάρκα μου ταύτην. Herm. Sim. V. 7 2: βλέπε μήποτε ἀναβῇ ἐπὶ τὴν καρδίαν σου
τὴν σάρκα σου ταύτην φθαρτὴν εἶναι. Barn. 5. 6 f.: 21. 1: 2 Clem. 9. 1: καὶ μή
λεγέτω τις ὑμῶν ὅτι αὕτη ἡ σὰρξ οὐ κρίνεται οὐδὲ ἀνίσταται Polyc. Ep. 7. 2:
Justin, Dial. 80 etc,) finds its place originally in the hope of a share in the
glorious kingdom of Christ. It therefore disappears or is modified wherever
that hope itself falls into the background. But it finally asserted itself throughout and became of independent importance, in a new structure of eschatological expectations, in which it attained the significance of becoming the
specific conviction of Christian faith. With the hope of the resurrection
of the body was originally connected the hope of a happy life in easy
blessedness, under green trees in magnificent fields with joyous feeding
flocks, and flying angels clothed in white. One must read the Revelation
of Peter, the Shepherd, or the Acts of Perpetua and Felicitas, in order
to see how entirely the fancy of many Christians, and not merely of those
who were uncultured, dwelt in a fairyland in which they caught sight now
of the Ancient of days, and now of the Youthful Shepherd, Christ The most
fearful delineations of the torments of Hell formed the reverse side to this. We
now know, through the Apocalypse of Peter, how old these delineations are.

of eternal life, and all conceivable spiritual blessings. [1] Of
these the community, so far as it is a community of saints,
that is, so far as it is ruled by the Spirit of God, already
possesses forgiveness of sins and righteousness. But, as a rule,
neither blessing was understood in a strictly religious sense, that
is to say, the effect of their religious sense was narrowed.
✓ The moralistic view, in which eternal life is the wages and
reward of a perfect moral life wrought out essentially by one's
own power, took the place of first importance at a very early
period. On this view, according to which the righteousness
of God is revealed in punishment and reward alike, the forgiveness of sin only meant a single remission of sin in connection with entrance into the Church by baptism, [2] and

1 The perfect knowledge of the truth and eternal life are connected
in the closest way (see p. 144, note 1) because the Father of truth is
also Prince of life (see Diognet. 12: οὐδὲ γὰρ ζωὴ ἄνευ γνώσεως οὐδὲ γνῶσις
ἀσφαλὴς ἄνευ ζωῆς ἀληθοῦς· διὸ πλησίον ἑκάτερον πεφύτευται, see also what follows).
The classification is a Hellenic one, which has certainly penetrated also
into Palestinian Jewish theology. It may be reckoned among the great
intuitions, which in the fulness of the times, united the religious and
reflective minds of all nations. The Pauline formula, "Where there is forgiveness of sin, there also is life and salvation", had for centuries no distinct
history. But the formula, "Where there is truth, perfect knowledge, there also
is eternal life", has had the richest history in Christendom from the beginning.
Quite apart from John, it is older than the theology of the Apologists (see,
for example, the Supper prayer in the Didache, 9. 10, where there is no mention of the forgiveness of sin, but thanks are given, ὑπὲρ τῆς γνώσεως καὶ
πίστεως καὶ ἀθανασίας ἧς ἐγνώρισεν ἡμῖν ὁ θεὸς διὰ Ἰησοῦ, or ὑπὲρ τῆς ζωῆς καὶ
γνώσεως, and 1 Clem. 36. 2: διὰ τούτο ἠθέλησεν ὁ δεσπότης τῆς ἀθανάτου γνωσεως
ἡμᾶς γεύσασθαι). It is capable of a very manifold content, and has never made
its way in the Church without reservations, but so far as it has we may
speak of a hellenising of Christianity. This is shewn most clearly in the
fact that the ἀθανασία, identical with ἀφθαρσία and ζωὴ αἰώνιος, as is proved by
their being often interchanged, gradually supplanted the βασιλεία τοῦ θεοῦ
(χριστοῦ) and thrust it out of the sphere of religious intuition and hope into
that of religious speech. It should also be noted, at the same time, that in the
hope of eternal life which is bestowed with the knowledge of the truth, the
resurrection of the body is by no means with certainty included. It is rather
added to it (see above) from another series of ideas. Conversely, the words
ζωὴν αἰώνιον were first added to the words σαρκὸς ἀνάστασιν in the western
Symbols at a comparatively late period, while in the prayers they are
certainly very old.
2 Even the assumption of such a remission is fundamentally in contradiction with moralism; but that solitary remission of sin was not called in question, was rather regarded as distinctive of the new religion,
and was established by an appeal to the omnipotence and special goodness of God, which appears just in the calling of sinners. In this calling,
grace as grace is exhausted (Barn. 5. 9; 2 Clem. 2. 4-7). But this grace

righteousness became identical with virtue. The idea is indeed still operative, especially in the oldest Gentile-Christian writings known to us, that sinlessness rests upon a new creation (regeneration) which is effected in baptism ; [1] but, so far as dissimilar eschatological hopes do not operate, it is everywhere in danger of being supplanted by the other idea, which maintains that there is no other blessing in the Gospel than the perfect truth and eternal life. All else is but a sum of obligations in which the Gospel is presented as a new law. The christianising of the Old Testament supported this conception. There was indeed an opinion that the Gospel, even so far as it is a law, comprehends a gift of salvation which is to be grasped by faith (νόμος ἄνευ ζυγοῦ ἀνάγκης, [2] νόμος τ. ἐλευθερίας [3] Christ himself the law); [4] but this notion, as it is obscure in itself, was also an uncertain one and was gradually lost. Fur-

itself seems to be annulled, inasmuch as the sins committed before baptism were regarded as having been committed in a state of ignorance (Tertull. de bapt. I.: delicta pristinæ cæcitatis), on account of which it seemed worthy of God to forgive them, that is, to accept the repentance which followed on the ground of the new knowledge. So considered, everything, in point of fact, amounts to the gracious gift of knowledge, and the memory of the saying, "Jesus receiveth sinners", is completely obscured. But the tradition of this saying and many like it, and above all, the religious instinct, where it was more powerfully stirred, did not permit a consistent development of that moralistic conception. See for this, Hermas. Sim. V. 7. 3 : περὶ τῶν προτέρων ἀγνοημάτων τῷ θεῷ μόνῳ δυνατὸν ἴασιν δοῦναι αὐτοῦ γὰρ ἐστι πᾶσα ἐξουσία. Præd. Petri ap. Clem. Strom. VI. 6. 48 : ὅσα ἐν ἀγνοίᾳ τις ὑμῶν ἐποίησεν μὴ εἰδὼς σαφῶς τὸν θεόν, ἐὰν ἐπιγνοὺς μετανοήσῃ, πάντα αὐτῷ ἀφεθήσεται τὰ ἁμαρτήματα. Aristides, Apol. 17: "The Christians offer prayers (for the unconverted Greeks) that they may be converted from their error. But when one of them is converted he is ashamed before the Christians of the works which he has done. And he confesses to God, saying: 'I have done these things in ignorance. And he cleanses his heart, and his sins are forgiven him, because he had done them in ignorance, in the earlier period when he mocked and jeered at the true knowledge of the Christians." Exactly the same in Tertull. de pudic. 10. init. The statement of this same writer (i. c. fin), "Cessatio delicti radix est veniæ, ut venia sit pænitentiæ fructus", is a pregnant expression of the conviction of the earliest Gentile Christians

1 This idea appears with special prominence in the Epistle of Barnabas (see 6. 11. 14) ; the new formation (ἀναπλάσσειν) results through the forgiveness of sin. In the moralistic view the forgiveness of sin is the result of the renewal that is spontaneously brought about on the ground of knowledge shewing itself in penitent feeling.

2 Barn. 2. 6, and my notes on the passage.

3 James I 25.

4 Hermas. Sim. VIII. 3. 2 ; Justin Dial. II. 43 ; Præd. Petri in Clem., Strom. I. 29. 182 ; II. 15. 68.

ther, by the "law" was frequently meant in the first place, not the law of love, but the commandments of ascetic holiness, or an explanation and a turn were given to the law of love, according to which it is to verify itself above all in asceticism. [1]

The expression of the contents of the Gospel in the concepts ἐπαγγελία (ζωὴ αἰώνιος) γνῶσις (ἀλήθεια) νόμος (ἐγκράτεια), seemed quite as plain as it was exhaustive, and the importance of faith which was regarded as the basis of hope and knowledge and obedience in a holy life, was at the same time in every respect perceived. [2]

Supplement I. — The moralistic view of sin, forgiveness of sin, and righteousness, in Clement, Barnabas, Polycarp and Ignatius, gives place to Pauline formulæ; but the uncertainty with which these are reproduced, shews that the Pauline idea has not been clearly seen. [3] In Hermas, however, and in the second Epistle of Clement, the consciousness of being under grace, even after baptism, almost completely disappears behind the demand to fulfil the tasks which baptism imposes. [4] The idea that serious sins, in the case of the baptised, no longer should or can be forgiven, except under special circumstances, appears to have prevailed in wide circles, if not everywhere. [5]

---

1 Didache, c. I., and my notes on the passage (Prolegg. p. 45 f.).

2 The concepts, ἐπαγγελία, γνῶσις, νόμος, form the Triad on which the later catholic conception of Christianity is based, though it can be proved to have been in existence at an earlier period. That πίστις must everywhere take the lead was undoubted, though we must not think of the Pauline idea of πίστις. When the Apostolic Fathers reflect upon faith, which, however, happens only incidentally, they mean a holding for true of a sum of holy traditions, and obedience to them, along with the hope that their consoling contents will yet be fully revealed. But Ignatius speaks like a Christian who knows what he possesses in faith in Christ, that is. in confidence in him. In Barn. I.: Polyc. Ep. 2, we find "faith, hope, love"; in Ignatius, "faith and love". Tertullian, in an excellent exposition, has shewn how far patience is a temper corresponding to Christian faith (see besides the Epistle of James).

3 See Lipsius De Clementis. R. ep. ad. Cor. priore disquis. 1855. It would be in point of method inadmissible to conclude from the fact that in 1 Clem. Pauline formulæ are relatively most faithfully produced, that Gentile Christianity generally understood Pauline theology at first, but gradually lost this understanding in the course of two generations.

4 Formally: τηρήσατε τὴν σάρκα ἁγνὴν καὶ τὴν σφραγῖδα ἄσπιλον (2 Clem. 8. 6.)

5 Hermas (Mand. IV. 3) and Justin presuppose it. Hermas of course sought and found a way of meeting the results of that idea which were threatening

It reveals the earnestness of those early Christians and their elevated sense of freedom and power; but it might be united either with the highest moral intensity, or with a lax judgment on the little sins of the day. The latter, in point of fact, threatened to become more and more the presupposition and result of that idea—for there exists here a fatal reciprocal action.

Supplement 2. — The realisation of salvation — as βασιλεία τοῦ θεοῦ and as ἀφθαρσία — being expected from the future, the whole present possession of salvation might be comprehended under the title of vocation (κλῆσις): see, for example, the second Epistle of Clement. In this sense *gnosis* itself was regarded as something only preparatory.

Supplement 3.— In some circles the Pauline formula about righteousness and salvation by faith alone, must, it would appear, not infrequently (as already in the Apostolic age itself) have been partly misconstrued, and partly taken advantage of as a cloak for laxity. Those who resisted such a disposition, and therefore also the formula in the post-Apostolic age, shew indeed by their opposition how little they have hit upon or understood the Pauline idea of faith: for they not only issued the watchword "faith and works" (though the Jewish ceremonial law was not thereby meant), but they admitted, and not only hypothetically, that one might have the true faith even though in his case that faith remained dead or united with immorality. See, above all, the Epistle of James and the Shepherd of Hermas; though the first Epistle of John comes also into consideration (III. 7: "He that doeth righteousness is righteous").[1]

Supplement 4.—However similar the eschatological expectations of the Jewish Apocalyptists and the Christians may

---

the Church with decimation; but he did not question the idea itself. Because Christendom is a community of saints which has in its midst the sure salvation, all its members—this is the necessary inference – must lead a sinless life.

1 The formula, "righteousness by faith alone", was really repressed in the second century; but it could not be entirely destroyed: see my Essay, "Gesch. d. Seligkeit allein durch den Glauben in der alten K." Ztsch. f. Theol. u. Kirche. I. pp. 82-105.

seem, there is yet in one respect an important difference between them. The uncertainty about the final consummation was first set aside by the Gospel. It should be noted as highly characteristic of the Jewish hopes of the future, even of the most definite, how the beginning of the end, that is, the overthrow of the world-powers and the setting up of the earthly kingdom of God, was much more certainly expressed than the goal and the final end. Neither the general judgment, nor what we, according to Christian tradition, call heaven and hell, should be described as a sure possession of Jewish faith in the primitive Christian period. It is only in the Gospel of Christ, where everything is subordinated to the idea of a higher righteousness and the union of the individual with God, that the general judgment and the final condition after it are the clear, firmly grasped goal of all meditation. No doctrine has been more surely preserved in the convictions and preaching of believers in Christ than this. Fancy might roam ever so much and, under the direction of the tradition, thrust bright and precious images between the present condition and the final end, the main thing continued to be the great judgment of the world, and the certainty that the saints would go to God in heaven, the wicked to hell. But while the judgment, as a rule, was connected with the Person of Jesus himself (see the Romish Symbol: the words κριτὴς ζώντων καὶ νεκρῶν, were very frequently applied to Christ in the earliest writings), the moral condition of the individual, and the believing recognition of the Person of Christ were put in the closest relation. The Gentile Christians held firmly to this. Open the Shepherd, or the second Epistle of Clement, or any other early Christian writing, and you will find that the judgment, heaven and hell, are the decisive objects. But that shews that the moral character of Christianity as a religion is seen and adhered to. The fearful idea of hell, far from signifying a backward step in the history of the religious spirit, is rather a proof of its having rejected the morally indifferent point of view, and of its having become sovereign in union with the ethical spirit.

§ 4. *The Old Testament as Source of the Knowledge of Faith.* [1]

The sayings of the Old Testament, the word of God, were believed to furnish inexhaustible material for deeper knowledge. The Christian prophets were nurtured on the Old Testament, the teachers gathered from it the revelation of the past, present and future (Barn. 1. 7), and were therefore able as prophets to edify the Churches; from it was further drawn the confirmation of the answers to all emergent questions, as one could always find in the Old Testament what he was in search of. The different writers laid the holy book under contribution in very much the same way; for they were all dominated by the presupposition that this book is a Christian book, and contains the explanations that are necessary for the occasion. There were several teachers, *e. g.*, Barnabas, who at a very early period boasted of finding in it ideas of special profundity and value — these were always an expression of the difficulties that were being felt. The plain words of the Lord as generally known, did not seem sufficient to satisfy the craving for knowledge, or to solve the problems that were emerging; [2] their origin and form also opposed difficulties at first to the attempt to obtain from them new disclosures by re-interpretation. But the Old Testament sayings and histories were in part unintelligible, or in their literal sense offensive; they were at the same time regarded as fun-

1 The only thorough discussion of the use of the Old Testament by an Apostolic Father, and of its authority, that we possess, is Wrede's "Untersuchungen zum 1 Clemensbrief" (1891). Excellent preliminary investigations, which, however, are not everywhere quite reliable, may be found in Hatch's Essays in Biblical Greek, 1889. Hatch has taken up again the hypothesis of earlier scholars, that there were very probably in the first and second centuries systematised extracts from the Old Testament (see p. 203-214). The hypothesis is not yet quite established (see Wrede, above work, p. 65), but yet it is hardly to be rejected. The Jewish catechetical and missionary instruction in the Diaspora needed such collections, and their existence seem to be proved by the Christian Apologies and the Sybilline books.

2 It is an extremely important fact that the words of the Lord were quoted and applied in their literal sense (that is chiefly for the statement of Christian morality) by Ecclesiastical authors, almost without exception, up to and inclusive of Justin. It was different with the theologians of the age, that is the Gnostics, and the Fathers from Irenæus.

damental words of God. This furnished the conditions for turning them to account in the way we have stated, The following are the most important points of view under which the Old Testament was used. (1) The Monotheistic cosmology and view of nature were borrowed from it (see, for example, 1 Clem.). (2) It was used to prove that the appearance and entire history of Jesus had been foretold centuries, nay, thousands of years beforehand, and that the founding of a new people gathered out of all nations had been predicted and prepared for from the very beginning. [1] (3) It was used as a means of verifying all principles and institutions of the Christian Church, — the spiritual worship of God without images, the abolition of all ceremonial legal precepts, baptism, etc. (4) The Old Testament was used for purposes of exhortation according to the formula *a minori ad majus;* if God then punished and rewarded this or that in such a way, how

---

[1] Justin was not the first to do so, for it had already been done by the so-called Barnabas (see especially c. 13) and others On the proofs from prophecy see my Texte und Unters. Bd. I. 3. pp. 56-74. The passage in the Praed. Petri (Clem. Strom. VI. 15. 128) is very complete : Ἡμεῖς ἀναπτίξαντες τὰς βίβλους ἃς εἴχομεν τῶν προφητῶν, ἃ μὲν διὰ παραβολῶν. ἃ δὲ διὰ αἰνιγμάτων, ἃ δὲ αὐθεντικῶς καὶ αὐτολεξεὶ τὸν Χριστὸν Ἰησοῦν ὀνομαζόντων, εὕρομεν καὶ τὴν παρουσίαν αὐτοῦ καὶ τὸν θάνατον καὶ τὸν σταυρὸν καὶ τὰς λοιπάς κολάσεις πάσας, ὃσας ἐποίησαν αὐτῷ οἱ Ἰουδαῖοι, καὶ τὴν ἔγερσιν καὶ τὴν εἰς οὐρανοὺς ἀνάληψιν πρὸ τοῦ Ἱεροσόλυμα κριθῆναι, καθὼς ἐγέγραπτο ταῦτα πάντα ἃ ἔδει αὐτὸν παθεῖν καὶ μετ' αὐτὸν ἃ ἔσται· ταῦτα οὖν ἐπιγνόντες ἐπιστεύσαμεν τῷ θεῷ διὰ τῶν γεγραμμένων εἰς αὐτόν. With the help of the Old Testament the teachers dated back the Christian religion to the beginning of the human race, and joined the preparations for the founding of the Christian community with the creation of the world. The Apologists were not the first to do so, for Barnabas and Hermas, and before these, Paul, the author of the Epistle to the Hebrews, and others had already done the same. This was undoubtedly to the cultured classes one of the most impressive articles in the missionary preaching. The Christian religion in this way got a hold which the others — with the exception of the Jewish—lacked. But for that very reason, we must guard against turning it into a formula, that the Gentile Christians had comprehended the Old Testament essentially through the scheme of prediction and fulfilment. The Old Testament is certainly the book of predictions, but for that very reason the complete revelation of God which needs no additions and excludes subsequent changes. The historical fulfilment only proves to the world the truth of those revelations. Even the scheme of shadow and reality is yet entirely out of sight. In such circumstances the question necessarily arises, as to what independent meaning and significance Christ's appearance could have, apart from that confirmation of the Old Testament. But, apart from the Gnostics, a surprisingly long time passed before this question was raised, that is to say, it was not raised till the time of Irenæus.

much more may we expect, who now stand in the last days, and have received the κλῆσις τῆς ἐπαγγελίας. (5) It was proved from the Old Testament that the Jewish nation is in error, and either never had a covenant with God or has lost it, that it has a false apprehension of God's revelations, and therefore has, now at least, no longer any claim to their possession. But beyond all this, (6) there were in the Old Testament books, above all, in the Prophets and in the Psalms, a great number of sayings—confessions of trust in God and of help received from God, of humility and holy courage, testimonies of a world-overcoming faith and words of comfort, love and communion—which were too exalted for any cavilling, and intelligible to every spiritually awakened mind. Out of this treasure which was handed down to the Greeks and Romans, the Church edified herself, and in the perception of its riches was largely rooted the conviction that the holy book must in every line contain the highest truth.

The point mentioned under (5) needs, however, further explanation. The self-consciousness of the Christian community of being the people of God, must have been, above all, expressed in its position towards Judaism, whose mere existence —even apart from actual assaults—threatened that consciousness most seriously. A certain antipathy of the Greeks and Romans towards Judaism co-operated here with a law of self-preservation. On all hands, therefore, Judaism as it then existed was abandoned as a sect judged and rejected by God, as a society of hypocrites,[1] as a synagogue of Satan,[2] as a people seduced by an evil angel,[3] and the Jews were declared to

1 See Διδαχή, 8.
2 See the Revelation of John II. 9 : III. 9; but see also the "Jews" in the Gospels of John and of Peter. The latter exonerates Pilate almost completely, and makes the Jews and Herod responsible for the crucifixion.
3 See Barn. 9. 4. In the second epistle of Clement the Jews are called: "οἱ δοκοῦντες ἔχειν θεὸν," cf. Præd. Petri in Clem., Strom. VI. 5. 41 : μηδὲ κατὰ Ἰουδαίους σέβεσθε· καὶ γὰρ ἐκεῖνοι μόνοι οἰόμενοι τὸν θεὸν γιγνώσκειν οὐκ ἐπίστανται, λατρεύοντες ἀγγέλοις καὶ ἀρχαγγέλοις, μηνὶ καὶ σελήνῃ, καὶ ἐὰν μὴ σελήνη φανῇ, σάββατον οὐκ ἄγουσι τὸ λεγόμενον πρῶτον, οὐδὲ νεομηνίαν ἄγουσιν, οὐδὲ ἄζυμα, οὐδὲ ἑορτήν, οὐδὲ μεγάλην ἡμέραν. (Cf. Diognet. 34.) Even Justin does not judge the Jews more favourably than the Gentiles, but less favourably; see Apol. I. 37, 39, 43, 34, 47, 53, 60. On the other hand, Aristides (Apol. c. 14, especially

have no further right to the possession of the Old Testament. Opinions differed, however, as to the earlier history of the nation and its relation to the true God. While some denied that there ever had been a covenant of salvation between God and this nation, and in this respect recognised only an intention of God,[1] which was never carried out because of the idolatry of the people, others admitted in a hazy way that a relation did exist; but even they referred all the promises of the Old Testament to the Christian people.[2] While the former saw in the observance of the letter of the law, in the case of circumcision, sabbath, precepts as to food, etc., a proof of the special devilish temptation to which the Jewish people succumbed,[3] the latter saw in circumcision a sign[4] given by God, and in virtue of certain considerations acknowledged that the literal observance of the law was for the time God's intention and command, though righteousness never came from such observance. Yet even they saw in the spiritual the alone true sense, which the Jews had denied, and were of opinion that the burden of ceremonies was a pædagogic necessity with reference to a people stiff-necked and prone to idolatry, *i. e.,* a defence of monotheism, and gave an interpretation to the sign of circumcision which made it no longer a blessing, but rather the mark for the execution of judgment on Israel.[5]

in the Syrian text) is much more friendly disposed to the Jews and recognises them more. The words of Pionius against and about the Jews, in the "Acta Pionii," c. 4, are very instructive.

1 Barn. 4. 6. f.: 14. 1 f. The author of Præd. Petri must have had a similar view of the matter.

2 Justin in the Dialogue with Trypho.

3 Barn. 9 f. It is a thorough misunderstanding of Barnabas' position towards the Old Testament to suppose it possible to pass over his expositions, c. 6-10, as oddities and caprices, and put them aside as indifferent or unmethodical. There is nothing here unmethodical, and therefore nothing arbitrary. Barnabas' strictly spiritual idea of God, and the conviction that all (Jewish) ceremonies are of the devil, compel his explanations. These are so little ingenious conceits to Barnabas that, but for them, he would have been forced to give up the Old Testament altogether. The account, for example, of Abraham having circumcised his slaves would have forced Barnabas to annul the whole authority of the Old Testament if he had not succeeded in giving it a particular interpretation. He does this by combining other passages of Genesis with the narrative, and then finding in it no longer circumcision, but a prediction of the crucified Christ.

4 Barn. 9. 6: ἀλλ' ἐρεῖς· καὶ μὴν περιτέτμηται ὁ λαὸς εἰς σφραγῖδα.

5 See the expositions of Justin in the Dial. (especially, 16, 18, 20, 30, 40-

Israel was thus at all times the pseudo-Church. The older people does not in reality precede the younger people, the Christians, even in point of time; for though the Church appeared only in the last days, it was foreseen and created by God from the beginning. The younger people is therefore really the older, and the new law rather the original law. [1] The Patriarchs, Prophets, and men of God, however, who were favoured with the communication of God's words, have nothing inwardly in common with the Jewish people. They are God's elect who were distinguished by a holy walk, and must be regarded as the forerunners and fathers of the Christian people. [2] To the question how such holy men appeared exclusively, or almost exclusively, among the Jewish people, the documents preserved to us yield no answer.

§ 5. The Knowledge of God and of the World. Estimate of the World.

The knowledge of faith was, above all, the knowledge of God as one, supramundane, spiritual, [3] and almighty ($\pi\alpha\nu\tau o$-$\kappa\rho\acute{\alpha}\tau\omega\rho$); God is creator and governor of the world and there-

---

46); Von Engelhardt, "Christenthum Justin's", p. 429. ff. Justin has the three estimates side by side. (1) That the ceremonial law was a pædagogic measure of God with reference to a stiff-necked people, prone to idolatry. (2) That it—like circumcision—was to make the people conspicuous for the execution of judgment, according to the Divine appointment. (3) That in the ceremonial legal worship of the Jews is exhibited the special depravity and wickedness of the nation. But Justin conceived the Decalogue as the natural law of reason, and therefore definitely distinguished it from the ceremonial law.

1 See Ztschr für K. G. I., p. 330 f.

2 This is the unanimous opinion of all writers of the post-Apostolic age. Christians are the true Israel; and therefore all Israel's predicates of honour belong to them. They are the twelve tribes, and therefore Abraham, Isaac and Jacob, are the Fathers of the Christians. This idea, about which there was no wavering, cannot everywhere be traced back to the Apostle Paul. The Old Testament men of God were in a certain measure Christians. See Ignat. Magn. 8. 2 : οἱ προφῆται κατὰ Χριστὸν Ἰησοῦν ἔζησαν.

3 God was naturally conceived and represented as corporeal by uncultured Christians, though not by these alone, as the later controversies prove (e. g., Orig. contra Melito; see also Tertull. De anima). In the case of the cultured, the idea of a corporeality of God may be traced back to Stoic influences; in the case of the uncultured, popular ideas co-operated with the sayings of the Old Testament literally understood, and the impression of the Apocalyptic images.

fore the Lord.[1] But as he created the world a beautiful
ordered whole (monotheistic view of nature)[2] for the sake
of man,[3] he is at the same time the God of goodness and
redemption (θεὸς σωτήρ), and the true faith in God and knowledge of him as the Father,[4] is made perfect only in the

---

1 See Joh. IV. 22; ἡμεῖς προσκυνοῦμεν ὃ οἴδαμεν. 1 Clem. 59. 3. 4; Herm.
Mand. I; Præd. Petri in Clem. Strom. VI. 5. 9: γινώσκετε ὅτι εἷς θεός ἐστιν,
ὃς ἀρχὴν πάντων ἐποίησεν, καὶ τέλους ἐξουσίαν ἔχων. Aristides Apol. 15 (Syr.):
" The Christians know and believe in God, the creator of heaven and
earth". Chap. 16: " Christians as men who know God, pray to him for
things which it becomes him to give and them to receive". (Similarly
Justin). From very many old Gentile Christian writings we hear it as a
cry of joy· " We know God the Almighty; the night of blindness is
past" (see, e. g., 2 Clem. c. 1). God is δεσπότης, a designation which is
very frequently used (it is rare in the New Testament). Still more frequently do we find κύριος. As the Lord and Creator, God is also called
the Father (of the world) so 1 Clem. 19. 2: ὁ πατὴρ καὶ κτίστης τοῦ σύμ-
παντος κόσμου. 35. 3: δημιουργὸς καὶ πατὴρ τῶν αἰώνων. This use of the name
Father for the supreme God, was, as is well known, familiar to the Greeks,
but the Christians alone were in earnest with the name The creation out of
nothing was made decidedly prominent by Hermas, see Vis. I. 1. 6, and my
notes on the passage. In the Christian Apocrypha, in spite of the vividness of
the idea of God, the angels play the same rôle as in the Jewish, and as in the
current Jewish speculations. According to Hermas, e. g., all God's actions are
mediated by special angels, nay, the Son of God himself is represented by a
special angel, viz , Michael, and works by him. But outside the Apocalypses
there seems to have been little interest in the good angels.
2 See, for example, 1 Clem. 20.
3 This is frequent in the Apologists; see also Diogn. 10. 2: but Hermas, Vis. II. 4. 1 (see also Cels. ap. Orig. IV. 23) says: διὰ τὴν ἐκκλησίαν
ὁ κόσμος κατηρτίσθη (cf. I. 1. 6. and my notes on the passage). Aristides
(Apol. 16) declares it as his conviction that "the beautiful things", that
is, the world, are maintained only for the sake of Christians; see, besides,
the words (I. c.); " I have no doubt, that the earth continues to exist
(only) on account of the prayers of the Christians." Even the Jewish
Apocalyptists wavered between the formulæ, that the world was created
for the sake of man, and for the sake of the Jewish nation. The two
are not mutually exclusive. The statement in the Eucharistic prayer of
Didache, 9. 3, ἔκτισας τὰ πάντα ἕνεκεν τοῦ ὀνόματός σου, is singular.
4 God is named the Father, (1) in relation to the Son (very frequent), (2) as
Father of the world (see above), (3) as the merciful one who has proved his
goodness, declared his will, and called Christians to be his sons (1 Clem. 23.
1; 29. 1; 2 Clem. 1. 4; 8. 4; 10. 1; 14. 1; see the index to Zahn's edition of
the Ignatian Epistles; Didache, 1. 5; 9. 2. 3; 10. 2). The latter usage is not
very common; it is entirely wanting, for example, in the Epistle of Barnabas.
Moreover, God is also called πατὴρ τῆς ἀληθείας, as the source of all truth (2
Clem. 3. 1 : 20. 5 : θεὸς τ. ἀληθείας). The identity of the Almighty God of creation with the merciful God of redemption is the tacit presupposition of all
declarations about God, in the case of both the cultured and the uncultured. It
is also frequently expressed (see above all the Pastoral Epistles), most frequently by Hermas (Vis. I. 3. 4), so far as the declaration about the creation
of the world is there united in the closest way with that about the creation

knowledge of the identity of the God of creation and the God of redemption. Redemption, however, was necessary, because at the beginning humanity and the world alike fell under the dominion of evil demons, [1] of the evil one. There was no

of the Holy Church. As to the designation of God in the Roman Symbol, as the " Father Almighty", that threefold exposition just given, may perhaps allow it.

1 The present dominion of evil demons, or of one evil demon, was just as generally presupposed as man's need of redemption, which was regarded as a result of that dominion. The conviction that the world's course (the πολιτεία ἐν τῷ κόσμῳ: the Latins afterwards used the word Sæculum) is determined by the devil, and that the dark one (Barnabas) has dominion, comes out most prominently where eschatological hopes obtain expression. But where salvation is thought of as knowledge and immortality, it is ignorance and frailty from which men are to be delivered. We may here also assume with certainty that these, in the last instance, were traced back by the writers to the action of demons. But it makes a very great difference whether the judgment was ruled by fancy which saw a real devil everywhere active, or whether, in consequence of theoretic reflection, it based the impression of universal ignorance and mortality on the assumption of demons who have produced them. Here again we must note the two series of ideas which intertwine and struggle with each other in the creeds of the earliest period; the traditional religious series, resting on a fanciful view of history—it is essentially identical with the Jewish Apocalyptic: see, for example, Barn. 4—and the empiric moralistic, (see 2 Clem. I. 2-7, as a specially valuable discussion, or Praed. Petri in Clem., Strom. VI. 5, 39, 40), which abides by the fact that men have fallen into ignorance, weakness and death (2 Clem. 1. 6: ὁ βίος ἡμῶν ὅλος ἄλλο οὐδὲν ἤν εἰ μὴ θάνατος). But, perhaps, in no other point, with the exception of the ἀνάστασις σαρκὸς, has the religious conception remained so tenacious as in this, and it decidedly prevailed, especially in the epoch with which we are now dealing. Its tenacity may be explained, among other things, by the living impression of the polytheism that surrounded the communities on every side. Even where the national gods were looked upon as dead idols—and that was perhaps the rule, see Praed. Petri, I. c.; 2 Clem. 3. 1; Didache, 6—one could not help assuming that there were mighty demons operative behind them, as otherwise the frightful power of idolatry could not be explained. But on the other hand, even a calm reflection and a temper unfriendly to all religious excess must have welcomed the assumption of demons who sought to rule the world and man. For by means of this assumption, which was wide-spread even among the Greeks, humanity seemed to be unburdened, and the presupposed capacity for redemption could therefore be justified in its widest range. From the assumption that the need of redemption was altogether due to ignorance and mortality, there was but one step, or little more than one step, to the assumption that the need of redemption was grounded in a condition of man for which he was not responsible, that is, in the flesh. But this step, which would have led either to dualism (heretical Gnosis) or to the abolition of the distinction between natural and moral, was not taken within the main body of the Church. The eschatological series of ideas with its thesis that death, evil and sin entered into humanity at a definite historical moment, when the demons took possession of the world, drew a limit which was indeed overstepped at particular points, but was in the end respected. We have therefore the remarkable fact that, on the one hand, early Christian

universally accepted theory as to the origin of this dominion;
but the sure and universal conviction was that the present
condition and course of the world is not of God, but is of
the devil. Those, however, who believed in God, the almighty creator, and were expecting the transformation of the
earth, as well as the visible dominion of Christ upon it, could
not be seduced into accepting a dualism in principle (God
and devil: spirit and matter). Belief in God, the creator,
and eschatological hopes, preserved the communities from the theoretic dualism that so readily suggested itself, which they
slightly touched in many particular opinions, and which threatened to dominate their feelings. The belief that the world
is of God and therefore good, remained in force A distinction was made between the present constitution of the
world, which is destined for destruction, and the future order
of the world which will be a glorious "restitutio in integrum".
The theory of the world as an articulated whole which had
already been proclaimed by the Stoics, and which was strengthened by Christian monotheism, would not, even if it had
been known to the uncultured, have been vigorous enough to
cope with the impression of the wickedness of the course of

(Jewish) eschatology called forth and maintained a disposition in which the
Kingdom of God, and that of the world, (Kingdom of the devil) were felt to be
absolutely opposed (practical dualism), while, on the other hand, it rejected
theoretic dualism. Redemption through Christ, however, was conceived in
the eschatological Apocalyptic series of ideas as essentially something entirely in the future, for the power of the devil was not broken, but rather increased (or it was virtually broken in believers and increased in unbelievers),
by the first advent of Christ, and therefore the period between the first and
second advent of Christ belongs to οὗτος ὁ αἰών (see Barn. 2. 4; Herm. Sim I;
2. Clem. 6. 3: ἔστιν δὲ οὗτος ὁ αἰὼν καὶ ὁ μέλλων δύο ἐχθροί· οὗτος λέγει μοιχείαν καὶ
φθορὰν καὶ φιλαργουρίαν καὶ ἀπάτην, ἐκεῖνος δὲ τούτοις ἀποστάσσεται; Ignat. Magn.
5. 2). For that very reason, the second coming of Christ must, as a matter of
course, be at hand, for only through it could the first advent get its full value.
The painful impression that nothing had been outwardly changed by Christ's
first advent (the heathen, moreover, pointed this out in mockery to the suffering Christians), must be destroyed by the hope of his speedy coming again.
But the first advent had its independent significance in the series of ideas
which regarded Christ as redeeming man from ignorance and mortality; for
the knowledge was already given, and the gift of immortality could only of
course be dispensed after this life was ended, but then immediately. The hope
of Christ's return was therefore a superfluity, but was not felt or set aside as
such, because there was still a lively expectation of Christ's earthly Kingdom.

this world, and the vulgarity of all things material. But the firm belief in the omnipotence of God, and the hope of the world's transformation grounded on the Old Testament, conquered the mood of absolute despair of all things visible and sensuous, and did not allow a theoretic conclusion, in the sense of dualism in principle, to be drawn from the practical obligation to renounce the world, or from the deep distrust with regard to the flesh.

§ 6. *Faith in Jesus Christ.*

1. As surely as redemption was traced back to God himself, so surely was Jesus (ὁ σωτὴρ ἡμῶν) held to be the mediator of it. Faith in Jesus was therefore, even for Gentile Christians, a compendium of Christianity. Jesus is mostly designated with the same name as God, [1] ὁ κύριος (ἡμῶν), for we must remember the ancient use of this title. All that has taken place or will take place with reference to salvation, is traced back to the "Lord." The carelessness of the early Christian writers about the bearing of the word in particular cases, [2] shews that in a religious relation, so far as there was reflection on the gift of salvation, Jesus could directly take the place of God. The invisible God is the author, Jesus the revealer and mediator, of all saving blessings. The final subject is presented in the nearest subject, and there is frequently no occasion for expressly distinguishing them, as the range and contents of the revelation of salvation in Jesus

---

1 No other name adhered to Christ so firmly as that of κύριος: see a specially clear evidence of this, Novatian de trinit. 30, who argues against the Adoptian and Modalistic heretics thus: " Et in primis illud retorquendum in istos, qui duorum nobis deorum controversiam facere præsumunt. Scriptum est, quod negare non possunt: " Quoniam unus est dominus." De Christo ergo quid sentiunt? Dominum esse, aut illum omnino non esse? Sed dominum illum omnino non dubitant. Ergo si vera est illorum ratiocinatio, jam duo sunt domini." On κύριος = δεσπότης, see above, p. 119, note.

2 Specially instructive examples of this are found in the Epistle of Barnabas and the second Epistle of Clement. Clement (Ep. 1) speaks only of faith in God.

coincide with the range and contents of the will of salvation
in God himself. Yet prayers, as a rule, were addressed to
God: at least, there are but few examples of direct prayers
to Jesus belonging to the first century (apart from the prayers in the Act. Joh. of the so-called Leucius). The usual
formula rather reads: θεῷ ἐξομολογούμεθα διὰ 'Ι. Χρ. — θεῷ
δόξα διὰ 'Ι. Χρ. [1]

2. As the Gentile Christians did not understand the significance of the idea that Jesus is the Christ (Messiah), the designation "χριστός" had either to be given up in their communities, or to subside into a mere name. [2] But even where,
through the Old Testament, one was reminded of the meaning of the word, and allowed a value to it, he was far
from finding in the statement that Jesus is the Lord's anointed, a clear expression of the dignity peculiar to him. That
dignity had therefore to be expressed by other means. Nevertheless the eschatological series of ideas connected the Gentile
Christians very closely with the early Christian ideas of faith,
and therefore also with the earliest ideas about Jesus. In the

---

1 See 1 Clem. 59-61. Διδαχή, c. 9. 10. Yet Novatian (de trinit. 14) exactly
reproduces the old idea, "Si homo tantummodo Christus, cur homo in
orationibus mediator invocatur, cum invocatio hominis ad præstandam
salutem inefficax judicetur." As the Mediator, High Priest, etc., Christ
is of course always and everywhere invoked by the Christians, but such
invocations are one thing and formal prayer another. The idea of the
congruence of God's will of salvation with the revelation of salvation
which took place through Christ, was further continued in the idea of
the congruence of this revelation of salvation with the universal preaching
of the twelve chosen Apostles (see above, p. 162 ff.), the root of the
Catholic principle of tradition. But the Apostles never became "οἱ κύριοι,"
though the concepts διδαχὴ (λόγος) κύριου, διδαχὴ (κήρυγμα) τῶν ἀποστόλων
were just as interchangeable as λόγος θεοῦ and λόγος χριστοῦ. The full
formula would be λόγος θεοῦ διὰ 'Ιησοῦ Χριστοῦ διὰ τῶν ἀποστόλων. But as the
subjects introduced by διὰ are chosen and perfect media, religious usage
permitted the abbreviation.
2 In the epistle of Barnabas "Jesus Christ" and "Christ" appear each
once, but "Jesus" twelve times: in the Didache "Jesus Christ" once, "Jesus"
three times. Only in the second half of the second century, if I am not
mistaken, did the designation "Jesus Christ", or "Christ", become the
current one, more and more crowding out the simple "Jesus". Yet the
latter designation—and this is not surprising—appears to have continued
longest in the regular prayers. It is worthy of note that in the Shepherd
there is no mention either of the name Jesus or of Christ. The Gospel
of Peter also says ὁ κύριος where the other Gospels use these names.

confession that God chose [1] and prepared [2] Jesus, that Jesus is the Angel [3] and the servant of God, [4] that he will judge the living and the dead, [5] etc., expression is given to ideas about Jesus, in the Gentile Christian communities, which are borrowed from the thought that he is the Christ called of God and entrusted with an office. [6] Besides, there was a

1 See 1 Clem. 64: ὁ θεὸς, ὁ ἐκλεξάμενος τὸν κύριον Ἰησοῦν Χριστὸν καὶ ἡμᾶς δι᾿ αὐτοῦ εἰς λαὸν περιούσιον δῷη, κ.τ.λ. (It is instructive to note that wherever the idea of election is expressed, the community is immediately thought of, for in point of fact the election of the Messiah has no other aim than to elect or call the community; Barn. 3. 6: ὁ λαὸς ὅν ἡτοίμασεν ἐν τῷ ἠγαπημένῳ αὐτοῦ). Herm. Sim. V. 2: ἐκλεξάμενος δοῦλόν τινα πιστὸν καὶ εὐάρεστον. V. 6. 5. Justin, Dial. 48: μὴ ἀρνεῖσθαι ὅτι οὗτός ἐστιν ὁ Χριστός, ἐὰν φαίνηται ὡς ἄνθρωπος ἐξ ἀνθρώπου γεννηθεὶς καὶ ἐκλογῇ γενόμενος εἰς τὸ Χριστὸν εἶναι ἀποδεικνύηται.

2 See Barn. 14. 5: Ἰησοῦς εἰς τοῦτο ἡτοιμάσθη, ἵνα.... ἡμᾶς λυτρωσάμενος ἐκ τοῦ σκότους διαθῆται ἐν ἡμῖν διαθήκην λόγῳ. The same word concerning the Church, l. c. 3. 6. and 5. 7: αὐτὸς ἑαυτῷ τὸν λαὸν τὸν καινὸν ἑτοιμάζων. 14. 6.

3 "Angel" is a very old designation for Christ (see Justin's Dial.) which maintained itself up to the Nicean controversy, and is expressly claimed for him in Novatian's treatise "de trinit." 11. 25 ff. (the word was taken from Old Testament passages which were applied to Christ). As a rule, however, it is not to be understood as a designation of the nature, but of the office of Christ as such, though the matter was never very clear. There were Christians who used it as a designation of the nature, and from the earliest times we find this idea contradicted (see the Apoc. Sophoniæ, ed. Stern, 1886, IV. fragment, p. 10: "He appointed no Angel to come to us, nor Archangel, nor any power, but he transformed himself into a man that he might come to us for our deliverance". Cf. the remarkable parallel, ep. ad. Diagn. 7. 2: .... οὐ, καθάπερ ἄν τις εἰκάσειεν ἄνθρωπος, ὑπηρέτην τινὰ πέμψας ἢ ἄγγελον ἢ ἄρχοντα ἤ τινα τῶν διεπόντων τὰ ἐπίγεια ἤ τινα τῶν πεπιστευμένων τὰς ἐν οὐρανοῖς διοικήσεις, ἀλλ᾿ αὐτὸν τὸν τεχνίτην καὶ δημιουργὸν τῶν ὅλων, κ.τ.λ.) Yet it never got the length of a great controversy, and as the Logos doctrine gradually made way, the designation "Angel" became harmless and then vanished.

4 Παῖς (after Isaiah): this designation, frequently united with Ἰησοῦς and with the adjectives ἅγιος and ἠγαπημένος (see Barn. 3, 6: 4, 3: 4, 8: Valent. ap. Clem. Alex., Strom. VI. 6. 52, and the Ascensio Isaiæ), seems to have been at the beginning a usual one. It sprang undoubtedly from the Messianic circle of ideas, and at its basis lies the idea of election. It is very interesting to observe how it was gradually put into the background and finally abolished It was kept longest in the liturgical prayers: see 1 Clem. 59. 2; Barn. 61: 9. 2; Acts iii. 13. 26; iv. 27. 30; Didache, 9. 2. 3; Mart. Polyc. 14. 20; Act. Pauli et Theclæ, 17. 24; Sibyl. I v. 324. 331 364; Diogn. 8, 9, 10: ὁ ἀγαπητὸς παῖς, 9. 1; also Ep. Orig. ad Afric. init; Clem. Strom. VII. 1. 4: ὁ μονογενὴς παῖς, and my note on Barn. 6. 1 In the Didache (9. 2) Jesus as well as David is in one statement called "Servant of God". Barnabas, who calls Christ the "Beloved", uses the same expression for the Church (4. 1. 9); see also Ignat. ad Smyrn. inscr.

5 See the old Roman Symbol and Acts X. 42; 2 Tim. IV 1; Barn. 7. 2; Polyc. Ep. 2. 1; 2 Clem. 2. 1; Hegesipp. in Euseb., H. E. III. 20. 6: Justin Dial. 118.

6 There could of course be no doubt that Christ meant the "anointed"

very old designation handed down from the circle of the disciples, and specially intelligible to Gentile Christians, though
not frequent and gradually disappearing, viz., "the Master". [1]

3. But the earliest tradition not only spoke of Jesus as
κύριος, σωτήρ, and διδάσκαλος, but as "ὁ υἱὸς τοῦ θεοῦ", and this
name was firmly adhered to in the Gentile Christian communities. [2] It followed immediately from this that Jesus belongs
to the sphere of God, and that, as is said in the earliest
preaching known to us, [3] one must think of him " ὡς περὶ θεοῦ ".
This formula describes in a classic manner the indirect "theologia Christi" which we find unanimously expressed in all
witnesses of the earliest epoch. [4] We must think about Christ

---

(even Aristides Apol. 2 fin , if Nestle's correction is right, Justin's Apol.
I. 4. and similar passages do not justify doubt on that point). But the
meaning and the effect of this anointing was very obscure. Justin says
(Apol. II. 6): Χριστὸς μὲν κατὰ τὸ κεχρῖσθαι καὶ κοσμῆσαι τὰ πάντα δι᾽ αὐτοῦ
τὸν θεὸν λέγεται, and therefore (see Dial 76 fin.) finds in this designation
an expression of the cosmic significance of Christ.

1 See the Apologists Apost. K O. (Texte v. Unters. II. 5. p. 25).
προορῶντας τοὺς λόγους τοῦ διδασκάλου ἡμῶν, ibid, p. 28: ὅτε ἤτησεν ὁ διδάσκαλος
τὸν ἄρτον, ibid. p. 30: προέλεγεν, ὅτε ἐδίδασκεν. Apost. Constit. (original writing) III. 6: αὐτὸς ὁ διδάσκαλος ἡμῶν καὶ κύριος. III. 7: ὁ κύριος καὶ διδάσκαλος
ἡμῶν εἶπεν. III. 19: III. 20: V. 12: 1 Clem. 13. 1 .... τῶν λόγων τοῦ κυρίου
Ἰησοῦ, οὓς ἐλάλησεν διδάσκων. Polyc. Ep 2: μνημονεύοντες ὧν εἶπεν ὁ κυρίος
διδάσκων Ptolem. ad Floram. 5: ἡ διδασκαλία τοῦ σωτῆρος.

2 The baptismal formula, which had been naturalised everywhere in
the communities at this period, preserved it above all. The addition of
ἴδιος, πρωτότοκος is worthy of notice. Μονογενής (= the only begotten and
also the beloved) is not common; it is found only in John, in Justin, in
the Symbol of the Romish Church, and in Mart. Polyc. (Diogn. 10 3).

3 The so-called second Epistle of Clement begins with the words:
Ἀδελφοί, οὕτως δεῖ ἡμᾶς φρονεῖν περὶ Ἰησοῦ, ὡς περὶ θεοῦ, ὡς περὶ κριτοῦ ζώντων
καὶ νεκρῶν, (this order in which the Judge appears as the higher is also
found in Barn. 7. 2), καὶ οὐ δεῖ ἡμᾶς μικρὰ φρονεῖν περὶ τῆς σωτηρίας ἡμῶν· ἐν τῷ
γὰρ φρονεῖν ἡμᾶς μικρὰ περὶ αὐτοῦ, μικρὰ καὶ ἐλπίζομεν λαβεῖν. This argumen-
tation (see also the following verses up to II. 7) is very instructive; for
it shews the grounds on which the φρονεῖν περὶ αὐτοῦ ὡς περὶ θεοῦ, was
based. H. Schultz (L. v. d. Gottheit Christi, p. 25 f.) very correctly
remarks: "In the second Epistle of Clement, and in the Shepherd, the
Christological interest of the writer ends in obtaining the assurance, through
faith in Christ as the world-ruling King and Judge, that the community of
Christ will receive a glory corresponding to its moral and ascetic works.

4 Pliny in his celebrated letter (96), speaks of a "Carmen dicere Christo
quasi deo" on the part of the Christians. Hermas has no doubt that the Chosen
Servant, after finishing his work, will be adopted as God's Son, and therefore
has been destined from the beginning, εἰς ἐξουσίαν μεγάλην καὶ κυριότητα (Sim. V.
6. 1). But that simply means that he is now in a Divine sphere, and that one
must think of him as of God But there was no unanimity beyond that. The for-

as we think about God, because, on the one hand, God had
exalted him, and committed to him as Lord, judgment over

mula says nothing about the nature or constitution of Jesus. It might indeed
appear from Justin's dialogue that the direct designation of Jesus as θεός (not
as ὁ θεός) was common in the communities; but not only are there some passages in Justin himself to be urged against this, but also the testimony of
other writers. Θεός, even without the article, was in no case a usual designation
for Jesus. On the contrary, it was always quite definite occasions which led
them to speak of Christ as of a God, or as God In the first place there were
Old Testament passages such as Ps. XLV. 8 : CX. 1 f., etc., which, as soon as
they were interpreted in relation to Christ, led to his getting the predicate θεός.
These passages, with many others taken from the Old Testament, were used
in this way by Justin. Yet it is very well worth noting, that the author of the
Epistle of Barnabas avoided this expression, in a passage which must have
suggested it. (12, 10, 11 on Ps. CX. 4). The author of the Didache calls him
"ὁ θεὸς Δάβιδ" on the basis of the above psalm. It is manifestly therefore in
liturgical formulæ of exalted paradox, or living utterances of religious feeling
that Christ is called God. See Ignat. ad Rom. 6. 3 ; ἐπιτρέψατέ μοι μιμητὴν εἶναι
τοῦ πάθους τοῦ θεοῦ μου (the μου here should be observed); ad. Eph. 1. 1 :
ἀναζωπυρήσαντες ἐν αἵματι θεοῦ : Tatian Orat. 13 : διάκονος τοῦ πεπονθότος θεοῦ. As to
the celebrated passage 1 Clem ad Cor. 2. 10 : τὰ παθήματα αὐτοῦ (the αὐτοῦ
refers to θεός) we may perhaps observe that that ὁ θεός stands far apart. However, such a consideration is hardly in place. The passages just adduced
shew that precisely the union of suffering (blood, death) with the concept
"God"—and only this union—must have been in Christendom from a very
early period; see Acts XX. 28 . . . . τὴν ἐκκλησίαν τοῦ θεοῦ ἣν περιεποιήσατο διὰ τοῦ
αἵματος τοῦ ἰδίου, and from a later period, Melito, Fragm. (in Routh Rel. Sacra
I. 122); ὁ θεὸς πέπονθεν ὑπὸ δεξιᾶς Ἰσραηλιτίδος ; Anonym. ap. Euseb. H E. V. 28.
11 ; ὁ εὔσπλαγχνος θεὸς καὶ κύριός ἡμῶν Ἰησοῦς Χριστὸς οὐκ ἐβούλετο ἀπολέσθαι μάρτυρα
τῶν ἰδίων παθημάτων ; Test. XII. Patriarch. (Levi 4) : ἐπὶ τῷ πάθει τοῦ ὑψίστου ; Tertull. de carne 5 ; "passiones dei", ad Uxor. II. 3 : "sanguine dei". Tertullian also
speaks frequently of the crucifying of God, the flesh of God, the death of God
(see Lightfoot, Clem. of Rome, p. 400 sq.). These formulæ were first subjected
to examination in the Patripassian controversy. They were rejected by
Athanasius, for example, in the fourth century (cf Apollin. II. 13 14; Opp I.
p 758); πῶς οὖν γεγράφατε ὅτι θεὸς ὁ διὰ σάρκος παθὼν καὶ ἀναστάς, ... οὐδαμοῦ
δὲ αἷμα θεοῦ δίχα σαρκὸς παραδεδώκασιν αἱ γραφαὶ ἢ θεὸν διὰ σαρκὸς παθόντα καὶ
ἀναστάντα. They continued in use in the west and became of the utmost significance in the christological controversies of the fifth century. It is not quite
certain whether there is a "theologia Christi" in such passages as Tit. II. 13 :
2 Pet. I. 1 (see the controversies on Rom. IX. 5) Finally, θεός and Christus were
often interchanged in religious discourse (see above) In the so-called second
Epistle of Clement (c. 1. 4) the dispensing of light, knowledge, is traced back
to Christ. It is said of him that, like a Father, he has called us children, he has
delivered us, he has called us into existence out of non-existence, and in this
God himself is not thought of. Indeed he is called (2. 2. 3) the hearer of
prayer and the controller of history; but immediately thereon a saying of the
Lord is introduced as a saying of God (Matt IX. 13). On the contrary, Isaiah
XXIX. 13, is quoted 3. 5) as a declaration of Jesus, and again (13. 4) a saying
of the Lord with the formula : λέγει ὁ θεός. It is Christ who pitied us (3. 1 : 16.
2); he is described simply as the Lord who hath called and redeemed us
(5. 1 : 8. 2 : 9. 5 : etc.). Not only is there frequent mention of the ἐντολαί

the living and the dead, and because, on the other hand, he has brought the knowledge of the truth, called sinful men, delivered them from the dominion of demons, and hath led, or will lead them, out of the night of death and corruption to eternal life. Jesus Christ is "our faith", "our hope", "our

(ἐντάλματα) of Christ, but 6, 7 (see 14. 1) speak directly of a ποιεῖν τὸ θέλημα τοῦ Χριστοῦ. Above all, in the entire first division (up to 9. 5) the religious situation is for the most part treated as if it were something essentially between the believer and Christ. On the other hand, (10. 1), the Father is he who calls (see also 16. 1), who brings salvation (9. 7), who accepts us as Sons (9. 10: 16. 1); he has given us promises (11. 1. 6. 7.); we expect his kingdom, nay, the day of his appearing (12. 1 f.: 6. 9: 9. 6: 11. 7: 12. 1). He will judge the world, etc.; while in 17. 4. we read of the day of Christ's appearing, of his kingdom and of his function of Judge, etc. Where the preacher treats of the relation of the community to God, where he describes the religious situation according to its establishment or its consummation, where he desires to rule the religious and moral conduct, he introduces, without any apparent distinction, now God himself, and now Christ. But this religious view, in which acts of God coincide with acts of Christ, did not, as will be shewn later on, influence the theological speculations of the preacher. We have also to observe that the interchanging of God and Christ is not always an expression of the high dignity of Christ, but, on the contrary, frequently proves that the personal significance of Christ is misunderstood, and that he is regarded only as the dependent revealer of God. All this shews that there cannot have been many passages in the earliest literature where Christ was roundly designated θεός. It is one thing to speak of the blood (death, suffering) of God, and to describe the gifts of salvation brought by Christ as gifts of God, and another thing to set up the proposition that Christ is a God (or God). When, from the end of the second century, one began to look about in the earlier writings for passages ἐν οἷς θεολογεῖται ὁ χριστός, because the matter had become a subject of controversy, one could, besides the Old Testament, point only to the writings of authors from the time of Justin (to apologists and controversialists) as well as to Psalms and odes (see the Anonym. in Euseb. H. E. V. 28. 4-6). In the following passages of the Ignatian Epistles "θεός" appears as a designation of Christ; he is called ὁ θεὸς ἡμῶν in Ephes. inscript.; Rom. inscr. bis 3. 2; Polyc. 8. 3; Eph. 1. 1, αἷμα θεοῦ; Rom. 6. 3, τὸ πάθος τοῦ θεοῦ μου; Eph. 7. 2, ἐν σαρκὶ γενόμενος θεός, in another reading, ἐν ἀνθρώπῳ θεός, Smyrn. I. 1, Ἰ. Χρ. ὁ θεός ὁ οὕτως ὑμᾶς σοφίσας. The latter passage, in which the relative clause must he closely united with "ὁ θεός", seems to form the transition to the three passages (Trall. 7. 1; Smyrn. 6. 1; 10. 1), in which Jesus is called θεος without addition But these passages are critically suspicious, see Lightfoot *in loco*. In the same way the "deus Jesus Christus" in Polyc. Ep 12. 2, is suspicious, and indeed in both parts of the verse. In the first, all Latin codd. have "dei filius," and in the Greek codd. of the Epistle, Christ is nowhere called θεός. We have a keen polemic against the designation of Christ as θεός in Clem. Rom. Homil. XVI. 15 sq.; Ὁ Πέτρος ἀπεκρίθη· ὁ κύριος ἡμῶν οὔτε θεοὺς εἶναι ἐφθέγξατο παρὰ τὸν κτίσαντα τὰ πάντα οὔτε ἑαυτὸν θεὸν εἶναι ἀνηγόρευσεν, υἱὸν δὲ θεοῦ τοῦ τὰ πάντα διακοσμήσαντος τὸν εἰπόντα αὐτὸν εὐλόγως ἐμακάρισεν, καὶ ὁ Σίμων ἀπεκρίνατο· οὐ δοκεῖ σοι οὖν τὸν ἀπὸ θεοῦ θεὸν εἶναι; καὶ ὁ Πέτρος ἔφη· πῶς τοῦτο εἶναι δύναται, φράσον ἡμῖν, τοῦτο γὰρ ἡμεῖς εἰπεῖν σοι οὐ δυνάμεθα, ὅτι μὴ ἠκούσαμεν παρ' αὐτοῦ.

life", and in this sense "our God". The religious assurance
that he is this, for we find no wavering on this point, is the
root of the "theologia Christi"; but we must also remember that the formula "θεός" was inserted beside "χύριος,"
that the "dominus ac deus," was very common at that time,[1]
and that a Saviour (σωτήρ) could only be represented somehow as
a Divine being.[2] Yet Christ never was, as "θεός", placed
on an equality with the Father,[3] — monotheism guarded
against that. Whether he was intentionally and deliberately
identified with Him the following paragraph will shew.

4. The common confession did not go beyond the statements
that Jesus is the Lord, the Saviour, the Son of God, that
one must think of him as of God, that dwelling now with

---

[1] On the further use of the word θεός in antiquity, see above, § 8, p.
120 f.; the formula "θεός ἐκ θεοῦ for Augustus, even 24 years before Christ's
birth; on the formula "dominus ac deus", see John XX. 28; the interchange of these concepts in many passages beside one another in the
anonymous writer (Euseb. H. E. V. 28. 11). Domitian first allowed himself to be called "dominus ac deus". Tertullian, Apol. 10. 11, is very instructive as to the general situation in the second century. Here are brought
forward the different causes which then moved men, the cultured and the
uncultured, to give to this or that personality the predicate of Divinity.
In the third century the designation of "dominus ac deus noster" for
Christ, was very common, especially in the west. (see Cyprian, Pseudo-
Cyprian, Novatian; in the Latin Martyrology a Greek ὁ χύριος is also frequently so translated). But only at this time had the designation come
to be in actual use even for the Emperor. It seems at first sight to follow
from the statements of Celsus (in Orig. c. Cels. III. 22-43) that this Greek
had and required a very strict conception of the Godhead; but his whole
work shews how little that was really the case. The reference to these
facts of the history of the time is not made with the view of discovering
the "theologia Christi" itself in its ultimate roots – these roots lie elsewhere,
in the person of Christ and Christian experience; but that this experience,
before any technical reflection, had so easily and so surely substituted
the new formula instead of the idea of Messiah, can hardly be explained
without reference to the general religious ideas of the time.

[2] The combination of θεός and σωτήρ in the Pastoral Epistles is very
important. The two passages in the New Testament in which perhaps a
direct "theologia Christi" may be recognised, contain likewise the concept
σωτήρ; see Tit. II. 13; προσδεχόμενοι τὴν μακαρίαν ἐλπίδα καὶ ἐπιφάνειαν τῆς δόξης
τοῦ μεγάλου θεοῦ καὶ σωτῆρος ἡμῶν Χριστοῦ Ἰησοῦ (cf. Abbot, Journal of the
Society of Bibl. Lit., and Exeg. 1881. June. p. 3 sq.): 2 Pet. I. 1: ἐν δικαιοσύνῃ
τοῦ θεοῦ ἡμῶν καὶ σωτῆρος. Ἰ. Χρ. In both cases the ἡμῶν should be specially
noted. Besides, θεὸς σωτήρ is also an ancient formula.

[3] A very ancient formula ran "θεὸς καὶ θεὸς υἱός", see Cels. ap. Orig II.
30; Justin, frequently: Alterc. Sim. et Theoph. 4, etc The formula is
equivalent to θεὸς μονογενής (see Joh. I. 18).

God in heaven, he is to be adored as προστάτης καὶ βοηθὸς τῆς ἀσθενείας, and as ἀρχιερεὺς τῶν προσΦορῶν ἡμῶν [as guardian and helper of the weak and as High Priest of our oblations], to be feared as the future Judge, to be esteemed most highly as the bestower of immortality, that he is our hope and our faith. There are found rather, on the basis of that confession, very diverse conceptions of the Person, that is, of the nature of Jesus, beside each other, [1] which collectively exhibit a certain analogy with the Greek theologies, the naive and the philosophic. [2] There was as yet no such thing here as ecclesiastical "doctrines" in the strict sense of the word, but rather conceptions more or less fluid, which were not seldom fashioned *ad hoc*. [3] These may be reduced collectively to two. [4] Jesus was either regarded as the man whom God hath chosen, in whom the Deity or the Spirit of God dwelt, and who, after being tested, was adopted by God and invested with

[1] Such conceptions are found side by side in the same writer. See, for example, the second Epistle of Clement, and even the first.

[2] See § 6, p. 120. The idea of a θεοποίησις was as common as that of the appearances of the gods. In wide circles, however, philosophy had long ago naturalised the idea of the λόγος τοῦ θεοῦ. But now there is no mistaking a new element everywhere. In the case of the Christologies which include a kind of θεοποίησις, it is found in the fact that the deified Jesus was to be recognised not as a Demigod or Hero, but as Lord of the world, equal in power and honour to the Deity. In the case of those Christologies which start with Christ as the heavenly spiritual being, it is found in the belief in an actual incarnation These two articles. as was to be expected, presented difficulties to the Gentile Christians, and the latter more than the former.

[3] This is usually overlooked. Christological doctrinal conceptions are frequently constructed by a combination of particular passages, the nature of which does not permit of combination. But the fact that there was no universally recognised theory about the nature of Jesus till beyond the middle of the second century, should not lead us to suppose that the different theories were anywhere declared to be of equal value, etc., therefore more or less equally valid; on the contrary, everyone, so far as he had a theory at all, included his own in the revealed truth. That they had not yet come into conflict is accounted for, on the one hand, by the fact that the different theories ran up into like formulæ, and could even frequently be directly carried over into one another, and on the other hand, by the fact that their representatives appealed to the same authorities But we must, above all, remember that conflict could only arise after the enthusiastic element, which also had a share in the formation of Christology, had been suppressed, and problems were felt to be such, that is, after the struggle with Gnosticism, or even during that struggle.

[4] Both were clearly in existence in the Apostolic age.

dominion, (Adoptian Christology); [1] or Jesus was regarded as a heavenly spiritual being (the highest after God) who took

1 Only one work has been preserved entire which gives clear expression to the Adoptian Christology, viz., the Shepherd of Hermas (see Sim V. and IX. 1. 12). According to it, the Holy Spirit—it is not certain whether he is identified with the chief Archangel—is regarded as the pre-existent Son of God, who is older than creation, nay, was God's counsellor at creation. The Redeemer is the virtuous man (σάρξ) chosen by God, with whom that Spirit of God was united. As he did not defile the Spirit, but kept him constantly as his companion, and carried out the work to which the Deity had called him, nay, did more than he was commanded, he was in virtue of a Divine decree adopted as a son and exalted to μεγάλη ἐξουσία καὶ κυριότης. That this Christology is set forth in a book which enjoyed the highest honour and sprang from the Romish community, is of great significance. The representatives of this Christology, who in the third century were declared to be heretics, expressly maintained that it was at one time the ruling Christology at Rome and had been handed down by the Apostles. (Anonym. in Euseb. H. E. V. 28. 3, concerning the Artemonites: φασὶ τοὺς μὲν προτέρους ἅπαντας καὶ αὐτοὺς τοὺς ἀποστόλους παρειληφέναι τε καὶ δεδιδαχέναι ταῦτα, ἃ νῦν οὗτοι λέγουσι, καὶ τετηρῆσθαι τὴν ἀλήθειαν τοῦ κηρύγματος μέχρι τῶν χρόνων τοῦ Βίκτορος . .. ἀπὸ δὲ τοῦ διαδόχου αὐτοῦ Ζεφυρίνου παρακεχαράχθαι τὴν ἀλήθειαν). This assertion, though exaggerated, is not incredible after what we find in Hermas. It cannot, certainly, be verified by a superficial examination of the literary monuments preserved to us, but a closer investigation shews that the Adoptian Christology must at one time have been very widespread, that it continued here and there undisturbed up to the middle of the third century (see the Christology in the Acta Archelai. 49, 50), and that it continued to exercise great influence even in the fourth and fifth centuries (see Book II c. 7). Something similar is found even in some Gnostics, e g., Valentinus himself (see Iren. I. 11. 1: καὶ τὸν Χριστὸν δὲ οὐκ ἀπὸ τῶν ἐν τῷ πληρώματι αἰώνων προβεβλῆσθαι. ἀλλὰ ὑπὸ τῆς μητρὸς, ἔξω δὲ γενομένης, κατὰ τὴν γνώμην τῶν κρειττόνων ἀποκεκυῆσθαι μετὰ σκιᾶς τινός Καὶ τοῦτον μέν, ἅτε ἄρρενα ὑπάρχοντα, ἀποκόψαντα ὑφ᾽ ἑαυτοῦ τὴν σκιὰν, ἀναδραμεῖν εἰς τὸ πλήρωμα. The same in the Exc. ex Theodot §§ 22, 23, 32, 33), and the Christology of Basilides presupposes that of the Adoptians. Here also belongs the conception which traces back the genealogy of Jesus to Joseph. The way in which Justin (Dialog. 48, 49, 87 ff.) treats the history of the baptism of Jesus, against the objection of Trypho that a pre-existent Christ would not have needed to be filled with the Spirit of God, is instructive. It is here evident that Justin deals with objections which were raised within the communities themselves to the pre-existence of Christ, on the ground of the account of the baptism. In point of fact, this account (it had, according to very old witnesses, see Resch, Agrapha Christi, p. 307, according to Justin, for example, Dial. 88. 103, the wording: ἅμα τῷ ἀναβῆναι αὐτὸν ἀπὸ τοῦ ποταμοῦ τοῦ Ἰορδάνου, τῆς φωνῆς αὐτοῦ λεχθείσης υἱός μου εἶ σύ, ἐγὼ σήμερον γεγέννηκά σε; see the Cod. D. of Luke. Clem. Alex. etc.) forms the strongest foundation of the Adoptian Christology, and hence it is exceedingly interesting to see how one compounds with it from the second to the fifth century, an investigation which deserves a special monograph. But, of course, the edge was taken off the report by the assumption of the miraculous birth of Jesus from the Holy Spirit, so that the Adoptians in recognising this, already stood with one foot in the camp of their opponents. It is now instructive to see here how the history of the baptism, which originally formed the beginning of the proclamation of Jesus' history, is suppressed in the earliest formulæ, and

flesh, and again returned to heaven after the completion of his work on earth (pneumatic Christology). [1] These two

therefore also in the Romish Symbol, while the birth from the Holy Spirit is expressly stated. Only in Ignatius (ad Smyrn. I; cf. ad Eph. 18. 2) is the baptism taken into account in the confession; but even he has given the event a turn by which it has no longer any significance for Jesus himself (just as in the case of Justin, who concludes from the *resting* of the Spirit in his fulness upon Jesus, that there will be no more prophets among the Jews, spiritual gifts being rather communicated to Christians; compare also the way in which the baptism of Jesus is treated in Joh. I.). Finally, we must point out that in the Adoptian Christology, the parallel between Jesus and all believers who have the Spirit and are Sons of God, stands out very clearly (Cf. Herm. Sim. V. with Mand. III. V. 1 : X. 2 : most important is Sim. V. 6. 7). But this was the very thing that endangered the whole view. Celsus, I. 57, addressing Jesus, asks; " If thou sayest that every man whom Divine Providence allows to be born (this is of course a formulation for which Celsus alone is responsible), is a son of God, what advantage hast thou then over others?" We can see already in the Dialogue of Justin, the approach of the later great controversy, whether Christ is Son of God κατὰ γνώμην, or κατὰ φύσιν, that is, had a pre-existence : "καὶ γὰρ εἰσί τινες, he says, ἀπὸ τοῦ ὑμετέρου γένους ὁμολογοῦντες αὐτὸν Χριστὸν εἶναι, ἄνθρωπον δὲ ἐξ ἀνθρώπων γενόμενον ἀποφαινόμενοι, οἷς οὐ συντίθεμαι" (c. 48).

1 This Christology which may be traced back to the Pauline, but which can hardly have its point of departure in Paul alone, is found also in the Epistle to the Hebrews and in the writings of John, including the Apocalypse, and is represented by Barnabas, 1 and 2. Clem., Ignatius, Polycarp, the author of the Pastoral Epistles, the Authors of Praed. Petri, and the Altercatio Jasonis et Papisci, etc. The Classic formulation is in 2 Clem. 9. 5 : Χριστὸς ὁ κύριος ὁ σώσας ἡμᾶς ὢν μὲν τὸ πρῶτον πνεῦμα ἐγένετο σὰρξ καὶ οὕτως ἡμᾶς ἐκάλεσεν. According to Barnabas (5. 3), the pre-existent Christ is παντὸς τοῦ κόσμου κύριος; to him God said, ἀπὸ καταβολῆς κόσμου, "Let us make man, etc." He is (5. 6) the subject and goal of all Old Testament revelation. He is οὐχὶ υἱὸς ἀνθρώπου ἀλλ: υἱὸς τοῦ θεοῦ, τύπῳ δὲ ἐν σαρκὶ φανερωθείς (12. 10); the flesh is merely the veil of the Godhead, without which man could not have endured the light (5. 10). According to 1 Clement, Christ is τὸ σκῆπτρον τῆς μελαγοσύνης τοῦ θεοῦ (16. 2), who if he had wished could have appeared on earth ἐν κόμπῳ ἀλαζονείας; he is exalted far above the angels (32), as he is the Son of God (παθήματα τοῦ θεοῦ, 2. 1); he hath spoken through the Holy Spirit in the Old Testament (22. 1). It is not certain whether Clement understood Christ under the λόγος μεγαλοσύνης τοῦ θεοῦ (27. 4). According to 2 Clem., Christ and the church are heavenly spiritual existences which have appeared in the last times. Gen. 1. 27 refers to their creation (c. 14; see my note on the passage: We learn from Origen that a very old Theologoumenon indentified Jesus with the ideal of Adam, the church with that of Eve. Similar ideas about Christ are found in Gnostic Jewish Christians); one must think about Christ as about God (I. 1). Ignatius writes (Eph. 7. 2): Εἷς, ἰατρός ἐστιν σαρκικός τε καὶ πνευματικός, γεννητὸς ακὶ ἀγέννητος, ἐν σαρκὶ γενόμενος θεός, ἐν θανάτῳ ζωὴ ἀληθινή, καὶ ἐκ Μαρίας καὶ ἐκ θεοῦ, πρῶτον παθητὸς καὶ τότε ἀπαθής Ἰησοῦς Χριστὸς ὁ κύριος ἡμῶν. As the human predicates stand here first, it might appear as though, according to Ignatius, the man Jesus first became God (ὁ θεός ἡμῶν, Cf. Eph. inscr.: 18. 2). In point of fact, he regards Jesus as Son of God only by his birth from the Spirit; but on the other hand, Jesus is ἀφ' ἑνὸς πατρός προελθῶν (Magn. 7. 2), is λόγος θεοῦ (Magn.

Christologies which are, strictly speaking, mutually exclusive—
the man who has become a God, and the Divine being who
has appeared in human form—yet came very near each other
when the Spirit of God implanted in the man Jesus was conceived as the pre-existent Son of God, [1] and when, on the
other hand, the title, Son of God, for that pneumatic being,
was derived only from the miraculous generation in the flesh;

---

8. 2,) and when Ignatius so often emphasises the truth of Jesus' history
against Docetism (Trall. 9. for example), we must assume that he shares
the thesis with the Gnostics that Jesus is by nature a spiritual being. But
it is well worthy of notice that Ignatius, as distinguished from Barnabas and
Clement, really gives the central place to the historical Jesus Christ, the Son
of God and the Son of Mary, and his work. The like is found only in Irenæus.
The pre-existence of Christ is presupposed by Polycarp. (Ep. 7. 1); but, like
Paul, he strongly emphasises a real exaltation of Christ (2. 1). The author of
Praed. Petri calls Christ the λόγος (Clem. Strom. I. 29, 182). As Ignatius calls
him this also, as the same designation is found in the Gospel, Epistles, and
Apocalypse of John (the latter a Christian adaptation of a Jewish writing), in
the Act. Joh (see Zahn, Acta Joh. p. 220), finally, as Celsus (II. 31) says quite
generally, "The Christians maintain that the Son of God is at the same time
his incarnate Word", we plainly perceive that this designation for Christ was
not first started by professional philosophers (see the Apologists, for example,
Tatian, Orat. 5, and Melito Apolog. fragm. in the Chron. pasch. p. 483, ed.
Dindorf: Χριστὸς ὤν θεοῦ λόγος πρὸ αἰώνων). We do not find in the Johannine
writings such a Logos speculation as in the Apologists, but the current
expression is taken up in order to shew that it has its truth in the appearing
of Jesus Christ. The ideas about the existence of a Divine Logos were very
widely spread; they were driven out of philosophy into wide circles. The
author of the Alterc. Jas. et Papisci conceived the phrase in Gen. 1. 1, ἐν ἀρχῇ,
as equivalent to ἐν υἱῷ (χριστῷ) Jerome. Quæst. hebr. in Gen. p. 3; see Tatian
Orat. 5: θεὸς ἦν ἐν ἀρχῇ τὴν δὲ ἀρχὴν λόγου δύναμιν παρειλήφαμεν. Ignatius
(Eph. 3) also called Christ ἡ γνώμη τοῦ πατρός (Eph. 17: ἡ γνῶσις τοῦ θεοῦ);
that is a more fitting expression than λόγος. The subordination of Christ
as a heavenly being to the Godhead, is seldom or never carefully emphasised, though it frequently comes plainly into prominence. Yet the author of the second Epistle of Clement does not hesitate to place the pre-
existent Christ and the pre-existent church on one level, and to declare
of both that God created them (c. 14). The formulæ φανεροῦσθαι ἐν σαρκί,
or, γίγνεσθαι σάρξ, are characteristic of this Christology It is worthy of
special notice that the latter is found in all those New Testament writers,
who have put Christianity in contrast with the Old Testament religions,
and proclaimed the conquest of that religion by the Christian, viz., Paul,
John, and the author of the Epistle to the Hebrews.

1 Hermas, for example, does this (therefore Link; Christologie des
Hermas, and Weizsäcker, Gott. Gel. Anz. 1886, p. 830, declare his Christology to be directly pneumatic): Christ is then identified with this Holy
Spirit (see Acta Archel. 50), similarly Ignatius (ad Magn. 15): κεκτημένοι
ἀδιάκριτον πνεῦμα, ὅς ἐστιν Ἰησοῦς Χριστὸς. This formed the transition to Gnostic
conceptions on the one hand, to pneumatic Christology on the other.
But in Hermas the real substantial thing in Jesus Christ is the σάρξ.

yet both these seem to have been the rule. [1] Yet, in spite
of all transitional forms, the two Christologies may be clearly
distinguished. Characteristic of the one is the development
through which Jesus is first to become a Godlike Ruler, [2]
and connected therewith, the value put on the miraculous
event at the baptism; of the other, a naive docetism. [3] For
no one as yet thought of affirming two natures in Jesus: [4]

1 Passages may indeed be found in the earliest Gentile Christian literature, in which Jesus is designated Son of God, independently of his
human birth and before it (so in Barnabas, against Zahn), but they are
not numerous. Ignatius very clearly deduces the predicate "Son" from
the birth in the flesh. Zahn, Marcellus, p. 216 ff.

2 The distinct designation "θεοποίησις" is not found, though that may be an
accident Hermas has the thing itself quite distinctly (See Epiph. c. Alog. H.
51. 18: νομίζοντες ἀπὸ Μαρίας καὶ δεῦρο Χριστὸν αὐτὸν καλεῖσθαι καὶ υἱὸν θεοῦ, καὶ εἶναι
μὲν πρότερον ψιλὸν ἄνθρωπον, κατὰ προκοπὴν δὲ εἰληφέναι τὴν τοῦ υἱοῦ τοῦ θεοῦ
προσηγορίαν). The stages of the προκοπή were undoubtedly the birth, baptism
and resurrection. Even the adherents of the pneumatic Christology, could not
at first help recognising that Jesus, through his exaltation, got more than he
originally possessed. Yet in their case, this conception was bound to become
rudimentary, and it really did so.

3 The settlement with Gnosticism prepared a still always uncertain end
for this naive Docetism. Apart from Barn 5. 12, where it plainly appears,
we have to collect laboriously the evidences of it which have not
accidentally either perished or been concealed. In the communities of the
second century there was frequently no offence taken at Gnostic docetism
(see the Gospel of Peter, Clem. Alex., Adumbrat. in Joh. Ep. I. c 1,
[Zahn, Forsch. z Gesch. des N. T.-lichen Kanons, III. p. 87]; "Fertur ergo
in traditionibus, quoniam Johannes ipsum corpus. quod erat extrinsecus,
tangens manum suam in profunda misisse et duritiam carnis nullo modo
reluctatam esse. sed locum manui præbuisse discipuli." Also Acta Joh.
p. 219, ed. Zahn). In spite of all his polemic against "δόκησις" proper,
one can still perceive a "moderate docetism" in Clem Alex., to which
indeed certain narratives in the Canonical Gospels could not but lead.
The so-called Apocryphal literature (Apocryphal Gospels and Acts of
Apostles), lying on the boundary between heretical and common Christianity, and preserved only in scanty fragments and extensive alterations,
was, it appears, throughout favourable to Docetism. But the later recensions
attest that it was read in wide circles.

4 Even such a formulation as we find in Paul (e. g., Rom. I. 3 f. κατὰ σάρκα —
κατὰ πνεῦμα), does not seem to have been often repeated (yet see 1 Clem 32.
2). It is of value to Ignatius only, who has before his mind the full Gnostic
contrast. But even to him we cannot ascribe any doctrine of two natures: for
this requires as its presupposition, the perception that the divinity and humanity are equally essential and important for the personality of the Redeemer Christ. Such insight. however, presupposes a measure and a direction
of reflection which the earliest period did not possess The expression "δύο
οὐσίαι Χριστοῦ" first appears in a fragment of Melito, whose genuineness is not.
however. generally recognised (see my Texte u. Unters. I. 1. 2. p. 257).
Even the definite expression for Christ θεὸς ὢν ὁμοῦ τε καὶ ἄνθρωπος was
fixed only in consequence of the Gnostic controversy.

the Divine dignity appeared rather, either as a gift,[1] or the human nature (σάρξ) as a veil assumed for a time, or as the metamorphosis of the Spirit.[2] The formula that Jesus was a mere man (ψιλὸς ἄνθρωπος), was undoubtedly always, and from the first, regarded as offensive.[3] But the converse formulæ, which identified the person of Jesus in its essence with the Godhead itself, do not seem to have been rejected

---

1 Hermas (Sim. V. 6. 7) describes the exaltation of Jesus, thus: ἵνα καὶ ἡ σάρξ αὕτη, δουλεύσασα τῷ πνεύματι ἀμέμπτως, σχῇ τόπον τινὰ κατασκηνώσεως, καὶ μὴ δόξῃ τὸν μισθὸν τῆς δουλείας αὐτῆς ἀπολωλεκέναι. The point in question is a reward of grace which consists in a position of rank (see Sim. V. 6. 1). The same thing is manifest from the statements of the later Adoptians. (Cf. the teaching of Paul Samosata).

2 Barnabas, e. g., conceives it as a veil (5. 10: εἰ γὰρ μὴ ἦλθεν εν σαρκί, οὐδ᾽ ἄν πως οἱ ἄνθρωποι ἐσώθησαν βλέποντες αὐτόν· ὅτε τὸν μέλλοντα μὴ εἶναι ἥλιον ἐμβλέποντες οὐκ ἰσχύουσιν εἰς τὰς ἀκτῖνας αὐτοῦ ἀντοφθαλμῆσαι). The formulation of the Christian idea in Celsus is instructive (c. Cels. VI. 69): "Since God is great and not easily accessible to the view, he put his spirit in a body which is like our own, and sent it down in order that we might be instructed by it". To this conception corresponds the formula: ἔρχεσθαι (φανεροῦσθαι) εν σαρκί (Barnabas, frequently; Polyc. Ep. 7. 1). But some kind of transformation must also have been thought of (See 2 Clem. 9. 5, and Celsus IV. 18: "Either God, as these suppose, is really transformed into a mortal body...." Apoc. Sophon. ed. Stern. 4 fragm. p. 10; " He has transformed himself into a man who comes to us to redeem us"). This conception might grow out of the formula σάρξ ἐγένετο (Ignat. ad. Eph. 7, 2 is of special importance here). One is almost throughout here satisfied with the σάρξ of Christ. that is the ἀληθεία τῆς σαρκός, against the Heretics (so Ignatius, who was already antignostic in his attitude) There is very seldom any mention of the humanity of Jesus. Barnabas (12), the author of the Didache (c. 10 6. See my note on the passage). and Tatian questioned the Davidic Sonship of Jesus, which was strongly emphasised by Ignatius; nay, Barnabas even expressly rejects the designation "Son of Man" (12. 10;'ίδε πάλιν Ἰησοῦς, οὐχὶ υἱὸς ἀνθρώπου ἀλλὰ υἱὸς τοῦ θεοῦ, τύπῳ δὲ ἐν σαρκὶ φανερωθείς). A docetic thought, however. lies in the assertion that the spiritual being Christ only assumed human flesh, however much the reality of the flesh may be emphasised. The passage 1 Clem. 49. 6, is quite unique: τὸ αἷμα αὐτοῦ ἔδωκεν ὑπὲρ ἡμῶν Ἰησοῦς Χριστὸς ... καὶ τὴν σάρκα ὑπὲρ τῆς σαρκὸς ἡμῶν καὶ τὴν ψυχὴν ὑπὲρ τῶν ψυχῶν ἡμῶν. One would fain believe this an interpolation; the same idea is first found in Irenæus. (V. 1. 1).

3 Even Hermas does not speak of Jesus as ἄνθρωπος (see Link). This designation was used by the representatives of the Adoptian Christology only after they had expressed their doctrine antithetically and developed it to a theory, and always with a certain reservation. The " ἄνθρωπος Χριστὸς Ἰησοῦς" in 1 Tim. II. 5 is used in a special sense The expression ἄνθρωπος for Christ appears twice in the Ignatian Epistles (the third passage Smyrn. 4 2: αὐτοῦ με ἐνδυναμοῦντος τοῦ τελείου ἀνθρώπου γενομένου, apart from the γενομένου, is critically suspicious, as well as the fourth, Eph. 7. 2; see above), in both passages, however, in connections which seem to modify the humanity; see Eph. 20 1: οἰκονομία εἰς τὸν καινὸν ἄνθρωπον Ἰησοῦν Χριστόν; Eph. 20. 2: τῷ υἱῷ ἀνθρώπου καὶ υἱῷ θεοῦ.

with the same decision. [1] Yet such formulæ may have been very rare, and even objects of suspicion, in the leading ecclesiastical circles, at least until after the middle of the second century we can point to them only in documents which hardly found approbation in wide circles. The assumption of the existence of at least one heavenly and eternal spiritual being beside God, was plainly demanded by the Old Testament

[1] See above p. 185, note; p. 189, note. We have no sure evidence that the later so-called Modalism (Monarchianism) had representatives before the last third of the second century; yet the polemic of Justin, Dial. 128, seems to favour the idea, (the passage already presupposes controversies about the personal independence of the pre-existent pneumatic being of Christ beside God; but one need not necessarily think of such controversies within the communities; Jewish notions might be meant, and this, according to Apol. 1. 63, is the more probable) The judgment is therefore so difficult, because there were numerous formulæ in practical use which could be so understood, as if Christ was to be completely identified with the Godhead itself (see Ignat. ad Eph. 7. 2, besides Melito in Otto. Corp. Apol. IX. p. 419, and Noëtus in the Philos. IX. 10, p. 448). These formulæ may, in point of fact, have been so understood, here and there, by the rude and uncultivated. The strongest again is presented in writings whose authority was always doubtful: see the Gospel of the Egyptians (Epiph. H. 62. 2), in which must have stood a statement somewhat to this effect: τὸν αὐτὸν εἶναι πατέρα, τὸν αὐτὸν εἶναι υἱὸν, τὸν αὐτὸν εἶναι ἄγιον πνεῦμα, and the Acta Joh. (ed Zahn, p. 220 f., 240 f.: ὁ ἀγαθὸς ἡμῶν θεὸς ὁ εὔσπλαγχνος, ὁ ἐλεήμων, ὁ ἄγιος, ὁ καθαρός, ὁ ἀμίαντος, ὁ μόνος, ο εἷς, ὁ ἀμετάβλητος, ὁ εἰλικρινής, ὁ ἄδολος, ὁ μὴ ὀργιζόμενος, ὁ πάσης ἡμῖν λεγομένης ἢ νοουμένης προσηγορίας ἀνώτερος καὶ ὑψηλότερος ἡμῶν θεὸς Ἰησοῦς). In the Act. Joh. are found also prayers with the address θεὲ Ἰησοῦ Χριστέ (pp. 242. 247) Even Marcion and a part the Montanists—both bear witness to old traditions—put no value on the distinction between God and Christ; cf. the Apoc. Sophon. A witness to a naive Modalism is found also in the Acta Pionii 9: "Quem deum colis? Respondit: Christum. Polemon (judex): Quid ergo? iste alter est? [the co-defendant Christians had immediately before confessed God the Creator]. Respondit: Non; sed ipse quem et ipsi paullo ante confessi sunt; cf. c. 16. Yet a reasoned Modalism may perhaps be assumed here. See also the Martyr Acts; e. g, Acta Petri, Andræ, Pauli et Dionysiæ 1 (Ruinart, p. 205): ἡμεῖς οἱ Χριστὸν τὸν βασιλέα ἔχομεν, ὅτι ἀληθινὸς θεός ἐστιν καὶ ποιητὴς οὐρανοῦ καὶ γῆς καὶ θαλάσσης. "Oportet me magis deo vivo et vero, regi sæculorum omnium Christo, sacrificium offerre." Act. Nicephor. 3 (p. 285). I take no note of the Testament of the twelve Patriarchs, out of which one can, of course, beautifully verify the strict Modalistic, and even the Adoptian Christology. But the Testamenta are not a primitive or Jewish Christian writing which Gentile Christians have revised, but a Jewish writing christianised at the end of the second century by a Catholic of Modalistic views But he has given us a very imperfect work, the Christology of which exhibits many contradictions. It is instructive to find Modalism in the theology of the Simonians, which was partly formed according to Christian ideas; see Irenæus I 23 1. "hic igitur a multis quasi deus glorificatus est, et docuit semetipsum esse qui inter Judæos quidem quasi filius apparuerit, in Samaria autem quasi pater descenderit, in reliquis vero gentibus quasi Spiritus Sanctus adventaverit.

writings, as they were understood; so that even those whose
Christology did not require them to reflect on that heavenly
being were forced to recognise it.[1] The pneumatic Christology, accordingly, meets us wherever there is an earnest occupation with the Old Testament, and wherever faith in Christ
as the perfect revealer of God, occupies the foreground, therefore not in Hermas, but certainly in Barnabas, Clement, etc.
The future belonged to this Christology, because the current
exposition of the Old Testament seemed directly to require
it, because it alone permitted the close connection between
creation and redemption, because it furnished the proof that
the world and religion rest upon the same Divine basis,
because it was represented in the most valuable writings of
the early period of Christianity, and finally, because it had
room for the speculations about the Logos. On the other
hand, no direct and natural relation to the world and to
universal history could be given to the Adoptian Christology,
which was originally determined eschatologically. If such a

[1] That is a very important fact which clearly follows from the Shepherd.
Even the later school of the Adoptians in Rome, and the later Adoptians
in general, were forced to assume a divine hypostasis beside the Godhead,
which of course sensibly threatened their Christology. The adherents of
the pneumatic Christology partly made a definite distinction between the
pre-existent Christ and the Holy Spirit (see, e. g., 1 Clem. 22. 1), and partly
made use of formulæ from which one could infer an identity of the two.
The conceptions about the Holy Spirit were still quite fluctuating; whether
he is a power of God, or personal, whether he is identical with the pre-
existent Christ, or is to be distinguished from him, whether he is the servant
of Christ (Tatian Orat. 13), whether he is only a gift of God to believers, or
the eternal Son of God, was quite uncertain. Hermas assumed the latter, and
even Origen (de princip. præf. c. 4) acknowledges that it is not yet decided
whether or not the Holy Spirit is likewise to be regarded as God's Son The
baptismal formula prevented the identification of the Holy Spirit with the
pre-existent Christ, which so readily suggested itself. But so far as Christ was
regarded as a πνεῦμα, his further demarcation from the angel powers was
quite uncertain, as the Shepherd of Hermas proves (though see 1 Clem. 36).
For even Justin, in a passage, no doubt, in which his sole purpose was to shew
that the Christians were not ἄθεοι, could venture to thrust in between God, the
Son and the Spirit, the good angels as beings who were worshipped and
adored by the Christians (Apol 1 6. [if the text be genuine and not an inter-
polation]; see also the Suppl. of Athanagoras). Justin, and certainly most of
those who accepted a pre-existence of Christ, conceived of it as a real pre-
existence. Justin was quite well acquainted with the controversy about the
independent quality of the power which proceeded from God To him it is not
merely, "Sensus, motus, affectus dei", but a "personalis substantia" (Dial. 128).

relation, however, were added to it, there resulted formulæ such as that of two Sons of God, one natural and eternal, and one adopted, which corresponded neither to the letter of the Holy Scriptures, nor to the Christian preaching. Moreover, the revelations of God in the Old Testament made by Theophanies, must have seemed, because of this their form, much more exalted than the revelations made through a man raised to power and glory, which Jesus constantly seemed to be in the Adoptian Christology. Nay, even the mysterious personality of Melchisedec, without father or mother, might appear more impressive than the Chosen Servant, Jesus, who was born of Mary, to a mode of thought which, in order to make no mistake, desired to verify the Divine by outer marks. The Adoptian Christology, that is, the Christology which is most in keeping with the self-witness of Jesus (the Son as the chosen Servant of God), is here shewn to be unable to assure to the Gentile Christians those conceptions of Christianity which they regarded as of highest value. It proved itself insufficient when confronted by any reflection on the relation of religion to the cosmos, to humanity, and to its history. It might, perhaps, still have seemed doubtful about the middle of the second century, as to which of the two opposing formulæ, "Jesus is a man exalted to a Godlike dignity", and "Jesus is a divine spiritual being incarnate", would succeed in the Church. But one only needs to read the pieces of writing which represent the latter thesis, and to compare them, say, with the Shepherd of Hermas, in order to see to which view the future must belong. In saying this, however, we are anticipating; for the Christological reflections were not yet vigorous enough to overcome enthusiasm and the expectation of the speedy end of all things, and the mighty practical tendency of the new religion to a holy life did not allow any theory to become the central object of attention. But, still, it is necessary to refer here to the controversies which broke out at a later period; for the pneumatic Christology forms an essential article, which cannot be dispensed with, in the expositions of Barnabas, Clement and Ignatius, and Justin shews that he cannot conceive of a Christianity without the belief in a real pre-existence of Christ. On the other hand, the liturgical formulæ, the prayers, etc., which have been preserved, scarcely ever take notice of the pre-existence of Christ. They either comprise statements which are borrowed from the Adoptian Christology, or they testify in an unreflective way to the Dominion and Deity of Christ.

5. The ideas of Christ's work which were influential in the communities—Christ as Teacher: creation of knowledge, setting up of the new law; Christ as Saviour: creation of life, overcoming of the demons, forgiveness of sins committed in the time of error,—were by some, in conformity with Apostolic tradition and following the Pauline Epistles, positively connected with the death and resurrection of Christ, while others maintained them without any connection with these events. But one nowhere finds independent thorough reflections on the connection of Christ's saving work with the facts proclaimed in the preaching, above all, with the death on the cross and the resurrection as presented by Paul. The reason of this undoubtedly is that in the conception of the work of salvation, the procuring of forgiveness fell into the background, as this could only be connected by means of the notion of sacrifice, with a definite act of Jesus, viz., with the surrender of his life. Consequently, the facts of the destiny of Jesus combined in the preaching, formed, only for the religious fancy, not for reflection, the basis of the conception of the work of Christ, and were therefore by many writers, Hermas, for example, taken no notice of. Yet the idea of suffering freely accepted, of the cross and of the blood of Christ, operated in wide circles as a holy mystery, in which the deepest wisdom and power of the Gospel must somehow lie concealed. [1] The peculiarity and uniqueness of the work of the historical Christ seemed, however, to be prejudiced by the assumption that Christ, essentially as the same person, was already in the Old Testament the Revealer of God. All

[1] See the remarkable narrative about the cross in the fragment of the Gospel of Peter, and in Justin, Apol. I. 55.

emphasis must therefore fall on this—without a technical reflection which cannot be proved—that the Divine revelation has now, through the historical Christ, become accessible and intelligible to all, and that the life which was promised will shortly be made manifest. ¹

1 We must, above all things, be on our guard here against attributing dogmas to the churches, that is to say, to the writers of this period. The difference in the answers to the question, How far and by what means, Jesus procured salvation? was very great, and the majority undoubtedly never at all raised the question, being satisfied with recognising Jesus as the revealer of God's saving will (Didache, 10. 2: εὐχαριστοῦμέν σοι, πάτερ ἅγιε, ὑπὲρ τοῦ ἁγίου ὀνόματός σου, οὗ κατεσκήνωσας ἐν ταῖς καρδίαις ἡμῶν καὶ ὑπὲρ τῆς γνώσεως καὶ πίστεως αὶ ἀθανασίας, ἧς ἐγνώρισας ἡμῖν διὰ 'Ιησοῦ τοῦ παιδός σου), without reflecting on the fact that this saving will was already revealed in the Old Testament. There is nowhere any mention of a saving work of Christ in the whole Didache, nay, even the *Kerygma* about him is not taken notice of. The extensive writing of Hermas shews that this is not an accident. There is absolutely no mention here of the birth. death, resurrection, etc., of Jesus, although the author in Sim. V. had an occasion for mentioning them. He describes the work of Jesus as (1) preserving the people whom God had chosen. (2) purifying the people from sin, (3) pointing out the path of life and promulgating the Divine law (c. c. 5. 6). This work. however, seems to have been performed by the whole life and activity of Jesus; even to the purifying of sin the author has only added the words: (καὶ αὐτὸς τὰς ἁμαρτίας αὐτῶν ἐκαθάρισε) πολλὰ κοπιάσας καὶ πολλοὺς κόπους ἠντληκώς (Sim. V. 6. 2). But we must further note that Hermas held the proper and obligatory work of Jesus to be only the preservation of the chosen people (from demons in the last days, and at the end), while in the other two articles he saw a performance in excess of his duty, and wished undoubtedly to declare therewith, that the purifying from sin and the giving of the law are not, strictly speaking. integral parts of the Divine plan of salvation, but are due to the special goodness of Jesus (this idea is explained by Moralism). Now, as Hermas, and others, saw the saving activity of Jesus in his whole labours, others saw salvation given and assured in the moment of Jesus' entrance into the world, and in his personality as a spiritual being become flesh. This mystic conception, which attained such wide-spread recognition later on. has a representative in Ignatius, if one can at all attribute clearly conceived doctrines to this emotional confessor. That something can be declared of Jesus, κατὰ πνεῦμα and κατὰ σάρκα—this is the mystery on which the significance of Jesus seems to Ignatius essentially to rest, but how far is not made clear. But the πάθος (αἷμα, σταυρός) and ἀνάστασις of Jesus are to the same writer of great significance, and by forming paradoxical formulæ of worship. and turning to account reminiscences of Apostolic sayings, he seems to wish to base the whole salvation brought by Christ on his suffering and resurrection (see Lightfoot on Eph. inscr. Vol. II. p. 25) In this connection also, he here and there regards all articles of the *Kerygma* as of fundamental significance. At all events. we have in the Ignatian Epistles the first attempt in the post-Apostolic literature, to connect all the theses of the *Kerygma* about Jesus as closely as possible with the benefits which he brought. But only the will of the writer is plain here, all else is confused, and what is mainly felt is that the attempt to conceive the blessings of salvation as the fruit of the sufferings and resurrection, has deprived

As to the facts of the history of Jesus, the real and the supposed, the circumstance that they formed the ever repeat-them of their definiteness and clearness. In proof we may adduce the following: If we leave out of account the passages in which Ignatius speaks of the necessity of repentance for the Heretics, or the Heathen, and the possibility that their sins may be forgiven (Philad. 3. 2 : 8. 1 ; Smyrn. 4 1 : 5. 3 ; Eph. 10. 1), there remains only one passage in which the forgiveness of sin is mentioned, and that only contains a traditional formula (Smyrn. 7. 1 : σάρξ Ἰησοῦ Χριστοῦ, ἡ ὑπὲρ τῶν ἁμαρτιῶν ἡμῶν παθοῦσα). The same writer, who is constantly speaking of the πάθος and ἀνάστασις of Christ, has nothing to say, to the communities to which he writes, about the forgiveness of sin Even the concept "sin", apart from the passages just quoted, appears only once, viz., Eph. 14. 2 : οὐδεὶς πίστιν ἐπαγγελλόμενος ἁμαρτάνει. Ignatius has only once spoken to a community about repentance (Smyrn. 9. 1). It is characteristic that the summons to repentance runs exactly as in Hermas and 2 Clem, the conclusion only being peculiarly Ignatian. It is different with Barnabas. Clement and Polycarp. They (see 1 Clem. 7. 4 : 12. 7 : 21 6 : 49. 6 ; Barn. 5 1 ff.) place the forgiveness of sin procured by Jesus in the foreground, connect it most definitely with the death of Christ. and in some passages seem to have a conception of that connection, which reminds us of Paul. But this just shews that they are dependent here on Paul (or on 1st Peter), and on a closer examination we perceive that they very imperfectly understand Paul, and have no independent insight into the series of ideas which they reproduce That is specially plain in Clement. For. in the first place, he everywhere passes over the resurrection (he mentions it only twice, once as a guarantee of our own resurrection, along with the Phoenix and other guarantees, 24. 1. and then as a means whereby the Apostles' were convinced that the kingdom of God will come, 42. 3). In the second place, he in one passage declares that the χάρις μετανοίας was communicated to the world through the shedding of Christ's blood (7. 4.) But this transformation of the ἄφεσις ἁμαρτιῶν into χάρις μετανοίας plainly shews that Clement had merely taken over from tradition the special estimate of the death of Christ as procuring salvation; for it is meaningless to deduce the χάρις μετανοίας from the blood of Christ. Barnabas testifies more plainly that Christ behoved to offer the vessel of his spirit as a sacrifice for our sins (4 3 : 5. 1), nay, the chief aim of his letter is to harmonise the correct understanding of the cross, the blood, and death of Christ in connection with baptism, the forgiveness of sin, and sanctification (application of the idea of sacrifice). He also unites the death and resurrection of Jesus (5. 6 : αὐτὸς δὲ ἵνα καταργήσῃ τὸν θάνατον καὶ τὴν ἐκ νεκρῶν ἀνάστασιν δείξῃ. ὅτι ἐν σαρκὶ ἔδει αὐτὸν φανερωθῆναι, ὑπέμεινεν, ἵνα καὶ τοῖς πατράσιν τὴν ἐπαγγελίαν ἀποδῷ καὶ αὐτὸς ἑαυτῷ τὸν λαὸν τὸν καινὸν ἑτοιμάζων ἐπιδείξῃ, ἐπὶ τῆς γῆς ὤν. ὅτι τὴν ἀνάστασιν αὐτὸς ποιήσας κρινεῖ): but the significance of the death of Christ is for him at bottom, the fact that it is the fulfilment of prophecy. But the prophecy is related, above all, to the significance of the tree, and so Barnabas on one occasion says with admirable clearness (5. 13); αὐτὸς δὲ ἠθέλησεν οὕτω παθεῖν· ἔδει γὰρ ἵνα ἐπὶ ξύλου πάθῃ. The notion which Barnabas entertains of the σάρξ of Christ suggests the supposition that he could have given up all reference to the death of Christ, if it had not been transmitted as a fact and predicted in the Old Testament. Justin shews still less certainty To him also, as to Ignatius. the cross (the death) of Christ is a great, nay, the greatest mystery, and he sees all things possible in it (see Apol. 1. 35, 55). He knows, further, as a man acquainted with the Old Testament. how to borrow from it very many points of view for the significance of Christ's death, (Christ the sacri-

ed proclamation about Christ gave them an extraordinary significance. In addition to the birth from the Holy Spirit and the Virgin, the death, the resurrection, the exaltation to the right hand of God, and the coming again, there now appeared more definitely the ascension to heaven, and also, though more uncertainly, the descent into the kingdom of the dead. The belief that Jesus ascended into heaven forty days after the resurrection, gradually made way against the older conception, according to which resurrection and ascension really coincided, and against other ideas which maintained a longer period between the two events. That probably is the result of a reflection which sought to distinguish the first from the later manifestations of the exalted Christ, and it is of the utmost importance as the beginning of a demarcation of the times. It is also very probable that the acceptance of an actual *ascensus in cœlum*, not a mere *assumptio*, was favourable to the idea of an actual descent of Christ *de cœlo*, therefore to the pneumatic Christology and vice versa. But there is also closely connected with the *ascensus in cœlum*, the notion of a *descensus ad inferna*, which commended itself on the ground of Old Testament prediction. In the first century, however, it still remained uncertain, lying on the borders of those productions of religious fancy which were not able at once to acquire a right of citizenship in the communities.[1]

fice, the Paschal lamb; the death of Christ the means of redeeming men; death as the enduring of the curse for us; death as the victory over the devil; see Dial 44, 90, 91, 111, 134). But in the discussions which set forth in a more intelligible way the significance of Christ, definite facts from the history have no place at all, and Justin nowhere gives any indication of seeing in the death of Christ more than the mystery of the Old Testament, and the confirmation of its trustworthiness. On the other hand, it cannot be mistaken that the idea of an individual righteous man being able effectively to sacrifice himself for the whole, in order through his voluntary death to deliver them from evil, was not unknown to antiquity. Origen (c. Celsum 1. 31) has expressed himself on this point in a very instructive way. The purity and voluntariness of him who sacrifices himself are here the main things. Finally, we must be on our guard against supposing that the expressions σωτηρία, ἀπολύτρωσις and the like, were as a rule related to the deliverance from sin. In the superscription of the Epistle from Lyons, for example, (Euseb. H. E. V. 1. 3: οἱ αὐτὴν τῆς ἀπολυτρώσεως ἡμῖν πίστιν καὶ ἐλπίδα ἔχοντες) the future redemption is manifestly to be understood by ἀπολύτρωσις.

1 On the Ascension, see my edition of the Apost. Fathers I. 2, p. 138.

One can plainly see that the articles contained in the *Kerygma* were guarded and defended in their reality (κατ' ἀληθείαν) by the professional teachers of the Church, against sweeping attempts at explaining them away, or open attacks on them. [1] But they did not yet possess the value of dogmas, for they were neither put in an indissoluble union with the idea of salvation, nor were they stereotyped in their extent, nor were fixed limits set to the imagination in the concrete delineation and conception of them. [2]

1 Paul knows nothing of an Ascension, nor is it mentioned by Clement, Ignatius, Hermas, or Polycarp. In no case did it belong to the earliest preaching. Resurrection and sitting at the right hand of God are frequently united in the formulæ (Eph I. 20 : Acts. II. 32 ff.) According to Luke XXIV. 51, and Barn. 15. 9, the ascension into heaven took place on the day of the resurrection (probably also according to Joh. XX. 17; see also the fragment of the Gosp. of Peter), and is hardly to be thought of as happening but once. (Joh III. 13 : VI 62; see also Rom X. 6 f.; Eph IV. 9 f.; 1 Pet. III. 19 f.; very instructive for the origin of the notion). According to the Valentinians and Ophites, Christ ascended into heaven 18 months after the resurrection (Iren. I. 3. 2 : 30. 14); according to the Ascension of Isaiah, 545 days (ed. Dillmann, pp. 43. 57 etc.); according to Pistis Sophia 11 years after the resurrection. The statement that the Ascension took place 40 days after the resurrection is first found in the Acts of the Apostles. The position of the ἀνελήμφθη ἐν δόξῃ, in the fragment of an old Hymn, 1 Tim. III. 16, is worthy of note, in so far as it follows the ὤφθη ἀγγέλοις, ἐκηρύχθη ἐν ἔθνεσιν, ἐπιστεύθη ἐν κόσμῳ. Justin speaks very frequently of the Ascension into heaven (see also Aristides). It is to him a necessary part of the preaching about Christ. On the descent into hell. see the collection of passages in my edition of the Apost. Fathers, III. p. 232. It is important to note that it is found already in the Gospel of Peter (ἐκήρυξας τοῖς κοιμωμένοις; ναί), and that even Marcion recognised it (in Iren. I. 27. 3), as well as the Presbyter of Irenæus (IV. 27 2), and Ignatius (ad Magn. 9. 3), see also Celsus in Orig. II. 43. The witnesses to it are very numerous, see Huidekoper, "The belief of the first three centuries concerning Christ's Mission to the under-world." New York, 1876.

1 See the Pastoral Epistles, and the Epistles of Ignatius and Polycarp.

2 The "facts" of the history of Jesus were handed down to the following period as mysteries predicted in the Old Testament, but the idea of sacrifice was specially attached to the death of Christ, certainly without any closer definition. It is very noteworthy that in the Romish baptismal confession, the Davidic Sonship of Jesus. the baptism, the descent into the under-world, and the setting up of a glorious Kingdom on the earth, are not mentioned. These articles do not appear even in the parallel confessions which began to be formed. The hesitancy that yet prevailed here with regard to details, is manifest from the fact, for example, that instead of the formula, "Jesus was born of (ἐκ) Mary," is found the other, "He was born through (διὰ) Mary (see Justin, Apol I. 22 31-33. 54. 63; Dial. 23, 43, 45. 48, 57. 54, 63, 66, 75, 85, 87, 100, 105, 120, 127). Iren. (I. 7. 2) and Tertull. (de carne 20) first contested the διὰ against the Valentinians.

§ 7. *The Worship, the Sacred Ordinances, and the Organisation of the Churches.*

It is necessary to examine the original forms of the worship and constitution, because of the importance which they acquired in the following period even for the development of doctrine.

1. In accordance with the purely spiritual idea of God, it was a fixed principle that only a spiritual worship is well pleasing to Him, and that all ceremonies are abolished, ἵνα ὁ καινὸς νόμος τοῦ κυρίου ἡμῶν Ἰησοῦ Χριστοῦ μὴ ἀνθρωποποίητον ἔχῃ τὴν προσφοράν.[1] But as the Old Testament and the Apostolic tradition made it equally certain that the worship of God is a sacrifice, the Christian worship of God was set forth under the aspect of the spiritual sacrifice. In the most general sense it was conceived as the offering of the heart and of obedience, as well as the consecration of the whole personality, body and soul (Rom. XIII. 1) to God.[2] Here, with a change of the figure, the individual Christian and the whole community were described as a temple of God.[3] In a more special sense, prayer as thanksgiving and intercession,[4] was regarded as the sacrifice which was to be accompanied, without constraint or ceremony, by fasts and acts of compassionate love.[5] Finally,

---

1 This was strongly emphasised: see my remarks on Barn. 2. 3. The Jewish cultus is often brought very close to the heathen by Gentile Christian writers. Praed. Petri (Clem. Strom. VI. 5. 41): καινῶς τὸν θεὸν διὰ τοῦ Χριστοῦ σεβόμεθα. The statement in Joh. IV. 24, πνεῦμα ὁ θεός, καὶ τοὺς προσκυνοῦντας αὐτὸν ἐν πνεύματι καὶ ἀληθείᾳ δεῖ προσκυνεῖν, was for long the guiding principle for the Christian worship of God.

2 Ps. LI. 19, is thus opposed to the ceremonial system (Barn. 2. 10). Polycarp consumed by fire is Mart. 14. 1) compared to a κριὸς ἐπίσημος ἐκ μεγάλου ποιμνίου εἰς προσφοράν, ὁλοκαύτωμα δεκτὸν τῷ θεῷ ἡτοιμασμένον.

3 See Barn. 6. 15: 16. 7-9; Tatian Orat. 15; Ignat. ad Eph. 9. 15; Herm. Mand. V. etc. The designation of Christians as priests is not often found.

4 Justin, Apol. 1. 9: Dial. 117: Ὅτι μὲν οὖν καὶ εὐχαὶ καὶ εὐχαριστίαι, ὑπὸ τῶν ἀξίων γινόμεναι. τέλειαι μόναι καὶ εὐάρεστοί εἰσι τῷ θεῷ θυσίαι. καὶ αὐτός φημι; see also still the later Fathers; Clem. Strom. VII. 6. 31: ἡμεῖς δι' εὐχῆς τιμῶμεν τὸν θεὸν, καὶ ταύτην τὴν θυσίαν ἀρίστην, καὶ ἁγιωτάτην μετὰ δικαιοσύνης ἀναπέμπομεν τῷ δικαίῳ λόγῳ; Iren. III. 18. 3; Ptolem. ad Floram. 3: προσφορὰς προσφέρειν προσέταξεν ἡμῖν ὁ σωτήρ, ἀλλὰ οὐχὶ τὰς δι' ἀλόγων ζώων ἢ τούτων τῶν θυμιαμάτων ἀλλὰ διὰ πνευματικῶν αἴνων καὶ δοξῶν καὶ εὐχαριστίας καὶ διὰ τῆς εἰς τοὺς πλησίον κοινωνίας καὶ εὐποιίας.

5 The Jewish regulations about fastings, together with the Jewish system of sacrifice were rejected: but on the other hand, in virtue of words of the Lord,

prayers offered by the worshipper in the public worship of the community, and the gifts brought by them, out of which were taken the elements for the Lord's supper, and which were used partly in the common meal, and partly in support of the poor, were regarded as sacrifice in the most special sense ($\pi\rho\sigma\phi\rho\dot{\alpha}$, $\delta\tilde{\omega}\rho\alpha$).[1] For the following period, however, it became of the utmost importance, (1) that the idea of sacrifice ruled the whole worship, (2) that it appeared in a special manner in the celebration of the Lord's supper, and consequently invested that ordinance with a new meaning, (3) that the support of the poor, alms, especially such alms as had been gained by prayer and fasting, was placed under the category of sacrifice (Heb. XIII. 16); for this furnished the occasion for giving the widest application to the idea of sacrifice, and thereby substituting for the original Semitic Old Testament idea of sacrifice with its spiritual interpretation, the Greek idea with its interpretation.[2] It may, however, be maintained that the

fasts were looked upon as a necessary accompaniment of prayer, and definite arrangements were already made for them (see Barn. 3; Didache 8; Herm. Sim. V. 1 ff.). The fast is to have a special value from the fact that whatever one saved by means of it, is to be given to the poor (see Hermas and Aristides, Apol. 15; "And if any one among the Christians is poor and in want, and they have not overmuch of the means of life, they fast two or three days, in order that they may provide those in need with the food they require"). The statement of James I. 27: θρησκεία καθαρὰ καὶ ἀμίαντος παρὰ τῷ θεῷ καὶ πατρὶ αὕτη ἐστίν, ἐπισκέπτεσθαι ὀρφάνους καὶ χήρας ἐν τῇ θλίψει αὐτῶν, was again and again inculcated in diverse phraseology (Polycarp, Ep. 4, called the Widows θυσιαστήριον of the community). Where moralistic views preponderated, as in Hermas and 2 Clement, good works were already valued in detail; prayers, fasts, alms appeared separately, and there was already introduced, especially under the influence of the so-called deutero-canonical writings of the Old Testament, the idea of a special meritoriousness of certain performances in fasts and alms (see 2 Clem. 16, 4). Still, the idea of the Christian moral life as a whole occupied the foreground (see Didache, cc. 1-5), and the exhortations to love God and one's neighbour, which, as exhortations to a moral life, were brought forward in every conceivable relation, supplemented the general summons to renounce the world, just as the official diaconate of the churches originating in the cultus, prevented the decomposition of them into a society of ascetics.

1 For details, see below in the case of the Lord's Supper. It is specially important that even charity, through its union with the cultus, appeared as sacrificial worship (see. e. g., Polyc. Ep. 4. 3).

2 The idea of sacrifice adopted by the Gentile Christian communities, was that which was expressed in individual prophetic sayings and in the Psalms, a spiritualising of the Semitic Jewish sacrificial ritual, which.

changes imposed on the Christian religion by Catholicism, are at no point so obvious and far-reaching, as in that of sacrifice, and especially in the solemn ordinance of the Lord's supper, which was placed in such close connection with the idea of sacrifice.

2. When in the "Teaching of the Apostles," which may be regarded here as a classic document, the discipline of life in accordance with the words of the Lord, Baptism, the order of fasting and prayer, especially the regular use of the Lord's prayer, and the Eucharist are reckoned the articles on which the Christian community rests, and when the common Sunday offering of a sacrifice made pure by a brotherly disposition, and the mutual exercise of discipline are represented as decisive for the stability of the individual community, [1] we perceive that the general idea of a pure spiritual worship of God has nevertheless been realised in definite institutions, and that, above all, it has included the traditional sacred ordinances, and adjusted itself to them as far as that was possible. [2] This could only take effect under the idea of the symbolical, and therefore this idea was most firmly attached to these ordinances. But the symbolical of that time is not to be considered as the opposite of the objectively real, but as the mysterious, the God produced ($\mu\nu\sigma\tau\eta\rho\iota\nu$), as contrasted with the natural, the profanely clear. As to Baptism, which was administered in the name of the Father, Son and Spirit, though Cyprian, Ep. 73. 16-18, felt compelled to oppose the custom of baptising in the name of Jesus, we noted above (Chap. III. p. 161 f.) that it was regarded as the bath of regeneration, and as renewal of life, inasmuch as it was assumed that by it the sins of the

however, had not altogether lost its original features. The entrance of Greek ideas of sacrifice cannot be traced before Justin. Neither was there as yet any reflection as to the connection of the sacrifice of the Church with the sacrifice of Christ upon the cross.

1 See my Texte und Unters. z. Gesch. d. Altchristl. Lit. II. 1. 2, p. 88 ff., p. 137 ff.

2 There neither was a "doctrine" of Baptism and the Lord's Supper, nor was there any inner connection presupposed between these holy actions. They were here and there placed together as actions by the Lord.

past state of blindness were blotted out. [1] But as faith was looked upon as the necessary condition, [2] and as on the other hand, the forgiveness of the sins of the past was in itself deemed worthy of God, [3] the asserted specific result of baptism remained still very uncertain, and the hard tasks which it imposed, might seem more important than the merely retrospective gifts which it proffered. [4] Under such circumstances the rite could not fail to lead believers about to be baptized, to attribute value here to the mysterious as such. [5] But that always creates a state of things which not only facilitates, but positively prepares for the introduction of new and strange ideas. For neither fancy nor reflection can long continue in the vacuum of mystery. The names σφραγίς and φωτισμός, which at that period came into fashion for baptism, are instructive, inasmuch as neither of them is a direct designation of the presupposed effect of baptism, the forgiveness of sin, and as besides, both of them evince a Hellenic conception. Baptism

1. Melito, Fragm. XII. (Otto. Corp. Apol. IX. p. 418). Δύο συνέστη τὰ ἄφεσιν ἁμαρτημάτων παρεχόμενα, πάθος διὰ Χριστὸν καὶ βάπτισμα.

2 There is no sure trace of infant baptism in this epoch; personal faith is a necessary condition (see Hermas, Vis. III. 7. 3; Justin, Apol. I. 61). "Prius est prædicare posterius tinguere" (Tertull. "de bapt." 14).

3 On the basis of repentance. See Praed. Petri in Clem. Strom. VI. 5. 43, 48.

4 See especially the second Epistle of Clement; Tertull. "de bapt." 15 : "Felix aqua quæ semel abluit, quæ ludibrio peccatoribus non est".

5 The sinking and rising in baptism, and the immersion, were regarded as significant, but not indispensable symbols (see Didache. 7). The most important passages for baptism are Didache 7 : Barn. 6. 11 : 11. 1. 11 (the connection in which the cross of Christ is here placed to the water is important; the tertium comp. is that forgiveness of sin is the result of both); Herm. Vis. III. 3, Sim. IX. 16, Mand. IV. 3 (ἑτέρα μετάνοια οὐκ ἔστιν εἰ μὴ ἐκείνη, ὅτε εἰς ὕδωρ κατέβημεν καὶ ἐλάβομεν ἄφεσιν ἁμαρτιῶν ἡμῶν τῶν προτέρων); 2 Clem. 6. 9: 7. 6: 8. 6. Peculiar is Ignat. ad. Polyc. 6. 2 : τὸ βάπτισμα ὑμῶν μενέτω ὡς ὅπλα. Specially important is Justin, Apol. I. 61. 65. To this also belong many passages from Tertullian's treatise "de bapt."; a Gnostic baptismal hymn in the third pseudo-Solomonic ode in the Pistis Sophia, p. 131, ed. Schwartze ; Marcion's baptismal formula in Irenæus 1. 21. 3. It clearly follows from the seventh chapter of the Didache, that its author held that the pronouncing of the sacred names over the baptised, and over the water, was essential, but that immersion was not; see the thorough examination of this passage by Schaff, "The oldest church manual called the teaching of the twelve Apostles" pp. 29-57. The controversy about the nature of John's baptism in its relation to Christian baptism. is very old in Christendom ; see also Tertull. "de bapt." 10. Tertullian sees in John's baptism only a baptism to repentance, not to forgiveness.

in being called the seal, [1] is regarded as the guarantee of a
blessing, not as the blessing itself, at least the relation to it
remains obscure; in being called enlightenment, [2] it is placed
directly under an aspect that is foreign to it. It would be
different if we had to think of $\varphi\omega\tau\iota\sigma\mu\acute{o}\varsigma$ as a gift of the Holy
Spirit, which is given to the baptised as real principle of a
new life and miraculous powers. But the idea of a necessary
union of baptism with a miraculous communication of the
Spirit, seems to have been lost very early, or to have become
uncertain, the actual state of things being no longer favourable
to it; [3] at any rate, it does not explain the designation of
baptism as $\varphi\omega\tau\iota\sigma\mu\acute{o}\varsigma$.

1 In Hermas and 2 Clement. The expression probably arose from the
language of the mysteries: see Appuleius, "de Magia", 55: "Sacrorum ple-
raque initia in Græcia participavi. Eorum quædam signa et monumenta
tradita mihi a sacerdotibus sedulo conservo." Ever since the Gentile
Christians conceived baptism (and the Lord's Supper) according to the
mysteries, they were of course always surprised by the parallel with the
mysteries themselves. That begins with Justin. Tertullian, "de bapt." 5,
says: "Sed enim nationes extraneæ, ab omni intellectu spiritalium potes-
tatum eadem efficacia idolis suis subministrant. Sed viduis aquis sibi
mentiuntur. Nam et sacris quibusdam per lavacrum initiantur, Isidis
alicujus aut Mithræ; ipsos etiam deos suos lavationibus efferunt. Ceterum
villas, domos, templa totasque urbes aspergine circumlatæ aquæ expiant passim. Certe ludis Apollinaribus et Eleusiniis tinguuntur, idque se in regenerationem et impunitatem periuriorum suorum agere præsumunt. Item penes
veteres, quisquis se homicidio infecerat, purgatrices aquas explorabat." De
praescr. 40: "Diabolus ipsas quoque res sacramentorum divinorum idolorum
mysteriis æmulatur. Tingit et ipse quosdam, utique credentes et fideles suos;
expositionem delictorum de lavacro repromittit, et si adhuc memini, Mithras
signat illic in frontibus milites suos, celebrat et panis oblationem et imaginem
resurrectionis inducit .... summum pontificem in unius nuptiis statuit, habet
et virgines, habet et continentes." The ancient notion that matter has a mysterious influence on spirit, came very early into vogue in connection with
baptism. We see that from Tertullian's treatise on baptism and his speculations about the power of the water (c. 1 ff.). The water must, of course, have
been first consecrated for this purpose (that is, the demons must be driven
out of it). But then it is holy water with which the Holy Spirit is united, and
which is able really to cleanse the soul. See Hatch, "The influence of Greek
ideas, etc.," p. 19. The consecration of the water is certainly very old: though
we have no definite witnesses from the earliest period. Even for the exorcism
of the baptised before baptism I know of no earlier witness than the Sentent.
LXXXVII. episcoporum (Hartel. Opp. Cypr. I. p. 450, No. 37 : "primo per
manus impositionem in exorcismo, secundo per baptismi regenerationem").
2 Justin is the first who does so (I. 61). The word comes from the
Greek mysteries. On Justin's theory of baptism, see also I. 62. and Von
Engelhardt, "Christenthum Justin's," p. 102 f.
3 Paul unites baptism and the communication of the Spirit; but they were
very soon represented apart, see the accounts in the Acts of the Apostles,

As regards the Lord's Supper, the most important point is that its celebration became more and more the central point, not only for the worship of the Church, but for its very life as a Church. The form of this celebration, the common meal, made it appear to be a fitting expression of the brotherly unity of the community (on the public confession before the meal, see Didache, 14, and my notes on the passage). The prayers which it included presented themselves as vehicles for bringing before God, in thanksgiving and intercession, every thing that affected the community; and the presentation of the elements for the holy ordinance was naturally extended to the offering of gifts for the poor brethren, who in this way received them from the hand of God himself. In all these respects, however, the holy ordinance appeared as a sacrifice of the community, and indeed, as it was also named, εὐχαριστία, a sacrifice of thanksgiving. [1] As an act of sacrifice, all the

which are certainly very obscure, because the author has evidently never himself observed the descent of the Spirit, or anything like it. The ceasing of special manifestations of the Spirit in and after baptism, and the enforced renunciation of seeing baptism accompanied by special shocks, must be regarded as the first stage in the sobering of the churches.

2 The idea of the whole transaction of the Supper as a sacrifice, is plainly found in the Didache, (c. 14), in Ignatius, and, above all, in Justin (I. 65 f.) But even Clement of Rome presupposes it, when in (cc. 40-44) he draws a parallel between bishops and deacons and the Priests and Levites of the Old Testament, describing as the chief function of the former (44. 4) προσφέρειν τὰ δῶρα. This is not the place to enquire whether the first celebration had, in the mind of its founder, the character of a sacrificial meal; but, certainly, the idea, as it was already developed at the time of Justin, had been created by the churches. Various reasons tended towards seeing in the Supper a sacrifice. In the first place, Malachi I. 11, demanded a solemn Christian sacrifice: see my notes on Didache, 14. 3. In the second place, all prayers were regarded as sacrifice, and therefore the solemn prayers at the Supper must be specially considered as such. In the third place, the words of institution τοῦτο ποιεῖτε, contained a command with regard to a definite religious action. Such an action, however, could only be represented as a sacrifice, and this the more that the Gentile Christians might suppose that they had to understand ποιεῖν in the sense of θύειν. In the fourth place, payments in kind were necessary for the "agapæ" connected with the Supper, out of which were taken the bread and wine for the Holy celebration; in what other aspect could these offerings in the worship be regarded than as προσφοραί for the purpose of a sacrifice? Yet the spiritual idea so prevailed that only the prayers were regarded as the θυσία proper, even in the case of Justin (Dial. 117). The elements are only δῶρα, προσφοραί, which obtain their value from the prayers, in which thanks are given for the gifts of creation and redemption,

termini technici which the Old Testament applied to sacrifice could be applied to it, and all the wealth of ideas which the Old Testament connects with sacrifice, could be transferred to it. One cannot say that anything absolutely foreign was therewith introduced into the ordinance, however doubtful it may be whether in the idea of its founder the meal was thought of as a sacrificial meal. But it must have been of the most wide-reaching significance, that a wealth of ideas was in this way connected with the ordinance, which had nothing what-ever in common, either with the purpose of the meal as a memorial of Christ's death, [1] or with the mysterious symbols of the body and blood of Christ. The result was that the one transaction obtained a double value. At one time it appeared as the προσφορά and θυσία of the Church, [2] as the pure sacrifice which is presented to the great king by Christians scattered over the world, as they offer to him their prayers, and place before him again what he has bestowed in order to receive it back with thanks and praise. But there is no reference in this to the mysterious words that the bread and wine are the body of Christ broken, and the blood of Christ shed for the for-giveness of sin. These words, in and of themselves, must have challenged a special consideration. They called forth the recognition in the sacramental action, or rather in the con-secrated elements, of a mysterious communication of God, a gift of salvation, and this is the second aspect. But on a purely

as well as for the holy meal, and entreaty is made for the introduction of the community into the Kingdom of God (see Didache, 9 10). Therefore, even the sacred meal itself is called εὐχαριστία (Justin, Apol. I. 66: ἡ τροφὴ αὕτη καλεῖται παρ᾽ ἡμῖν εὐχαριστία. Didache, 9. 1: Ignat.,, because it is τροφὴ εὐχαριστηθεῖσα. It is a mistake to suppose that Justin already understood the body of Christ to be the object of ποιεῖν, and therefore thought of a sacrifice of this body (1. 66) The real sacrificial act in the Supper consists rather, according to Justin, only in the εὐχαριστίαν ποιεῖν, whereby the κοινὸς ἄρτος becomes the ἄρτος τῆς εὐχαριστίας. The sacrifice of the Supper in its essence, apart from the offering of alms, which in the practice of the Church was closely united with it, is nothing but a sacrifice of prayer: the sacrificial act of the Christian here also is nothing else than an act of prayer (see Apol. I. 13, 65-67; Dial. 28, 29, 41, 70, 116-118).

1 Justin lays special stress on this purpose. On the other hand, it is wanting in the Supper prayers of the Didache, unless c. 9. 2 be regarded as an allusion to it.

2 The designation θυσία is first found in the Didache, c. 14.

spiritual conception of the Divine gift of salvation, the blessings mediated through the Holy Supper could only be
thought of as spiritual (faith, knowledge, or eternal life), and
the consecrated elements could only be recognised as the
mysterious vehicles of these blessings. There was yet no
reflection on the distinction between symbol and vehicle; the
symbol was rather regarded as the vehicle, and vice versa.
We shall search in vain for any special relation of the par-
taking of the consecrated elements to the forgiveness of sin.
That was made impossible by the whole current notions of
sin and forgiveness. That on which value was put was the
strengthening of faith and knowledge, as well as the guarantee of eternal life, and a meal in which there was appropriated not merely common bread and wine, but a τροφὴ
πνευματική, seemed to have a bearing upon these. There
was as yet little reflection; but there can be no doubt that
thought here moved in a region bounded, on the one hand,
by the intention of doing justice to the wonderful words of
institution which had been handed down, and on the other
hand, by the fundamental conviction that spiritual things can
only be got by means of the Spirit.[1] There was thus at-

---

1 The Supper was regarded as a "Sacrament" in so far as a blessing was represented in its holy food. The conception of the nature of
this blessing as set forth in John VI. 27-58, appears to have been the
most common. It may be traced back to Ignatius, ad Eph. 20. 2 : ἕνα ἄρτον
κλῶντες ὅς ἐστιν φάρμακον ἀθανασίας, ἀντίδοτος τοῦ μὴ ἀποθανεῖν ἀλλὰ ζῆν ἐν Ἰησοῦ
Χριστοῦ διὰ παντός; Cf. Didache, 10. 3 : ἡμῖν ἐχαρίσω πνευματικὴν τροφὴν καὶ
ποτὸν καὶ ζωὴν αἰώνιον; also 10. 21 : εὐχαριστοῦμέν σοι ὑπὲρ τῆς γνώσεως καὶ πίστεως
καὶ ἀθανασίας. Justin Apol. I. 66: ἐκ τῆς τροφῆς ταύτης αἷμα καὶ σάρκες κατὰ
μεταβολὴν τρέφονται ἡμῶν (κατὰ μεταβολήν, that is, the holy food, like all
nourishment, is completely transformed into our flesh; but what Justin
has in view here is most probably the body of the resurrection. The
expression, as the context shews, is chosen for the sake of the parallel
to the incarnation). Iren. IV. 18. 5 : V. 2. 2 f. As to how the elements are
related to the body and blood of Christ, Ignatius seems to have expressed
himself in a strictly realistic way in several passages, especially ad. Smyr.
7. 1 : εὐχαριστίας καὶ προσευχῆς ἀπέχονται διὰ τὸ μὴ ὁμολογεῖν, τὴν εὐχαριστίαν
σάρκα εἶναι τοῦ σωτῆρος ἡμῶν Ἰησοῦ Χριστοῦ, τὴν ὑπὲρ τῶν ἁμαρτιῶν ἡμῶν παθοῦσαν.
But many passages shew that Ignatius was far from such a conception,
and rather thought as John did. In Trall. 8, faith is described as the flesh,
and love as the blood of Christ; in Rom. 7, in one breath the flesh of
Christ is called the bread of God, and the blood ἀγάπη ἄφθαρτος. In Philad.
1, we read: αἷμα Ἰ Χρ. ἥτις ἐστὶν χαρὰ αἰώνιος καὶ παράμονος. In Philad. 5, the
Gospel is called the flesh of Christ, etc. Höfling is therefore right in

tached to the Supper the idea of sacrifice, and of a sacred gift
guaranteed by God. The two things were held apart, for
there is as yet no trace of that conception, according to which
the body of Christ represented in the bread[1] is the sacrifice
offered by the community. But one feels almost called upon
here to construe from the premises the later development of
the idea, with due regard to the ancient Hellenic ideas of sacrifice.

3. The natural distinctions among men, and the differences
of position and vocation which these involve, were not to be
abolished in the Church, notwithstanding the independence
and equality of every individual Christian, but were to be
consecrated: above all, every relation of natural piety was to
be respected. Therefore the elders also acquired a special
authority, and were to receive the utmost deference and due

saying (Lehre v. Opfer, p. 39): "The Eucharist is to Ignatius σάρξ of
Christ, as a visible Gospel, a kind of Divine institution attesting the
content of πίστις, viz., belief in the σάρξ παθοῦσα, an institution which is
at the same time, to the community, a means of representing and preserving its unity in this belief." On the other hand, it cannot be mistaken
that Justin (Apol. I. 66) presupposed the identity, miraculously produced
by the Logos, of the consecrated bread and the body he had assumed.
In this we have probably to recognise an influence on the conception of
the Supper, of the miracle represented in the Greek Mysteries: Οὐχ ὡς
κοινὸν ἄρτον οὐδὲ κοινὸν πόμα ταῦτα λαμβάνομεν, ἀλλ' ὅν τρόπον διὰ λόγου θεοῦ
σαρκοποιηθεὶς Ἰησοῦς Χριστὸς ὁ σωτὴρ ἡμῶν καὶ σάρκα καὶ αἷμα ὑπὲρ σωτηρίας ἡμῶν
ἔσχεν, οὕτως καὶ τὴν δι' εὐχῆς λόγου τοῦ παρ' αὐτοῦ εὐχαριστηθεῖσαν τροφήν, ἐξ
ἧς αἷμα καὶ σάρκες κατὰ μεταβολὴν τρέφονται ἡμῶν, ἐκείνου τοῦ σαρκοποιηθέντος
Ἰησοῦ καὶ σάρκα καὶ αἷμα ἐδιδάχθημεν εἶναι (See Von Otto on the passage). In
the Texte u. Unters. VII. 2. p. 117 ff., I have shewn that in the different
Christian circles of the second century, water and only water was often
used in the Supper instead of wine, and that in many regions this custom
was maintained up to the middle of the third century (see Cypr. Ep.
63). I have endeavoured to make it further probable, that even Justin in
his Apology describes a celebration of the Lord's Supper with bread and
water. The latter has been contested by Zahn, "Bread and wine in the
Lord's Supper, in the early Church," 1892, and Jülicher, Zur Gesch. der
Abendmahlsfeier in der aeltesten Kirche (Abhandl. f. Weiszäcker, 1892, p.
217 ff.)

1 Ignatius calls the thank-offering the flesh of Christ, but the concept
"flesh of Christ" is for him itself a spiritual one. On the contrary, Justin
sees in the bread the actual flesh of Christ, but does not connect it
with the idea of sacrifice. They are thus both as yet far from the later
conception. The numerous allegories which are already attached to the
Supper (one bread equivalent to one community; many scattered grains
bound up in the one bread, equivalent to the Christians scattered abroad
in the world, who are to be gathered together into the Kingdom of God;
one altar, equivalent to one assembly of the community, excluding private
worship, etc.), cannot as a group be adduced here.

obedience. But, however important the organisation that was based on the distinction between πρεσβύτεροι and νεώτεροι, it ought not to be considered as characteristic of the Churches, not even where there appeared at the head of the community a college of chosen elders, as was the case in the greater communities and perhaps soon everywhere. On the contrary, only an organisation founded on the gifts of the Spirit (χαρίσματα), bestowed on the Church by God, [1] corresponded to the original peculiarity of the Christian community. The Apostolic age therefore transmitted a twofold organisation to the communities. The one was based on the διακονία τοῦ λόγου, and was regarded as established directly by God; the other stood in the closest connection with the economy of the church, above all with the offering of gifts, and so with the sacrificial service. In the first were men speaking the word of God, commissioned and endowed by God, and bestowed on Christendom, not on a particular community, who as ἀπόστολοι, προφῆται, and διδάσκαλοι had to spread the Gospel, that is to edify the Church of Christ. They were regarded as the real ἡγούμενοι in the communities, whose words given them by the Spirit all were to accept in faith. In the second were ἐπίσκοποι, and διάκονοι, appointed by the individual congregation and endowed with the charisms of leading and helping, who had to receive and administer the gifts, to perform the sacrificial service (if there were no prophets present), and take charge of the affairs of the community. [2] It lay in the

1 Cf. for the following my arguments in the larger edition of the " Teaching of the Apostles" Chap. 5, (Texte u. Unters. II. 1. 2). The numerous recent enquiries (Loening, Loofs, Réville etc.) will be found referred to in Sohm's Kirchenrecht. Vol. I. 1892, where the most exhaustive discussions are given.

2 That the bishops and deacons were, primarily, officials connected with the cultus, is most clearly seen from 1 Clem. 40-44, but also from the connection in which the 14th Chap. of the Didache stands with the 15th (see the οὖν 15.1) to which Hatch in conversation called my attention. The φιλοξενία, and the intercourse with other communities (the fostering of the "unitas") belonged, above all, to the affairs of the church. Here, undoubtedly, from the beginning lay an important part of the bishop's duties. Ramsay ("The Church in the Roman Empire," p. 361 ff.) has emphasised this point exclusively, and therefore one-sidedly. According to him, the monarchical Episcopate sprang from the officials who were appointed *ad hoc* and for a time, for the purpose of promoting intercourse with other churches.

nature of the case that as a rule the ἐπίσκοποι, as independent
officials, were chosen from among the elders, and might thus
coincide with the chosen πρεσβύτεροι. But a very important
development takes place in the second half of our epoch.
The prophets and teachers—as the result of causes which
followed the naturalising of the Churches in the world—fell
more and more into the background, and their function, the
solemn service of the word, began to pass over to the officials of the community, the bishops, who already played a
great rôle in the public worship. At the same time, however,
it appeared more and more fitting to entrust one official, as
chief leader (superintendent of public worship), with the reception of gifts and their administration, together with the care
of the unity of public worship, that is, to appoint one bishop
instead of a number of bishops, leaving, however, as before, the
college of presbyters, as προϊστάμενοι τῆς ἐκκλησίας, a kind of
senate of the community. ¹ Moreover, the idea of the chosen
bishops and deacons as the antitypes of the Priests and Levites, had been formed at an early period in connection with
the idea of the new sacrifice. But we find also the idea, which
is probably the earlier of the two, that the prophets and
teachers, as the commissioned preachers of the word, are the
priests. The hesitancy in applying this important allegory
must have been brought to an end by the disappearance of
the latter view. But it must have been still more important
that the bishops, or bishop, in taking over the functions of
the old λαλοῦντες τὸν λόγον, who were not Church officials, took

    1 Sohm (in the work mentioned above) seeks to prove that the mo-
narchical Episcopate originated in Rome and is already presupposed by
Hermas. I hold that the proof for this has not been adduced. and I
must also in great part reject the bold statements which are
fastened on to the first Epistle of Clement. They may be comprehended
in the proposition which Sohm, p. 158, has placed at the head of his
discussion of the Epistle. "The first Epistle of Clement makes an epoch
in the history of the organisation of the Church. It was destined to put
an end to the early Christian constitution of the Church." According to
Sohm (p. 165), another immediate result of the Epistle was a change of
constitution in the Romish Church, the introduction of the monarchical
Episcopate. That, however, can only be asserted, not proved; for the
proof which Sohm has endeavoured to bring from Ignatius' Epistle to.
the Romans and the Shepherd of Hermas, is not convincing.

over also the profound veneration with which they were regarded as the special organs of the Spirit. But the condition
of the organisation in the communities about the year 140,
seems to have been a very diverse one. Here and there, no
doubt, the convenient arrangement of appointing only one
bishop was carried out, while his functions had not perhaps
been essentially increased, and the prophets and teachers were
still the great spokesmen. Conversely, there may still have
been in other communities a number of bishops, while the
prophets and teachers no longer played regularly an important rôle. A fixed organisation was reached, and the Apostolic
episcopal constitution established, only in consequence of the
so-called Gnostic crisis, which was epoch-making in every
respect. One of its most important presuppositions, and one
that has struck very deep into the development of doctrine must,
however, be borne in mind here. As the Churches traced
back all the laws according to which they lived, and all the
blessings they held sacred, to the tradition of the twelve
Apostles, because they regarded them as Christian only on
that presupposition, they also in like manner, as far as we
can discover, traced back their organisation of presbyters,
i. e., of bishops and deacons, to Apostolic appointment. The
notion which followed quite naturally, was that the Apostles themselves had appointed the first church officials. [1] That idea may
have found support in some actual cases of the kind, but this
does not need to be considered here; for these cases would
not have led to the setting up of a theory. But the point
in question here is a theory, which is nothing else than an
integral part of the general theory, that the twelve Apostles
were in every respect the middle term between Jesus and
the present Churches (see above, p. 158). This conception is
earlier than the great Gnostic crisis, for the Gnostics also
shared it. But no special qualities of the officials, but only of
the Church itself, were derived from it, and it was believed that
the independence and sovereignty of the Churches were in no way

---

1 See, above all, 1 Clem. 42, 44, Acts of the Apostles, Pastoral Epistles, etc.

endangered by it, because an institution by Apostles was considered equivalent to an institution by the Holy Spirit, whom they possessed, and whom they followed. The independence of the Churches rested precisely on the fact that they had the Spirit in their midst. The conception here briefly sketched, was completely transformed in the following period by the addition of another idea—that of Apostolic succession,[1] and then became, together with · the idea of the specific priesthood of the leader of the Church, the most important means of exalting the office above the community.[2]

SUPPLEMENTARY.

This review of the common faith and the beginnings of knowledge, worship and organisation, in the earliest Gentile Christianity, will have shewn that the essential premises for the development of Catholicism were already in existence before the middle of the second century, and before the burning conflict with Gnosticism. We may see this, whether we look

[1] This idea is Romish. See Book II. chap. II. C.
[2] We must remember here, that besides the teachers, elders, and deacons, the ascetics (virgins, widows, celibates, abstinentes) and the martyrs (confessors) enjoyed a special respect in the Churches, and frequently laid hold of the government and leading of them. Hermas enjoins plainly enough the duty of esteeming the confessors higher than the presbyters (Vis. III. 1. 2). The widows were soon entrusted with diaconal tasks connected with the worship, and received a corresponding respect. As to the limits of this there was, as we can gather from different passages, much disagreement. One statement in Tertullian shews that the confessors had special claims to be considered in the choice of a bishop (adv. Valent. 4: "Speraverat Episcopatum Valentinus, quia et ingenio poterat et eloquio. Sed alium ex martyrii prærogativa loci potitum indignatus de ecclesia authenticæ regulæ abrupit"). This statement is strengthened by other passages; see Tertull. de fuga; 11: "Hoc sentire et facere omnem servum dei oportet, etiam minoris loci, ut maioris fieri possit, si quem gradum in persecutionis tolerantia ascenderit"; see Hippol. in the Arab. canons, and also Achelis, Texte u. Unters. VI. 4. pp. 67, 220: Cypr. Epp. 38. 39. The way in which confessors and ascetics, from the end of the second century, attempted to have their say in the leading of the Churches. and the respectful way in which it was sought to set their claims aside, shew that a special relation to the Lord, and therefore a special right with regard to the community, was early acknowledged to these people, on account of their achievements. On the transition of the old prophets and teachers into wandering ascetics, later into monks, see the Syriac Pseudo-Clementine Epistles, "de virginitate," and my Abhandl i d. Sitzungsberichten d. K. Pr. Akad. d. Wissensch. 1891, p. 361 ff.

at the peculiar form of the *Kerygma,* or at the expression of the idea of tradition, or at the theology with its moral and philosophic attitude. We may therefore conclude that the struggle with Gnosticism hastened the development, but did not give it a new direction. For the Greek spirit, the element which was most operative in Gnosticism, was already concealed in the earliest Gentile Christianity itself: it was the atmosphere which one breathed; but the elements peculiar to Gnosticism were for the most part rejected. [1] We may even go back a step further (see above, pp. 41, 76). The great Apostle to the Gentiles himself, in his epistle to the Romans, and in those to the Corinthians, transplanted the Gospel into Greek modes of thought. He attempted to expound it with Greek ideas, and not only called the Greeks to the Old Testament and the Gospel, but also introduced the Gospel as a leaven into the religious and philosophic world of Greek ideas. Moreover, in his pneumatico-cosmic Christology he gave the Greeks an impulse towards a theologoumenon, at whose service they could place their whole philosophy and mysticism. He preached the foolishness of Christ crucified, and yet in doing so, proclaimed the wisdom of the nature-vanquishing Spirit, the heavenly Christ. From this moment was established a development which might indeed assume very different forms, but in which all the forces and ideas of Hellenism must gradually pass over to the Gospel. But even with this the last word has not been said; on the contrary, we must remember that the Gospel itself belonged to the fulness of the times, which is indicated by the inter-action of the Old Testament and the Hellenic religions (see above, pp. 41, 56).

The documents which have been preserved from the first century of the Gentile Church are, in their relation to the history of Dogma, very diverse. In the Didache we have a Catechism for Christian life, dependent on a Jewish Greek Catechism, and giving expression to what was specifically Christian

---

[1] See Weizsäcker. Gött. Gel. Anz. 1886, No. 21, whose statements I can almost entirely make my own.

in the prayers, and in the order of the Church. The Epistle
of Barnabas, probably of Alexandrian origin, teaches the cor·
rect, Christian, interpretation of the Old Testament, rejects
the literal interpretation and Judaism as of the devil, and in
Christology essentially follows Paul. The Romish first Epistle
of Clement, which also contains other Pauline reminiscences
(reconciliation and justification) represents the same Christology, but it set it in a moralistic mode of thought. This is
a most typical writing in which the spirit of tradition, order,
stability, and the universal ecclesiastical guardianship of Rome
is already expressed. The moralistic mode of thought is
classically represented by the Shepherd of Hermas, and the
second Epistle of Clement, in which, besides, the eschatological element is very prominent. We have in the Shepherd
the most important document for the Church Christianity of
the age, reflected in the mirror of a prophet who, however,
takes into account the concrete relations. The theology of
Ignatius is the most advanced, in so far as he, opposing the
Gnostics, brings the facts of salvation into the foreground,
and directs his Gnosis not so much to the Old Testament as
to the history of Christ. He attempts to make Christ $\varkappa \alpha \tau \grave{\alpha}$
$\pi \nu \epsilon \tilde{\upsilon} \mu \alpha$ and $\varkappa \alpha \tau \grave{\alpha} \, \sigma \acute{\alpha} \rho \varkappa \alpha$ the central point of Christianity. In this
sense his theology and speech is Christocentric, related to
that of Paul and the fourth Evangelist, (specially striking is
the relationship with Ephesians), and is strongly contrasted
with that of his contemporaries. Of kindred spirit with him
are Melito and Irenæus, whose forerunner he is. He is related
to them as Methodius at a later period was related to the
classical orthodox theology of the fourth and fifth centuries.
This parallel is appropriate, not merely in point of form: it
is rather one and the same tendency of mind which passes
over from Ignatius to Melito, Irenæus, Methodius, Athanasius,
Gregory of Nyssa (here, however, mixed with Origenic elements),
and to Cyril of Alexandria. Its characteristic is that not
only does the person of Christ as the God-man form the central point and sphere of theology, but also that all the main points
of his history are mysteries of the world's redemption. (Ephes.

19). But Ignatius is also distinguished by the fact that behind all that is enthusiastic, pathetic, abrupt, and again all that pertains to liturgical form, we find in his epistles a true devotion to Christ (ὁ θεός μου). He is laid hold of by Christ: Cf. Ad. Rom. 6: ἐκεῖνον ζητῶ, τὸν ὑπὲρ ἡμῶν ἀποθανόντα, ἐκεῖνον θέλω, τὸν δι' ἡμᾶς ἀναστάντα; Rom. 7: ὁ ἐμὸς ἔρως ἐσταύρωται καὶ οὐκ ἔστιν ἐν ἐμοὶ πῦρ φιλοῦλον. As a sample of his theological speech and his rule of faith, see ad. Smyrn. 1: ἐνόησα ὑμᾶς κατηρτισμένους ἐν ἀκινήτῳ πίστει, ὥσπερ καθηλωμένους ἐν τῷ σταυρῷ τοῦ κυρίου Ἰησοῦ Χριστοῦ σαρκί τε καὶ πνεύματι καὶ ἡδρασμένους ἐν ἀγάπῃ ἐν τῷ αἵματι Χριστοῦ, πεπληροφορημένους εἰς τὸν κυρίου ἡμῶν, ἀληθῶς ὄντα ἐκ γένους Δαβὶδ κατὰ σάρκα, υἱὸν θεοῦ κατὰ θέλημα καὶ δύναμιν θεοῦ, γεγενημένον ἀληθῶς ἐκ παρθένου, βεβαπτισμένον ὑπὸ Ἰωάννου, ἵνα πληρωθῇ πᾶσα δικαιοσύνη ὑπ' αὐτοῦ, ἀληθῶς ἐπὶ Ποντίου Πιλάτου καὶ Ἡρώδου τετράρχου καθηλωμένον ὑπὲρ ἡμῶν ἐν σαρκί — ἀφ' οὗ καρποῦ ἡμεῖς, ἀπὸ τοῦ θεομακαρίτου αὐτοῦ πάθους — ἵνα ἄρῃ σύσσημον εἰς τοὺς αἰῶνας διὰ τῆς ἀναστάσεως εἰς τοὺς ἁγίους καὶ πιστοὺς αὐτοῦ εἴτε ἐν Ἰουδαίοις εἴτε ἐν ἔθνεσιν ἐν ἑνὶ σώματι τῆς ἐκκλησίας αὐτοῦ. The Epistle of Polycarp is characterised by its dependence on earlier Christian writings (Epistles of Paul, 1 Peter, 1 John), consequently, by its conservative attitude with regard to the most valuable traditions of the Apostolic period. The *Kerygma* of Peter exhibits the transition from the early Christian literature to the apologetic (Christ as νόμος and as λόγος).

It is manifest that the lineage, "Ignatius, Polycarp, Melito, Irenæus", is in characteristic contrast with all others, has deep roots in the Apostolic age, as in Paul and in the Johannine writings, and contains in germ important factors of the future formation of dogma, as it appeared in Methodius, Athanasius, Marcellus, Cyril of Jerusalem. It is very doubtful therefore, whether we are justified in speaking of an Asia Minor theology. (Ignatius does not belong to Asia Minor). At any rate, the expression, Asia Minor-Romish Theology, has no justification. But it has its truth in the correct observation, that the standards by which Christianity and Church matters were measured and defined, must have been similar in Rome and Asia Minor during the second century. We

lack all knowledge of the closer connections. We can only
again refer to the journey of Polycarp to Rome, to that of
Irenæus by Rome to Gaul, to the journey of Abercius and
others (cf. also the application of the Montanist communities in
Asia Minor for recognition by the Roman bishop). In all probability, Asia Minor, along with Rome, was the spiritual centre
of Christendom from about 60-200: but we have but few
means for describing how this centre was brought to bear on
the circumference. What we do know belongs more to the
history of the Church than to the special history of dogma.

Literature.—The writings of the so-called Apostolic Fathers.
See the edition of v. Gebhardt, Harnack, Zahn, 1876. Hilgenfeld, Nov. Test. extra Can. recept. fasc. IV. 2 edit. 1884,
has collected further remains of early Christian literature. The
Teaching of the twelve Apostles. Fragments of the Gospel
and Apocalypse of Peter (my edition, 1893). Also the writings
of Justin and other apologists, in so far as they give disclosures about the faith of the communities of his time, as well
as statements in Celsus Ἀληθὴς Λόγος, in Irenæus, Clement of
Alexandria, and Tertullian. Even Gnostic fragments may be
cautiously turned to profit. Ritschl, Entstehung der altkath.
Kirche 2 Aufl. 1857. Pfleiderer, Das Urchristenthum, 1887.
Renan, Origins of Christianity, vol. V. V. Engelhardt, Das Chris-
tenthum Justin's, d. M. 1878, p. 375 ff. Schenkel, Das Christus-
bild der Apostel, etc., 1879. Zahn, Gesch. des N.-Tlichen
Kanons, 2 Bde. 1888. Behm, Das Christliche Gesetzthum der
Apostolischen Väter (Zeitschr. f. kirchl. Wissensch. 1886).
Dorner, History of the doctrine of the Person of Christ, 1845.
Schultz, Die Lehre von der Gottheit Christi, 1881, p. 22 ff.
Höfling. Die Lehre der ältesten Kirche vom Opfer, 1851.
Höfling, Das Sacrament d. Taufe, 1848. Kahnis, Die Lehre
vom Abendmahl, 1851. Th. Harnack, Der Christliche Gemeinde-
gottedienst im Apost. u. Altkath. Zeitalter, 1854. Hatch,
Organisation of the Early Church, 1883. My Prolegomena
to the Didache (Texte u. Unters. II. Bd. H. 1, 2). Diestel,
Gesch. des A. T. in der Christl. Kirche, 1869. Sohm, Kir-
chenrecht, 1892, Monographs on the Apostolic Fathers: on 1

Clem.: Lipsius, Lightfoot (most accurate commentary), Wrede;
on 2 Clem.: A. Harnack (Ztschr. f. K. Gesch. 1887); on Barnabas:
J. Müller; on Hermas: Zahn, Hückstädt, Link; on Papias: Weiffenbach, Leimbach, Zahn, Lightfoot; on Ignatius and Polycarp:
Lightfoot (accurate commentary) and Zahn; on the Gospel and
Apocalypse of Peter: A. Harnack: on the Kerygma of Peter:
von Dobschütz; on Acts of Thecla: Schlau.

CHAPTER IV

THE ATTEMPTS OF THE GNOSTICS TO CREATE AN APOSTOLIC DOGMATIC, AND A CHRISTIAN THEOLOGY; OR, THE ACUTE SECULARISING OF CHRISTIANITY.

§ 1. *The Conditions for the Rise of Gnosticism.*

THE Christian communities were originally unions for a holy life, on the ground of a common hope, which rested on the belief that the God who has spoken by the Prophets has sent his Son Jesus Christ, and through him revealed eternal life, and will shortly make it manifest. Christianity had its roots in certain facts and utterances, and the foundation of the Christian union was the common hope, the holy life in the Spirit according to the law of God, and the holding fast to those facts and utterances. There was, as the foregoing chapter will have shewn, no fixed Didache beyond that.[1] There was abundance of fancies, ideas, and knowledge, but these had not yet the value of being the religion itself. Yet the belief that Christianity guarantees the perfect knowledge, and leads from one degree of clearness to another, was in opera-tion from the very beginning. This conviction had to be im-mediately tested by the Old Testament, that is, the task was imposed on the majority of thinking Christians, by the cir-cumstances in which the Gospel had been proclaimed to them, of making the Old Testament intelligible to themselves, in other words, of using this book as a Christian book, and of

---

1 We may consider here once more the articles which are embraced in the first ten chapters of the recently discovered Διδαχὴ τῶν ἀποστόλων, after enumerating and describing which, the author continues (11. 1): ὃς ἂν οὖν ἐλθών διδάξῃ ὑμᾶς ταῦτα πάντα τὰ προειρημένα, δέξασθε αὐτόν.

finding the means by which they might be able to repel the Jewish claim to it, and refute the Jewish interpretation of it. This task would not have been imposed, far less solved, if the Christian communities in the Empire had not entered into the inheritance of the Jewish propaganda, which had already been greatly influenced by foreign religions (Babylonian and Persian, see the Jewish Apocalypses), and in which an extensive spiritualising of the Old Testament religion had already taken place. This spiritualising was the result of a philosophic view of religion, and this philosophic view was the outcome of a lasting influence of Greek philosophy and of the Greek spirit generally on Judaism. In consequence of this view, all facts and sayings of the Old Testament in which one could not find his way, were allegorised. "Nothing was what it seemed, but was only the symbol of something invisible. The history of the Old Testament was here sublimated to a history of the emancipation of reason from passion." It describes, however, the beginning of the historical development of Christianity, that as soon as it wished to give account of itself, or to turn to advantage the documents of revelation which were in its possession, it had to adopt the methods of that fantastic syncretism. We have seen above that those writers who made a diligent use of the Old Testament, had no hesitation in making use of the allegorical method. That was required not only by the inability to understand the verbal sense of the Old Testament, presenting diverging moral and religious opinions, but, above all, by the conviction, that on every page of that book Christ and the Christian Church must be found. How could this conviction have been maintained, unless the definite concrete meaning of the documents had been already obliterated by the Jewish philosophic view of the Old Testament?

This necessary allegorical interpretation, however, brought into the communities an intellectual philosophic element, a γνῶσις, which was perfectly distinct from the Apocalyptic dreams, in which were beheld angel hosts on white horses, Christ with eyes as a flame of fire, hellish beasts, conflict and victory. [1] In this γνῶσις, which attached itself to the Old Testament, many began to see the specific blessing which was promised to mature faith, and through which it was to attain perfection. What a wealth of relations, hints, and intuitions seemed to disclose itself, as soon as the Old Testament was considered allegorically, and to what extent had the way been prepared here by the Jewish philosophic teachers! From the simple narratives of the Old Testament had already been developed a theosophy, in which the most abstract ideas had acquired reality, and from which sounded forth the Hellenic canticle of the power of the Spirit over matter and sensuality, and of the true home of the soul. Whatever in this great adaptation still remained obscure and unnoticed, was now lighted up by the history of Jesus, his birth, his life, his sufferings and triumph. The view of the Old Testament as a document of the deepest wisdom, transmitted to those who knew how to read it as such, unfettered the intellectual interest which would not rest until it had entirely transferred the new religion from the world of feelings, actions and hopes, into the world of Hellenic conceptions, and transformed it into a metaphysic. In that exposition of the Old Testament which we find, for example, in the so-called Barnabas, there is already concealed an important philosophic, Hellenic element, and in that sermon which bears the name of Clement (the so-called second Epistle of Clement), conceptions such as that of the Church, have already assumed a bodily form and been joined in marvellous connections, while, on the contrary, things concrete have been transformed into things invisible.

1 It is a good tradition, which designates the so-called Gnosticism, simply as Gnosis, and yet uses this word also for the speculations of non-Gnostic teachers of antiquity (*e. g.*, of Barnabas). But the inferences which follow have not been drawn. Origen says truly (c. Celsus III. 12). "As men, not only the labouring and serving classes, but also many from the cultured classes of Greece, came to see something honourable in Christianity, sects could not fail to arise, not simply from the desire for controversy and contradiction, but because several scholars endeavoured to penetrate deeper into the truth of Christianity. In this way sects arose, which received their names from men who indeed admired Christianity in its essence, but from many different causes had arrived at different conceptions of it."

But once the intellectual interest was unfettered, and the new religion had approximated to the Hellenic spirit by means of a philosophic view of the Old Testament, how could that spirit be prevented from taking complete and immediate possession of it, and where, in the first instance, could the power be found that was able to decide whether this or that opinion was incompatible with Christianity? This Christianity, as it was, unequivocally excluded all polytheism, and all national religions existing in the Empire. It opposed to them the one God, the Saviour Jesus, and a spiritual worship of God. But, at the same time, it summoned all thoughtful men to knowledge, by declaring itself to be the only true religion, while it appeared to be only a variety of Judaism. It seemed to put no limits to the character and extent of the knowledge, least of all to such knowledge as was able to allow all that was transmitted to remain, and at the same time, abolish it by transforming it into mysterious symbols. That really was the method which every one must and did apply who wished to get from Christianity more than practical motives and super-earthly hopes. But where was the limit of the application? Was not the next step to see in the Evangelic records also new material for spiritual interpretations, and to illustrate from the narratives there, as from The Old Testament, the conflict of the spirit with matter, of reason with sensuality? Was not the conception that the traditional deeds of Christ were really the last act in the struggle of those mighty spiritual powers whose conflict is delineated in the Old Testament, at least as evident as the other, that those deeds were the fulfilment of mysterious promises? Was it not in keeping with the consciousness possessed by the new religion of being the universal religion, that one should not be satisfied with mere beginnings of a new knowledge, or with fragments of it, but should seek to set up such knowledge in a complete and systematic form, and so to exhibit the best and universal system of life as also the best and universal system of knowledge of the world? Finally, did not the free and yet so rigid forms in which the Christian communities were organised, the union of the mysterious with a wonderful publicity, of the spiritual with significant rites (baptism and the Lord's Supper), invite men to find here the realisation of the ideal which the Hellenic religious spirit was at that time seeking, viz., a communion which in virtue of a Divine revelation, is in possession of the highest knowledge, and therefore leads the holiest life, a communion which does not communicate this knowledge by discourse, but by mysterious efficacious consecrations, and by revealed dogmas? These questions are thrown out here in accordance with the direction which the historical progress of Christianity took. The phenomenon called Gnosticism gives the answer to them.[1]

§ 2. *The Nature of Gnosticism.*

The Catholic Church afterwards claimed as her own those writers of the first century (60-160) who were content with turning speculation to account only as a means of spiritual-ising the Old Testament, without, however, attempting a systematic reconstruction of tradition. But all those who in the first century undertook to furnish Christian practice with the foundation of a complete systematic knowledge, she declared false Christians, Christians only in name. Historical enquiry cannot accept this judgment. On the contrary, it sees in Gnosticism a series of undertakings, which in a certain way is analogous to the Catholic embodiment of Christianity, in doctrine, mo-rals, and worship. The great distinction here consists essen-tially in the fact that the Gnostic systems represent the acute secularising or hellenising of Christianity, with the rejection of the Old Testament,[2] while the Catholic system, on the

[1] The majority of Christians in the second century belonged no doubt to the uncultured classes, and did not seek abstract knowledge, nay, were distrustful of it; see the λόγος ἀληθής of Celsus, especially III 44, and the writings of the Apologists. Yet we may infer from the treatise of Origen against Celsus that the number of "Christiani rudes" who cut themselves off from theological and philosophic knowledge, was about the year 240 a very large one; and Tertullian says (Adv. Prax. 3): "Simplices quique, ne dixerim imprudentes et idiotæ, quæ major semper credentium pars est," cf. de jejun. 11: "Major pars imperitorum apud gloriosissimam multitudinem psychicorum."

[2] Overbeck (Stud. z. Gesch. d. alten Kirche. p. 184) has the merit of having first given convincing expression to this view of Gnosticism.

other hand, represents a gradual process of the same kind with the conservation of the Old Testament. The traditional religion on being, as it were, suddenly required to recognise itself in a picture foreign to it, was yet vigorous enough to reject that picture; but to the gradual, and one might say indulgent remodelling to which it was subjected, it offered but little resistance, nay, as a rule, it was never conscious of it. It is therefore no paradox to say that Gnosticism, which is just Hellenism, has in Catholicism obtained half a victory. We have, at least, the same justification for that assertion— the parallel may be permitted—as we have for recognising a triumph of 18th century ideas in the first Empire, and a continuance, though with reservations, of the old régime.

From this point of view the position to be assigned to the Gnostics in the history of dogma, which has hitherto been always misunderstood, is obvious. *They were, in short, the Theologians of the first century.*[1] They were the first to transform Christianity into a system of doctrines (dogmas). They were the first to work up tradition systematically. They undertook to present Christianity as the absolute religion, and therefore placed it in definite opposition to the other religions, even to Judaism. But to them the absolute religion, viewed in its contents, was identical with the result of the philosophy of religion for which the support of a revelation was to be sought. They are therefore those Christians who, in a swift advance, attempted to capture Christianity for Hellenic culture, and Hellenic culture for Christianity, and who gave up the Old Testament in order to facilitate the conclusion of the covenant between the two powers, and make it possible to

1 The ability of the prominent Gnostic teachers has been recognised by the Church Fathers: see Hieron. Comm. in Osee. II. 10, Opp. VI. 1: "Nullus potest hæresim struere, nisi qui ardens ingenii est et habet dona naturæ quæ a deo artifice sunt creata: talis fuit Valentinus, talis Marcion, quos doctissimos legimus, talis Bardesanes, cujus etiam philosophi admirantur ingenium." It is still more important to see how the Alexandrian theologians (Clement and Origen) estimated the exegetic labours of the Gnostics, and took account of them. Origen undoubtedly recognised Herakleon as a prominent exegete, and treats him most respectfully even where he feels compelled to differ from him All Gnostics cannot, of course, be regarded as theologians. In their totality they form the Greek society with a Christian name.

assert the absoluteness of Christianity.—But the significance of
the Old Testament in the religious history of the world, lies just
in this, that, in order to be maintained at all, it required the
application of the allegoric method, that is, a definite proportion
of Greek ideas, and that, on the other hand, it opposed the strongest barrier to the complete hellenising of Christianity. Neither
the sayings of Jesus, nor Christian hopes, were at first capable of forming such a barrier. If, now, the majority of Gnostics
could make the attempt to disregard the Old Testament, that
is a proof that, in wide circles of Christendom, people were
at first satisfied with an abbreviated form of the Gospel, containing the preaching of the one God, of the resurrection and
of continence,—a law and an ideal of practical life. [1] In this
form, as it was realised in life, the Christianity which dispensed
with "doctrines" seemed capable of union with every form
of thoughtful and earnest philosophy, because the Jewish
foundation did not make its appearance here at all. But the
majority of Gnostic undertakings may also be viewed as
attempts to transform Christianity into a theosophy, that is,
into a revealed metaphysic and philosophy of history, with a
complete disregard of the Jewish Old Testament soil on which
it originated, through the use of Pauline ideas, [2] and under
the influence of the Platonic spirit. Moreover, comparison is
possible between writers such as Barnabas and Ignatius, and
the so-called Gnostics, to the effect of making the latter appear in possession of a completed theory, to which fragmentary,
ideas in the former exhibit a striking affinity.

We have hitherto tacitly presupposed that in Gnosticism
the Hellenic spirit desired to make itself master of Christianity, or more correctly of the Christian communities. This
conception may be, and really is still contested. For according to the accounts of later opponents, and on these we are
almost exclusively dependent here, the main thing with the
Gnostics seems to have been the reproduction of Asiatic My-

---

[1] Otherwise the rise of Gnosticism cannot at all be explained.
[2] Cf. Bigg, "The Christian Platonists of Alexandria," p. 83 : "Gnosticism
was in one respect distorted Paulinism."

thologoumena of all kinds, so that we should rather have to see in Gnosticism a union of Christianity with the most remote Oriental cults and their wisdom. But with regard to the most important Gnostic systems the words hold true, "The hands are the hands of Esau, but the voice is the voice of Jacob". There can be no doubt of the fact, that the Gnosticism which has become a factor in the movement of the history of dogma, was ruled in the main by the Greek spirit, and determined by the interests and doctrines of the Greek philosophy of religion, [1] which doubtless had already assumed a syncretistic character. This fact is certainly concealed by the circumstance that the material of the speculations was taken now from this, and now from that Oriental religious philosophy, from astrology and the Semitic cosmologies. But that is only in keeping with the stage which the religious development had reached among the Greeks and Romans of that time. [2] The cultured, and these primarily come into consideration here, no longer had a religion in the sense of a national religion, but a philosophy of religion. They were, however, in search of a religion, that is, a firm basis for the results of their speculations, and they hoped to obtain it by turning themselves towards the very old Oriental cults, and seeking to fill them with the religious and moral knowledge which had been gained by the Schools of Plato and of Zeno. The union of the traditions and rites of the Oriental religions, viewed as mysteries, with the spirit of Greek philosophy is the characteristic of the epoch. The needs, which asserted themselves with equal strength, of a complete knowledge of the All, of

1 Joel, "Blick in die Religionsgesch." Vol. I. pp. 101-170, has justly emphasised the Greek character of Gnosis, and insisted on the significance of Platonism for it. "The Oriental element did not always in the case of the Gnostics, originate at first hand, but had already passed through a Greek channel."

2 The age of the Antonines was the flourishing period of Gnosticism. Marquardt (Römische Staatsverwaltung. Vol. 3, p. 81) says of this age: "With the Antonines begins the last period of the Roman religious development, in which two new elements enter into it. These are the Syrian and Persian deities, whose worship at this time was prevalent not only in the city of Rome, but in the whole empire, and, at the same time, Christianity, which entered into conflict with all ancient tradition, and in this conflict exercised a certain influence even on the Oriental forms of worship.

a spiritual God, a sure, and therefore very old revelation, atonement and immortality, were thus to be satisfied at one and the same time. The most sublimated spiritualism enters here into the strangest union with a crass superstition based on Oriental cults. This superstition was supposed to insure and communicate the spiritual blessings. These complicated tendencies now entered into Christianity.

We have accordingly to ascertain and distinguish in the prominent Gnostic schools, which, in the second century on Greek soil, became an important factor in the history of the Church, the Semitic-cosmological foundations, the Hellenic philosophic mode of thought, and the recognition of the redemption of the world by Jesus Christ. Further, we have to take note of the three elements of Gnosticism, viz., the speculative and philosophical, the mystic element connection with worship, and the practical, ascetic. The close connection in which these three elements appear, [1] the total transformation of all ethical into cosmological problems, the upbuilding of a philosophy of God and the world on the basis of a combination of popular Mythologies, physical observations belonging to the Oriental (Babylonian) religious philosophy, and historical events, as well as the idea that the history of religion is the last act in the drama-like history of the Cosmos—all this is not peculiar to Gnosticism, but rather corresponds to a definite stage of the general development. It may, however, be asserted that

[1] It is a special merit of Weingarten (Histor. Ztschr. Bd 45. 1881. p. 441 f.) and Koffmane (Die Gnosis nach ihrer Tendenz und Organisation, 1881) to have strongly emphasised the mystery character of Gnosis, and in connection with that, its practical aims. Koffmane, especially, has collected abundant material for proving that the tendency of the Gnostics was the same as that of the ancient mysteries, and that they thence borrowed their organisation and discipline. This fact proves the proposition that Gnosticism was an acute hellenising of Christianity. Koffmane has, however, undervalued the union of the practical and speculative tendency in the Gnostics, and, in the effort to obtain recognition for the mystery character of the Gnostic communities, has overlooked the fact that they were also schools. The union of mystery-cultus and school is just, however, their characteristic. In this also they prove themselves the forerunners of Neoplatonism and the Catholic Church. Moehler in his programme of 1831 (Urspr. d. Gnosticismus Tübingen), vigorously emphasised the practical tendency of Gnosticism, though not in a convincing way. Hackenschmidt (Anfänge des katholischen Kirchenbegriffs, p. 83 f.) has judged correctly.

Gnosticism anticipated the general development, and that not only with regard to Catholicism, but also with regard to Neoplatonism, which represents the last stage in the inner history of Hellenism. [1] The Valentinians have already got as far as Jamblichus.

The name Gnosis, Gnostics, describes excellently the aims of Gnosticism, in so far as its adherents boasted of the absolute knowledge, and faith in the Gospel was transformed into a knowledge of God, nature and history. This knowledge, however, was not regarded as natural, but in the view of the Gnostics was based on revelation, was communicated and guaranteed by holy consecrations, and was accordingly cultivated by reflection supported by fancy. A mythology of ideas was created out of the sensuous mythology of any Oriental religion, by the conversion of concrete forms into speculative and moral ideas, such as "Abyss," "Silence," "Logos," "Wisdom," "Life," while the mutual relation and number of these abstract ideas were determined by the data supplied by the corresponding concretes. Thus arose a philosophic dramatic poem, similar to the Platonic, but much more complicated, and therefore more fantastic, in which mighty powers, the spiritual and good, appear in an unholy union with the material and wicked, but from which the spiritual is finally delivered by the aid of those kindred powers which are too exalted to be ever drawn down into the common. The good and heavenly which has been drawn down into the material, and therefore really non-existing, is the human spirit, and the exalted power who delivers it is Christ. The Evangelic history as handed down is not the history of Christ, but a collection of allegoric representations of the great history of God and the world. Christ has really no history. His appearance in this world of mixture

1 We have also evidence of the methods by which ecstatic visions were obtained among the Gnostics, see the Pistis Sophia, and the important rôle which prophets and Apocalypses played in several important Gnostic communities (Barcoph and Barcabbas, prophets of the Basilideans; Martiades and Marsanes among the Ophites; Philumene in the case of Apelles; Valentinian prophecies; Apocalypses of Zostrian, Zoroaster, etc.) Apocalypses were also used by some under the names of Old Testament men of God and Apostles.

and confusion is his deed, and the enlightenment of the spirit about itself is the result which springs out of that deed. This enlightenment itself is life. But the enlightenment is dependent on revelation, asceticism and surrender to those mysteries which Christ founded, in which one enters into communion with a *præsens numen*, and which in mysterious ways promote the process of raising the spirit above the sensual. This rising above the sensual is, however, to be actively practised. Abstinence therefore, as a rule, is the watchword. Christianity thus appears here as a speculative philosophy which redeems the spirit by enlightening it, consecrating it, and instructing it in the right conduct of life. The Gnosis is free from the rationalistic interest in the sense of natural religion. Because the riddles about the world which it desires to solve are not properly intellectual, but practical, because it desires to be in the end γνῶσις σωτηρίας, it removes into the region of the suprarational the powers which are supposed to confer vigour and life on the human spirit. Only a μάθησις, however, united with μυσταγωγία, resting on revelation, leads thither, not an exact philosophy. Gnosis starts from the great problem of this world, but occupies itself with a higher world, and does not wish to be an exact philosophy, but a philosophy of religion. Its fundamental philosophic doctrines are the following: (1) The indefinable, infinite nature of the Divine primeval Being exalted above all thought. (2) Matter as opposed to the Divine Being, and therefore having no real being, the ground of evil. (3) The fulness of divine potencies, Æons, which are thought of partly as powers, partly as real ideas, partly as relatively independent beings, presenting in gradation the unfolding and revelation of the Godhead, but at the same time rendering possible the transition of the higher to the lower. (4) The Cosmos as a mixture of matter with divine sparks, which has arisen from a descent of the latter into the former, or, as some say, from the perverse, or, at least, merely permitted undertaking of a subordinate spirit. The Demiurge, therefore, is an evil, intermediate, or weak, but penitent being; the best thing therefore in the world is aspiration. (5) The deliverance of the spiritual element from its union with matter, or the separation of the good from the world of sensuality by the Spirit of Christ which operates through knowledge, asceticism, and holy consecration: thus originates the perfect Gnostic, the man who is free from the world, and master of himself, who lives in God and prepares himself for eternity. All these are ideas for which we find the way prepared in the philosophy of the time, anticipated by Philo, and represented in Neoplatonism as the great final result of Greek philosophy. It lies in the nature of the case that only some men are able to appropriate the Christianity that is comprehended in these ideas, viz , just as many as are capable of entering into this kind of Christianity, those who are spiritual. The others must be considered as non-partakers of the Spirit from the beginning, and therefore excluded from knowledge as the *profanum vulgus.* Yet some, the Valentinians, for example, made a distinction in this *vulgus,* which can only be discussed later on, because it is connected with the position of the Gnostics towards Jewish Christian tradition.

The later opponents of Gnosticism preferred to bring out the fantastic details of the Gnostic systems, and thereby created the prejudice that the essence of the matter lay in these. They have thus occasioned modern expounders to speculate about the Gnostic speculations in a manner that is marked by still greater strangeness. Four observations shew how unhistorical and unjust such a view is, at least with regard to the chief systems. (1) The great Gnostic schools, wherever they could, sought to spread their opinions. But it is simply incredible that they should have expected of all their disciples, male and female, an accurate knowledge of the details of their system. On the contrary, it may be shewn that they often contented themselves with imparting consecration, with regulating the practical life of their adherents, and instructing them in the general features of their system. [1] (2) We see how in one and the same school, for example, the Valen-

---

1 See Koftmane, before-mentioned work. p. 5 f.

tinian, the details of the religious metaphysic were very various and changing. (3) We hear but little of conflicts between
the various schools. On the contrary, we learn that the
books of doctrine and edification passed from one school to
another. ¹ (4) The fragments of Gnostic writings which have
been preserved, and this is the most important consideration
of the four, shew that the Gnostics devoted their main strength
to the working out of those religious, moral, philosophical
and historical problems, which must engage the thoughtful
of all times. ² We only need to read some actual Gnostic
document, such as the Epistle of Ptolemæus to Flora, or certain paragraphs of the Pistis Sophia, in order to see that the
fantastic details of the philosophic poem can only, in the case
of the Gnostics themselves, have had the value of liturgical
apparatus, the construction of which was not of course
matter of indifference, but hardly formed the principle interest.
The things to be proved, and to be confirmed by the aid of this
or that very old religious philosophy, were certain religious
and moral fundamental convictions, and a correct conception
of God, of the sensible, of the creator of the world, of Christ,

---

1 See Fragm. Murat. V. 81 f.; Clem. Strom. VII. 17. 108; Orig. Hom. 34.
The Marcionite Antitheses were probably spread among other Gnostic
sects. The Fathers frequently emphasise the fact that the Gnostics were
united against the church: Tertullian de præscr 42: "Et hoc est, quod
schismata apud hæreticos fere non sunt, quia cum sint, non parent. Schisma
est enim unitas ipsa." They certainly also delight in emphasising the contradictions of the different schools; but they cannot point to any earnest
conflict of these schools with each other. We know definitely that Bardasanes
argued against the earlier Gnostics, and Ptolemæus against Marcion.

2 See the collection, certainly not complete, of Gnostic fragments by Grabe
(Spicileg.) and Hilgenfeld (Ketzergeschichte.) Our books on the history of
Gnosticism take far too little notice of these fragments as presented to us,
above all, by Clement and Origen, and prefer to keep to the doleful
accounts of the Fathers about the "Systems", (better in Heinrici: Valent.
Gnosis, 1871). The vigorous efforts of the Gnostics to understand the
Pauline and Johannine ideas, and their in part surprisingly rational and
ingenious solutions of intellectual problems, have never yet been systematically estimated. Who would guess, for example, from what is currently
known of the system of Basilides, that, according to Clement, the following
proceeds from him, (Strom. IV. 12. 18): ὡς αὐτὸς φησιν ὁ Βασιλείδης, ἓν μέρος
ἐκ τοῦ λεγομένου θελήματος τοῦ θεοῦ ὑπειλήφαμεν, τὸ ἠγαπηκέναι ἅπαντα, ὅτι λόγον
ἀποσώζουσι πρὸς τὸ πᾶν ἅπαντα· ἕτερον δὲ τὸ μηδενὸς ἐπιθυμεῖν, καὶ τὸ τρίτον μισεῖν
μηδὲ ἕν, and where do we find, in the period before Clement of Alexandria,
faith in Christ united with such spiritual maturity and inner freedom as in
Valentinians, Ptolemæus and Heracleon?

of the Old Testament, and the evangelic tradition. Here were
actual dogmas. But how the grand fantastic union of all the
factors was to be brought about, was, as the Valentinian
school shews, a problem whose solution was ever and again
subjected to new attempts. [1] No one to-day can in all respects distinguish what to those thinkers was image and what
reality, or in what degree they were at all able to distinguish
image from reality, and in how far the magic formulæ of their
mysteries were really objects of their meditation. But the
final aim of their endeavours, the faith and knowledge of
their own hearts which they instilled into their disciples, the
practical rules which they wished to give them, and the view
of Christ which they wished to confirm them in, stand out
with perfect clearness. Like Plato, they made their explanation of the world start from the contradiction between sense
and reason, which the thoughtful man observes in himself.
The cheerful asceticism, the powers of the spiritual and the
good which were seen in the Christian communities, attracted
them and seemed to require the addition of theory to practice.
Theory without being followed by practice had long been in
existence, but here was the as yet rare phenomenon of a moral
practice which seemed to dispense with that which was regarded
as indispensable, viz., theory. The philosophic life was already
there; how could the philosophic doctrine be wanting, and after
what other model could the latent doctrine be reproduced than
that of the Greek religious philosophy? [2] That the Hellenic

1 Testament of Tertullian (adv. Valent. 4) shews the difference between
the solution of Valentinus, for example, and his disciple Ptolemæus.
"Ptolemæus nomina et numeros Æonum distinxit in personales substantias,
sed extra deum determinatas, quas Valentinus in ipsa summa divinitatis
ut sensus et affectus motus incluserat." It is, moreover, important that
Tertullian himself should distinguish this so clearly

2 There is nothing here more instructive than to hear the judgments
of the cultured Greeks and Romans about Christianity, as soon as they
have given up the current gross prejudices. They shew with admirable
clearness, the way in which Gnosticism originated Galen says (quoted
by Gieseler, Church Hist. 1. 1. 4): "Hominum plerique orationem demon-
strativam continuam mente assequi nequeunt, quare indigent. ut institu-
antur parabolis Veluti nostro tempore videmus, homines illos, qui Christiani
vocantur, fidem suam e parabolis petiisse. Hi tamen interdum talia
faciunt, qualia qui vere philosophantur. Nam quod mortem contemnunt,
id quidem omnes ante oculos habemus; item quod verecundia quadam

spirit in Gnosticism turned with such eagerness to the Christian
communities and was ready even to believe in Christ in order
to appropriate the moral powers which it saw operative in
them, is a convincing proof of the extraordinary impression
which these communities made. For what other peculiarities
and attractions had they to offer to that spirit than the certainty of their conviction (of eternal life), and the purity of
their life? We hear of no similar edifice being erected in
the second century on the basis of any other Oriental cult—
even the Mithras cult is scarcely to be mentioned here—as
the Gnostic was on the foundation of the Christian. [1] The
Christian communities, however, together with their worship
of Christ, formed the real solid basis of the greater number
and the most important of the Gnostic systems, and in this fact we
have, on the very threshold of the great conflict, a triumph
of Christianity over Hellenism. The triumph lay in the recognition of what Christianity had already performed as a moral
and social power. This recognition found expression in bring-

ducti ab usu rerum venerearum abhorrent. Sunt enim inter eos feminæ et
viri, qui per totam vitam a concubitu abstinuerint ; sunt etiam qui in animis
regendis coërcendisque et in accerrimo honestatis studio eo progressi sint,
ut nihil cedant vere philosophantibus." Christians, therefore, are philosophers
without philosophy. What a challenge for them to produce such, that is to
seek out the latent philosophy! Even Celsus could not but admit a certain
relationship between Christians and philosophers. But as he was convinced
that the miserable religion of the Christians could neither include nor endure
a philosophy, he declared that the moral doctrines of the Christians were
borrowed from the philosophers (I. 4) In course of his presentation (V. 65 : VI.
12. 15-19, 42 ; VII. 27-35) he deduces the most decided marks of Christianity,
as well as the most important sayings of Jesus from (misunderstood)
statements of Plato and other Greek philosophers. This is not the place
to shew the contradictions in which Celsus was involved by this. But it
is of the greatest significance that even this intelligent man could only
see philosophy where he saw something precious. The whole of Christianity
from its very origin appeared to Celsus (in one respect) precisely as
the Gnostic systems appear to us, that is, these really are what Christianity
as such seemed to Celsus to be. Besides, it was constantly asserted up
to the fifth century that Christ had drawn from Plato's writings. Against
those who made this assertion, Ambrosius (according to Augustine, Ep.
31. c 8) wrote a treatise which unfortunately is no longer in existence.

1 The Simonian system at most might be named, on the basis of the syncretistic religion founded by Simon Magus. But we know little about it, and
that little is uncertain Parallel attempts are demonstrable in the third century
on the basis of various "revealed" fundamental ideas (ἡ ἐκ λογίων φιλοσοφία).

ing the highest that one possessed as a gift to be consecrated by the new religion, a philosophy of religion whose end was plain and simple, but whose means were mysterious and complicated.

§ 3. *History of Gnosticism and the forms in which it appeared.*

In the previous section we have been contemplating Gnosticism as it reached its prime in the great schools of Basilides and Valentinus, and those related to them, [1] at the close of the period we are now considering, and became an important factor in the history of dogma. But this Gnosticism had (1) preliminary stages, and (2) was always accompanied by a great number of sects, schools and undertakings which were only in part related to it, and yet, reasonably enough, were grouped together with it.

To begin with the second point, the great Gnostic schools were flanked on the right and left by a motley series of groups which at their extremities can hardly be distinguished from popular Christianity on the one hand, and from the Hellenic and the common world on the other. [1] On the right were communities such as the Encratites, which put all stress on a strict asceticism, in support of which they urged the example of Christ, but which here and there fell into dualistic ideas. [3] There were further, whole communities which, for decennia, drew their

1 Among these I reckon those Gnostics whom Irenæus (I. 29-31) has portrayed, as well as part of the so-called Ophites, Peratæ, Sethites and the school of the Gnostic Justin (Hippol. Philosoph. V. 6-28). There is no reason for regarding them as earlier or more Oriental than the Valentinians, as is done by Hilgenfeld against Baur, Möller, and Gruber (the Ophites, 1864). See also Lipsius, "Ophit. Systeme", i. d. Ztschr. f. wiss. Theol. 1863. IV, 1864, I. These schools claimed for themselves the name Gnostic (Hippol. Philosoph. V. 6). A part of them, as is specially apparent from Orig c. Celsum. VI., is not to be reckoned Christian. This motley group is but badly known to us through Epiphanius, much better through the original Gnostic writings preserved in the Coptic language. (Pistis Sophia and the works published by Carl Schmidt Texte u. Unters. Bd. VIII.). Yet these original writings belong, for the most part, to the second half of the third century (see also the important statements of Porphyry in the Vita Plotini. c. 16), and shew a Gnosticism burdened with an abundance of wild speculations, formulæ, mysteries, and ceremonial. However, from these very monuments it becomes plain that Gnosticism anticipated Catholicism as a ritual system (see below).

2 On Marcion, see the following Chapter.

3 We know that from the earliest period (perhaps we might refer even to

views of Christ from books which represented him as a heavenly spirit who had merely assumed an apparent body. ¹ There were also individual teachers who brought forward peculiar opinions without thereby causing any immediate stir in the Churches. ² On the left there were schools such as the Carpocratians, in which the philosophy and communism of Plato

the Epistle to the Romans) there were circles of ascetics in the Christian communities who required of all, as an inviolable law, under the name of Christian perfection, complete abstinence from marriage, renunciation of possessions, and a vegetarian diet. (Clem. Strom III. 6. 49: ὑπὸ διαβόλου ταύτην παραδίδοσθαι δογματίζουσι, μιμεῖσθαι δ᾽ αὐτοὺς οἱ μεγάλαυχοί φασι τὸν κύριον μήτε γήμαντα, μήτε τι ἐν τῷ κόσμῳ κτησάμενον, μᾶλλον παρὰ τοὺς ἄλλους νενοηκέναι τὸ εὐαγγέλιον καυχόμενοι. — Here then, already, imitation of the poor life of Jesus, the "Evangelic" life, was the watchword Tatian wrote a book, περὶ τοῦ κατὰ τὸν σωτῆρα καταρτισμοῦ, that is, on perfection according to the Redeemer: in which he set forth the irreconcilability of the worldly life with the Gospel). No doubt now existed in the Churches that abstinence from marriage, from wine and flesh, and from possessions, was the perfect fulfilling of the law of Christ (βαστάζειν ὅλον τὸν ζυγὸν τοῦ κυρίου). But in wide circles strict abstinence was deduced from a special charism, all boastfulness was forbidden, and the watchword given out: ὅσον δύνασαι ἀγνεύσεις. which may be understood as a compomise with the worldly life as well as a reminiscence of a freer morality (see my notes on Didache, c. 6: 11, 11 and Prolegg. p. 42 ff.). Still, the position towards asceticism yielded a hard problem, the solution of which was more and more found in distinguishing a higher and a lower though sufficient morality, yet repudiating the higher morality as soon as it claimed to be the alone authoritative one. On the other hand, there were societies of Christian ascetics who persisted in applying literally to all Christians the highest demands of Christ, and thus arose, by secession, the communities of the Encratites and Severians. But in the circumstances of the time even they could not but be touched by the Hellenic mode of thought, to the effect of associating a speculative theory with asceticism, and thus approximating to Gnosticism. This is specially plain in Tatian, who connected himself with the Encratites, and in consequence of the severe asceticism which he prescribed, could no longer maintain the identity of the supreme God and the creator of the world (see the fragments of his later writings in the Corp. Apol. ed Otto. T. VI). As the Pauline Epistles could furnish arguments to either side, we see some Gnostics such as Tatian himself, making diligent use of them, while others such as the Severians, rejected them. (Euseb. H. E. IV. 29. 5, and Orig. c. Cels. V. 65). The Encratite controversy was, on the one hand, swallowed up by the Gnostic, and on the other hand, replaced by the Montanistic. The treatise written in the days of Marcus Aurelius by a certain Musanus (where?) which contains warnings against joining the Encratites (Euseb. H. E. IV. 28) we unfortunately no longer possess.

   1 See Eusebius, H. E. VI. 12. Docetic elements are apparent even in the fragment of the Gospel of Peter recently discovered
   2 Here, above all, we have to remember Tatian, who in his highly praised Apology, had already rejected altogether the eating of flesh (c. 23) and set up very peculiar doctrines about the spirit, matter, and the nature of man (c. 12 ff.). The fragments of the Hypotyposes of Clem. of Alex. show how much one had to bear in some rural Churches at the end of the second century.

were taught, the son of the founder and second teacher Epiphanes honoured as a God (at Cephallenia), as Epicurus was in his school, and the image of Jesus crowned along with those of Pythagoras, Plato and Aristotle.[1] On this left flank are, further, swindlers who take their own way, like Alexander of Abonoteichus, magicians, soothsayers, sharpers and jugglers, under the sign-board of Christianity, deceivers and hypocrites who appear using mighty words with a host of unintelligible formulæ, and take up with scandalous ceremonies, in order to rob men of their money and women of their honour.[2] All this was afterwards called "Heresy" and "Gnosticism," and is still so called.[3] And these names may be retained, if we will understand by them nothing else than the world taken into Christianity, all the manifold formations which resulted from the first contact of the new religion with the

---

[1] See Clem. Strom III. 2. 5; Ἐπιφάνης, υἱὸς Καρποκράτους, ἔζησε τὰ πάντα ἔτη ἑπτακαίδεκα καὶ θεὸς ἐν Σάμῃ τῆς Κεφαλληνίας τετίμηται, ἔνθα αὐτῷ ἱερὸν ῥυτῶν λίθων, βωμοί, τεμένη, μουσεῖον, ᾠκοδόμηταί τε καὶ καθιέρωται, καὶ συνιόντες εἰς τὸ ἱερὸν οἱ Καφαλλῆνες κατὰ νουμηνίαν γενέθλιον ἀποθέωσιν θύουσιν Ἐπιφάνει, σπένδουσί τε καὶ εὐωχοῦνται καὶ ὕμνοι λέγονται. Clement's quotations from the writings of Epiphanes shew him to be a pure Platonist: the proposition that property is theft is found in him. Epiphanes and his father, Çarpocrates, were the first who attempted to amalgamate Plato's State with the Christian ideal of the union of men with each other. Christ was to them, therefore, a philosophic Genius like Plato, see Irenæus. I. 25. 5: "Gnosticos autem se vocant, etiam imagines, quasdam quidem depictas, quasdam autem et de reliqua materia fabricatas habent . . . . . et has coronant, et proponent eas cum imaginibus mundi philosophorum, videlicet cum imagine Pythagoræ et Platonis et Aristotelis et reliquorum, et reliquam observationem circa eas similiter ut gentes faciunt."

[2] See the "Gnostics" of Hermas, especially the false prophet whom he portrays, Mand. XI., Lucian's Peregrinus, and the Marcus, of whose doings Irenæus (I 13 ff.) gives such an abominable picture. To understand how such people were able to obtain a following so quickly in the Churches, we must remember the respect in which the "prophets" were held (see Didache XI.). If one had once given the impression that he had the Spirit, he could win belief for the strangest things, and could allow himself all things possible (see the delineations of Celsus in Orig. c. Cels. VII. 9. 11). We hear frequently of Gnostic prophets and prophetesses, see my notes on Herm. Mand. XI. 1 and Didache XI 7 If an early Christian element is here preserved by the Gnostic schools, it has undoubtedly been hellenised and secularised as the reports shew. But that the prophets altogether were in danger of being secularised is shewn in Didache XI. In the case of the Gnostics the process is again only hastened.

[3] The name Gnostic originally attached to schools which had so named themselves. To these belonged, above all, the so-called Ophites, but not the Valentinians or Basilideans.

society into which it entered. To prove the existence of that
left wing of Gnosticism is of the greatest interest for the
history of dogma, but the details are of no consequence. On
the other hand, in the aims and undertakings of the Gnostic
right, it is just the details that are of greatest significance,
because they shew that there was no fixed boundary between
what one may call common Christian and Gnostic Christian.
But as Gnosticism, in its contents, extended itself from the
Encratites and the philosophic interpretation of certain articles
of the Christian proclamation, as brought forward without offence
by individual teachers in the communities, to the complete
dissolution of the Christian element by philosophy, or the
religious charlatanry of the age, so it exhibits itself formally
also in a long series of groups which comprised all imaginable
forms of unions. There were churches, ascetic associations,
mystery cults, strictly private philosophic schools,[1] free unions
for edification, entertainments by Christian charlatans and
deceived deceivers, who appeared as magicians and prophets,
attempts at founding new religions after the model and under
the influence of the Christian, etc. But, finally, the thesis that
Gnosticism is identical with an acute secularising of Christianity, in the widest sense of the word, is confirmed by the
study of its own literature. The early Christian production
of Gospel and Apocalypses was indeed continued in Gnosticism,
yet so that the class of "Acts of the Apostles" was added
to them, and that didactic, biographic and "belles lettres"

---

1 Special attention should be given to this form, as it became in later
times of the very greatest importance for the general development of doctrine in the Church. The sect of Carpocrates was a school. Of Tatian Irenæus
says (I. 28. 1): Τατίανος Ἰουστίνου ἀκροατὴς γεγονώς .... μετὰ δὲ τὴν ἐκείνου
μαρτυρίαν ἀποστὰς τῆς ἐκκλησίας, οἰήματι διδασκάλου ἐπαρθεὶς .... ἴδιον χαρακτῆρα
διδασκαλείου συνεστήσατο. Rhodon (in Euseb. H. E. V 13. 4) speaks of a
Marcionite διδασκαλεῖον. Other names were, "Collegium" (Tertull. ad Valent.
1) "Secta", the word had not always a bad meaning, αἵρεσις, ἐκκλησία
(Clem. Strom. VII. 16. 98, on the other hand, VII. 15. 92: Tertull. de præscr.
42: plerique nec Ecclesias habent), θίασος (Iren. I 13. 4, for the Marcosians),
συναγωγή, σύστημα, διατριβή, αἱ ἀθρώπιναι ςυνηλύσεις, factiuncula, congregatio,
conciliabulum, conventiculum The mystery-organisation most clearly
appears in the Naassenes of Hippolytus, the Marcosians of Irenæus, and
the Elkasites of Hippolytus, as well as in the Coptic-Gnostic documents
that have been preserved. (See Koffmane, above work, pp. 6-22).

elements were received into them, and claimed a very important place. If this makes the Gnostic literature approximate
to the profane, that is much more the case with the scientific theological literature which Gnosticism first produced. Dog-
matico-philosophic tracts, theologico-critical treatises, historical
investigations and scientific commentaries on the sacred books,
were, for the first time in Christendom, composed by the
Gnostics, who in part occupied the foremost place in the
scientific knowledge, religious earnestness and ardour of the
age. They form, in every respect, the counterpart to the
scientific works which proceeded from the contemporary philosophic schools. Moreover, we possess sufficient knowledge of
Gnostic hymns and odes, songs for public worship, didactic
poems, magic formulæ, magic books, etc., to assure us that
Christian Gnosticism took possession of a whole region of the
secular life in its full breadth, and thereby often transformed
the original forms of Christian literature into secular. [1] If,

1 The particulars here belong to church history. Overbeck ("Ueber die
Anfänge der patristischen Litteratur" in d. hist. Ztschr. N. F. Bd. XII. p. 417
ff.) has the merit of being the first to point out the importance, for the history
of the Church, of the forms of literature as they were gradually received in
Christendom. Scientific, theological literature has undoubtedly its origin in
Gnosticism. The Old Testament was here, for the first time, systematically
and also in part, historically criticised; a selection was here made from the
primitive Christian literature; scientific commentaries were here written
on the sacred books (Basilides and especially the Valentinians, see Heracleon's comm. on the Gospel of John [in Origen]; the Pauline Epistles were
also technically expounded; tracts were here composed on dogmatico-phil-
osophic problems (for example, περὶ δικαιοσύνης — περὶ προσφυοῦς ψυχῆς — ἠθικὰ
-- περὶ ἐγκρατείας ἢ περὶ εὐνουχίας), and systematic doctrinal systems already
constructed (as the Basilidean and Valentinian); the original form of the
Gospel was here first transmuted into the Greek form of sacred novel and
biography (see, above all, the Gospel of Thomas, which was used by the
Marcosians and Naassenes, and which contained miraculous stories from the
childhood of Jesus); here, finally, psalms, odes and hymns were first composed (see the Acts of Lucius, the psalms of Valentinus, the psalms of Alexander the disciple of Valentinus, the poems of Bardesanes). Irenæus, Tertullian
and Hippolytus have indeed noted, that the scientific method of interpretation followed by the Gnostics, was the same as that of the philosophers
(e. g., of Philo). Valentinus, as is recognised even by the Church Fathers,
stands out prominent for his mental vigour and religious imagination,
Heracleon for his exegetic theological ability, Ptolemy for his ingenious
criticism of the Old Testament and his keen perception of the stages of
religious development (see his Epistle to Flora in Epiphanius, hær. 33. c. 7).
As a specimen of the language of Valentinus one extract from a homily may
suffice (in Clem. Strom. IV. 13. 89). Ἀπ᾽ ἀρχῆς ἀθάνατοί ἐστε καὶ τέκνα ζωῆς ἐστε

however, we bear in mind how all this at a later period was gradually legitimised in the Catholic Church, philosophy, the science of the sacred books, criticism and exegesis, the ascetic associations, the theological schools, the mysteries, the sacred formulæ, the superstition, the charlatanism, all kinds of profane literature, etc., it seems to prove the thesis that the victorious epoch of the gradual hellenising of Christianity followed the abortive attempts at an acute hellenising.

The traditional question as to the origin and development of Gnosticism, as well as that about the classification of the Gnostic systems, will have to be modified in accordance with the foregoing discussion. As the different Gnostic systems might be contemporary, and in part were undoubtedly contemporary, and as a graduated relation holds good only between some few groups, we must, in the classification, limit ourselves essentially to the features which have been specified in the foregoing paragraph, and which coincide with the position of the different groups to the early Christian tradition in its connection with the Old Testament religion, both as a rule of practical life, and of the common cultus. [1]

As to the origin of Gnosticism, we see how, even in the earliest period, all possible ideas and principles foreign to Christianity force their way into it, that is, are brought in under Christian rules, and find entrance, especially in the consideration of the Old Testament. [2] We might be satisfied

---

αἰωνίας, καὶ τὸν θάνατον ἠθέλετε μερίσασθαι εἰς ἑαυτούς, ἵνα δαπανήσητε αὐτὸν καὶ ἀναλώσητε, καὶ ἀποθάνῃ ὁ θάνατος ἐν ὑμῖν καὶ δι᾽ ὑμῶν, ὅταν γὰρ τὸν μὲν κόσμον λύητε, αὐτοὶ δὲ μὴ καταλύητθε, κυριεύετε τῆς κρίσεως καὶ τῆς φθορᾶς ἀπάσης. Basilides falls into the background behind Valentinus and his school. Yet the Church Fathers, when they wish to summarise the most important Gnostics, usually mention Simon Magus, Basilides, Valentinus, Marcion (even Apelles). On the relation of the Gnostics to the New Testament writings, and to the New Testament, see Zahn, Gesch des N. T-lichen Kanons I. 2, p 718.

1 Baur's classification of the Gnostic systems, which rests on the observation of how they severally realised the idea of Christianity as the absolute religion, in contrast to Judaism and Heathenism, is very ingenious, and contains a great element of truth. But it is insufficient with reference to the whole phenomenon of Gnosticism, and it has been carried out by Baur by violent abstractions.

2 The question, therefore, as to the time of the origin of Gnosticism, as a complete phenomenon, cannot be answered The remarks of Hegesippus (Euseb. H. E. IV. 22) refer to the Jerusalem Church, and have not even for

with the observation that the manifold Gnostic systems were produced by the increase of this tendency. In point of fact we must admit that in the present state of our sources, we can reach no sure knowledge beyond that. These sources, however, give certain indications which should not be left unnoticed. If we leave out of account the two assertions of opponents, that Gnosticism was produced by demons [1] and —this, however, was said at a comparatively late period—that it originated in ambition and resistance to the ecclesiastical office, the episcopate, we find in Hegesippus, one of the earliest writers on the subject, the statement that the whole of the heretical schools sprang out of Judaism or the Jewish sects; in the later writers, Irenæus, Tertullian and Hippolytus, that these schools owe most to the doctrines of Pythagoras, Plato, Aristotle, Zeno, etc. [2] But they all agree in this, that a definite personality, viz., Simon the Magician, must be regarded as the original source of the heresy. If we try it by these statements of the Church Fathers, we must see at once that the problem in this case is limited—certainly in a proper way. For after Gnosticism is seen to be the acute secularising of Christianity the only question that remains is, how are we to account for the origin of the great Gnostic schools, that is, whether it is possible to indicate their preliminary stages. The following may be asserted here with some confidence: Long before the appearance of Christianity, combinations of religion had taken place in Syria and Palestine, [3] especially in Samaria, in so far, on the one hand, as the Assyrian and Babylonian religious philosophy, together with its myths, as

that the value of a fixed datum. The only important question here is the point of time at which the expulsion or secession of the schools and unions took place in the different national churches.

1 Justin Apol. 1. 26.

2 Hegesippus in Euseb. H. E. IV. 22, Iren. II. 14. 1 f., Tertull. de præscr. 7, Hippol. Philosoph. The Church Fathers have also noted the likeness of the cultus of Mithras and other deities.

3 We must leave the Essenes entirely out of account here, as their teaching, in all probability, is not to be considered syncretistic in the strict sense of the word, (see Lucius, "Der Essenismus", 1881), and as we know absolutely nothing of a greater diffusion of it. But we need no names here, as a syncretistic, ascetic Judaism could and did arise everywhere in Palestine and the Diaspora.

well as the Greek popular religion, with its manifold interpretations, had penetrated as far as the eastern shore of the Mediterranean, and been accepted even by the Jews, and, on the
other hand, the Jewish Messianic idea had spread and called
forth various movements. [1] The result of every mixing of
national religions, however, is to break through the traditional,
legal and particular forms. [2] For the Jewish religion syncretism signified the shaking of the authority of the Old
Testament by a qualitative distinction of its different parts,
as also doubt as to the identity of the supreme God with
the national God. These ferments were once more set in
motion by Christianity. We know that in the Apostolic age
there were attempts in Samaria to found new religions, which
were in all probability influenced by the tradition and preaching concerning Jesus. Dositheus, Simon Magus, Cleobius,
and Menander appeared as Messiahs or bearers of the Godhead, and proclaimed a doctrine in which the Jewish faith
was strangely and grotesquely mixed with Babylonian myths,
together with some Greek additions. The mysterious worship,
the breaking up of Jewish particularism, the criticism of the
Old Testament, which for long had had great difficulty in
retaining its authority in many circles, in consequence of the
widened horizon and the deepening of religious feeling, finally,
the wild syncretism, whose aim, however, was a universal
religion, all contributed to gain adherents for Simon. [3] His

1 Freudenthal's "Hellenistische Studien" informs us as to the Samaritan
syncretism; see also Hilgenfeld's " Ketzergeschichte ", p. 149 ff. As to the
Babylonian mythology in Gnosticism, see the statements in the elaborate
article, "Manichäismus ", by Kessler (Real-Encycl. für protest. Theol., 2 Aufl.).
    2 Wherever traditional religions are united under the badge of philosophy
a conservative syncretism is the result, because the allegoric method,
that is, the criticism of all religion, veiled and unconscious of itself, is
able to blast rocks and bridge over abysses. All forms may remain here,
under certain circumstances, but a new spirit enters into them. On the
other hand, where philosophy is still weak, and the traditional religion
is already shaken by another, there arises the critical syncretism in which
either the gods of one religion are subordinated to those of another, or
the elements of the traditional religion are partly eliminated and replaced
by others. Here, also, the soil is prepared for new religious formations,
for the appearance of religious founders.
    3 It was a serious mistake of the critics to regard Simon Magus as a fiction,
which, moreover, has been given up by Hilgenfeld (Ketzergeschichte, p. 163 ff.),

enterprise appeared to the Christians as a diabolical caricature
of their own religion, and the impression made by the success
which Simonianism gained by a vigorous propaganda even
beyond Palestine into the West, supported this idea. [1] We can
therefore understand how, afterwards, all heresies were traced
back to Simon. To this must be added that we can actually
trace in many Gnostic systems the same elements which were
prominent in the religion proclaimed by Simon (the Babylonian and Syrian), and that the new religion of the Simonians,
just like Christianity, had afterwards to submit to be transformed into a philosophic, scholastic doctrine. [2] The formal
parallel to the Gnostic doctrines was therewith established.
But even apart from these attempts at founding new religions,
Christianity in Syria, under the influence of foreign religions
and speculation on the philosophy of religion, gave a powerful
impulse to the criticism of the law and the prophets which
had already been awakened. In consequence of this, there
appeared, about the transition of the first century to the second,
a series of teachers, who, under the impression of the Gospel,
sought to make the Old Testament capable of furthering the
tendency to a universal religion, not by allegorical interpre-

and Lipsius (Apocr. Apostelgesch. I I. 1),—the latter, however, not decidedly. The whole figure, as well as the doctrines attributed to Simon
(see Acts of the Apostles, Justin, Irenæus, Hippolytus), not only have
nothing improbable in them, but suit very well the religious circumstances
which we must assume for Samaria. The main point in Simon is his
endeavour to create a universal religion of the supreme God. This explains his success among the Samaritans and Greeks. He is really a
counterpart to Jesus, whose activity can just as little have been unknown
to him as that of Paul. At the same time, it cannot be denied, that the
later tradition about Simon was the most confused and biassed imaginable,
or that certain Jewish Christians at a later period may have attempted
to endow the magician with the features of Paul in order to discredit
the personality and teaching of the Apostle. But this last assumption
requires a fresh investigation.

1 Justin. Apol. I. 26: Καὶ σχεδὸν πάντες μὲν Σαμαρεις, ὀλίγοι δὲ καὶ ἐν ἄλλοις
ἔθνεσιν, ὡς τὸν πρῶτον θεὸν Σίμωνα ὁμολογοῦντες, ἐκεῖνον καὶ προσκυνοῦσιν (besides
the account in the Philos. and Orig. c. Cels. I. 57: VI. 11). The positive
statement of Justin that Simon came even to Rome (under Claudius) can
hardly be refuted from the account of the Apologist himself, and therefore not at all (See Renan, "Antichrist").

2 We have it as such in the Μεγάλη Ἀπόφασις which Hippolytus (Philosoph.
VI. 19. 20) made use of. This Simonianism may perhaps have been related
to the original, as the doctrines of the Christian Gnostics to the Apostolic
preaching.

tation, but by a sifting criticism. These attempts were of very different kinds. Teachers such as Cerinthus, clung to the notion that the universal religion revealed by Christ was identical with undefiled Mosaism, and therefore maintained even such articles as circumcision and the Sabbath commandment, as well as the earthly kingdom of the future. But they rejected certain parts of the law, especially, as a rule, the sacrificial precepts, which were no longer in keeping with the spiritual conception of religion. They conceived the creator of the world as a subordinate being distinct from the supreme God, which is always the mark of a syncretism with a dualistic tendency; introduced speculations about Æons and angelic powers, among whom they placed Christ, and recommended a strict asceticism. When, in their Christology, they denied the miraculous birth, and saw in Jesus a chosen man on whom the Christ, that is, the Holy Spirit, descended at the baptism, they were not creating any innovation, but only following the earliest Palestinian tradition. Their rejection of the authority of Paul is explained by their efforts to secure the Old Testament as far as possible for the universal religion. [1] There were others who rejected all ceremonial commandments as proceeding from the devil, or from some intermediate being, but yet always held firmly that the God of the Jews was the supreme God. But alongside of these stood also decidedly anti-Jewish groups, who seem to have been influenced in part by the preaching of Paul. They advanced much further in the criticism of the Old Testament and perceived the impossibility of saving it for the Christian universal religion. They rather connected this religion with the cultus-wisdom of Babylon and Syria, which seemed more adapted for allegorical interpretations, and opposed this formation to the Old Testament religion. The God of the Old Testament appears here at best as a subordinate Angel of limited power, wisdom and

---

[1] The Heretics opposed in the Epistle to the Colossians may belong to these. On Cerinthus, see Polycarp, in Iren. III. 3. 2, Irenæus (I 26. I.: III. 11. 1), Hippolytus and the redactions of the Syntagma, Cajus in Euseb. III. 28. 2, Hilgenfeld, Ketzergeschichte, p. 411 ff. To this category belong also the Ebionites and Elkasites of Epiphanius (See Chap. 6).

goodness. In so far as he was identified with the creator of the world, and the creation of the world itself was regarded as an imperfect or an abortive undertaking, expression was given both to the anti-Judaism and to that religious temper of the time, which could only value spiritual blessing in contrast with the world and the sensuous. These systems appeared more or less strictly dualistic, in proportion as they did or did not accept a slight co-operation of the supreme God in the creation of man; and the way in which the character and power of the world-creating God of the Jews was conceived, serves as a measure of how far the several schools were from the Jewish religion and the Monism that ruled it. All possible conceptions of the God of the Jews, from the assumption that he is a being supported in his undertakings by the supreme God, to his identification with Satan, seem to have been exhausted in these schools. Accordingly, in the former case, the Old Testament was regarded as the revelation of a subordinate God, in the latter as the manifestation of Satan, and therefore the ethic—with occasional use of Pauline formulæ — always assumed an antinomian form, compared with the Jewish law, in some cases antinomian even in the sense of libertinism. Correspondingly, the anthropology exhibits man as bipartite, or even tripartite, and the Christology is strictly docetic and anti-Jewish. The redemption by Christ is always, as a matter of course, related only to that element in humanity which has an affinity with the Godhead. [1]

1 The two Syrian teachers, Saturninus and Cerdo, must in particular be mentioned here. The first (See Iren. I. 24. 1. 2, Hippolyt. and the redactions of the Syntagma) was not strictly speaking a dualist, and therefore allowed the God of the Old Testament to be regarded as an Angel of the supreme God, while at the same time he distinguished him from Satan. Accordingly, he assumed that the supreme God co-operated in the creation of man by angel powers—sending a ray of light, an image of light, that should be imitated as an example and enjoined as an ideal. But all men have not received the ray of light. Consequently, two classes of men stand in abrupt contrast with each other. History is the conflict of the two Satan stands at the head of the one, the God of the Jews at the head of the other. The Old Testament is a collection of prophecies out of both camps The truly good first appears in the Æon Christ, who assumed nothing cosmic. did not even submit to birth. He destroys the works of Satan (generation. eating of flesh), and delivers the men who have within them a spark of light. The Gnosis of

It is uncertain whether we should think of the spread of these doctrines in Syria in the form of a school, or of a cultus; probably it was both. From the great Gnostic systems as formed by Basilides and Valentinus they are distinguished by the fact, that they lack the peculiar philosophic, that is Hellenic element, the speculative conversion of angels and Æons into real ideas, etc. We have almost no knowledge of their effect. This Gnosticism has never directly been a historical factor of striking importance, and the great question is whether it was so indirectly.[1] That is to say, we do not know whether this Syrian Gnosticism was, in the strict sense, the preparatory stage of the great Gnostic schools, so that these schools should be regarded as an actual reconstruction of it. But there can be no doubt that the appearance of the great Gnostic schools in the Empire, from Egypt to Gaul, is contemporaneous with the vigorous projection of Syrian cults westwards, and therefore the assumption is suggested, that the Syrian Christian syncretism was also spread in connection with that projection, and underwent a change corresponding to the new conditions. We know definitely that the Syrian Gnostic, Cerdo, came to Rome, wrought there, and exercised an influence on Marcion. But no less probable is the assumption that the great Hellenic Gnostic schools arose spontaneously, in the sense of having been independently developed out of the elements to which undoubtedly the Asiatic cults also belonged, without being influenced in any way by Syrian syncretistic efforts. The conditions for the growth of such

Cerdo was much coarser. (Iren. I. 27. 1, Hippolyt. and the redactions). He contrasted the good God and the God of the Old Testament as two primary beings. The latter he identified with the creator of the world. Consequently, he completely rejected the Old Testament and everything cosmic and taught that the good God was first revealed in Christ. Like Saturninus he preached a strict docetism; Christ had no body, was not born, and suffered in an unreal body. All else that the Fathers report of Cerdo's teaching has probably been transferred to him from Marcion, and is therefore very doubtful.

1 This question might perhaps be answered if we had the Justinian Syntagma against all heresies; but, in the present condition of our sources, it remains wrapped in obscurity. What may be gathered from the fragments of Hegesippus, the Epistles of Ignatius, the Pastoral Epistles and other documents, such as, for example, the Epistle of Jude, is in itself so obscure, so detached, and so ambiguous, that it is of no value for historical construction.

formations were nearly the same in all parts of the Empire. The great advance lies in the fact that the religious material as contained in the Gospel, the Old Testament, and the wisdom connected with the old cults, was philosophically, that is, scientifically, manipulated by means of allegory, and the aggregate of mythological powers translated into an aggregate of ideas. The Pythagorean and Platonic, more rarely the Stoic philosophy, were compelled to do service here. Great Gnostic schools, which were at the same time unions for worship, first enter into the clear light of history in this form, (see previous section), and on the conflict with these, surrounded as they were by a multitude of dissimilar and related formations, depends the progress of the development. [1]

We are no longer able to form a perfectly clear picture of how these schools came into being, or how they were related to the Churches. It lay in the nature of the case that the heads of the schools, like the early itinerant heretical teachers, devoted attention chiefly, if not exclusively, to those who were already Christian, that is, to the Christian communities. [2] From the Ignatian Epistles, the Shepherd of

[1] There are, above all, the schools of the Basilideans, Valentinians and Ophites. To describe the systems in their full development lies, in my opinion, outside the business of the history of dogma and might easily lead to the mistake that the systems as such were controverted, and that their construction was peculiar to Christian Gnosticism. The construction, as remarked above, is rather that of the later Greek philosophy, though it cannot be mistaken that, for us, the full parallel to the Gnostic systems first appears in those of the Neoplatonists. But only particular doctrines and principles of the Gnostics were really called in question, their critique of the world, of providence, of the resurrection, etc.; these therefore are to be adduced in the next section. The fundamental features of an inner development can only be exhibited in the case of the most important, viz., the Valentinian school. But even here, we must distinguish an Eastern and a Western branch. (Tertull. adv. Valent. I.: "Valentiniani frequentissimum plane collegium inter hæreticos". Iren. l. l.; Hippol. Philos. VI. 35; Orig. Hom. II. 5 in Ezech. Lomm. XIV. p. 40: "Valentini robustissima secta").

[2] Tertull. de præscr. 42: "De verbi autem administratione quid dicam, cum hoc sit negotium illis, non ethnicos convertendi, sed nostros evertendi? Hanc magis gloriam captant, si stantibus ruinam, non si jacentibus elevationem operentur. Quoniam et ipsum opus eorum non de suo proprio ædificio venit, sed de veritatis destructione; nostra suffodiunt, ut sua ædificent. Adime illis legem Moysis et prophetas et creatorem deum, accusationem eloqui non habent" (See adv. Valent. I init.). This is hardly a malevolent accusation. The philosophic interpretation of a religion will always impress those only on whom the religion itself has already made an impression.

Hermas (Vis. III. 7. 1 : Sim. VIII. 6. 5 : IX. 19. and especially 22),
and the Didache (XI. 1. 2) we see that those teachers who
boasted of a special knowledge, and sought to introduce
"strange" doctrines, aimed at gaining the entire churches.
The beginning, as a rule, was necessarily the formation of
conventicles. In the first period therefore, when there was
no really fixed standard for warding off the foreign doctrines—
Hermas is unable even ·to characterise the false doctrines—
the warnings were commonly exhausted in the exhortation:
κολλᾶσθε τοῖς ἁγίοις, ὅτι οἱ κολλώμενοι αὐτοῖς ἁγιασθήσονται,
["connect yourselves with the saints, because those who are
connected with them shall be sanctified"]. As a rule, the
doctrines may really have crept in unobserved, and those
gained over to them may for long have taken part in a twofold worship, the public worship of the churches, and the
new consecration. Those teachers must of course have assumed a more aggressive attitude who rejected the Old Testament. The attitude of the Church, when it enjoyed competent
guidance, was one of decided opposition towards unmasked or
recognised false teachers. Yet Irenæus' account of Cerdo in
Rome shews us how difficult it was at the beginning to get
rid of a false teacher. [1] For Justin, about the year 150, the
Marcionites, Valentinians, Basilideans and Saturninians, are
groups outside the communities, and undeserving of the name
"Christians". [2] There must therefore have been at that time,
in Rome and Asia Minor at least, a really perfect separation
of those schools from the Churches (it was different in Alexandria). Notwithstanding, this continued to be the region
from which those schools obtained their adherents. For the

3 Iren. III. 4. 2 : Κέρδων εἰς τὴν ἐκκλησίαν ἐλθὼν καὶ ἐξομολογούμενος, οὕτως
διετέλεσε, ποτὲ μὲν λαθροδιδασκαλῶν ποτὲ δὲ πάλιν ἐξομολογούμενος, ποτὲ δὲ ἐλεγ-
χόμενος ἐφ᾽ οἷς ἐδίδασκε κακῶς, καὶ ἀφιστάμενος τῆς τῶν ἀδελφῶν συνοδίας ; see,
besides, the valuable account of Tertull. de præscr. 30. The account of
Irenæus (I. 13) is very instructive as to the kind of propaganda of Marcus,
and the relation of the women he deluded to the Church. Against actually
recognised false teachers the fixed rule was to renounce all intercourse
with them (2 Joh. 10. 11 ; Iren. ep. ad. Florin on Polycarp's procedure,
in Euseb. H. E. V. 20. 7 ; Iren. III. 3. 4). But how were the heretics to
be surely known?

2 Among those who justly bore this name he distinguishes those οἱ
ὀρθογνώμενες κατὰ πάντα χριστανοί εἰσιν (Dial. 80).

Valentinians recognised that the common Christians were much
better than the heathen, that they occupied a middle position
between the "pneumatic" and the "hylic", and might look
forward to a kind of salvation. This admission, as well as
their conforming to the common Christian tradition, enabled
them to spread their views in a remarkable way, and they
may not have had any objection in many cases, to their
converts remaining in the great Church. But can this community have perceived everywhere and at once, that the
Valentinian distinction of "psychic" and "pneumatic" is not
identical with the scriptural distinction of children and men
in understanding? Where the organisation of the school (the
union for worship) required a long time of probation, where
degrees of connection with it were distinguished, and a strict
asceticism demanded of the perfect, it followed of course that
those on the lower stage should not be urged to a speedy
break with the Church. [1] But after the creation of the
catholic confederation of churches, existence was made more
and more difficult for these schools. Some of them lived on
somewhat like our freemason-unions, some, as in the East,
became actual sects (confessions), in which the wise and the
simple now found a place, as they were propagated by families.
In both cases they ceased to be what they had been at the
beginning. From about 210, they ceased to be a factor of

---

1 Very important is the description which Irenæus (III. 15. 2) and
Tertullian have given of the conduct of the Valentinians as observed by
themselves (adv. Valent. 1). " Valentiniani nihil magis curant quam occultare,
quod prædicant; si tamen prædicant qui occultant. Custodiæ officium
conscientiæ officium est (a comparison with the Eleusinian mysteries
follows.) Si bona fide quæras, concreto vultu. suspenso supercilio, Altum
est, aiunt. Si subtiliter temptes per ambiguitates bilingues communem
fidem adfirmant. Si scire te subostendas negant quidquid agnoscunt.
Si cominus certes, tuam simplicitatem sua cæde dispergunt. Ne discipulis
quidem propriis ante committunt quam suos fecerint. Habent artificium
quo prius persuadeant quam edoceant." At a later period Dionysius
of Alex. (in Euseb. H. E. VII. 7· speaks of Christians who maintain
an apparent communion with the brethren. but resort to one of the
false teachers (cf. as to this Euseb. H E. VI. 2. 13). The teaching
of Bardesanes influenced by Valentinus, who, moreover, was hostile to
Marcionitism, was tolerated for a long time in Edessa (by the Christian
kings), nay, was recognised. The Bardesanites and the "Palutians" (catholics)
were differentiated only after the beginning of the third century.

the historical development, though the Church of Constantine
and Theodosius was alone really able to suppress them.

§ 4. *The most important Gnostic Doctrines.*

We have still to measure and compare with the earliest
tradition those Gnostic doctrines which, partly at once and
partly in the following period, became important. Once more,
however, we must expressly refer to the fact, that the epoch-
making significance of Gnosticism for the history of dogma,
must not be sought chiefly in the particular doctrines, but
rather in the whole way in which Christianity is here conceived
and transformed. The decisive thing is the conversion of the
Gospel into a doctrine, into an absolute philosophy of religion,
the transforming of the *disciplina Evangelii* into an asceticism
based on a dualistic conception, and into a practice of mysteries. [1] We have now briefly to shew, with due regard to
the earliest tradition, how far this transformation was of positive or negative significance for the following period, that is,
in what respects the following development was anticipated by
Gnosticism, and in what respects Gnosticism was disavowed
by this development. [2]

[1] There can be no doubt that the Gnostic propaganda was seriously
hindered by the inability to organise and discipline churches, which is
characteristic of all philosophic systems of religion. The Gnostic organisation
of schools and mysteries was not able to contend with the episcopal
organisation of the churches; see Ignat. ad Smyr. 6. 2; Tertull. de præscr.
41. Attempts at actual formations of churches were not altogether wanting
in the earliest period; at a later period they were forced on some schools.
We have only to read Iren. III. 15. 2 in order to see that these associations
could only exist by finding support in a church. Irenæus expressly remarks
that the Valentinians designated the common Christians καθολικοί (communes)
καὶ ἐκκλησιαστικοί, but that they, on the other hand, complained that "we
kept away from their fellowship without cause, as they thought like ourselves."
[2] The differences between the Gnostic Christianity and that of the Church,
that is, the later ecclesiastical theology, were fluid, if we observe the following
points. (1) That even in the main body of the Church, the element of knowledge was increasingly emphasised, and the Gospel began to be converted into
a perfect knowledge of the world (increasing reception of Greek philosophy,
development of πίστις to γνῶσις). (2) That the dramatic eschatology began
to fade away. (3) That room was made for docetic views, and value put upon
a strict asceticism. On the other hand, we must note: (1) That all this existed
only in germ or fragments within the great Church during the flourishing

(1) Christianity, which is the only true and absolute religion, embraces a revealed system of doctrine (positive).

(2) This doctrine contains mysterious powers, which are communicated to men by initiation (mysteries).

(3) The revealer is Christ (positive), but Christ alone, and only in his historical appearance — no Old Testament Christ (negative); this appearance is itself redemption: the doctrine is the announcement of it and of its presuppositions (positive). [1]

(4) Christian doctrine is to be drawn from the Apostolic tradition, critically examined. This tradition lies before us in a series of Apostolic writings, and in a secret doctrine derived from the Apostles, (positive). [2] As exoteric it is compre-

period of Gnosticism. (2) That the great Church held fast to the facts fixed in the baptismal formula (in the *Kerygma*), and to the eschatological expectations, further, to the creator of the world as the supreme God, to the unity of Jesus Christ, and to the Old Testament, and therefore rejected dualism. (3) That the great Church defended the unity and equality of the human race, and therefore the uniformity and universal aim of the Christian salvation. (4) That it rejected every introduction of new, especially of Oriental Mythologies, guided in this by the early Christian consciousness and a sure intelligence. A deeper, more thorough distinction between the Church and the Gnostic parties hardly dawned on the consciousness of either. The Church developed herself instinctively into an imperial Church, in which office was to play the chief rôle. The Gnostics sought to establish or conserve associations in which the genius should rule, the genius in the way of the old prophets or in the sense of Plato, or in the sense of a union of prophecy and philosophy. In the Gnostic conflict, at least at its close, the judicial priest fought with the virtuoso and overcame him.

1 The absolute significance of the person of Christ was very plainly expressed in Gnosticism (Christ is not only the teacher of the truth, but the manifestation of the truth), more plainly than where he was regarded as the subject of Old Testament revelation. The pre-existent Christ has significance in some Gnostic schools, but always a comparatively subordinate one. The isolating of the person of Christ, and quite as much the explaining away of his humanity, is manifestly out of harmony with the earliest tradition. But, on the other hand, it must not be denied that the Gnostics recognised redemption in the historical Christ: Christ personally procured it (see under 6. h.).

2 In this thesis, which may be directly corroborated by the most important Gnostic teachers, Gnosticism shews that it desires *in thesi* (in a way similar to Philo) to continue on the soil of Christianity as a positive religion. Conscious of being bound to tradition, it first definitely raised the question, what is Christianity? and criticised and sifted the sources for an answer to the question. The rejection of the Old Testament led it to that question and to this sifting. It may be maintained with the greatest probability, that the idea of a canonical collection of Christian writings first emerged among the Gnostics (see also Marcion). They really needed such a collection, while all those who recognised the Old Testament as a document of revelation, and gave it a Christian interpretation, did not at first need a new document, but simply joined on the new to the old, the Gospel to the Old Testament. From

the numerous fragments of Gnostic commentaries on New Testament writings which have been preserved, we see that these writings there enjoyed canonical authority, while at the same period, we hear nothing of such authority, nor of commentaries in the main body of Christendom (see Heinrici, " Die Valentinianische Gnosis, u. d. h Schrift", 1871). Undoubtedly, sacred writings were selected according to the principle of apostolic origin. This is proved by the inclusion of the Pauline Epistles in the collections of books. There is evidence of such having been made by the Naassenes, Peratæ, Valentinians, Marcion, Tatian and the Gnostic Justin. The collection of the Valentinians, and the Canon of Tatian must have really coincided with the main parts of the later Ecclesiastical Canon. The later Valentinians accommodated themselves to this Canon, that is, recognised the books that had been added (Tertull. de præscr. 38). The question as to who first conceived and realised the idea of a Canon of Christian writings, Basilides, or Valentinus, or Marcion, or whether this was done by several at the same time, will always remain obscure, though many things favour Marcion. If it should even be proved that Basilides (see Euseb. H. E. IV. 7. 7) and Valentinus himself, regarded the Gospels only as authoritative, yet the full idea of the Canon lies already in the fact of their making these the foundation and interpreting them allegorically. The question as to the extent of the Canon afterwards became the subject of an important controversy between the Gnostics and the Catholic Church. The Catholics throughout took up the position that their Canon was the earlier, and the Gnostic collection the corrupt revision of it (they were unable to adduce proof, as is attested by Tertullian's de præscr.). But the aim of the Gnostics to establish themselves on the uncorrupted apostolic tradition, gathered from writings, was crossed by three tendencies, which, moreover, were all jointly operative in the Christian communities, and are therefore not peculiar to Gnosticism. (1) By faith in the continuance of prophecy, in which new things are always revealed by the Holy Spirit (the Basilidean and Marcionite prophets). (2) By the assumption of an esoteric secret tradition of the Apostles (see Clem. Strom. VII. 17. 106. 108; Hipp. Philos. VII. 20; Iren. I. 25. 5 : III. 2. 1; Tertull. de præscr. 25. Cf. the Gnostic book, Πίστις Σοφία, which in great part is based on doctrines said to be imparted by Jesus to his disciples after his resurrection). (3) By the inability to oppose the continuous production of Evangelic writings, in other words, by the continuance of this kind of literature and the addition of Acts of the Apostles (Gospel of the Egyptians (?), other Gospels, Acts of John, Thomas. Philip, etc. We know absolutely nothing about the conditions under which these writings originated. the measure of authority which they enjoyed. or the way in which they gained that authority). In all these points, which in Gnosticism hindered the development of Christianity to the "religion of a new book", the Gnostic schools shew that they stood precisely under the same conditions as the Christian communities in general (see above Chap. 3. § 2). If all things do not deceive us, the same inner development may be observed even in the Valentinian school, as in the great Church, viz , the production of sacred Evangelic and Apostolic writings, prophecy and secret gnosis, falling more and more into the background, and the completed Canon becoming the most important basis of the doctrine of religion. The later Valentinians (see Tertull. de præscr. and adv. Valent) seem to have appealed chiefly to this Canon, and Tatian no less (about whose Canon, see my Texte u. Unters I. 1. 2. pp. 213-218). But finally, we must refer to the fact that it was the highest concern of the Gnostics to furnish the historical proof of the Apostolic origin of their doctrine by an exact reference to the links of the tradition (see Ritschl, Entstehung der altkath. Kirche 2nd ed. p. 338. f.) Here again it appears that Gnosticism shared with Christendom the universal presupposition that the valuable thing is the Apostolic origin

hended in the *regula fidei* (positive),[1] as esoteric it is propagated by chosen teachers.[2]

(5) The documents of revelation (Apostolic writings), just because they are such, must be interpreted by means of allegory, that is, their deeper meaning must be extracted in this way (positive).[3]

(see above. p. 160 f.), but that it first created artifical chains of tradition, and that this is the first point in which it was followed by the Church: (see the appeals to the Apostle Matthew, to Peter and Paul, through the mediation of "Glaukias", and "Theodas", to James and the favourite disciples of the Lord, in the case of the Naassenes, Ophites, Basilideans and Valentinians, etc.; see, further, the close of the Epistle of Ptolemy to Flora in Epiphan. H. 33. 7: Μαθήσῃ ἑξῆς καὶ τὴν τούτου ἀρχήν τε καὶ γέννησιν, ἀξιουμένη τῆς ἀποστολικῆς παραδόσεως, ἣ ἐκ διαδοχῆς καὶ ἡμεῖς παρειλήφαμεν, μετὰ καιροῦ [sic] κανονίσαι πάντας τοὺς λόγους τῇ τοῦ σωτῆρος διδασκαλίᾳ, as well as the passages adduced above under 2). From this it further follows that the Gnostics may have compiled their Canon solely according to the principle of Apostolic origin. Upon the whole we may see here, how foolish it is to seek to dispose of Gnosticism with the phrase, "lawless fancies". On the contrary, the Gnostics purposely took their stand on the tradition; nay, they were the first in Christendom who determined the range, contents and manner of propagating the tradition. They are thus the first Christian theologians.

1 Here also we have a point of unusual historical importance. As we first find a new Canon among the Gnostics, so also among them (and in Marcion) we first meet with the traditional complex of the Christian *Kerygma* as a doctrinal confession (*regula fidei*), that is, as a confession, which, because it is fundamental, needs a speculative exposition, but is set forth by this exposition as the summary of all wisdom. The hesitancy about the details of the *Kerygma* only shews the general uncertainty which at that time prevailed. But again, we see that the later Valentinians completely accommodated themselves to the later development in the Church (Tertull. adv. Valent. I.: "communem fidem adfirmant"), that is. attached themselves, probably even from the first, to the existing forms, while in the Marcionite Church a peculiar *regula* was set up by a criticism of the tradition. The *regula*, as a matter of course, was regarded as Apostolic. On Gnostic *regulæ*, see Iren. I. 21. 5, 31. 3: II. præf.: II. 19. 8: III. 11. 3. III 16. 1. 5: Ptolem. ap. Epiph. h. 33. 7; Tertull. adv. Valent. 1. 4: de præscr. 42: adv. Marc. I. 1: IV. 5. 17; Ep. Petri ad Jacob in Clem. Hom. c. 1. We still possess, in great part verbatim, the *regula* of Apelles, in Epiphan. h. 44 2. Irenæus (I. 7. 2) and Tertull. (de carne, 20) state that the Valentinian *regula* contained the formula; "γεννηθέντα διὰ Μαρίας"; see on this p. 203. In noting that the two points so decisive for Catholicism, the Canon of the New Testament and the Apostolic *regula*, were first, in the strict sense, set up by the Gnostics on the basis of a definite fixing and systematising of the oldest tradition, we may see that the weakness of Gnosticism here consisted in its inability to exhibit the publicity of tradition and to place its propagation in close connection with the organisation of the churches.

2 We do not know the relation in which the Valentinians placed the public Apostolic *regula fidei* to the secret doctrine derived from one Apostle. The Church, in opposition to the Gnostics, strongly emphasised the publicity of all tradition. Yet afterwards, though with reservations, she gave a wide scope to the assumption of a secret tradition.

3 The Gnostics transferred to the Evangelic writings, and demanded as simply necessary, the methods which Barnabas and others used in

(6) The following may be noted as the main points in the Gnostic conception of the several parts of the *regula fidei*.

(*a*) The difference between the supreme God and the creator of the world, and therewith the opposing of redemption and creation, and therefore the separation of the Mediator of revelation from the Mediator of creation. [1]

(*b*) The separation of the supreme God from the God of the Old Testament, and therewith the rejection of the Old Testament, or the assertion that the Old Testament contains no revelations of the supreme God, or at least only in certain parts. [2]

(*c*) The doctrine of the independence and eternity of matter.

(*d*) The assertion that the present world sprang from a fall

---

expounding the Old Testament (see the samples of their exposition in Irenæus and Clement. Heinrici, l. c.). In this way, of course, all the specialties of the systems may be found in the documents. The Church at first condemned this method (Tertull. de præscr. 17-19. 39; Iren. I. 8. 9), but applied it herself from the moment in which she had adopted a New Testament Canon of equal authority with that of the Old Testament. However, the distinction always remained, that in the confrontation of the two Testaments with the views of getting proofs from prophecy, the history of Jesus described in the Gospels was not at first allegorised. Yet afterwards, the Christological dogmas of the third and following centuries demanded a docetic explanation of many points in that history.

1 In the Valentinian, as well as in all systems not coarsely dualistic, the Redeemer Christ has no doubt a certain share in the constitution of the highest class of men, but only through complicated mediations. The significance which is attributed to Christ in many systems for the production or organisation of the upper world, may be mentioned. In the Valentianian system there are several mediators. It may be noted that the abstract conception of the divine primitive Being seldom called forth a real controversy. As a rule, offence was taken only at the expression.

2 The Epistle of Ptolemy to Flora is very instructive here. If we leave out of account the peculiar Gnostic conception, we have represented in Ptolemy's criticism the later Catholic view of the Old Testament, as well as also the beginning of a historical conception of it. The Gnostics were the first critics of the Old Testament in Christendom. Their allegorical exposition of the Evangelic writings should be taken along with their attempts at interpreting the Old Testament literally and historically. It may be noted, for example, that the Gnostics were the first to call attention to the significance of the change of name for God in the Old Testament; see Iren. II 35. 3. The early Christian tradition led to a procedure directly the opposite. Apelles, in particular, the disciple of Marcion, exercised an intelligent criticism on the Old Testament, see my treatise, "de Apellis gnosi." p. 71 sq., and also Texte u. Unters. VI. 3. p. 111 ff. Marcion himself recognised the historical contents of the Old Testament as reliable, and the criticism of most Gnostics only called in question its religious value.

of man, or from an undertaking hostile to God, and is therefore the product of an evil or intermediate being. [1]

(e) The doctrine, that evil is inherent in matter, and therefore is a physical potence. [2]

(f) The assumption of Æons, that is, real powers and heavenly persons in whom is unfolded the absoluteness of the
Godhead. [3]

[1] Ecclesiastical opponents rightly put no value on the fact, that some
Gnostics advanced to Pan-Satanism with regard to the conception of
the world, while others beheld a certain *justitia civilis* ruling in the
world. For the standpoint which the Christian tradition had marked out,
this distinction is just as much a matter of indifference, as the other,
whether the Old Testament proceeded from an evil, or from an intermediate being. The Gnostics attempted to correct the judgment of faith
about the world and its relation to God, by an empiric view of the world.
Here again they are by no means "visionaries", however fantastic the
means by which they have expressed their judgment about the condition
of the world, and attempted to explain that condition. Those, rather are
"visionaries" who give themselves up to the belief that the world is the
work of a good and omnipotent Deity, however apparently reasonable
the arguments they adduce. The Gnostic (Hellenistic) philosophy of religion,
at this point, comes into the sharpest opposition to the central point of
the Old Testament Christian belief, and all else really depends on this.
Gnosticism is antichristian so far as it takes away from Christianity its Old
Testament foundation, and belief in the identity of the creator of the world
with the supreme God. That was immediately felt and noted by its opponents.
[2] The ecclesiastical opposition was long uncertain on this point. It is
interesting to note that Basilides portrayed the sin inherent in the child
from birth, in a way that makes one feel as though he were listening to
Augustine (see the fragment from the 23rd book of the Ἐξηγητικά, in
Clem., Strom. VI. 12. 83). But it is of great importance to note how even
very special later terminologies, dogmas, etc., of the Church, were in a
certain way anticipated by the Gnostics. Some samples will be given
below; but meanwhile we may here refer to a fragment from Apelles'
Syllogisms in Ambrosius (de Parad. V. 28): "Si hominem non perfectum
fecit deus, unusquisque autem per industriam propriam perfectionem sibi
virtutis adsciscit: nonne videtur plus sibi homo adquirere, quam ei deus
contulit?" One seems here to be transferred into the fifth century.
[3] The Gnostic teaching did not meet with a vigorous resistance even
on this point, and could also appeal to the oldest tradition. The arbitrariness
in the number, derivation and designation of the Æons was contested. The
aversion to barbarism also co-operated here, in so far as Gnosticism delighted
in mysterious words borrowed from the Semites. But the Semitic element
attracted as well as repelled the Greeks and Romans of the second century. The Gnostic terminologies within the Æon speculations were partly
reproduced among the Catholic theologians of the third century; most
important is it that the Gnostics have already made use of the concept
"ὁμοούσιος"; see Iren., I. 5. 1: ἀλλὰ τὸ μὲν πνευματικὸν μὴ δεδυνῆσθαι αὐτὴν
μορφῶσαι, ἐπειδὴ ὁμοούσιον ὑπῆρχεν αὐτῇ (said of the Sophia): L 5. 4, καὶ
τοῦτον εἶναι τὸν κατ᾽ εἰκόνα καὶ ὁμοίωσιν γεγονότα· κατ᾽ εἰκόνα μὲν τὸν ὑλικὸν
ὑπάρχειν, παραπλήσιον μὲν, ἀλλ᾽ οὐχ ὁμοούσιον τῷ θεῷ καθ᾽ ὁμοίωσιν δὲ τὸν ψυχικόν.

(*g*) The assertion that Christ revealed a God hitherto unknown.

(*h*) The doctrine that in the person of Jesus Christ — the Gnostics saw in it redemption, but they reduced the person to the physical nature — the heavenly Æon, Christ, and the human appearance of that Æon must be clearly distinguished, and a "distincte agere" ascribed to each. Accordingly, there were some, such as Basilides, who acknowledged no real union between Christ and the man Jesus, whom, besides, they regarded as an earthly man. Others, *e. g.*, part of the Valentinians, among whom the greatest differences prevailed — see Tertull. adv. Valent. 39 — taught that the body of Jesus was a heavenly psychical formation, and sprang from the womb of Mary only in appearance. Finally, a third party, such as Saturninus, declared that the whole visible appearance of Christ was a phantom, and therefore denied the birth of Christ. [1]

I. 5. 5: τὸ δὲ κύημα τῆς μητρὸς τῆς "'Αχαμώθ", ὁμοούσιον ὑπάρχον τῇ μητρί. In all these cases the word means "of one substance". It is found in the same sense in Clem., Hom. 20. 7: See also Philos. VII. 22 ; Clem., Exc. Theod. 42. Other terms also which have acquired great significance in the Church since the days of Origen, (*e g.*, ἀγέννητος), are found among the Gnostics, see Ep. Ptol. ad Floram, 5 ; and Bigg. (l. c. p. 58, note 3) calls attention to the appearance of τριάς in Excerpt. ex. Theod. § 80, perhaps the earliest passage.

1 The characteristic of the Gnostic Christology is not Docetism, in the strict sense, but the doctrine of the two natures, that is, the distinction between Jesus and Christ, or the doctrine that the Redeemer as Redeemer was not a man. The Gnostics based this view on the inherent sinfulness of human nature, and it was shared by many teachers of the age without being based on any principle (see above, p. 195 f.). The most popular of the three Christologies briefly characterised above was undoubtedly that of the Valentinians. It is found, with great variety of details, in most of the nameless fragments of Gnostic literature that have been preserved, as well as in Apelles. This Christology might be accommodated to the accounts of the Gospels and the baptismal confession (how far is shewn by the *regula* of Apelles, and that of the Valentinians may have run in similar terms). It was taught here that Christ had passed through Mary as a channel; from this doctrine very easily the notion of the Virginity of Mary, uninjured even after the birth — it was already known to Clem. Alex. (Strom. VII. 16. 93). The Church also, later on, accepted this view. It is very difficult to get a clear idea of the Christology of Basilides, as very diverse doctrines were afterwards set up in his school as is shewn by the accounts. Among them is the doctrine, likewise held by others, that Christ in descending from the highest heaven took to himself something from every sphere through which he passed. Something similar is found among the Valentinians, some of whose prominent leaders made a very complicated phenomenon of Christ, and gave him also a direct relation to the demiurge. There is

Christ separates that which is unnaturally united, and thus leads everything back again to himself; in this redemption consists (full contrast to the notion of the ἀνακεφαλαίωσις).

further found here the doctrine of the heavenly humanity, which was afterwards accepted by ecclesiastical theologians. Along with the fragments of Basilides the account of Clem. Alex. seems to me the most reliable. According to this, Basilides taught that Christ descended on the man Jesus at the baptism. Some of the Valentinians taught something similar : the Christology of Ptolemy is characterised by the union of all conceivable Christology theories. The different early Christian conceptions may be found in him. Basilides did not admit a real union between Christ and Jesus; but it is interesting to see how the Pauline Epistles caused the theologians to view the sufferings of Christ as necessarily based on the assumption of sinful flesh, that is, to deduce from the sufferings that Christ has assumed sinful flesh. The Basilidean Christology will prove to be a peculiar preliminary stage of the later ecclesiastical Christology. The anniversary of the baptism of Christ was to the Basilideans, as the day of the ἐπιφάνεια, a high festival day (see Clem., Strom. I 21. 146) : they fixed it for the 6th (2nd) January. And in this also the Catholic Church has followed the Gnosis. The real docetic Christology as represented by Saturninus (and Marcion) was radically opposed to the tradition, and struck out the birth of Jesus, as well as the first 30 years of his life. An accurate exposition of the Gnostic Christologies, which would carry us too far here, (see especially Tertull., de carne Christi), would shew, that a great part of the questions which occupy Church theologians till the present day, were already raised by the Gnostics; for example, what happened to the body of Christ after the resurrection? (see the doctrines of Apelles and Hermogenes); what significance the appearance of Christ had for the heavenly and Satanic powers? what meaning belongs to his sufferings, although there was no real suffering for the heavenly Christ, but only for Jesus? etc. In no other point do the anticipations in the Gnostic dogmatic stand out so plainly (see the system of Origen; many passages bearing on the subject will be found in the third and fourth volumes of this work, to which readers are referred). The Catholic Church has learned but little from the Gnostics, that is, from the earliest theologians in Christendom, in the doctrine of God and the world, but very much in Christology, and who can maintain that she has ever completely overcome the Gnostic doctrine of the two natures, nay, even Docetism? Redemption viewed in the historical person of Jesus, that is, in the appearance of a Divine being on the earth, but the person divided and the real history of Jesus explained away and made inoperative, is the signature of the Gnostic Christology—this, however, is also the danger of the system of Origen and those systems that are dependent on him (Docetism) as well as, in another way, the danger of the view of Tertullian and the Westerns (doctrine of two natures). Finally, it should be noted that the Gnosis always made a distinction between the supreme God and Christ, but that, from the religious position, it had no reason for emphasising that distinction. For to many Gnostics, Christ was in a certain way the manifestation of the supreme God himself, and therefore in the more popular writings of the Gnostics (see the Acta Johannis) expressions are applied to Christ which seem to identify him with God. The same thing is true of Marcion and also of Valentinus (see his Epistle in Clem., Strom. II. 20. 114: εἷς δὲ ἐστιν ἀγαθός, οὗ παρουσία ἡ διὰ τοῦ υἱοῦ φανέρωσις). This Gnostic estimate of Christ has undoubtedly had a mighty influence on the later Church development of Christology. We might say without hesitation that to

(i) The conversion of the ἐκκλησία (it was no innovation to regard the heavenly Church as an Æon) into the college of the pneumatic, who alone, in virtue of their psychological endowment, are capable of Gnosis and the divine life, while the others, likewise in virtue of their constitution, as hylic perish. The Valentinians, and probably many other Gnostics also, distinguished between pneumatic, psychic and hylic. They regarded the psychic as capable of a certain blessedness, and of a corresponding certain knowledge of the supersensible, the latter being obtained through Pistis, that is, through Christian faith. [1]

most Gnostics Christ was a πνεῦμα ὁμοούσιον τῷ πατρί. The details of the life, sufferings and resurrection of Jesus are found in many Gnostics, transformed, complemented and arranged in the way in which Celsus (Orig., c. Cels. I. II.) required for an impressive and credible history. Celsus indicates how everything must have taken place if Christ had been a God in human form. The Gnostics in part actually narrate it so. What an instructive coincidence! How strongly the docetic view itself was expressed in the case of Valentinus, and how the exaltation of Jesus above the earthly was thereby to be traced back to his moral struggle, is shewn in the remarkable fragment of a letter (in Clem., Strom. III. 7. 59): Πάντα ὑπομείνας ἐγκρατὴς τὴν θεότητα Ἰησοῦς εἰργάζετο. ἤσθιεν γὰρ καὶ ἔπιεν ἰδίως οὐκ ἀποδιδοὺς τὰ βρώματα, τοσαύτη ἦν αὐτῷ τῆς ἐγκρατείας δύναμις, ὥστε καὶ μὴ φθαρῆναι τὴν τροφὴν ἐν αὐτῷ ἐπεὶ τὸ φθείρεσθαι αὐτὸς οὐκ εἶχεν. In this notion, however, there is more sense and historical meaning than in that of the later ecclesiastical aphtharto-docetism.

1 The Gnostic distinction of classes of men was connected with the old distinction of stages in spiritual understanding, but has its basis in a law of nature. There were again empirical and psychological views—they must have been regarded as very important, had not the Gnostics taken them from the traditions of the philosophic schools—which made the universalism of the Christian preaching of salvation, appear unacceptable to the Gnostics. Moreover, the transformation of religion into a doctrine of the school, or into a mystery cult, always resulted in the distinction of the knowing from the *profanum vulgus*. But in the Valentinian assumption that the common Christians as psychical occupy an intermediate stage, and that they are saved by faith, we have a compromise which completely lowered the Gnosis to a scholastic doctrine within Christendom. Whether and in what way the Catholic Church maintained the significance of Pistis as contrasted with Gnosis, and in what way the distinction between the knowing (priests) and the laity was there reached, will be examined in its proper place. It should be noted, however, that the Valentinian, Ptolemy, ascribes freedom of will to the psychic (which the pneumatic and hylic lack), and therefore has sketched by way of by-work a theology for the psychical beside that for the pneumatic, which exhibits striking harmonies with the exoteric system of Origen. The denial by Gnosticism of free will, and therewith of moral responsibility, called forth very decided contradiction. Gnosticism, that is, the acute hellenising of Christianity, was wrecked in the Church on free will, the Old Testament and eschatology.

(*k*) The rejection of the entire early christian eschatology, especially the second coming of Christ, the resurrection of the body, and Christ's Kingdom of glory on the earth, and, in connection with this, the assertion that the deliverance of the spirit from the sensuous can be expected only from the future, while the spirit enlightened about itself already possesses immortality, and only awaits its introduction into the pneumatic pleroma.[1]

1 The greatest deviation of Gnosticism from tradition appears in eschatology, along with the rejection of the Old Testament and the separation of the creator of the world from the supreme God. Upon the whole our sources say very little about the Gnostic eschatology. This, however, is not astonishing; for the Gnostics had not much to say on the matter, or what they had to say found expression in their doctrine of the genesis of the world, and that of redemption through Christ. We learn that the *regula* of Apelles closed with the words: ἀνέπτη εἰς οὐρανὸν ὅθεν καὶ ἧκε, instead of ὅθεν ἔρχεται κρῖναι ζῶντας καὶ νεκρούς. We know that Marcion, who may already be mentioned here, referred the whole eschatological expectations of early Christian times to the province of the god of the Jews, and we hear that Gnostics (Valentinians) retained the words σαρκος ἀνάστασιν, but interpreted them to mean that one must rise in this life, that is perceive the truth (thus the "resurrectio a mortuis", that is, exaltation above the earthly, took the place of the "resurrectio mortuorum"; See Iren. II. 31. 2: Tertull., de resurr. carnis, 19). While the Christian tradition placed a great drama at the close of history, the Gnostics regard the history itself as the drama, which virtually closes with the (first) appearing of Christ. It may not have been the opinion of all Gnostics that the resurrection has already taken place, yet for most of them the expectations of the future seem to have been quite faint, and above all without significance. The life is so much included in knowledge, that we nowhere in our sources find a strong expression of hope in a life beyond (it is different in the earliest Gnostic documents preserved in the Coptic language), and the introduction of the spirits into the Pleroma appears very vague and uncertain. But it is of great significance that those Gnostics who, according to their premises, required a real redemption from the world as the highest good, remained finally in the same uncertainty and religious despondency with regard to this redemption, as characterised the Greek philosophers. A religion which is a philosophy of religion remains at all times fixed to this life, however strongly it may emphasise the contrast between the spirit and its surroundings, and however ardently it may desire redemption. The desire for redemption is unconsciously replaced by the thinker's joy in his knowledge, which allays the desire (Iren., III. 15. 2: "Inflatus est iste [scil. the Valentinian proud of knowledge] neque in cœlo, neque in terra putat se esse, sed intra Pleroma introisse et complexum jam angelum suum, cum institorio et supercilio incedit gallinacei elationem habens.... Plurimi, quasi jam perfecti, semetipsos spiritales vocant, et se nosse jam dicunt eum qui sit intra Pleroma ipsorum refrigerii locum"). As in every philosophy of religion, an element of free thinking appears very plainly here also. The eschatological hopes can only have been maintained in vigour by the conviction that the world is of God. But we must finally refer to the fact, that even in eschatology, Gnosticism only drew the inferences

In addition to what has been mentioned here, we must finally fix our attention on the ethics of Gnosticism. Like the ethics of all systems which are based on the contrast between the sensuous and spiritual elements of human nature, that of the Gnostics took a twofold direction. On the one hand, it sought to suppress and uproot the sensuous, and thus became strictly ascetic (imitation of Christ as motive of asceticism; [1] Christ and the Apostles represented as ascetics); [2] on the other hand, it treated the sensuous element as indifferent, and so became libertine, that is, conformed to the world. The former was undoubtedly the more common, though there are credible witnesses to the latter; the *frequentissimum collegium* in particular, the Valentinians, in the days of Irenæus and Tertullian, did not vigorously enough prohibit a lax and world-conforming morality; [3] and among the Syrian and Egyptian Gnostics there were associations which celebrated the most revolting orgies. [4] As the early Christian tradition summoned to a strict renunciation of the world and to self-control, the Gnostic asceticism could not but make an impression at the first; but the dualistic basis on which it rested could not fail to excite suspicion as soon as one was capable of examining it. [5]

from views which were pressing into Christendom from all sides, and were in an increasing measure endangering its hopes of the future Besides, in some Valentinian circles, the future life was viewed as a condition of education, as a progress through the series of the (seven) heavens; *i. e.*, purgatorial experiences in the future were postulated. Both afterwards, from the time of Origen, forced their way into the doctrine of the Church (purgatory, different ranks in heaven), Clement and Origen being throughout strongly influenced by the Valentinian eschatology.

1 See the passage Clem.. Strom. III. 6, 49, which is given above, p. 238.

2 Cf. the Apocryphal Acts of Apostles and diverse legends of Apostles (*e. g.*, in Clem. Alex.).

3 More can hardly be said: the heads of schools were themselves earnest men. No doubt statements such as that of Heracleon seem to have led to laxity in the lower sections of the collegium: ὁμολογίαν εἶναι τὴν μὲν ἐν τῇ πίστει καὶ πολιτείᾳ, τὴν δὲ ἐν φωνῇ· ἡ μὲν οὖν ἐν φωνῇ ὁμολογία καὶ ἐπὶ τῶν ἐξουσιῶν γίνεται, ἥν μόνην ὁμολογίαν ἡγοῦνται εἶναι οἱ πολλοί, οὐχ ὑγιῶς δύνανται δὲ ταύτην τὴν ὁμολογίαν καὶ οἱ ὑποκριταὶ ὁμολογεῖν.

4. See Epiph. h. 26, and the statements in the Coptic Gnostic works. (Schmidt, Texte u Unters. VIII. 1. 2, p. 566 ff.).

5 There arose in this way an extremely difficult theoretical problem, but practically a convenient occasion for throwing asceticism altogether overboard, with the Gnostic asceticism, or restricting it to easy exercises.

Literature.—The writings of Justin (his syntagma against heresies has not been preserved), Irenæus, Tertullian, Hip-

This is not the place for entering into the details. Shibboleths, such as φεύγετε οὐ τὰς φύσεις ἀλλὰ τὰς γνώμας τῶν κακῶν, may have soon appeared. It may be noted here, that the asceticism which gained the victory in Monasticism, was not really that which sprang from early Christian, but from Greek impulses, without, of course, being based on the same principle. Gnosticism anticipated the future even here. That could be much more clearly proved in the history of the worship. A few points which are of importance for the history of dogma may be mentioned here : (1) The Gnostics viewed the traditional sacred actions (Baptism and the Lord's Supper) entirely as mysteries, and applied to them the terminology of the mysteries (some Gnostics set them aside as psychic); but in doing so they were only drawing the inferences from changes which were then in process throughout Christendom. To what extent the later Gnosticism in particular was interested in sacraments, may be studied especially in the Pistis Sophia and the other Coptic works of the Gnostics, which Carl Schmidt has edited; see, for example, Pistis Sophia, p. 233. "Dixit Jesus ad suos μαθήτας: ἀμήν, dixi vobis, haud adduxi quidquam in κόσμον veniens nisi hunc ignem et hanc aquam et hoc vinum et hunc sanguinem." (2) They increased the holy actions by the addition of new ones, repeated baptisms (expiations), anointing with oil, sacrament of confirmation (ἀπολύτρωσις); see, on Gnostic sacraments, Iren. I. 20, and Lipsius, Apokr. Apostelgesch. I. pp. 336—343, and cf. the πυκνῶς μετανοοῦσι in the delineation of the Shepherd of Hermas. Mand. XI. (3) Marcus represented the wine in the Lord's Supper as actual blood in consequence of the act of blessing : see Iren., I. 13. 2 : ποτήρια οἴνῳ κεκραμένα προσποιούμενος εὐχαριστεῖν, καὶ ἐπὶ πλέον ἐκτείνων τὸν λόγον τῆς ἐπικλήσεως, πορφύρεα καὶ ἐρυθρὰ ἀναφαίνεσθαι ποιεῖ, ὡς δοκεῖν τὴν ἀπὸ τῶν ὑπὲρ τὰ ὅλα χάριν τὸ αἷμα τὸ ἑαυτῆς στάζειν ἐν ἐκείνῳ τῷ ποτηρίῳ διὰ τῆς ἐπικλήσεως αὐτοῦ, καὶ ὑπεριμείρεσθαι τοὺς παρόντας ἐξ ἐκείνου γεύσασθαι τοῦ πόματος, ἵνα καὶ εἰς αὐτοὺς ἐπομβρήσῃ ἡ διὰ τοῦ μάγου τούτου κληϊζομένη χάρις. Marcus was indeed a charlatan; but religious charlatanry afterwards became very earnest, and was certainly taken earnestly by many adherents of Marcus. The transubstantiation idea, in reference to the elements in the mysteries, is also plainly expressed in the Excerpt. ex. Theodot. § 82 : καὶ ὁ ἄρτος καὶ τὸ ἔλαιον ἁγιάζεται τῇ δυνάμει τοῦ ὀνόματος οὐ τὰ αὐτὰ ὄντα κατὰ τὸ φαινόμενον οἷα ἐλήφθη, ἀλλὰ δυνάμει εἰς δύναμιν πνευματικὴν μεταβέβληται (that is, not into a new super-terrestrial material, not into the real body of Christ, but into a spiritual power). οὕτως καὶ τὸ ὕδωρ καὶ τὸ ἐξορκιζόμενον καὶ τὸ βάπτισμα γινόμενον οὐ μόνον χωρεῖ τὸ χεῖρον, ἀλλὰ καὶ ἁγιασμὸν προσλαμβάνει. Irenæus possessed a liturgical handbook of the Marcionites, and communicates many sacramental formulæ from it (I. c. 13 sq.). In my treatise on the Pistis Sophia (Texte u. Unters. VII. 2. pp. 59—94) I think I have shewn ("The common Christian and the Catholic elements of the Pistis Sophia") to what extent Gnosticism anticipated Catholicism as a system of doctrine and an institute of worship. These results have been strengthened by Carl Schmidt (Texte u. Unters. VIII. 1. 2). Even purgatory, prayers for the dead, and many other things, raised in speculative questions and definitely answered, are found in those Coptic Gnostic writings, and are then met with again in Catholicism. One general remark may be permitted in conclusion. The Gnostics were not interested in apologetics, and that is a very significant fact. The πνεῦμα in man was regarded by them as a supernatural principle, and on that account they are free from all rationalism and moralistic dogmatism. For that very reason they are in earnest with the idea of revelation, and do not attempt to prove

polytus, Clement of Alexandria, Origen, Epiphanius, Philastrius and Theodoret; cf. Volkmar, Die Quellen der Ketzergeschichte, 1885.

Lipsius, Zur Quellenkritik des Epiphanios, 1875; also Die Quellen der ältesten Ketzergeschichte, 1875.

Harnack, Zur Quellenkritik d. Gesch. d. Gnostic, 1873 (continued i. D. Ztschr. f. d. hist. Theol. 1874, and in Der Schrift de Apellis gnosi monarch. 1874).

Of Gnostic writings we possess the book Pistis Sophia, the writings contained in the Coptic Cod. Brucianus, and the Epistle of Ptolemy to Flora; also numerous fragments, in connection with which Hilgenfeld especially deserves thanks, but which still require a more complete selecting and a more thorough discussion (see Grabe, Spicilegium T. I. II. 1700. Heinrici, Die Valentin. Gnosis, u. d. H. Schrift, 1871).

On the (Gnostic) Apocryphal Acts of the Apostles, see Zahn, Acta Joh. 1880, and the great work of Lipsius, Die apokryphen Apostelgeschichten, I. Vol., 1883; II. Vol., 1887. (See also Lipsius, Quellen d. röm. Petrussage, 1872).

Neander, Genet. Entw. d. vornehmsten gnostischen Systeme, 1818.

Matter, Hist. crit. du gnosticisme, 2 Vols., 1828.

Baur, Die Christl. Gnosis, 1835.

Lipsius, Der Gnosticismus, in Ersch. und Gruber's Allg. Encykl. 71 Bd. 1860.

Moeller, Geschichte d. Kosmologie i. d. Griech. K. bis auf Origenes. 1860.

King, The Gnostics and their remains, 1873.

Mansel, The Gnostic heresies, 1875.

Jacobi, Art. "Gnosis" in Herzog's Real Encykl. 2nd Edit.

---

it or convert its contents into natural truths. They did endeavour to prove that their doctrines were Christian, but renounced all proof that revelation is the truth (proofs from antiquity). One will not easily find in the case of the Gnostics themselves, the revealed truth described as philosophy, or morality as the philosophic life If we compare therefore, the first and fundamental system of Catholic doctrine, that of Origen, with the system of the Gnostics, we shall find that Origen, like Basilides and Valentinus, was a philosopher of revelation, but that he had besides a second element which had its origin in apologetics.

Hilgenfeld, Die Ketzergeschichte des Urchristenthums, 1884, where the more recent special literature concerning individual Gnostics is quoted.

Lipsius, Art. "Valentinus" in Smith's Dictionary of Christian Biography.

Harnack, Art. "Valentinus" in the Encycl. Brit.

Harnack, Pistis Sophia in the Texte und Unters. VII. 2.

Carl Schmidt, Gnostische Schriften in koptischer Sprache aus dem Codex Brucianus (Texte und Unters. VIII. 1. 2).

Joël, Blicke in die Religionsgeschichte zu Anfang des 2 Christl. Jahrhunderts, 2 parts, 1880, 1883.

Renan, History of the Origins of Christianity. Vols. V. VI. VII.

CHAPTER V.

MARCION'S ATTEMPT TO SET ASIDE THE OLD TESTAMENT
FOUNDATION OF CHRISTIANITY,
TO PURIFY TRADITION, AND TO REFORM CHRISTENDOM ON
THE BASIS OF THE PAULINE GOSPEL.

MARCION cannot be numbered among the Gnostics in the
strict sense of the word.[1] For (1) he was not guided by any
speculatively scientific, or even by an apologetic, but by a so-
teriological interest.[2] (2) He therefore put all emphasis on
faith, not on Gnosis.[3] (3) In the exposition of his ideas he
neither applied the elements of any Semitic religious wisdom,

1 He belonged to Pontus and was a rich shipowner: about 139 he
came to Rome, already a Christian, and for a short time belonged to
the church there. As he could not succeed in his attempt to reform it,
he broke away from it about 144. He founded a church of his own and
developed a very great activity. He spread his views by numerous jour-
neys, and communities bearing his name very soon arose in every province of the Empire (Adamantius, de recta in deum fide, Origen, Opp.
ed. Delarue I. p. 809: Epiph. h. 42. p. 668. ed. Oehler). They were
ecclesiastically organised (Tertull, de præscr. 41, and adv. Marc IV. 5)
and possessed bishops, presbyters. etc. (Euseb., H. E. IV. 15. 46 : de
Mart. Palaest. X. 2: Les Bas and Waddington, Inscript. Grecq. et Latines
rec. en Grêce et en Asie Min. Vol. III. No. 2558). Justin (Apol. 1. 26)
about 150 tells us that Marcion's preaching had spread κατὰ πᾶν γένος
ἀνθρώπων, and by the year 155, the Marcionites were already numerous in
Rome (Iren. III. 34). Up to his death, however, Marcion did not give up
the purpose of winning the whole of Christendom, and therefore again
and again sought connection with it (Iren. l. c.; Tertull., de præscr. 30),
likewise his disciples (see the conversation of Apelles with Rhodon in
Euseb., H. E. V. 13. 5, and the dialogue of the Marcionites with Adamantius). It is very probable that Marcion had fixed the ground features
of his doctrine, and had laboured for its propagation, even before he
came to Rome. In Rome the Syrian Gnostic Cerdo had a great influence
on him, so that we can even yet perceive, and clearly distinguish, the
Gnostic element in the form of the Marcionite doctrine transmitted to us.
2 "Sufficit," said the Marcionites, "unicum opus deo nostro, quod hominem liberavit summa et præcipua bonitate sua. (Tertull., adv. Marc. I 17).
3 Apelles, the disciple of Marcion, declared (Euseb., H. E. V. 13. 5) σωθήσεσθαι
τοὺς ἐπὶ τὸν ἐσταυρωμένον ἠλπικότας, μόνον ἐὰν ἐν ἔργοις ἀγαθοῖς εὑρίσκωνται.

nor the methods of the Greek philosophy of religion.[1] (4)
He never made the distinction between an esoteric and an
exoteric form of religion. He rather clung to the publicity
of the preaching, and endeavoured to reform Christendom, in
opposition to the attempts at founding schools for those who
knew and mystery cults for such as were in quest of initiation. It was only after the failure of his attempts at reform
that he founded churches of his own, in which brotherly

---

[1] This is an extremely important point. Marcion rejected all allegories.
(See Tertull., adv. Marc. II. 19. 21. 22: III. 5. 6. 14 19: IV. 15. 20: V. 1;
Orig., Comment. in Matth. T. XV. 3 Opp. III. p. 655: in. ep. ad. Rom. Opp.
IV. p. 494 sq.: Adamant., Sect. I, Orig. Opp. I. pp. 808. 817; Ephr. Syrus.
hymn. 36 Edit. Benedict, p. 520 sq.) and describes this method as an arbitrary
one. But that simply means that he perceived and avoided the transformation
of the Gospel into Hellenic philosophy. No philosophic formulæ are found in
any of his statements that have been handed down to us. But what is still
more important, none of his early opponents have attributed to Marcion a
system, as they did to Basilides and Valentinus There can be no doubt that
Marcion did not set up any system (the Armenian, Esnik, first gives a Marcionite system, but that is a late production, see my essay in the Ztschr. f. wiss.
Theol. 1896. p. 80 f.). He was just as far from having any apologetic or
rationalistic interest. Justin (Apol. I. 58) says of the Marcionites; ἀποδειξιν
μηδεμίαν περὶ ὧν λέγουσιν ἔχουσιν, ἀλλὰ ἀλόγως ὡς ὑπὸ λύκου ἄρνες συνηρπασμένοι
κτλ. Tertullian again and again casts in the teeth of Marcion that he has
adduced no proof. See I. 11 sq.: III. 2. 3. 4: IV. 11: "Subito Christus, subito
et Johannes Sic sunt omnia apud Marcionem, quæ suum et plenum habent
ordinem apud creatorem". Rhodon (Euseb., H. E. V. 13. 4) says of two prominent genuine disciples of Marcion: μὴ εὑρίσκοντες τὴν διαίρεσιν τῶν πραγμάτων,
ὡς οὐδὲ ἐκεῖνος, δυὸ ἀρχὰς ἀπεφήναντο ψιλῶς καὶ ἀναποδείκτως. Of Apelles, the
most important of Marcion's disciples, who laid aside the Gnostic borrows of
his master, we have the words (l. c.): μὴ δεῖν ὅλως ἐξετάζειν τὸν λόγον, ἀλλ'
ἔκαστον, ὡς πεπίστευκε, διαμένειν. Σωθήσεσθαι γὰρ τοὺς ἐπὶ τὸν ἐσταρωμένον ἠλπικότας ἀπεφαίνετο, μόνον ἐὰν ἐν ἔργοις ἀγαθοῖς εὑρίσκωνται . . . . τὸ δὲ πῶς ἔστι
μία ἀρχή. μὴ γινώσκειν ἔλεγεν, οὕτω δὲ κινεῖσθαι μόνον . . . . μὴ ἐπίστασθαι πῶς
εἷς ἐστιν ἀγέννητος θεός, τοῦτο δὲ πιστεύειν. It was Marcion's purpose therefore
to give all value to faith alone, to make it dependent on its own convincing
power, and avoid all philosophic paraphrase and argument. The contrast in
which he placed the Christian blessing of salvation, has in principle nothing
in common with the contract in which Greek philosophy viewed the *summum
bonum*. Finally, it may be pointed out that Marcion introduced no new elements (Æons, Matter, etc.) into his evangelic views, and leant on no Oriental religious science. The later Marcionite speculations about matter (see the
account of Esnik) should not be charged upon the master himself, as is manifest from the second book of Tertullian against Marcion. The assumption that
the creator of the world created it out of a *materia subjacens*, is certainly found
in Marcion (see Tertull., 1. 15; Hippol., Philos. X. 19); but he speculated no
further about it, and that assumption itself was not rejected, for example, by
Clem. Alex. (Strom. II. 16. 74 : Photius on Clement's Hypotyposes). Marcion did
not really speculate even about the good God; yet see Tertull., adv. Marc. I.
14. 15 : IV. 7 : "Mundus ille superior" — "coelum tertium".

equality, freedom from all ceremonies, and strict evangelical discipline were to rule. [1] Completely carried away with the novelty, uniqueness and grandeur of the Pauline Gospel of the grace of God in Christ, Marcion felt that all other conceptions of the Gospel, and especially its union with the Old Testament religion, was opposed to, and a backsliding from the truth. [2] He accordingly supposed that it was necessary to make the sharp antitheses of Paul, law and gospel, wrath and grace, works and faith, flesh and spirit, sin and righteousness, death and life, that is the Pauline criticism of the Old Testament religion, the foundation of his religious views, and to refer them to two principles, the righteous and wrathful god of the Old Testament, who is at the same time identical with the creator of the world, and the God of the Gospel, quite unknown before Christ, who is only love and mercy. [3] This Paulinism in its religious strength, but without dialectic, without the Jewish Christian view of history, and detached from the soil of the Old Testament, was to him the true Christianity. Marcion, like Paul, felt that the religious value of a statutory law with commandments and ceremonies, was very different from that of a uniform law of love. [4] Accordingly, he had a capacity for appreciating the Pauline idea of faith; it is to him reliance on the unmerited grace of God which is revealed in Christ. But Marcion shewed himself to be a Greek,

---

1 Tertull., de præscr. 41. sq.; the delineation refers chiefly to the Marcionites (see Epiph. h. 42. c. 3. 4, and Esnik's account), on the Church system of Marcion, see also Tertull., adv. Marc. I. 14, 21, 23, 24, 28, 29: III. 1, 22: IV. 5, 34: V. 7, 10, 15, 18.

2 Marcion himself originally belonged to the main body of the Church, as is expressly declared by Tertullian and Epiphanius, and attested by one of his own letters.

3 Tertull., adv. Marc. I. 2, 19: "Separatio legis et evangelii proprium et principale opus est Marcionis . . . ex diversitate sententiarum utriusque instrumenti diversitatem quoque argumentatur deorum". II. 28, 29: IV. 1. I. 6: "dispares deos, alterum, judicem, ferum, bellipotentem; alterum mitem, placidum et tantummodo bonum atque optimum." Iren. I. 27. 2.

4 Marcion maintained that the good God is not to be feared. Tertull., adv. Marc. I. 27: "Atque adeo præ se ferunt Marcionitæ quod deum suum omnino non timeant. Malus autem, inquiunt, timebitur; bonus autem diligitur." To the question why they did not sin if they did not fear their God, the Marcionites answered in the words of Rom. VI. 1 2. (l. c).

influenced by the religious spirit of the time, by changing the
ethical contrast of the good and legal into the contrast between
the infinitely exalted spiritual and the sensible which is subject to the law of nature, by despairing of the triumph of
good in the world and, consequently, correcting the traditional
faith that the world and history belong to God, by an empirical view of the world and the course of events in it,[1] a
view to which he was no doubt also led by the severity of
the early Christian estimate of the world. Yet to him
systematic speculation about the final causes of the contrast
actually observed, was by no means the main thing. So far
as he himself ventured on such a speculation he seems to
have been influenced by the Syrian Cerdo. The numerous
contradictions which arise as soon as one attempts to reduce
Marcion's propositions to a system, and the fact that his disciples tried all possible conceptions of the doctrine of principles, and defined the relation of the two Gods very differently,
are the clearest proof that Marcion was a religious character,
that he had in general nothing to do with principles, but with
living beings whose power he felt, and that what he ultimately
saw in the Gospel was not an explanation of the world,
but redemption from the world,[2]—redemption from a world,
which even in the best that it can offer, has nothing that
can reach the height of the blessing bestowed in Christ.[3]
Special attention may be called to the following particulars.

1. Marcion explained the Old Testament in its literal sense
and rejected every allegorical interpretation. He recognised

1 Tertull., adv. Marc. I. 2 : II. 5.

2 See the passage adduced, p. 266, note 2, and Tertull., I. 19: "Immo
inquiunt Marcionitæ, deus noster, etsi non ab initio, etsi non per conditio-
nem, sed per semetipsum revelatus est in Christi Jesu". The very fact
that different theological tendencies (schools) appeared within Marcionite
Christianity and were mutually tolerant, proves that the Marcionite Church
itself was not based on a formulated system of faith. Apelles expressly
conceded different forms of doctrine in Christendom, on the basis of faith
in the Crucified and a common holy ideal of life (see p. 267).

3 Tertull., I, 13. "Narem contrahentes impudentissimi Marcionitæ con-
vertuntur ad destructionem operum creatoris. Nimirum, inquiunt, grande
opus et dignum deo mundus"? The Marcionites (Iren., IV. 34. 1) put the
question to their ecclesiastical opponents, "Quid novi attulit dominus
veniens?" and therewith caused them no small embarrassment.

it as the revelation of the creator of the world and the god
of the Jews, but placed it, just on that account, in sharpest
contrast to the Gospel. He demonstrated the contradictions
between the Old Testament and the Gospel in a voluminous
work (the ἀντιθέσεις).[1] In the god of the former book he saw
a being whose character was stern justice, and therefore anger,
contentiousness and unmercifulness. The law which rules nature
and man appeared to him to accord with the characteristics
of this god and the kind of law revealed by him, and therefore it seemed credible to him that this god is the creator
and lord of the world (κοσμοκράτωρ). As the law which governs
the world is inflexible, and yet, on the other hand, full of
contradictions, just and again brutal, and as the law of the
Old Testament exhibits the same features, so the god of creation was to Marcion a being who united in himself the whole
gradations of attributes from justice to malevolence, from ob-
stinacy to inconsistency.[2] Into this conception of the creator
of the world, the characteristic of which is that it cannot be
systematised, could easily be fitted the Syrian Gnostic theory
which regards him as an evil being, because he belongs to this
world and to matter. Marcion did not accept it in principle,[3]
but touched it lightly and adopted certain inferences.[4] On

1 On these see Tertull, I. 19; II. 28. 29: IV. 1, 4, 6: Epiph.; Hippol.,
Philos. VII. 30; the book was used by other Gnostics also (it is very
probable that 1 Tim. VI. 20 an addition to the Epistle—refers to Marcion's
Antitheses). Apelles, Marcion's disciple, composed a similar work under
the title of "Syllogismi". Marcion's Antitheses, which may still in part be
reconstructed from Tertullian, Epiphanius, Adamantius, Ephraem, etc.,
possessed canonical authority in the Marcionite church, and therefore took
the place of the Old Testament. That is quite clear from Tertull., I. 19
(cf. IV. 1): Separatio legis et Evangelii proprium et principale opus est
Marcionis, nec poterunt negare discipuli ejus, quod in summo (suo) in-
strumento habent, quo denique initiantur et indurantur in hanc hæresim.
2 Tertullian has frequently pointed to the contradictions in the Marcionite
conception of the god of creation. These contradictions, however, vanish
as soon as we regard Marcion's god from the point of view that he is
like his revelation in the Old Testament.
3 The creator of the world is indeed to Marcion "malignus", but not
"malus".
4 Marcion touched on it when he taught that the "visibilia" belonged
to the god of creation, but the "invisibilia" to the good God (I. 16).
He adopted the consequences, inasmuch as he taught docetically about
Christ, and only assumed a deliverance of the human soul.

the basis of the Old Testament and of empirical observation, Marcion divided men into two classes, good and evil, though he regarded them all, body and soul, as creatures of the demiurge. The good are those who strive to fulfil the law of the demiurge. These are outwardly better than those who refuse him obedience. But the distinction found here is not the decisive one. To yield to the promptings of Divine grace is the only decisive distinction, and those just men will shew themselves less susceptible to the manifestation of the truly good than sinners. As Marcion held the Old Testament to be a book worthy of belief, though his disciple, Apelles, thought otherwise, he referred all its predictions to a Messiah whom the creator of the world is yet to send, and who, as a warlike hero, is to set up the earthly kingdom of the "just" God. [1]

2. Marcion placed the good God of love in opposition to the creator of the world. [2] This God has only been revealed in Christ. He was absolutely unknown before Christ, [3] and men were in every respect strange to him. [4] Out of pure goodness and mercy, for these are the essential attributes of this God who judges not and is not wrathful, he espoused the cause of those beings who were foreign to him, as he could not bear to have them any longer tormented by their just and yet malevolent lord. [5] The God of love appeared in Christ and proclaimed a new kingdom (Tertull., adv. Marc. III. 24. fin.). Christ called to himself the weary and heavy laden, [6] and proclaimed to them that he would deliver them

1 See especially the third book of Tertull., adv. Marcion.

2 "Solius bonitatis", "deus melior", were Marcion's standing expressions for him.

3 "Deus incognitus" was likewise a standing expression. They maintained against all attacks the religious position that, from the nature of the case, believers only can know God, and that this is quite sufficient (Tertull., I. 11).

4 Marcion firmly emphasised this and appealed to passages in Paul; see Tertull., I. 11, 19, 23: "scio dicturos, atquin hanc esse principalem et perfectam bonitatem, cum sine ullo debito familiaritatis in extraneos voluntaria et libera effunditur, secundum quam inimicos quoque nostros et hoc nomine jam extraneos deligere jubeamur". The Church Fathers therefore declared that Marcion's good God was a thief and a robber. See also Celsus, in Orig. VI. 53.

5 See Esnik's account, which, however, is to be used cautiously.

6 Marcion has strongly emphasised the respective passages in Luke's Gospel: see his Antitheses, and his comments on the Gospel, as presented by Tertullian (l. IV).

from the fetters of their lord and from the world. He shewed mercy to all while he sojourned on the earth, and did in every respect the opposite of what the creator of the world had done to men. They who believed in the creator of the world nailed him to the cross. But in doing so they were unconsciously serving his purpose, for his death was the price by which the God of love purchased men from the creator of the world. [1] He who places his hope in the Crucified can now be sure of escaping from the power of the creator of the world, and of being translated into the kingdom of the good God. But experience shews that, like the Jews, men who are virtuous according to the law of the creator of the world, do not allow themselves to be converted by Christ; it is rather sinners who accept his message of redemption. Christ, therefore, rescued from the under-world, not the righteous men of the Old Testament (Iren. I. 27. 3), but the sinners who were disobedient to the creator of the world. If the determining thought of Marcion's view of Christianity is here again very clearly shewn, the Gnostic woof cannot fail to be seen in the proposition that the good God delivers only the souls, not the bodies of believers. The antithesis of spirit and matter, appears here as the decisive one, and the good God of love becomes the God of the spirit, the Old Testament god the god of the flesh. In point of fact, Marcion seems to have given such a turn to the good God's attributes of love, and incapability of wrath, as to make Him the apathetic, infinitely exalted Being, free from all affections. The contradiction in which Marcion is here involved is evident, because he taught expressly that the spirit of man is in itself just as foreign to the good God as his body. But the strict asceticism which Marcion demanded as a Christian, could have had no motive, without the Greek assumption of a metaphysical contrast of

---

[1] That can be plainly read in Esnik, and must have been thought by Marcion himself, as he followed Paul (see Tertull., l. V. and I. 11). Apelles also emphasised the death upon the cross. Marcion's conception of the purchase can indeed no longer be ascertained in its details. But see Adamant., de recta in deum fide, sect. I. It is one of his theoretic contradictions that the good God who is exalted above righteousness should yet purchase men.

flesh and Spirit, which in fact was also apparently the doctrine of Paul.

3. The relation in which Marcion placed the two Gods, appears at first sight to be one of equal rank.[1] Marcion himself, according to the most reliable witnesses, expressly asserted that both were uncreated, eternal, etc. But if we look more closely we shall see that in Marcion's mind there can be no thought of equality. Not only did he himself expressly declare that the creator of the world is a self-contradictory being of limited knowledge and power, but the whole doctrine of redemption shews that he is a power subordinate to the good God. We need not stop to enquire about the details, but it is certain that the creator of the world formerly knew nothing of the existence of the good God, that he is in the end completely powerless against him, that he is overcome by him, and that history in its issue with regard to man, is determined solely by its relation to the good God. The just god appears at the end of history, not as an independent being, hostile to the good God, but as one subordinate to him,[2] so that some scholars, such as Neander, have attempted to claim for Marcion a doctrine of one principle, and to deny that he ever held the complete independence of the creator of the world, the creator of the world being simply an angel of the good God. This inference may certainly be drawn with

1 Tertull. I. 6: "Marcion non negat creatorem deum esse."
2 Here Tertull., I. 27, 28, is of special importance; see also II. 28: IV. 29 (on Luke XII. 41—46): IV. 30. Marcion's idea was this. The good God does not judge or punish; but He judges in so far as he keeps evil at a distance from Him: it remains foreign to Him. "Marcionitæ interrogati quid fiet peccatori cuique die illo? respondent abici illum quasi ab oculis". "Tranquilitas est et mansuetudinis segregare solummodo et partem ejus cum infidelibus ponere". But what is the end of him who is thus rejected? "Ab igne, inquiunt, creatoris deprehendetur". We might think with Tertullian that the creator of the world would receive sinners with joy: but this is the god of the law who punishes sinners. The issue is twofold: the heaven of the good God, and the hell of the creator of the world. Either Marcion assumed with Paul that no one can keep the law, or he was silent about the end of the "righteous" because he had no interest in it. At any rate, the teaching of Marcion closes with an outlook in which the creator of the world can no longer be regarded as an independent god. Marcion's disciples (see Esnik) here developed a consistent theory: the creator of the world violated his own law by killing the righteous Christ, and was therefore deprived of all his power by Christ.

little trouble, as the result of various considerations, but it is forbidden by reliable testimony. The characteristic of Marcion's teaching is just this, that as soon as we seek to raise his ideas from the sphere of practical considerations to that of a consistent theory, we come upon a tangled knot of contradictions. The theoretic contradictions are explained by the different interests which here cross each other in Marcion. In the first place, he was consciously dependent on the Pauline theology, and was resolved to defend everything which he held to be Pauline. Secondly, he was influenced by the contrast in which he saw the ethical powers involved. This contrast seemed to demand a metaphysical basis, and its actual solution seemed to forbid such a foundation. Finally, the theories of Gnosticism, the paradoxes of Paul, the recognition of the duty of strictly mortifying the flesh, suggested to Marcion the idea that the good God was the exalted God of the spirit, and the just god the god of the sensuous, of the flesh. This view, which involved the principle of a metaphysical dualism, had something very specious about it, and to its influence we must probably ascribe the fact that Marcion no longer attempted to derive the creator of the world from the good God. His disciples who had theoretical interests in the matter, no doubt noted the contradictions. In order to remove them, some of these disciples advanced to a doctrine of three principles, the good God, the just creator of the world, the evil god, by conceiving the creator of the world sometimes as an independent being, sometimes as one dependent on the good God. Others reverted to the common dualism, God of the spirit and god of matter. But Apelles, the most important of Marcion's disciples, returned to the creed of the one God ($\mu i\alpha\ \dot{\alpha}\rho\chi\dot{\eta}$), and conceived the creator of the world and Satan as his angels, without departing from the fundamental thought of the master, but rather following suggestions which he himself had given.[1] Apart from Apelles,

---

[1] Schools soon arose in the Marcionite church, just as they did later on in the main body of Christendom (see Rhodon in Euseb , H. E. V. 13. 2-4). The different doctrines of principles which were here developed (two, three, four

who founded a Church of his own, we hear nothing of the
controversies of disciples breaking up the Marcionite church.
All those who lived in the faith for which the master had
worked—viz., that the laws ruling in nature and history, as
well as the course of common legality and righteousness, are
the antitheses of the act of Divine mercy in Christ, and that
cordial love and believing confidence have their proper contrasts in self-righteous pride and the natural religion of the
heart,—those who rejected the Old Testament and clung solely
to the Gospel proclaimed by Paul, and finally, those who considered that a strict mortification of the flesh and an earnest
renunciation of the world were demanded in the name of the
Gospel, felt themselves members of the same community, and
to all appearance allowed perfect liberty to speculations about
final causes.

4. Marcion had no interest in specially emphasising the
distinction between the good God and Christ, which according to the Pauline Epistles, could not be denied. To him
Christ is the manifestation of the good God himself.[1] But

principles; the Marcionite Marcus's doctrine of two principles in which the
creator of the world is an evil being, diverges furthest from the Master),
explain the different accounts of the Church Fathers about Marcion's
teaching. The only one of the disciples who really seceded from the
Master, was Apelles (Tertull., de præscr. 30). His teaching is therefore the
more important, as it shews that it was possible to retain the fundamental
ideas of Marcion without embracing dualism. The attitude of Apelles to
the Old Testament is that of Marcion, in so far as he rejects the book.
But perhaps he somewhat modified the strictness of the Master. On the
other hand, he certainly designated much in it as untrue and fabulous.
It is remarkable that we meet with a highly honoured prophetess in the
environment of Apelles: in Marcion's church we hear nothing of such,
nay, it is extremely important as regards Marcion, that he has never
appealed to the Spirit and to prophets. The "sanctiores feminæ" Tertull.
V. 8, are not of this nature, nor can we appeal even to V. 15. Moreover,
it is hardly likely that Jerome ad Eph. III. 5, refers to Marcionites. In
this complete disregard of early Christian prophecy, and in his exclusive
reliance on literary documents, we see in Marcion a process of despiritual-
ising, that is, a form of secularisation peculiar to himself. Marcion no longer
possessed the early Christian enthusiasm as, for example, Hermas did.

1 Marcion was fond of calling Christ "Spiritus salutaris" From the
treatise of Tertullian we can prove both that Marcion distinguished Christ
from God, and that he made no distinction (see, for example, I. 11, 14:
II. 27: III. 8, 9, 11 : IV 7). Here again Marcion did not think theologically.
What he regarded as specially important was that God has revealed
himself in Christ, "per semetipsum" Later Marcionites expressly taught

Marcion taught that Christ assumed absolutely nothing from the creation of the Demiurge, but came down from heaven in the 15th year of the Emperor Tiberius, and after the assumption of an apparent body, began his preaching in the synagogue of Capernaum.[1] This pronounced docetism which denies that Jesus was born, or subjected to any human process of development,[2] is the strongest expression of Marcion's abhorrence of the world. This aversion may have sprung from the severe attitude of the early Christians toward the world, but the inference which Marcion here draws, shews, that this feeling was, in his case, united with the Greek estimate of spirit and matter. But Marcion's docetism is all the more remarkable that, under Paul's guidance, he put a high value on the fact of Christ's death upon the cross. Here also is a glaring contradiction which his later disciples laboured to remove. This much, however, is unmistakable, that Marcion succeeded in placing the greatness and uniqueness of redemption through Christ in the clearest light and in beholding this redemption in the person of Christ, but chiefly in his death upon the cross.

5. Marcion's eschatology is also quite rudimentary. Yet be assumed with Paul that violent attacks were yet in store for the Church of the good God on the part of the Jewish Christ of the future, the Antichrist. He does not seem to have taught a visible return of Christ, but, in spite of the omnipotence and goodness of God, he did teach a twofold issue of history. The idea of a deliverance of all men, which seems to follow from his doctrine of boundless grace, was quite foreign to him. For this very reason, he could not help actually making the good God the judge, though in theory he rejected the idea,

Patripassianism, and have on that account been often grouped with the Sabellians. But other Christologies also arose in Marcion's church, which is again a proof that it was not dependent on scholastic teaching, and therefore could take part in the later development of doctrines.

1 See the beginning of the Marcionite Gospel.

2 Tertullian informs us sufficiently about this. The body of Christ was regarded by Marcion merely as an "umbra", a "phantasma". His disciples adhered to this, but Apelles first constructed a "doctrine" of the body of Christ.

in order not to measure the will and acts of God by a human standard. Along with the fundamental proposition of Marcion, that God should be conceived only as goodness and grace, we must take into account the strict asceticism which he prescribed for the Christian communities, in order to see that that idea of God was not obtained from antinomianism. We know of no Christian community in the second century which insisted so strictly on renunciation of the world as the Marcionites. No union of the sexes was permitted. Those who were married had to separate ere they could be received by baptism into the community. The sternest precepts were laid down in the matter of food and drink. Martyrdom was enjoined; and from the fact that they were ταλαίπωροι καὶ μισούμενοι in the world, the members were to know that they were disciples of Christ. [1] With all that, the early Christian enthusiasm was wanting.

6. Marcion defined his position in theory and practice towards the prevailing form of Christianity, which, on the one hand, shewed throughout its connection with the Old Testament, and, on the other, left room for a secular ethical code, by assuming that it had been corrupted by Judaism, and therefore needed a reformation. [2] But he could not fail to note that this corruption was not of recent date, but belonged to the oldest tradition itself. The consciousness of this moved him to a historical criticism of the whole Christian tradition. [3]

[1] The strict asceticism of Marcion and the Marcionites is reluctantly acknowledged by the Church Fathers; see Tertull., de præscr. 30: "Sanctissimus magister"; I. 28, "carni imponit sanctitem". The strict prohibition of marriage: I. 29: IV. 11, 17, 29, 34, 38: V. 7, 8, 15, 18; prohibition of food: 1. 14 cynical life: Hippol., Philos. VII. 29; numerous martyrs: Euseb, H. E. V. 16. 21, and frequently elsewhere. Marcion named his adherents (Tertull. IV. 9 36) "συνταλαίπωροι καὶ συμμισούμενοι". It is questionable whether Marcion himself allowed the repetition of baptism; it arose in his church. But this repetition is a proof that the prevailing conception of baptism was not sufficient for a vigorous religious temper.

[2] Tertull. I. 20. "Aiunt, Marcionem non tam innovasse regulam separatione legis et evangelii quam retro adulteratam recurrasse"; See the account of Epiphanius, taken from Hippolytus, about the appearance of Marcion in Rome (h. 42. 1. 2).

[3] Here again we must remember that Marcion appealed neither to a secret tradition, nor to the "Spirit", in order to appreciate the epoch-making nature of his undertaking.

Marcion was the first Christian who undertook such a task.
Those writings to which he owed his religious convictions,
viz., the Pauline Epistles, furnished the basis for it. He found
nothing in the rest of Christian literature that harmonised
with the Gospel of Paul. But he found in the Pauline Epistles
hints which explained to him this result of his observations.
The twelve Apostles whom Christ chose did not understand
him, but regarded him as the Messiah of the god of creation. [1]
And therefore Christ inspired Paul by a special revelation,
lest the Gospel of the grace of God should be lost through
falsifications. [2] But even Paul had been understood only by

---

[1] In his estimate of the twelve Apostles Marcion took as his stand-
point Gal. II. See Tertull. I. 20: IV. 3 (generally IV. 1—6), V. 3; de
præscr. 22. 23. He endeavoured to prove from this chapter that from a
misunderstanding of the words of Christ, the twelve Apostles had proclaimed a different Gospel than that of Paul; they had wrongly taken
the Father of Jesus Christ for the god of creation. It is not quite clear
how Marcion conceived the inward condition of the Apostles during the
lifetime of Jesus (See Tertull. III. 22: IV. 3. 39). He assumed that they
were persecuted by the Jews as the preachers of a new God. It is
probable, therefore, that he thought of a gradual obscuring of the preaching of Jesus in the case of the primitive Apostles. They fell back into
Judaism; see Iren. III. 2. 2. "Apostolos admiscuisse ea quæ sunt legalia salvatoris verbis"; III. 12. 12: "Apostoli quæ sunt Judæorum sentientes scripser-
unt" etc.; Tertull V. 3: "Apostolos vultis Judaismi magis adfines subintelligi."
The expositions of Marcion in Tertull. IV. 9, 11, 13, 21, 24, 39: V. 13, shew
that he regarded the primitive Apostles as out and out real Apostles of Christ.

[2] The call of Paul was viewed by Marcion as a manifestation of Christ,
of equal value with His first appearance and ministry; see the account of
Esnik. "Then for the second time Jesus came down to the lord of the
creatures in the form of his Godhead, and entered into judgment with him
on account of his death .... And Jesus said to him: ' Judgment is between
me and thee, let no one be judge but thine own laws .... hast thou not
written in this thy law, that he who killeth shall die?' And he answered,
'I have so written' .. Jesus said to him, 'Deliver thyself therefore into
my hands'... The creator of the world said, 'Because I have slain thee
I give thee a compensation, all those who shall believe on thee, that thou
mayest do with them what thou pleasest.' Then Jesus left him and carried away Paul, and shewed him the price, and sent him to preach that
we are bought with this price, and that all who believe in Jesus are sold
by this just god to the good one." This is a most instructive account;
for it shews that in the Marcionite schools the Pauline doctrine of reconciliation was transformed into a drama, and placed between the death of
Christ and the call of Paul, and that the Pauline Gospel was based, not
directly on the death of Christ upon the cross, but on a theory of it converted
into history. On Paul as the one apostle of the truth; see Tertull. I. 20 : III.
5, 14: IV. 2 sq.: IV. 34: V. I. As to a Marcionite theory that the promise
to send the Spirit was fulfilled in the mission of Paul, an indication of the
want of enthusiasm among the Marcionites, see the following page, note 2.

few (by none?). His Gospel had also been misunderstood nay, his Epistles had been falsified in many passages, [1] in order to make them teach the identity of the god of creation and the God of redemption. A new reformation was therefore necessary. Marcion felt himself entrusted with this commission, and the church which he gathered recognised this vocation of his to be the reformer. [2] He did not appeal to a new revelation such as he presupposed for Paul. As the Pauline Epistles and an authentic εὐαγγέλιον κυρίου were in existence, it was only necessary to purify these from interpolations, and restore the genuine Paulinism which was just the Gospel itself. But it was also necessary to secure and preserve this true Christianity for the future. Marcion, in all probability, was the first to conceive and, in great measure, to realise the idea of placing Christendom on the firm foundation of a definite theory of what is Christian—but not of basing it on a theological doctrine—and of establishing this theory by a fixed

1 Marcion must have spoken *ex professo* in his Antitheses about the Judaistic corruptions of Paul's Epistles and the 'Gospel. He must also have known Evangelic writings bearing the names of the original Apostles, and have expressed himself about them (Tertull. IV. 1—6).
2 Marcion's self-consciousness of being a reformer, and the recognition of this in his church is still not understood, although his undertaking itself and the facts speak loud enough. (1) The great Marcionite church called itself after Marcion (Adamant., de recta in deum fide. I. 809 ; Epiph. h. 42, p. 668, ed. Oehler: Μαρκίων σοῦ τὸ ὄνομα ἐπικέκληνται οἱ ὑπὸ σοῦ ἠπατημένοι, ὡς σεαυτὸν κηρύξαντος καὶ οὐχὶ Χριστόν. We possess a Marcionite inscription which begins: συναγωγὴ Μαρκιωνιστῶν). As the Marcionites did not form a school, but a church, it is of the greatest value for shewing the estimate of the master in this church, that its members called themselves by his name. (2) The Antitheses of Marcion had a place in the Marcionite canon (see above, p. 270). This canon therefore embraced a book of Christ, Epistles of Paul, and a book of Marcion, and for that reason the Antitheses were always circulated with the canon of Marcion (3) Origen (in Luc. hom. 25. T. III. p. 962) reports as follows: "Denique in tantam quidam dilectionis audaciam proruperunt, ut nova quædam et inaudita super Paulo monstra confingerent. Alii enim aiunt, hoc quod scriptum est, sedere a dextris salvatoris et sinistris, de Paulo et de Marcione dici, quod Paulus sedet a dextris, Marcion sedet a sinistris. Porro alii legentes: Mittam vobis advocatum Spiritum veritatis, nolunt intelligere tertiam personam a patre et filio, sed Apostolum Paulum." The estimate of Marcion which appears here is exceedingly instructive. (4) An Arabian writer, who, it is true, belongs to a later period, reports that Marcionites called their founder "Apostolorum principem." (5) Justin, the first opponent of Marcion, classed him with Simon Magus and Menander, that is, with demonic founders of religion These testimonies may suffice.

collection of Christian writings with canonical authority.[1] He was not a systematic thinker; but he was more, for he was not only a religious character, but at the same time a man with an organising talent, such as has no peer in the early Church. If we think of the lofty demands he made on Christians, and, on the other hand, ponder the results that accompanied his activity, we cannot fail to wonder. Wherever Christians were numerous about the year 160, there must have been Marcionite communities with the same fixed but free organisation, with the same canon and the same conception of the essence of Christianity, pre-eminent for the strictness of their morals and their joy in martyrdom.[2] The Catholic Church was then only in process of growth, and it was long ere it reached the solidity won by the Marcionite church through the activity of one man, who was animated by a faith so strong that he was able to oppose his conception of Christianity to all others as the only right one, and who did not shrink from making selections from tradition instead of explaining it away. He was the first who laid the firm found-

---

1 On Marcion's Gospel see the Introductions to the New Testament and Zahn's Kanonsgeschichte, Bd. I., p. 585 ff. and II., p. 409. Marcion attached no name to his Gospel, which, according to his own testimony, he produced from the third one of our Canon (Tertull, adv. Marc. IV. 2. 3. 4). He called it simply εὐαγγέλιον (κυρίου), but held that it was the Gospel which Paul had in his mind when he spoke of his Gospel. The later Marcionites ascribed the authorship of the Gospel partly to Paul, partly to Christ himself, and made further changes in it. That Marcion chose the Gospel called after Luke should be regarded as a makeshift; for this Gospel, which is undoubtedly the most Hellenistic of the four Canonical Gospels, and therefore comes nearest to the Catholic conception of Christianity, accommodated itself in its traditional form but little better than the other three to Marcionite Christianity. Whether Marcion took it for a basis because in his time it had already been connected with Paul (or really had a connection with Paul), or whether the numerous narratives about Jesus as the Saviour of sinners, led him to recognise in this Gospel alone a genuine kernel, we do not know.

2 The associations of the Encratites and the community founded by Apelles stood between the main body of Christendom and the Marcionite church. The description of Celsus (especially V. 61—64 in Orig.) shews the motley appearance which Christendom presented soon after the middle of the second century He there mentions the Marcionites, and a little before (V. 59), the "great Church." It is very important that Celsus makes the main distinction consist in this, that some regarded their God as identical with the God of the Jews, whilst others again declared that "theirs was a different Deity who is hostile to that of the Jews, and that it was he who had sent the Son." (V. 61).

ation for establishing what is Christian, because, in view of
the absoluteness of his faith, [1] he had no desire to appeal
either to a secret evangelic tradition, or to prophecy, or to
natural religion.

Remarks. — The innovations of Marcion are unmistakable.
The way in which he attempted to sever Christianity from
the Old Testament was a bold stroke which demanded the
sacrifice of the dearest possession of Christianity as a religion,
viz., the belief that the God of creation is also the God of
redemption. And yet this innovation was partly caused by a
religious conviction, the origin of which must be sought not
in heathenism, but on Old Testament and Christian soil. For
the bold Anti-judaist was the disciple of a Jewish thinker,
Paul, and the origin of Marcion's antinomianism may be
ultimately found in the prophets. It will always be the glory
of Marcion in the early history of the Church that he, the
born heathen, could appreciate the religious criticism of the
Old Testament religion as formerly exercised by Paul. The
antinomianism of Marcion was ultimately based on the strength
of his religious feeling, on his personal religion as contrasted
with all statutory religion That was also its basis in the
case of the prophets and of Paul, only the statutory religion
which was felt to be a burden and a fetter was different in
each case. As regards the prophets, it was the outer sacrificial worship, and the deliverance was the idea of Jehovah's
righteousness. In the case of Paul, it was the pharisaic treatment of the law, and the deliverance was righteousness by
faith. To Marcion it was the sum of all that the past had
described as a revelation of God: only what Christ had given
him was of real value to him. In this conviction he founded
a Church. Before him there was no such thing in the sense

---

[1] One might be tempted to comprise the character of Marcion's religion
in the words, "The God who dwells in my breast can profoundly excite my
inmost being. He who is throned above all my powers can move nothing outwardly." But Marcion had the firm assurance that God has done something
much greater than move the world: he has redeemed men from the world,
and given them the assurance of this redemption, in the midst of all oppression and enmity which do not cease.

of a community, firmly united by a fixed conviction, harmo-
niously organised, and spread over the whole world. Such a
Church the Apostle Paul had in his mind's eye, but he was
not able to realise it.   That in the century of the great
mixture of religion the greatest apparent paradox was actually
realised: namely, a Paulinism with two Gods and without the
Old Testament; and that this form of Christianity first resulted
in a church which was based not only on intelligible words,
but on a definite conception of the essence of Christianity as
a religion, seems to be the greatest riddle which the earliest
history of Christianity presents.   But it only seems so. The
Greek, whose mind was filled with certain fundamental features
of the Pauline Gospel (law and grace), who was therefore convinced that in all respects the truth was there, and who on
that account took pains to comprehend the real sense of
Paul's statements, could hardly reach any other results than
those of Marcion. The history of Pauline theology in the
Church, a history first of silence, then of artificial interpretation,
speaks loudly enough.   And had not Paul really separated
Christianity as religion from Judaism and the Old Testament?
Must it not have seemed an inconceivable inconsistency, if
he had clung to the special national relation of Christianity
to the Jewish people, and if he had taught a view of history
in which for pædagogic reasons indeed, the Father of mercies
and God of all comfort had appeared as one so entirely
different? He who was not capable of translating himself
into the consciousness of a Jew, and had not yet learned the
method of special interpretation, had only the alternative, if
he was convinced of the truth of the Gospel of Christ as
Paul had proclaimed it, of either giving up this Gospel against
the dictates of his conscience, or striking out of the Epistles
whatever seemed Jewish.   But in this case the god of creation
also disappeared, and the fact that Marcion could make this
sacrifice proves that this religious spirit, with all his energy,
was not able to rise to the height of the religious faith which
we find in the preaching of Jesus.

In basing his own position and that of his church on Paulinism, as he conceived and remodelled it, Marcion connected himself with that part of the earliest tradition of Christianity which is best known to us, and has enabled us to understand his undertaking historically as we do no other. Here we have the means of accurately indicating what part of this structure of the second century has come down from the Apostolic age and is really based on tradition, and what does not. Where else could we do that? But Marcion has taught us far more. He does not impart a correct understanding of early Christianity, as was once supposed, for his explanation of that is undoubtedly incorrect, but a correct estimate of the reliability of the traditions that were current in his day alongside of the Pauline. There can be no doubt that Marcion criticised tradition from a dogmatic stand-point. But would his undertaking have been at all possible, if at that time a reliable tradition of the twelve Apostles and their teaching had existed and been operative in wide circles? We may venture to say no. Consequently, Marcion gives important testimony against the historical reliability of the notion that the common Christianity was really based on the tradition of the twelve Apostles. It is not surprising that the first man who clearly put and answered the question, "What is Christian?" adhered exclusively to the Pauline Epistles, and therefore found a very imperfect solution. When more than 1600 years later the same question emerged for the first time in scientific form, its solution had likewise to be first attempted from the Pauline Epistles, and therefore led at the outset to a one-sidedness similar to that of Marcion. The situation of Christendom in the middle of the second century was not really more favourable to a historical knowledge of early Christianity, than that of the 18th century, but in many respects more unfavourable. Even at that time, as attested by the enterprise of Marcion, its results, and the character of the polemic against him, there were besides the Pauline Epistles, no reliable documents from which the teaching of the twelve Apostles could have been gathered. The position which the Pauline Epistles occupy in the history of the world is, however, described by the fact that every tendency in the Church which was unwilling to introduce into Christianity the power of Greek mysticism, and was yet no longer influenced by the early Christian eschatology, learned from the Pauline Epistles a Christianity which, as a religion, was peculiarly vigorous. But that position is further described by the fact that every tendency which courageously disregards spurious traditions, is compelled to turn to the Pauline Epistles, ·which, on the one hand, present such a profound type of Christianity, and on the other, darken and narrow the judgment about the preaching of Christ himself, by their complicated theology. Marcion was the first, and for a long time the only Gentile Christian who took his stand on Paul. He was no moralist, no Greek mystic, no Apocalyptic enthusiast, but a religious character, nay, one of the few pronouncedly typical religious characters whom we know in the early Church before Augustine. But his attempt to resuscitate Paulinism is the first great proof that the conditions under which this Christianity originated do not repeat themselves, and that therefore Paulinism itself must receive a new construction if one desires to make it the basis of a Church. His attempt is a further proof of the unique value of the Old Testament to early Christendom, as the only means at that time of defending Christian monotheism. Finally, his attempt confirms the experience that a religious community can only be founded by a religious spirit who expects nothing from the world.

Nearly all ecclesiastical writers, from Justin to Origen, opposed Marcion. He appeared already to Justin as the most wicked enemy. We can understand this, and we can quite as well understand how the Church Fathers put him on a level with Basilides and Valentinus, and could not see the difference between them. Because Marcion elevated a better God above the god of creation, and consequently robbed the Christian God of his honour, he appeared to be worse than a heathen (Sentent. episc. LXXXVII., in Hartel's edition of Cyprian, I. p. 454; "Gentiles quamvis idola colant, tamen summum deum patrem creatorem cognoscunt et confitentur [!];

in hunc Marcion blasphemat, etc."), as a blaspheming emissary
of demons, as the first-born of Satan (Polyc., Justin, Irenæus).
Because he rejected the allegoric interpretation of the Old
Testament, and explained its predictions as referring to a Messiah of the Jews who was yet to come, he seemed to be a
Jew (Tertull., adv. Marc. III.). Because he deprived Christianity of the apologetic proof (the proof from antiquity) he
seemed to be a heathen and a Jew at the same time (see my
Texte u. Unters. I. 3, p. 68; the antitheses of Marcion became very important for the heathen and Manichæan assaults
on Christianity). Because he represented the twelve Apostles
as unreliable witnesses, he appeared to be the most wicked
and shameless of all heretics. Finally, because he gained so
many adherents, and actually founded a church, he appeared
to be the ravening wolf (Justin, Rhodon), and his church as
the spurious church. (Tertull., adv. Marc. IV. 5). In Marcion
the Church Fathers chiefly attacked what they attacked in
all Gnostic heretics, but here error shewed itself in its worst
form. They learned much in opposing Marcion (see Bk. II.).
For instance, their interpretation of the *regula fidei* and of
the New Testament received a directly Antimarcionite expression in the Church. One thing, however, they could not learn
from him, and that was how to make Christianity into a philosophic system. He formed no such system, but he has
given a clearly outlined conception, based on historic documents, of Christianity as the religion which redeems the world.

Literature.—All anti-heretical writings of the early Church,
but especially Justin, Apol. I. 26, 58; Iren. I. 27; Tertull.,
adv. Marc. I—V.; de præscr.; Hippol., Philos.; Adamant., de
recta in deum fidei; Epiph. h. 42; Ephr. Syr.; Esnik. The
older attempts to restore the Marcionite Gospel and Aposto-
licum have been antiquated by Zahn's Kanonsgeschichte, l. c.
Hahn (Regimonti, 1823) has attempted to restore the Antitheses. We are still in want of a German monograph on Marcion
(see the whole presentation of Gnosticism by Zahn, with his
Excursus, l. c.). Hilgenfeld, Ketzergesch. p. 316 f. 522 f.; cf. my
works, Zur Quellenkritik des Gnosticismus, 1873; de Apelles

Gnosis Monarchia, 1874; Beiträge z. Gesch. der Marcionit-
ischen Kirchen (Ztschr. f. wiss. Theol. 1876). Marcion's Commentar zum Evangelium (Ztschr. f. K. G. Bd. IV. 4). Apelles
Syllogismen in the Texte u. Unters. VI. H. 3. Zahn, die
Dialoge des Adamantius in the Ztschr. f. K.-Gesch. IX. p.
193 ff. Meyboom, Marcion en de Marcionieten, Leiden, 1888.

———

CHAPTER VI.

APPENDIX: THE CHRISTIANITY OF THE JEWISH CHRISTIANS.

1. ORIGINAL Christianity was in appearance Christian Judaism, the creation of a universal religion on Old Testament soil. It retained therefore, so far as it was not hellenised, which never altogether took place, its original Jewish features. The God of Abraham, Isaac and Jacob was regarded as the Father of Jesus Christ, the Old Testament was the authoritative source of revelation, and the hopes of the future were based on the Jewish ones. The heritage which Christianity took over from Judaism, shews itself on Gentile Christian soil, in fainter or distincter form, in proportion as the philosophic mode of thought already prevails, or recedes into the background.[1] To describe the appearance of the Jewish, Old Testament, heritage in the

---

[1] The attitude of the recently discovered "Teaching of the twelve Apostles" is strictly universalistic, and hostile to Judaism as a nation, but shews us a Christianity still essentially uninfluenced by philosophic elements. The impression made by this fact has caused some scholars to describe the treatise as a document of Jewish Christianity. But the attitude of the Didache is rather the ordinary one of universalistic early Christianity on the soil of the Græco-Roman world. If we describe this as Jewish Christian, then from the meaning which we must give to the words "Christian" and "Gentile Christian", we tacitly legitimise an undefined and undefinable aggregate of Greek ideas, along with a specifically Pauline element, as primitive Christianity, and this is perhaps not the intended, but yet desired, result of the false terminology. Now, if we describe even such writings as the Epistle of James and the Shepherd of Hermas as Jewish Christian, we therewith reduce the entire early Christianity, which is the creation of a universal religion on the soil of Judaism, to the special case of an indefinable religion. The same now appears as one of the particular values of a completely indeterminate magnitude. Hilgenfeld (Judenthum und Juden-christenthum, 1886; cf. also Ztschr. f. wiss. Theol. 1886, H. 4) advocates another conception of Jewish Christianity in opposition to the following account. Zahn, Gesch. des N.T-lich. Kanons, II. p. 668 ff. has a different view still.

Christian faith, so far as it is a religious one, by the name
Jewish Christianity, beginning at a certain point quite arbitrarily chosen, and changeable at will, must therefore necessarily lead to error, and it has done so to a very great extent.
For this designation makes it appear as though the Jewish
element in the Christian religion were something accidental,
while it is rather the case that all Christianity, in so far as
something alien is not foisted into it, appears as the religion
of Israel perfected and spiritualised. We are therefore not
justified in speaking of Jewish Christianity, where a Christian
community, even one of Gentile birth, calls itself the true
Israel, the people of the twelve tribes, the posterity of Abraham; for this transfer is based on the original claim of Christianity and can only be forbidden by a view that is alien to
it. Just as little may we designate Jewish Christian the mighty
and realistic hopes of the future which were gradually repressed
in the second and third centuries. They may be described
as Jewish, or as Christian; but the designation Jewish Christian
must be rejected; for it gives a wrong impression as to the
historic right of these hopes in Christianity. The eschatological ideas of Papias were not Jewish Christian, but Christian;
while, on the other hand, the eschatological speculations of
Origen were not Gentile Christian, but essentially Greek. Those
Christians who saw in Jesus the man chosen by God and
endowed with the Spirit, thought about the Redeemer not in
a Jewish Christian, but in a Christian manner. Those of Asia
Minor who held strictly to the 14th of Nisan as the term of
the Easter festival, were not influenced by Jewish Christian,
but by Christian or Old Testament, considerations. The author
of the "Teaching of the Apostles," who has transferred the
rights of the Old Testament priests with respect to the first
fruits, to the Christian prophets, shews himself by such transference not as a Jewish Christian, but as a Christian. There
is no boundary here; for Christianity took possession of the
whole of Judaism as religion, and it is therefore a most arbitrary view of history which looks upon the Christian appropriation of the Old Testament religion, after any point, as no

longer Christian, but only Jewish Christian. Wherever the
universalism of Christianity is not violated in favour of the
Jewish nation, we have to recognise every appropriation of
the Old Testament as Christian. Hence this proceeding
could be spontaneously undertaken in Christianity, as was in
fact done.

2. But the Jewish religion is a national religion, and Christianity burst the bonds of nationality, though not for all who
recognised Jesus as Messiah. This gives the point at which
the introduction of the term " Jewish Christianity " is appropriate. [1]
It should be applied exclusively to those Christians who really
maintained in their whole extent, or in some measure, even
if it were to a minimum degree, the national and political
forms of Judaism and the observance of the Mosaic law in
its literal sense, as essential to Christianity, at least to the
Christianity of born Jews, or who, though rejecting these forms,
nevertheless assumed a prerogative of the Jewish people even
in Christianity (Clem., Homil. XI. 26: ἐὰν ὁ ἀλλόφυλος τὸν νόμον
πράξῃ, Ἰουδαῖός ἐστιν, μὴ πράξας δέ Ἕλλην; "If the foreigner
observe the law he is a Jew, but if not he is a Greek.") [2]
To this Jewish Christianity is opposed, not Gentile Christianity, but the Christian religion, in so far as it is conceived
as universalistic and anti-national in the strict sense of the
term (Presupp. § 3), that is, the main body of Christendom in
so far as it has freed itself from Judaism as a nation. [3]

It is not strange that this Jewish Christianity was subject

---

1 Or even Ebionitism; the designations are to be used as synonymous.

2 The more rarely the right standard has been set up in the literature
of Church history, for the distinction of Jewish Christianity, the more
valuable are those writings in which it is found. We must refer, above
all, to Diestel, Geschichte des A. T. in der Christl. Kirche, p. 44, note 7.

3 See Theol. Lit. Ztg. 1883. Col. 409 f. as to the attempt of Joël to
make out that the whole of Christendom up to the end of the first century was strictly Jewish Christian, and to exhibit the complete friendship
of Jews and Christians in that period ("Blicke in die Religionsgesch."
2 Abth. 1883). It is not improbable that Christians like James, living in
strict accordance with the law, were for the time being respected even
by the Pharisees in the period preceding the destruction of Jerusalem.
But that can in no case have been the rule. We see from, Epiph., h.
29. 9. and from the Talmud, what was the custom at a later period.

to all the conditions which arose from the internal and external position of the Judaism of the time; that is, different tendencies were necessarily developed in it, according to the measure of the tendencies (or the disintegrations) which asserted themselves in the Judaism of that time. It lies also in the nature of the case that, with one exception, that of Pharisaic Jewish Christianity, all other tendencies were accurately parallelled in the systems which appeared in the great, that is, anti-Jewish Christendom. They were distinguished from these, simply by a social and political, that is, a national element. Moreover, they were exposed to the same influences from without as the synagogue, and as the larger Christendom, till the isolation to which Judaism as a nation, after severe reverses condemned itself, became fatal to them also. Consequently, there were besides Pharisaic Jewish Christians, ascetics of all kinds who were joined by all those over whom Oriental religious wisdom and Greek philosophy had won a commanding influence (see above, p. 242 f.).

In the first century these Jewish Christians formed the majority in Palestine, and perhaps also in some neighbouring provinces. But they were also found here and there in the West.

Now the great question is, whether this Jewish Christianity as a whole, or in certain of its tendencies, was a factor in the development of Christianity to Catholicism. This question is to be answered in the negative, and quite as much with regard to the history of dogma as with regard to the political history of the Church. From the stand-point of the universal history of Christianity, these Jewish Christian communities appear as rudimentary structures which now and again, as objects of curiosity, engaged the attention of the main body of Christendom in the East, but could not exert any important influence on it, just because they contained a national element.

The Jewish Christians took no considerable part in the Gnostic controversy, the epoch-making conflict which was raised within the pale of the larger Christendom about the decisive question, whether, and to what extent, the Old Testament should remain a basis of Christianity, although they themselves were no less occupied with the question. [1] The issue of this conflict in favour of that party which recognised the Old Testament in its full extent as a revelation of the Christian God, and asserted the closest connection between Christianity and the Old Testament religion, was so little the result of any influence of Jewish Christianity, that the existence of the latter would only have rendered that victory more difficult, unless it had already fallen into the background, as a phenomenon of no importance. [2] How completely insignificant it was is shewn not only by the limited polemics of the Church Fathers, but perhaps still more by their silence, and the new import which the reproach of Judaising obtained in Christendom after the middle of the second century. In proportion as the Old Testament, in opposition to Gnosticism, became a more conscious and accredited possession in the Church, and at the same time, in consequence of the naturalising of Christianity in the world, the need of regulations, fixed rules, statutory enactments etc., appeared as indispensable, it must have been natural to use the Old Testament as a holy code of such enactments. This procedure was no falling away from the original anti-Judaic attitude, provided nothing national was taken from the book, and some kind of spiritual interpretation given to what had been borrowed. The "apostasy" rather lay simply in the changed needs. But one now sees how those parties in the Church, to which for any reason this progressive legislation was distasteful, raised the reproach of "Judaising," [3] and

1 There were Jewish Christians who represented the position of the great Church with reference to the Old Testament religion, and there were some who criticised the Old Testament like the Gnostics. Their contention may have remained as much an internal one, as that between the Church Fathers and Gnostics (Marcion) did, so far as Jewish Christianity is concerned. There may have been relations between Gnostic Jewish Christians and Gnostics, not of a national Jewish type, in Syria and Asia Minor, though we are completely in the dark on the matter.

2 From the mere existence of Jewish Christians, those Christians who rejected the Old Testament might have argued against the main body of Christendom and put before it the dilemma: either Jewish Christian or Marcionite. Still more logical indeed was the dilemma: either Jewish, or Marcionite Christian.

3 So did the Montanists and Antimontanists mutually reproach each other with Judaising (see the Montanist writings of Tertullian). Just in the same way the arrangements as to worship and organisation, which were ever being

further, how conversely the same reproach was hurled at
those Christians who resisted the advancing hellenising of
Christianity, with regard, for example, to the doctrine of God,
eschatology, Christology, etc. [1] But while this reproach is
raised, there is nowhere shewn any connection between those
described as Judaising Christians and the Ebionites. That they
were identified off-hand is only a proof that "Ebionitism"
was no longer known. That "Judaising" within Catholicism
which appears, on the one hand, in the setting up of a Catholic
ceremonial law (worship, constitution, etc.), and on the other,
in a tenacious clinging to less hellenised forms of faith and
hopes of faith, has nothing in common with Jewish Christianity, which desired somehow to confine Christianity to the
Jewish nation. [2] Speculations that take no account of history
may make out that Catholicism became more and more Jewish
Christian. But historical observation, which reckons only with
concrete quantities, can discover in Catholicism, besides Christianity, no element which it would have to describe as Jewish

more richly developed, were described by the freer parties as Judaising,
because they made appeal to the Old Testament, though, as regards their
contents, they had little in common with Judaism. But is not the method of
claiming Old Testament authority for the regulations rendered necessary
by circumstances nearly as old as Christianity itself? Against whom the lost
treatise of Clement of Alexandria " κανὼν ἐκκλησιαστικὸς ἢ πρὸς τοὺς Ἰουδαίζοντας "
(Euseb., H. E. VI. 13. 3) was directed, we cannot tell. But as we read, Strom.,
VI. 15, 125, that the Holy Scriptures are to be expounded according to the
ἐκκλησιαστικὸς κανὼν, and then find the following definition of the Canon:
κανὼν δὲ ἐκκλησιαστικὸς ἡ συνωδία καὶ συμφωνία νόμου τε καὶ προφητῶν τῇ κατὰ
τὴν τοῦ κυρίου παρουσίαν παραδιδομένῃ διαθήκῃ, we may conjecture that the
Judaisers were those Christians, who, in principle, or to some extent,
objected to the allegorical interpretation of the Old Testament. We have
then to think either of Marcionite Christians or of "Chiliasts", that is,
the old Christians who were still numerous in Egypt about the middle
of the third century (see Dionys. Alex. in Euseb., H. E. VII. 24). In the
first case, the title of the treatise would be paradoxical But perhaps
the treatise refers to the Quarto-decimans, although the expression κανὼν
ἐκκλησιαστικός seems too ponderous for them (see, however, Orig., Comm.
in Matth. n. 76, ed. Delarue III. p. 895). Clement may possibly have had
Jewish Christians before him. See Zahn, Forschungen, vol. III. p. 37 f.

1 Cases of this kind are everywhere, up to the fifth century, so
numerous that they need not be cited We may only remind the reader
that the Nestorian Christology was described by its earliest and its
latest opponents as Ebionitic.

2 Or were those western Christians Ebionitic who, in the fourth century, still clung to very realistic Chiliastic hopes, who, in fact, regarded
their Christianity as consisting in these?

Christian. It observes only a progressive hellenising, and in consequence of this, a progressive spiritual legislation which utilizes the Old Testament, a process which went on for centuries according to the same methods which had been employed in the larger Christendom from the beginning. ¹ Baur's brilliant attempt to explain Catholicism as a product of the mutual conflict and neutralising of Jewish and Gentile Christianity, (the latter according to Baur being equivalent to Paulinism) reckons with two factors, of which, the one had no significance at all, and the other only an indirect effect, as regards the formation of the Catholic Church. The influence of Paul in this direction is exhausted in working out the universalism of the Christian religion, for a Greater than he had laid the foundation for this movement, and Paul did not realise it by

---

1 The hellenising of Christianity went hand in hand with a more extensive use of the Old Testament; for, according to the principles of Catholicism, every new article of the Church system must be able to legitimise itself as springing from revelation. But, as a rule, the attestation could only be gathered from the Old Testament, since religion here appears in the fixed form of a secular community Now the needs of a secular community for outward regulations gradually became so strong in the Church as to require palpable ceremonial rules. But it cannot be denied, that from a certain point of time, first by means of the fiction of Apostolic constitutions (see my edition of the Didache, Prolegg. p. 239 ff.), and then without this fiction, not, however, as a rule, without reservations, ceremonial regulations were simply taken over from the Old Testament. But this transference (See Bk. II) takes place at a time when there can be absolutely no question of an influence of Jewish Christianity. Moreover, it always proves itself to be catholic by the fact that it did not in the least soften the traditional anti-Judaism. On the contrary, it attained its full growth in the age of Constantine. Finally, it should not be overlooked that at all times in antiquity, certain provincial churches were exposed to Jewish influences, especially in the East and in Arabia, that they were therefore threatened with being Judaised, or with apostasy to Judaism, and that even at the present day, certain Oriental Churches shew tokens of having once been subject to Jewish influences. (see Serapion in Euseb , H. E. VI. 12. 1, Martyr. Pion., Epiph. de mens. et pond. 15. 18; my Texte u. Unters. I. 3. p. 73 f., and Wellhausen, Skizzen und Vorarbeiten, Part. 3. p 197 ff.; actual disputations with Jews do not seem to have been common, though see Tertull , adv. Jud and Orig. c. Cels. I. 45, 49, 55: II, 31. Clement also keeps in view Jewish objections.) This Jewish Christianity, if we like to call it so, which in some regions of the East was developed through an immediate influence of Judaism on Catholicism, should not, however, be confounded with the Jewish Christianity which is the most original form in which Christianity realised itself. This was no longer able to influence the Christianity which had shaken itself free from the Jewish nation (as to futile attempts, see below), any more than the protecting covering stripped from the new shoot, can ever again acquire significance for the latter.

himself alone. Placed on this height Catholicism was certainly
developed by means of conflicts and compromises, not, however, by conflicts with Ebionitism, which was to all intents
and purposes discarded as early as the first century, but as
the result of the conflict of Christianity with the united
powers of the world in which it existed, on behalf of its own
peculiar nature as the universal religion based on the Old
Testament. Here were fought triumphant battles, but here
also compromises were made which characterise the essence
of Catholicism as Church and as doctrine. [1]

A history of Jewish Christianity and its doctrines does not
therefore, strictly speaking, belong to the history of dogma,
especially as the original distinction between Jewish Christianity and the main body of the Church lay, as regards its
principle, not in doctrine, but in policy. But seeing that the
opinions of the teachers in this Church regarding Jewish
Christianity, throw light upon their own stand-point, also that
up till about the middle of the second century Jewish Christians

---

1 What is called the ever-increasing "legal" feature of Gentile Christianity
and the Catholic Church, is conditioned by its origin, in so far as its theory
is rooted in that of Judaism spiritualised and influenced by Hellenism. As
the Pauline conception of the law never took effect, and a criticism of the Old
Testament religion which is just law, neither understood nor ventured upon in
the larger Christendom—the forms were not criticised, but the contents spiritualised—so the theory that Christianity is promise and spiritual law, is
to be regarded as the primitive one. Between the spiritual law and the national law there stand indeed ceremonial laws, which, without being spiritually interpreted, could yet be freed from the national application. It cannot
be denied that the Gentile Christian communities and the incipient Catholic Church were very careful and reserved in their adoption of such laws
from the Old Testament, and that the later Church no longer observed this
caution. But still it is only a question of degree, for there are many examples
of that adoption in the earliest period of Christendom. The latter had no
cause for hurry in utilizing the Old Testament so long as there was no external
or internal policy, or so long as it was still in embryo. The decisive factor lies
here again in enthusiasm and not in changing theories The basis for these
was supplied from the beginning. But a community of individuals under spiritual excitement builds on this foundation something different from an associ-
ation which wishes to organise and assert itself as such on earth. (The
history of Sunday is specially instructive here; see Zahn, Gesch. des Sonn-
tags, 1878, as well as the history of the discipline of fasting, see Linsenmayr,
Entwickelung der Kirchl. Fastendisciplin. 1877, and Die Abgabe des Zehnten.
In general, Cf. Ritschl., Entstehung der Altkath. Kirche, 2 edit. pp. 312 ff. 331
ff. 1 Cor IX. 9, may be noted).

were still numerous and undoubtedly formed the great majority of believers in Palestine, [1] and finally, that attempts— unsuccessful ones indeed—on the part of Jewish Christianity to bring Gentile Christians under its sway, did not cease till about the middle of the third century, a short sketch may be appropriate here. [2]

1 Justin, Apol. I. 53, Dial. 47; Euseb., H. E. IV. 5; Sulpic. Sev., Hist. Sacr II. 31; Cyrill, Catech. XIV. 15. Important testimonies in Origen, Eusebius, Epiphanius and Jerome.

2 No Jewish Christian writings have been transmitted to us, even from the earliest period; for the Apocalypse of John which describes the Jews as a synagogue of Satan, is not a Jewish Christian book (III. 9 especially, shews that the author knows of only one covenant of God, viz., that with the Christians) Jewish Christian sources lie at the basis of our synoptic Gospels, but none of them in their present form is a Jewish Christian writing. The Acts of the Apostles is so little Jewish Christian, its author seemingly so ignorant of Jewish Christianity, at least so unconcerned with regard to it, that to him the spiritualised Jewish law, or Judaism as a religion which he connects as closely as possible with Christianity, is a factor already completely detached from the Jewish people (see Overbeck's Commentar z. Apostelgesch. and his discussion in the Ztschr. f. wiss. Theol. 1872. p. 305 ff.). Measured by the Pauline theology we may indeed, with Overbeck, say of the Gentile Christianity, as represented by the author of the Acts of the Apostles, that it already has germs of Judaism, and represents a falling off from Paulinism, but these expressions are not correct, because they have at least the appearance of making Paulinism the original form of Gentile Christianity. But as this can neither be proved nor believed, the religious attitude of the author of the Acts of the Apostles must have been a very old one in Christendom. The Judaistic element was not first introduced into Gentile Christianity by the opponents of Paul, who indeed wrought in the national sense, and there is even nothing to lead to the hypothesis that the common Gentile Christian view of the Old Testament and of the law should be conceived as resulting from the efforts of Paul and his opponents, for the consequent effect here would either have been null, or a strengthening of the Jewish Christian thesis. The Jewish element, that is, the total acceptance of the Jewish religion *sub specie aeternitatis et Christi*, is simply the original Christianity of the Gentile Christians itself considered as theory. Contrary to his own intention, Paul was compelled to lead his converts to this Christianity, for only for such Christianity was "the time fulfilled" within the empire of the world. The Acts of the Apostles gives eloquent testimony to the pressing difficulties which, under such circumstances, stand in the way of a historical understanding of the Gentile Christians in view of the work and the theology of Paul. Even the Epistle to the Hebrews is not a Jewish Christian writing: but there is certainly a peculiar state of things connected with this document. For, on the one hand, the author and his readers are free from the law, a spiritual interpretation is given to the Old Testament religion which makes it appear to be glorified and fulfilled in the work of Christ, and there is no mention of any prerogative of the people of Israel. But, on the other hand, because the spiritual interpretation, as in Paul, is here teleological, the author allows a temporary significance to the cultus as literally understood, and therefore, by his criti-

Justin vouches for the existence of Jewish Christians, and distinguishes between those who would force the law even on Gentile-
Christians, and would have no fellowship with such as did not

cism he conserves the Old Testament religion for the past, while declaring
that it was set aside, as regards the present, by the fulfilment of Christ.
The teleology of the author, however, looks at everything only from the
point of view of shadow and reality, an antithesis which is at the service
of Paul also, but which in his case vanishes behind the antithesis of law
and grace. This scheme of thought, which is to be traced back to a way
of looking at things which arose in Christian Judaism, seeing that it really
distinguishes between old and new, stands midway between the conception
of the Old Testament religion entertained by Paul, and that of the common
Gentile Christian as it is represented by Barnabas. The author of the
Epistle to the Hebrews undoubtedly knows of a twofold convenant of God.
But the two are represented as stages, so that the second is completely
based on the first. This view was more likely to be understood by the
Gentile Christians than the Pauline, that is, with some seemingly slight
changes, to be recognised as their own. But even it at first fell to the
ground, and it was only in the conflict with the Marcionites that some
Church Fathers advanced to views which seem to be related to those
of the Epistle to the Hebrews. Whether the author of this Epistle was
a born Jew or a Gentile — in the former case he would far surpass the
Apostle Paul in his freedom from the national claims — we cannot, at
any rate, recognise in it a document containing a conception which still
prizes the Jewish nationality in Christianity, nay, not even a document to prove
that such a conception was still dangerous. Consequently, we have no Jewish
Christian memorial in the New Testament at all, unless it be in the Pauline
Epistles. But as concerns the early Christian literature outside the Canon, the
fragments of the great work of Hegesippus are even yet by some investigators
claimed for Jewish Christianity. Weizsäcker (Art. "Hegesippus" in Herzog's
R. E. 2 edit) has shewn how groundless this assumption is. That Hegesippus
occupied the common Gentile Christian position is certain from unequivocal
testimony of his own. If, as is very improbable, we were obliged to ascribe to
him a rejection of Paul, we should have to refer to Eusebius, H. E. IV. 29, 5.
(Σευηριανοὶ βλασφημοῦντες Παῦλον τὸν ἀπόστολον ἀθετοῦσιν αὐτοῦ τὰς ἐπιστολὰς
μηδὲ τὰς πράξεις τῶν ἀποστόλων καταδεχόμενοι, but probably the Gospels ; these
Severians therefore, like Marcion, recognised the Gospel of Luke, but rejected
the Acts of the Apostles), and Orig. c. Cels. V. 65 (εἰσὶ γὰρ τινες αἱρέσεις τὰς
Παύλου ἐπιστολὰς τοῦ ἀποστόλου μὴ προσιέμεναι ὥσπερ Ἐβιωναῖοι ἀμφότεροι καὶ οι
καλούμενοι Ἐγκρατηταί). Consequently, our only sources of knowledge of Jewish
Christianity in the post-Pauline period are merely the accounts of the Church
Fathers, and some additional fragments (see the collection of fragments of the
Ebionite Gospel and that to the Hebrews in Hilgenfeld, Nov. Test. extra can.
rec. fasc. IV. Ed. 2, and in Zahn, l. c. II. p. 642 ff.). We know better, but
still very imperfectly, certain forms of the syncretistic Jewish Christianity,
from the Philosoph. of Hippolytus and the accounts of Epiphanius, who is certainly nowhere more incoherent than in the delineation of the Jewish Christians, because he could not copy original documents here, but was forced to
piece together confused traditions with his own observations See below on
the extensive documents which are even yet as they stand, treated as records
of Jewish Christianity, viz., the Pseudo-Clementines. Of the pieces of writing whose Jewish Christian origin is controverted, in so far as they may be
simply Jewish, I say nothing.

observe it, and those who considered that the law was binding only on people of Jewish birth, and did not shrink from fellowship with Gentile Christians who were living without the law. How the latter could observe the law and yet enter into intercourse with those who were not Jews, is involved in obscurity, but these he recognises as partakers of the Christian salvation and therefore as Christian brethren, though he declares that there are Christians who do not possess this large heartedness. He also speaks of Gentile Christians who allowed themselves to be persuaded by Jewish Christians into the observance of the Mosaic law, and confesses that he is not quite sure of the salvation of these. This is all we learn from Justin,[1] but it is instructive enough. In the first place, we can see that the question is no longer a burning one: "Justin here represents only the interests of a Gentile Christianity whose stability has been secured." This has all the more meaning that in the Dialogue Justin has not in view an individual Christian community, or the communities of a province, but speaks as one who surveys the whole situation of Christendom.[2] The very fact that Justin has devoted to the whole question only one chapter of a work containing 142, and the magnanimous way in which he speaks, shew that the phenomena in question have no longer any importance for the main body of Christendom. Secondly, it is worthy of notice that Justin distinguishes two tendencies in Jewish Christianity. We observe these two tendencies in the Apostolic age (Presupp. § 3); they had therefore maintained themselves to his time. Finally, we must not overlook the circumstance that he adduces only the ἔννομος πολιτεία, "legal polity," as characteristic of this Jewish Christianity. He speaks only incidentally of a difference in doctrine, nay, he manifestly presupposes that the διδάγματα Χριστοῦ, "teachings of Christ," are essentially found among them just as among the Gentile Christians; for he regards the more liberal among them as friends and brethren.[3]

1 As to the chief localities where Jewish Christians were found, see Zahn, Kanonsgesch. II. p. 648 ff.

2 Dialogue 47.

3 Yet it should be noted that the Christians who, according to Dial. 48,

The fact that, even then, there were Jewish Christians here and there who sought to spread the ἔννομος πολιτεία among Gentile Christians, has been attested by Justin and also by other contemporary writers.[1] But there is no evidence of this propaganda having acquired any great importance. Celsus also knows Christians who desire to live as Jews according to the Mosaic law (V. 61), but he mentions them only once, and otherwise takes no notice of them in his delineation of, and attack on, Christianity. We may perhaps infer that he knew of them only from hearsay, for he simply enumerates them along with the numerous Gnostic sects. Had this keen observer really known them he would hardly have passed them over, even though he had met with only a small

---

denied the pre-existence of Christ and held him to be a man, are described as Jewish Christians. We should read in the passage in question, as my recent comparison of the Parisian codex shews, ἀπὸ τοῦ ὑμετέρου γένους. Yet Justin did not make this a controversial point of great moment.

[1] The so-called Barnabas is considerably older than Justin. In his Epistle (4. 6) he has in view Gentile Christians who have been converted by Jewish Christians, when he utters a warning against those who say ὅτι ἡ διαθήκη ἐκείνων (the Jews) καὶ ἡμῶν (ἐστιν). But how great the actual danger was cannot be gathered from the Epistle. Ignatius in two Epistles (ad Magn. 8—10 : ad Philad. 6. 9) opposes Jewish Christian intrigues, and characterises them solely from the point of view that they mean to introduce the Jewish observance of the law. He opposes them with a Pauline idea (Magn. 8. 1 : εἰ γὰρ μέχρι νῦν κατὰ νόμον. Ἰουδαϊσμὸν ζῶμεν ὁμολογοῦμεν χάριν μὴ εἰληφέναι), as well as with the common Gentile Christian assumption that the prophets themselves had already lived κατὰ Χριστόν. These Judaists must be strictly distinguished from the Gnostics whom Ignatius elsewhere opposes (against Zahn, Ignat. v. Ant. p. 356 f.). The dangers from this Jewish Christianity cannot have been very serious, even if we take Magn. 11. 1, as a phrase. There was an active Jewish community in Philadelphia (Rev. III. 9), and so Jewish Christian plots may have continued longer there. At the first look it seems very promising that in the old dialogue of Aristo of Pella, a Hebrew Christian, Jason, is put in opposition to the Alexandrian Jew, Papiscus. But as the history of the little book proves, this Jason must have essentially represented the common Christian and not the Ebionite conception of the Old Testament and its relation to the Gospel, etc ; see my Texte u. Unters. I. 1. 2. p. 115 ff. ; I. 3 p. 115 - 130. Testimony as to an apostasy to Judaism is occasionally though rarely given; see Serapion in Euseb., H. E. VI. 12, who addresses a book to one Domninus, ἐκπεπτωκότα παρὰ τὸν τοῦ διωγμοῦ καιρὸν ἀπὸ τῆς εἰς Χριστὸν πίστεως ἐπὶ τὴν Ἰουδαϊκὴν ἐθελοθρησκείαν ; see also Acta Pionii, 13. 14. According to Epiphanius, de mens. et pond. 14. 15, Acquila, the translator of the Bible, was first a Christian and then a Jew. This account is perhaps derived from Origen, and is probably reliable. Likewise according to Epiphanius (l. c. 17. 18), Theodotion was first a Marcionite and then a Jew. The transition from Marcionitism to Judaism (for extremes meet) is not in itself incredible.

number of them.[1] Irenæus placed the Ebionites among the heretical schools,[2] but we can see from his work that in his day they must have been all but forgotten in the West.[3] This was not yet the case in the East. Origen knows of them. He knows also of some who recognise the birth from the Virgin. He is sufficiently intelligent and acquainted with history to judge that the Ebionites are no school, but as believing Jews are the descendants of the earliest Christians, in fact he seems to suppose that all converted Jews have at all times observed the law of their fathers. But he is far from judging of them favourably. He regards them as little better than the Jews ('Ιουδαῖοι καὶ οἱ ὀλίγῳ διαφέροντες αὐτῶν 'Εβιωναῖοι, "Jews and Ebionites who differ little from them"). Their rejection of Paul destroys the value of their recognition of Jesus as Messiah. They appear only to have assumed

---

1 It follows from c. Cels. II. 1—3, that Celsus could hardly have known Jewish Christians.

2 Iren. I. 26. 2: III. 11. 7: III. 15. 1, 21. 1: IV. 33 4: V. 1. 3. We first find the name Ebionæi, the poor, in Irenæus. We are probably entitled to assume that this name was given to the Christians in Jerusalem as early as the Apostolic age, that is, they applied it to themselves (poor in the sense of the prophets and of Christ, fit to be received into the Messianic kingdom). It is very questionable whether we should put any value on Epiph. h 30. 17.

3 When Irenæus adduces as the points of distinction between the Church and the Ebionites, that besides observing the law and repudiating the Apostle Paul, the latter deny the Divinity of Christ and his birth from the Virgin, and reject the New Testament Canon (except the Gospel of Matthew), that only proves that the formation of dogma has made progress in the Church The less was known of the Ebionites from personal observation, the more confidently they were made out to be heretics who denied the Divinity of Christ and rejected the Canon. The denial of the Divinity of Christ and the birth from the Virgin was, from the end of the second century, regarded as the Ebionite heresy *par excellence,* and the Ebionites themselves appeared to the Western Christians, who obtained their information solely from the East, to be a school like those of the Gnostics, founded by a scoundrel named Ebion for the purpose of dragging down the person of Jesus to the common level. It is also mentioned incidentally, that this Ebion had commanded the observance of circumcision and the Sabbath; but that is no longer the main thing (see Tertull, de carne 14, 18, 24: de virg. vel. 6: de præscr. 10. 33; Hippol, Syntagma, [Pseudo-Tertull, 11; Philastr. 37; Epiph h. 30]; Hippol, Philos. VII. 34. The latter passage contains the instructive statement that Jesus by his perfect keeping of the law became the Christ). This attitude of the Western Christians proves that they no longer knew Jewish Christian communities Hence it is all the more strange that Hilgenfeld (Ketzergesch. p. 422 ff.) has in all earnestness endeavoured to revive the Ebion of the Western Church Fathers.

Christ's name, and their literal exposition of the Scripture is meagre and full of error. It is possible that such Jewish Christians may have existed in Alexandria, but it is not certain. Origen knows nothing of an inner development in this Jewish Christianity.[1] Even in Palestine, Origen seems to have occupied himself personally with these Jewish Christians, just as little as Eusebius.[2] They lived apart by themselves and were not aggressive. Jerome is the last who gives us a clear and certain account of them [3] He, who associated with them, assures us that their attitude was the same as in the second century, only they seem to have made progress in the recognition of the birth from the Virgin and in their more friendly position towards the Church.[4] Jerome

1 See Orig. c. Cels. II. 1 : V. 61, 65 : de princip. IV. 22; hom. in Genes. III. 15 (Opp. II. p. 65); hom. in Jerem XVII. 12 (III. p. 254); in Matth. T. XVI. 12 (III. p. 494), T. XVII 12 (III. p 733); cf. Opp. III. p. 895 : hom. in Lc. XVII. (III. p. 952). That a portion of the Ebionites recognised the birth from the Virgin was according to Origen frequently attested That was partly reckoned to them for righteousness and partly not, because they would not admit the pre-existence of Christ. The name "Ebionites" is interpreted as a nickname given them by the Church ("beggarly" in the knowledge of scripture, and particularly of Christology).

2 Eusebius knows no more than Origen (H E. III 27), unless we specially credit him with the information that the Ebionites keep along with the Sabbath also the Sunday. What he says of Symmachus, the translator of the Bible, and an Ebionite, is derived from Origen (H. E. VI. 17) The report is interesting, because it declares that Symmachus *wrote* against Catholic Christianity, especially against the Catholic Gospel of Matthew (about the year 200. But Symmachus is to be classed with the Gnostics, and not with the common type of Jewish Christianity (see below). We have also to thank Eusebius (H. E. III. 5. 3) for the information that the Christians of Jerusalem fled to Pella, in Peræa, before the destruction of that city. In the following period the most important settlements of the Ebionites must have been in the countries east of the Jordan, and in the heart of Syria (see Jul. Afric. in Euseb., H. E I 7. 14: Euseb, de loc. hebr. in Lagarde, Onomast. p. 301; Epiph., h. 29. 7: h. 30 2). This fact explains how the bishops in Jerusalem and the coast towns of Palestine came to see very little of them. There was a Jewish Christian community in Beroea with which Jerome had relations (Jerom., de Vir. inl. 3).

3 Jerome correctly declares (Ep. ad. August. 122 c 13, Opp. I. p. 746), "(Ebionitæ) credentes in Christo propter hoc solum a patribus anathematizati sunt. quod legis cæremonias Christi evangelio miscuerunt, et sic nova confessi sunt, ut vetera non omitterent."

4 Ep. ad August. l. c.; Quid dicam de Hebionitis, qui Christianos esse se simulant? usque hodie per totas orientis synagogas inter Judæos(!) hæresis est, que dicitur Minæorum et a Pharisæis nunc usque damnatur, quos vulgo Nazaræos nuncupant, qui credunt in Christum filium dei natum de Virgine Maria et eum dicunt esse, qui sub pontio Pilato passus est et resurrexit, in quem et nos

at one time calls them Ebionites and at another Nazarenes,
thereby proving that these names were used synonymously. [1]
There is not the least ground for distinguishing two clearly
marked groups of Jewish Christians, or even for reckoning
the distinction of Origen and the Church Fathers to the account of Jewish Christians themselves, so as to describe as
Nazarenes those who recognised the birth from the Virgin,
and who had no wish to compel the Gentile Christians to
observe the law, and the others as Ebionites. Apart from
syncretistic or Gnostic Jewish Christianity, there is but one
group of Jewish Christians holding various shades of opinion,
and these from the beginning called themselves Nazarenes
as well as Ebionites. From the beginning, likewise, one
portion of them was influenced by the existence of a great
Gentile Church which did not observe the law. They acknowledged the work of Paul and experienced in a slight degree
influences emanating from the great Church. [2] But the gulf
which separated them from that Church did not thereby become narrower. That gulf was caused by the social and
political separation of these Jewish Christians, whatever mental
attitude, hostile or friendly, they might take up to the
great Church. This Church stalked over hem with iron feet,

credimus; sed dum volunt et Judæi esse et Christiani, nec Judæi sunt nec
Christiani." The approximation of the Jewish Christian conception to that
of the Catholics shews itself also in their exposition of Isaiah IX. 1. f.
(see Jerome on the passage). But we must not forget that there were
such Jewish Christians from the earliest times. It is worthy of note that
the name Nazarenes, as. applied to Jewish Christians, is found in the
Acts of the Apostles XXIV. 5, in the Dialogue of Jason and Papiscus,
and then first again in Jerome.

   1 Zahn, 1 c. p. 648 ff. 668 ff. has not convinced me of the contrary,
but I confess that Jerome's style of expression is not everywhere clear.

   2 Zahn, (l. c.) makes a sharp distinction between the Nazarenes, on the
one side, who used the Gospel of the Hebrews, acknowledged the birth
from the Virgin, and in fact the higher Christology to some extent, did
not repudiate Paul, etc., and the Ebionites on the other, whom he simply
identifies with the Gnostic Jewish Christians, if I am not mistaken. In
opposition to this, I think I must adhere to the distinction as given
above in the text and in the following: (1) Non-Gnostic, Jewish Christians
(Nazarenes, Ebionites), who appeared in various shades, according to
their doctrine and attitude to the Gentile Church, and whom, with the
Church Fathers, we may appropriately classify as strict or tolerant (exclusive or liberal). (2) Gnostic or syncretistic Judæo-Christians who are
also termed Ebionites.

as over a structure which in her opinion was full of contradictions throughout (" Semi-christiani "), and was disconcerted
neither by the gospel of these Jewish Christians nor by anything else about them. [1] But as the Synagogue also vigorously
condemned them, their position up to their extinction was a
most tragic one. These Jewish Christians, more than any other
Christian party, bore the reproach of Christ.

The Gospel, at the time when it was proclaimed among
the Jews, was not only law, but theology, and indeed syncretistic theology. On the other hand, the temple service
and the sacrificial system had begun to lose their hold in
certain influential circles. [2] We have pointed out above
(Presupp. §§. 1. 2. 5) how great were the diversities of Jewish sects,
and that there was in the Diaspora, as well as in Palestine
itself, a Judaism which, on the one hand, followed ascetic
impulses, and on the other, advanced to a criticism of the
religious tradition without giving up the national claims. It
may even be said that in theology the boundaries between
the orthodox Judaism of the Pharisees and a syncretistic
Judaism were of an elastic kind. Although religion, in those
circles, seemed to be fixed in its legal aspect, yet on its theological side it was ready to admit very diverse speculations,
in which angelic powers especially played a great rôle. [3]

1 This Gospel no doubt greatly interested the scholars of the Catholic
Church from Clement of Alexandria onwards But they have almost all
contrived to evade the hard problem which it presented. It may be noted,
incidentally, that the Gospel of the Hebrews, to judge from the remains
preserved to us, can neither have been the model nor the translation of
our Matthew, but a work independent of this, though drawing from the
same sources, representing perhaps to some extent an earlier stage of
the tradition. Jerome also knew very well that the Gospel of the Hebrews
was not the original of the canonical Matthew, but he took care not to
correct the old prejudice. Ebionitic conceptions, such as that of the
female nature of the Holy Spirit, were of course least likely to convince
the Church Fathers. Moreover, the common Jewish Christians hardly
possessed a Church theology, because for them Christianity was something entirely different from the doctrine of a school. On the Gospel
of the Hebrews, see Handmann (Texte u. Unters. V 3), Resch, Agrapha
(l. c. V. 4), and Zahn, l. c. p. 642 ff.

2 We have as yet no history of the sacrificial system, and the views as to sacrifice in the Græco-Roman epoch, of the Jewish Nation. It is urgently needed.

3 We may remind readers of the assumptions, that the world was
created by angels, that the law was given by angels, and similar ones

That introduced into Jewish monotheism an element of differentiation, the results of which were far-reaching. The field was prepared for the formation of syncretistic sects. They present themselves to us on the soil of the earliest Christianity, in the speculations of those Jewish Christian teachers who are opposed in the Epistle to the Colossians, and in the Gnosis of Cerinthus (see above, p. 246). Here cosmological ideas and myths were turned to profit. The idea of God was sublimated by both. In consequence of this, the Old Testament records were subjected to criticism, because they could not in all respects be reconciled with the universal religion which hovered before men's minds. This criticism was opposed to the Pauline in so far as it maintained, with the common Jewish Christians, and Christendom as a whole, that the genuine Old Testament religion was essentially identical with the Christian. But while those common Jewish Christians drew from this the inference that the whole of the Old Testament must be adhered to in its traditional sense and in all its ordinances, and while the larger Christendom secured for itself the whole of the Old Testament by deviating from the ordinary interpretation, those syncretistic Jewish Christians separated from the Old Testament, as interpolations, whatever did not agree with their purer moral conceptions and borrowed speculations. Thus, in particular, they got rid of the sacrificial ritual, and all that was connected with it, by putting ablutions in their place. First the profanation, and afterwards, the abolition of the temple worship, after the destruction of Jerusalem, may have given another new and welcome impulse to this by coming to be regarded as its Divine confirmation (Presupp. § 2). Christianity now appeared as purified Mosaism. In these Jewish Christian undertakings we have undoubtedly before us a series of peculiar attempts to elevate the Old Testament religion into the uni-

which are found in the theology of the Pharisees. Celsus (in Orig. I. 26: V. 6) asserts generally that the Jews worshipped angels, so does the author of the Prædicatio Petri, as well as the apologist Aristides. Cf. Joël, Blicke in die Religionsgesch. I. Abth., a book which is certainly to be used with caution (see Theol. Lit. Ztg. 1881. Coll. 184 ff.).

v̇ersal one, under the impression of the person of Jesus; attempts, however, in which the Jewish religion, and not the Jewish people, was to bear the costs by curtailment of its distinctive features. The great inner affinity of these attempts with the Gentile Christian Gnostics has already been set forth. The firm partition wall between them, however, lies in the claim of these Jewish Christians to set forth the pure Old Testament religion, as well as in the national Jewish colouring which the constructed universal religion was always to preserve. This national colouring is shewn in the insistance upon a definite measure of Jewish national ceremonies as necessary to salvation, and in the opposition to the Apostle Paul, which united the Gnostic Judæo-Christians with the common type, those of the strict observance. How the latter were related to the former, we do not know, for the inner relations here are almost completely unknown to us. [1]

Apart from the false doctrines opposed in the Epistle to the Colossians, and from Cerinthus, this syncretistic Jewish Christianity which aimed at making itself a universal religion, meets us in tangible form only in three phenomena: [2] in the Elkesaites of Hippolytus and Origen, in the Ebionites with their associates of Epiphanius, sects very closely connected, in fact to be viewed as one party of manifold shades, [3] and

---

[1] No reliance can be placed on Jewish sources, or on Jewish scholars, as a rule. What we find in Joël, l. c. I. Abth. p. 101 ff. is instructive. We may mention Grätz, Gnosticismus und Judenthum (Krotoschin, 1846), who has called attention to the Gnostic elements in the Talmud, and dealt with several Jewish Gnostics and Antignostics, as well as with the book of Jezira. Grätz assumes that the four main dogmatic points in the book Jezira, viz., the strict unity of the deity, and, at the same time, the negation of the demiurgic dualism, the creation out of nothing with the negation of matter, the systematic unity of the world and the balancing of opposites, were directed against prevailing Gnostic ideas.

[2] We may pass over the false teachers of the Pastoral Epistles, as they cannot be with certainty determined, and the possibility is not excluded that we have here to do with an arbitrary construction; see Holtzman, Pastoralbriefe, p. 150 f.

[3] Orig. in Euseb. VI. 38; Hippol., Philos. IX 13 ff., X. 29; Epiph., h. 30, also h. 19. 53; Method , Conviv. VIII. 10. From the confused account of Epiphanius, who called the common Jewish Christians Nazarenes, the Gnostic type Ebionites and Sampsæi. and their Jewish forerunners Osseni, we may conclude, that in many regions where there were Jewish Christians they yielded

in the activity of Symmachus.[1] We observe here a form of
religion as far removed from that of the Old Testament as from
the Gospel, subject to strong heathen influences, not Greek, but
Asiatic, and scarcely deserving the name " Christian," because it
appeals to a new revelation of God which is to complete that
given in Christ. We should take particular note of this in
judging of the whole remarkable phenomenon. The question
in this Jewish Christianity is not the formation of a philosophic
school, but to some extent the establishment of a kind of
new religion, that is, the completion of that founded by Christ,
undertaken by a particular person basing his claims on a
revealed book which was delivered to him from heaven. This
book which was to form the complement of the Gospel, possessed, from the third century, importance for all sections of
Jewish Christians so far as they, in the phraseology of Epiphanius, were not Nazarenes.[2] The whole system reminds
one of Samaritan Christian syncretism;[3] but we must be on

to the propaganda of the Elkesaite doctrines, and that in the fourth
century there was no other syncretistic Jewish Christianity besides the
various shades of Elkesaites.

1 I formerly reckoned Symmachus, the translator of the Bible, among
the common Jewish Christians; but the statements of Victorinus Rhetor
on Gal. I. 19. II. 26 (Migne T. VIII. Col. 1155. 1162) shew that he has a
close affinity with the Pseudo-Clementines, and is also to be classed with
the Elkesaite Alcibiades. "Nam Jacobum apostolum Symmachiani faciunt
quasi duodecimum et hunc secuntur, qui ad dominum nostrum Jesum
Christum adjungunt Judaismi observationem, quamquam etiam Jesum Christum fatentur; dicunt enim eum ipsum Adam esse et esse animam genera-
lem, et aliæ hujusmodi blasphemiæ." The account given by Eusebius,
H. E. VI. 17 (probably on the authority of Origen, see also Demonstr.
VII. 1) is important: Τῶν γε μὲν ἑρμηνευτῶν αὐτῶν δὴ τούτων ἰστέον, Ἐβιωναῖον
τὸν Σύμμαχον γεγονέναι..... καὶ ὑπομνήματα δὲ τοῦ Συμμάχου εἰσέτι νῦν φέρεται,
ἐν οἷς δοκεῖ πρὸς τὸ κατὰ Ματθαῖον ἀποτεινόμενος εὐαγγέλιον τὴν δεδηλωμένην αἵρεσιν
κρατύνειν. Symmachus therefore adopted an aggressive attitude towards the
great Church, and hence we may probably class him with Alcibiades who
lived a little later. Common Jewish Christianity was no longer aggressive
in the second century

2 Wellhausen (l. c. Part III. p. 206) supposes that Elkesaï is equivalent
to Alexius. That the receiver of the "book" was a historical person is
manifest from Epiphanius' account of his descendants (h. 19 2: 53. 1).
From Hipp., Philosoph. IX. 16, p 468, it is certainly probable, though not
certain, that the book was produced by the unknown author as early as the
time of Trajan. On the other hand, the existence of the sect itself can be
proved only at the beginning of the third century, and therefore we have
the possibility of an ante-dating of the "book." This seems to have been
Origen's opinion.

3 Epiph. (h. 53. 1) says of the Elkesaites: οὔτε χριστιανοὶ ὑπάρχοντες οὔτε

our guard against identifying the two phenomena, or even regarding them as similar. These Elkesaite Jewish Christians held fast by the belief that Jesus was the Son of God, and saw in the "book" a revelation which proceeded from him. They did not offer any worship to their founder,[1] that is, to the receiver of the "book," and they were, as will be shewn, the most ardent opponents of Simonianism.[2]

Alcibiades of Apamea, one of their disciples, came from the East to Rome about 220-230, and endeavoured to spread the doctrines of the sect in the Roman Church. He found the soil prepared, inasmuch as he could announce from the "book" forgiveness of sins to all sinful Christians, even the grossest transgressors, and such forgiveness was very much needed. Hippolytus opposed him, and had an opportunity of seeing the book and becoming acquainted with its contents. From his account and that of Origen we gather the following: (1) The sect is a Jewish Christian one, for it requires the νόμου πολιτεία (circumcision and the keeping of the Sabbath), and repudiates the Apostle Paul; but it criticises the Old Testament and rejects a part of it. (2) The objects of its faith are the "Great and most High God", the Son of God (the "Great King"), and the Holy Spirit (thought of as female); Son and Spirit appear as angelic powers. Considered outwardly, and according to his birth, Christ is a mere man, but with this peculiarity, that he has already been frequently born and manifested (πολλάκις γεννηθέντα καὶ γεννώμενον πεφηνέναι καὶ φύεσθαι, ἀλλάσ-

---

Ἰουδαῖοι οὔτε Ἕλληνες, ἀλλὰ μέσον ἁπλῶς ὑπάρχοντες. He pronounces a similar judgment as to the Samaritan sects (Simonians), and expressly (h. 30. 1) connects the Elkesaites with them.

1 The worship paid to the descendants of this Elkesai, spoken of by Epiphanius, does not, if we allow for exaggerations, go beyond the measure of honour which was regularly paid to the descendants of prophets and men of God in the East. Cf. the respect enjoyed by the blood relations of Jesus and Mohammed.

2 If the "book" really originated in the time of Trajan, then its production keeps within the frame-work of common Christianity, for at that time there were appearing everywhere in Christendom revealed books which contained new instructions and communications of grace. The reader may be reminded, for example, of the Shepherd of Hermas. When the sect declared that the "book" was delivered to Elkesai by a male and a female angel, each as large as a mountain, that these angels were the Son of God and the Holy Spirit, etc., we have, apart from the fantastic colouring, nothing extraordinary.

σοντα γενέσεις καὶ μετενσωματούμενον, cf. the testimony of Victorinus as to Symmachus). From the statements of Hippolytus we cannot be sure whether he was identified with the Son of God,[1] at any rate the assumption of repeated births of Christ shews how completely Christianity was meant to be identified with what was supposed to be the pure Old Testament religion. (3) The "book" proclaimed a new forgiveness of sin, which, on condition of faith in the "book" and a real change of mind, was to be bestowed on every one, through the medium of washings, accompanied by definite prayers which are strictly prescribed. In these prayers appear peculiar Semitic speculations about nature ("the seven witnesses: heaven, water, the holy spirits, the angels of prayer, oil, salt, earth"). The old Jewish way of thinking appears in the assumption that all kinds of sickness and misfortune are punishments for sin, and that these penalties must therefore be removed by atonement. The book contains also astrological and geometrical speculations in a religious garb. The main thing, however, was the possibility of a forgiveness of sin, ever requiring to be repeated, though Hippolytus himself was unable to point to any gross laxity. Still, the appearance of this sect represents the attempt to make the religion of Christian Judaism palatable to the world. The possibility of repeated forgiveness of sin, the speculations about numbers, elements, and stars, the halo of mystery, the adaptation to the forms of worship employed in the "mysteries", are worldly means of attraction which shew that this Jewish Christianity

---

[1] It may be assumed from Philos. X. 29, that, in the opinion of Hippolytus, the Elkesaites identified the Christ from above with the Son of God, and assumed that this Christ appeared on earth in changing and purely human forms, and will appear again (αὐτὸν δὲ μεταγγιζόμενον ἐν σώμασι πολλοῖς πολλάκις, καὶ νῦν δὲ ἐν τῷ Ἰησοῦ, ὁμοίως ποτὲ μὲν ἐκ τοῦ θεοῦ γεγενῆσθαι, ποτὲ δὲ πνεῦμα γεγονέναι, ποτὲ δὲ ἐκ παρθένου, ποτὲ δὲ οὐ καὶ τοῦτον δὲ μετέπειτα ἀεὶ ἐν σώματι μεταγγίζεσθαι καὶ ἐν πολλοῖς κατὰ καιροὺς δείκνυσθαι). As the Elkesaites (see the account by Epiphanius) traced back the incarnations of Christ to Adam, and not merely to Abraham, we may see in this view of history the attempt to transform Mosaism into the universal religion. But the Pharisaic theology had already begun with these Adam-speculations, which are always a sign that the religion in Judaism is feeling its limits too narrow. The Jews in Alexandria were also acquainted with these speculations.

was subject to the process of acute secularization. The Jewish mode of life was to be adopted in return for these concessions. Yet its success in the West was of small extent and short-lived.

Epiphanius confirms all these features, and adds a series of new ones. In his description, the new forgiveness of sin is not so prominent as in that of Hippolytus, but it is there. From the account of Epiphanius we can see that these syncretistic Judæo-Christian sects were at first strictly ascetic and rejected marriage as well as the eating of flesh, but that they gradually became more lax. We learn here that the whole sacrificial service was removed from the Old Testament by the Elkesaites and declared to be non-Divine, that is non-Mosaic, and that fire was consequently regarded as the impure and dangerous element, and water as the good one.[1] We learn further, that these sects acknowledged no prophets and men of God between Aaron and Christ, and that they completely adapted the Hebrew Gospel of Matthew to their own views.[2] In addition to this book, however, (the Gospel of the 12 Apostles), other writings, such as Περίοδοι Πέτρου διὰ Κλήμεντος, Ἀναβαθμοὶ Ἰακώβου and similar histories of Apostles, were held in esteem by them. In these writings the Apostles were represented as zealous ascetics, and, above all, as vegetarians, while the Apostle Paul was most bitterly opposed. They called him a Tarsene, said he was a Greek, and heaped on him gross abuse. Epiphanius also dwells strongly upon their Jewish mode of life (circumcision, Sabbath), as well as their daily washings,[3] and gives some information about the constitution and form of worship of these sects (use of baptism : Lord's Supper with bread and water). Finally, Epiphanius

---

1 In the Gospel of these Jewish Christians Jesus is made to say (Epiph. h. 30. 16) ἦλθον καταλῦσαι τὰς θυσίας, καὶ ἐὰν μὴ παύσησθε τοῦ θύειν, οὐ παύσεται ἀφ' ὑμῶν ἡ ὀργὴ. We see the essential progress of this Jewish Christianity within Judaism, in the opposition in principle to the whole sacrificial service (vid. also Epiph., h. 19. 3).

2 On this new Gospel see Zahn, Kanongesch. II. p. 724 ff.

3 It is incorrect to suppose that the lustrations were meant to take the place of baptism, or were conceived by these Jewish Christians as repeated baptisms Their effect was certainly equal to that of baptism. But it is nowhere hinted in our authorities that they were on that account made equivalent to the regular baptism.

gives particulars about their Christology. On this point there were differences of opinion, and these differences prove that there was no Christological dogma. As among the common Jewish Christians, the birth of Jesus from the Virgin was a matter of dispute. Further, some identified Christ with Adam, others saw in him a heavenly being (ἄνωθεν ὄν), a spiritual being, who was created before all, who was higher than all angels and Lord of all things, but who chose for himself the upper world; yet this Christ from above came down to this lower world as often as he pleased. He came in Adam, he appeared in human form to the patriarchs, and at last appeared on earth as a man with the body of Adam, suffered, etc. Others again, as it appears, would have nothing to do with these speculations, but stood by the belief that Jesus was the man chosen by God, on whom, on account of his virtue, the Holy Spirit—ὅπερ ἐστὶν ὁ Χριστός—descended at the baptism. [1] (Epiph. h. 30. 3, 14, 16). The account which Epiphanius gives of the doctrine held by these Jewish Christians regarding the Devil, is specially instructive (h. 30. 16): Δύο δέ τινας συνιστῶσιν ἐκ θεοῦ τεταγμένους, ἕνα μὲν τὸν Χριστόν, ἕνα δὲ τὸν διάβολον· καὶ τὸν μὲν Χριστὸν λέγουσι τοῦ μέλλοντος αἰῶνος εἰληφέναι τὸν κλῆρον, τὸν δὲ διάβολον τοῦτον πεπιστεῦσθαι ὃν αἰῶνα, ἐκ προσταγῆς δῆλον τοῦ παντοκράτορος κατὰ αἴτησιν ἑκατέρων αὐτῶν. Here we have a very old Semitico-Hebraic idea preserved in a very striking way, and therefore we may probably assume that in other respects also, these Gnostic Ebionites preserved that which was ancient. Whether they did so in their criticism of the Old Testament, is a point on which we must not pronounce judgment.

We might conclude by referring to the fact that this syncretistic Jewish Christianity, apart from a well-known mission-

---

[1] The characteristic here, as in the Gentile Christian Gnosis, is the division of the person of Jesus into a more or less indifferent medium, and into the Christ Here the factor constituting his personality could sometimes be placed in that medium, and sometimes in the Christ spirit, and thus contradictory formulæ could not but arise. It is therefore easy to conceive how Epiphanius reproaches these Jewish Christians with a denial, sometimes of the Divinity, and sometimes of the humanity of Christ (see h. 30. 14).

ary effort at Rome, was confined to Palestine and the neighbouring countries, and might consider it proved that this
movement had no effect on the history and development of
Catholicism, [1] were it not for two voluminous writings which
still continue to be regarded as monuments of the earliest
epoch of syncretistic Jewish Christianity. Not only did Baur
suppose that he could prove his hypothesis about the origin
of Catholicism by the help of these writings, but the attempt
has recently been made on the basis of *the Pseudo-Clementine
Recognitions and Homilies*, for these are the writings in question,
to go still further and claim for Jewish Christianity the glory
of having developed by itself the whole doctrine, worship and
constitution of Catholicism, and of having transmitted it to
Gentile Christianity as a finished product which only required
to be divested of a few Jewish husks. [2] It is therefore necessary to subject these writings to a brief examination. Everything depends on the time of their origin, and the tendencies
they follow. But these are just the two questions that are
still unanswered. Without depreciating those worthy men
who have earnestly occupied themselves with the Pseudo-Clementines, [3] it may be asserted, that in this region everything

1 This syncretistic Judaism had indeed a significance for the history
of the world, not, however, in the history of Christianity, but for the
origin of Islam. Islam, as a religious system, is based partly on syncretistic Judaism (including the Zabians, so enigmatic in their origin), and,
without questioning Mohammed's originality, can only be historically
understood by taking this into account. I have endeavoured to establish
this hypothesis in a lecture printed in MS. form, 1877. Cf. now the con-
clusive proofs in Wellhausen, l. c. Part III. p. 197—212. On the Mandeans,
see Brandt, Die Mandäische Religion, 1889; (also Wellhausen in d. deut-
schen Lit. Ztg., 1890 No. I. Lagarde i. d. Gött. Gel. Anz., 1890, No. 10).

2 See Bestmann, Gesch. der Christl. Sitte Bd. II. 1 Part: Die juden-
christliche Sitte, 1883; also, Theol. Lit. Ztg, 1883. Col. 269 ff The same
author, Der Ursprung des Katholischen Christenthums und des Islams,
1884; also Theol. Lit. Ztg. 1884, Col. 291 ff

3 See Schliemann, Die Clementinen etc., 1844; Hilgenfeld, Die Clemen-
tinischen Recogn. u. Homil, 1848; Ritschl, in d. Allg. Monatschrift f.
Wissensch. u. Litt., 1852. Uhlhorn, Die Homil. u. Recogn., 1854; Lehmann,
Die Clement. Schriften, 1869; Lipsius, in d. Protest. K. Ztg., 1869, p. 477
ff.; Quellen der Römische Petrussage, 1872. Uhlhorn, in Herzog's R.
Encykl. (Clementinen) 2 Edit III p. 286, admits: "There can be no
doubt that the Clementine question still requires further discussion. It
can hardly make any progress worth mentioning until we have collected
better the material, and especially till we have got a corrected edition

is as yet in darkness, especially as no agreement has been reached even in the question of their composition. No doubt such a result appears to have been pretty nearly arrived at as far as the time of composition is concerned, but that estimate (150-170, or the latter half of the second century) not only awakens the greatest suspicion, but can be proved to be wrong. The importance of the question for the history of dogma does not permit the historian to set it aside, while, on the other hand, the compass of a manual does not allow us to enter into an exhaustive investigation. The only course open in such circumstances is briefly to define one's own position.

1. The Recognitions and Homilies, in the form in which we have them, do not belong to the second century, but at the very earliest to the first half of the third. There is nothing, however, to prevent our putting them a few decades later. [1]

with an exhaustive commentary. The theory of the genesis, contents and aim of the pseudo-Clementine writings, unfolded by Renan (Orig. T. VII p. 74 – 101) is essentially identical with that of German scholars. Langen (die Clemensromane, 1890) has set up very bold hypotheses, which are also based on the assumption that Jewish Christianity was an important church factor in the second century, and that the pseudo-Clementines are comparatively old writings

1 There is no external evidence for placing the pseudo-Clementine writings in the second century. The oldest witness is Origen (IV. p. 401, Lommatzsch); but the quotation: "Quoniam opera bona, quæ fiunt ab infidelibus, in hoc sæculo iis prosunt," etc., is not found in our Clementines, so that Origen appears to have used a still older version. The internal evidence all points to the third century (canon, composition, theological attitude. etc.). Moreover, Zahn (Gött. Gel. Anz 1876. No. 45) and Lagarde have declared themselves in favour of this date; while Lipsius (Apokr. Apostelgesch. II. 1) and Weingarten (Zeittafeln, 3 Edit. p 23) have recently expressed the same opinion. The Homilies presuppose (1) Marcion's Antitheses, (2) Apelles' Syllogisms, (3) perhaps Callistus' edict about penance (see III. 70), and writings of Hippolytus (see also the expression ἐπίσκοπος ἐπισκόπων. Clem. ep. ad. Jacob I., which is first found in Tertull, de pudic I.). (4) The most highly developed form of polemic against heathen mythology. (5) The complete development of church apologetics, as well as the conviction that Christianity is identical with correct and absolute knowledge. They further presuppose a time when there was a lull in the persecution of Christians, for the Emperor. though pretty often referred to, is never spoken of as a persecutor, and when the cultured heathen world was entirely disposed in favour of an eclectic monotheism Moreover, the remarkable Christological statement in Hom. XVI. 15, 16. points to the third century, in fact probably even presupposes the theology of Origen; Cf. the sentence:

2. They were not composed in their present form by heretical Christians, but most probably by Catholics. Nor do they aim at forming a theological system, [1] or spreading the views of a sect. Their primary object is to oppose Greek polytheism, immoral mythology, and false philosophy, and thus to promote edification. [2]

3. In describing the authors as Catholic, we do not mean that they were adherents of the theology of Irenæus or Origen. The instructive point here rather, is that they had as yet no fixed theology, and therefore could without hesitation regard and use all possible material as means of edification. In like manner, they had no fixed conception of the Apostolic age, and could therefore appropriate motley and dangerous material. Such Christians, highly educated and correctly trained too, were still to be found, not only in the third century, but even later. But the authors do not seem to have been free from a bias, inasmuch as they did not favour the Catholic, that is, the Alexandrian apologetic theology which was in process of formation.

4. The description of the Pseudo-Clementine writings, naturally derived from their very form, as " edifying, didactic romances for the refutation of paganism", is not inconsistent with the idea, that the authors, at the same time, did their utmost to oppose heretical phenomena, especially the Marcionite church and Apelles, together with heresy and heathenism in general, as represented by Simon Magus.

5. The objectionable materials which the authors made use of were edifying for them, because of the position assigned

---

τοῦ πατρὸς τὸ μὴ γεγεννῆσθαι ἐστιν, υἱοῦ δὲ τὸ γεγεννῆσθαι γεννητὸν δὲ ἀγεννήτῳ ἤ καὶ αὐτογεννήτῳ οὐ συνκρίνεται. Finally, the decided repudiation of the awakening of Christian faith by visions and dreams, and the polemic against these is also no doubt of importance for determining the date; see XVII. 14—19. Peter says, § 18 : τὸ ἀδιδάκτως ἄνευ ὀπτασίας καὶ ὀνείρων μαθεῖν ἀποκάλυψίς ἐστιν, he had already learned that at his confession (Matt. XVI.). The question, εἴ τις δὲ ὀπτασίαν πρὸς διδασκαλίαν σοφισθῆναι δύναται, is answered in the negative, §. 19.

1 This is also acknowledged in Koffmane. Die Gnosis, etc, p 33

2 The Homilies, as we have them, are mainly composed of the speeches of Peter and others. These speeches oppose polytheism, mythology and the doctrine of demons, and advocate monotheism, ascetic morality and rationalism. The polemic against Simon Magus almost appears as a mere accessory.

therein to Peter, because of the ascetic and mysterious elements they contained, and the opposition offered to Simon, etc. The offensive features, so far as they were still contained in these sources, had already become unintelligible and harmless. They were partly conserved as such and partly removed.

6. The authors are to be sought for perhaps in Rome, perhaps in Syria, perhaps in both places, certainly not in Alexandria

7. The main ideas are: (1) The monarchy of God. (2) the syzygies (weak and strong). (3) Prophecy (the true Prophet). (4) Stoical rationalism, belief in providence, good works. φιλαν- θρωπία, etc. = Mosaism. The Homilies are completely saturated with stoicism, both in their ethical and metaphysical systems, and are opposed to Platonism, though Plato is quoted in Hom. XV. 8, as Ἑλλήνων σοφός τις (a wise man of the Greeks). In addition to these ideas we have also a strong hierarchical tendency. The material which the authors made use of was in great part derived from syncretistic Jewish Christian tradition, in other words, those histories of the Apostles were here utilised which Epiphanius reports to have been used by the Ebionites (see above). It is not probable, however, that these writings in their original form were in the hands of the narrators; the likelihood is that they made use of them in revised forms.

8. It must be reserved for an accurate investigation to ascertain whether those modified versions which betray clear marks of Hellenic origin, were made within syncretistic Judaism itself, or whether they are to be traced back to Catholic writers. In either case, they should not be placed earlier than about the beginning of the third century, but in all probability one or two generations later still.

9. If we adopt the first assumption, it is most natural to think of that propaganda which, according to the testimony of Hippolytus and Origen, Jewish Christianity attempted in Rome in the age of Caracalla and Heliogabalus, through the medium of the Syrian, Alcibiades. This coincides with the last great advance of Syrian cults into the West, and is, at the

same time, the only one known to us historically. But it is
further pretty generally admitted that the immediate sources
of the Pseudo-Clementines already presuppose the existence of
Elkesaite Christianity. We should accordingly have to assume
that in the West, this Christianity made greater concessions
to the prevailing type, that it gave up circumcision and accommodated itself to the Church system of Gentile Christianity, at the same time withdrawing its polemic against Paul.

10. Meanwhile the existence of such a Jewish Christianity
is not as yet proved, and therefore we must reckon with the
possibility that the remodelled form of the Jewish Christian
sources, already found in existence by the revisers of the
Pseudo-Clementine Romances, was solely a Catholic literary
product. In this assumption, which commends itself both as
regards the aim of the composition and its presupposed conditions, we must remember that, from the third century
onwards, Catholic writers systematically corrected, and to a
great extent reconstructed, the heretical histories which were
in circulation in the churches as interesting reading, and that
the extent and degree of this reconstruction varied exceedingly, according to the theological and historical insight of
the writer. The identifying of pure Mosaism with Christianity
was in itself by no means offensive when there was no further
question of circumcision. The clear distinction between the
ceremonial and moral parts of the Old Testament, could no
longer prove an offence after the great struggle with Gnosticism. [1] The strong insistance upon the unity of God, and the
rejection of the doctrine of the Logos, were by no means
uncommon in the beginning of the third century ; and in the

---

[1] This distinction can also be shewn elsewhere in the Church of the third
century. But I confess I do not know how Catholic circles got over the fact
that, for example, in the third book of the Homilies many passages of the old
Testament are simply characterised as untrue, immoral and lying. Here the
Homilies remind one strongly of the Syllogisms of Apelles, the author of
which, in other respects, opposed them in the interest of his doctrine of creating angels. In some passages the Christianity of the Homilies really looks
like a syncretism composed of the common Christianity, the Jewish Christian
Gnosticism, and the criticism of Apelles. Hom. VIII. 6—8 is also highly
objectionable.

speculations about Adam and Christ, in the views about God and the world and such like, as set before us in the immediate sources of the Romances, the correct and edifying elements must have seemed to outweigh the objectionable. At any rate, the historian who, until further advised, denies the existence of a Jewish Christianity composed of the most contradictory elements, lacking circumcision and national hopes, and bearing marks of Catholic and therefore of Hellenic influence, judges more prudently than he who asserts, solely on the basis of Romances which are accompanied by no tradition and have never been the objects of assault, the existence of a Jewish Christianity accommodating itself to Catholicism which is entirely unattested.

11. Be that as it may, it may at least be regarded as certain that the Pseudo-Clementines contribute absolutely nothing to our knowledge of the origin of the Catholic Church and doctrine, as they shew at best in their immediate sources a Jewish Christianity strongly influenced by Catholicism and Hellenism.

12. They must be used with great caution even in seeking to determine the tendencies and inner history of syncretistic Jewish Christianity. It cannot be made out with certainty, how far back the first sources of the Pseudo-Clementines date, or what their original form and tendency were. As to the first point, it has indeed been said that Justin, nay, even the author of the Acts of the Apostles, presupposes them, and that the Catholic tradition of Peter, in Rome, and of Simon Magus, are dependent on them (as is still held by Lipsius); but there is so little proof of this adduced, that in Christian literature up to the end of the second century (Hegesippus?) we can only discover very uncertain traces of acquaintance with Jewish Christian historical narrative. Such indications can only be found, to any considerable extent, in the third century, and I do not mean to deny that the contents of the Jewish Christian histories of the Apostles contributed materially to the formation of the ecclesiastical legends about Peter. As is shewn in the Pseudo-Clementines, these

histories of the Apostles especially opposed Simon Magus and his adherents (the new Samaritan attempt at a universal religion), and placed the authority of the Apostle Peter against them. But they also opposed the Apostle Paul, and seem to have transferred Simonian features to Paul, and Pauline features to Simon. Yet it is also possible that the Pauline traits found in the magician were the outcome of the redaction, in so far as the whole polemic against Paul is here struck out, though certain parts of it have been woven into the polemic against Simon. But probably the Pauline features of the magician are merely an appearance. The Pseudo-Clementines may, to some extent, be used, though with caution, in determining the doctrines of syncretistic Jewish Christianity. In connection with this we must take what Epiphanius says as our standard. The Pantheistic and Stoic elements which are found here and there must of course be eliminated. But the theory of the genesis of the world from a change in God himself (that is from a $\pi\rho o\beta o\lambda\acute{\eta}$), the assumption that all things emanated from God in antitheses (Son of God—·Devil; heaven— earth; male—female; male and female prophecy), nay, that these antitheses are found in God himself (goodness, to which corresponds the Son of God — punitive justice, to which corresponds the Devil), the speculations about the elements which have proceeded from the one substance, the ignoring of freedom in the question about the origin of evil, the strict adherence to the unity and absolute causality of God, in spite of the dualism, and in spite of the lofty predicates applied to the Son of God—all this plainly bears the Semitic-Jewish stamp.

We must here content ourselves with these indications. They were meant to set forth briefly the reasons which forbid our assigning to syncretistic Jewish Christianity, on the basis of the Pseudo-Clementines, a place in the history of the genesis of the Catholic Church and its doctrine.

Bigg, The Clementine Homilies (Studia Biblica et Eccles. II., p. 157 ff.), has propounded the hypothesis that the Homilies are an Ebionitic revision of an older Catholic original (see p. 184:

"The Homilies as we have it, is a recast of an orthodox work by a highly unorthodox editor." P. 175 : "The Homilies are surely the work of a Catholic convert to Ebionitism, who thought he saw in the doctrine of the two powers the only tenable answer to Gnosticism. We can separate his Catholicism from his Ebionitism, just as surely as his Stoicism"). This is the opposite of the view expressed by me in the text. I consider Bigg's hypothesis well worth examining, and at first sight not improbable; but I am not able to enter into it here.

APPENDIX I.

On the Conception of Pre-existence.

On account of the importance of the question we may be here permitted to amplify a few hints given in Chap. II., § 4, and elsewhere, and to draw a clearer distinction between the Jewish and Hellenic conceptions of pre-existence.

According to the theory held by the ancient Jews and by the whole of the Semitic nations, everything of real value that from time to time appears on earth has its existence in heaven. In other words it exists with God, that is, God possesses a knowledge of it; and for that reason it has a real being. But it exists beforehand with God in the same way as it appears on earth, that is with all the material attributes belonging to its essence. Its manifestation on earth is merely a transition from concealment to publicity ($\varphi\alpha\nu\epsilon\rho o\tilde{\nu}\sigma\theta\alpha\iota$). In becoming visible to the senses, the object in question assumes no attribute that it did not already possess with God. Hence its material nature is by no means an inadequate expression of it, nor is it a second nature added to the first. The truth rather is that what was in heaven before is now revealing itself upon earth, without any sort of alteration taking place in the process. There is no *assumptio naturæ novæ*, and no change or mixture. The old Jewish theory of pre-existence is founded on the religious idea of the omniscience and omnipotence of God, that God to whom the events of history do not come as a surprise, but who guides their course. As the whole history of the world and the destiny of each individual are recorded on his tablets or books, so also each thing is ever present before him. The decisive contrast is between

God and the creature. In designating the latter as "foreknown" by God, the primary idea is not to ennoble the creature, but rather to bring to light the wisdom and power of God. The ennobling of created things by attributing to them a pre-existence is a secondary result (see below).

According to the Hellenic conception, which has become associated with Platonism, the idea of pre-existence is independent of the idea of God; it is based on the conception of the contrast between spirit and matter, between the infinite and finite, found in the cosmos itself. In the case of all spiritual beings, life in the body or flesh is at bottom an inadequate and unsuitable condition, for the spirit is eternal, the flesh perishable. But the pre-temporal existence, which was only a doubtful assumption as regards ordinary spirits, was a matter of certainty in the case of the higher and purer ones. They lived in an upper world long before this earth was created, and they lived there as spirits without the "polluted garment of the flesh". Now if they resolved for some reason or other to appear in this finite world, they cannot simply become visible, for they have no "visible form". They must rather "assume flesh", whether they throw it about them as a covering, or really make it their own by a process of transformation or mixture. In all cases—and here the speculation gave rise to the most exciting problems—the body is to them something inadequate which they cannot appropriate without adopting certain measures of precaution, but this process may indeed pass through all stages, from a mere seeming appropriation to complete union. The characteristics of the Greek ideas of pre-existence may consequently be thus expressed. First, the objects in question to which pre-existence is ascribed are meant to be ennobled by this attribute. Secondly, these ideas have no relation to God. Thirdly, the material appearance is regarded as something inadequate. Fourthly, speculations about *phantasma, assumptio naturæ humanæ, transmutatio, mixtura, duæ naturæ*, etc., were necessarily associated with these notions.

We see that these two conceptions are as wide apart as the

poles. The first has a religious origin, the second a cosmological and psychological; the first glorifies God, the second
the created spirit.

However, not only does a certain relationship in point of
form exist between these speculations, but the Jewish conception is also found in a shape which seems to approximate still
more to the Greek one.

Earthly occurrences and objects are not only regarded as
"foreknown" by God before being seen in this world, but
the latter manifestation is frequently considered as the copy
of the existence and nature which they possess in heaven, and
which remains unalterably the same, whether they appear upon
earth or not. That which is before God experiences no change.
As the destinies of the world are recorded in the books, and God
reads them there, it being at the same time a matter of indifference, as regards this knowledge of his, when and how they
are accomplished upon earth, so the Tabernacle and its furniture, the Temple, Jerusalem, etc., are before God, and continue
to exist before him in heaven, even during their appearance
on earth and after it.

This conception seems really to have been the oldest one.
Moses is to fashion the Temple and its furniture according to
the pattern he saw on the Mount (Exod. XXV. 9. 40: XXVI.
30: XXVII. 8: Num. VIII. 4). The Temple and Jerusalem
exist in heaven, and they are to be distinguished from the
earthly Temple and the earthly Jerusalem; yet the ideas of
a φανεροῦσθαι of the thing which is in heaven and of its copy
appearing on earth, shade into one another and are not always
clearly separated.

The classing of things as original and copy was at first no more
meant to glorify them than was the conception of a pre-
existence they possessed within the knowledge of God. But
since the view which in theory was true of everything earthly,
was, as is naturally to be expected, applied in practice to
nothing but valuable objects—for things common and ever
recurring give no impulse to such speculations—the objects
thus contemplated were ennobled, because they were raised

above the multitude of the commonplace. At the same time
the theory of original and copy could not fail to become a
starting-point for new speculations, as soon as the contrast
between the spiritual and material began to assume importance among the Jewish people.

That took place under the influence of the Greek spirit;
and was perhaps also the simultaneous result of an intellectual or moral development which arose independently of that
spirit. Accordingly, a highly important advance in the old
ideas of pre-existence appeared in the Jewish theological literature belonging to the time of the Maccabees and the following decades. To begin with, these conceptions are now
applied to persons, which, so far as I know, was not the case
before this (individualism). Secondly, the old distinction of original and copy is now interpreted to mean that the copy is
the inferior and more imperfect, that in the present æon of
the transient it cannot be equivalent to the original, and that
we must therefore look forward to the time when the original
itself will make its appearance, (contrast of the material and
finite and the spiritual).

With regard to the first point, we have not only to consider
passages in Apocalypses and other writings in which pre-
existence is attributed to Moses, the patriarchs, etc., (see above,
p. 102), but we must, above all, bear in mind utterances like
Ps. CXXXIX. 15, 16. The individual saint soars upward to
the thought that the days of his life are in the book of God,
and that he himself was before God, whilst he was still un-
perfect. But, and this must not be overlooked, it was not
merely his spiritual part that was before God, for there is
not the remotest idea of such a distinction, but the whole man,
although he is בָּשָׂר.

As regards the second point, the distinction between a
heavenly and an earthly Jerusalem, a heavenly and an earthly
Temple, etc., is sufficiently known from the Apocalypses and
the New Testament. But the important consideration is that
the sacred things of earth were regarded as objects of less
value, instalments, as it were, pending the fulfilment of the

whole promise. The desecration and subsequent destruction of sacred things must have greatly strengthened this idea. The hope of the heavenly Jerusalem comforted men for the desecration or loss of the earthly one. But this gave at the same time the most powerful impulse to reflect whether it was not an essential feature of this temporal state, that everything high and holy in it could only appear in a meagre and inadequate form. Thus the transition to Greek ideas was brought about. The fulness of the time had come when the old Jewish ideas, with a slightly mythological colouring, could amalgamate with the ideal creations of Hellenic philosophers.

These, however, are also the general conditions which gave rise to the earliest Jewish speculations about a personal Messiah, except that, in the case of the Messianic ideas within Judaism itself, the adoption of specifically Greek thoughts, so far as I am able to see, cannot be made out.

Most Jews, as Trypho testifies in Justin's Dialogue, 49, conceived the Messiah as a man. We may indeed go a step further and say that no Jew at bottom imagined him otherwise; for even those who attached ideas of pre-existence to him, and gave the Messiah a supernatural background, never advanced to speculations about assumption of the flesh, incarnation, two natures and the like. They only transferred in a specific manner to the Messiah the old idea of pre-terrestrial existence with God, universally current among the Jews. Before the creation of the world the Messiah was hidden with God, and, when the time is fulfilled, he makes his appearance. This is neither an incarnation nor a humiliation, but he appears on earth as he exists before God, viz., as a mighty and just king, equipped with all gifts. The writings in which this thought appears most clearly are the Apocalypse of Enoch (Book of Similitudes, Chap. 46-49) and the Apocalypse of Esra (Chap. 12-14). Support to this idea, if anything more of the kind had been required, was lent by passages like Daniel VII. 13 f. and Micah, V. 1. Nowhere do we find in Jewish writings a conception which advances beyond the notion that the Messiah is the man who is with God in heaven; and who will make his appearance at his own time. We are merely entitled to say that, as the same idea was not applied to all persons with the same certainty, it was almost unavoidable that men's minds should have been led to designate the Messiah as the man from heaven. This thought was adopted by Paul (see below), but I know of no *Jewish* writing which gave clear expression to it.

Jesus Christ designated himself as the Messiah, and the first of his disciples who recognised him as such were native Jews. The Jewish conceptions of the Messiah consequently passed over into the Christian community. But they received an impulse to important modifications from the living impression conveyed by the person and destiny of Jesus. Three facts were here of pre-eminent importance. First, Jesus appeared in lowliness, and even suffered death. Secondly, he was believed to be exalted through the resurrection to the right hand of God, and his return in glory was awaited with certainty. Thirdly, the strength of a new life and of an indissoluble union with God was felt issuing from him, and therefore his people were connected with him in the closest way.

In some old Christian writings found in the New Testament and emanating from the pen of native Jews, there are no speculations at all about the pre-temporal existence of Jesus as the Messiah, or they are found expressed in a manner which simply embodies the old Jewish theory and is merely distinguished from it by the emphasis laid on the exaltation of Jesus after death through the resurrection. I. Pet. 1. 18 ff. is a classic passage : ἐλυτρώθητε τιμίῳ αἵματι ὡς ἀμνοῦ ἀμώμου καὶ ἀσπίλου Χριστοῦ, προεγνωσμένου μὲν πρὸ καταβολῆς κόσμου, φανερωθέντος δὲ ἐπ᾽ἐσχάτου τῶν χρόνων δι᾽ ὑμᾶς τοὺς δι᾽ αὐτοῦ πιστοὺς εἰς θεὸν τὸν ἐγείραντα αὐτὸν ἐκ νεκρῶν καὶ δόξαν αὐτῷ δόντα, ὥστε τὴν πίστιν ὑμῶν καὶ ἐλπίδα εἶναι εἰς θεόν. Here we find a conception of the pre-existence of Christ which is not yet affected by cosmological or psychological speculation, which does not overstep the boundaries of a purely religious contemplation, and which arose from the Old Testament way of thinking, and the living impression derived from the person of Jesus. He is "fore-

known (by God) before the creation of the world", not as a
spiritual being without a body, but as a Lamb without blemish
and without spot; in other words, his whole personality together with the work which it was to carry out, was within God's
eternal knowledge. He "was manifested in these last days for
our sake", that is, he is now visibly what he already was
before God. What is meant here is not an incarnation, but
a *revelatio*. Finally, he appeared in order that our faith and
hope should now be firmly directed to the living God, *that*
God who raised him from the dead and gave him honour.
In the last clause expression is given to the specifically
Christian thought, that the Messiah Jesus was *exalted* after
crucifixion and death; from this, however, no further conclusions
are drawn.

But it was impossible that men should everywhere rest
satisfied with these utterances, for the age was a theological
one. Hence the paradox of the suffering Messiah, the certainty
of his glorification through the resurrection, the conviction of
his specific relationship to God, and the belief in the real
union of his Church with him did not seem adequately expressed
by the simple formulæ προεγνωσμένος, φανερωθείς. In reference
to all these points, we see even in the oldest Christian writings,
the appearance of formulæ which fix more precisely the nature
of his pre-existence, or in other words his heavenly existence.
With regard to the first and second points there arose the view
of humiliation and exaltation, such as we find in Paul and in
numerous writings after him. In connection with the third
point the concept "Son of God" was thrust into the foreground, and gave rise to the idea of the image of God (2
Cor. IV. 4; Col. I. 15; Heb. I. 2; Phil. II. 6). The fourth
point gave occasion to the formation of theses, such as we
find in Rom. VIII. 29: πρωτότοκος ἐν πολλοῖς ἀδελφοῖς, Col. I.
18: πρωτότοκος ἐκ τῶν νεκρῶν (Rev. I. 5), Eph. II. 6: συνήγειρεν
καὶ συνεκάθισεν ἐν τοις ἐπουρανίοις ἡμᾶς ἐν Χριστῷ Ἰησοῦ, I. 4:
ὁ θεὸς ἐξελέξατο ἡμᾶς ἐν Χριστῷ πρὸ καταβολῆς κόσμου, I. 22: ὁ
θεὸς ἔδωκεν τὸν Χριστὸν κεφαλὴν υπὲρ πάντα τῇ ἐκκλησίᾳ ἥτις ἐστὶν
τὸ σῶμα αὐτοῦ, etc. This purely religious view of the Church,

according to which all that is predicated of Christ is also applied to his followers, continued a considerable time. Hermas declares that the Church is older than the world, and that the world was created for its sake (see above, p. 103), and the author of the so-called 2nd Epistle of Clement declares (Chap. 14) .... ἐσόμεθα ἐκ τῆς ἐκκλησίας τῆς πρώτης τῆς πνευματικῆς, τῆς πρὸ ἡλίου καὶ σελήνης ἐκτισμένης ...... οὐκ οἴομαι δὲ ὑμᾶς ἀγνοεῖν, ὅτι ἐκκλησία ζῶσα σῶμα ἐστι Χριστοῦ. λέγει γὰρ ἡ γραφή. Ἐποίησεν ὁ θεὸς τὸν ἄνθρωπον ἄρσεν καὶ θῆλυ. τὸ ἄρσεν ἐστιν ὁ Χριστὸς τὸ θῆλυ ἡ ἐκκλησία. Thus Christ and his Church are inseparably connected. The latter is to be conceived as pre-existent quite as much as the former; the Church was also created before the sun and the moon, for the world was created for its sake. This conception of the Church illustrates a final group of utterances about the pre-existent Christ, the origin of which might easily be misinterpreted unless we bear in mind their reference to the Church. In so far as he is προεγνωσμένος πρὸ καταβολῆς κόσμου, he is the ἀρχὴ τῆς κτίσεως τοῦ θεοῦ (Rev. III. 14), the πρωτότοκος πάσης κτίσεως, etc. According to the current conception of the time, these expressions mean exactly the same as the simple προεγνωσμένος πρὸ καταβολῆς κόσμου, as is proved by the parallel formulæ referring to the Church. Nay, even the further advance to the idea that the world was created by him (Cor. Col. Eph. Heb.) need not yet necessarily be a μετάβασις εἰς ἄλλο γένος; for the beginning of things (ἀρχή) and their purpose form the real force to which their origin is due (principle ἀρχή). Hermas indeed calls the Church older than the world simply because "the world was created for its sake".

All these further theories which we have quoted up to this time need in no sense alter the original conception, so long as they appear in an isolated form and do not form the basis of fresh speculations. They may be regarded as the working out of the original conception attaching to Jesus Christ, προεγνωσμένος πρὸ καταβολῆς κόσμου, φανερωθείς κ. τ. λ.; and do not really modify this religious view of the matter. Above all, we find in them as yet no certain transition to the Greek view which

splits up his personality into a heavenly and an earthly portion; it still continues to be the complete Christ to whom all
the utterances apply. But, beyond doubt, they already reveal
the strong impulse to conceive the Christ that had appeared as a
divine being. He had not been a transitory phenomenon, but has
ascended into heaven and still continues to live. This post-exis-
tence of his gave to the ideas of his pre-existence a support and
a concrete complexion which the earlier Jewish theories lacked.

We find the transition to a new conception in the writings
of Paul. But it is important to begin by determining the relationship between his Christology and the views we have been
hitherto considering. In the Apostle's clearest trains of thought
everything that he has to say of Christ hinges on his
death and resurrection. For this we need no proofs, but see,
more especially Rom. I. 3 f.: περὶ τοῦ υἱοῦ αὐτοῦ, τοῦ γενομένου
ἐκ σπέρματος Δαυεὶδ κατὰ σάρκα, τοῦ ὁρισθέντος υἱοῦ θεοῦ ἐν δυνάμει
κατὰ πνεῦμα ἁγιωσύνης ἐκ ἀναστάσεως νεκρῶν, Ἰησοῦ Χριστοῦ τοῦ
κυρίου ἡμῶν. What Christ became and his significance for us
now are due to his death on the cross and his resurrection.
He condemned sin in the flesh and was obedient unto death.
Therefore he now shares in the δόξα of God. The exposition
in 1 Cor. XV. 45, also (ὁ ἔσχατος Ἀδὰμ εἰς πνεῦμα ζωοποιοῦν,
ἀλλ' οὐ πρῶτον τὸ πνευματικὸν ἀλλὰ τὸ ψυχικόν, ἔπειτα τὸ πνευ-
ματικόν. ὁ πρῶτος ἄνθρωπος ἐκ γῆς χοϊκός ὁ δεύτερος ἄνθρωπος ἐξ
οὐρανοῦ) is still capable of being understood, as to its fundamental features, in a sense which agrees with the conception
of the Messiah, as κατ' ἐξοχήν, the man from heaven who was
hidden with God. There can be no doubt, however, that this
conception as already shewn by the formulæ in the passage
just quoted, formed to Paul the starting-point of a speculation,
in which the original theory assumed a completely new shape.
The decisive factors in this transformation were the Apostle's
doctrine of "spirit and flesh", and the corresponding conviction that the Christ who is not be known "after the flesh",
is a spirit, namely, the mighty spiritual being (πνεῦμα ζωοποιοῦν),
who has condemned sin in the flesh, and thereby enabled
man to walk not after the flesh, but after the spirit.

According to one of the Apostle's ways of regarding the matter, Christ, after the accomplishment of his work, became the πνεῦμα ζωοποιοῦν through the resurrection. But the belief that Jesus always stood before God as the heavenly man, suggested to Paul the other view, that Christ was always a "spirit", that he was sent down by God, that the flesh is consequently something inadequate and indeed hostile to him, that he nevertheless assumed it in order to extirpate the sin dwelling in the flesh, that he therefore humbled himself by appearing, and that this humiliation was the deed he performed.

This view is found in 2 Cor. VIII. 9: Ἰησοῦς Χριστὸς δἰ ὑμᾶς ἐπτώχευσεν πλούσιος ὤν; in Rom. VIII. 3: ὁ θεὸς τὸν ἑαυτοῦ υἱὸν πέμψας ἐν ὁμοιώματι σαρκὸς ἁμαρτίας καὶ περὶ ἁμαρτίας κατέκρινε τὴν ἁμαρτίαν ἐν τῇ σαρκί; and in Phil. II. 5 f.: Χριστὸς Ἰησους ἐν μορΦῇ θεοῦ ὑπάρχων ..... ἑαυτὸν ἐκένωσεν μόρΦην δούλον λαβών, ἐν ὁμοιώματι ἀνθρώπων γενόμενος, καὶ σχήματι εὑρεθεὶς ὡς ἄνθρωπος ἐταπείνωσεν ἑαυτὸν κ. τ. λ. In both forms of thought Paul presupposes a real exaltation of Christ. Christ receives after the resurrection more than he ever possessed (τὸ ὄνομα τὸ ὑπὲρ πᾶν ὄνομα). In this view Paul retains a historical interpretation of Christ, even in the conception of the πνεῦμα Χριστός. But whilst many passages seem to imply that the work of Christ began with suffering and death, Paul shews in the verses cited, that he already conceives the appearance of Christ on earth as his moral act, as a humiliation, purposely brought about by God and] Christ himself, which reaches its culminating point in the death on the cross. Christ, the divine spiritual being, is sent by the Father from heaven to earth, and of his own free will he obediently takes this mission upon himself. He appears in the ὁμοίωμα σαρκὸς ἁμαρτίας, dies the death of the cross, and then, raised by the Father, ascends again into heaven in order henceforth to act as the κύριος ζώντων and νεκρῶν, and to become to his own people the principle of a new life in the spirit.

Whatever we may think about the admissibility and justification of this view, to whatever source we may trace its origin and however strongly we may emphasise its divergencies from the contemporaneous Hellenic ideas, it is certain that it approaches very closely to the latter; for the distinction of spirit and flesh is here introduced into the concept of pre-existence, and this combination is not found in the Jewish notions of the Messiah.

Paul was the first who limited the idea of pre-existence by referring it solely to the spiritual part of Jesus Christ, but at the same time gave life to it by making the pre-existing Christ (the spirit) a being who, even during his pre-existence, stands independently side by side with God.

He was also the first to designate Christ's σάρξ as "assumpta", and to recognise its assumption as in itself a humiliation. To him the appearance of Christ was no mere φανεροῦσθαι, but a κενοῦσθαι, ταπεινοῦσθαι, and πτωχεύειν.

These outstanding features of the Pauline Christology must have been intelligible to the Greeks, but, whilst embracing these, they put everything else in the system aside. Χριστὸς ὁ κύριος ὁ σώσας ἡμᾶς, ὢν μὲν τὸ πρῶτον πνεῦμα, ἐγένετο σὰρξ καὶ οὕτως ἡμᾶς ἐκάλεσεν, says 2 Clem. (9. 5), and that is also the Christology of 1 Clement, Barnabas and many other Greeks. From the sum total of Judæo-Christian speculations they only borrowed, in addition, the one which has been already mentioned: the Messiah as προεγνωσμένος πρὸ καταβολῆς κόσμου is for that very reason also ἡ ἀρχὴ τῆς κτίσεως τοῦ θεοῦ, that is the beginning, purpose and principle of the creation. The Greeks, as the result of their cosmological interest, embraced this thought as a fundamental proposition. The complete Greek Christology then is expressed as follows: Χριστὸς, ὁ σώσας ἡμᾶς, ὢν μὲν τὸ πρῶτον πνεῦμα καὶ πάσης κτίσεως ἀρχὴ, ἐγένετο σὰρξ καὶ οὕτως ἡμᾶς ἐκάλεσεν. *That is the fundamental theological and philosophical creed on which the whole Trinitarian and Christological speculations of the Church of the succeeding centuries are built, and it is thus the root of the orthodox system of dogmatics;* for the notion that Christ was the ἀρχὴ πάσης κτίσεως necessarily led in some measure to the conception of Christ as the Logos. For the Logos had long been regarded by cultured men as the beginning and principle of the creation.[1]

1 These hints will have shewn that Paul's theory occupies a middle position between the Jewish and Greek ideas of pre-existence. In the canon, however, we have another group of writings which likewise gives evidence of a middle position with regard to the matter, I mean the Johannine writings. If we only possessed the prologue to the Gospel of John with its "ἐν ἀρχῇ ἦν ὁ λόγος" the "πάντα δι' αὐτοῦ ἐγένετο" and the "ὁ λόγος σάρξ ἐγένετο" we could indeed point to nothing but Hellenic ideas. But the Gospel itself, as is well known, contains very much that must have astonished a Greek, and is opposed to the philosophical idea of the Logos. This occurs even in the thought, ὁ λόγος σάρξ ἐγένετο" which in itself is foreign to the Logos conception. Just fancy a proposition like the one in VI. 44, οὐδεὶς δύναται ἐλθεῖν πρὸς με, ἐὰν μὴ ὁ πατὴρ ὁ πέμψας με ἑλκύσῃ αὐτὸν, or in V. 17. 21, engrafted on Philo's system, and consider the revolution it would have caused there. No doubt the prologue to some extent contains the themes set forth in the presentation that follows, but they are worded in such a way that one cannot help thinking the author wished to prepare Greek readers for the paradox he had to communicate to them, by adapting his prologue to their mode of thought Under the altered conditions of thought which now prevail, the prologue appears to us the mysterious part, and the narrative that follows seems the portion that is relatively more intelligible. But to the original readers, if they were educated Greeks, the prologue must have been the part most easily understood. As nowadays a section on the nature of the Christian religion is usually prefixed to a treatise on dogmatics, in order to prepare and introduce the reader, so also the Johannine prologue seems to be intended as an introduction of this kind. It brings in conceptions which were familiar to the Greeks, in fact it enters into these more deeply than is justified by the presentation which follows; for the notion of the incarnate Logos is by no means the dominant one here. Though faint echoes of this idea may possibly be met with here and there in the Gospel—I confess I do not notice them—the predominating thought is essentially the conception of Christ as the Son of God, who obediently executes what the Father has shewn and appointed him. The works which he does are allotted to him, and he performs them in the strength of the Father. The whole of Christ's farewell discourses and the intercessory prayer evince no Hellenic influence and no cosmological speculation whatever, but shew the inner life of a man who knows himself to be one with God to a greater extent than any before him, and who feels the leading of men to God to be the task he had received and accomplished In this consciousness he speaks of the glory he had with the Father before the world was (XVII. 4 f.: ἐγώ σε ἐδόξασα ἐπὶ τῆς γῆς, τὸ ἔργον τελειώσας ὁ δέδωκάς μοι ἵνα ποιήσω· καὶ νῦν δόξασόν με σύ, πάτερ, παρὰ σεαυτῷ τῇ δόξῃ ᾗ εἶχον πρὸ τοῦ τὸν κόσμον εἶναι, παρὰ σοί). With this we must compare verses like III. 13: οὐδεὶς ἀναβέβηκεν εἰς τὸν οὐρανὸν εἰ μὴ ὁ ἐκ τοῦ οὐρανοῦ καταβάς, ὁ υἱὸς τοῦ ἀνθρώπου, and III. 31: ὁ ἄνωθεν ἐρχόμενος ἐπάνω πάντων ἐστιν. ὁ ὢν ἐκ τῆς γῆς ἐκ τῆς γῆς ἐστὶν καὶ ἐκ τῆς γῆς λαλεῖ ὁ ἐκ τοῦ οὐρανοῦ ἐρχόμενος ἐπάνω πάντων ἐστιν (see also I. 30: VI. 33, 38, 41 f. 50 f. 58, 62: VIII. 14, 58; XVII. 24). But though the pre-existence is strongly expressed in these passages, a separation of πνεῦμα (λόγος) and σάρξ in Christ is nowhere assumed in the Gospel except in the prologue. It is always Christ's whole personality to which every sublime attribute is ascribed. The same one who "can do nothing of himself", is also the one who was once glorious and will yet be glorified. This idea, however, can still be referred to the προεγνωσμένος πρὸ καταβολῆς

With this transition the theories concerning Christ are removed from Jewish and Old Testament soil, and also that of religion (in the strict sense of the word), and transplanted to the Greek one. Even in his pre-existent state Christ is an independent power existing side by side with God. The pre-existence does not refer to his whole appearance, but only to a part of his essence; it does not primarily serve to glorify the wisdom and power of the God who guides history, but only glorifies Christ, and thereby threatens the monarchy of God.[1] The appearance of Christ is now an "assumption of flesh", and immediately the intricate questions about the connection of the heavenly and spiritual being with the flesh simultaneously arise and are at first settled by the theories of a naive docetism. But the flesh, that is the human nature created by God, appears depreciated, because it was reckoned as something unsuitable for Christ, and foreign to him as a spiritual being. Thus the Christian religion was mixed up with the refined asceticism of a perishing civilization, and a foreign substructure given to its system of morality, so earnest in its simplicity.[2] But the most questionable result was the following. Since the predicate "Logos", which at first, and for a long time, coincided with the idea of the reason ruling in the cosmos, was considered as the highest that could be given to Christ, the holy and divine element, namely, the power of a new life, a power to be viewed and laid hold of

κόσμου, although it gives a peculiar δόξα with God to him who was foreknown of God, and the oldest conception is yet to be traced in many expressions, as, for example, I. 31: κάγὼ οὐκ ᾔδειν αὐτόν, ἀλλ' ἵνα φανερωθῇ τῷ Ἰσραὴλ διὰ τοῦτο ἦλθον, V. 19: οὐ δύναται ὁ υἱὸς ποιεῖν ἀφ' ἑαυτοῦ οὐδὲν ἄν μή τι βλέπῃ τὸν πατέρα ποιοῦνται, V. 36: VIII. 38: ἃ ἐγὼ ἑώρακα παρὰ τῷ πατρὶ λαλῶ, VIII. 40: τὴν ἀλήθειαν ὑμῖν λελάληκα ἣν ἤκουσα παρὰ τοῦ θεοῦ, XII. 49: XV. 15: πάντα ἃ ἤκουσα παρὰ τοῦ πατρός μου ἐγνώρισα ὑμῖν.

1 This is indeed counterbalanced in the fourth Gospel by the thought of the complete community of love between the Father and the Son, and the pre-existence and descent of the latter here also tend to the glory of God. In the sentence "God so loved the world" etc., that which Paul describes in Phil. II. becomes at the same time an act of God, in fact the act of God. The sentence "God is love" sums up again all individual speculations, and raises them into a new and most exalted sphere.

2 If it had been possible for speculation to maintain the level of the Fourth Gospel, nothing of that would have happened; but where were there theologians capable of this?

in Christ, was transformed into a cosmic force and thereby secularised.

In the present work I have endeavoured to explain fully how the doctrine of the Church developed from these premises into the doctrine of the Trinity and of the two natures. I have also shewn that the imperfect beginnings of Church doctrine, especially as they appear in the Logos theory derived from cosmology, were subjected to wholesome corrections—by the Monarchians, by Athanasius, and by the influence of biblical passages which pointed in another direction. Finally, the Logos doctrine received a form in which the idea was deprived of nearly all cosmical content. Nor could the Hellenic contrast of "spirit" and "flesh" become completely developed in Christianity, because the belief in the bodily resurrection of Christ, and in the admission of the flesh into heaven, opposed to the principle of dualism a barrier which Paul as yet neither knew nor felt to be necessary. The conviction as to the resurrection of the flesh proved the hard rock which shattered the energetic attempts to give a completely Hellenic complexion to the Christian religion.

The history of the development of the ideas of pre-existence is at the same time the criticism of them, so that we need not have recourse to our present theory of knowledge which no longer allows such speculations. The problem of determining the significance of Christ through a speculation concerning his natures, and of associating with these the concrete features of the historical Christ, was originated by Hellenism. But even the New Testament writers, who appear in this respect to be influenced in some way by Hellenism, did not really speculate concerning the different natures, but, taking Christ's spiritual nature for granted, determined his religious significance by his moral qualities—Paul by the moral act of humiliation and obedience unto death, John by the complete dependence of Christ upon God and hence also by his obedience, as well as the unity of the love of Father and Son. There is only one idea of pre-existence which no empiric contemplation of history and no reason can uproot. This is identical with the

most ancient idea found in the Old Testament, as well as that
prevalent among the early Christians, and consists in the religious thought that God the Lord directs history. In its application to Jesus Christ, it is contained in the words we read
in 1 Pet. I. 20: προεγνωσμένος μὲν πρὸ καταβολῆς κόσμου, φανε-
ρωθεὶς δὲ δι᾽ ὑμᾶς τοὺς δι᾽ αὐτοῦ πιστοὺς εἰς θεὸν τὸν ἐγείραντα
αὐτὸν ἐκ νεκρῶν καὶ δόξαν αὐτῷ δόντα, ὥστε τὴν πίστιν ὑμῶν καὶ
ἐλπίδα εἶναι εἰς θεόν.

APPENDIX II.

Liturgy and the Origin of Dogma.

THE reader has perhaps wondered why I have made so little reference to Liturgy in my description of the origin of dogma. For according to the most modern ideas about the history of religion and the origin of theology, the development of both may be traced in the ritual. Without any desire to criticise these notions, I think I am justified in asserting that this is another instance of the exceptional nature of Christianity. For a considerable period it possessed no ritual at all, and the process of development in this direction had been going on, or been completed, a long time before ritual came to furnish material for dogmatic discussion.

The worship in Christian Churches grew out of that in the synagogues, whereas there is no trace of its being influenced by the Jewish Temple service (Duchesne, Origines du Culte Chrétien, p. 45 ff.). Its oldest constituents are accordingly prayer, reading of the scriptures, application of scripture texts, and sacred song. In addition to these we have, as specifically Christian elements, the celebration of the Lord's Supper, and the utterances of persons inspired by the Spirit. The latter manifestations, however, ceased in the course of the second century, and to some extent as early as its first half. The religious services in which a ritual became developed were prayer, the Lord's Supper and sacred song. The Didache had already prescribed stated formulæ for prayer. The ritual of the Lord's Supper was determined in its main features by the memory of its institution. The sphere of sacred song remained the most unfettered, though here also, even at an early period

—no later in fact than the end of the first and beginning of the second century—a fixed and a variable element were distinguished; for responsory hymns, as is testified by the Epistle of Pliny and the still earlier Book of Revelation, require to follow a definite arrangement. But the whole, though perhaps already fixed during the course of the second century, still bore the stamp of spirituality and freedom. It was really worship in spirit and in truth, and this and no other was the light in which the Apologists, for instance, regarded it. Ritualism did not begin to be a power in the Church till the end of the second century; though it had been cultivated by the " Gnostics " long before, and traces of it are found at an earlier period in some of the older Fathers, such as Ignatius.

Among the liturgical fragments still preserved to us from the first three centuries two strata may be distinguished. Apart from the responsory hymns in the Book of Revelation, which can hardly represent fixed liturgical pieces, the only portions of the older stratum in our possession are the Lord's Prayer, originating with Jesus himself and used as a liturgy, together with the sacramental prayers of the. Didache. These prayers exhibit a style unlike any of the liturgical formulæ of later times; the prayer is exclusively addressed to God, it returns thanks for knowledge and life; it speaks of Jesus the $\pi\alpha\tilde{\imath}\varsigma\ \theta\varepsilon o\tilde{\upsilon}$ (Son of God) as the mediator; the intercession refers exclusively to the Church, and the supplication is for the gathering together of the Church, the hastening of the coming of the kingdom and the destruction of the world. No direct mention is made of the death and resurrection of Christ. These prayers are the peculiar property of the Christian Church. It cannot, however, be said that they exercised any important influence on the history of dogma. The thoughts contained in them perished in their specific shape; the measure of permanent importance they attained in a more general form, was not preserved to them through these prayers.

The second stratum of liturgical pieces dates back to the great prayer with which the first Epistle of Clement ends, for in many respects this prayer, though some expressions in it remind us of the older type (διά τοῦ ἠγαπημένου παιδός σου Ἰησοῦν Χριστοῦ, "through thy beloved son Jesus Christ"), already exhibits the characteristics of the later liturgy, as is shewn, for example, by a comparison of the liturgical prayer in the Constitutions of the Apostles (see Lightfoot's edition and my own). But this piece shews at the same time that the liturgical prayers, and consequently the liturgy also, sprang from those in the synagogue, for the similarity is striking. Here we find a connection resembling that which exists between the Jewish "Two Ways" and the Christian instruction of catechumens. If this observation is correct, it clearly explains the cautious use of historical and dogmatic material in the oldest liturgies—a precaution not to their disadvantage. As in the prayers of the synagogue, so also in Christian Churches, all sorts of matters were not submitted to God or laid bare before Him, but the prayers serve as a religious ceremony, that is, as. adoration, petition and intercession. Σὺ εἶ ὁ θεὸς μόνος καὶ Ἰησοῦς Χριστὸς ὁ παῖς σου καὶ ἡμεῖς λαός σου καὶ πρόβατα τῆς νομῆς σου, (thou art God alone and Jesus Christ is thy son, and we are thy people and the sheep of thy pasture). In this confession, an expressive Christian modification of that of the synagogue, the whole liturgical ceremony is epitomised. So far as we can assume and conjecture from the scanty remains of Ante-Nicene liturgy, the character of the ceremony was not essentially altered in this respect. Nothing containing a specific dogma or theological speculation was admitted. The number of sacred ceremonies, already considerable in the second century (how did they arise?), was still further increased in the third; but the accompanying words, so far as we know, expressed nothing but adoration, gratitude, supplication, and intercession. The relations expressed in the liturgy became more comprehensive, copious and detailed; but its fundamental character was not changed. The history of dogma in the first three centuries is not reflected in their liturgy.

APPENDIX III.

NEOPLATONISM.

The historical significance and position of Neoplatonism.

THE political history of the ancient world ends with the
Empire of Diocletian and Constantine, which has not only
Roman and Greek, but also Oriental features. The history of
ancient philosophy ends with the universal philosophy of Neoplatonism, which assimilated the elements of most of the
previous systems, and embodied the result of the history of
religion and civilisation in East and West. But as the Roman
Byzantine Empire is at one and the same time a product of
the final effort and the exhaustion of the ancient world, so
also Neoplatonism is, on one side, the completion of ancient
philosophy, and, on another, its abolition. Never before in the
Greek and Roman theory of the world did the conviction of
the dignity of man and his elevation above nature, attain so
certain an expression as in Neoplatonism; and never before
in the history of civilisation did its highest exponents, notwithstanding all their progress in inner observation, so much under-
value the sovereign significance of real science and pure knowledge as the later Neoplatonists did. Judged from the stand-point
of pure science, of empirical knowledge of the world, the
philosophy of Plato and Aristotle marks a momentous turning-
point, the post-Aristotelian a retrogression, the Neoplatonic a
complete declension. But judging from the stand-point of religion
and morality, it must be admitted that the ethical temper which
Neoplatonism sought to beget and confirm, was the highest
and purest which the culture of the ancient world produced.

This necessarily took place at the expense of science: for on the soil of polytheistic natural religions, the knowledge of nature must either fetter and finally abolish religion, or be fettered and abolished by religion. Religion and ethic, however, proved the stronger powers. Placed between these and the knowledge of nature, philosophy, after a period of fluctuation, finally follows the stronger force. Since the ethical itself, in the sphere of natural religions, is unhesitatingly conceived as a higher kind of "nature", conflict with the empirical knowledge of the world is unavoidable. The higher "physics", for that is what religious ethics is here, must displace the lower or be itself displaced. Philosophy must renounce its scientific aspect, in order that man's claim to a supernatural value of his person and life may be legitimised.

It is an evidence of the vigour of man's moral endowments that the only epoch of culture which we are able to survey in its beginnings, its progress, and its close, ended not with materialism, but with the most decided idealism. It is true that in its way this idealism also denotes a bankruptcy; as the contempt for reason and science, and these are contemned when relegated to the second place, finally leads to barbarism, because it results in the crassest superstition, and is exposed to all manner of imposture. And, as a matter of fact, barbarism succeeded the flourishing period of Neoplatonism. Philosophers themselves no doubt found their mental food in the knowledge which they thought themselves able to surpass; but the masses grew up in superstition, and the Christian Church, which entered on the inheritance of Neoplatonism, was compelled to reckon with that and come to terms with it. Just when the bankruptcy of the ancient civilisation and its lapse into barbarism could not have failed to reveal themselves, a kindly destiny placed on the stage of history barbarian nations, for whom the work of a thousand years had as yet no existence. Thus the fact is concealed, which, however, does not escape the eye of one who looks below the surface, that the inner history of the ancient world must necessarily have degenerated into barbarism of its own accord, because it ended with the renunciation of this world. There is no desire either to enjoy it, to master it, or to know it as it really is. A new world is disclosed for which everything is given up, and men are ready to sacrifice insight and understanding, in order to possess this world with certainty; and, in the light which radiates from the world to come, that which in this world appears absurd becomes wisdom, and wisdom becomes folly.

Such is Neoplatonism. The pre-Socratic philosophers, declared by the followers of Socrates to be childish, had freed themselves from theology, that is, the mythology of the poets, and constructed a philosophy from the observation of nature, without troubling themselves about ethics and religion. In the systems of Plato and Aristotle physics and ethics were to attain to their rights, though the latter no doubt already occupied the first place; theology, that is popular religion, continues to be thrust aside. The post-Aristotelian philosophers of all parties were already beginning to withdraw from the objective world. Stoicism indeed seems to fall back into the materialism that prevailed before Plato and Aristotle; but the ethical dualism which dominated the mood of the Stoic philosophers, did not in the long run tolerate the materialistic physics; it sought and found help in the metaphysical dualism of the Platonists, and at the same time reconciled itself to the popular religion by means of allegorism, that is, it formed a new theology. But it did not result in permanent philosophic creations. A one-sided development of Platonism produced the various forms of scepticism which sought to abolish confidence in empirical knowledge. Neoplatonism, which came last, learned from all schools. In the first place, it belongs to the series of post-Aristotelian systems and, as the philosophy of the subjective, it is the logical completion of them. In the second place, it rests on scepticism; for it also, though not at the very beginning, gave up both confidence and pure interest in empirical knowledge. Thirdly, it can boast of the name and authority of Plato; for in metaphysics it consciously went back to him and expressly opposed the metaphysics of the Stoics. Yet on this very point it also learned something from the Stoics; for the

Neoplatonic conception of the action of God on the world, and of the nature and origin of matter, can only be explained by reference to the dynamic pantheism of the Stoics. In other respects, especially in psychology, it is diametrically opposed to the Stoa, though superior. Fourthly, the study of Aristotle also had an influence on Neoplatonism. That is shewn not only in the philosophic methods of the Neoplatonists, but also, though in a subordinate way, in their metaphysics. Fifthly, the ethic of the Stoics was adopted by Neoplatonism, but this ethic necessarily gave way to a still higher view of the conditions of the spirit. Sixthly and finally, Christianity also, which Neoplatonism opposed in every form (especially in that of the Gnostic philosophy of religion), seems not to have been entirely without influence. On this point we have as yet no details, and these can only be ascertained by a thorough examination of the polemic of Plotinus against the Gnostics.

Hence, with the exception of Epicureanism, which Neoplatonism dreaded as its mortal enemy, every important system of former times was drawn upon by the new philosophy. But we should not on that account call Neoplatonism an eclectic system in the usual sense of the word. For in the first place, it had one pervading and all predominating interest, the religious; and in the second place, it introduced into philosophy a new supreme principle, the super-rational, or the super-essential. This principle should not be identified with the "Ideas" of Plato or the "Form" of Aristotle. For as Zeller rightly says: "In Plato and Aristotle the distinction of the sensuous and the intelligible is the strongest expression for belief in the truth of thought; it is only sensuous perception and sensuous existence whose relative falsehood they presuppose; but of a higher stage of spiritual life lying beyond idea and thought, there is no mention. In Neoplatonism, on the other hand, it is just this super-rational element which is regarded as the final goal of all effort, and the highest ground of all existence; the knowledge gained by thought is only an intermediate stage between sensuous perception and the super-rational intuition; the intelligible forms are not that which is highest and last, but only the media by which the influences of the formless original essence are communicated to the world. This view therefore presupposes not merely doubt of the reality of sensuous existence and sensuous notions, but absolute doubt, aspiration beyond all reality. The highest intelligible is not that which constitutes the real content of thought, but only that which is presupposed and earnestly desired by man as the unknowable ground of his thought." Neoplatonism recognised that a religious ethic can be built neither on sense-perception nor on knowledge gained by the understanding, and that it cannot be justified by these; it therefore broke both with intellectual ethics and with utilitarian morality. But for that very reason, having as it were parted with perception and understanding in relation to the ascertaining of the highest truth, it was compelled to seek for a new world and a new function in the human spirit, in order to ascertain the existence of what it desired, and to comprehend and describe that of which it had ascertained the existence. But man cannot transcend his psychological endowment. An iron ring incloses him. He who does not allow his thought to be determined by experience falls a prey to fancy, that is, thought, which cannot be suppressed, assumes a mythological aspect: superstition takes the place of reason, dull gazing at something incomprehensible is regarded as the highest goal of the spirit's efforts, and every conscious activity of the spirit is subordinated to visionary conditions artificially brought about. But that every conceit may not be allowed to assert itself, the gradual exploration of every region of knowledge according to every method of acquiring it, is demanded as a preliminary —the Neoplatonists did not make matters easy for themselves,—and a new and mighty principle is set up which is to bridle fancy, viz., *the authority of a sure tradition.* This authority must be superhuman, otherwise it would not come under consideration; it must therefore be divine. On divine disclosures, that is revelations, must rest both the highest super-rational region of knowledge and the possibility of knowledge itself. In a word, the philosophy which Neoplatonism

represents, whose final interest is the religious, and whose
highest object is the super-rational, must be a *philosophy of
revelation*.

In the case of Plotinus himself and his immediate disciples, this
does not yet appear plainly. They still shew confidence in the
objective presuppositions of their philosophy, and have, especially
in psychology, done great work and created something new. But
this confidence vanishes in the later Neoplatonists. Porphyry, before he became a disciple of Plotinus, wrote a book περὶ τῆς ἐκλογίων
φιλοσοφίας; as a philosopher he no longer required the "λόγια".
But the later representatives of the system sought for their philosophy revelations of the Godhead. They found them in the religious traditions and cults of all nations. Neoplatonism learned from
the Stoics to rise above the political limits of nations and states,
and to widen the Hellenic consciousness to a universally human
one. The spirit of God has breathed throughout the whole
history of the nations, and the traces of divine revelation are
to be found everywhere. The older a religious tradition or
cultus is, the more worthy of honour, the more rich in thoughts
of God it is. Therefore the old Oriental religions are of special
value to the Neoplatonists. The allegorical method of interpreting myths, which was practised by the Stoics in particular,
was accepted by Neoplatonism also. But the myths, spiritually
explained, have for this system an entirely different value from
what they had for the Stoic philosophers. The latter adjusted themselves to the myths by the aid of allegorical explanation; the later Neoplatonists, on the other hand, (after
a selection in which the immoral myths were sacrificed, see,
e. g. Julian) regarded them as *the proper material and sure
foundation of philosophy*. Neoplatonism claims to be not only
the absolute *philosophy*, completing all systems, but, at the
same time, the absolute *religion*, confirming and explaining all
earlier religions. A rehabilitation of all ancient religions is
aimed at (see the philosophic teachers of Julian and compare his
great religious experiment); each was to continue in its traditional form, but, at the same time, each was to communicate
the religious temper and the religious knowledge which Neo-

platonism had attained, and each cultus is to lead to the high morality which it behoves man to maintain. In Neoplatonism the psychological fact of the longing of man for something higher, is exalted to the all-predominating principle which explains the world. Therefore the religions, though they are to be purified and spiritualised, become the foundation of philosophy. The Neoplatonic philosophy therefore presupposes the religious syncretism of the third century, and cannot be understood without it. The great forces which were half unconsciously at work in this syncretism, were reflectively grasped by Neoplatonism. It is the final fruit of the developments resulting from the political, national and religious syncretism which arose from the undertakings of Alexander the Great, and the Romans.

Neoplatonism is consequently a stage in the history of religion; nay, its significance in the history of the world lies in the fact that it is so. In the history of science and enlightenment it has a position of significance only in so far as it was the necessary transition stage through which humanity had to pass, in order to free itself from the religion of nature and the depreciation of the spiritual life, which oppose an insurmountable barrier to the highest advance of human knowledge. But as Neoplatonism in its philosophical aspect means the abolition of ancient philosophy, which, however, it desired to complete, so also in its religious aspect it means the abolition of the ancient religions which it aimed at restoring. For in requiring these religions to mediate a definite religious knowledge, and to lead to the highest moral disposition, it burdened them with tasks to which they were not equal, and under which they could not but break down. And in requiring them to loosen, if not completely destroy, the bond which was their only stay, namely, the political bond, it took from them the foundation on which they were built. But could it not place them on a greater and firmer foundation? Was not the Roman Empire in existence, and could the new religion not become dependent on this in the same way as the earlier religions had been dependent on the lesser states and nations? It might be thought so, but it was no longer possible. No doubt the political history of the

nations round the Mediterranean, in their development into the
universal Roman monarchy, was parallel to the spiritual history
of these nations in their development into monotheism and a
universal system of morals; but the spiritual development in
the end far outstripped the political: even the Stoics attained
to a height which the political development could only partially
reach. Neoplatonism did indeed attempt to gain a connection
with the Byzantine Roman Empire: one noble monarch, Julian,
actually perished as a result of this endeavour: but even before
this the profounder Neoplatonists discerned that their lofty
religious philosophy would not bear contact with the despotic
Empire, because it would not bear any contact with the "world"
(plan of the founding of Platonopolis). Political affairs are at
bottom as much a matter of indifference to Neoplatonism as
material things in general. The idealism of the new philosophy
was too high to admit of its being naturalised in the despirit-
ualised, tyrannical and barren creation of the Byzantine Empire,
and this Empire itself needed unscrupulous and despotic police
officials, not noble philosophers. Important and instructive,
therefore, as the experiments are, which were made from time
to time by the state and by individual philosophers, to unite the
monarchy of the world with Neoplatonism, they could not but
be ineffectual.

But, and this is the last question which one is justified in
raising here, why did not Neoplatonism create an independent
religions community? Since it had already changed the ancient
religions so fundamentally, in its purpose to restore them, since
it had attempted to fill the old naive cults with profound
philosophic ideas, and to make them exponents of a high morality, why did it not take the further step and create a
religious fellowship of its own? why did it not complete and
confirm the union of gods by the founding of a church which
was destined to embrace the whole of humanity, and in which,
beside the one ineffable Godhead, the gods of all nations could
have been worshipped? Why not? The answer to this question
is at the same time the reply to another, viz., why did the
christian church supplant Neoplatonism? Neoplatonism lacked,

three elements to give it the significance of a new and permanent
religious system. Augustine in his confessions (Bk. VII. 18—21)
has excellently described these three elements. First and above
all, it lacked a religious founder; secondly, it was unable to give
any answer to the question, how one could permanently maintain
the mood of blessedness and peace: thirdly, it lacked the means
of winning those who could not speculate. The "people" could
not learn the philosophic exercises which it recommended as
the condition of attaining the enjoyment of the highest good;
and the way on which even the "people" can attain to the
highest good was hidden from it. Hence these "wise and
prudent" remained a school. When Julian attempted to interest
the common uncultured man in the doctrines and worship of
this school, his reward was mockery and scorn.

Not as philosophy and not as a new religion did Neoplatonism
become a decisive factor in history, but, if I may say so, as a
frame of mind. [1] The feeling that there is an eternal highest
good which lies beyond all outer experience and is not even
the intelligible, this feeling, with which was united the conviction
of the entire worthlessness of everything earthly, was produced
and fostered by Neoplatonism. But it was unable to describe
the contents of that highest being and highest good, and therefore
it was here compelled to give itself entirely up to fancy and
æsthetic feeling. Therefore it was forced to trace out "mys-

---

[1] Excellent remarks on the nature of Neoplatonism may be found in
Eucken, Gött. Gel. Anz., 1 März, 1884. p. 176 ff.: this sketch was already
written before I saw them. "We find the characteristic of the Neoplatonic
epoch in the effort to make the inward, which till then had had alongside
of it an independent outer world as a contrast, the exclusive and all-
determining element. The movement which makes itself felt here, outlasts
antiquity and prepares the way for the modern period; it brings about
the dissolution of that which marked the culminating point of ancient life,
that which we are wont to call specifically classic. The life of the spirit,
till then conceived as a member of an ordered world and subject to its
laws, now freely passes beyond these bounds, and attempts to mould, and
even to create, the universe from itself. No doubt the different attempts
to realise this desire reveal, for the most part, a deep gulf between will
and deed; usually ethical and religious requirements of the naive human
consciousness must replace universally creative spiritual power, but all
the insufficient and unsatisfactory elements of this period should not obscure
the fact that, in one instance, it reached the height of a great philosophic
achievement, in the case of Plotinus".

terious ways to that which is within", which, however, led nowhere. It transformed thought into a dream of feeling; it immersed
itself in the sea of emotions; it viewed the old fabled world
of the nations as the reflection of a higher reality, and transformed reality into poetry; but in spite of all these efforts it
was only able, to use the words of Augustine, to see from afar
the land which it desired. It broke this world into fragments;
but nothing remained to it, save a ray from a world beyond,
which was only an indescribable "something".

And yet the significance of Neoplatonism in the history of
our moral culture has been, and still is, immeasurable. Not only
because it refined and strengthened man's life of feeling and
sensation, not only because it, more than anything else, wove
the delicate veil which even to-day, whether we be religious or
irreligious, we ever and again cast over the offensive impression
of the brutal reality, but, above all, because it begat the consciousness that the blessedness which alone can satisfy man, is
to be found somewhere else than in the sphere of knowledge.
That man does not live by bread alone, is a truth that was
known before Neoplatonism; but it proclaimed the profounder
truth, which the earlier philosophy had failed to recognise, that
man does not live by knowledge alone. Neoplatonism not only
had a propadeutic significance in the past, but continues to be,
even now, the source of all the moods which deny the world
and strive after an ideal, but have not power to raise themselves
above æsthetic feeling, and see no means of getting a clear notion
of the impulse of their own heart and the land of their desire.

Historical Origin of Neoplatonism.

The forerunners of Neoplatonism were, on the one hand,
those Stoics who recognise the Platonic distinction of the sensible and supersensible world, and on the other, the so-called
Neopythagoreans and religious philosophers, such as Posidonius,
Plutarch of Chæronea, and especially Numenius of Apamea. [1]

---

[1] Plotinus, even in his lifetime, was reproached with having borrowed
most of his system from Numenius. Porphyry, in his "Vita Plotini",
defended him against this reproach.

Nevertheless, these cannot be regarded as the actual Fathers of Neoplatonism; for the philosophic method was still very imperfect in comparison with the Neoplatonic, their principles were uncertain, and the authority of Plato was not yet regarded as placed on an unapproachable height. The Jewish and Christian philosophers of the first and second centuries stand very much nearer the later Neoplatonism than Numenius. We would probably see this more clearly if we knew the development of Christianity in Alexandria in the second century. But, unfortunately, we have only very meagre fragments to tell us of this. First and above all, we must mention Philo. This philosopher, who interpreted the Old Testament religion in terms of Hellenism, had, in accordance with his idea of revelation, already maintained that the Divine Original Essence is supra-rational, that only ecstasy leads to Him, and that the materials for religious and moral knowledge are contained in the oracles of the Deity. The religious ethic of Philo, a combination of Stoic, Platonic, Neopythagorean and Old Testament gnomic wisdom, already bears the marks which we recognise in Neoplatonism. The acknowledgment that God was exalted above all thought, was a sort of tribute which Greek philosophy was compelled to pay to the national religion of Israel, in return for the supremacy which was here granted to the former. The claim of positive religion to be something more than an intellectual conception of the universal reason, was thereby justified. Even religious syncretism is already found in Philo; but it is something essentially different from the later Neoplatonic, since Philo regarded the Jewish cult as the only valuable one, and traced back all elements of truth in the Greeks and Romans to borrowings from the books of Moses.

The earliest Christian philosophers, especially Justin and Athenagoras, likewise prepared the way for the speculations of the later Neoplatonists by their attempts, on the one hand, to connect Christianity with Stoicism and Platonism, and on the other, to exhibit it as supra-Platonic. The method by which Justin, in the introduction to the Dialogue with Trypho, attempts to establish the Christian knowledge of God, that is, the knowledge of the truth, on Platonism, Scepticism and "Revelation", strikingly reminds us of the later methods of the Neoplatonists. Still more is one reminded of Neoplatonism by the speculations of the Alexandrian Christian Gnostics, especially of Valentinus and the followers of Basilides. The doctrines of the Basilidians (?) communicated by Hippolytus (Philosoph. VII. c. 20 sq.), read like fragments from the didactic writings of the Neoplatonists: Ἐπεὶ οὐδὲν ἦν οὐχ ὕλη, οὐκ οὐσία, οὐκ ἀνούσιον, οὐχ ἁπλοῦν, οὐ σύνθετον, οὐκ ἀνόητον, οὐκ ἀναίσθητον, οὐκ ἄνθρωπος......οὐκ ἂν θεὸς ἀνοήτως, ἀναισθήτως ἀβούλως ἀπροαιρέτως, ἀπαθῶς, ἀνεπιθυμήτιος κόσμον ἠθέλησε ποιῆσαι.....Οὕτως οὐκ ἂν θεὸς ἐποίησε κόσμον οὖκ ὄντα ἐξ οὐκ ὄντων, καταβαλόμενος καὶ ὑποστήσας σπερμα τι ἐν ἔχον πᾶσαν ἐν ἑαυτῷ τῆς τοῦ κόσμου πανσπερμίαν. Like the Neoplatonists, these Basilidians did not teach an emanation from the Godhead, but a dynamic mode of action of the Supreme Being. The same can be asserted of Valentinus who also places an unnamable being above all, and views matter not as a second principle, but as a derived product. The dependence of Basilides and Valentinus on Zeno and Plato is, besides, undoubted. But the method of these Gnostics in constructing their mental picture of the world and its history, was still an uncertain one. Crude primitive myths are here received, and naively realistic elements alternate with bold attempts at spiritualising. While therefore, philosophically considered, the Gnostic systems are very unlike the finished Neoplatonic ones, it is certain that they contained almost all the elements of the religious view of the world, which we find in Neoplatonism.

But were the earliest Neoplatonists really acquainted with the speculations of men like Philo, Justin, Valentinus and Basilides? were they familiar with the Oriental religions, especially with the Jewish and the Christian? and, if we must answer these questions in the affirmative, did they really learn from these sources?

Unfortunately, we cannot at present give certain, and still less detailed answers to these questions. But, as Neoplatonism originated in Alexandria, as Oriental cults confronted every one there, as the Jewish philosophy was prominent in the literary market of Alexandria, and that was the very place where scientific Christianity had its headquarters, there can, generally speaking, be no doubt that the earliest Neoplatonists had some acquaintance with Judaism and Christianity. In addition to that, we have the certain fact that the earliest Neoplatonists had discussions with (Roman) Gnostics (see Carl Schmidt, Gnostische Schriften in koptischer Sprache, pp. 603—665), and that Porphyry entered into elaborate controversy with Christianity. In comparison with the Neoplatonic philosophy, the system of Philo and the Gnostics appears in many respects an anticipation, which had a certain influence on the former, the precise nature of which has still to be ascertained. But the anticipation is not wonderful, for the religious and philosophic temper which was only gradually produced on Greek soil, existed from the first in such philosophers as took their stand on the ground of a revealed religion of redemption. Iamblichus and his followers first answer completely to the Christian Gnostic schools of the second century; that is to say, Greek philosophy, in its immanent development, did not attain till the fourth century the position which some Greek philosophers, who had accepted Christianity, had already reached in the second. The influence of Christianity—both Gnostic and Catholic—on Neoplatonism was perhaps very little at any time, though individual Neoplatonists since the time of Amelius employed Christian sayings as oracles, and testified their high esteem for Christ.

Sketch of the History and Doctrines of Neoplatonism.

Ammonius Saccas (died about 245), who is said to have been born a Christian, but to have lapsed into heathenism, is regarded as the founder of the Neoplatonic school in Alexandria. As he has left no writings, no judgment can be formed as to his teaching. His disciples inherited from him the prominence which they gave to Plato and the attempts to prove the harmony between the latter and Aristotle. His most important disciples were; Origen the Christian, a second heathen Origen, Longinus, Herennius, and, above all, Plotinus. The latter was born in the year 205, at Lycopolis in Egypt, laboured from 224 in Rome, and found numerous adherents and admirers, among others the Emperor Galienus and his consort, and died in lower Italy about 270. His writings were arranged by his disciple, Porphyry, and edited in six Enneads.

The Enneads of Plotinus are the fundamental documents of Neoplatonism. The teaching of this philosopher is mystical, and, like all mysticism, it falls into two main portions. The first and theoretic part shews the high origin of the soul, and how it has departed from this its origin. The second and practical part points out the way by which the soul can again be raised to the Eternal and the Highest. As the soul with its longings aspires beyond all sensible things and even beyond the world of ideas, the Highest must be something above reason. The system therefore has three parts. I. The Original Essence. II. The world of ideas and the soul. III. The world of phenomena. We may also, in conformity with the thought of Plotinus, divide the system thus: A. The supersensible world (1. The Original Essence; 2. the world of ideas; 3. the soul). B. The world of phenomena. The Original Essence is the One in contrast to the many; it is the Infinite and Unlimited in contrast to the finite; it is the source of all being, therefore the absolute causality and the only truly existing; but it is also the Good, in so far as everything finite is to find its aim in it and to flow back to it. Yet moral attributes cannot be ascribed to this Original Essence, for these would limit it. It has no attributes at all: it is a being without magnitude, without life, without thought; nay, one should not, properly speaking, even call it an existence; it is something above existence, above goodness, and at the same time the operative force without any substratum. As operative force the Original Essence is continually begetting something else, without itself being changed or moved or diminished. This creation is not a physical process, but an emanation of force; and because that which is produced has any existence only in so far as the originally Existent works in it, it may be said that Neoplatonism is dynamical Pantheism. Everything

that has being is directly or indirectly a production of the
"One". In this "One" everything so far as it has being, is
Divine, and God is all in all. But that which is derived is
not like the Original Essence itself. On the contrary, the
law of decreasing perfection prevails in the derived. The latter
is indeed an image and reflection of the Original Essence,
but the wider the circle of creations extends the less their
share in the Original Essence. Hence the totality of being
forms a gradation of concentric circles which finally lose themselves almost completely in non-being, in so far as in the last
circle the force of the Original Essence is a vanishing one.
Each lower stage of being is connected with the Original
Essence only by means of the higher stages; that which is
inferior receives a share in the Original Essence only through
the medium of these. But everything derived has one feature,
viz., a longing for the higher; it turns itself to this so far as
its nature allows it.

The first emanation of the Original Essence is the Νοῦς;
it is a complete image of the Original Essence and archetype
of all existing things; it is being and thought at the same time,
World of ideas and Idea. As image the Νοῦς is equal to the
Original Essence, as derived it is completely different from it.
What Plotinus understands by Νοῦς is the highest sphere which
the human spirit can reach (κόσμος νοητός) and at the same
time pure thought itself.

The soul which, according to Plotinus, is an immaterial substance like the Νοῦς, [1] is an image and product of the immov-
able Νοῦς. It is related to the Νοῦς as the latter is to the
Original Essence. It stands between the Νοῦς and the world
of phenomena. The Νοῦς penetrates and enlightens it, but it
itself already touches the world of phenomena. The Νοῦς is
undivided, the soul can also preserve its unity and abide in
the Νοῦς; but it has at the same time the power to unite
itself with the material world and thereby to be divided.
Hence it occupies a middle position. In virtue of its nature

[1] On this sort of Trinity, see Bigg, " The Christian Platonists of Alexandria," p. 248 f.

and destiny it belongs, as the single soul (soul of the world), to the supersensible world; but it embraces at the same time the many individual souls; these may allow themselves to be ruled by the Νοῦς, or they may turn to the sensible and be lost in the finite.

The soul, an active essence, begets the corporeal or the world of phenomena. This should allow itself to be so ruled by the soul that the manifold of which it consists may abide in fullest harmony. Plotinus is not a dualist like the majority of Christian Gnostics. He praises the beauty and glory of the world. When in it the idea really has dominion over matter, the soul over the body, the world is beautiful and good. It is the image of the upper world, though a shadowy one, and the gradations of better or worse in it are necessary to the harmony of the whole. But, in point of fact, the unity and harmony in the world of phenomena disappear in strife and opposition. The result is a conflict, a growth and decay, a seeming existence. The original cause of this lies in the fact that a substratum, viz., matter, lies at the basis of bodies. Matter is the foundation of each (τὸ βάθος ἑκάστου ἡ ὕλη); it is the obscure, the indefinite, that which is without qualities, the μὴ ὄν. As devoid of form and idea it is the evil, as capable of form the intermediate.

The human souls that are sunk in the material have been ensnared by the sensuous, and have allowed themselves to be ruled by desire. They now seek to detach themselves entirely from true being, and striving after independence fall into an unreal existence. Conversion therefore is needed, and this is possible, for freedom is not lost.

Now here begins the practical philosophy. The soul must rise again to the highest on the same path by which it descended: it must first of all return to itself. This takes place through virtue which aspires to assimilation with God and leads to Him. In the ethics of Plotinus all earlier philosophic systems of virtue are united and arranged in graduated order. Civic virtues stand lowest, then follow the purifying, and finally the deifying virtues. Civic virtues only adorn the life, but do

not elevate the soul as the purifying virtues do; they free
the soul from the sensuous and lead it back to itself and
thereby to the Νοῦς. Man becomes again a spiritual and permanent being, and frees himself from every sin, through asceticism. But he is to reach still higher; he is not only to be
without sin, but he is to be "God". That takes place through
the contemplation of the Original Essence, the One, that is
through ecstatic elevation to Him. This is not mediated by
thought, for thought reaches only to the Νοῦς, and is itself
only a movement. Thought is only a preliminary stage towards
union with God. The soul can only see and touch the Original
Essence in a condition of complete passivity and rest. Hence,
in order to attain to this highest, the soul must subject itself
to a spiritual "Exercise". It must begin with the contemplation of material things, their diversity and harmony, then
retire into itself and sink itself in its own essence, and thence
mount up to the Νοῦς, to the world of ideas; but, as it still
does not find the One and Highest Essence there, as the call
always comes to it from there: "We have not made ourselves"
(Augustine in the sublime description of Christian, that is,
Neoplatonic exercises), it must, as it were, lose sight of itself
in a state of intense concentration, in mute contemplation and
complete forgetfulness of all things. It can then see God, the
source of life, the principle of being, the first cause of all
good, the root of the soul. In that moment it enjoys the
highest and indescribable blessedness; it is itself, as it were,
swallowed up by the deity and bathed in the light of eternity.

Plotinus, as Porphyry relates, attained to this ecstatic union
with God four times during the six years he was with him.
To Plotinus this religious philosophy was sufficient; he did not
require the popular religion and worship. But yet he sought
their support. The Deity is indeed in the last resort only the
Original Essence, but it manifests itself in a fulness of eman-
ations and phenomena. The Νοῦς is, as it were, the second
God; the λόγοι, which are included in it, are gods; the stars
are gods, etc. A strict monotheism appeared to Plotinus a
poor thing. The myths of the popular religion were interpreted

by him in a particular sense, and he could justify even magic, soothsaying and prayer. He brought forward reasons for the worship of images, which the Christian worshippers of images subsequently adopted. Yet, in comparison with the later Neo-platonists, he was free from gross superstition and wild fanat-icism. He cannot, in the remotest sense, be reckoned among the "deceivers who were themselves deceived," and the restor-ation of the ancient worships of the Gods was not his chief aim.

Among his disciples the most important were Amelius and Porphyry. Amelius changed the doctrine of Plotinus in some points, and even made use of the prologue of the Gospel of John. Porphyry has the merit of having systematized and spread the teaching of his master, Plotinus. He was born at Tyre, in the year 233; whether he was for some time a Christ-ian is uncertain; from 263-268 he was a pupil of Plotinus at Rome; before that he wrote the work περὶ τῆς ἐκ λογίων φιλο-σοφίας, which shews that he wished to base philosophy on revelation; he lived a few years in Sicily (about 270) where he wrote his "fifteen books against the Christians"; he then returned to Rome where he laboured as a teacher, edited the works of Plotinus, wrote himself a series of treatises, married, in his old age, the Roman Lady Marcella, and died about the year 303. Porphyry was not an original, productive thinker, but a diligent and thorough investigator, characterized by great learning, by the gift of an acute faculty for philological and historical criticism, and by an earnest desire to spread the true philosophy of life, to refute false doctrines, especially those of the Christians, to ennoble man and draw him to that which is good. That a mind so free and noble surrendered itself entirely to the philosophy of Plotinus and to polytheistic mysticism, is a proof that the spirit of the age works almost irresistibly, and that religious mysticism was the highest possession of the time. The teaching of Porphyry is distinguished from that of Plotinus by the fact that it is still more practical and religious. The aim of philosophy, according to Porphyry, is the salvation of the soul. The origin and the guilt of evil lie not in the body, but in the desires of the soul. The strictest asceticism (ab-

stinence from cohabitation, flesh and wine) is therefore required
in addition to the knowledge of God. During the course of
his life Porphyry warned men more and more decidedly against
crude popular beliefs and immoral cults. " The ordinary notions
of the Deity are of such a kind that it is more godless to
share them than to neglect the images of the gods". But
freely as he criticised the popular religions, he did not wish to
give them up. He contended for a pure worship of the many
gods, and recognised the right of every old national religion,
and the religious duties of their professors. His work against
the Christians is not directed against Christ, or what he regarded
as the teaching of Christ, but against the Christians of his day
and against the sacred books which, according to Porphyry, were
written by impostors and ignorant people. In his acute criticism of the genesis or what was regarded as Christianity in
his day, he spoke bitter and earnest truths, and therefore acquired
the name of the fiercest and most formidable of all the enemies
of Christians. His work was destroyed (condemned by an edict
of Theodosius II. and Valentinian, of the year 448), and even
the writings in reply (by Methodius, Eusebius, Apollinaris,
Philostorgius, etc.,) have not been preserved. Yet we possess
fragments in Lactantius, Augustine, Macarius Magnes and
others, which attest how thoroughly Porphyry studied the
Christian writings and how great his faculty was for true historical criticism.

Porphyry marks the transition to the Neoplatonism which
subordinated itself entirely to the polytheistic cults, and which
strove, above all, to defend the old Greek and Oriental religions
against the formidable assaults of Christianity. Iamblichus, the
disciple of Porphyry (died 330), transformed Neoplatonism "from
a philosophic theorem into a theological doctrine". The doctrines
peculiar to Iamblichus can no longer be deduced from scientific,
but only from practical motives. In order to justify superstition
and the ancient cults, philosophy in Iamblichus becomes a
theurgic, mysteriosophy, spiritualism. Now appears that series
of "Philosophers", in whose case one is frequently unable to
decide whether they are deceivers or deceived, " decepti decept-

ores", as Augustine says. A mysterious mysticism of numbers
plays a great rôle. That which is absurd and mechanical is
surrounded with the halo of the sacramental; myths are proved
by pious fancies and pietistic considerations with a spiritual
sound; miracles, even the most foolish, are believed in and
are performed. The philosopher becomes the priest of magic,
and philosophy an instrument of magic. At the same time,
the number of Divine Beings is infinitely increased by the further
action of unlimited speculation But this fantastic addition which
Iamblichus makes to the inhabitants of Olympus, is the very
fact which proves that Greek philosophy has here returned to
mythology, and that the religion of nature was still a power.
And yet no one can deny that, in the fourth century, even the
noblest and choicest minds were found among the Neoplatonists.
So great was the declension, that this Neoplatonic philosophy
was still the protecting roof for many influential and earnest
thinkers, although swindlers and hypocrites also concealed themselves under this roof. In relation to some points of doctrine,
at any rate, the dogmatic of Iamblichus marks an advance.
Thus, the emphasis he lays on the idea that evil has its seat
in the will, is an important fact; and in general the significance
he assigns to the will is perhaps the most important advance
in psychology, and one which could not fail to have great
influence on dogmatic also (Augustine). It likewise deserves
to be noted that Iamblichus disputed Plotinus' doctrine of the
divinity of the human soul.

The numerous disciples of Iamblichus (Aedesius, Chrysantius,
Eusebius, Priscus, Sopater, Sallust and especially Maximus, the
most celebrated) did little to further speculation; they occupied
themselves partly with commenting on the writings of the earlier
philosophers (particularly Themistius), partly as missionaries of
their mysticism. The interests and aims of these philosophers
are best shewn in the treatise "De mysteriis Ægyptiorum".
Their hopes were strengthened when their disciple Julian, a
man enthusiastic and noble, but lacking in intellectual originality, ascended the imperial throne, 361 to 363. This emperor's
romantic policy of restoration, as he himself must have seen,

had, however, no result, and his early death destroyed every hope of supplanting Christianity.

But the victory of the Church, in the age of Valentinian and Theodosius, unquestionably purified Neoplatonism. The struggle for dominion had led philosophers to grasp at and unite themselves with everything that was hostile to Christianity. But now Neoplatonism was driven out of the great arena of history. The Church and its dogmatic, which inherited its estate, received along with the latter superstition, polytheism, magic, myths and the apparatus of religious magic. The more firmly all this established itself in the Church and succeeded there, though not without finding resistance, the freer Neoplatonism becomes. It does not by any means give up its religious attitude or its theory of knowledge, but it applies itself with fresh zeal to scientific investigations and especially to the study of the earlier philosophers. Though Plato remains the divine philosopher, yet it may be noticed how, from about 400, the writings of Aristotle were increasingly read and prized. Neoplatonic schools continue to flourish in the chief cities of the empire up to the beginning of the fifth century, and in this period they are at the same time the places where the theologians of the Church are formed. The noble Hypatia, to whom Synesius, her enthusiastic disciple, who was afterwards a bishop, raised a splendid monument, taught in Alexandria. But from the beginning of the fifth century ecclesiastical fanaticism ceased to tolerate heathenism. The murder of Hypatia put an end to philosophy in Alexandria, though the Alexandrian school maintained itself in a feeble form till the middle of the sixth century. But in one city of the East, removed from the great highways of the world, which had become a provincial city and possessed memories which the Church of the fifth century felt itself too weak to destroy, viz., in Athens, a Neoplatonic school continued to flourish. There, among the monuments of a past time, Hellenism found its last asylum. The school of Athens returned to a more strict philosophic method and to learned studies. But as it clung to religious philosophy and undertook to reduce the whole Greek tradition, viewed in the light of Plotinus' theory, to a comprehensive and strictly articulated system, a philosophy arose here which may be called scholastic. For every philosophy is scholastic which considers fantastic and mythological material as a *noli me tangere*, and treats it in logical categories and distinctions by means of a complete set of formulæ. But to these Neoplatonists the writings of Plato, certain divine oracles, the Orphic poems, and much else which were dated back to the dim and distant past, were documents of standard authority, and inspired divine writings. They took from them the material of philosophy, which they then treated with all the instruments of dialectic.

The most prominent teachers at Athens were Plutarch (died 433), his disciple Syrian (who, as an exegete of Plato and Aristotle, is said to have done important work, and who deserves notice also, because he very vigorously emphasised the freedom of the will), but, above all, Proclus (411-485). Proclus is the great scholastic of Neoplatonism. It was he "who fashioned the whole traditional material into a powerful system with religious warmth and formal clearness, filling up the gaps and reconciling the contradictions by distinctions and speculations," "Proclus," says Zeller, "was the first who, by the strict logic of his system, formally completed the Neoplatonic philosophy and gave it, with due regard to all the changes it had undergone since the second century, that form in which it passed over to the Christian and Mohammedan middle ages. Forty-four years after the death of Proclus the school of Athens was closed by Justinian (in the year 529); but in the labours of Proclus it had completed its work, and could now really retire from the scene. It had nothing new to say; it was ripe for death, and an honourable end was prepared for it. The words of Proclus, the legacy of Hellenism to the Church and to the middle ages, attained an immeasurable importance in the thousand years which followed. They were not only one of the bridges by which the philosophy of the middle ages returned to Plato and Aristotle, but they determined the scientific method of the next thirty generations, and they partly produced, partly strengthened and brought to maturity the mediæval Christian mysticism in East and West.

The disciples of Proclus, Marinus, Asclepiodotus, Ammonius, Zenodotus, Isidorus, Hegias, Damascius, are not regarded as prominent. Damascius was the last head of the school at Athens. He, Simplicius, the masterly commentator on Aristotle, and five other Neoplatonists, migrated to Persia after Justinian had issued the edict closing the school. They lived in the illusion that Persia, the land of the East, was the seat of wisdom, righteousness and piety. After a few years they returned with blasted hopes to the Byzantine kingdom.

At the beginning of the sixth century Neoplatonism died out as an independent philosophy in the East; but almost at the same time, and this is no accident, it conquered new regions in the dogmatic of the Church through the spread of the writings of the pseudo-Dionysius; it began to fertilize Christian mysticism, and filled the worship with a new charm.

In the West, where, from the second century, we meet with few attempts at philosophic speculation, and where the necessary conditions for mystical contemplation were wanting, Neoplatonism only gained a few adherents here and there. We know that the rhetorician, Marius Victorinus, (about 350) translated the writings of Plotinus. This translation exercised decisive influence on the mental history of Augustine, who borrowed from Neoplatonism the best it had, its psychology, introduced it into the dogmatic of the Church, and developed it still further. It may be said that Neoplatonism influenced the West at first only through the medium or under the cloak of ecclesiastical theology. Even Boethius—we can now regard this as certain— was a Catholic Christian. But in his mode of thought he was certainly a Neoplatonist. His violent death in the year 525, marks the end of independent philosophic effort in the West. This last Roman philosopher stood indeed almost completely alone in his century, and the philosophy for which he lived was neither original, nor firmly grounded and methodically carried out.

Neoplatonism and Ecclesiastical Dogmatic.

The question as to the influence which Neoplatonism had on the history of the development of Christianity, is not easy to answer; it is hardly possible to get a clear view of the relation between them. Above all, the answers will diverge according as we take a wider or a narrower view of so-called "Neoplatonism". If we view Neoplatonism as the highest and only appropriate expression for the religious hopes and moods which moved the nations of Græco-Roman Empire from the second to the fifth centuries, the ecclesiastical dogmatic which was developed in the same period, may appear as a younger sister of Neoplatonism which was fostered by the elder one, but which fought and finally conquered her. The Neoplatonists themselves described the ecclesiastical theologians as intruders who appropriated Greek philosophy, but mixed it with foreign fables. Hence Porphyry said of Origen (in Euseb., H. E. VI. 19): "The outer life of Origen was that of a Christian and opposed to the law; but, in regard to his views of things and of the Deity, he thought like the Greeks, inasmuch as be introduced their ideas into the myths of other peoples" This judgment of Porphyry is at any rate more just and appropriate than that of the Church theologians about Greek philosophy, that it had stolen all its really valuable doctrines from the ancient sacred writings of the Christians. It is, above all, important that the affinity of the two sides was noted. So far, then, as both ecclesiastical dogmatic and Neoplatonism start from the feeling of the need of redemption, so far as both desire to free the soul from the sensuous, so far as they recognise the inability of man to attain to blessedness and a certain knowledge of the truth without divine help and without a revelation, they are fundamentally related. It must no doubt be admitted that Christianity itself was already profoundly affected by the influence of Hellenism when it began to outline a theology; but this influence must be traced back less to philosophy than to the collective culture, and to all the conditions under which the spiritual life was enacted. When

Neoplatonism arose ecclesiastical Christianity already possessed the fundamental features of its theology, that is, it had developed these, not by accident, contemporaneously and independent of Neoplatonism. Only by identifying itself with the whole history of Greek philosophy, or claiming to be the restoration of pure Platonism, was Neoplatonism able to maintain that it had been robbed by the church theology of Alexandria. But that was an illusion. Ecclesiastical theology appears, though our sources here are unfortunately very meagre, to have learned but little from Neoplatonism even in the third century, partly because the latter itself had not yet developed into the form in which the dogmatic of the church could assume its doctrines, partly because ecclesiastical theology had first to succeed in its own region, to fight for its own position and to conquer older notions intolerable to it. Origen was quite as independent a thinker as Plotinus; but both drew from the same tradition. On the other hand, the influence of Neoplatonism on the Oriental theologians was very great from the fourth century. The more the Church expressed its peculiar ideas in doctrines which, though worked out by means of philosophy, were yet unacceptable to Neoplatonism (the christological doctrines), the more readily did theologians in all other questions resign themselves to the influence of the latter system. The doctrines of the incarnation, of the resurrection of the body, and of the creation of the word, in time formed the boundary lines between the dogmatic of the Church and Neoplatonism; in all else ecclesiastical theologians and Neoplatonists approximated so closely that many among them were completely at one. Nay, there were Christian men, such as Synesius, for example, who in certain circumstances were not found fault with for giving a speculative interpretation of the specifically Christian doctrines. If in any writing the doctrines just named are not referred to, it is often doubtful whether it was composed by a Christian or a Neoplatonist. Above all, the ethical rules, the precepts of the right life, that is, asceticism, were always similar. Here Neoplatonism in the end celebrated its greatest triumph. It introduced into the church its entire mysticism, its mystic exercises, and even the magical ceremonies, as expounded by Iamblichus. The writings of the pseudo-Dionysius contain a Gnosis in which, by means of the doctrines of Iamblichus and doctrines like those of Proclus, the dogmatic of the church is changed into a scholastic mysticism with directions for practical life and worship. As the writings of this pseudo-Dionysius were regarded as those of Dionysius the disciple of the Apostle, the scholastic mysticism which they taught was regarded as apostolic, almost as a divine science. The importance which these writings obtained first in the East, then from the ninth or the twelfth century also in the West, cannot be too highly estimated. It is impossible to explain them here. This much only may be said, that the mystical and pietistic devotion of to-day, even in the Protestant Church, draws its nourishment from writings whose connection with those of the pseudo-Areopagitic can still be traced through its various intermediate stages.

In antiquity itself Neoplatonism influenced with special directness one Western theologian, and that the most important, viz., Augustine. By the aid of this system Augustine was freed from Manichæism, though not completely, as well as from scepticism. In the seventh Book of his confessions he has acknowledged his indebtedness to the reading of Neoplatonic writings. In the most essential doctrines, viz., those about God, matter, the relation of God to the world, freedom and evil, Augustine always remained dependent on Neoplatonism; but at the same time, of all theologians in antiquity he is the one who saw most clearly and shewed most plainly wherein Christianity and Neoplatonism are distinguished. The best that has been written by a Father of the Church on this subject, is contained in Chapters 9-21 of the seventh Book of his confessions.

The question why Neoplatonism was defeated in the conflict with Christianity, has not as yet been satisfactorily answered by historians. Usually the question is wrongly stated. The point here is not about a Christianity arbitrarily fashioned, but only about Catholic Christianity and Catholic theology. This conquered Neoplatonism after it had assimilated nearly everything it possessed. Further, we must note the place where the

victory was gained. The battle-field was the empire of Constantine, Theodosius and Justinian. Only when we have considered these and all other conditions, are we entitled to enquire
in what degree the specific doctrines of Christianity contributed
to the victory, and what share the organisation of the church
had in it. Undoubtedly, however, we must always give the
chief prominence to the fact that the Catholic dogmatic excluded
polytheism in principle, and at the same time found a means
by which it could represent the faith of the cultured mediated
by science as identical with the faith of the multitude resting
on authority.

In the theology and philosophy of the middle ages, mysticism
was the strong opponent of rationalistic dogmatism; and, in
fact, Platonism and Neoplatonism were the sources from which
in the age of the Renaissance and in the following two centuries, empiric science developed itself in opposition to the
rationalistic dogmatism which disregarded experience. Magic,
astrology, alchemy, all of which were closely connected with
Neoplatonism, gave an effective impulse to the observation of
nature and, consequently, to natural science, and finally prevailed over formal and barren rationalism. Consequently, in
the history of science, Neoplatonism has attained a significance
and performed services of which men like Iamblichus and
Proclus never ventured to dream. In point of fact, actual
history is often more wonderful and capricious than legends
and fables.

Literature. — The best and fullest account of Neoplatonism,
to which I have been much indebted in preparing this sketch,
is Zeller's, Die Philosophie der Griechen, III. Theil, 2 Abthei-
lung (3 Auflage, 1881) pp. 419-865. Cf. also Hegel, Gesch. d.
Philos. III. 3 ff. Ritter, IV. pp. 571-728: Ritter et Preller,
Hist. phil. græc. et rom. § 531 ff. The Histories of Philosophy
by Schwegler, Brandis, Brucker, Thilo, Strümpell, Ueberweg
(the most complete survey of the literature is found here),
Erdmann, Cousin, Prantl. Lewes. Further: Vacherot, Hist. de
l'école d'Alexandria, 1846, 1851. Simon, Hist. de l'école

d'Alexandria, 1845. Steinhart, articles "Neuplatonismus", "Plotin", "Porphyrius", "Proklus" in Pauly, Realencyclop. des klass. Alterthums. Wagenmann, article "Neuplatonismus" in Herzog, Realencyklopädie f. protest. Theol. T. X. (2 Aufl.) pp. 519-529. Heinze, Lehre vom Logos, 1872, p. 298 f. Richter, Neuplatonische Studien, 4 Hefte.

Heigl, Der Bericht des Porphyrios über Origenes, 1835. Redepenning, Origenes I. p. 421 f. Dehaut, Essai historique sur la vie et la doctrine d'Ammonius Saccas, 1836. Kirchner, Die Philosophie des Plotin, 1854. (For the biography of Plotinus, cf. Porphyry, Eunapius, Suidas; the latter also in particular for the later Neoplatonists). Steinhart, De dialectica Plotini ratione, 1829, and Mèletemata Plotiniana, 1840. Neander, Ueber die welthistorische Bedeutung des 9ten Buchs in der 2ten Enneade des Plotinos, in the Abhandl. der Berliner Akademie, 1843. p. 299 f. Valentiner, Plotin u. s. Enneaden, in the Theol. Stud. u. Kritiken, 1864, H. 1. On Porphyrius, see Fabricius, Bibl. gr. V. p. 725 f. Wolff, Porph. de philosophia ex oraculis haurienda librorum reliquiæ, 1856. Müller, Fragmenta hist. gr. III. 688 f. Mai, Ep. ad Marcellam, 1816. Bernays, Theophrast. 1866. Wagenmann, Jahrbücher für Deutsche Theol. Th. XXIII. (1878) p. 269 f. Richter, Zeitschr. f. Philos. Th. LII. (1867) p. 30 f. Hebenstreit, de Iamblichi doctrina, 1764. Harless, Das Buch von den ägyptischen Mysterien, 1858. Meiners, Comment. Societ. Gotting IV. p. 50 f. On Julian, see the catalogue of the rich literature in the Realencyklop. f. prot Theol. Th. VII. (2 Aufl.) p. 287, and Neumann, Juliani libr. c. Christ. quæ supersunt, 1880. Hoche, Hypatia, in "Philologus" Th. XV. (1860) p. 435 f. Bach, De Syriano philosopho, 1862. On Proclus, see the Biography of Marinus and Freudenthal in "Hermes" Th. XVI. p. 214 f. On Boethius, cf. Nitzsch, Das System des Boëthius, 1860. Usener, Anecdoton Holderi, 1877.

On the relation of Neoplatonism to Christianity and its significance in the history of the world, cf. the Church Histories of Mosheim, Gieseler, Neander, Baur; also the Histories of Dogma by Baur and Nitzsch. Also Löffler, Der Platonismus der Kirchenväter, 1782. Huber, Die Philosophie der Kirchen-

väter, 1859. Tzschirner, Fall des Heidenthums, 1829. Burckhardt, Die Zeit Constantin's des Grossen, p. 155 f. Chastel,
Hist. de la destruction du Paganisme dans l'empire d'Orient,
1850. Beugnot, Hist. de la destruction du Paganisme en Occi-
dent, 1835. E, v. Lasaulx, Der Untergang des Hellenismus,
1854. Bigg, The Christian Platonists of Alexandria 1886.
Réville, La réligion à Rome sous les Sévères, 1886. Vogt,
Neuplatonismus und Christenthum, 1836. Ullmann, Einfluss
des Christenthums auf Porphyrius, in Stud. und Krit., 1832 On
the relation of Neoplatonism to Monasticism, cf. Keim, Aus dem
Urchristenthum, 1178, p. 204 f. Carl Schmidt, Gnostische Schriften in Koptischer Sprache, 1892 (Texte u. Unters. VIII. 1. 2).
See, further, the Monographs on Origen, the later Alexandrians.
the three Cappadocians, Theodoret, Synesius, Marius Victorinus,
Augustine, Pseudo-Dionysius, Maximus, Scotus Erigena and
the Mediæval Mystics. Special prominence is due to: Jahn,
Basilius Plotinizans, 1838. Dorner, Augustinus, 1875. Bestmann,
Qua ratione Augustinus notiones philos. Græcæ adhibuerit, 1877.
Loesche, Augustinus `Plotinizans, 1881. Volkmann, Synesios,
1869. On the after effects of Neoplatonism on Christian Dog-
matic, see Ritschl, Theologie und Metaphysik. 2 Aufl. 1887.